Robert Mimpriss

The Gospel treasury, and expository harmony of the four evangelists:

In the words of the authorised version, having Scripture illustrations; expository notes form the most aproved commentators; practical reflections

Robert Mimpriss

The Gospel treasury, and expository harmony of the four evangelists:
In the words of the authorised version, having Scripture illustrations; expository notes form the most aproved commentators; practical reflections

ISBN/EAN: 9783337714345

Printed in Europe, USA, Canada, Australia, Japan

Cover: Foto ©ninafisch / pixelio.de

More available books at **www.hansebooks.com**

TRUBSHAW'S EDITION.

THE GOSPEL TREASURY,

AND

EXPOSITORY HARMONY OF THE FOUR EVANGELISTS,

IN THE WORDS OF THE AUTHORIZED VERSION,

HAVING

SCRIPTURE ILLUSTRATIONS; EXPOSITORY NOTES FROM THE MOST APPROVED COMMENTATORS; PRACTICAL REFLECTIONS; GEOGRAPHICAL NOTICES; COPIOUS INDEX, ETC.

COMPILED BY

ROBERT MIMPRISS,

AUTHOR OF "THE SYSTEM OF GRADUATED SIMULTANEOUS INSTRUCTION," ETC., ETC.

TWO VOLUMES IN ONE

VOL. I.

NEW YORK:
DODD & MEAD, No. 751 BROADWAY,
SUCCESSORS TO M. W. DODD.
1870.

⁎ FOR METHOD OF READING THE HARMONY OF THE FOUR EVANGELICAL NARRATIVES AS A CONTINUOUS HISTORY, SEE SECTION VII., P. 49. (SEE ALSO REVIEW IN "THE SUNDAY-SCHOOL TIMES," AS AT THE END, VOL. II., OF THIS WORK.)

PREFACE TO AMERICAN EDITION.

HE who is so fortunate as to possess a copy of *The Gospel Treasury*, is furnished with one of the most valuable aids to the study of the Life of Jesus Christ that is to be had. It is not an ordinary "commentary." Nor is it a dry skeleton of facts and dates to be referred to only as one would refer to the directory, the dictionary, or the census report.

Mr. Mimpriss has shown a remarkable amount of patient and untiring industry in the compilation of this valuable aid to the study of the Sacred Word. He has arranged it with faultless system, and with great accuracy and completeness of detail. The book introduces itself at once to the student who would use it, and in such a companionable manner forces upon him its ability to afford him the help he needs, that he is fascinated by it, and led on from step to step to closer acquaintance with the life and ministry of the God-man on earth. The four gospel narratives are placed so as to chant a harmonious song of praise to Him whose record they are. The Old Testament is brought, with all its rich stores of prophecy, to add the light of the ancient dispensation to that of the new, and to show that the " Wonderful, Counsellor " of Isaiah is the same with the Babe of Bethlehem ; that the " man of sorrows and acquainted with grief" is the same as He " who his own self bare our sins in his own body on the tree." The Old Testament brings, too, its history and topography, to assist in an understanding of the scenes and events of the New. There are few books that so completely carry out the idea of studying the Bible *as a whole*, as this does.

the above will suffice to illustrate the importance of attending to every word of the Gospel narratives, and the desirableness of having each distinct narrative in juxta-position, for consultation at sight.

"The insertion of many of the original words in the text serves, not only to show the agreement, or actual difference of expression used by the sacred writers, in the several narratives of the same event, but also to remedy the want of precision which sometimes occurs in our excellent translation—the same word in the original is often variously rendered into English; and, in some cases, various words in the original correspond to the *same* English expression. This was inevitable in the hands of different translators, and detracts nothing from the general excellence of our present Authorized Version.

"The same division of labour occasioned a want of uniform marking of those words, by *italics*, which are not included in the original: to remedy this, many words appear in italics which are not so distinguished in the Authorized Version."*

With reference to the hyphens which are introduced in the text, it is only necessary to inform the English reader, that their use is to connect two or more words which, in the original, are expressed by one word: as Luke i. 1, "which-are-most-surely-believed:" here five English words are used to express the meaning of one Greek word, πεπληροφορημένων (*peplerophoremenon*).—Verse 3, "in-order;" two words to express one, καθεξῆς (*kathexes*). This use of the hyphen will often considerably help, even the scholar, "to a better understanding of a sentence or expression—will frequently recall the original to the mind, and prevent it from laying hold of a meaning which has no warrant but in the idiom of our own language.

"One suggestion, which may be useful to all readers, whether acquainted with the original language or not, is here submitted as inviting their attention. The hyphen will serve to mark the degree of emphasis any expression may have; as, for instance, in that often repeated affirmation of Him who spake as the Divine Logos, whether it stands thus, 'Verily, verily, I say unto you;' or, 'Verily, verily, I-say unto-you:' since in the first instance there are, in addition to the words contained in the other, the originals of 'I' and 'unto,' as we have 'Αμὴν ἀμὴν ἐγω λέγω πρὸς ὑμας, instead of only 'Αμὴν ἀμὴν λέγω ὑμίν. Another example may suffice to justify the importance of the hyphen: 'And ye will not come unto me, that ye might have life;' where it will appear that 'ye-will' is the rendering of θέλετε, and not the form of the verb *come*."†

The hyphens having *dots*, indicate that the words, entering into combination, are separated from each other, by the words that come between the dotted ends of the hyphens: as Matt. ii. 12, § v.

---

* See Preface to the first edition. † *Ibid.*

PLAN OF THE GOSPEL TREASURY. v

p. 33, "they-should-·not·-return:" "not" is therefore a distinct word in the original, while the words " they-should-return" are, in the original, expressed by one, ἀνακάμψαι (anakampsai)

In the SCRIPTURE ILLUSTRATIONS, ample use has been made of what was already available; but in no case without a careful revision: while much has been added calculated to lead into an intelligent acquaintance with the whole inspired volume.

The NOTES have been very carefully selected, and it is hoped will prove gems of Biblical literature. The best expositor of the Scriptures is unquestionably God's own word; and in the "SCRIPTURE ILLUSTRATIONS," we anticipate, the children of God will most delight. "To the law and to the testimony," Isa. viii. 20. "Prove all things; hold fast that which is good," 1 Thess. v. 21.

The PRACTICAL REFLECTIONS will, it is trusted, be found well chosen, and helpful to a useful application of the text.

The GEOGRAPHICAL NOTICES, which are from the most recent authorities, are as complete as our limits allow, and sufficient for all practical purposes.

In the ADDENDA is given extra matter, which it may be good to consult; but which it was not necessary to introduce under any of these specific heads.

In the CHART of OUR LORD'S LIFE AND MINISTRY every event recorded in the Gospel Narratives is Geographically localized and numbered, agreeing with the one hundred lessons in *The System of Graduated Simultaneous Instruction.*—See note.

The ANALYTICAL AND HISTORICAL TABLE, p. xiii—xxvii, exhibits the most prominent subjects in each Section; and the parallels which occur in other portions of the Evangelical History [within brackets] will, with the column of illustrations, be usefully suggestive.

The "GOSPEL TREASURY" will, it is expected, be found serviceable to all who are engaged in spreading abroad the knowledge of our LORD JESUS CHRIST, and in promoting the interests of HIS kingdom, whether by exertions in the pulpit, or in the Bible class; whether as Catechists, as Sabbath School Teachers, as Conductors of Seminaries, or as Heads of Families.

FINALLY, whatever excellence there is in the book, the Compiler most unfeignedly acknowledges is due, not to himself, but to others; especially to the valuable contributions, and disinterested and laborious revision and superintendence of a dear Christian brother.*

---

* The flattering and nearly unanimous commendation given to THE GOSPEL TREASURY, by all who have used it, makes it my very grateful duty now, to record, with unfeigned thanks, that the Christian brother above referred to, is John Wilson, Esq., author of "*Lectures on the Israelitish Origin of the English Nation,*" without whose serviceable and almost gratuitous aid, and most valuable contributions, in Notes, Practical Reflections, etc., the volume would, probably, have had no existence.

THE GOSPEL TREASURY FOR TEACHERS.

To save expense, the book is adapted to the teachers of the Fourth and Fifth Grades of "*The Mimpriss System of Graduated Simultaneous Instruction.*" The distinctions to be observed are:—

First.—In the "SCRIPTURE ILLUSTRATIONS," only such as refer to the Gospels, the Acts, and the Epistles, are to be taken by the teacher of the FOURTH GRADE.

Second.—In the "NOTES," only such portions as are *not* within brackets are to be taken by the same.

Third.—In the "PRACTICAL REFLECTIONS," the same selection is to be made by the same teacher.

For the "Bible," or "Fifth Grade Teacher," there is presented in this volume, it is believed, considerable help to a profitable searching of the entire word of God. Previous to assembling his class, the lesson should be carefully studied, and a suitable selection made by the teacher. A Note at Sect. vii. p. 49 will explain the use of a Harmony of the Gospel narratives, in realizing a Continuous History of our Lord's life and ministry; and, on comparison, will be seen to agree with the book prepared for the scholars in Sabbath Schools and Catechumen Classes.*

The Sections† agree with the arrangement of the One Hundred Lessons, in the First, Second, and Third Grades of the "*System of Graduated Simultaneous Instruction:*" but it will very often occur, that a Section in THE GOSPEL TREASURY embraces more than can be gone through at one time: in such cases the *lower* grades must be accommodated to the *higher;* and in the *lower* grades beneficial results will follow the recapitulation of the last lesson, and the preceding, whether on one or more Sabbaths in continuance.

It is not expected that ALL that is provided in a Section of "THE GOSPEL TREASURY" can be imparted to any class in a Sabbath or other school at one sitting; but we have furnished "A TREASURY," from which every diligent teacher may obtain valuable aid, for training the rising generation to ascribe, "TO THE ONLY WISE GOD OUR SAVIOUR, GLORY AND MAJESTY, DOMINION AND POWER." AMEN.

---

* A Narrative Harmony of the Four Gospels, or The Steps of Jesus, arranged as a Continuous History, pp. 288.

† NOTE.—When the *Section* differs from the *Lesson,* the foot-note will explain it; as Section 20, p. 153: this, with Section 21, p. 159, constitutes Lesson 21. The Sections and Lessons henceforward to Section 29, p. 221—8, agree. Lesson 30 embraces Section 29, p. 229, and Sections 30—1, p. 232—241. After this, Section 32, p. 242, to Section 36, p. 285 and the Lessons, are the same. Sections 37, 8, pp. 286—293, form Lesson 37. Section 39, p. 293—303, is Lesson 38. Section 40, p. 304, the death of John Baptist, to p. 308, is Lesson 39. Lesson 40 is the same as the Section, from p. 309 to 316. Sections 41, 2, p. 317—324, is Lesson 41. Section 43 is Lesson 42. In VOL. II. the Lessons are always signified in the heading, immediately after the Section.

AN INTRODUCTORY SKETCH

OF

A JOURNEY FROM LONDON TO JERUSALEM.

JERUSALEM.—Is the most renowned city in the world; whether we consider its antiquity (see GEOG. NOTICES, § v. p. 36; § vi. p. 42; § xxiii. pp. 181—.4); Hebron and Damascus being the only cities claiming earlier origin; or whether we consider its vast wealth, accumulated in the time of David and of his son Solomon, when '*the king made silver and gold at Jerusalem as plenteous as stones, and cedar trees made he as the sycamore trees that are in the vale for abundance.*' 2 Chron. i. 15; or whether we contemplate its earlier history, in which was manifested the obedience of faithful Abraham, in preparing to offer up his only son there, on mount Moriah. In looking back upon the history of Jerusalem, we become acquainted with patriarchs, prophets, priests, and kings, who lived and died and are buried there; and with the stupendous exhibition of God's love in delivering up his dear and only begotten Son, to die for the sin of the world. From thence the gospel flowed unto us. There the blessed Saviour proclaimed salvation through his death; and, after ages have rolled by, and Jerusalem has been trodden down by the Gentiles, the time is fast approaching when the place in which he was abased shall witness his glory. Jerusalem . . . . is accessible to the people of Asia on the north, and to those of the east by the Euphrates, the Persian gulf, and the Red sea; to our own nation and Europe generally, and America in the far west, by the Mediterranean or Great sea; and to the people of Africa and Arabia, on the south. Jerusalem is '*the city of the great King!*' Matt. v. 35. '*They shall call Jerusalem the throne of the LORD;*'—see Jer. iii. 17; and to it all nations shall flow, to worship the Lord in Jerusalem. —See Isa. lx. 1—4. '*The word that Isaiah the son of Amos saw concerning Judah and Jerusalem.* 2 *And it shall come to pass in the last days, that the mountain of the LORD's house shall be established in the top of the mountains, and shall be exalted above the hills; and all nations shall flow unto it.* 3 *And many people shall go and say, Come ye, and let us go up to the mountain of the LORD, to the house of the God of Jacob; and he will teach us of his ways, and we will walk in his paths: for out of Zion shall go forth the law, and the word of the LORD from Jerusalem.* 4 *And he shall judge among the nations, and shall rebuke many people: and they shall beat their swords into ploughshares, and their spears into pruning-hooks: nation shall not lift up sword against nation, neither shall they learn war any more.*'—'*Therefore they shall come and sing in the height of Zion, and shall flow together to the goodness of the LORD, for wheat, and for wine, and for oil, and for the young of the flock and of the herd: and their soul shall be as a watered garden; and they shall not sorrow any more at all,*' Jer. xxxi. 12. See also Mic. iv. 2; Zech. viii. 20—23. '*Thus saith the LORD of hosts; It shall yet come to pass, that there shall come people, and the inhabitants of many cities:* 21 *and the inhabitants of one city shall go to another, saying, Let us go speedily to pray before the LORD, and to seek the LORD of hosts: I will go also.* 22 *Yea, many people and strong nations shall come to seek the LORD of hosts in Jerusalem, and to pray before the LORD.* 23 *Thus saith the LORD of hosts; In those days it shall come to pass, that ten men shall take hold out of all languages of the nations, even shall take hold of the skirt of him that is a Jew, saying, We will go with you; for we have heard that God is with you.*'

It is gratifying to trace our proximity to this Holy land: that land, which heretofore was considered only approachable after a long and tedious pilgrimage, is now brought within a holiday trip for recreation.

The following brief outline is presented for the gratification of those who are looking with hope to the land of their fathers.

Every thing being prepared, three hours' run by the railway to Southampton, and a few minutes for embarkation, will secure the traveller comfortably on board a gigantic steamer, which shortly after will be majestically cleaving the placid bosom of Southampton Water; and after passing the venerable pile of Netley Abbey, and Calshot Castle, the Isle of Wight is coasted, and soon the vast Atlantic entered.

In three or four days the Spanish coast is made; and shepherds' and fishermen's huts are seen dispersed on the rocky shore, and the sea is animated by fishing boats 'skimming along the water like things of life.' Instead of the toil and danger experienced by ancient pilgrims, in the soft evening, music charms the ear, and the deck is promenaded by ladies and gentlemen, as at the Spas and watering places of home: the difference being the vessel's deck instead of lawns and gravel walks; and for flowering shrubs is the smooth sea; and instead of variegated lamps devised, the silvery beams of the moon fantastically dancing upon the water. And in the morning, the sun emerging from his ocean bed, amply repays him who witnesses the gorgeous display of its early beams, and brings in view the coast of Portugal; and, perhaps, a finny inhabitant of the deep sportively spouting water in the air. Then comes the evening, and sweet music again refreshens and enlivens the gay scene. Another day the artificial monster of the deep foams onward, and having neared the barren and mountainous coast, the evening brings its former delights. On the seventh day, the impetuous vessel progresses through Gibraltar's straits, affording a distinct view of the Spanish mountains, richly cultivated from the base almost to their summits; and the mountains on the African side are visible also. This, perhaps, is the Lord's day, and its decent observance is felt in the mustering of all hands for prayer and praise. Isaiah lvi. 2. Soon the delightful passage is varied by a walk on terra firma; and what has been glowingly set forth, beautiful, in the picture, is

GOD IS LOVE.—1 Jno. iv. 8.

vii

surpassed in personal experience. The houses are clean and neat, standing out in pleasing relief from the steep bold mountain side which flanks the town. All those plants which, in England, can be reared only in the hot-house, here grow in open air. The finest grapes are sold for one penny per pound, and every other fruit proportionably cheap. GIBRALTAR is defended in an almost impregnable manner. The inhabitants consist of Jews, Spaniards, Turks, &c., wearing the costumes of their different countries; presenting a grotesque appearance; and which, to a stranger only a few days' removed from English society, makes the place appear to him another world. After a few hours, the boiling steam is again plied, and the calm evening renews its music and its graceful charms. On the eighth day, the blue waters of the Mediterranean are stemmed, and the playful porpoise gambols on its surface. The day following, the blazing sun asserts his power, and is acknowledged by all who expose themselves to his influence. The Algerine coast is neared; the town is clearly seen, nearly surrounding the harbour, as an amphitheatre: the curious sails of its small craft affording scope for the pencil's mimic art. Hitherto all has been smooth, calm, and delightful; but another day dawns with storm, and tempest, and angry billows; and, instead of the pleasant evening cool, sickness is an unwelcome visiter. The eleventh day, the power of steam quails to Almightiness;—trembling and rolling, like a drunken man, before the lashing of the surge. Onward still, she passes one island after another. On the morning of the twelfth, MALTA, the island on which St. Paul was shipwrecked, opens its capacious harbour, and boatmen clamouring for engagement surround the vessel; others present shells and curiosities for sale; others carry in their skiffs brown naked boys, who sportively dive for money, or other things thrown into the water, which they never fail to reach ere it touches the bottom; and for applause, frequently descend under the ship to the other side. The houses are built of white and yellow stone; which the beautiful light and clear atmosphere of the Mediterranean strikes, and causes all the designs of the cornices, corners of the angles, balustrades of the terraces, and carved work of the balconies, to be articulated fully and clearly in the blue horizon. This quality of the air, this white, yellow, golden colour of the stone, imparts to the meanest edifice a firmness and neatness which revive and gladden the sight. As at Gibraltar, the inhabitants are dressed in the most diversified colours, and seemingly are from all parts of the world, amid a melancholy exhibition of squalid disease and mendicity. Another day, the thirteenth, at Malta, will afford an opportunity to witness the illustration of our Lord's beautiful description, Jno. x. 4, of a shepherd going before his flock, leading them out to pasture, '*And when he putteth forth his own sheep, 'e goeth before them, and the sheep follow him: for they know his voice.*' Some of the streets are named after the craftsmen who occupy them; as the Tailor Street, where, almost at every door, may be seen two or three tailors, cutting and sewing. Further on may be seen cobblers, shoemakers, and others, following their handicraft with might and main, in the middle of the street. Grapes, of the most luscious kind, are sold at one halfpenny per pound, and are seen everywhere hanging from the trees in large clusters. Some of the Roman Catholic churches are magnificent in their structure, and richly adorned; that of St. John has two gates, as large as those of a gentleman's mansion, of solid silver. The gates were formerly of solid gold, but Buonaparte unceremoniously removed them. After an agreeable detention of, sometimes, two days for the Marseilles mail, a bustle pervades the vicinity of the packet, and again the passenger for the Holy Land and the Holy City sleeps on the bosom of old Ocean. The fourteenth day, only the broad and blue sea, besprinkled with a few vessels gracefully gliding along, and the canopy of heaven, can now be seen. This brings again the heavenly blessing, '*the Lord's day,*' mercifully appointed a day of rest for man and beast. Again the bell tolls; and all bow down to the Lord God Almighty, meekly bending upon their knees. The sixteenth—The refreshing sweetness of the early breeze is delightful to him who can forego the luxury of slumber. The seventeenth—The nevertiring vessel now approaches land; the coast of Africa is beheld; preparations are made, by assorting the passengers' luggage, for disembarkation on the following day; the eighteenth. Awaking in the morning, Alexandria, the seaport of the land of the Pharaohs, is entered; where Turk and Arab boatmen contend, and on shore hundreds of brawny natives with camels and donkeys squabble for employment. Dr. Robinson describes the scene, vol. i. p. 20. thus:—

'The moment we set foot on shore, we needed no further conviction that we had left Europe and were now in the Oriental world: we found ourselves in the midst of a dense crowd, through which we made our way with difficulty; Egyptians, Turks, Arabs, Copts, Negroes, Franks; complexions of white, black, olive, bronze, brown, and almost all other colours; long beards and no beards at all; all costumes and no costumes; silks and rags; wide robes and no robes; women muffled in shapeless black mantles, their faces wholly covered except peep-holes for the eyes; endless confusion, and a clatter and medley of tongues, Arabic, Turkish, Greek, Italian, French, German, and English, as the case might be; strings of huge camels in single file, with high loads; little donkeys, bridled and saddled, each guided by a sore-eyed Arab boy, with a few words of sailor-English, who thrusts his little animal, *nolens volens*, almost between your legs.'

All travellers to Jerusalem must proceed from Alexandria to Joppa, or across the desert by Suez, Sinai, &c. The mail leaves Alexandria for Beyrout, calling at Joppa, within 48 hours after the arrival of the English packet. Beyrout is a sea-port on the coast of Palestine, about 250 miles from Alexandria. Joppa is a port on the same coast, about half-way. Passengers, by other vessels, for Jerusalem, must go to Beyrout, and return thence in a hired vessel to Joppa; which materially increases the length of the journey to such as cannot afford to go by land from Beyrout to Jerusalem. The following description of the passage from Alexandria to Beyrout is from an interesting modern publication:—

'It was blowing very fresh as we ran out to sea under a close-reefed mainsail, but the sun shone brightly, and the waves were of the purple hue that they wore to Homer's eyes; their foam flew from them in rainbow fragments; and the gallant little craft darted from wave to wave, like the joyous sea birds that flew around her. Now she hovers for a moment on the watery precipice, now flings herself into the bosom of old Neptune, whose next throb sent her aloft again into the golden sunshine and the diamond spray, till the merry gale catches her drapery, and she plunges once more into the watery valley, as if at hide and seek with her invisible playfellow, the wind.

'We never saw a sail, or caught sight of land, but now and then we had a glimpse of a dolphin; several flying-fish fluttered on board with their iridescent wings, and lay panting, and apparently quite contented. Our voyage savoured more of a cruise in a yacht than a passage in a packet.

'On the fourth morning, the coast of Syria rose over the horizon; and the clearness of the atmosphere, together with the speed of our yacht bounding before a southerly gale, made the magnificent panorama of Lebanon start into sight, and develop its complicated beauty, as if by magic. At sunrise, a faint wavy line announced our approach to land; at eight o'clock, we seemed in the very shadow of its mountains, and that country before us was the HOLY LAND.

'For 1,800 years, the Western world, in all its prosperous life and youthful energy, has looked with reverence and hope towards that hopeless and stricken, but yet honoured land. After ages of obscurity and oblivion, as a mere province of a fallen empire, that country suddenly became invested with a glory till then unknown to earth. A few poor fishermen went forth from those shores among the nations, and announced such tidings, as changed their destiny for ever. Human life became an altered state; new motives, sympathies, and principles arose, new humanities became developed; new hopes, no longer bounded by, but enlarging from, the grave, animated our race. God had been amongst us, and spoken to us, like brethren, of our glorious inheritance.

'NARROW AS ARE ITS BOUNDARIES, WE HAVE ALL A SHARE IN THE POSSESSION. WHAT .. CHURCH IS TO A CITY, PALESTINE IS TO THE W....D.

'Phœnician fleets once covered these silent waters: wealthy cities once fringed those lonely shores; and, during 3,000 years, war has led all the nations of the earth in terrible procession along those historic plains: yet it is not mere history that thrills the pilgrim to the Holy Land with such feelings, as no other spot on the wide earth inspires; but the belief that on yonder

FROM LONDON TO JERUSALEM.

earth the Creator once trod with human feet, bowed down with human suffering, linked to humanity by its closest sympathy of sorrow, bedewing our tombs with his tears, and consecrating our world with his blood. Such thoughts will influence the most thoughtless traveller on his first view of Palestine, and convert into a pilgrim, for the time, the most reckless wanderer: even the infidel, in his lonely and desecrated heart, must feel a reverence for the *human* character of one who lived and died like him of Nazareth.

'And now we can recognise Tyre and Sidon; now the pine forest and the garden-covered promontory; and now we open the city of Beyrout, with its groves and dismantled towers, and the magnificent scenery that surrounds it.

'The promontory of Beyrout is of a triangular form, and the town lies on the N.W. coast, about an hour distant from the cape, directly on the shore. A broad plain or valley extends from S. to N. across the promontory, full of cultivation, and containing the largest olive grove in Syria.* All around Beyrout is covered with mulberry groves:' the culture of silk being the chief employment of all the inhabitants. The plain and adjacent mountain side swarms with villages. The port is now filled up; so that vessels can anchor only in the open road. The town is surrounded, on the land side, by a wall of no great strength, with towers. The houses are high, and solidly built of stone. The streets are narrow and gloomy, badly paved, or rather laid, with large stones, with a deep channel in the middle for animals, in which water often runs. The city lies on a gradual slope, so that the streets have a descent towards the sea; but back of the town, the ground rises towards the south, with considerable elevation.

'In the valley that lies between the promontory and the mountains, spreads one of the richest and most varied tracts of verdure in the world. Gardens, groves, the gleams of a winding river, white cottages, half covered by creeping shrubs, lanes of flowering cactus, alternating tracts of yellow sands, and clumps of pine trees, afford a delightful range for the searching eye. For those who have any time to spare, few places in the East afford so desirable a resting place as this, combining, with many resources, such opportunities of acquiring information. A tolerably clean and comfortable boarding-house is in the vicinity. All Beyrout seem to be perpetually bathing in the delicious sea: little pyramids of red, and blue, and white garments, may be seen all along the shore, and the shaved heads of their owners dotting the surface of the water. Little children, almost as soon as they can sprawl upon the ground, are to be seen kicking among the waves.'—*Crescent and the Cross*, pp. 4—26.

'The dwellings of the Franks are scattered upon the hills towards the south, each in the midst of its garden; they are built of stone, in the European style, and exhibit many of the comforts of the West, heightened by the luxuries of the East. On the right, the mighty wall of Lebanon rises in indescribable majesty, teeming with villages, and more or less cultivated to the very top. Beyrout is the centre of European trade, and the port for Damascus. From the convenience of its communication with the interior, it is made the chief seat of the American mission in Syria; having flourishing schools, and doing good according to their means. The population is supposed to be about 10,000.'—*See also* Lowthian's Journal, pp. 26—40, for a short residence at Beyrout.

The passage by sea from Beyrout to Joppa introduces many places of Old Testament interest. A few hours' sail brings SIDON close at hand, Lebanon continuing long in sight, a magnificent and sublime object. *From a distance*, Sidon looks clean and neat; and many small villages are seen on the sides, and even on the summits of the mountains.† About 6 miles south of Sidon is TYRE, a city of ancient renown, but now poor and miserable, 'a place for the *spreading of nets in the midst of the sea*. Multitudes of ruins mark its former greatness. The sin of Tyre was '*pride.*'‡ Coasting southward CARMEL is reached. The village of KISHON, about two miles and a half north of Carmel, is mean and dirty, but on the mount is a convent of great magnificence: the seat of superstition and idolatry, as in the days when Elijah slew there the false prophets of Baal. CÆSAREA, the town where Herod was eaten of worms, is south of Carmel; after which is JOPPA. This is the coast of PALESTINE—THE HOLY LAND—THE LAND OF CANAAN—THE LAND OF JUDEA: but the most pleasing name by which we recognise it, is 'THE LAND OF PROMISE;' for to Abraham, and to his seed, God gave it for an everlasting possession. Situated at the extremity of the *Mediterranean sea*, having the Euphrates and the Persian gulf on the east, and the Red sea on the south, it is the centre of all lands; and in it is situated JERUSALEM, of which it is said, '*The* LORD *of hosts shall reign in mount Zion, and in Jerusalem, and before his ancients gloriously.*' —*See* Isa. xxiv. 23. Travellers from Europe to the Holy City usually land at JAFFA, anciently *Joppa*, the principal sea-port in Palestine; and to which the cedar, employed by king Solomon in the building of 'the temple,' was brought from mount Lebanon. It is a small fortified town, standing on a promontory: having for its harbour a miserable enclosure of rocks. The town is a labyrinth of khans, convents, narrow lanes, deserted ruins, and waste places with a few dirty streets leading from one quarter to another. The Franciscan convent often shelters 1,000 pilgrims at Easter, and other seasons of pilgrimage. The bazaars and markets look very gay with Syrian silks, and shining arms, and a profusion of fruit and flowers. From Jaffa to Jerusalem is about 40 miles. The road for nearly 3 miles is through cultivated gardens, well filled with fig, orange, lemon, pomegranate, and palm trees. The Indian fig, with its prickles, is used for and makes a durable fence. The road then opens on the highly fertile, but almost deserted and uncultivated plain of Sharon. *Ramleh* is about 10 miles distant, and is ordinarily made the resting place for the night, the remainder of the journey being performed the following day. *Ramleh* stands on a slight elevation, and is a mean straggling town, without fortification, and surrounded with gardens and orchards. From *Ramleh* the road continues for several miles through a luxuriant but almost waste plain, with scarcely an inhabitant; after which it enters a narrow defile of rocky mountains, rising almost perpendicularly, with toppling precipices all around, and obstructed with huge stones. Slippery rocks, yawning into deep fissures, and almost impracticable footing, is the only road, and this for 4,000 years probably the highway from Jaffa to Jerusalem. When at length the last acclivity is reached, emerging on a wide and sterile plain, and the first glimpse of the Holy City is gained, the leading pilgrims sink on their knees, and a shout of enthusiasm bursts from each traveller, and Arab, Italian, Greek, and Englishman exclaims, each in his own tongue, 'El Khuds!' 'Gerusalemma!' 'Hagiopolis!' 'The Holy City!' From this height not a tree or green spot is visible; no sign of life breaks the solemn stillness. To the right and left, as far as the eye can reach, vague undulations of colourless rocks extend to the horizon. A broken and desolate plain in front is bounded by a wavy battlemented wall, over which are seen towers, minarets, and mosque domes, intermingled with church turrets and terraced roofs. High over the city, to the left, rises the mount of Olives; and the distant hills of Moab afford a background to the picture. As the city is approached, nothing but the bare walls are visible, with the massive gates and lofty towers; and Jerusalem is entered under a high archway called the Jaffa or Pilgrim's gate. Pilgrims find lodgings in the various convents; and others, accommodation in a hotel kept by a Maltese, a relation of the late bishop's dragoman.—*See* Sect. v. p. 36, and [§ 23, pp. 181—4.

---

* Since the above was written, this is said to have been destroyed in the fierce contests of the Druses and the Maronites.

† *See* Sect. 45, 'Harmony of the Holy Gospel.' ‡ Ibid.

Who is able to stand before this h ly LORD God?—1 Sam. vi. 20.

ix

The LORD is King for ever and ever.—Psalm x. 16.

AN HISTORICAL SKETCH OF THE LAND OF PROMISE.

THE LAND OF ISRAEL—PALESTINE, OR JUDÆA.—Was given in an everlasting covenant to Abraham and his seed for ever.—*See* Gen. xii. 6, 7; xiii. 14—.7. It was washed on the W. by the Mediterranean, or *Great sea*, as it is called in the Bible: Nu. xxxiv. 6, 'And *as far* the western border, ye shall even have the *great sea* for a border: this shall be your west border.' Josh. i. 4, 'From the wilderness and this Lebanon, even unto the great river, the river Euphrates, all the land of the Hittites, and unto the *great sea* toward the going down of the sun, shall be your coast.' NORTHWARD, it reached along the Mediterranean sea to *Mount Casius* at the mouth of the *Orontes*, which is the entrance into *Hamath*. Numb. xxxiv. 7—9, 'This shall be your *north* border; from the great sea ye shall point out for you MOUNT HOR (Heb. *Hor-ha-hor*).* From mount Hor ye shall point out unto the entrance into *Hamath*,' &c. Its SOUTH border—is the 'River of Egypt,'—*see* Gen. xv. 18, 'Unto thy seed have I given this land, from the *river of Egypt* unto the great river. the *river Euphrates*.' And the EAST border,—*see* Deut. xi. 24, 'Every place whereon the soles of your feet shall tread shall be yours: ... from the river, the *river Euphrates*, even unto the uttermost sea shall your coast be.'

'The difference of latitude and longitude in the land actually occupied by ancient Israel, and that which was promised in the everlasting covenant, and still remains to be fulfilled, is as follows:—*see* 1 Kings iv. 25, "Judah and Israel dwelt safely from Dan even to Beersheba, all the days of Solomon." (But Solomon, like his father David, exercised a nominal or real sovereignty over all the regions which the Lord had given to the seed of Jacob.—*See* 1 Ki. iv. 21.)

'The latitude of Beersheba is 31 deg. 15 min.; of Dan, 33 deg. 15 min.;—the south point of the Dead sea, the ancient border of Israel, is 31 deg. 7 min. in the same longitude with Dan, the intervening distance, in a line from north to south, being 128 geographical, or about 150 English, miles.

'The latitude of the north point of the Elanitic gulf of the Red sea, on which *Ezion-geber*, a port of Solomon's, stood, is 29 deg. 31 min. This is the *south* border promised to Abraham. The mouth of the *Orontes*, or the entrance into Hamath from the Mediterranean, is 36 deg., and that of Beer, or Berothah on the Euphrates, 37 deg. But the range of Amanus lies beyond it, and the medium longitude of the *north* boundary is more than 36 deg. 31 min. N.; or in an ideal line, from south to north, the length of the land is upwards of seven degrees, or 500 miles, instead of 150 as of old.

'The breadth of IMMANUEL'S land, instead of its anciently contracted span, from the Mediterranean sea on the west, to a few miles on the east of Jordan, stops not short of a navigable frontier everywhere, and on every side. The longitude of the river Nile is 30 deg. 2 min.; that of the Euphrates, as it flows through the Persian Gulf, 48 deg. 25 min.; or a difference of nearly 18 deg. and a half, or more than 1,100 miles.

'On the northern extremity of the land, the range of Amanus mountains from the river Euphrates, to the uttermost sea, or extremity of the Mediterranean, scarcely exceeds 100 miles. In round numbers, the average breadth of the PROMISED LAND is 600 miles, which, multiplied by its length 500 miles, gives an area of 300,000 square miles, or more than that of any kingdom or empire in Europe, Russia alone excepted.

'Separated as Israel is from other lands, such are its borders, that it has unequalled freedom of access to all ... and is still fitted for becoming "the glory of all lands," the heritage of a people blessed of the LORD.'†

THE LAND OF PROMISE was so called from God's having given it by promise to the seed of Abraham, Gen. xii. 7; *see also* Gen. xiii. 14—.7, 'And the Lord said unto Abraham, after that Lot was separated from him, Lift up now thine eyes, and look from the place where thou art, northward, and southward, and eastward, and westward: for all the land which thou seest, to thee will I give it, and to thy seed for ever. And I will make thy seed as the dust of the earth; so that if a man can number the dust of the earth, *then* shall thy seed also be numbered. Arise, walk through the land, in the length of it, and in the breadth of it: for I will give it unto thee.'—xvii. 8, 'And I will give unto thee, and to thy seed after thee, the land wherein thou art a stranger, all the land of Canaan, for an everlasting possession; and I will be their God.'

It was called the LAND OF CANAAN, because, upon the dispersion of the three great families of mankind, the country lying at the south-eastern extremity of the *Mediterranean*, from Sidon to Gaza, was usurped by Canaan, the eldest son of Ham. And the name of PALESTINE was derived from the Philistines, whose ancestors were the Philistim, or children of the Caphtorim and Casluhim, who were descendants of Mizraim, (*see* Gen. x. 13, .4,) and came from Egypt. They passed into Canaan, whence they drove out the ancient inhabitants, and they possessed a considerable tract of country at the time Abraham sojourned in Canaan.—*See* Gen. xxi. 34, 'And Abraham sojourned in the Philistines' land many days.'—*See also* xxvi. 14, .5. They extended their conquests as far northward as Ekron, and nearly to Joppa, and divided their territory into five lordships, called after their principal cities, viz. Ekron, Ashdod, Gath, Ascalon, and Gaza.—*See* Josh. xiii. 3, 'From Sihor, which *is* before Egypt, even unto the borders of Ekron northward, *which* is counted to the Canaanite: five lords of the Philistines; the Gazathites, and the Ashdothites, the Eshkalonites, the Gittites, and the Ekronites; also the Avites.' These dwelt in the western or maritime part of it, bordering on Egypt; and, though they were subjected by David, and kept in obedience by some of his successors, they became afterwards so powerful as to furnish the Greek and Latin writers, as well as the neighbouring people, with a general appellation for the whole country.

The Israelites left Egypt B.C. 1560,‡ and after wandering forty years in the wilderness, two tribes and a half of them were settled E. of the Jordan by Moses, who died shortly afterwards: the children of Israel crossed over the river, under the conduct of Joshua, and, after six years' successful fighting against the Canaanites, divided their land amongst the nine tribes and a half. The southern part of the country, between the *Dead sea* and the *Mediterranean*, from the *Torrent of Egypt* to Jabneel, now called Yebna, was at first allotted to the tribe of Judah: but as it was subsequently found that this was too much for them, the western part of it was given to the tribes of Simeon and Dan, and that to the north was bestowed upon Benjamin. The last-mentioned tribe, on whose southern limits was the city of Jerusalem, touched to the E. on a small part of the Jordan, and to the W. upon Dan.—After the death of Joshua, the Israelites became subject to the surrounding nations; but under Saul and David they regained their independence.

The name of JUDAH, or JUDÆA, was first applied to the southern part of Palestine, when ten of the tribes revolted from the house of David. Upon the death of Solomon, B. C. 974, the kingdom was divided; Rehoboam, his son, being chosen by the tribes of Judah and Benjamin, and Jeroboam by the remaining ten tribes: the former was henceforward called The kingdom of Judah; the latter, The kingdom of Israel.—(1 Ki. xii. 16, .7, 'So when all Israel saw that the king hearkened not unto them, the people answered the king, saying, What portion have we in David? neither *have we* inheritance in the son of Jesse: to your tents, O Israel: now see to thine own house, David. So Israel departed unto their tents. But *as for* the children of Israel which dwelt in the cities of Judah, Rehoboam reigned over them.' 20 ver. 'And it came to pass, when all Israel heard that Jeroboam was come again, that they sent and called him unto the congregation, and made him king over all Israel: there was none that followed the house of David, but the tribe of Judah only.') Judah, and the children of Israel, his companions, were

* A very high mountain. † *See* Keith's 'Land of Israel.' ‡ *See* Greswell, vol. iii., p. 443.

The kingdom is the LORD'S; and He .. the Governor among the nations.—Psalm xxii. 28.

HISTORICAL SKETCH OF THE LAND OF PROMISE.

from that time called the 'kingdom of Judah. After the defection of the ten tribes from under Rehoboam, the two kingdoms maintained their freedom for many years, amidst the continual wars by which they were harassed; but Hazael, king of Syria, at last subdued Israel, and for a long time kept it in subjection. The king of Assyria next invaded them, and having besieged their city Samaria for three years, reduced it to ashes.—*See* SAMARIA.

Such of the inhabitants as survived the dreadful carnage which ensued, were carried away captive into Assyria, B. C. 719; and the kingdom of Israel, which had stood divided from that of Judah for more than 250 years, was now at an end. After this, Judah also was attacked by the Babylonians, and subsequently by the Egyptians, the latter of whom reduced it to subjection; but upon the defeat of the Egyptians by the Babylonians, Nebuchadnezzar seized upon Jerusalem, and, after having tyrannized over the people for some years, at last levelled the city and the temple with the ground, and carried away the inhabitants to Babylon, and thus put an end to the kingdom of Judah, about B. C. 588, or 476 years from the time that David began to reign over it.—*See* 2 Chr. xxxvi. Seventy years after, when Cyrus was king of Persia, a remnant of the Jews returned, and built again their city and temple, around which they settled; and the southern part of PALESTINE was henceforth called JUDÆA. To the N. of them, in the former inheritance of Ephraim and the half tribe of Manasseh, sate a mixed race of people, among whom may have been some families casually left behind in the great captivity. More certain are we, that colonies of idolatrous heathen were placed there by the Assyrian monarch, 2 Ki. xvii. 24—34; and that these were subsequently joined by some Jews, such as Joiada, mentioned Neh. xiii. 28. They were called *Samaritans*, from their dwelling round the old capital of the kingdom of Israel; and were looked upon by the Jews as so impure, that they had no dealings with them. Alexander the Great subdued Palestine, and at his death its possession was disputed by Antigonus and the Egyptians, until Antiochus the Great, king of Syria, united it to his dominions. The Jews, under Judas Maccabæus, revolted, and established their freedom. They over-ran Samaria, and planted colonies in the northern part of the country, which assumed henceforward the name of GALILEE; and raised up a king about B.C. 107. His successors called in the Romans to settle their disputes; and the Roman general, Pompey, irritated by the little respect shewn to him, marched against Jerusalem and reduced it, B.C. 63, and soon after completed the subjugation of the whole country. In the time of Marc Antony, Herod was made king of Judæa; and it was during his reign that our Saviour was born. Judæa remained subject to the Romans till A.D. 66, when a contest arose between the Jews and Syrians respecting the possession of Cæsarea: the case being referred to Nero, he decided in favour of the latter; upon which the Jews took up arms, and, after committing some dreadful massacres, succeeded in driving all the Romans and Syrians from Judæa. Vespasian was sent against them with a powerful army, and would soon have brought them to subjection, but, on his march to Jerusalem, he received the intelligence of his having been chosen emperor: he accordingly left the command of the army to his son Titus, who, A.D. 70, reduced the city to ashes, and put an end to the Jewish nation, as had been prophesied for ages beforehand.

The name of the HOLY LAND is applied to it by Christians in nearly all the languages of Europe; chiefly and eminently from its having been the scene of our Blessed Lord's life, death, and resurrection.

In the time of the events recorded in the history of the New Testament, Palestine was divided into five principal parts. These were Galilee, Samaria, Judæa, properly so called, Batanæa, and Peræa; the three first of which were on this side Jordan, and the two last beyond it; over all of which Herod, surnamed 'the Great,' was king.—*See* Luc. v. 'Herod.'

GALILEE—Was the northernmost province of Palestine, and was exceedingly fertile and populous, having 204 towns and villages, containing, on an average, 15,000 souls, making in all above 3,000,000 inhabitants. It touched to the W. on *Phœnice*, to the N. on *Cœlo-Syria*, to the E. on *Batanæa*, and to the S. on *Samaria*. It contained 530 square miles. It was subdivided into Upper and Lower, so named with respect to the river Jordan, the former being also called '*Galilee of the Gentiles*,' from its being inhabited not only by Jews, but by Syrians, Greeks, Phœnicians, and Egyptians. This province was, above all, honoured with our Saviour's presence. It was here that he was conceived; and here, in an obscure village, he lived with his reputed parents until he began to be about thirty years of age, and was baptized of John. And though he visited the other provinces and Judæa at the stated feasts, when the male Israelites were commanded to go up to worship in Jerusalem, yet, in fulfilment of prophecy, (see § 16,) he fixed upon Capernaum to dwell in: and after his resurrection the disciples went away into Galilee, into a mountain, where they saw and worshipped him; the same probably on which he had been seen by Peter, James, and John, in glory, along with Moses and Elias.* And they were 'men of Galilee' whom he commissioned, saying, ' Go into all the world, and preach the gospel to every creature.'—UPPER GALILEE belonged formerly to the tribe of Naphtali. It bordered on *Tyre* and *Sidon*, and extended E. of the river Jordan. In its northern part, close to the W. source of the Jordan, stood *Dan*, which was formerly *Laish*, until it was wrested by conquest from the Sidonians, when it received the name of the tribe which took it. It was the northernmost town occupied by the children of Israel, in the same way that Beersheba was the southernmost: hence the frequent definition of the land of Israel—'from Dan to Beersheba.' LOWER GALILEE lay between *lake Gennesaret* and the Mediterranean sea. The northern part belonged to the tribe of Zebulun, and the southern part to the tribe of Issachar.

SAMARIA.—Touched to the W. on the Mediterranean, to the N. on Phœnice and Galilee, to the E. on Peræa, and to the S. on Judæa: it contained 1,330 square miles. It occupied the whole country between the Jordan and the sea; and therefore such as travelled from Judæa into Galilee 'must needs go through Samaria.'

Samaria derived its name from its metropolis Samaria, which was so called after one Shemer, of whom Omri, king of Israel, bought the ground, for the building of the city; and from the circumstance of this city having become the subsequent capital of the kingdom of Israel, the name of *Samaria* is frequently used by the sacred writers of the Old Testament, to denote the whole of that kingdom. Samaria is intersected by a range of mountains connected with Mnt. Hermon of Galilee: where this range enters the provinces it is called Gilboa. Mount Gilboa, celebrated for the death of Saul and Jonathan, and for the defeat of the Israelites by the Philistines, was in the northern part of Samaria, and formed part of that range of hills which traverses the whole province from north to south; towards the city of Samaria, it is known by the names of Phinehas, Ebal, and Gerizim, and upon the borders of Judæa as the mountains of Ephraim.

Upon the division of the tribes into the two kingdoms of Judah and Israel, Jeroboam, king of the latter, built Sichem, or Sheehem, in mount Ephraim, about the centre of Samaria, and made it the capital of his dominions.—*See* Sect. 13.

Samaria, the subsequent metropolis of the kingdom of Israel till the time of the Assyrian captivity, was only a few miles to the north of Sichem; it was nearly destroyed by the Assyrians, but was restored by the colonists, whom they sent into the country; and who, from this city, first assumed the name of Samaritans. It was very flourishing under the Maccabees, but being once more destroyed, it was again rebuilt and beautified by Herod, who named it *Sebaste*, in honour of Augustus; it is still called *Sebaste*, or *Kalaat Samour*.

JUDÆA, properly so called.—Was bounded on the N. by Samaria, on the E. by the Dead sea, on the S. by Arabia Petræa, and on the W. by the Mediterranean sea. It contained 3,135 square miles, and constituted the inheritance of four out of the twelve tribes, viz. of Benjamin, Dan, Judah, and Simeon, the two last being in the southern part of the province. The frontier between *Judæa* and *Arabia Propria* is formed by a range of mountains, connected with mount Seir, and known by the names of *Halak* and *Madeh Acrabbin*; this latter gives the adjacent district the

* See Sections 1. & xevi. † Page viii. first paragraph, *et seq.*

HISTORICAL SKETCH OF THE LAND OF PROMISE.

name of *Acrabattene*. These mountains separated the possessions of the children of Israel from the land of Edom, or Idumea, as the Greeks called it: but when the Jews were carried captive to Babylon, the southern part of their country, being left destitute, was seized by the Idumæans, who became so strong as to be able to maintain possession of it long after the Jews returned from their bondage. They were conquered at last by the Maccabees, but, having embraced Judaism, they were incorporated with the Jewish nation, and allowed to retain possession of the country they had seized upon, which from them was called Idumea; it extended as far northward as Hebron, and was noted, as was the whole of Judæa, for its fine palm trees. To the northward of this, lay the district Daromas, which still preserves its name in *Darom*: between it and Samaria stretches a range of hills, which caused the district they traversed to be called *Orine*, or 'The hill country of Judæa.'—See Sect. 2, p. 14.

Judæa is celebrated above all other divisions of Palestine. The chief city of the whole land—even Jerusalem, the 'city of the Great King,' was there. In *Jerusalem* was the temple of the LORD, to which the Jews were commanded to go up three times every year to worship JEHOVAH, the LORD their God. In JUDÆA was *Bethlehem*, the city of David, out of which, although it was little among the thousands of Judah, came forth 'HE *that is to be* ruler in Israel; whose goings forth have been from of old, from everlasting.' He who was David's son, is David's Lord, was born there. Jerusalem was the scene of his sufferings; for there he offered himself, 'a Lamb without spot,' without the gate: there he burst the bonds of death; and from OLIVET, on the east, he ascended into heaven. In *Judæa* were the disciples to remain until they were endued with power from on high, and from thence was the gospel to go forth unto the uttermost parts of the earth.

BATANÆA.—Was bounded on the W. by Galilee, on the N. and E. by Syria, and on the S. by Peræa, and corresponded nearly with the inheritance of the half tribe of Manasseh beyond Jordan; it contained 1000 square miles. It derived its name from *Basan*, or *Bashan*, of the Bible, and was noted for its fine cattle and good pasturage; its lofty hills were likewise much celebrated for their beautiful oaks. In the northern part of the province was mount Hermon,—*Heish*, called by the Sidonians, *Sirion* or *Sion*, and by the Amorites *Shenir*. In its western part was Cæsarea Philippi.—*See* Sect. 50. In the south-western corner was Gadara—*Om Keis.—See* Sect. 35.

PERÆA.—Was bounded on the N. by *Batanæa*, on the W. by *Samaria*, on the S. by *Arabia*, and on the E. by *Syria*; it contained 1,505 square miles. It derived its name from the Greek word *weραν, ultra*, from its lying beyond Jordan. The southern part of Peræa, between the two rivers *Arnon* and *Jabok*, formed the kingdom of the Amorites, whose king, Sihon, was defeated by the Israelites. In the centre of Peræa rose the lofty *mount Gilead*, or Galeed, still called *Djelaoud*, near which Jacob and Laban raised a heap of stones in token of friendship; 'therefore was the name of it called *Galeed*,' i. e. ' *The heap of witness*.'—Gen. xxxi. 48.

Of the LAND OF PROMISE Moses said, Deut. xi. 10—2, 'The land, whither thou goest in to possess it, *is* not as the land of Egypt, from whence ye came out, where thou sowedst thy seed, and wateredst *it* with thy foot, as a garden of herbs: but the land, whither ye go to possess it, *is* a land of hills and valleys, *and* drinketh water of the rain of heaven: a land which the LORD thy God careth for: the eyes of the LORD thy God *are* always upon it, from the beginning of the year even unto the end of the year.'

The *Jordan* is the principal river.—*See* Sect. 8.

Few of the HILLS approach to the character of mountains.

QUARANTINA, north of Jericho, rises an almost perpendicular rock, 1200 or 1500 feet.

HERMON.—In the N.E. of Galilee is the majestic HERMON, or SION, of the Old Testament. The usual estimate of the height of Hermon (*Jebel Esh-Sheikh*) is 10,000 feet above the Mediterranean. The top is partially crowned with snow, or rather ice, during the whole year, which however lies only in the ravines, and thus presents at a distance the appearance of radiant stripes around and below the summit. North-westward of Hermon is *Lebanon*, so full of interesting associations.

TABOR.—Although undeserving of the name of Mountain, for height, yet is prominent in Scripture for many important transactions. In its neighbourhood, Sisera, the captain of Jabin's army, with his chariots and his multitude, were delivered into the hand of Barak, Judg. iv. 6—15; and by many it has been regarded as the place of our Lord's transfiguration. The beauty of the mountain, and its conspicuous position, rendered it a favourite subject of poetic contemplation; and when the Psalmist (lxxxix. 12) exclaims, ' Tabor and Hermon shall rejoice in thy name,' he selects these two as the representatives of all the mountains of Palestine; the former as the most graceful, and the latter as the loftiest.—*See* Sect. 51.

MOUNT CARMEL.—Is often mentioned by the sacred writers; it forms one of the most remarkable headlands on the whole coast of the Mediterranean sea, and is about 1,500 feet high.

The prophecies concerning the LAND OF ISRAEL have been so exactly accomplished, *that they may be used as history*. The traveller, however careless of divine revelation, and even the scorner, abundantly testifies to the present desolation of the land: the once strong forts and towers are become dens—defenced cities are destroyed, uninhabited, and laid waste. The once productive and well-watered plains are become barren, and the herbs of every field wither. The infidel *Volney* bears witness to the truth of prophecy; for as it had been foretold, he writes, ' The temples are thrown down, the palaces are demolished, the ports are filled up, the towns destroyed, and the earth, stripped of its inhabitants, seems a dreary burying place.' Almost daily, accounts reach us, vividly portraying the curse that is upon it. Jerusalem, the City of our God, has become heaps; and Zion, as was predicted, is plowed as a field; and the place of the temple of the Most High is desecrated by the erection of a Muhammedan mosque, where death awaits the true worshipper that dares intrude within the polluted place. The ancient population was, for the limits of the country, greater than that of any other part of the then known world. In the time of David, the population must have amounted to several millions, as the men able to bear arms were numbered, at the lowest computation, and after an imperfect census, at 1,300,000. In the time of Jehoshaphat, the men of war, in Judah alone, amounted to 1,060,000. Josephus tells us that at one celebration of the Passover, in the reign of Nero, there were present at Jerusalem 2,700,000 persons. The valleys are composed of a deep rich soil, free from stones. The rocks are principally of grey limestone, and they contributed greatly towards the sustenance of a large population, as they were terraced in all directions with embankments built up with loose stones, on which grew melons, cucumbers, and other creeping plants, as well as the vine, the fig, and the olive, as now seen on a few cultivated spots. It would be wrong to argue the former capabilities of the Holy Land from its present appearance, as it is now under the curse of God, and its general barrenness is in full accordance with prophetic denunciation.

But the time is fast approaching, when, as said Moses, Deut. xxx. 3—5, ' That then the LORD thy God will turn thy captivity, and have compassion upon thee, and will return and gather thee from all the nations, whither the LORD thy God hath scattered thee. If any of thine be driven out unto the utmost *parts* of heaven, from thence will the LORD thy God gather thee, and from thence will he fetch thee: and the LORD thy God will bring thee into the land which thy fathers possessed, and thou shalt possess it; and he will do thee good, and multiply thee above thy fathers.'—*See also* Isa. lxi. 4; Ezek. xxxvi. 8; Amos ix. 13—5.

To the antiquary, to the lover of the sublime and beautiful, and, above all, to the child of God, no land abounds with so many attractions as ' The Land of Israel.' We have connected therewith the earliest and most faithful records of the wonderful providence of God, from the beginning of creation, to the redemption of man. Magnificent remains of the oldest cities in the world are there: its scenery is of the most diversified beauty. The position is best fitted for its becoming what it was appointed to be, ' *the glory of all lands*.' IMMANUEL'S LAND may be the earthly centre of MESSIAH'S KINGDOM, when its bounds are extended according to the description of prophecy, as Psalm lxxii.

For the LORD's portion *is* his people; Jacob *is* the lot of his inheritance.—Deut. xxxii. 9.

INDEX TO THE GOSPELS,

CHAPTERS AND VERSES.

MATTHEW.

Verse.	Page.	Sect.
I.		
1—16	23	4
17	24	..
18—21	13	2
22—.5	14	..
II.		
1, 2	31	5
3—8	32	..
9—12	33	..
13—.8	34	..
19—23	35	..
III.		
1, 2	50	7
3, 4	51	..
5—8	52	..
9, 10	53	..
11, .2	54	..
13—.5	58	8
16, .7	59	..
IV.		
1, 2	63	9
3—6	64	..
7, 8	65	..
9—11	66	..
12—.6	107	16
17—.9	108	..
20—.2	109	..
23	115	18
24, .5	116	..
V.		
1—6	120	19
7—9	121	..
10—.4	122	..
15—.9	123	..
20—.2	124	..
23—.9	125	..
30—.7	126	..
38—43	127	..
44—.8	128	..
VI.		
1—7	131	19
8—11	132	..
12—.7	133	..
18—24	134	..
25—32	135	..
33, .4	136	..
VII.		
1, 2	137	19
3—8	138	..
9—14	139	..
15—21	140	..
22—.7	141	..
28, .9	142	..
VIII.		
1	142	19
2	159	21
3, 4	160	..
5—7	218	28
8—10	219	..
11—.3	220	..
14—.6	112	17
17	113	..
18, .9	264	34
20—.3	265	..
24—.6	266	..
27	267	..
28	269	35
29	270	..
30—.2	271	..
33, .4	272	..
IX.		
1	274	35
2	164	22
3	165	..
4—7	166	..
8, 9	167	..
10—.2	277	36
13—.5	278	..
16—.8	279	..
19—21	280	..
22	281	..
IX. (continued).		
23, .4	283	36
25	284	..
26—34	285	..
35	293	38
36—.8	294	39
X.		
1	294	39
2	206	27
3, 4	207	..
5, 6	295	39
7—10	296	..
11—.3	297	..
14—.7	298	..
18—22	299	..
23—.7	300	..
28—35	301	..
36—41	302	..
42	303	..
XI.		
1	303	39
2, 3	222	29
4—6	223	..
7—10	224	..
11—.5	225	..
16—.9	226	..
20—.5	227	..
26—30	228	..
XII.		
1—4	188	24
5, 6	189	..
7, 8	190	..
9, 10	195	25
11, .2	196	..
13, .4	197	..
15	200	26
16—.8	201	..
19, 20	202	..
21	203	..
22, .3	234	31
24—.7	235	..
28—31	236	..
XII. (continued).		
32—.5	237	31
36—41	238	..
42—.5	239	..
46—50	240	..
XIII.		
1, 2	242	32
3, 4	243	..
5—11	244	..
12—.4	245	..
15—.7	246	..
18, .9	254	33
20, .1	255	..
22	256	..
23	257	..
24, .5	246	32
26—30	247	..
31—.3	248	..
34, .5	249	..
36	253	33
37, .8	259	..
39—43	260	..
44—.6	261	..
47—52	262	..
53	264	34
54	286	37
55—.7	287	..
58	288	..
XIV.		
1	304	40
2, 3	305	..
4—6	306	..
7—9	307	..
10—.2	308	..
13, .4	310	..
15	311	..
16, .7	312	..
18, .9	313	..
20, .1	314	..
22	317	41
23, .4	318	..
25, .6	319	..
27—31	320	..

INDEX TO THE GOSPELS.

XIV. (continued).			XIX.			XXIII.			XXVI. (continued).		
Verse.	Page.	Sect.	Verse.	Page.	Sect.	Verse.	Page.	Sect.	Verse.	Page.	Sect.
32, .3	321	41	1, 2	209	71	1—3	312	85	30	405	87
34, .5	322	42	3	218	74	4, 5	313	..	31—.5	406	..
36	323	..	4—9	219	..	6—11	314	..	36	412	88
			10—.3	220	..	12—.5	315	..	37, .8	413	..
VOL. II.			14	221	..	16—22	316	..	39	414	..
XV.			15	222	..	23—.6	317	..	40—.2	415	..
			16	223	75	27—32	318	..	43—.6	416	..
1	4	44	17, .8	224	..	33—.5	319	..	47	417	..
2, 3	5	..	19—21	225	..	36—.8	320	..	48, .9	418	..
4—6	6	..	22, .3	226	..	39	321	..	50, .1	419	..
7—9	7	..	24—.6	227	..				52, .3	420	..
10—.3	8	..	27, .8	228	..				54—.6	421	..
14—.8	9	..	29	229	..	XXIV.			57	425	89
19	10	..	30	230	..	1	323	86	58	426	..
20	11	..				2—4	324	..	59—61	427	..
21, .2	13	45	XX.			5—7	325	..	62, .3	428	..
23—.5	14	..	1—4	231	76	8, 9	326	..	64—.6	429	..
26—.8	15	..	5—12	232	..	10	328	..	67—.9	430	..
29	24	46	13—.6	233	..	11—.3	329	..	70, .1	431	..
30, .1	25	..	17—.9	235	77	14	330	..	72—.4	432	..
32—.4	26	..	20—.2	237	..	15	331	..	75	433	..
35—.8	27	..	23—.5	238	..	16—21	332	..			
39	28	47	26—.8	239	..	22	333	..	XXVII.		
			29, 30	242	79	23	334	..	1	434	89
XVI.			31—.3	243	..	24—.7	335	..	2—5	435	..
1	28	47	34	244	..	28, .9	336	..	6—8	436	..
2—4	29	..				30, .1	338	..	9, 10	437	..
5—7	32	48	XXI.			32, .3	339	..	11	445	90
8—10	33	..	1, 2	260	82	34, .5	340	..	12—.4	446	..
11, .2	34	49	3—5	261	..	36—.8	341	..	15, .6	449	..
13	35	50	6, 7	262	..	39—44	342	..	17—.9	450	..
14—.6	36	..	8	263	..	45—.8	343	..	20—.2	451	..
17, .8	37	..	9	264	..	49—51	344	..	23, .4	452	..
19, 20	39	..	10, .1	265	..				25, .6	453	..
21	40	..	12	270	..				27—.9	455	91
22, .3	41	..	13	278	..	XXV.			30—.2	456	..
24—.6	42	..	14—.7	266	82	1—9	346	86	33	458	..
27	43	..	18, .9	275	83	10—.5	347	..	34	459	..
28	44	..	20—.2	276	..	16—22	348	..	35, .6	461	..
			23	282	84	23—.7	349	..	37, .8	462	..
XVII			24, .5	283	..	28—30	350	..	39—42	463	..
1	51	51	26, .7	284	..	31—.3	351	..	43, .4	464	..
2, 3	53	..	28—32	285	..	34—.7	352	..	45, .6	466	..
4	54	..	33	286	..	38—44	353	..	47—.9	467	..
5	55	..	34, .5	287	..	45, .6	354	..	50	468	..
6—8	56	..	36	288	..				51	470	92
9—11	57	..	37—41	289	..				52—.4	471	..
12—.4	58	..	42—.4	290	..	XXVI.			55, .6	472	..
15—.7	59	..	45, .6	291	..	1—3	355	86	57	474	..
18	60	..				4, 5	356	..	58	475	..
19—21	61	..	XXII.			6, 7	253	81	59, 60	476	..
22	70	52	1, 2	291	84	8	254	..	61—.3	477	..
23	71	..	3—8	292	..	9, 10	255	..	64—.6	478	..
24, .5	72	..	9—12	293	..	11, .2	256	..			
26 .7	73	..	13, 4	294	..	13	257	..			
			15, .6	295	..	14	356	86	XXVIII.		
XVIII.			17, .8	296	..	15, .6	357	..	1	484	93
1	74	52	19—22	297	..	17, .8	362	87	2—4	485	..
2—5	75	..	23, .4	300	85	19	363	..	5—7	486	..
6	76	..	25—.9	301	..	20	364	..	8	487	..
7, 8	77	..	30	302	..	21	370	..	9, 10	501	95
9, 10	78	..	31, .2	303	..	22—.4	371	..	11—.3	487	93
11—.3	82	53	33—.7	304	..	25	372	..	14, .5	488	..
14—.9	83	..	38—40	305	..	26	368	..	16—.8	502	96
20—.4	84	..	41—.3	306	..	27, .8	378	..	19	503	..
25—35	85	..	44—.6	307	..	29	379	..	20	504	..

BLESSED ARE THEY THAT HAVE NOT SEEN, AND YET HAVE BELIEVED.—John xx. 29.

IF YE KNOW THESE THINGS, HAPPY ARE YE IF YE DO THEM.—John xiii. 17.

LORD, INCREASE OUR FAITH.—Luke xvii. 5.

MARK.

Verse.	Page.	Sect.	Verse.	Page.	Sect.	Verse.	Page.	Sect.	Verse.	Page.	Sect.
I.			**IV. (continued).**			**VII. (continued).**			**X. (continued).**		
1—3	49	7	33, .4	249	32	25, .6	14	45	34	236	77
4	50	..	35	264	34	27—.9	15	..	35—.8	237	..
5	52	..	36	265	..	30	16	..	39—42	238	..
6	51	..	37—.9	266	..	31—.3	24	46	43—.5	239	..
7, 8	54	..	40, .1	267	..	34—.7	25	..	46	242	79
9	58	8							47—51	243	..
10, .1	59	..	**V.**			**VIII.**			52	244	..
12, .3	63	9	1—5	269	35	1—5	26	46			
14	107	16	6—8	270	..	6—9	27	..	**XI.**		
15—.7	108	..	9—13	271	..	10, .1	28	47	1, 2	260	82
18—20	109	..	14—.6	272	..	12	30	..	3	261	..
21—.4	110	17	17—20	273	..	13	31	48	4—7	262	..
25—.8	111	..	21	274	..	14—.6	32	..	8	263	..
29—34	112	..	22, .3	279	36	17—.21	33	..	9, 10	264	..
35—.8	114	18	24—.8	280	..	22—.6	34	49	11	265	..
39	115	..	29—33	281	..	27	35	50	12—.4	275	83
40	159	21	34—.6	282	..	28, .9	36	..	15	276	..
41—.4	160	..	37—.9	283	..	30	39	..	16	277	..
45	161	..	40—.3	284	..	31	40	..	17—.9	278	..
						32, .3	41	..	20—.2	281	84
II.			**VI.**			34—.6	42	..	23—.7	282	..
1—3	164	22	1, 2	286	37	37, .8	43	..	28—30	283	..
4—7	165	..	3, 4	287	..				31—.3	284	..
8—12	166	..	5, 6	288	..	**IX.**					
13	167	..	7	294	39	1	44	50	**XII.**		
14	168	..	8, 9	296	..	2	51	51	1	266	81
15—.7	168	..	10	297	..	3, 4	53	..	2, 3	287	..
18—22	169	..	11	298	..	5	54	..	4—6	288	..
23—.6	188	24	12, .3	303	..	6, 7	55	..	7—9	289	..
27, .8	190	..	14	304	40	8	56	..	10, .1	290	..
			15—.7	305	..	9—12	57	..	12	291	..
III.			18—22	306	..	13—.7	58	..	13	295	..
1, 2	195	25	23—.6	307	..	18, .9	59	..	14—.5	296	..
3, 4	196	..	27—.9	308	..	20—.5	60	..	16, .7	297	..
5, 6	197	..	30	309	..	26—.9	61	..	18, .9	300	85
7, 8	200	26	31—.4	310	..	30	70	52	20—.4	301	..
9—12	201	..	35	311	..	31, .2	71	..	25	302	..
13	205	27	36—.8	312	..	33	72	..	26, .7	303	..
14—.7	206	..	39—41	313	..	34, .5	74	..	28—.9	304	..
18, .9	207	..	42—.4	314	..	36—.8	75	..	30—.3	305	..
19	233	30	45	317	41	39—42	76	..	34	306	..
20, .1	233	..	40, .7	318	..	43—.6	77	..	35—.7	307	..
22—.6	235	31	48—50	319	..	47—50	78	..	38—41	308	..
27, .8	236	..	51, .2	321	..				42—.4	309	..
29, 30	237	..	53—.6	322	42	**X.**					
31—.5	240	..				1	209	71	**XIII.**		
			VOL. II.			2—4	218	74	1	323	86
IV.			**VII.**			5—9	219	..	2—5	324	..
1	242	32	1—4	4	44	10—.3	220	..	6—8	325	..
2—4	243	..	5	5	..	14, .5	221	..	9	326	..
5—9	244	..	6—8	7	..	16	222	..	10, .1	327	..
10, 1	253	33	9	5	..	17	223	75	12, .3	328	..
12—.5	254	..	10, .1	6	..	18, .9	224	..	14	331	..
16	255	..	12, .3	7	..	20, .1	225	..	15—.9	332	..
17	255	..	14—.7	8	..	22—.4	226	..	20	333	..
18, .9	256	..	18—20	9	..	25—.7	227	..	21	334	..
20	257	..	21, .2	10	..	28, .9	228	..	22, .3	335	..
21, .2	258	..	23	11	..	30	229	..	24	336	..
23—.5	259	..	24	13	45	31	230	..	25	337	..
26—.9	247	32				32, .3	235	77	26, .7	338	..
30—2	248	..									

THE SAME LORD OVER ALL IS RICH UNTO ALL THAT CALL UPON HIM.—Rom. x. 12.

ONLY LET YOUR CONVERSATION BE AS IT BECOMETH THE GOSPEL OF CHRIST.—Phil. i. 27.

BE NOT AFRAID, ONLY BELIEVE.—Mark v. 36.

INDEX TO THE GOSPELS.

XIII. (continued).			XIV. (continued).			XIV. (continued).			XV. (continued).		
Verse.	Page.	Sect.	Verse.	Page.	Sect.	Verse.	Page.	Sect.	Verse.	Page.	Sect.
28, .9	339	86	22	368	87	70, .1	432	89	38	470	92
30, .1	340	..	23, .4	378	..	72	433	..	39	471	..
32, .3	341	..	25	379	..	XV.			40, .1	472	..
34—.7	342	..	26	405	..				42, .3	474	..
			27—31	406	..	1	434	89	44, .5	475	..
			32	412	88	2	445	90	46	476	..
XIV.			33, .4	413	..	3—5	446	..	47	477	..
			35, .6	414	..	6, 7	449	..			
1	355	86	37 –.9	415	..	8—10	450	..	XVI.		
2	356	..	40—.2	416	..	11, .2	451	..			
3	253	81	43	417	..	13, .4	452	..	1, 2	484	93
4	254	..	44, .5	418	..	15	453	..	3, 4	485	..
5, 6	255	..	46, .7	419	..	16, .7	455	91	5—7	486	..
7, 8	256	..	48—50	421	..	18—21	456	..	8	487	..
9	257	..	51, .2	422	..	22	458	..	9	491	..
10	356	86	53	425	89	23	459	..	10, .1	492	..
11	357	..	54	426	..	24, .5	461	..	12	493	94
12, .3	362	87	55—.8	427	..	26—.8	462	..	13	497	95
14—.6	363	..	59—61	428	..	29—32	463	..	14	500	..
17	364	..	62—.4	429	..	33, .4	466	..	15, .6	515	98
18	370	..	65—.7	430	..	35, .6	467	..	17—.9	516	..
19—21	371	..	68, .9	431	..	37	468	..	20	518	100

LUKE.

I.			III. (continued).			V. (continued).			VIII. (continued).		
1—3	1	1	9—14	53	7	22—.5	166	22	4	242	32
4, 5	2	..	15—.7	54	..	26, .7	167	..	5	243	..
6—11	3	..	18—20	55	..	28—32	168	..	6—8	244	..
12—.7	4	..	21, .2	59	8	33—.9	169	..	9, 10	253	33
18—20	5	..	23	60	..				11, .2	254	..
21—.5	6	..	23—36	23	4	VI.			13	255	..
26—31	9	2	37, .8	24	..	1—4	188	24	14	256	..
32—.8	10	..				5	190	..	15	257	..
39—49	11	..	IV.			6, 7	195	25	16, .7	258	..
50—.5	12	..				8, 9	196	..	18	259	..
56	14	..	1, 2	63	9	10, .1	197	..	19—21	262	..
57—.9	15	3	3, 4	64	..	12	205	27	22	265	34
60—.8	16	..	5	65	..	13, .4	206	..	23, .4	266	..
69—75	17	..	6—8	66	..	15—22	207	..	25	267	..
76—.9	18	..	9	64	..	23—34	208	..	26, .7	269	35
80	19	..	10—.2	65	..	35—40	209	..	28, .9	270	..
			13	66	..	41—.9	210	..	30—.2	271	..
II.			14—.8	102	15				33—.6	272	..
			19	103	..	VII.			37—.9	273	..
1—4	19	4	20—.7	104	..	1 –6	218	28	40	274	..
5—10	20	..	28—30	105	..	7 –9	219	..	41	279	36
11—.5	21	..	31	107	16	10	220	..	42—.4	280	..
16—21	22	..	32—.4	110	17	11—.3	221	29	45—.7	281	..
22—.6	24	..	35—.7	111	..	14—.6	222	..	48—50	282	..
27—33	25	..	38—41	112	..	17—.9	222	..	51, .2	283	..
34, .5	26	..	42	114	18	20—.3	223	..	53—.6	284	..
36—.8	27	..	43, .4	115	..	24—.7	224	..			
39	35	5				28—30	225	..			
40—.3	40	6	V.			31—.5	226	..	IX.		
44—.9	41	..				36	229	..	1	294	39
50—.2	42	..	1—3	153	20	37—.9	230	..	2	295	..
			4—8	154	..	40—.7	231	..	3	296	..
III.			9—11	155	..	48—50	232	..	4	297	..
			12	159	21				5	298	..
1, 2	49	7	13, .4	160	..	VIII.			6	303	..
3	50	..	15, .6	161	..				7	304	40
4—6	51	..	17, .8	164	22	1, 2	232	30	8, 9	305	..
7, 8	52	..	19—21	165	..	3	233	..			

HERE HAVE WE NO CONTINUING CITY.—Heb. xiii. 14.

INDEX TO THE GOSPELS.

Verse	Page	Sect.	Verse	Page	Sect.	Verse	Page	Sect.	Verse	Page	Sect.
IX. (continued).			**XIII.**			**XIX.**			**XXII. (continued).**		
10	309	40	1—5	173	64	1	242	79	20	378	87
11	310	..	6—9	174	..	2—8	246	..	21, 2	369	..
12	311	..	10—.5	175	65	9—11	247	80	23	371	..
13	312	..	16—21	176	..	12—.5	248	..	24—.8	375	..
14—.6	313	..	22—.5	177	66	16—22	249	..	29—33	376	..
17	314	..	26—32	178	..	23—.7	250	..	34—.8	377	..
			33—.5	179	..	28	252	81	39	405	..
VOL. II.						29, 30	260	82	40, 1	413	88
			XIV.			31	261	..	42—.4	414	..
IX. (continued).			1—6	181	67	32—.5	262	..	45, 6	416	..
18	35	50	7—14	182	..	36—40	263	..	47	417	..
19, 20	36	..	15—20	183	..	41—.3	264	..	48—50	419	..
21	39	..	21—.7	184	..	44	265	..	51	420	..
22	40	..	28—34	185	..	45	276	83	52, .3	421	..
23—.5	42	..	35	186	..	46—.8	278	..	54	425	89
26	43	..							55	427	..
27	44	..	**XV.**			**XX.**			56	430	..
28	51	51	1	188	68	1	282	84	57, .8	431	..
29	52	..	2—7	189	..	2—4	283	..	59	432	..
30	53	..	8—12	190	..	5—8	284	..	60—.2	433	..
31—.3	54	..	13—.5	191	..	9	286	..	63	429	..
34, .5	55	..	16—20	192	..	10	287	..	64, .5	430	..
36	56	..	21—.4	193	..	11—.3	288	..	66—71	434	..
37	57	..	25—31	194	..	14—.6	289	..			
38	58	..	32	195	..	17, .8	290	..	**XXIII.**		
39—41	59	..				19	291	..	1	435	89
42	60	..				20	295	..	2, 3	445	90
43—.5	71	52	**XVI.**			21—.3	296	..	4, 5	446	..
46	72	..	1—5	196	69	24—.6	297	..	6—8	447	..
47	74	..	6—10	197	..	27, .8	300	85	9—12	448	..
48, .9	75	..	11—.5	198	..	29—34	301	..	13—.7	449	..
50	76	..	16—.9	199	..	35, .6	302	..	18—20	451	..
51—.3	135	59	20—.3	200	..	37, .8	303	..	21—.3	452	..
54—60	136	..	24—.8	201	..	39, 40	304	..	24, .5	453	..
61, .2	137	..	29—31	202	..	41—.4	307	..	26	456	91
						45—.7	308	..	27—.9	457	..
X.									30—.3	458	..
1—6	141	60	**XVII.**			**XXI.**			34	459	..
7—15	142	..	1—4	206	70	1	308	85	35	463	..
16—.9	143	..	5—9	207	..	2—4	309	..	36—40	464	..
20—.2	144	..	10—.6	208	..	5	323	86	41—.3	465	..
23—.8	145	..	17—.9	209	..	6—8	324	..	44, .5	466	..
29—33	146	..	20	210	72	9, 10	325	..	46	468	..
34—.7	147	..	21—.5	211	..	11, .2	326	..	47	471	92
38, .9	149	61	26—34	212	..	13	327	..	48, .9	472	..
40—.2	150	..	35—.7	213	..	14—.7	328	..	50, .1	474	..
						18, .9	329	..	52	475	..
XI.						20	331	..	53	476	..
1, 2	151	62	**XVIII.**			21—.3	332	..	54—.6	477	..
3—13	152	..	1, 2	214	73	24	334	..			
14—23	153	..	3—8	215	..	25, .6	337	..	**XXIV.**		
24—32	154	..	9—11	216	..	27	338	..	1—6	488	93
33—.8	155	..	12—.4	217	..	28—31	339	..	7—11	489	..
39—45	156	..	15	220	74	32—.5	340	..	12	490	..
46—54	157	..	16, .7	221	..	36	341	..	13—.5	493	94
			18	223	75	37, .8	357	..	16—25	494	..
XII.			19, 20	224	..				26—.8	495	..
1—3	163	63	21, .2	225	..	**XXII.**			29—32	496	..
4—15	164	..	23, .4	226	..	1	355	86	33—.5	497	95
16—27	165	..	25—.7	227	..	2—4	356	..	36—41	498	..
28—36	166	..	28, .9	228	..	5, 6	357	..	42, .3	499	..
37—42	167	..	30	229	..	7—10	362	87	44—.7	512	98
43—.7	168	..	31—.2	235	77	11—.3	363	..	48, .9	513	..
48—52	169	..	33, .4	236	..	14—.8	364	..	50	515	..
53—.9	170	..	35—43	240	78	19	369	..	51	516	..
									52, .3	517	99

LET US . . . FOLLOW AFTER THE THINGS WHICH MAKE FOR PEACE, AND THINGS WHEREWITH ONE MAY EDIFY ANOTHER.—Rom. xiv. 19.

THY KINGDOM COME:

JOHN.

I.			VI. (continued).			XI. (continued).			XVII. (continued).		
Verse.	Page.	Sect.	Verse.	Page.	Sect.	Verse.	Page.	Sect.	Verse.	Page.	Sect.
1—5	46	7	32—.6	328	43	55,.6	252	81	14—.9	402	87
6—13	47	..	37—40	329	..	5"	253	..	20—.2	403	..
14—.8	48	..	41—.5	330	..	XII.			23—.6	404	..
19—25	68	10	46—53	331	..	1—3	253	81	XVIII.		
26—30	69	..	54—61	332	..	4	254	..	1	405	87
31—.8	70	..	62—.5	333	..	5—7	255	..	2—4	417	88
39—42	71	..	66—71	334	..	8	256	..	5—9	418	..
43—.8	72	..				9—11	257	..	10	419	..
49—51	73	..	VOL. II.			12,.3	259	82	11	420	..
II.			VII.			14—.6	262	..	12—.6	425	89
1—4	76	11	1	70	52	17,.8	263	..	17	430	..
5—9	77	..	2—7	87	54	19—21	266	..	18	431	..
10—.2	78	..	8,9	88	..	22—.8	267	..	19—24	426	..
13—.8	81	12	10—.7	91	55	29—34	268	..	25	431	..
19—25	82	..	18—20	92	..	35,.6	260	..	26	432	..
			21—.7	93	..	37,.8	309	85	27	433	..
III.			28—34	94	..	39—42	310	..	28	435	..
1—5	83	12	35—.8	95	..	43—.7	311	..	29—31	440	90
6—11	84	..	39—48	96	..	48—50	312	..	32—36	441	..
12—.5	85	..	49—53	97	..	XIII.			37—.9	442	..
16—.9	86	..				1—3	365	87	40	443	..
20,21	87	..	VIII.			4—10	366	..	XIX.		
22—.9	89	13	2—11	97	55	11—.7	367	..	1—7	443	00
30—.3	90	..	12—.4	99	..	18—21	370	..	8—12	444	..
34—.6	91	..	15—22	101	..	22—.4	371	..	13,.4	445	..
IV.			23—.7	102	..	25—30	372	..	15	418	..
1—3	91	13	28—32	103	..	31—.3	373	..	16	453	..
4—12	92	..	33—.9	104	..	34—.7	374	..	17	458	91
13—21	93	..	40—.3	105	..	38	375	..	18	459	..
22—.6	94	..	44—50	106	..	XIV.			19—21	460	..
27—37	95	..	51—.8	107	..	1—3	380	87	22—.4	461	..
38—42	96	..	59	108	..	4—9	381	..	25,.6	465	..
43—.9	100	14	IX.			10—.4	382	..	27	466	..
50—.4	101	..	1—6	109	55	15—.9	383	..	28,.9	467	..
V.			7—16	110	..	20—.5	384	..	30	468	..
1—8	175	23	17—25	111	..	26—.9	385	..	31—.6	473	92
9—17	176	..	26—33	112	..	30,.1	386	..	37,.8	474	..
18—24	177	..	34—41	113	..				39	475	..
25—30	178	..	X.			XV.			40—.2	476	..
31—.8	179	..	1—6	114	55	1—3	387	87	XX.		
39—47	180	..	7—12	115	..	4—11	388	..	1,2	489	93
VI.			13—.7	116	..	12—.6	389	..	3—11	490	..
1,2	310	40	18—21	117	..	17—22	390	..	12—.7	491	..
3—7	311	..	22,.3	120	56	23—.7	391	..	18	492	..
8,9	312	..	24—.8	121	..	XVI.			19,20	498	95
10,.1	313	..	29—34	122	..	1—3	392	87	21—.3	499	..
12,.3	314	..	35—.9	123	..	4—10	393	..	24—.6	500	..
14,.5	317	..	40—.2	125	57	11—.3	394	..	27—.9	501	..
16,.7	318	41	XI.			14—21	395	..	30,.1	518	100
18,.9	319	..	1—4	127	58	22—.8	396	..	XXI.		
20	320	..	5—16	128	..	29—33	397	..	1,2	505	97
21	321	..	17—26	129	..	XVII.			3—7	506	..
22—.4	322	42	27—37	130	..	1,2	398	87	8—15	507	..
25,.6	325	43	38—43	131	..	3—6	399	..	16,.7	508	..
27	326	..	44—.9	132	..	7—10	400	..	18—20	509	..
28—31	327	..	50—.4	133	..	11—.3	401	..	21—.4	510	..
									25	518	100

ANALYTICAL AND HISTORICAL TABLE.

PART I. MATTHEW I., II. LUKE I., II., III. 23—38.

ARRANGED IN THE ORDER OF TIME.

Comprehending the space of 31 years; viz.—From the prediction of the birth of John the Baptist, B.C. 6, to the commencement of his public ministry, A.D. 26.*

SECTION I.—THE BIRTH OF JOHN FORETOLD. Luke i. 1—25. p. 1—8.

No. 1. *The Preface according to Luke. ch. i. 1—4. p. 1.*

	MATT.	MARK.	LUKE.	JOHN.	ILLUSTRATIONS.
Luke's preface: eye-witnesses, Theophilus .	—	—	1. 1-4	—	Ac. 1. 1; 10. 39-41.

John's birth foretold. ver. 5—23. Jerusalem. p. 2—6.

	MATT.	MARK.	LUKE.	JOHN.	ILLUSTRATIONS.
Zacharias ('Course of Abia') and Elisabeth, ('Daughter of Aaron') . . .			1. 5-7		1 Ch. 24. 7, 10, .9. Ex.28; Lev.t.9; Nu.18.
Zacharias executes priest's office in temple .	—	—	— 8-10	—	Ex. 28. 1; 1 Ki. 6.
An angel appears at the altar of incense .	—	—	— 11, .2	—	Ex. 30. 1-10; Rev. 8. 3.
And predicts the birth of John . . .	—	—	— 13, .4	—	
His charac. and mini. [*Elias*, 1 Ki. 17, &c.]	—	—	— 15-.7	—	Mal. 3. 1; 4. 5, 6.
Zacharias struck dumb for unbelief . .	—	—	— 18-23	—	Gabriel, Dn. 8. 16.

The conception of John the Baptist. ver. 24, .5. Hill country of Judæa. p. 6.

	MATT.	MARK.	LUKE.	JOHN.	ILLUSTRATIONS.
Elisabeth humbled because of her husband's case while given occasion to rejoice . .			1. 24, .5		Ver. 13—20, p. 4, 5.

SECT. II.—THE BIRTH OF JESUS FORETOLD. Matt. i. 18—25. Luke i. 26—56. p. 9—15.

No. 2. *The birth of Jesus foretold. Luke i. 26—38. At Nazareth. p. 9, 10.*

	MATT.	MARK.	LUKE.	JOHN.	ILLUSTRATIONS.
Mary saluted by an angel . . .			1. 26-.9		Ver. 11, .2, p. 3, 4.
The birth of Jesus foretold. David .	—	—	— 30-.3	—	2 Sa. 7. 11, .2.
'With God nothing shall be impossible' .	[19. 20]	—	— 34-.7	—	Comp.ver.18; Je. 32. 17.
'Be it unto me according to thy word' .	—	—	— 38	—	

Mary visits Elisabeth. ch. i. 39—55. Hill country of Judæa. p. 11, .2.

	MATT.	MARK.	LUKE.	JOHN.	ILLUSTRATIONS.
Mary salutes Elisabeth . . .			1. 39, 40		Jos. 21. 11.
Elisabeth filled with the Holy Ghost .	—	—	— 41	—	Ver. 67-79, p. 16-.8.
'Blessed .. thou among women' . .	—	—	— 42-.5	—	[Ver. 28] ch. 11. 27, .8.
Song of Mary, 'My soul doth magnify,' &c.	—	—	— 46-55	—	1 Sa. 2. 1-10.

Mary returns home, and is taken into the house of Joseph as his espoused wife. Matt. i. 18—25. Luke i. 56. At Nazareth. p. 13, .4.

	MATT.	MARK.	LUKE.	JOHN.	ILLUSTRATIONS.
Case of Mary made known to Joseph .	1. 18-20		[1. 31-.7]	—	De. 24. 1, 2.
The names, 'Jesus' and 'Immanuel' .	— 21-.3	—	—	—	Is. 7. 14.
Joseph obedient to the vision . .	— 24, .5	—	—	—	Job 23. 14-.7.
Mary returns home to Nazareth . .	—	—	— 56	—	Ver. 26, 39, p. 9, 11.

SECT. III.—JOHN THE BAPTIST BORN AND BROUGHT UP. Luke i. 57—80. p. 15—.9.

No. 3. *The birth, &c., of John the Baptist. Luke i. 57—79. Hill country of Judæa. p. 15—.8.*

	MATT.	MARK.	LUKE.	JOHN.	ILLUSTRATIONS.
John Baptist born. Elisab.'s cousins rejoice			1. 57, .8	—	See ver. 14, p. 4.
John named and circumcised . .	—	—	— 59-66	—	Ge. 17. 12.
ZACHARIAS' SONG, ver. 67-79:—					
'Blessed be the Lord God of Israel' . .	—	—	— 67-71	—	— 35. 9-13.
'To remember his holy covenant' . .	—	—	— 72	—	— 22. 16-.8.
'The oath which he sware' . . .	—	—	— 73-.5	—	Ps. 105. 8-10.
John to 'go bef. the fa. of the Lord,'[ver.17]	—	—	— 76	—	Mt. 3. 11, .2; 11. 12-.5.
'To give knowledge of salvation,' &c. .	—	—	— 77-.9	[1. 29-36.]	
The residue of John's private history, p. 19 .	—	—	— 80	—	Lev. 8. 33-.5.

* *See* the Table of Supposed Chronology of the Gospel History, p. xxvi.

TEACH ME, O LORD, THE WAY OF THY STATUTES.—Psa. cxix. 33.

ANALYTICAL AND HISTORICAL TABLE.

	MATT.	MARK.	LUKE.	JOHN.	ILLUSTRATIONS
1. Distrust—'Command these,' &c.	4. 3, 4	1.—	4. 3, 4		De. 8. 3.
2. Presumption—'Cast thyself,' &c. (*Temple*)	—5-7		—9-12		Ps. 91. 11, .2; De. 6. 16.
3. Covetousness—'All these,' &c. (*N. of Jeric.*)	—8-10		—5-8		De. 10. 12, .3, 20.
The devil departs	—11		—13		Lu. 4. 33—b [22. 43, .4].
Angels minister to Jesus.	—11	—13			Ps. 91. 11.

SECTION X.—JOHN'S TESTIMONY TO JESUS. John i. 19—51. p. 68—76.

No. 10. *Deputies are sent by the council of the Jews to question John the Baptist; John renders his second testimony to the Messiah or Christ. John i. 19—28. Bethabara, or Bethany, opposite Scythopolis. p. 68.*

	MATT.	MARK.	LUKE.	JOHN.	ILLUSTRATIONS
John answers the priests and Levites				1. 19-24	Mal. 3. 1.
Why he baptized				—25-.9	

Particulars of two days spent at Bethabara; during which John renders a double testimony to Jesus. John i. 29—36. Ibid. p. 69, 70.

	MATT.	MARK.	LUKE.	JOHN.	ILLUSTRATIONS
John points to Jesus as 'the Lamb of God'.				1. 29	Ex.12; La.16.21,.2; Re.5
Refers to his former testimony concer. Jesus				—30, .1	Mt. 3. 11, .2; Lu. 3. 16, .7.
Bears record of descent of the Spirit on Jesus				—32-.4	Mt. 3. 16; Mk. 1. 10;
Again points to Jesus as the Lamb of God				—35, .6	(Lu. 3. 22.

Andrew and Simon follow Jesus. ver. 37—42. Ibid. p. 70, .1.

	MATT.	MARK.	LUKE.	JOHN.	ILLUSTRATIONS
Andrew & another follow Jesus, 'Come & see'				1. 37-.9	
Andrew brings his brother Simon (Cephas).	[16.17,.8]	——		—40-.2	1 Pe. 2. 4-8.

The next day Jesus returns into Galilee. Jesus findeth Philip; Philip bringeth Nathanael to Jesus; Jesus' testimony to Nathanael. ver. 43—51. Ibid. p. 72, .3.

	MATT.	MARK.	LUKE.	JOHN.	ILLUSTRATIONS
Jesus findeth Philip (Lover of the horse)				1. 43, .4	Rev. 19. 11-.6.
Philip findeth Nathanael: 'Come and see'				—45, .6	Rev. 6. 1, 3, 5, 7.
Jesus' recognition of Nathanael				—47, .8	Ge. 32. 24-30.
Nathanael's confession, 'Thou art the Son'	[16. 16]			—49	Ps. 2.
Promise, to Nathanael, of the Apocalypse				—50, .1	Ge. 28. 11-22; Rev. 1; 4.

SECTION XI.—BEGINNING OF MIRACLES. WATER TURNED INTO WINE. John ii. 1—11, .2. Cana. p. 76—80.

No. 11. *Jesus is present at a marriage feast in Cana; he turns water into wine, which is the beginning of his miracles. He goes down to Capernaum.*

	MATT.	MARK.	LUKE.	JOHN.	ILLUSTRATIONS
Marriage in Cana of Galilee				2. 1	Is.62.5; Je.3.14; Hos.2.
Jesus & his disciples (see ch. 1. 37-47) invited				—2	(14-20); Eph. 5. 25-33.
Mary's request and Jesus' reply (ch. 7. 6)				—3, 4	Comp. Joe. 19. 26.
She bids the servant obey Jesus				—5	
The vessels filled with water		[7. 2-5]		—6, 7	2 Ki. 4. 1-7.
When drawn out is the best wine				—8-10	Is. 55. 1.
'The beginning of miracles,' &c.				—11	
Goes down to Capernaum		[4. 13]		—12	

SECTION XII.—JESUS AT THE FIRST PASSOVER. CLEANSES THE TEMPLE. CONVERSES WITH NICODEMUS. John ii. 13—iii. 21. p. 81—.8.

No. 12. *Jesus attends the passover at the commencement of his public ministry; he casts the buyers and sellers out of the temple. John ii. 13—22. Jerusalem. p. 81, .2.*

	MATT.	MARK.	LUKE.	JOHN.	ILLUSTRATIONS
Jesus goes up to Jerusalem				2. 13	1 Co. 5. 7, 8.
Cleanses the temple. 'Make not,' &c.	[21. 12, .3	11. 15-.7	19. 45, .6]	—14-.7	Mal. 3. 1; Ps. 69. 9.
A sign asked, predicts his resurrection.	[26. 61	14. 58, .9	24. 6, 9]	—18-22	Ho. 6. 2.

Miracles wrought during the passover. Many believe upon Jesus. ver. 23—.5. p. 82.

	MATT.	MARK.	LUKE.	JOHN.	ILLUSTRATIONS
Many believe his miracles				2. 23	
Jesus knew the Jews were not to be trusted.				—24, .5	Je. 3. 11.

Nicodemus visits Jesus by night. John iii. 1—21. p. 83—.7.

	MATT.	MARK.	LUKE.	JOHN.	ILLUSTRATIONS
Nicodemus comes to Jesus. 'Rabbi,' &c.				3. 1, 2	[Jno. 7. 50, .1.]
Necessity of the new birth				—3	[Jno. 1. 13] 1 Pe. 1. 23.
Nicodemus asks, 'How can a man be,' &c.				—4	
Jesus' reply, must 'be born of water,' &c.				—5-8	Eze.36.25—8; He.10.22.
Nicodemus asks, 'How can these things be?'				—9	[Jno. 6. 52-60.]
They were things Nicod. should have known				—10-.2	[Jno. 16. 28.]
The Son of man on earth and in heaven				—13	Pr. 30. 4.
The saving truth, 'As Moses lifted,' &c.				—14, .5	Nu. 21. 7-9.
'God so loved the world,' &c.		[9. 5, 6]		—16	[Jno. 6. 47; Ac. 16. 31]
The Son was sent not to condemn.				—17	(Rom. 8. 32.
Rejection of the light aggravates guilt .				—18, .9	Jno. 15. 24.
Of hating and loving the light				—20, .1	Eph. 5. 8-17.

SECTION XIII.—JOHN'S LAST TESTIMONY. WOMAN OF SAMARIA. John iii. 22—iv. 42. Ænon and Sychar. p. 89—99.

No. 13. *Jesus' disciples begin to baptize; John also continues baptizing. John iii. 22—.4. Ænon, near to Salim. p. 89.*

	MATT.	MARK.	LUKE.	JOHN.	ILLUSTRATIONS
Jesus' disciples baptize				3. 22.	[Jno. 4. 1, 2.]
John continues to baptize				—23, .4.	Mt. 3. 5, 6; Mk. 1, 5.

QUICKEN ME, O LORD, FOR THY NAME'S SAKE.—Psalm cxliii. 11

ANALYTICAL AND HISTORICAL TABLE.

A dispute having arisen between the Jews and the disciples of John, concerning purification, John renders the last, and the most explicit, of his testimonies to Jesus Christ. John iii. 25—36. Ænon, near to Salim. p. 89—91.

	MATT.	MARK.	LUKE.	JOHN.	ILLUSTRATIONS.
The Jews seek to provoke John to envy	—	—	—	3. 25, .6	[Jno. 1. 7, 15, 27-34.]
John, the friend of the Bridegroom	—	—	—	— 27-.9	Mal. 3. 1.
—— bears increased testimony to Jesus	—	—	—	— 30..6	1 Co. 15. 47.

Jesus departs into Galilee: and, on his way, abides two days at Sychar in Samaria, John not being yet cast into prison. John iv. 1—42. p. 91—.6.

Jesus leaves Judæa for Galilee	—	—	4. 1-3	—	1 Ki.16.23,.4;2Ki.17.24-.6.
Comes to Jacob's well	—	—	—	— 4-6	Ge. 33.18,.9; Josh.24.32.
Converses with a woman of Samaria	—	—	—	— 7-9	
Concerning 'the living water'	—	—	—	— 10-.5	Is. 44. 3.
Intimates his knowledge of her character, &c.	—	—	—	— 16..9	[Jno. i. 48.] (2. 8.
Shews how the Father is to be worshipped	—	—	—	— 20,-4	Gerizim, Dɔ.27.12; 1 Ti.
Messias—' I that speak unto thee am He'	—	—	—	— 25,.6	[Jno. 9. 37] De. 18. 18.
The disciples return to Jesus	—	—	—	— 27	
'Come see,' &c. ' Is not this the Christ ?'	—	—	—	— 28-30	De. 18. 15.
Jesus' meat—'the harvest'—sowing & reaping	—	—	—	— 31-8	[Jno. vi. 38] Ps. 40. 8.
Jesus . . . 'the Saviour of the world'	—	—	—	— 39-42	1 Jno. 4. 14; Is. 45. 22-.5.

SECTION XIV.—HEALING OF THE NOBLEMAN'S SON. John iv. 43—54. p. 100, ..1.

No. 14. *From Sychar Jesus proceeds to Galilee; John being now cast into prison. Jesus again visits Cana. John iv. 43—.6. p. 100.*

Jesus leaves Sychar, and goes into Galilee	—	—	—	4. 43	
A prophet hath no honour in his own country	[13. 57	—	4. 24]	— 44	
The Galilæans receive him	—	—	[9. 40]	— 45, .6	Jno. 2. 1; 2. 23.

Jesus heals a nobleman's son lying sick at Capernaum. John iv. 46—54. Cana. p. 100, ..1.

Requested to heal a nobleman's son	[8. 5, 6	—	7. 2-5]	4. 47	
Jesus gives a token of his power	[— 7-13	—	— 6-9]	— 48-50	
It is found as Jesus had said—who thus manifests his Omniscience, Omnipotence, and Omnipresence	—	—	[— 10]	— 51-.4	

SECTION XV.—JESUS PREACHES; IS REJECTED OF HIS TOWNSMEN. Luke iv. 14—30. At Nazareth. p. 102—..6.

No. 15. *Jesus visits Nazareth, and preaches there in the synagogue on the sabbath day, and is threatened. Luke iv. 14—30. p. 102—..5.*

Jesus in the power of the Spirit	—	—	4. 14	—	Lu. 3 22; Is. 11. 2; 42. 1.
There goes forth a fame of him, &c.	[4. 24	1. 28]	— 14	—	Ge. 12. 2.
Jesus in the synagogue reads Is. lxi. 1—3	[13. 54	6. 1, 2]	— 15-21	[18. 20]	
His townsmen expect much for themselves	—	—	— 22, .3	—	[Lu. 2. 47.]
No prophet is accepted in his own country	[13. 57	— 4]	— 24	[4. 44]	
Jesus speaks of Elias and Eliseus	—	—	— 25-.7	—	1 Ki. 17; 2 Ki. 5. 1-5, 14.
The hearers filled with wrath	—	—	— 28	—	[Lu. 6. 11; Jno. 8. 37]
They seek to kill him	—	—	— 29	[11. 53]	Ps. 37. 14, 32, .3.
He passes through the midst of them	—	—	— 30	[8. 59 10. 39]	

SECTION XVI.—JESUS MAKES CHOICE OF CAPERNAUM. SECOND CALL OF JESUS' FIRST DISCIPLES. Matt. iv. 12—22. Mark i. 14—20. Luke iv. 31. p. 107—..9.

No. 16. *Jesus makes choice of Capernaum as his place of abode, and prepares to enter there on his public ministry. Matt. iv. 12—.7. Mk. i. 14,.5. Lu. iv. 31. p. 107,..8.*

Jesus dwells at Capernaum	4. 12, .3	1. 14	4. 31	—	(Jos. 19. 32-.9.
On the sea coast in the borders of Zabulon and Nephthalim	— 13	—	—	—	Zeb.Jos.19.10-.6; Neph. Is. 9. 1, 2.
In fulfilment of prophecy	— 14-.6	—	—	—	[Mt. 3. 2, 8.]
Proclaims the kingdom, & calls to repentance	— 17	— 14, .5	—	—	

The four disciples, Simon and Andrew, James and John, are called by Jesus. Matt. iv. 18— 22. Mark i. 16—20. Sea of Galilee. p. 108, ..9.

Jesus walks by the sea of Galilee	4. 18	1. 16	[5. 1	21. 1]	[Mt. 13. 1, p. 242.]
Calls Simon and Andrew, the second time	— 19-20	— 16-.8	[—1-11	1. 35-42]	
And two sons of Zebedee	— 21, .2	— 19, 20	—	—	Lu.9.54-.6; Mk.10.35-45.

SECTION XVII.—A SABBATH IN CAPERNAUM. A DEMONIAC, ETC., HEALED. Matt. viii. 14—.7. Mark i. 21—34. Luke iv. 31—41. p. 110—..3.

No. 17. *Jesus teaches for the first time in the synagogue of Capernaum on the sabbath day; the people are astonished at his manner of teaching; he casts out a devil. Mark i. 21—.8. Luke iv. 31—.7. p. 110, ..1.*

Jesus teaches with power in the synagogue	—	1. 21, .2	4. 31, .2	—	[Mt. 7. 28, .9; 13. 54.] [Lu. ver. 41]Jaa. 2. 19.
Forbids an unclean spirit to speak of him	—	— 23-.5	— 33-.5	—	[Mk. 5. 7, 8; 9. 25-7.]
Casts out the unclean spirit	—	— 25, .6	— 35	—	[Lu. 4. 14; Mt.4. 24.]
His fame spread abroad	—	— 27, .8	— 36, .7	—	

ANALYTICAL AND HISTORICAL TABLE.

The same day, Jesus heals Simon's mother-in-law. Matt. viii. 14, .5. Mark i. 29—31. Luke iv. 38, .9. *At Capernaum.* p. 112.

	MATT.	MARK.	LUKE.	JOHN	ILLUSTRATIONS.
Simon's mother-in-law sick of a fever	8. 14	1. 29, 30	4. 38		
Jesus touches her hand, and she is healed	— 15	— 31	— 39		[Mt. 9. 25.]

After sunset Jesus performs divers miracles of healing and dispossession. Matt. viii. 16, .7. Mark i. 32—.4. Luke iv. 40, .1. p. 112, ..3.

	MATT.	MARK.	LUKE.	JOHN	ILLUSTRATIONS.
At even he heals and dispossesses many	8. 16	1. 32..4	4. 40, .1	—	[Mt. 4. 24] 1 Pe. 2. 24.
Fulfilment of prophecy (Is. 53. 4)	— 17	—	—		[19. 36, .7 Mt. 2. 23; 4. 14.]

SECTION XVIII.—JESUS' FIRST GENERAL CIRCUIT OF GALILEE. Matt. iv. 23—.5. Mark i. 35—.9. Luke iv. 42—.4. p. 114—..8.

Early in the morning of the next day, that is, of the first day of the week, Jesus departs from Capernaum to a desert place to pray: his disciples follow him thither: attended by whom, he sets out on the first general circuit of Galilee, preaching the gospel of the kingdom, teaching, and working miracles of healing and dispossession everywhere.

No. 18. *See line from Capernaum going northward, westward, southward, eastward, and to the north of the lake of Galilee.*

	MATT.	MARK.	LUKE.	JOHN	ILLUSTRATIONS.
Jesus is early at secret prayer	[Mt. 6. 6]	1. 35	4. 42		Ps. 5. 3.
Simeon, &c., follow after and find him		— 36, .7			
His special mission was to preach		— 38			Is. 61. 1.
The people find and wish to detain him		[— 36, .7]	— 42	[4. 40]	(Comp. Mt. 8. 34, § 35,
He must preach the kingd. to other cities also		[— 38]	— 43		p. 272.)
First general circuit of Galilee	4. 23	— 39	— 44		
Performs sundry miracles	— 23				
His fame goes throughout Syria, &c.	— 24				See on Mk. 1. 27, § 17.
Is followed from many quarters	25	[3. 7-12	6. 17-.9]		

SECTION XIX.—SERMON ON THE MOUNT. Matthew v.—viii. 1. p. 119—..52.

No. 19. *When the circuit was drawing to an end, and the concourse of the people was greatest, Jesus teaches his disciples from a mountain in the neighbourhood of Capernaum.* Matt. v.—viii. 1.

	MATT.	MARK.	LUKE.	JOHN	ILLUSTRATIONS.
1. The Beatitudes	5. 3-12		[6. 20-.3]		Ps. 37. 11; Ge. 12. 1-3.
2. 'Salt of the earth,' 'Light of the world'	— 13-.6	[9. 50	8.16; 11.33]		Pr. 4. 18; Ph. 2. 15.
3. The law and prophets, Christ came to fulf.	— 17-20				Is. 42. 21; Rom. 3. 21.
4. 'Ye have heard,' 'But I say unto,' ve. 21—48					He. 4. 7-11.
Of Killing—'anger without cause'	— 21..6				Ex. 20. 13; 1 Jno. 3. 15.
„ Adultery and putting away	— 27-32				Ex.20.14; Job 31. 1; Mt.
„ Oaths or vows	— 33-.7				Nu. 30. 2. (18. 8, 9.
„ Retaliation—suing at the law	— 38-42				Ex. 21, 24.
Love your enemies	— 43, .4		[6. 27, .8]		Rom. 12. 14-20.
Be ye ... perfect ... as your Father in heaven	— 45-.8		[— 36..7]		Job 25. 3.
5. *How to honour our Father, &c.*, ch. 6. 1—18			[8. 17]		
'When thou doest alms'	6. 1-4				Mt. 25. 34; Lu. 14. 14.
'When thou prayest'	— 5, 6				Pr. 20. 6; Rom. 12. 8.
'Use not vain repetitions'	— 7, 8				Ps. 34. 15; Is. 65. 24.
'Our Father which art in heaven'	— 9-13		[11. ,2,&c.]		1 Ki. 18. 26-.9.
We must forgive, as we seek forgiveness	— 14, .5	[11. 25, .6]			Is. 66. 1; Rom. 8. 15.
'Moreover when ye fast,' &c.	— 16-8				Ja. 2. 13; Mt. 18. 35. Is. 58. 5; Job 2. 12.
6. *To have the first care for the spiritual life,* ver. 19—34					
To lay up treasure in heaven	— 19-21		[18. 24, .5]		Mt. 19. 21.
We must be single eyed	— 22..4		[11. 34-.6;16 13]		1 Ti. 6. 9, 17-.9; 1 Pe.1.4.
The Christian has God to care for him	— 25-30		[12. 22,&c.]		1 Jno. 2. 15. Ps. 104. 27, .8; 1 Ti. 6. 8.
Not to be like the Gentiles, 'Seek first,' &c.	— 31-.4	[10. 30	12. 31	6. 27]	Ps. 37. 25.
7. 'Judge not,' 'First cast out the beam'	7. 1-6	[11. 24	6. 37]		Rom.14.3,4,10; Jn.1.6,7.
8. 'Ask,' 'Seek,' 'Knock,' &c.	— 7-14		11. 9, 10]		Is. 55. 6; 58. 9; 65. 24.
'Beware of false prophets,' &c.	— 15-20		[6. 43-.5	15. 26]	Je. 23. 16.
9. 'Not every one that saith,' &c.	— 21-.3	[13. 27]			
10. Of building on the rock, and on the sand	— 24..7		[6. 47,.9	13. 17]	
His teaching is with authority	— 28, .9	[1. 22	4. 32	7. 46]	Tit. 2. 15.
Followed by multitudes	8. 1				

SECTION XX.*—THE MIRACULOUS DRAUGHT OF FISHES. Luke v. 1—11. p. 153—..8.

No. 20. *Jesus teaches the people from the lake of Gennesaret: Simon Peter and his partners having let down their nets at Jesus' command, enclose a great draught of fishes.*

	MATT.	MARK.	LUKE.	JOHN	ILLUSTRATIONS.
Jesus by the lake of Gennesaret			5. 1, 2		
— teaches the people out of a ship	[13. 1-9	4. 1-9]	— 3		
Bids Simon launch out into the deep, &c.			— 4, 5		
A miraculous draught of fishes			— 6, 7	[21. 13, .4]	
Simon Peter's confession			— 8-10		
Jesus' reply			— 10		
Jesus' first disciples forsake all & follow him	[4. 19, 20	1. 16-.8]	— 11	[1. 42]	

* Sections xx., xxi., form Lesson 21 in the Course Graduated for Simultaneous Instruction.

IS THERE INIQUITY IN MY TONGUE?—Job vi. 30.

xxiv

ANALYTICAL AND HISTORICAL TABLE.

SECTION XXI.—A LEPER HEALED, ETC. Matthew viii. 2—4. Mark i. 40—.5.
Luke v. 12—.6. Probably near Caorazin. p. 159—.62.

No. 21. *Jesus heals a leper. Matt. viii. 2—4. Mark i. 40—.4. Luke v. 12—.4. p. 159,.60.*

	MATT.	MARK.	LUKE.	JOHN.	ILLUSTRATIONS.
A leper beseeches Jesus to heal him	8. 2	1. 40	5. 12	—	Ja. 5. 11; 1 Pe. 3. 8.
Jesus is moved with compassion	—	— 41	—	—	Comp. Lu.5.12; Mt.9.29.
He heals the leper	— 3	— 42	— 13	—	
And charges him to tell no man [Mt.9.30; 17.9]	— 4	— 43,.4	— 14	—	
But to make an offering for a testimony	— 4	— 44	— 14	—	Le. 14. 3, 4, 10, .1.

To avoid the publicity occasioned by the preceding miracle, Jesus withdraws into the desert, and spends some time there in prayer to God. Mark i. 45. Luke v. 15, .6. p. 161.

The leper publishes the matter	—	1. 45	5. 15	—	Ecc. 3. 7.
Multitudes come to Jesus [Mt. 4. 25; Lu. 5. 1]	—	— 45	— 15	—	
Jesus withdraws to the wilderness to pray	—	[1. 35]	— 16	—	1 Ki. 18. 31-46.

SECTION XXII.—A MAN SICK OF THE PALSY HEALED. MATTHEW CALLED. SUPPER WITH LEVI. Matt. ix. 2—9. Mark ii. 1—22. Luke v. 17—39. Capernaum. p. 163—.70.

No. 22. *Jesus returns to Capernaum, where he heals a man sick of the palsy. Matt. ix. 2—8. Mark ii. 1—12. Luke v. 17—26. p. 163—..7.*

Jesus enters Capernaum after some days	—	2. 1	—	—	Lu. 8. 1; Is. 61. 1.
Many gath. together. Jesus preaches to them	—	— 2	—	—	[Mt. 3. 7.]
'Pharisees and doctors of the law sitting by'	—	—	5. 17	—	(10. 9.
Men bring one sick of the palsy	9. 2	— 3	— 18	—	De. 22. 8; Mt 10. 27; Ac.
And let him down through the tiling	—	— 4	— 19	—	Ps. 103. 13.
Jesus pron. the man's sins forg. [Lu. 7. 47-50]	— 2	— 5	— 20	—	Da. 9. 9; 1 Ti. 3. 16.
Jesus is thought guilty of blasphemy	— 3	— 6, 7	— 21	—	1 Ch. 28. 9; He. 4. 13;
He knows their thoughts [Mt. 12. 25; Lu. 6. 8]	— 4	— 8	— 22	[2. 25]	(Rev. 2. 23.
Proves his power to forgive by healing, &c.	— 5-7	— 9-12	— 23-.5	[10.37,.8]	
The people glorify God	— 8	— 12	— 26	—	

Jesus teaches the people again by the lake; he calls Levi, or Matthew, to be his disciple. Matt. ix. 9. Mark ii. 13, .4. Luke v. 27, .8. p. 167.

Jesus teaches the people by the sea side	[13. 1]	2. 13	[5. 1-3]	—	
Jesus calls Matthew (Levi) to follow him	9. 9	— 14	5. 27, .8	—	Pr. 27. 2.

Jesus is entertained in the house of Levi, where he makes answer to the Pharisees why he ate with publicans and sinners; and excuses his disciples for not observing fastings. Mark i. 15—22. Luke v. 29—39. p. 168, ..9.

Levi makes a great feast for Jesus	[9. 10]	2. 15	5. 29	—	
Why Jesus went among publicans & sinners	[—11,.3]	— 16, .7	— 30..2	—	Lu. 7. 34.
Why his disciples did not fast	[—14,.5]	— 18-20	— 33..5	—	
Parable of new cloth on an old garment	[— 16]	— 21	— 36	—	
—— of new wine in old bottles	[— 17]	— 22	— 37, .8	—	
—— of having drunk old wine	—	—	— 39	—	

SECTION XXIII.—JESUS, AT THE SECOND PASSOVER, HEALS A LAME MAN. ADVERTS TO THE PROOFS OF HIS MESSIAHSHIP. John ch. v. Jerusalem. p. 174—.87.

No. 23. *On the approach of the second passover Jesus goes up to Jerusalem; he heals a sick man at the pool of Bethesda on the sabbath day, for which supposed breach of the sabbath the Jews thenceforward go about to kill him. John v. 1—18. p. 174—..7.*

Jesus goes up to the feast	—	—	—	5. 1	Lu. 2. 41,.2; Jno. 2. 13;
At Bethesda, he heals an impotent man	—	—	—	— 2-9	Mt. 9. 6. (De. 16. 1.
The man blamed for carrying his bed	[12. 2	3. 4	13. 14]	— 10..3	Je. xvii. 21.
The Jews seek to kill Jesus	[12. 14		4. 28-30]	— 14..8	Ph. 2. 6.

The discourse of Jesus respecting his oneness with the Father, his life-giving power, and the proofs of his Messiahship. ver. 19—47. p. 177—.80.

JESUS DECLARES HIS ONENESS WITH THE FATHER. ver. 19—30.

He is—					
in working	1. 'The Wonderful'	—	—	5. 19	
in knowledge	2. 'Counsellor'	—	—	— 20	
power and honour	3. 'Mighty God'	—	—	— 21—.3	[Jno. 17. 2] 2 Co. 5. 10.
bestowing everlast. life	4. 'Everlast. Father'	—	—	— 24	1 Jno. 5. 11.
first resurrection and executing judgment	5. 'Prince of Peace'	—	—	— 25-.7	Da. 7. 13, .4.
general resurrection	—	—	—	— 28, .9	Da. 12. 1; 1 Th. 4. 16.
Jesus is one with the Father as to will	—	—	—	— 30	Ps. 40. 7, 8.

a Matthew records a feast or meal, ch. ix. 10—.7, § 36, pp. 277—..9, very similar to this, and which Mr. Greswell refers to a much later period in our Lord's ministry.

BLESSED IS HE THAT CONSIDERETH THE POOR, ETC.—Psalm xli. 1.

ANALYTICAL AND HISTORICAL TABLE.

ADVERTS TO THE PROOFS OF HIS MESSIAHSHIP. ver. 31—.9.

	MATT.	MARK.	LUKE.	JOHN.	ILLUSTRATIONS.
Witness of 'another,' (" the Spirit of truth ")	—	—	—	5. 31,.2	1 Jno. 5. 6, 7, 9.
—— Jesus' forerunner, John	—	—	—	— 33—.5	Jno. 1 6, 7.
—— Jesus' own works	—	—	—	— 36	Ac. 2 22.
—— the Father	[3.17; 17.5	1.11	3. 12]	— 37	Lu. 3. 22.
—— 'his word abiding in you'	—	—	—	— 38	1 Jno. 2. 14.
—— the Holy Scriptures	—	—	—	[24.27,44—.7]—39	Is. 8. 20; Ps. 19. 7-14

WHY THEY DID NOT RECEIVE THE WITNESS TO HIS MESSIAHSHIP. ver. 40—.4.

	MATT.	MARK.	LUKE.	JOHN.	ILLUSTRATIONS.
It was not their will to come to Jesus	—	—	—	5. 40	
He received not honour from men	—	—	—	— 41	1 Thess. 2. 6.
They had not in them the love of God	—	—	—	— 42	
They disliked to hear God	—	—	—	— 43	
They sought not hon. from God only	—	—	—	— 44	Rom. 2: 10, 29.
The testimony of Moses	—	—	[16. 31]	— 45—.7	— 12

SECTION XXIV.—THE DISCIPLES, ON THE SABBATH, PLUCK EARS OF CORN.
Matthew xii. 1—8. Mark ii. 23—.8. Luke vi. 1—5. p. 187—.94.

No. 24. *In the neighbourhood of Jerusalem.*

	MATT.	MARK.	LUKE.	JOHN.	ILLUSTRATIONS.
The disciples an hungered, and pluck corn	12. 1	2. 23	6. 1	—	
Are accused by the Pharisees [Mt. 15. 1, 2]	— 2	— 24	— 2	—	Ex. 31. 15; De. 23. 25.
Jesus alludes to the case of David	— 3, 4	— 25. .6	— 3, 4	—	1 Sa. 21. 6.
The shewbread only for the priests	— 4	— 26	— 4	—	Le. 24. 5-8, 9.
The priests in the temple .... blameless	— 5	—	—	—	Nu. 28. 9, 10.
' One greater than the temple'	— 6	—	—	[7. 22, 31]	(Mic. 6. 6-8.
Mercy, and not sacrifice . [Mt. ix. 13]	— 7	—	—	—	Hos. 6. 6; Pr. 21. 3;
The sabbath made for the benefit of man	—	— 27	—	—	Eze. 20. 12, 20.
The Lord of the sabbath	— 8	— 28	— 5	—	Rev. 1. 10.

SECTION XXV.—THE WITHERED HAND RESTORED. Matt. xii. 9—14. Mark iii. 1—6.
Luke vi. 6—11. At Capernaum. p. 195—.9.

No. 25. *On another sabbath day, in a synagogue, Jesus heals a withered hand. The Pharisees conspire with the Herodians to put Jesus to death.*

	MATT.	MARK.	LUKE.	JOHN.	ILLUSTRATIONS.
Jesus teaches in the synagogue [Mt. 4. 23]	12. 9	3. 1	6. 6	[6. 25-71]	
A man there with a withered hand	— 10	— 1	— 6	—	
Jesus is watched [Lu. 11. 53, .4; 14. 1; 20. 20]	— 10	— 2	— 7	—	Psa. 37. 32; 38.12; 62. 4.
—— knows their thoughts	[9. 4	2. 8]	— 8	—	Is. 11. 3; Ac. 5. 1-11.
Confounds his enemies	—	— 3, 4	— 8, 9	—	[Lu. 20. 26.]
Parable of one sheep, fallen into a pit	— 11, .2	—	[14. 5]	—	
Jesus grieved for the hardness of their hearts	—	— 5	—	—	Rom. 2. 5.
—— saith to the man, 'Stretch,' &c. [Mt.9.6,7]	— 13	— 5	— 10	[5. 8, 9]	
The withered hand healed	— 13	— 5	— 10	—	
The Pharisees, &c., seek his death [Mt. 27. 1]	— 14	— 6	— 11	[11. 53]	Mt. 2. 16-.8; Jno.5.16-.8.

SECTION XXVI.—JESUS' FIRST PARTIAL CIRCUIT BY THE SEA.
Matthew xii. 15—21. Mark iii. 7—12. p. 200—.4.

No. 26. *Jesus withdraws to the lake of Gennesaret; and, attended by his disciples and the multitude, begins a partial circuit of that part of it which bordered on Galilee; working miracles, and teaching the people, when there was occasion, from a ship.*

	MATT.	MARK.	LUKE.	JOHN.	ILLUSTRATIONS.
Jesus withdraws with his disciples	12. 15	3. 7			
To the sea	[4. 13-.8]	— 7	[5. 1-11	6. 1]	
Is followed by multitudes	— 15	— 7,.8	.6. 17]	—	
A small ship to wait on him	—	— 9	—	—	Lu. 5. 3.
Many press upon him to be healed	—	— 10	—	—	Lu. 5. 1, 2, to hear.
Unclean spirits fall down and cry out, &c.	—	— 11	[4. 41]	—	[Mk. 1. 23,.4] Ja. 2. 19.
Jesus charges them not to make him known	— 16	— 12	—	—	[Mt. 8. 4] Jno. 15. 26.
In fulfilment of Esaias, xlii. 1-4	— 17	—	—	—	See Ps. 40. 7-9.
' Behold my servant, whom I have chosen '	— 18	—	—	—	Ph. 2. 7.
My beloved, in whom my soul is well pleased	— 18	—	—	—	[Mt. 3. 16,.7; 17. 5.]
My spirit upon him [Mt. 3. 16; Jno.1.32,.4]	— 18	—	—	—	Is. 11. 2; 61. 1; Ac. 2.
He shall shew judgment	— 18	—	—	[2. 32]	Ac. 3. 23; 1 Co. 12. 7,8.
—— shall not strive, nor cry, &c.	— 19	—	—	—	Is. 53. 7; 1 Pe. 2. 23.
—— shall not break the bruised reed, &c.	— 20	—	—	—	Is. 42. 1-4.
Till he send forth judgment, &c.	— 20	—	—	—	2 Pe. 1. 19; Is. 42. 13,.4.
In his name shall the Gentiles trust	— 21	—	—	—	Is. 9. 6; 52. 6; He. 19.11, (.2, .3, .6.

SECTION XXVII.—JESUS CHOOSES TWELVE APOSTLES. SERMON IN THE PLAIN.
Matt. x. 2—4. Mark iii. 13—.9. Luke vi. 12—49. North of Capernaum. p. 205—.17.

No. 27. *Immediately before his return to Capernaum, Jesus passes a night in prayer upon a certain mountain: in the morning he ordains twelve of his disciples to be apostles. Matt. x. 2—4. Mark iii. 13—.9. Luke vi. 12—.6. N. of Capernaum. p. 205—.7.*

	MATT.	MARK.	LUKE.	JOHN.	ILLUSTRATIONS.
Jesus passes the night in prayer	—	3. 13	6. 12	—	(Lu. 9. 28.) [Mk. 1. 35; Mt. 14. 23;
Chooses twelve apostles	—	— 13—.5	—	—	Mt.19.28; Jno.15.16; Ac.
Names of the apostles	10. 2-4	— 16—.9	— 14—.6	—	[Ac. 1. 13.] (10. 40,.1.

WHERE IS THY GOD?—Psalm xlii. 3.

ANALYTICAL AND HISTORICAL TABLE.

Jesus descends from the mountain to the people, and then delivers a sermon to his disciples in the presence of the multitude. Luke vi. 17—49. p. 207—.10.

	MATT.	MARK.	LUKE.	JOHN.	ILLUSTRATIONS.
Jesus descends to the plain, and heals many	—	—	6. 17–.9	—	

SERMON ON THE PLAIN.

Four beatitudes	[5. 3-12]	—	— 20–.3	—	Ps. 107. 9; Jas. 2. 5.
Four woes .	—	—	— 24–.6	[10. 19]	1 Ti. 6. 9; Pr. 14. 13.
'Love your enemies'	[— 43–.8]	—	— 27–36	—	1 Co. 6. 7; Pr. 25. 21.
'Judge not,' &c.	[7. 1–5]	—	— 37–42	—	Jas. 2. 13.
Of good and evil fruit	[— 16-23]	—	— 43–.5	—	
Of building upon the rock and on the earth.	[— 24–.7]	—	— 46–.9	—	

SECTION XXVIII.—JESUS HEALS A CENTURION'S SERVANT. Matthew viii. 5—13. Luke vii. 1—10. Capernaum. p. 217—.20.

No. 28. After the sermon on the plain, Jesus enters Capernaum, and heals of his sickness the servant of a certain centurion.

Jesus enters Capernaum [Mt. 4. 13; Lu. 4. 31]	8. 5	—	7. 1	—	
A centurion, whose servant is ready to die	—	—	— 2	—	
Sends to Jesus, beseeching him	— 5, 6	—	— 3	—	[4. 47-54] Mt. 9. 18; 15. 22, 25–.7.]
Jesus saith, 'I will come and heal him'	— 7	—	—	—	
Intercession of the Jewish elders	—	—	— 4, 5	—	1 Jno. 3. 14.
The centurion's humility and trust	— 8, 9	—	— 6-8	—	Ge. 32. 10.
Jesus admires the centurion's faith	— 10	—	— 9	—	
Who are to be heirs with Abraham	— 11, .2	—	—	—	
Weeping and gnashing of teeth [Mt. 13.41.&c.]	— 12	—	—	—	[Mt. 22. 13; 21.51; 25.30.]
'As thou hast believed, so be it done,' &c.	— 13	—	— 10	—	[4. 50–.3] Lu. 7. 50] Mt. 17. 20; 1 Co. 13. 2.

SECTION XXIX.—JESUS RAISES THE WIDOW'S SON TO LIFE. REPLIES TO JOHN'S MESSENGER. A WOMAN WASHES JESUS' FEET. Matt. xi. 2—30. Luke vii. 11—50. Nain. p. 221—232.

No. 29. The next day Jesus departs to Nain; and as he approaches the gate of the city, he raises to life the son of a widow woman. Luke vii. 11—.6. p. 221, ..2.

The dead son of a widow carried out	—	—	7. 11, .2	—	
Jesus has compassion on her	[9. 36]	. 41]	— 13	—	
He raises the young man to life [Lu. 8. 54]	—	—	— 14, .5	[11. 43]	Ac. 9. 40.
Fear on all, and they glorify God [Lu. 1. 65–.8]	—	—	— 16	[6. 14]	De. 18. 15.

John the Baptist, being in prison, sends two of his disciples to question Jesus. Jesus dismisses them to John with his answer. Matt. xi. 2—6. Luke vii. 17—23. p. 222, ..3.

John is informed of the works of Jesus	[14, 3]	—	— 17, .8	—	[Lu.1.13,57-63; 3.19,20.]
—— sends to ask, 'Art thou he that,' &c.	11. 2, 3	—	— 19, 20	[6. 14]	Ge. 49. 10; Nu. 24. 17; Mi. 5. 2; Mal. 3. 1; Ps. (146, 7-10; Da.9.24.
Jesus cures many of their plagues, &c.	—	—	— 21	—	
And answers, 'Go . . . Tell John what,' &c.	— 4, 5	—	— 22	—	[Lu. 4. 18] Is. 61. 1.
'Blessed is he, whosoever shall not be' &c.	— 6	—	— 23	[6. 66]	1 Co. 1. 23; Mt. 5. 3-12

Jesus takes occasion, from the message to John, to discourse to the people concerning him. Matt. xi. 7—30. Luke vii. 24—35. p. 224—.9.

John not one likely to be shaken	11. 7	—	7. 24	—	See Mt.3.7-12; Lu.3.19.
Considering, 1st, How he had been brought up	— 8	—	— 25	—	[Lu. 1. 80; Mt. 3, 4.]
" 2nd, His spiritual advantages	— 9, 10	—	— 26, .7	—	[Lu. 1. 76] Mal. 3. 1.
The least in the kingdom is greater than he	— 11	—	— 28	—	[Lu.22.24–.7] Ph.2.5-11.
In what case John would have been Elias	— 12–.5	—	—	—	[Mt.17.12,.3] Lu.1.15–.7
The baptized and unbap. [Mt.3.5,6; Lu.3.12]	—	—	— 29, 30	—	
Like children playing in the markets	— 16–.9	[1. 6]	— 31–.5	—	[Lu. 1. 15; Mt. 3. 4.]
Jesus laments over Chora., Bethsai., & Caper.	— 20–.4	—	[10.13–.5]	—	
Thanks the Father for revealing unto babes	— 25, .6	—	[— 21]	—	
Only through the Son is the Father revealed	— 27	—	[— 22]	—	
'Come unto me, all ye that labour,' &c.	— 28-30	—	—	—	[Mt. 23. 1, 4, 37.]

The same day Jesus eats bread in the house of a certain Pharisee. A woman, who was a sinner, anoints his feet; what ensued thereupon. Luke vii. 36—50. p. 229—.32.

Jesus eats with a Pharisee	—	—	7. 36	—	
A woman, a sinner, anoints the feet of Jesus	[26. 6, 7]	14. 3]	— 37, .8	[12. 3]	1 Ti. 1. 15.
Simon supposes Jesus ignorant of her charac.	—	—	— 39	—	
He knows both her and the Pharisee	[9. 4]	—	— 40	[1, 45–.8]	2. 25] He. 4. 13.
Parable of the two debtors	[18.23-25]	—	— 41–.3	—	Rom. 3. 24.
Evidence of being forgiven	—	—	— 44–.7	—	1 Jno. 4. 19.
'Thy faith hath saved thee; go in peace'	[9. 22]	5. 34]	— 48-50	—	Hab. 2. 4.

HE DISCOVERETH DEEP THINGS OUT OF DARKNESS.—Job xii. 22.

ANALYTICAL AND HISTORICAL TABLE.

Jesus calms a violent storm on the lake. Matt. viii. 24—.7. *Mark* iv. 37—41.
Luke viii. 23—.5. p. 266, ..7.

	MATT.	MARK.	LUKE.	JOHN.	ILLUSTRATIONS.
A great tempest—the waves beat into the ship	8. 24	4. 37	8. 23	—	Ps. 107. 25-.7.
Jesus asleep on a pillow	— 24	— 38		—	Ecc. 5. 12.
The cry of distress	— 25	— 38	— 24	—	Ps. 107. 28.
Jesus rebukes the winds and sea	— 26	— 39	— 24	—	Ex. 14. 21-31 ; Ps. 65. 7.
Reproaches the disciples for want of faith	— 26	— 40	— 25	—	[Mt. vi. 30 ; 14. 31.]
They fear exceed., & say, 'What manner,' &c.	— 27	— 41	25	—	[Mt. 14. 32, .3] Ps. 9. 7-9.

SECTION XXXV.—JESUS CASTS OUT DEVILS. HE RETURNS TO CAPERNAUM.
Matt. viii. 28—34; ix. 1. Mark v. 1—21. Luke viii. 26—40. East of the sea of Galilee, and West of the same. p. 268—.76.

No. 35. *Jesus lands in the country of the Gadarenes, and casts devils out of two men who dwelt among the tombs. Matt.* viii. 28—33. *Mark* v. 1—14. *Luke* viii. 26—34. p. 269—272.

Jesus is met by two possessed with devils	8. 28	5. 1-3	8. 26, .7		
Their character and abode	— 28	— 3-5	— 27		1 Ki. 18. 28. (Mt. 26. 53.]
They confess Jesus to be the Son of God	— 29	— 6, 7	— 28		[Mk.]. 24; Lu. 4. 41 ;
Legion commanded to leave the man		— 8, 9	— 29, 30		[Mk. 1. 25; ix. 25] Rev.
They request not to be sent out, &c.		— 10			(18. 2, 4.
—————— not to be sent into the deep			— 31		Rev. 20. 3.
But to enter the swine	— 30, .1.	— 11, 2.	— 32		De. 14. 8.
The swine perish in the lake	— 32	— 13	— 33		Rev. 18. 21
They that feed them spread the alarm	— 33	— 14	— 34		

The people of the city and neighbourhood request Jesus to depart out of their coasts. Matt. viii. 34. *Mark* v. 14—20. *Luke* viii. 35—.9. p. 272—.4.

They find the dem. cloth. & in his right m.	—	5. 14-.6	8. 35-.6		2 Ti. 1. 7.
They request Jesus to depart from them	8. 34	— 17	— 37		Comp. Mk. 4. 39 ; 5. 2,
The man asks to follow Jesus		— 18	— 38		(8, 9.
Jesus' answer		— 19	— 39		
The man publishes in Decapolis		— 20	— 39		

Jesus returns to Capernaum. Matt. ix. 1. *Mark* v. 21. *Luke* viii. 40. p. 274.

Jesus passes over into his own city	9. 1	5. 21	8. 40		
The people gladly receive him	—	— 21	— 40	[i. 45]	

SECTION XXXVI.—JESUS EATS WITH PUBLICANS AND SINNERS. RESTORES JAIRUS' DAUGHTER TO LIFE, ETC. Matthew ix. 10—34. Mark v. 22—43. Luke viii. 41—56. Capernaum. p. 277—.86.

No. 36. *Jesus sits at meat ; the Pharisees murmur that he eats with publicans, &c. ; the disciples of John inquire why the disciples of Jesus did not fast : Jesus replies. Matt.* ix. 10—17. p. 277—.9.

Jesus eats with publicans and sinners	9. 10-.7	[2. 15-22	5. 29-39]	—	

Jairus applies to Jesus to visit his daughter, who is at the point of death. Matt. ix. 18, .9. *Mark* v. 22—.4. *Luke* viii. 41, .2. p. 279, .80.

Jairus falls at Jesus' feet and worships him	9. 18	5. 22	8. 41		[Mt. 8. 2; 15. 25.]
Beseeches him to heal his daughter	— 18	— 23	— 41	[4. 46-.9]	Comp. Lu. 7. 1-3, 6-8.
Who was about twelve years old, and dying			— 42		
Jesus going with Jairus is thronged	— 19	— 24	— 42		

On the way a woman is healed who had an issue of blood twelve years. Matt. ix. 20—.2. *Mark* v. 25—34. *Luke* viii. 43—.8. p. 280—.2.

A woman who had been long diseased	9. 20	5. 25	8. 43		
Having spent all upon phys. & noth. bettered	—	— 26	— 43		Job 13. 4.
In faith touches the hem of Jesus' garment	— 20, .1	— 27 , .8	— 44		[Lu. 6 19] ; Ac. 19. 11, .2.
And feels she is healed		— 29		[4.50, .2, .3]	
Jesus knowing, &c., asks, 'Who touched me?'		30. .2	— 45, .6		Nah. 1. 7 ; Ac. 5. 12-.6.
The woman decl. bef. all what she had done		— 33	— 47		Ps. 103.
Jesus comforts her, and commends her faith	— 22	— 34	— 48	[Comp.11:40	See Mt. 8. 13, § 28, p.xix.]

In the mean time the daughter of Jairus expires, whom Jesus raises to life again. Matt. ix. 23—.6. *Mark* v. 35—43. *Luke* viii. 49—56. p. 282—.5.

Jairus encouraged to exercise faith	[Co. 9. 18]	5. 35, .6	8. 49, 50		Rev. 1. 17, .8.
Jesus (with the three) enters Jairus' house	9. 23	— 37, .8	— 51		Mt. 17. 1-7 ; 26. 36, .7.
The scorners excluded	— 24, .5	— 39, 40	— 52, .3		2 Ch. 35. 25 ; comp. Je.
					22. 18.
The damsel raised to life	— 25	— 41, .2	— 54	[11. 43, .4	Mk. 1. 31 ; Lu. 7. 14, .5.]
Commands it not to be told	—	— 43	— 56		[Mk. 1. 43, .4 ; 9. 9.]
His fame goes abroad	— 26				[Mt. 4. 24; 9. 31; Lu. 4. 14.]

THE LORD IS MERCIFUL AND GRACIOUS.—Psalm ciii. 8.

ANALYTICAL AND HISTORICAL TABLE.

Jesus heals two blind men. Matt. ix. 27—31. p. 285.

	MATT.	MARK.	LUKE.	JOHN.	ILLUSTRATIONS.
Two blind men cry out after Jesus [Mt. 20. 30]	9. 27, .8	[10. 47, .8 18. 38-40]			Is. 35, 5, 6; 42. 5-7.
He touches their eyes	— 29, 30	[— 42, .3]			[See on Mk.8. .3, supra.
Charges them, 'See that no man know it'	— 30				
But they spread abroad his fame, &c.	— 31				

Dispossesses a dumb demoniac. Matt. ix. 32—4. p. 285.

Jesus casts out a dumb devil	9. 32				
The multitudes marvel [Mt. 12. 22, .3]	— 33	[3. 22	11. 14]		
The Pharisees blaspheme — 24]	— 34		[—15, .6 8. 48-52]		Is. 35. 6.

SECTION XXXVII.—JESUS REVISITS HIS OWN COUNTRY. Nazareth. p. 286—..8.

No. 37. *Matt. xiii. 54—.8. Mark vi. 1—6.*

Jesus comes into his own country	[4.13; 9.1] 6. 1	[4. 16			
Teaches in a synagogue	13. 54 — 2	[— 16-22			
'Whence hath this man this wisdom?'	— 54 — 2	[— 22			Mt. 13.14,.5; Is. 6. 9, 10.
'Is not this the carpenter?'	— 55, .6 — 3		[6. 42]		
Where a prophet is without honour	— 57 — 4		[— 25]		Lu. 2. 34.
The cause of Jesus doing no mighty work there	— 58 — 5, 6				[Mk. 3. 5.]

SECTION XXXVIII.—JESUS' THIRD GENERAL CIRCUIT OF GALILEE

No. 38. *See line from Nazareth going through Galilee. p. 293.*

| Jesus goes teaching in the synagogues | 9. 35 | 6. 6 | | | [Mt. 4. 23; Lu. 8. 1-3.] |
| Preaching the gospel, &c. and healing | — 35 | | [8. 1-3] | | [— 23; Mk. 1. 39.] |

SECTION XXXIX.—THE TWELVE APOSTLES SENT OUT. Matthew ix. 36—.8; x. 1, 5—xi. 1. Mark vi. 7—13. Luke ix. 1—6. Capernaum. p. 293—303.

No. 39. *The twelve apostles are sent out in companies of two and two. Jesus departs also on his second partial circuit. Matt. ix. 36—.8; x. 1, 5—xi. 1. Mark vi. 7—13. Luke ix. 1—6. Capernaum. p. 294—303.*

Why Jesus is moved with compassion	9. 36		[7.13;19.41-.4]	[11. 35	Mt. 14. 14] 1 Pe. 3. 8.
Directs to pray for labourers for the harvest	— 37, .8		[10. 2	]	2 Th.3.1. (Ecc.4.9.12.
Sends forth the twelve, two and two	10. 1	6. 7	9. 1, 2		[Mk. 3. 14,.5] Nu.13.23;
Sent to lost sheep of the house of Israel	— 5, 6				[Mt. 15. 24] Ja. 1. 1.
To preach and heal	— 7, 8		— 2		[Lu. 10. 9.]
Provision for the journey	— 9, 10	— 8, 9	— 3		[— 10. 4.]
With whom to lodge	— 11	— 10	— 4		[— 10. 5-7]; Ac. 16. 15.
How to enter an house	— 12, .3				
How to act when rejected	— 14, .5	— 11	— 5		[— 10. 10, .1]; Ac. 13. 50, .1.
'Be wise as serpents,' &c.	— 16		[10. 3]		Rom. 16. 19; Ep. 5. 15; Col. 4. 5; 1 Co. 14. 20; Ph. 2. 15, Ja. 3. 17.
What they might expect from men	— 17, .8				Ac. 25. 7, 23; 2 Co.11.24.
To trust God for their defence	— 19, 20	[13. 11	[12. 11-.3]		Je. 1. 7; Ac. 4. 8, 12, .3.
Persecution from relatives, &c., hated of all	— 21, .2	— 12, .3	21. 16]		Mic. 7. 6.
He that shall endure to the end [Mt. 24. 13]	— 22				
Not to court persecution	— 23	[3. 6, 7]			Ac. 14. 5, 6.
To expect it like their Master	— 24, .5	[3. 22	6. 40	13. 16]	
Boldly to proclaim the truth	— 26, .7		[12. 2, 3		Is. 51. 7, 12.
Whom to fear	— 28-31		[12. 4		Rom.10.9,10; 1Jno.2.23;
Such as confess Jesus he will confess	— 32, .3		[9.26; 12.8]		Ps. 41. 9. (Rev. 3. 5.
Dissensions in families to arise	— 34-.6		[12. 51-.3]		
Christ must be loved supremely	— 37-.9		[14. 26, .7 19. 25]		
Christ received in his messengers	— 40		[9. 48	13. 20]	
Who shall receive a prophet's reward	— 41				1 Kl. 17. 8-16.
A cup of cold water given for his sake, &c.	— 42	[9. 41]			Heb. 6. 10.
The apostles go forth preaching, &c.	[3. 2]	6. 12, .3	9. 6		
Jesus also departs to teach and to preach	11. 1				

SECTION XL.—THE DEATH OF JOHN THE BAPTIST RECORDED. FIVE THOUSAND FED. Matthew xiv. 1—21. Mark vi. 14—44. Luke ix. 7—17. John vi. 1—13. Capernaum and Desert of Bethsaida, in Decapolis. p. 304—.16.

No. 40. *The fame of Jesus reaches Herod the tetrarch of Galilee: particulars of the death of John the Baptist. Probably Capernaum. Matt. xiv. 1—12. Mark vi. 14—29. Luke ix. 7—9. p. 304—..8.*

The fame of Jesus reaches Herod	14. 1	6. 14	9. 7		Mal. 4. 5; Lu. 1. 17.
Herod's perplexity			— 7-9		Comp. Jne. 10. 41.
Jesus supposed to be John raised from dead	— 2	— 14			

KNOW YE THAT THE LORD HE IS GOD.—Psalm c. 3.

ANALYTICAL AND HISTORICAL TABLE

	MATT.	MARK.	LUKE.	JOHN.	ILLUSTRATIONS.
Herod's desire to see Jesus			9. 9		
Conjectures respecting Jesus	[16. 14]	6. 15	[— 8]		
Herod's saying, 'It is John'	14. 2	— 16			
Herod had laid hold on John	— 3	— 17			
Why John was apprehended	— 4	— 18, .9	[3. 19, 20]		Comp. Ge. 39. 14-20.
Why his death had been delayed	— 5	— 20			Ezek. 2. 5-7.
The occasion on which John was slain	— 6	— 21			Prov. 22. 14.
The dancing girl	— 6	— 22			
The rash oath	— 7	— 23			Est. 5. 6; 7. 2.
The girl instructed by her mother	— 8	— 24, .5			Prov. 29. 10.
The danger of evil company	— 9	— 26			Ecc. 5. 2; Da. 6. 14;
John beheaded	— 10	— 27			(Ja. 1. 15, .6.
His head presented to Herodias	— 11	— 28			
John's disciples bury him, and tell Jesus	— 12	— 29			Acts 8. 2

Upon the return of the apostles, they are taken by Jesus apart to the desert of Bethsaida; the multitudes follow them thither; five thousand men, besides women and children, are fed with five loaves of bread and two fishes. Matt. xiv. 13—21. Mark vi. 30—44. Luke ix. 10—.7. John vi. 1—13. Desert of Bethsaida in Decapolis. p. 309—.16.

					(6. 13, .4.
The apostles return from their mission		6. 30	9. 10		First called Apostles, Lu.
Jesus invites them to a desert place		— 31			[Mk. 3. 20.]
They go by ship, many follow on foot	14. 13	— 32, .3	— 10, .1	6. 1, 2	
Jesus compassionates the multitudes	— 14	— 34	— 11		
— speaks to Philip of providing bread				— 3-7	[Mt. 9. 36; 15. 32.]
— is advised to send the people away	— 15	— 35, .6	— 12	[6. 5]	
— says, 'Give ye them to eat'	— 16	— 37	— 13		Nu. 11. 13-22; 2 Kl. 4. 43.
Their stock of provisions	— 17	— 33	— 13	— 8, 9	[Mt. 15. 31; Mk. 8. 5.]
Arrangements for feeding the people	— 18, .9	— 39-41	— 14, .6	— 10, .1	[— 35, .6 — 6,7.]
They all eat, and are filled	— 20	— 42	— 17	— 12	[— 37 — 8.]
Twelve baskets of fragments taken up	— 20	— 43	— 17	— 13	[— 37 — 8.]
The number fed 5,000, &c.	— 21	— 44	[— 14	— 10	— 38 — 9.]

SECTION XLI.—JESUS DISMISSES HIS DISCIPLES TO CAPERNAUM. AVOIDS THE MULTITUDE. WALKS UPON THE WATER. Matthew xiv. 22—33. Mark vi. 45—52. John vi. 14—21. p. 317—.21.

No. 41. *Jesus dismisses his disciples. Matt. xiv. 22—.4. Mk. vi. 45—.7. Jno. vi. 14—.7.*

The men conclude Jesus is 'that prophet'			6. 14		[ch. 7. 40]; De. 18. 15-.8.
Jesus bids his disciples to cross the sea	14. 22	6. 45			
The multitude would by force make him king				— 15	Mt. 26. 52, .3; Jno. 18. 36;
Jesus' conduct thereupon	— 23	— 46	[9. 28]	— 15	(2 Co. 10. 4, 5.
The ship tossed with waves	— 24	— 47		— 16, .7	Mt. 8. 24, .5; Ps. 34. 15.

Jesus walks upon the water, and empowers Peter to do the same: the ship in which the disciples were is miraculously transported across the lake. Matthew xiv. 25—33. Mark vi. 48—52. John vi. 18—21. p. 319—.21.

Jesus walks upon the water		— 25	— 49	[24. 29]	— 19	Job 9. 8; Ps. 77. 19.
The disciples are alarmed at his appearance	— 26	— 49, 50	[24. 37]	— 19	Lu. 1. 12, .3; 28, .9; 2. 8-11.
'Be of good cheer, it is I'	— 27	— 50	[— 38]	— 20	[Mt. 9. 2]; Isa. 41. 10, .3, .4;
					Ac. 23. 11; Re. 1. 17, .8.
Peter asks to walk on the water	— 28, .9			[21. 7]	Ph. 4. 13.
His faith fails—is upheld by Jesus	— 30, 1				[Mt. 8. 26]; Ja. 1. 6.
They go up into the ship	— 32	— 51		— 21	[Mk. 4. 39.]
Immediately the ship is at the land, &c.				— 21	
Jesus is confessed to be the Son of God	— 33	[1. 1	1. 35	6. 68, .9	Mt. 16. 15, .6.]
Why the disciples were amazed		— 51, .2			[Mk. 16. 14]; Ps. 106. 13; He. 3. 8-13.

SECTION XLII.—JESUS RETURNS THROUGH THE REGION OF GENNESARET TO CAPERNAUM: THE MULTITUDE, WHICH HAD BEEN LEFT ON THE OTHER SIDE OF THE LAKE, ALSO RETURN TO CAPERNAUM IN QUEST OF JESUS.

No. 41, continued. *Matt. xiv. 34—.6. Mark vi. 53—.6. John vi. 22—.4. p. 322, ..3.*

Jesus and disciples come into land of Genn.	14. 34	6. 53	[5. 1	6. 17]	
The people know him	— 35	— 54			Mk. 3. 7-11; Mt. 9. 35.
They gather to him all who are diseased	— 35	— 55			Ac. 5. 15, .6.
These, by touching his garment, are healed	— 36	— 56			See on Mt. 9. 21, § 36; Ac.
The people who had been fed follow him				6 22—.4	See ver. 25, .6. (19. 12.

SECTION XLIII.—DISCOURSE WHICH ENSUED WITH THE MULTITUDE IN THE SYNAGOGUE OF CAPERNAUM: MANY OF THE DISCIPLES BEING OFFENDED THEREBY, JESUS TRIES THE FAITH OF THE TWELVE; AND A YEAR BEFORE THE EVENT, FORETELLS HIS OWN BETRAYAL BY ONE OF THEM. John vi. 25—71. p. 325—.35.

No. 42. *Jesus discourses of the bread of life.*

Those who had been fed find Jesus				6. 25	
Their worldly motives				— 26	

A WICKED DOER GIVETH HEED TO FALSE LIPS.—Prov. xvii. 4.

ANALYTICAL AND HISTORICAL TABLE.

	MATT.	MARK.	LUKE.	JOHN.	ILLUSTRATIONS.
For what men should labour	[6. 19, 20	—	10. 42]	6. 27	Is. 55. 2.
The sealed of the Father	—	—	—	— 27	— 55. 4; [Jno. 1. 32-4;
They ask, 'What shall we do?'	—	—	—	— 28	(3. 33.]
Jesus points out the work of God	—	—	—	— 29	Is. 55. 3; 1 Jno. 3. 23.
They ask, 'What sign shewest thou?'	[12.38;	16.1 8. 11	11. 16]	— 30	(Jno. 2. 18); Is. 55. 73.
Our fathers were given bread from heaven	—	—	—	— 31	Ex. 16. 14-36.
He who gave manna now gives the true bread	—	—	—	— 32	[Jno. 3. 16]; Ps.78.24,.5.
'Life unto the world'	—	—	—	— 33	[— 14. 6.]
'Lord, evermore give us this bread'	—	—	—	— 34	[— 4. 15.]
Jesus is 'the bread of life'	—	—	—	— 35	[— 4. 14; 7. 37];
					Is. 55. 6. 7.
The Jews saw, yet believed not	—	—	—	— 36	[— 12. 37] 8, 9.
Who they are that come to Jesus	—	—	—	— 37	[— 10.28,.9] — 5;
					Rom. 8 28-30.
Whence and wherefore Jesus had come	[26. 39]	—	—	— 38	[— 4. 31;5. 30]; Ps.40.
Of such as are given to Christ	[18. 14]	—	—	— 39	[— 18 9.] (7, 8.
They will be raised up at the last day	[11. 6]	—	—	— 40	[— 3. 15,.6; 11. 24,.5.]
The Jews, being disappointed, murmur	—	—	—	— 41	
Their ignorance of whence Jesus came	[13. 55	6. 3	4. 22]	— 42	See Mt. 22. 45.
Jesus alludes to his words, ver. 39, 40	—	—	—	— 43, .4	I's. 25. 8, 9, 14.
Those taught of God come to Christ	—	—	—	— 45	Is. 54. 13; Mic. 4. 2.
Who hath seen the Father	[11. 27]	—	—	— 46	[Jno. 1. 18.] (31.)
The bread of life and the manna contrasted	—	—	—	— 47-51	[— 16. 27—see on ver.
The Jews cannot understand	—	—	—	— 52	[— 3. 9.]
Christ the true passover	[26. 26]	—	—	— 53	
Such as have eter. life [ver. 27, 40,63, ch. 4. 14]	—	—	—	— 54	1 Co. 15. 45-9; Ep. 3. 17.
Excellence of the bread of life [Jno. 14. 21]	—	—	—	— 55-8	1 Co. 15. 45-9; Ep. 3. 17;
					1 Jno. 3. 24; 4. 13, .5, .6.
Not as their fathers ate	—	—	—	— 58	Ps. 78. 30, .1.
'An hard saying; who can bear it?'	—	—	—	— 59, 60	(Ep. 4. 8-10.
Jesus' pre-existence and future ascension	—	[16. 19]	—	— 61, .2	[Jno 3. 13; Ac. 1. 9];
Feeding on Jesus' words we have life	—	—	—	— 63	2 Co. 2. 15, .6; 3. 6.
Jesus' foreknowledge as to Judas—comp.					
ver. 71, and Jno. 2. 24, .5	—	—	—	— 64	[Jno. 13. 11.]
Those given of the Father come, &c.	—	—	—	— 65	[See ver. 37, 44, .5.]
Many forsake Jesus	—	—	—	— 66	Is. 1. 28; He. 10. 38.
To the twelve—'Will ye also go away?'	—	[14. 27-50	6. 13-.6]	— 67	
Peter's answer and confession [Mt. 14. 33	16. 16	8. 29	9. 20]	— 68, .9	[Jno. 1. 49]; Is. 55. 3.
Jesus speaks of Judas Iscariot the betrayer	[26. 48, .9]	—	—	— 70, .1	[— 12. 6; 13. 21-30.]

THEY THAT FORSAKE THE LORD SHALL BE CONSUMED.—Isaiah i. 28.

SUPPOSED CHRONOLOGY OF THE GOSPEL HISTORY.

(*Greswell*, Vol. IV. Part II. pp. 74¼—..6.)

B.C.*	
Vision of the angel to Zacharias, Thursday, Oct. 5	6
Birth of John Baptist, Saturday, October 5; Circumcision, October 12	b
Birth of Christ, Saturday, April 5, Nisan 10	4
Circumcision of Jesus, Saturday, April 12	ib.
Presentation in the Temple, Friday, May 16	ib.
Arrival of the Magi, about August 2	ib.
Flight of the Holy Family to Egypt, about Aug. 9	ib.
Return from Egypt, about March 31	3

A.D.	
Visit of Jesus to Jerusalem, in his twelfth year Passover, April 8	8
Beginning of the ministry of John, Monday, Oct. 5	26
Baptism of Jesus Christ, end of January	27
Beginning of the ministry of Jesus Christ, and first cleansing of the Temple, Monday, April 5, Nisan 10	ib.
First Passover, Friday, April 9	ib.
Arrival of Jesus at Sychar, Thursday, May 13	ib.
Imprisonment of John, Sunday, May 16	ib.
First feast of Pentecost, Sunday, May 30	ib.
Call of the four disciples, Friday, June 4	ib.
Beginning of the ministry at Capernaum, Saturday, June 5	ib.
Commencement of the first circuit of Galilee, Sunday, June 6	ib.
First feast of Tabernacles, Monday, October 4	ib.
Two hundred and twentieth sabbatic year, seed-time or autumn	ib.
First feast of Encœnia, Sunday, December 12	ib.
Miracle at the Pool of Bethesda, Saturday, March 25, Nisan 10	†28
Second Passover, Wednesday, March 29	ib.
Walking through the corn-fields, Saturday, April 1	ib.
First partial circuit of Galilee	ib.
Second Feast of Pentecost, Friday, May 19	ib.
Ordination of the Twelve	ib.
Second general circuit of Galilee	ib.
Second feast of Tabernacles, Saturday, Sept. 23	ib.

	A.D.
Death of John Baptist	28
Third general circuit of Galilee	ib.
Second feast of Dedication, Friday, December 1	ib.
Mission of the Twelve, February	29
Second partial circuit of Galilee	ib.
First miracle of feeding, Thursday, April 5	ib.
Discourse in the synagogue at Capernaum, Saturday, April 7	ib.
Third Passover, Monday, April 16	ib.
Confession of Peter, Sunday, May 20	ib.
Transfiguration, Sunday, May 27	ib.
Third feast of Pentecost, Wednesday, June 6	ib.
Third feast of Tabernacles, Thursday, Oct. 11	ib.
Appearance of Jesus at the feast, Monday, Oct. 15	ib.
Miracle on the blind man, Thursday, October 18	ib.
Third feast of Dedication, Wednesday, Dec. 19	ib.
Raising of Lazarus, and retreat to Ephraim, Jan.	30
Return to Capernaum, and mission of the Seventy, February	ib.
Fourth general circuit of Galilee, March	ib.
Passage through Jericho, Friday, March 29	ib.
Arrival at Bethany, Nisan 8, Saturday, March 30	ib.
Unction at Bethany, Saturday, March 30	ib.
Resort of the Jews to Bethany, Sunday, Nisan 9, March 31	ib
Procession to the Temple, afternoon of Monday, Nisan 10, April 1	ib.
Second cleansing of the Temple, morning of Tuesday, Nisan 11, April 2	ib.
Close of our Lord's public ministry, evening of Wednesday, Nisan 12, April 3	ib.
Prophecy on the Mount of Olives	ib.
Compact of Judas with the Sanhedrim	ib.
Celebration of the last supper, night of Thursday, Nisan 14, April 4	ib.
Fourth Passover, and Passion of Jesus, Friday, Nisan 14, April 5	ib.
Resurrection of Jesus, Sunday, Nisan 16, April 7	ib.
Ascension into heaven, Thursday, Zif or Jar 26, May 16	ib.

DATES AND PLACES OF THE GOSPELS.

		A.D.
Hebrew Gospel of St. Matthew	Judæa	42
Greek Gospel of St. Matthew	Rome	55
Gospel of St. Mark	Rome	55
Gospel of St. Luke	Rome	60
Gospel of St. John	Ephesus	101

* "The date adopted in the margin of the authorized English version of the Scriptures fixes the creation of the world at 4004 years before the birth of Jesus Christ. The chronology of that version was settled by Dr. Williams Lloyd, Bishop of St. Asaph: It is a modification of Archbishop Usher's chronology, who follows the computation of the Hebrew Bible, and fixes the creation of the world at 4000 years before the birth of Christ. The chronology followed here is that of Bishop Lloyd, which is that most generally received.

† This year was intercalated one day.

BEHOLD YOUR GOD!—Isaiah xl. 9

THE LORD SHALL JUDGE THE PEOPLE.—Psalm vii. 8.

INDEX TO THE GEOGRAPHICAL NOTICES.

	Section.	Page.
ABILENE	7	55
Batanea		ix
Bethabara, beyond Jordan	10	74
Bethesda, true site of the pool of	23	186
Bethlehem ... § 4. 27	5	37
Bethsaida in Galilee	11	80
———— in Decapolis	40	315
———— desert of	40	315
Cana	11	79
Capernaum ... § 11. 76, § 16. 109	25	198
Carmel, mount		x
Decapolis	18	117
Ænon	13	96
Galilee ... § 15. 105		ix
———— sea of ... § 26. 203	32	250
———— length of the sea of	42	324
Gennesaret, lake of	20	155
———— land of	42	323
Gergesenses, country of	35	274
Gadarenes		—
Hermon		x
Hill country of Judæa	2	14
Hinnom, valley of	19	129
Holy Land		ix
Idumea	26	203
Iturea	7	55
Jacob's Well	13	98
Jerusalem ... § 5. 36	6	42
———— outwardly	23	181
———— as approached from Jaffa	—	182
———— ———— mount of Olives	—	182
———— ———— Bethlehem	—	183
———— ———— the north	—	183
———— its Inhabitants	—	184
———— Pilgrims visiting	—	185
———— Sketch of a journey from London to		v, vi
Jordan, river	8	60
———— beyond ... § 10. 74, § 26. 200, Scrip. Illus.	18	118
Judæa		viii, ix
———— hill country of	2	14
Land of Promise, a sketch of the		vii—ix
———— Israel		vii
———— Canaan		vii
———— Holy		ix
———— Gennesaret ... (see lake of Gennesaret, § 20. 155)	42	323
Magdala ... (see land of Gennesaret)	42	323
Nain	29	229
Nazareth ... § 2. 14, § 6. 43	37	288
Nephthalim or Naphtali	16	109

THE RIGHTEOUS GOD TRIETH THE HEARTS AND REINS.—Psalm vii. 9.

INDEX TO THE GEOGRAPHICAL NOTICES.

	Section.	Page.
Peræa		x
Quarantania, mountain		x
Shechem, Sichem	13	96
Salem, or Salim	—	96
Samaria		ix
Sarepta	15	106
Sychar, Shechem, or Sichem	13	96
Syria	18	117
Tophet	19	129
Tabor		x
Trachonitis	7	55
Valley of Hinnom	19	129
Wilderness—scene of the temptation	9	67
Zarephath	15	106
Zebulun	16	109

PLACES MENTIONED IN THE GOSPEL NARRATIVES

Those marked thus † are not noticed in the Gospels.

ABILENE
Arimathea
Bethabara, opposite Scythopolis
Bethabara, opposite Jericho
Bethabara, beyond Jordan, probably Bethany, opposite Scythopolis—Greswell
Bethany
†Bethel
Bethesda
Bethlehem
Bethphage
Bethsaida in Decapolis
Ditto in Galilee
Calvary—See Greswell (p. 242, vol. 3)
Cana
†Ditto in the Plain of Tyre
Capernaum
Cæsarea Philippi
Chorazin
Dalmanutha—See Greswell (p 360, vol. 2)
Decapolis
Emmaus
Ænon
Ephraim
Gadara
Galilee, upper
Galilee, lower
Galilee, sea of
Gennesaret, region of
Gergesa
Gethsemane
Iturea

Idumea—too much to the south of Jerusalem to be seen in the Chart
Jericho
Jordan
Jordan, country round about
Jordan, beyond, where John at first baptized, 'Bethabara,' probably Bethany, opposite Scythopolis
Jerusalem
Judæa
Judæa, Wilderness of
Kedron
Magdala
Nain
Nazareth
Nephthalim
Olives, mount of
Phœnicia
Rama
Ditto, north of Jerusalem
Salim
Samaria
Sarepta
Sebaste, or Samaria
Sidon
Siloam
Sychar
†Tabor
Tiberias
Trachonitis
Tyre
Zebulun.

MY DEFENCE IS OF GOD.—Psalm vii. 10.

INDEX TO THE ADDENDA.

	Section.	Page.
AARON	1	8
Accuseth—'There is one that ... you'	23	187
Analysis of the Harmony of SECT. 25	25	199
Apostles—Ordination of	27	211
—— Name of the twelve, descriptive of the manner in which the disciples of Christ build upon him	27	215
—— See also 'The Twelve,' p. 213.		
Bethesda—Site of the pool of	23	186
Blasphemy against the Holy Ghost	31	241
Book	4	28
Brethren of our Lord	37	290
—— their unbelief	—	292
Circuit—First general	18	118
—— partial	26	204
Council—The	19	129
Deep—Into the	35	274
Demoniacs at Gergesa	—	275
Disciples—Comparison of call of four, Matt. iv. 18–22; Mark i. 16–20; and the miraculous draught of fishes, Luke v. 1—11	20	157
Evangelists	1	6
Except ye eat, &c. (John vi. 53)	43	335
Feast (John v. 1)	23	185
'Foxes have holes,' &c.	34	268
Genealogies according to Matthew and Luke	4	30
Gergesa, on the time of crossing to	34	268
Hagiographa and the Decalogue compared	—	172
Harmony, analysis of the	25	199
Herod	5	39
In order	1	7
John the Evangelist	1	7
John—On chap. i. 15, 27–30	10	74
—— Natural inference of ch. iv 35	13	99
—— ch. v. 1, 'Feast,'	23	185
—— ch. vi. 53, 'Except ye eat'	43	335
John the Baptist—Ministry of	7	56
Lake—Time of crossing ... to Gergesa	34	268
—— Incidents in the way, 'Foxes have holes,' &c.	—	268
—— Our Lord passing the night on the	35	276
Law and the prophets—recognition of, in the Sermon on the Mount	19	142
Levites	10	75
Leper—Of the locality of the cure of the	21	161
Leprosy	—	161
Luke	1	6
Magi—Visit of the	5	38
Mark—The Evangelist	1	6
Matthew——	1	6
—— Irregularities of his gospel	22	170
Ministry of John the Baptist	7	56

INDEX TO THE ADDENDA.

	Section.	Page.
Minor prophets and the Decalogue compared		171
Miracle	11	80
Mystery, 'Unto you is given to know the ... of the kingdom'	33	263
NAME—Exhibited in the books of the New Testament	19	149
Ordination of the twelve apostles	27	211
Order, in	1	7
Our Lord at twelve years old	6	43
—— Baptism of	8	62
—— Brethren of	37	290
—— Ministry in Judæa of	12	87
—— Manner of teaching of	17	113
—— Passing the night on the lake	35	276
—— Residence in Egypt of	5	39
—— Return to Nazareth of	5	39
—— Time of his birth	4	29
Parables. On Jesus beginning to teach in	52	251
Passover	6. 43. 12	88
Pharisees	7	56
Pontius Pilate	7	55
Priests	10	74
Rabbi	12	87
Rock—The (Matthew vii. 24)	19	149
Roof—They uncovered the	22	170
Ruler—A	36	286
Sabbath day	24	191
—————— Supposed change of ... at the time of the Exodus	—	191
—————— Restitution of the paradisiacal ... at our Lord's resurrection	—	192
—————— Jews' preparation for the	—	192
—————— Remember the ... day	—	193
—————— A day of rest	—	193
—————— Exercises	—	194
—————— The second .. after the first	—	194
Sadducees	7	56
Samaritans	13	98
Scribes	25	199
Sermon on the Mount, and the Law and the Prophets	19	142
—————— Introductory to St. Paul's Epistles	—	144-.9
—————— Tabular view of	—	152
—————— Matt. v.—viii. 1, and the Sermon in the Plain, Luke vi. 17—49, compared	27	211
Simon	10	75
Synagogue	15	106
Temple	1	8
Temptation—Scene of	9	67
—————— Order of	—	67
Time of our Saviour's birth	4	29
—————— feeding the 5,000	40	316
Time of crossing the lake	34	268
Timothy—Summary of Epistles to	19	147-.9
Tittle—One	—	128
Tophet	—	129
Twelve—The .. (see also p. 215, 'Names of the twelve Apostles')	27	213
Valley of Hinnom	19	129
Verbal differences	8	62
Wilderness—Scene of the Temptations	9	67
Work of God—The (Jno. vi. 29)	43	335
Zacharias	1	7

LABOUR NOT TO BE RICH: CEASE FROM THINE OWN WISDOM.—Prov. xxiii. 4.

GENERAL INDEX.

AA—AN	Sect.	Page.	Evang.
Aaron and see p. 3, Add	1	2	Lu. 1. 5
Abel, Th; blood of	62	157	— 11. 51
Abia, Course of	1	2	— 1. 5
Abiathar the high priest	24	189	Mk. 2. 26
Abide in me, and I in you	87	389	Jno. 15,4,7
Abideth. The Son a. ev.	55	104	— 8. 35
— Christ a. for ever	32	268	— 12. 34
Abilene . . Geog.	7	55	
Abode in Galilee, Jesus and his d	52	70	Mt. 17. 22
— not in the truth	55	106	Jno. 8. 44
— Will make our a. with him	87	384	— 14. 23
Able, I am a to destroy the tem	89	427	Mt. 26. 61
Ability, According to his several	80	347	— 25. 15
Above all, He that cometh from a.	13	90	Jn). 3. 31
— Except it were given thee fr	90	444	— 19. 11
Abomination in the sight of God	69	199	Lu. 16. 15
— of desolation, What	86	331	Mt. 24. 15
Abraham, Jesus Christ the Son of	4	27	— 1. 1
— and to his seed for ever	2	12	Lu. 1. 55
— (the Jews said) We be 4	55	104	Jno. 8. 33
— is our father,	ib.	105	— 39
— Works of A.	ib.	ib.	— 39
— saw my day and was	ib.	107	— 56
— Daughter of	65	176	Lu. 13. 16
— Son of (Zaccheus)	80	247	— 19. 9
— His bosom	69	200	— 16. 22
— Prayer to him unsuc	ib.	201	—16.24-31
— refers to Moses & the P	ib.	202	— 16. 29
— The God of	65	313	Mk. 12. 26
Acceptable year, Christ preached	15	103	Lu. 4. 19
Accomplish, The decease he sh	51	54	— 9. 31
Account of thy stewardship	69	195	— 16. 2
Accuse no one falsely	7	53	— 8. 14
Accuseth you, Moses	23	180	Jno. 5, 45
Accusation, Jesus'	91	462	Mt. 27. 37
Adjure, I a, thee by	89	428	— 26. 63
Adversary	63	170	Lu. 12. 58
Adultery	19	125	Mt. 5.27,.8
Adulteress	55	99	Jno. 8. 3
Afraid	86	349	Mt. 25. 25
— Pilate was the more	90	444	Jno. 19. 8
Afoot	40	310	Mk. 6. 33
Agree with thine adversary	19	125	Mt. 5. 25
Agreed not together	89	427	Mk. 14. 56
Ah	91	463	— 15, 29
Akra . . Geog.	92	481	
Alabaster box § 29 p. 230. Lu. 7. 37.	91	254	Mt. 26. 7
Alexander and Rufus	91	457	Mk. 15. 21
Alive again (The Prodigal Son)	63	193	Lu. 15. 24
All,Elias verily cometh first,and r	51	57	Mk. 9. 12
— I, if I be lifted up, will draw	82	268	Jno. 12. 32
— live unto him	85	303	Lu. 20. 38
— into his hand, The Father	13	91	Jno. 3. 35
— delivered unto me,§ 23, p. 223,'	60	144	Lu. 10. 22
— things that I have heard	87	389	Jno. 15. 15
— these things shall come	85	320	Mt. 21. 36
— &c., When shall	86	324	Mk. 13. 4
— Jesus' reply	ib.	340	— 30
— people, Good tidings of great	4	20	Lu. 2. 10
— the people	29	225	— 7. 29
— rejoiced	65	176	— 13. 17
— gave praise	73	241	— 18 43
— mine are thine	87	400	Jno.17. 10
— Come unto me a. ye that lab	29	378	Mt. 11. 28
— the kingdoms	9	65	4. 8
— Israel, Restoration of Ad	51	67	—
— nations, Hated of	86	327	— 24. 9
— — shall be gathered	ib.	351	25, 32
— — Go and teach	96	503	— 28. 19
Alms	19	130	6. 1
— Give	62	156	Lu. 11. 41
Alone, Let them	44	9	Mt. 15. 14
Altar of incense	1	4	Lu. 1. 11
— and the temple	62	157	— 11. 51
Always, Men ought a. to pray,	73	214	— 18. 1
Amazed, There were all	17	111	Mk. 1, 27
— in themselves	41	321	— 6. 51
— Began to be sore	88	413	— 14. 33
Am, Before Abraham was, I	55	107	Jno. 8. 58
Amen, Verily §19, p. 133. Mt. 6.	96	504	Mt. 28. 20
Amos . . Ad	22	171	—
Andrew follows Jesus	10	71	Jno. 1. 40
— brings Simon to Jesus	ib.	71	— 1.41,.2
— Jesus in the house of	17	112	Mk. 1. 29
— second of 12 apostles Ad	27	215	—
— and Philip tell Jesus	82	267	Jno. 12. 22
— one of the four on mount	86	324	Mk. 13. 3

AN—AS	Sect.	Page.	Evang.
Angel	2	9	Lu. 1. 26
— appears to Zacharias	1	3	— 11
— — to Mary at Nazar	3	9	— 26
— — to Joseph in a dr	ib.	13	Mt. 1. 20
— — to shepherds at B	4	20	Lu. 2. 9
— strengthening him (Jesus)	88	414	— 22. 43
Angels, Shall give his a. charge	9	65	Mt. 4. 6
— ministered to Jesus	ib.	66	— 11
— of God ascending and des	10	73	Jno. 1. 51
— of the little ones	53	82	Mt. 18. 10
— The holy	50	43	Lu. 9. 26
— Then shall he send his	86	338	Mt. 24. 31
— at Jesus' resurrection	93	485	— 28. 2
— called 'two men'	ib.	463	Lu. 24. 4
— Two seen by Mary	ib.	491	Jno. 20. 12
Angry without cause	19	124	Mt. 5. 22
— The elder brother was	68	194	Lu. 15. 28
Anise	83	317	Mt. 23, 23
Anna, a prophetess	4	27	Lu. 2. 36
Annas and Caiaphas	7	49	— 3. 2
— Jesus led to	89	425	Jno. 18. 13
Anoint thine head	19	133	Mt. 6. 17
Anointed	15	102	Lu. 4. 18
— Jesus' feet	29	230	— 7. 38
— The apostles a. many	39	303	Mk. 6. 13
— Eyes of the blind man	55	110	Jno. 9. 6
Anointing at Bethany	81	253	Mt. 26. 7
— Judas against the	ib.	254	Jno. 12. 4
Another that beareth witness	23	179	— 5. 32
— Do we look for	29	223	Mt. 11. 3
— man's	69	198	Lu. 16. 12
— Comforter	87	383	Jno.14.16
— maid	89	431	Mt. 26, 71
Annunciation to Mary	2	9	Lu. 1. 26
Answered nothing	90	446	Mt, 27. 12
—	ib.	448	Lu. 23. 9
Antichrist, The forerunner of	88	418	Mt. 27. 48
Antipas, Herod	40	304	— 14. 1
Apart to an high mountain	51	52	— 17. 1
— in the way	77	235	— 20. 17
Apocalypse promised	10	73	Jno. 1. 51
Apostles, The twelve . . Ad	27	206	Mt. 10. 2
— On their names . . d	ib.	213	— —
— — their ordination d	ib.	211	— —
— As built on the Rock d	ib.		— —
— ask to have the parable ex	33	253	Mk. 4. 10
— sent out to preach	39	294	Mt. 9. 38
— Their return	40	309	Mk. 6. 30
— employed in feeding 5000.	13	313	Mt. 14. 19
— — — 4000. 46	27	—	15. 36
— Course of their min. indi			
— cated by that of our Lord	45	13	— 21
— questioned concerning	50	39	— 16. 15
— forbid to speak of him until.			
— further instructed	ib.	39	— 20
— The 2 key doctrines giv	ib.	40	—16.21-8
— Which should be the gre	51,3	74	— 18. 1
— Their place in the kingd	75	223	— 19. 28
— not to exercise lordship	87	375	Lu. 22. 26
— Their privilege	ib.	389	Jno. 15. 15
— Their great commission	96	503	Mt.28.19,&c.
Appearance, Judge not according	55	93	Jno. 7. 24
Appearing, Christ's glorious	86	338	Mt. 24. 30
Appears, Jesus a. to the eleven	95	498	Lu. 24. 36
Appoint unto you a kingdom	87	376	— 22. 29
Appointed me	ib.	ib.	— —
Approaches to Jerusalem . Geog.	23	182,..3	—
Arabs, Their salutation	60	141	— 10. 4
— manner of eating	87	372	Jno.13. 26
Archelaus, Antipater	5	35	Mt. 2. 22
Arimathæa (see p. 479.	93	474	Mk. 15. 43
Arise, take up thy bed	22	166	Mk. 9. 6
— Said to Jairus' daughter	36	284	Lu. 8. 54
— I will (The Prodigal Son)	68	192	— 15. 18
— let us go hence	87	386	Jno. 14. 31
Arm of the Lord	85	309	— 12. 38
Armies, He sent forth his	84	293	Mt. 22. 7
Arose, The saints which slept	92	471	— 27. 52
Ascend (I) to my Father	93	492	Jno. 20. 17
Ashamed of me and my words	50	43	Mk. 8. 38
— Of him shall the Son of m	ib.	ib.	— —
— His adversaries were	65	176	Lu. 13. 17
Asher	4	27	— 2. 36
Asia, The Churches of Note	33	255	Mt. 13. 3
Ask, seek, knock	19	138	— 7.7,&c.
— in unity	53	84	— 18, 19
— what ye will	87	388	Jno. 15. 7

xxxix

AS—BE

	Sect.	Page.	Evang.
Asked, Thou wouldest have	13	92	Jno. 4. 10
— Hitherto have ye a. noth.	87	396	— 16. 24
Ass, or ox	67	181	Lu. 14. 5
— Disciples sent for an	82	260	Mt. 21. 2
— colt	ib.	262	Jno. 12. 15
Assembled, The chief priests, &c.	97	355	Mt. 26. 3
Astonished at his doct., §17, p. 110,	19	142	— 7. 28
Atonement—see on ' Suffer many	50	40	— 16, 21
— Ad	ib.	46	—
— My blood.. shed for	67	379	— 26. 28
Augustus Cæsar, Decree of	4	19	Lu. 2. 1
Austere man	60	249	— 19. 21
Authority, Jesus spake as having	17	110	Mk. 1. 22
— —	19	142	Mt. 7. 29
— of the Son	23	178	Jno.5.26,.7
— questioned	84	283	Lu. 20.
Avarice	83	275	Mt. 21. 13
Avenge me of mine adversary	73	215	Lu. 18. 3
Avoid worldly anxiety	63	165	— 12. 22
Awake him (Lazarus)	58	123	Jno. 11. 11
Axe, now also the a. is laid	7	53	Lu. 3. 9

B.

	Sect.	Page.	Evang.
Babes, Of revealing to	60	144	Lu. 10. 21
Backward, and fell to the ground	89	413	Jno. 18. 6
Bags which wax not old	63	166	Lu. 12. 33
Band which took Jesus	88	417	Jno. 18. 3
Banias . Geog.	50	44	—
Baptism with the Holy Ghost	7	54	Lu. 3. 16
— of Jesus by John p.62, Ad	8	58	Mt. 3. 13–7
— He had yet a b to be bap.	65	169	Lu. 12. 50
— Whence was the b. of Jo	84	283	Mt. 21, 25
— that I am baptized with	77	238	— 20. 22
Baptisms, The two contrasted	7	54	Lu. 3. 16
Baptist, His birth foretold	1	4	— 1. 13
— His birth	3	15	— 57
— Why so named	7	49	Mt. 3. 1
— His ministry Ad	ib.	56	—
— Diff. betw. his & Christ's	10	74	Jn.1.15,27–30
— Beheaded	40	308	Mk. 6. 27
— Christ supposed to be John	50	36	Mt. 16. 14
Baptizing them in name of the F	96	503	— 28. 19
Baptized, He that believeth and is	98	515	Mk. 16. 16
— Jesus b. not, but his dis	13	89	Jno.3.22—4.1
— Ye shall be b. with the .	93	513	Acts 1 5
Barachias	85	320	Mt. 23. 35
Bare the bag, Judas	81	255	Jno. 12. 6
Bar-jona	50	37	Mt. 16. 17
Bartholomew, 6th of 12 apostles Ad	27	214,.5	—
Baskets, Twelve	40	314	Mk. 6. 43
— Seven	46	27	Mt. 15. 37
— Twelve and seven	46	33	Mk. 8. 19
Be broken up	86	342	Mt. 24. 43
Bear his cross	67	185	Lu. 14. 27
— long with them	73	215	— 18. 7
— Ye cannot b. them now	87	394	Jno. 16. 12
— witness unto the truth	90	442	— 18. 37
Beast	60	147	Lu. 10. 34
Beaten with many stripes	63	169	— 12. 47
Beating and killing	84	288	Mk. 12. 5
Beatitudes, The eight	19	130–2	Mt. 5. 1–12
— Contrasted	85	315.-8	—23.13–30
Beckoned	87	371	Jno. 13. 24
Bed, The paralytic to carry his	22	166	Mt. 9. 6
— Take up thy b. and walk	23	175	Jno. 5. 8
Beelzebub	31	235	Mt. 12. 24
Beginning at Jerusalem	98	512	Lu. 24. 47
— from Galilee	90	446	— 23, 5
— From the b. of the er	74	219	Mk. 10. 6
— of the Gospel of Jesus C	7	49	Jno. 1. 1
— In the b. was the word	ib.	46	Jno. 1. 1
Begged the body of Jesus	92	475	Mt. 27. 58
Begging by the wayside	79	243	Mk. 10. 46
Behold the Bridegroom cometh	86	344	Mt. 25. 6
— — man !	90	442	Jno. 19. 5
— thy son !	91	466	— 26
— mother !	ib.	ib.	— 27
— my hands!	95	498	Lu. 24. 39
Believe, if thou canst	51	60	Mk. 9. 23
— also in me	87	380	Jno. 14. 1
— That ye might	ib.	385,.6	— 29
— it not	86	334	Mt, 24. 23
— on him should receive	55	96	Jno. 7. 39
— that ye receive	84	282	Mk. 11. 24
Believed, Many	55	103	Jno. 8. 30
— not on him	85	309	— 12. 37
— not for joy	95	498	Lu. 24. 41
— Who hath b. our report?	85	309	Jno, 12. 38
Believer's privilege	87	382	— 14. 13
Believeth, He that b. on me	43	387	— 6. 35
— on him	ib.	329	— 40
Believing on Christ, Perseverance	55	103	8. 31
XI.			

BE—BO

	Sect.	Page.	Evang.
Beloved Son Mk. 1 2. §3. p. 60.	51	55	Lu. 9. 35
— I will send my	84	289	— 20. 13
Fenefactors	87	375	— 22. 25
Beside himself, Said of Jesus	30	233	Mk. 3. 21
Besought him for her	17	112	Lu. 4. 38
Bethabara p.74 Geog.	10	69	Jno. 1. 28
Bethany, When Jesus was in	81	253	— 12. 1
— the town of Mary and M	58	127	— 11. 1
Bethany Geog.	58	134	Jno. 11. 1
— Time of arrival at	81	258	—
— Time of the unction at de	ib.	ib.	—
Bethesda p. 186, do	23	175	— 5. 2
Bethlehem, Jesus born in	4	20	Lu. 2. 4-7
— Geog.	ib.	27	—
— —	5	37	—
— Christ cometh	55	96	Jno. 7. 42
Bethphage	82	260	Mt. 21. 1
Bethsaida, .. of Andrew & Peter.	10	72	Jno. 1. 44
— To the other side before	41	317	Mk. 6. 45
— Jesus heals a blind man	49	34	— 8. 22
— in Decapolis Geog.	40	315	—
Bethshan, Bysan ditto	18	117	—
Bethulia Note.	19	122	Mt. 5. 14
Beware of men	32	296	— 10. 17
— leaven of the Pharisees	63	163	Lu. 12. 1
Bewrayeth thee	89	432	Mt. 26. 73
Bezetha . Geog.	92	481	—
Bidden	84	292	— 22. 8
Bill, Take thy	69	197	Lu. 16. 6
Bind, Whatsoever thou shalt	50	39	Mt. 16. 19
— him hand and foot	84	294	— 22. 13
Birth of Jesus foretold	2	9	Lu. 1. 31
— Jesus at Bethlehem	4	20	— 2. 6, 7
— Time of Jesus' Ad	ib.	29	—
— day, Herod's	40	308	Mt. 14. 6
Bitterly, Peter went out and wept	89	433	Lu. 22 62
Blasphemy against the Holy Ghost	31	237	Mt. 12. 31
— p. 24, Addenda, §31,	62	161	—
— —	63	164	Lu. 12. 10
— Son of man	31	237	Mt. 12. 32
— —	63	164	Lu. 12. 10
— Jesus accused of	89	429	Mt. 26. 65
— Jesus stoned for	56	123	Jno. 10. 33
Blessed are the poor in spirit, &c.	19	120	Mt. 5. 3
— be ye poor, &c.	27	207	Lu. 6. 20
— be the Lord God of Israel	3	16	— 1. 68
— and brake, &c.	40	313	Mt. 14. 19
— the fishes	46	27	Mk. 8. 7
— art thou, Simon	50	37	Mt. 16. 17
— is the womb, &c.	62	154	Lu. 11, 27
— Yea rather, b. are they	ib.	ib.	— 28
— See 'Gave thanks,' Lu 22. 19.	87	368	Mt. 26. 26
— little children	74	222	Mk. 10. 16
— is he that cometh. &c.	68	180	Lu. 13. 35
— Mt. 21, 9. §82, p. 264,	85	321	Mt. 23. 39
— of my Father	86	352	— 25. 34
— is that servant, &c.	ib.	343	— 24. 46
— While he b. them, &c.	98	516	Lu. 24. 51
Blessing, Pre-requisites to Prac. R	19	121	Mt. 5. 2-8
— two sons of Joseph Scr	11	74	Mt. 10. 16
Blind, Recovering of sight to the	15	103	Lu. 4. 18
— Can the b. lead the b. ?	27	209	— 6. 39
— Took the b. man by the hand	49	34	Mk. 8. 23
— to be feasted	67	182	Lu. 14. 13
— leaders of the b.	44	9	Mt. 15. 14
— at Jericho (East of)	78	240	Lu. 18. 35
— Bartimæus (West of)	79	242	Mk. 10. 46
— and lame in the temple	82	206	Mt. 21. 14
Blood, Born not of	7	47	Jno. 1. 13
— of the New Testament	87	378	Mt. 26. 28
— Innocent	89	435	— 27. 4
— His b. be upon us	90	453	— 25
— and water	92	473	Jno. 19. 34
Boats from Tiberias	42	322	— 6. 23
Body, This is my	87	369	Mt. 26. 26
— Wheresoever the b. is	73	213	Lu. 17. 37
Boisterous, The wind was	41	320	Mt. 14. 30
Boldness, People wonder at Jesus'	55	93	Jno. 7. 26
Boldly unto Pilate	92	475	Mk. 15. 43
Bondage, Never in b. to any man	55	104	Jno. 8. 33
Book Ad	4	28	Mt. 1. 1
Borders of his garment	36	280	Mk. 5. 27
Borders of their garments	85	315	Mt. 23. 5
Born again	12	83	Jno. 3. 3
— How can a man be b. when he	ib.	ib.	— 4
— of water and the Spirit	ib.	ib.	— 5
— of the flesh	ib.	84	— 6
— blind	55	109	9. 1
— His testimony	ib.	111	— 25
— On his cure	ib.	112	—30-.3
— To this end was I	90	442	— 18. 37
Bosom of the Father	7	48	1. 18

BO—CH

	Sect.	Page.	Evang.
Bosom Leaning on Jesus"	87	371	— 13 23
Bottles, New wine must be put	22	169	Lu. 5. 38
Brake it (the bread at supper)	57	363	Mt. 26. 26
Branches of palm trees	82	259	Jno. 12. 1
— Ye are the	67	389	— 15. 5
Bread, Man shall not live by b. al	9	64	Mt. 4. 4
— The true b. from heaven	43	328	Jno. 6. 32
— Whence so much?	46	26	Mt. 15. 33
— Blessed that shall eat b. in	67	183	Lu. 14. 15
— He that eateth b. with me	67	370	Jno. 13. 18
Break not the least commandment	19	123	Mt. 5. 19
Brethren, Behold my mother and	31	240	— 12. 49
— On the b. of our Lord Ad	37	290	— —
— See on Mary's children	91	469	— —
— Neither did his b. believe	54	87	Jno. 7. 5
— All ye are	85	314	Mt. 23. 8
Brethren, Strengthen thy	87	376	Lu. 22. 32
— Go tell my	95	501	Mt. 28. 10
— Go to my	93	492	Jno. 20. 17
Bride, He that hath the	13	89	— 3. 29
— chamber, Children of the	36	278	Mt. 9. 15
Bridegroom, Behold the b. cometh	66	346	— 25. 6
Broken hearted, Heal the	15	103	Lu. 4. 19
Brother, If thy b. trespass against	53	83	Mt. 18. 15
Bruised, Set at liberty them that	15	103	Lu. 4. 18
Build, I will b. my church	50	38	Mt. 16. 19
Builders, The stone rejected by	84	290	— 21. 42
Buildings of the temple	86	323	— 24. 1
Built a tower	84	287	— 21. 33
Burden—see 'Yoke'	29	228	— 11. 30
— and heat of the day	76	233	— 20. 12
Burdens, Ye lade men with	62	157	Lu. 11. 46
— They bind heavy	85	318	Mt. 23. 4
Burial, She did it for my	81	256	— 26. 12
Burn within us, Did not our	94	496	Lu. 24. 32
Bury, Manner of the Jews to	92	476	Jno. 19. 40
Bush, God spake to Moses in the	85	308	Mk 12. 26
Bushel, Light not to be hid under	19	128	Mt. 5. 15
Buy a sword	87	377	Lu. 22. 36
— for yourselves	86	347	Mt. 25. 9
— those things	87	372	Jno. 13. 29
By and by	70	207	Lu. 17. 7

C

	Sect.	Page.	Evang.
Caiaphas, Annas and	7	49	Lu. 3. 2
— His remarkable proph	58	132	Jno. 11. 49
— Account of	86	355	Mt. 26. 3
— Jesus led away to	89	425	Jno. 18. 13
— adjures Jesus	ib.	428	Mt. 26. 63
Calf, The fatted	68	193	Lu. 15. 23
Call his name, Meaning of names,	1	4	— 1. 13
— of the first disciples Ad	20	157	Mt. 26. 57
Called his name Jesus	4	22	— 2. 21
Calm, At Jesus' word a great	34	266	— 8. 26
Came I forth	18	114	Mk. 1. 38
— down from heaven	43	329	Jno. 6. 38
Camel, Easier for a	75	227	Mt. 19. 24
Camel's hair, John clothed with	7	51	— 3. 4
Cana, Marriage at	11	76	Jno. 2. 1
Canaan	45	13	Mt. 15. 22
Candle to be placed on a c. stick	62	155	Lu. 11. 33
Candlestick	19	123	Mt. 5. 15
Cannot hear my word	55	106	Jno. 8. 43
Capernaum, Jesus goes down to	11	78	— 2. 12
— Nobleman's son	14	100	— 4. 46
— Jesus resides at	16	107	Mt. 4. 13
— heals a centur	26	218	Lu. 7. 1-10
— Upbraided	29	227	Mt. 11. 23
— visited after Transfig	72	—	17. 24
Captains of the temple	88	421	Lu. 22. 52
Captives, Deliverance to the	15	103	— 4. 18
Carcase, Wheresoever the c. is	86	336	Mt 24. 28
Carpenter? Is not this the	37	287	Mk. 6. 3
Cast out the beam	19	138	Mt. 7. 5
— Will in no wise c. out.	43	329	Jno. 6. 37
— him into outer darkness	84	294	Mt. 22. 13
— The poor widow c. in more	85	309	Mk. 12. 43
— forth the unfruitful branch	87	388	Jno. 15. 6
Casting out of Satan	31	235	Mk. 3. 23
Catch men	20	155	Lu. 5. 10
Cedron, Over the brook	87	405	Jno. 18. 1
Centurion's serv. healed	26	220	Lu. 7. 4-10
Centurion at the Crucifixion	92	471	Mt. 27. 54
Cephas,	10	71	Jno. 1. 42
Certainty, Mightest know the	1	2	Lu. 1. 4
Certainly this was a righteous man	92	472	— 23. 47
Cæsar, Caesar's	4	19	— 2. 1
— 's image and superscription	84	297	Mt. 22. 20
— We have no king but	90	443	Jno. 19. 15
Cæsarea Philippi	50	35	Mt. 16. 13
Cestius Gallus Note	86	332	— 24. 16
Chaff	7	54	— 3. 12

CH—CO

	Sect.	Page.	Evang.
Chappers (Messengers) Note	19	127	Mt. 5. 41
Charged them straitly	36	284	Mk. 5. 43
Chastise, I will therefore ch. him	90	449	Lu. 23. 16
Cheer, Be of good	41	320	Mk. 6. 50
Chief priests and elders	84	282	Mt. 21. 23
—	86	355	— 26. 3
Child, And they had no	1	3	Lu. 1. 7
Children of God	19	122	Mt. 5. 9
— (God of Abraham)	85	303	Mk. 12. 26
— of your Father which is	19	128	Mt. 5. 45
— of the kingdom	23	220	— 8. 12
— in the markets	29	226	— 11. 16
— Then are the ch. free	52	73	— 17. 26
— Become as little	ib.	75	— 18. 3
— Suffer the little c. to c	74	221	Mk. 10. 14
— Ye are ch. of them	85	318	Mt. 23. 31
— Left no	ib.	301	Lu. 20. 31
— Weep . . . for your	91	457	— 23. 28
— have ye any meat?	97	506	Jno. 21. 5
— Zebedee's	92	472	Mt. 27. 56
Chorazin	60	142	Lu. 10. 13
Chosen, Many be called, but few Ad	76	233	Mt. 20. 16
— of God	91	463	Lu. 23. 35
Christ the Lord	4	21	— 2. 11
Christ, The Lord's	24		Lu. 2. 26
— The C. the Son of the lv.	50	35	Mt. 16. 16
— His sufferings foretold	ib.	40	— 21
— glory	ib.	43	— 27
— on the Holy Mount	51	52	— 17. 1-5
— Jews' notions of	55	93	Jno. 7. 27
— This is the	ib.	96	— 41
— the Son of God, § 58, p.			
130, Jno. 11. 27	89	428	Mt. 26. 63
— What think ye of?	85	306	— 22. 42
— Many shall say, I am	86	325	— 24. 5
— Son of the Blessed	89	428	Mk. 14. 61

John's Gospel gives an outline of the evidence that Jesus is the Christ.
See synopsis of, § 100, p. 519.

	Sect.	Page.	Evang.
Church, on this Rock I will build	50	38	Mt. 16. 18
— Tell it to the	53	83	— 18. 17
Circuit of Galilee, Jesus' first Ad	18	118	— —
— — First partial do	26	204	— —
— — Second general	30	232	Lu. 8. 1
— — Third general	38	293	Mt. 9. 35
Circumcision of John	15		Lu. 1. 59
— Jesus	4	22	— 2. 21
City of David	9	—	— 4
— The Holy	9	64	Mt. 4. 5
— His own	35	274	— 9. 1
Citizen of that country	68	191	Lu. 15 15
Clay, Anointing with	55	110	Jno. 9. 6-11
Clean, but not all	87	366	— 13. 10
— through the word	ib.	387	— 15. 3
Cleansing of the leper	21	159	Lu. 5. 12,.3
— temple	12	81	Jno.2.13-.7
— — second	83	277	Mt.21.12,.3
— — On the time of Ad	ib.	279	— —
Cloke, No c. for their sins	87	390	Jno. 15. 22
Cloth, New c unto an old garment	36	279	Mt. 9. 16
Clothes, The high priest rent his	89	429	— 26. 65
Coasts, Bethlehem and the	5	34	— 2. 16
— Depart from their	35	275	Mk. 5. 17
Coat, If any man . . . take away	19	127	Mt. 5. 40
— Jesus' c. was without seam	91	461	Jno. 19. 28
Coats, He that hath two	7	53	Lu. 3. 11
— shoes, staves	39	296	Mt. 10. 10
Cock-crowing, or in the morning see			
'Watch'	86	342	Mk. 13. 35
Cock crew, and Peter remembered	89	431	—14.68•72
Colossians, Epistle to the Ad	19	146	— —
Colt, Ye shall find an ass tied, and	82	260	— 21. 2
Come and see	10	71	Jno.1.39,46
— down, are my child die	14	100	— 4. 49
— The Son of man be	39	300	Mt. 10. 23
— That prophet that should	41	317	Jno. 6. 14
— Art thou he that should	29	222	Mt. 11. 3
— from God	87	365	Jno. 13. 3
— I c. to thee (the Father)	ib.	401	— 17. 11
— No man can c. unto me exc	43	330	— 6. 44
— unto me all ye that labour	29	228	Mt. 11. 28
— Then shall the end	86	330	— 24. 14
Comest in thy kingdom	91	465	Lu. 23. 42
Cometh, He that c. to me	43	329	Jno. 6. 35
— He that c. in the name of	66	180	Lu. 13. 35
— The Lord	82	264	Mt. 21. 9
— No man c. unto the F	87	381	Jno. 14. 6
Coming after me	10	69	— 1. 27

XLI

CO–DA

	Sect.	Page.	Evang.
Coming in his kingdom	50	44	Mt. 16, 28
— of the Son of man	86	335	— 24, 27
Comfort, Be of good	36	282	Lu. 8, 48
— them the sisters of Laza	58	129	Jno. 11. 19
Comforted, They that mourn sh	19	120	Mt. 5. 4
Comforter, Another	87	383	Jno. 14. 16
— The Spirit of truth	ib.	ib.	— 17
— The Holy Ghost	ib.	385	— 26
— If I depart, I will send	ib.	383	— 16. 7
Comfortless, I will not leave you	ib.	383	— 14, 18
Commandment of God	44	5	Mt. 15. 3
— He gave me a	85	312	Jno. 12. 49
— This c. have I rec	55	117	— 10. 18
— A new c. I give	87	374	— 13. 34
— This is my c., that	ib.	389	— 15. 12
Commandments, Keep the	75	224	Mt. 19. 17
— of men	44	7	— 15. 9
— The two great	85	304	Mk. 12.28-31
— and sermon on m	19	137	Recapitula.
Commended, Foresight	60	197	Lo. 16. 8
Committed much	63	169	— 12. 48
Companies on the green grass	40	313	Mk. 6. 39
Company, Danger of bad	ib.	308	Mt.14.9-11
Compassion, Jesus'	21	160	Mk. 1. 41
— on the widow of Nain	29	221	Lu. 7. 13
— on the multitudes	40	311	Mt. 14. 14
— — —	46	26	— 15. 32
— on the man born bl.	79	244	— 20. 34
Compel them to come in	67	184	Lu. 14. 23
Concord in prayer recommended	53	84	Mt. 18. 19
Condemn, Neither do I c. thee,	55	100	Jno. 8. 11
Condescension of Jesus,	37	287	Mk. 6. 3
Confessing their sins	7	42	— 1. 5
Considered not the loaves, &c.,	41	321	Mk. 6. 52
Consolation of Israel	4	24	Lu. 2. 25
Continue in my word	55	103	Jno. 8. 31
Continued with me in my temp	87	375	Lu. 22. 28
Converted, Except ye be	52	75	Mt. 18. 3
Convinceth me of sin	55	106	Jno. 8. 46
Corinthians, Epistles to	Ad	19	144, .5
Corn, Disciples plucked	24	188	Mt. 12. 1-8
Could not cast him out	51	59	Mk. 9. 18
Council, In danger of the	19	124	Mt. 5. 22
Counsel of God	29	226	Lu. 7. 30
Country, In the same c. shepherds	4	20	— 2. 8
— His own	37	286	Mk. 6. 1
— near to the wilderness	58	133	Jno. 11. 54
Covenant, His holy	3	17	Lu. 1. 72
Covetous, The Pharisees were	69	198	— 16. 14
Covetousness, Beware of	63	164	— 12. 15
Cross, Taketh not his	39	302	Mt. 10. 38
— Take up his	50	42	Mk. 8. 34
— Bear his	67	185	Lu. 14. 27
— Compelled to bear his	91	457	Mt. 27. 32
Crowned, Jesus c. with thorns	ib.	455	— 29
Crucify Mt. 20, 19 § 77, p. 236,	90	443	Jno. 19. 6
Crucified, Jesus delivered to be	ib.	453	Mt. 27. 26
— There they c. him	91	459	Lu. 23. 33
Cry of unclean spirit	17	110	Mk. 1. 24
Crumbs, The dogs eat of the	45	15	Mt. 15. 27
Cubit	19	135	— 6. 27
Cumin	85	317	— 23. 23
Cup of cold water only p.203. Mt. 10,42	52	76	Mk. 9. 41
— that I shall drink of	77	237	Mt. 20. 22
— given to the disciples	87	378	— 26.27,.8
— Let this c. pass from me	88	414	— 39
— which my Father hath given	ib.	420	Jno. 18. 11
Cursedst, The fig tree which thou	84	281	Mk. 11. 21
Curseth, He that c. father or m	44	6	Mt. 15. 4
Custom (reading the Scriptures	15	102	Lu. 4. 16
Cut him in sunder § 83, p.168. Lu.12.46.86		244	Mt. 24. 51

D

		Sect.	Page.	Evang.
Daniel, Book of	Ad	22	172	
— Abomination spoken of by		86	331	Mt. 24. 15
Daily bread		62	152	Lu. 11. 3
Danced, Herodias' daughter		40	307	Mk. 6. 22
Darkness, Have loved		12	86	Jno. 3. 19
— Not walk in		55	100	— 8. 12
— Not abide in		85	311	— 12. 46
— Outer		85	350	Mt. 25. 30
— at the crucifixion		91	446	Lu.23.44,.5
Darkened, Sun shall be		86	337	Mt. 24. 29
David, His eating shewbread		24	189	Mk. 2. 26
— The throne of		2	10	Lu. 1. 32
— Christ, the Son of		4	23	Mt. 1. 1
— Is not this the Son of		31	234	— 12. 23
— Son of D., have mercy		36	285	— 9. 27
— — — —		78	240	Lu. 18. 38
— Thou Son of		79	243	Mk. 10. 47

DA–DI

	Sect.	Page.	Evang.
David The son of	85	306	Mt. 22, 42
— The house and lineage of	4	19	Lu. 2. 4
— Christ cometh of the seed	55	96	Jno. 7. 42
Daughter, Jairus' d. restored	36	279	Mt. 9.18-25
— of the woman of Can	45	13	— 15. 22
Day, While it is	55	109	Jno. 9. 4
— Should raise it up at the last	48	329	— 6. 39
— I will — him	ib.	329	— 40
— Third	77	235	Mt. 20. 19
— In this thy	82	264	Lu. 19. 42
— time	86	357	— 21. 37
Days, When they had fulfilled	6	40	— 2. 43
— After three	ib.	41	— 46
— In those	7	50	Mt. 3. 1
— After two	14	100	Jno. 4. 43
— After six	51	52	Mt. 17. 1
— The d. will come	72	211	Lu. 17, 22
— of Noe	ib.	212	— 26
— of the Son of man	ib.	ib.	— 30
Dayspring	3	18	— 1. 79
Dead, Let the d. bury their	34	265	Mt. 8. 22
— Lazarus is	58	123	Jno. 11. 14
— Tho' he were d. yet shall he	ib.	129	— 25
— and is alive again	63	193	Lu. 15. 24
Deaf and impediment, &c.	46	24	Mk. 7. 32
Dealt with me	1	6	Lu. 1. 25
Death, Shadow of	3	18	— 79.
— Not see d. before he had	4	24	— 2. 26
— Jesus spake of his	87	395	Jno. 16. 16
— Not taste of d. till, &c.	50	44	Mt. 16. 28
— Never see	55	107	Jno. 8. 51
Debtors, The two,	29	231	Lu. 7. 41
Debts, Forgive us our,	19	183	Mt. 6. 12
Decalogue, and minor proph. comp	ib.	171	Addenda
Decapolis — Mt. 4, 25. § 18, p. 116,	46	24	Mk. 7. 31
Decease, which he should accom	51	54	Lu. 9. 31
Deceive, Take heed that no man,	86	324	Mt. 24. 4
— Jesus so called	92	477	— 27. 63
Decrease, I must	13	90	Jno. 3. 30
Decree from Cæsar Augustus	4	19	Lu. 2. 1
Dedication, Feast of	56	120	Jno. 10. 22
Deep, Into the	35	274	Addenda
Defiled	44	4	Mk. 7. 2
— Lest they should be	90	440	Jno. 18. 28
Defileth, What	44	8	Mt. 15. 11
Demoniac, One blind and dumb	31	234	— 12. 22
— Two dwelling among	35	269	— 8. 28
Den of thieves, The temple made	83	278	Mk. 11. 17
Denial, Peter's foretold	87	377	Lu. 22. 34
— Their accomplishment	89	430	Mt. 26. 69-75
— On the times of Peter's	ib.	437	Addenda
Departed from me	19	141	Mt. 7. 23
Departed from Galilee	71	209	— 19. 1
— from the temple	86	323	— 24. 1
Derided, The Pharis. who were cov	69	198	Lu. 16. 14
Deserts, In the d. until Isr	3	19	— 1. 80
Desolate, Your house is left	66	179	— 13. 35
Desolation of Jerusalem,	86	334	— 21. 24
Despise not one of these little	53	82	Mt. 18. 10
Despiseth, He that d. you, despis	60	143	Lu. 10. 16
Despised others,	73	216	— 18. 9
Destroy, He will miserably	84	289	Mt. 21. 41
Deuteronomy	19	143	Addenda
Devil, Jesus tempted of the	9	63	Mt. 4. 1-11
— An unclean d. cried, Let us	17	110	Lu. 4. 34
— One of you is a	43	334	Jno. 6. 70
— Hast a	55	92	— 7. 20
— Ye are of your father the	ib.	106	— 8. 44
Devils forbid to confess Christ	17	112	Mk. 1. 34
— Those possessed with d. h	18	116	Mt. 4. 24
Devour widows' houses	85	315	— 23. 14
Didymus (Thomas)	58	128	Jno. 11. 16
Die, And not	43	331	— 6. 50
— Shall never	58	130	— 11. 26
— Neither can they d. any more	65	302	Lu. 20. 36
Differences, on verbal	8	62	Addenda
Different destinations	86	348	Mt. 25. 20-30
Digged in the earth	ib.	348	— 18
Dilemma of the Pharisees and Her	84	295	— 22.15-22
Dines, Jesus d. with a Pharisee	29	229	Lu.7.36,&c.
— see 'Eat bread'	67	181	— 14. 1
Dinner, Prepared my	84	292	Mt. 22. 4
Discern, Ye can	47	29	— 16. 3
Disciples, Those first called	11	76	Jno. 2. 2
— What required in	50	42	Mt. 16. 24
— dispute concerning prec	52	80	Addenda
— refer the dispute to Jes	53	82	Mt. 18. 1
— to beware of the scribes	85	308	Mk. 12. 38
— taught to pray	62	151	Lu.11.2,&c.
— sent for an ass	82	260	Mt. 20,1-2

XLII

DI—EN

	Sect.	Page.	Evang.
Disciples, Jesus prays for his	87	400	Jno. 17. 9
— Jesus exhorts them to p	88	416	Lu. 22. 40
Disobedient to the wisdom of the	1	5	— 1.17
Dispersion, Sign of	86	381	— 21. 20
Dispossessions, On the	02	161	Addenda
Divided, House d. against itself	31	235	Mk. 3. 24
— unto them his living.	68	100	Lu. 15. 12
Divorcement, Writing of	19	126	Mt. 5. 31
— Bill of	74	219	Mk. 10. 4
— On	ib.	218	Mt. 19. 3
Do, Whatsoever ye would that men	19	139	— 7. 12
— the will of my Father	31	240	— 12. 50
— What shall we?	43	327	Jno. 6. 28
— and thou shalt live	60	145	Lu. 10. 28
Doctors, Jesus among the	0	41	— 2. 46
Doctrine, My d. is not mine	55	91	Jno. 7. 16
Doctrines, Teaching for	44	7	Mt. 15. 9
Dogs, Give not that which is holy	19	139	— 7. 6
— came and licked his sores	69	200	Lu. 16. 21
Door, Christ is the	55	115	Jno. 10. 9
Doors, Know that it is near, even	86	340	Mt. 24. 33
Doubt, How long make us to	56	121	Jno. 10. 24
Doves, Pair of turtle	4	24	Lu. 2. 24
— Harmless as	30	298	Mt. 10. 16
— sold in the temple	12	81	Jno. 2. 16
—	83	277	Mt. 21. 12
Draught, Miraculous d. of fishes	20	153	Lu. 5.1-11
— Second —	97	506	Jno. 21. 6
Draw him, Except the Father	43	330	— 6. 44
— all unto me	82	268	— 12. 32
Dream	2	13	Mt. 1. 20
— Wise men's	5	53	— 2. 12
Drink neither wine	1	4	Lu. 1. 15
— I will not	87	364	— 22. 18
— ye all of it	ib.	378	Mt. 26. 27
— Ye shall d. indeed of my cup	77	238	— 20. 23
Drops of blood, His sweat was as	88	414	Lu. 22. 44
Dropsy, Man cured of	67	181	— 14. 4
Drowned in the depth of the sea	52	81	Addenda
Dry, What shall be done in the	91	458	Lu. 23. 31
Dumb man possessed with a devil	36	285	Mt. 9. 32
— spirit cast out	62	153	Lu.11.14,&c.
Dust, Shake off the	39	298	Mt. 10. 14
Dwelleth in me	43	352	Jno. 6. 56

E

Eagles be gathered together	86	333	Mt. 24. 28
Early, Jesus at prayer	18	114	Mk. 1. 35
— in the temple teaching	55	99	Jno. 8. 2
Earnestly, He prayed the more	88	414	Lu. 22. 44
Earth, Meek shall inherit the	19	120	Mt. 5. 5
— Distress of nations on the	86	385	Lu. 21. 25
— The whole	ib.	340	— 35
Earth did quake	92	470	Mt. 27. 51
Earthly things	12	85	Jno. 3. 12
Earthquakes	86	326	Mt. 24. 7
Easier for a camel	75	227	— 19. 24
East and west	28	220	— 8. 11
— Out of the e. even to the west	86	335	— 24. 27
Eat, They have nothing to	40	312	Mk. 6. 36
— Our fathers did e. manna	43	327	Jno. 6. 31
— bread on the sabbath day	67	181	Lu. 14. 1
— in the kingdom of God	ib.	183	— 15
Eaten and drunk in thy presence	68	178	— 13. 26
Eateth bread with me	87	370	Mk. 14. 18
Eating, As they were	ib.	368	Mt. 26. 26
Ebal, Mount	13	93	Jno. 4. 20
Ecclesiastes	19	172	Addenda
Egg, If he shall ask an	62	152	Lu. 11. 12
Egypt, Jesus' sojourn in	5	34	— 2.13-.5
Eight days were accomplished	4	22	— 21
— about an	51	51	— 9. 28
Eighth day, John circumcised on	3	15	— 1. 50
Elders, Jesus predicts his rejection	50	40	Mk. 8. 31
— Tradition of the	44	4	— 7. 3
Elect's sake	86	333	Mt. 24. 22
— The very	ib.	335	— 31
— Gather together his	ib.	339	— 31
Eli, Eli, Lama, &c., &c.	91	466	— 27. 46
Elias sent to a widow of Sarepta	15	104	Lu. 4. 25
— John not E. of the past	10	63	Jno. 1. 21
— But the E. which was to c	29	225	Mt. 11. 14
— shall first come	57	—	17. 11
— is come already	ib.	58	— 12
Elisabeth	1	3	Lu. 1. 5
Eliseus, His healing Naaman	15	105	— 4. 27
Embalming (Anoint)	81	256	Mk. 14. 8
Emmanuel	2	14	Mt. 1. 23
Empty, Sent him away	84	288	Mk. 12. 3
Encouragement to ask of God	87	397	Jno. 16. 33
End, Then shall the e. come	86	330	Mt. 24. 14
— Loved them unto the	87	365	Jno. 13. 1

EN—FA

	Sect.	Page.	Evang.
End, Things concerning me have	ib.	377	Lu. 22. 37
— He that endureth to the	39	299	Mt. 10. 22
Endor	51	65	Geog. Not.
Endure to the end	86	329	— 24. 13
Enemies, Those mine	80	250	Lu. 19. 27
— shall cast a trench	82	265	— 43
English, Their origin	67	195	Addenda
— privileges and responsib	86	343	Mt.24,45,-6
— see 'Ephraim'			
Enough... Said of two swords	87	347	Lu. 22. 38
Enquire, Do ye	ib.	305	Jno. 10. 19
Entered, Satan e. into Judas	60	356	Lu. 22. 3
Entering into the ship again	48	31	Mk. 8. 13
Ephraim, the blessing on	74	222	— 10. 16
— appointed to bring forth the			
fruit of the kingdom	84	290	Mt. 21. 43
— see on 'Prodigal son'	68	187	Introduc.
— see 'City' and 'Mount			
Ephphatha	46	25	Mk. 7. 34
Epistles of Paul	19	144	Addenda
— Peter	50	47	ditto
Esaias, The book of	15	102	Lu. 4. 17
— quoted Mt. 12. 18 p. 201 § 26.	32	245	Mt. 12. 14
— Well did E. say	44	7	— 15. 7
Esoteric and exoteric	33	263	Addenda
Esther	19	172	ditto
Eternal life	12	86	Jno. 3. 15
— What... do to inh	75	224	Mt. 19. 16
— The righteous into life	86	354	— 25. 46
— And this is life e. to know	87	399	Jno. 17. 3
Everlasting Life	75	230	Lu. 18. 30
— punishment	86	354	Mt. 25. 46
Evangelists, The four	1	6	Addenda
Evening	40	311	— 14. 14
— When the e. was come	41	318	Jno. 6. 16
— it is e. ye say	47	29	Mt. 16. 2,3
Even, When e. was come	87	364	— 26. 20
Eucharist	ib.	369	Lu. 22. 19
Eunuchs	74	220	Mt. 19. 12
Evil thoughts	44	10	— 15. 19
— servant	86	343	— 24. 48
— Is thine eye?	76	234	— 20. 15
— Keep them from the	87	402	Jno. 17. 15
Exact no more than, &c.	7	53	Lu. 3. 13
Exalt himself	85	315	Mt. 23. 12
Exalteth himself	67	182	Lu. 14. 11
Example, Public	2	13	Mt. 1. 19
— Christ our e. in suff	50	47	Addenda
— of scribes, &c., not to b	85	312	— 23. 3
Excellent, Most	1	1	Lu. 1. 3
Exchangers	86	350	Mt. 25. 27
Excommunication versus Arguin	55	111	Jno.9.22,33
Excuse, Began to make	67	183	Lu. 14. 18
Exodus, Book of	19	142	Addenda
— Jesus'	51	54	— 9. 31
Expedient for us	58	133	Jno. 11. 50
— for you that I go away	87	393	— 16. 7
Extortion and excess	85	317	Mt. 23, 25
Extortioners	73	217	Lu. 18. 11
Eyes, having e., see ye not?	48	33	Mk. 8. 13
Eye witnesses and ministers	1	1	Lu. 1. 2
Eye for an eye	19	127	Mt. 5. 38
— be single	ib.	134	— 6. 22
— An evil	44	10	Mk. 7. 22
— If thine e. offend thee	52	78	— 9. 47
Ezra	19	172	Addenda

F.

Fail not, I have prayed that thy f	87	376	Lu. 22. 32
Faith, Medium of forgiveness	29	232	— 7. 50
— of receiving h	36	280	Mk.5,28,-9
— O woman, great is thy	45	15	Mt. 15. 28
— If ye have f. as a grain, &c.	70	207	Lu. 17. 6
— Shall he find f. on the e	73	216	— 18. 8
Faithful in that which is least	69	198	— 16. 10
— If ye have not been	ib.	ib.	— 10. 12
Fail and rising again of many, &c.	4	20	— 2. 34
— down and worship me	9	66	Mt. 4. 9
— Whosoever shall f. on this st	84	290	— 21. 44
False witnesses	91	458	Lu. 23. 30
— on us	44	10	Mt. 15. 20
— witnesses	89	427	— 26. 59
Fame of Jesus spread abroad	15	102	Lu. 4. 14
— Mk. 1. 28, 517, p. 111	18	116	Mt. 4. 24
Famines	86	326	— 24. 7
Father, I must be about my F. b	6	42	Lu. 2. 49
— The only begotten of the	7	48	Jno. 1. 14
— Our F., which art in h	10	132	Mt. 6. 9
— His witness to the Son	39	179	Jno. 5. 37
— All that the F. hath	43	329	— 6. 37
— And I live by the	ib.	332	— 57
— greater than all	56	122	— 10. 29

XLIII

FA—FO

	Sect.	Page.	Evang.
Father revealed in the Son	87	382	Jno. 14.10,.1
— greater than I	ib.	385	— 28
— Herein is my F. glorified	ib.	389	— 15. 8
— Because I go to my	ib.	394	— 16. 10
— Show you plainly of the	ib.	396	— 25
— I came forth from the	ib.	ib.	— 28
— The prodigal's return to	68	192	Lu. 15. 18
— Call no man	85	314	Mt. 23. 9
— forgive them	91	459	Lu. 23. 34
Fathers, As he spake to our	2	12	— 1. 55
— Not as your	43	232	Jno. 6. 58
Farthing, The uttermost	19	125	Mt. 5. 26
— Two sparrows sold for	39	301	— 10. 29
— Two mites, which in	85	309	Mk. 12. 42
Fast twice in the week	73	217	Lu. 18. 12
Fasted, Jesus f. forty days	9	63	Mk. 1. 13
— John's disciples f. often	22	169	— 2. 18
— The Pharisees f. oft	36	278	Mt. 9. 14
Fashion of Jesus' countenance alt	51	52	Lu. 9. 29
Favour with God	2	9	— 1. 30
Favoured, Hail, highly	ib.	ib.	— 28
Fear not to take unto thee Mary	ib.	12	Mt. 1. 20
— Serve him without	3	17	Lu. 1. 74
— them not	29	300	Mt. 10. 26
— him which is able	ib.	301	— 28
— of the Jews	55	91	Juo. 7. 13
Fearful sights	86	358	Addenda
Feast, The Passover, a f. of the J	23	175	— 5. 1
— On the f. of Tabernacles	54	89	Addenda
— Midst of the f. of Tabernacl	55	91	— 7. 14
— Last, that great day of the	ib.	95	— 37
— of the Dedication	56	124	Addenda
— Not on the f. day, lest, &c.	86	356	Mt. 26. 5
Feed, The Prodigal sent to f. sw	68	191	Lu. 15. 15
Feedeth, Your heavenly Father	19	135	Mt. 6. 26
Feeding of 5000, &c	40	313	—14.19-21
— Time of year	ib.	316	Addenda
— Locality of the	ib.	315	di. do
— of the 4000, &c.	46	27	— 15. 38
Feet of Jesus washed with tears	29	230	Lu. 7. 38
— Jesus washes his disciples'	87	366	Jno. 13. 4
Fell backward to the ground	88	418	— 18. 6
Fever, Peter's wife's mother	17	112	Mt. 8. 14
Few . . . that find it	19	139	— 7. 14
— Are there f. that be saved?	66	177	Lu. 13. 23
Field, The f. is the world	33	259	Mt. 13. 38
— Treasure hid in a	ib.	261	— 44
Fifty, Thou art not yet f. years	55	107	Jno. 8. 57
Fig tree, Jesus saw Nathanael	10	73	— 1. 48
— Parable of the barren	64	174	Lu. 13. 6-9
— afar off, having leaves	83	275	Mt. 21. 19
— having nothing but	ib.	ib.	Mk. 11. 13
— No man to eat fruit of	ib.	276	— 14
— No fruit to grow on it	ib.	275	Mt. 21. 19
— withered away	84	281	Mk. 11. 21
Fill ye up the measure	85	318	Mt. 23. 32
Filled, Let the children first be	45	15	Mk. 7. 27
Finger of God	62	153	Lu. 11. 20
— (Spirit of God)	31	236	Mt. 12. 28
Finished, It is	91	468	Jno. 19. 30
Fire, Wilt thou that we comm	59	136	Lu. 9. 54
— on the earth	63	169	— 12. 49
First-born	4	20	— 2. 7
Fish, If he ask a	19	139	Mt. 7. 10
— that first cometh up	52	73	— 17. 27
Fishes, Miraculous draught of	20	153	Lu 5. 1-11
— after Jesus' resur	97	506	Jno. 21. 6
Five loaves of the 5000	48	33	Mt. 16. 9
Flax, Smoking	26	202	— 12. 20
Flee ye into another city	39	300	Lu. 10. 23
Flesh and blood	50	37	— 16. 17
— No. f be saved	86	333	— 24. 22
Fold, One f. and one Shepherd	55	116	Jno. 10. 16
Followed, The two disciples f. J	10	70	— 1. 37
Follow me	16	108	Mt. 4. 19
Fool, a term of reproof	62	156	Lu. 11. 40
Foolish, who built on the sand	19	141	Mt. 7. 26
Foolishness	44	10	Mk. 7. 22
Foot, If thy f. offend thee	52	77	— 9. 45
Footstool	85	307	— 12. 36
Forbade, We f. him because	52	76	— 9. 38
Forbid him not	ib.	ib.	— 39
Force, by f. to make him a king	41	318	Jno. 6. 15
Forgive, Father f. them	91	459	Lu. 23. 34
Forgiveness enforced	19	133	Mt. 6. 14
— the ground of obed	29	231	Lu. 7. 41,.2
— Love a sign of	ib.	ib.	— 47
— Faith the Medium of	ib.	232	— 50
— How often to be exer	53	84	Mt. 18. 21,.2
— Prayer in the spirit f	84	262	Mk. 11. 25

XLIV

FO—GL

	Sect.	Page.	Evang.
Fornication, Not born of	55	105	Jno. 8. 41
Forsaken, My God, why, &c.	91	467	Mk. 15. 34
Forstook all, and followed him	20	155	Lu. 5. 11
Forswear thyself, Thou shalt not	19	126	Mt. 5. 33
Foundation laid in Sion, High M	51	52	Note.
— of the world	86	352	— 25. 34
Fourfold, I restore him	80	246	Lu. 19. 8
Fox, Herod so called	66	179	— 13. 32
Foxes have holes	59	136	— 9. 58
Fragments, Cather up the	34	265	Mt. 8. 20
Frankincense	40	314	Jno. 6. 12
Frankly forgave them both	5	33	Mt. 2. 11
Free, The truth shall make	29	231	Lu. 7. 42
Freely give	55	103	Jno. 8. 32
Friend, wherefore art thou come?	39	296	Mt. 10. 8
Friends, Make to yourselves	88	419	— 26. 50
— Ye are my	69	197	Lu. 16. 9
Fruit, If it bear f., well	87	389	Jno.15.14,.5
— Much	64	174	Lu. 13. 9
— Go and bring forth	87	388	Jno. 15. 8
— That your f. should remain	ib.	389	— 16
Fruits in their seasons	84	210	Mt. 21. 41
— Bringing forth the	ib.	290	— 43
— By their f. ye shall know th	19	140	— 7.16-20
Fruitfulness, Different degrees of	32	244	— 13. 5-8
Fuller, So as no f. on earth, &c.	51	53	Mk. 9. 3
Fulfilled, The time is	16	108	— 1. 15
Fulfilment of prophecy	17	113	Mt. 8. 17
Fulness, Of his	7	48	Jno. 1. 16

G.

	Sect.	Page.	Evang.
Gabbatha	90	445	Jno. 19. 13
Gadara	Note. 25	272	Mt. 8. 34
Gadarenes	ib.	269	Mk. 5. 1
Galatians, Ep.	19	145	Addenda
Galilee, Would go forth into	10	72	Jno. 1. 43
— Jesus goes into	14	100	— 4. 43
— of the Gentiles	10	107	Mt. 4. 15
— Multitudes followed Jesus	13	116	— 25
— On ministry near the sea	32	250	Geog. Not.
— Sea of	ib.	ib.	ibid.
— Passed through, after Trans. figuration	52	70	Mk. 9. 30
— Art thou also of	55	97	Jno. 7. 52
— On Jesus' departure from	71	209	Addenda
— Into G., into a mountain.	96	502	Mt. 28. 16
Galileans, whose blood Pilate, &c.	64	173	Lu. 13. 1
Garment, Hem of his	36	280	Mk. 5. 27
Garments, Spread their g, in the	82	263	Mt. 21. 8
— Laid aside his	87	366	Jno. 13. 4
Garner, Wheat into his	7	54	Mt. 3. 12
Gates of hell	50	39	— 16. 18
Gather together in one	63	133	Jno. 11. 52
— out of his kingdom	33	260	Mt. 13. 41
— together his elect	86	339	— 24. 31
Gave me no meat	ib.	339	— 25. 42
Genealogy of Jesus	4	20	— 1. 1-17
Genealogies of Matt. and Luke Ad	ib.	30	Lu.3.23-38
Generation, This wicked	31	239	Mt. 12. 45
— This adulterous	50	43	Mk. 8. 38
— Shall come upon this	85	320	Mt. 23 36
Genesis and first commandment	19	142	Addenda
Gennesaret, Lake of	20	153	Lu. 5. 1
Gentiles, Their example	19	135	Mt. 6. 32
— Go not into the way of	39	295	— 10. 5
— In his name shall the	26	209	— 12. 21
Gergesa, On the time of crossing	34	268	Addenda
Gergesenes, The country of	35	274	Geog. Not.
Gerizim	13	93	Jno. 4. 20
Get thee behind me	9	66	Lu. 4. 8
Gethsemane	89	412	Mt. 26. 36
—	ib.	42	Geog. Not.
Gift of God	13	92	Jno. 4. 10
— It is a	44	6	Mt. 15. 5
Gifts presented to Christ	5	33	— 2. 11
— Be just before presenting	19	125	— 5.23,.4
Girded, Let your loins be	63	166	Lu. 12. 35
Girdle about his loins	7	51	Mt. 3. 4
Give, What shall a man, &c.,	50	43	— 16. 26
— an account of thy stewardsh	69	196	Lu. 16. 2
— What will ye g. me?	86	357	Mt. 26. 15
Given me, Of all which he hath	43	329	Jno. 6. 39
Glorified, Now is the Son of man	87	373	— 13. 31
— I am g. in them	ib.	400	— 17. 10
Glorify, Straightway	ib.	373	— 13. 32
— thy Son	ib.	396	— 17. 1
— That thy Son also may g.	ib.	ib.	— —
— thou me with thine own	ib.	399	— 17. 5

GL–HA

	Sect.	Page.	Evang.
Glory of the Lord	4	20	Jn. 2. 9
— of thy people Israel	ib.	25	— 32
— to God in the highest	ib.	21	— 14
— of them (of all lands)	9	65	Mt. 4. 8
— Manifested forth his	11	78	Jno. 2. 11
— Shall come in the g. of his F	50	43	Lu. 9. 26
— his own	ib.	ib.	— 26
— Jesus appeared in	51	54	— 31
— Moses and Elias appeared in	ib.	53	Mt. 17. 3
— Pet. and Jas. and John saw J	ib.	54	Lu. 9. 32
— His own	55	92	Jno. 7. 18
— Thou shalt see the g. of God	58	131	— 11. 40
— Throne of his	75	228	Mt. 19. 28
— Esaias saw his	85	310	Jno. 12. 41
God, The Lord G. of Israel hath			
redeemed his people	2	16	Lu. 1. 68
— our Creator and Preserver	19	135	Mt.6.25,&c.
— Exam. of kindness and forb	19	128	— 5.45–.S
— so loved the world that he	12	86	Jno. 3. 16
— to be worship'd in spirit	13	94	— 4. 23
— to be served with our whole	85	304	Mk.12.29,30
— my G. and your G.	53	492	Jno. 20. 17
Godhead—see 'Father,' 'Son,' and			
Holy Ghost,	06	503	Mt. 23. 19
Gods, Rulers so called	56	122	Jno. 10. 34
Gold of the temple	85	310	Mt. 23. 16
Golgotha	91	458	— 27. 33
Gone out, When he was	57	373	Jno. 13. 31
Good, Can there any g. thing, &c.	10	72	— 1. 46
— works, May see your	19	128	Mt. 5. 16
— things, Your Father give	ib.	139	— 7. 11
— tree bringeth forth g. fruit	27	210	Lu. 6. 43
— ground, Received seed into	33	257	Mt 13. 23
— Shepherd, Parable of the	55	114	Jno.10.1-21
— part, Mary hath chosen the	61	150	Lu. 10. 42
— Master, what, &c.	75	222	Mt. 19. 16
— None g. but one	ib.	224	— 17
— Is thine eye evil, because I	76	233	— 20. 15
— for that man	87	371	— 26. 24
— man, and a just	92	474	Lu. 23. 50
Goods, Soul, thou hast much	63	165	— 12 19
— Delivered to them his	86	347	Mt. 25. 14
Goodman of the house	ib.	342	— 24. 43
Goodwill toward men	4	21	Lu. 2. 14
Gospel to the poor	15	103	— 4. 18
— Wherever this g. is preached.	81	257	Mt. 26. 13
— of the kingdom	10	108	Mk. 1. 14
	86	359	Addenda
Governor (Christ)	5	22	Mt. 2. 6
— (Pilate)	89	435	— 27. 2
Governors and kings	89	299	— 10. 18
Grace of God	6	40	Lu. 2. 40
— Full of	7	48	Jno. 1. 14
— for grace	ib.	ib.	— 16
— and truth	ib.	ib.	— 17
Gracious words,	15	104	Lu. 4. 22
Grain of mustard seed	32	248	Mt. 13. 31
Grass, If God so clothe the	19	135	6. 30
Graves were opened	92	471	— 27. 52
Great is your reward in the kingd	19	122	— 5. 19
— The g. commandment	85	304	— 22. 36
Greater things	10	73	Jno. 1. 50
— Whether is	87	375	Ln. 22. 27
Greatest, Which of them should	52	72	— 9. 46
— Who is	ib.	74	Mt. 18. 1
Greece, Pleasures of this life in	33	256	Lu. 8. 14
Greek, The women a	45	14	Mk. 7. 26
Greeks ask to see Jesus	82	266	Jno. 12. 20
Green tree	91	458	Lu. 23. 31
Groaned in the spirit	58	130	Jno. 11. 33
Ground, Good—and see Introd	32	244	Mt. 13. 8
Guests, Wedding furnished with	84	293	— 22. 10
Guide our feet	2	19	Lu. 1. 79
Guile, No	10	72	Jno. 1. 47
Guilty of death.	89	429	Mt. 26. 66

H

Habitations, Receive you into	69	197	Lu. 16. 9
Habakkuk	19	171	Addenda
Hades, On existence and locality	69	202	ditto
Haggai	19	171	ditto
Hagiographa	ib.	172	ditto
Hallowed be thy name	19	131	Mt. 6. 9
Hand of the Lord	3	16	Lu. 1. 66
— Jesus stretched his h. to Pe	41	320	Mt. 14. 31
— of him that betrayeth me	87	369	Lu. 22 21
Hands, Jesus put h. on blind m	49	54	Mk. 8. 25
— Put his h. on little	74	221	Mt. 19. 13
Hanged, Judas h. himself	89	436	— 27. 5
Hardness of your hearts	74	219	Mk. 10. 5
— only enter into the kingdom	75	226	— 23

HA–HU

	Sect.	Page.	Evang.
Harvest, And then cometh	15	95	Jno. 4. 35
Hate, Cannot h. you	54	87	— 7. 7
— not his, &c.	67	184	Lu. 14. 26
— If the world h. you	87	390	Jno. 15. 19
Head of the corner	84	290	Mt. 21. 42
Heal the broken-hearted	15	102	Lu. 4. 18
— the sick	39	296	Mt. 10. 8
Healing all manner of sickness	19	115	— 4. 23
Hear, Who hath ears to	32, 3	244	— 13.9,43
— Who can h. it	43	332	Jno. 6. 60
— ye him	51	56	Mt. 17. 5
— O Israel	85	304	Mk. 12. 29
— the word of God	62	154	Lu. 11. 28
Heard him gladly	40	316	— 6. 20
Heareth God's words	55	106	Jno. 8. 47
— God h. not sinners	ib.	113	— 9. 31
Heart of the earth	31	238	Mt. 12. 40
— Out of the	44	10	Mk. 7. 21
Heaven and earth to pass, &c.	69	199	Lu. 16. 17
	86	340	Mt. 24. 35
Heavenly Father	44	8	— 15. 13
— things	12	85	Jno. 3. 12
Heavens opened at Jesus' baptism	8	59	Mt. 3. 16
Heavy with sleep	51	54	Lu. 9. 32
— Began to be very	88	413	Mt. 26. 37
Hebrew, Greek, and Latin	91	460	Jno. 19. 20
Heed, Take	86	340	Lu. 21. 34
Hell fire, In danger of	19	124	Mt. 5. 22
— Gates of	50	38	— 16. 18
— Lift up his eyes in	69	200	Lu. 16. 23
Hen doth gather her brood	66	179	— 13. 34
— gathereth her chickens	85	320	Mt. 23. 37
Henceforth ye know him	87	381	Jno. 14. 7
— I will not drink,	ib.	370	Mk. 26. 29
— I call you not servants	87	389	Jno. 15. 15
Hereafter, Thou shalt know	13	366	— 18. 7
— I will not talk much	ib.	386	— 14. 30
Hermon—see 'High Mountain'	51	51	Mt. 17. 1
Herod the tetrarch	40	304	— 14. 1
Herodias	ib.	305	— 3
Herodians' question concerning	84	295	— 22. 16
Herod's steward	30	235	Lu. 8. 3
Hid from wise and prudent	20	228	Mt. 11, 25
— thy talent, &c.	86	349	— 25. 25
Hide himself from them	82	269	Jno. 12. 36
High, Exceeding h. mountain	9	65	Mt. 4. 8
— mountain—see 'Hermon'	51	52	— 17. 1
— ways, Go ye, therefore, into	84	293	— 22. 9
— day, That Sabbath was an-	92	473	Jno. 19. 31
Hill country of Judea	2	11	Lu. 1. 39
Himself, He that speaketh of	55	92	Jno. 7. 18
Hireling, Character of	ib.	115	— 10. 12
Holy is his name	2	12	Lu. 1. 49
— Ghost at Jesus' baptism	8	59	— 3. 22
— On the blasphemy ag	62	161	Addenda
Holy Ghost, The Comforter	87	385	Jno. 14. 26
— Father	ib.	401	— 17. 11
— One of God	17	110	Mk. 1. 24
— city	9	64	Mt. 4. 5.
— mount	51	52	— 17. 1
— Standing in the h. place	86	331	— 24. 15
Honour thy father and t.y mo	44	6	— 15. 4
— Him will my Father	82	267	Jno. 12. 26
Honoureth, It is my Father that	55	107	— 8. 54
Horn of salvation	3	17	Lu. 1. 69
Hosanna, Blessed is the King of I	82	260	Jno.12.13
— in the highest	ib.	264	Mt. 21. 9
— to the Son of David	ib.	ib.	ib.
Hosea	19	171	Addenda
Host, Multitude of the heavenly	4	21	Lu. 2. 13
— directed who to invite	67	182	— 14. 12
Hook, Cast an	52	73	Mt. 17. 27
Hour, Mine	11	77	Jno. 2. 4
Huse, Your,	85	320	Mt. 23. 38
Housetop Healing of the paraly	22	165	Lu. 5. 19
— Let him on the h. not	86	332	Mt. 24. 17
Housetops, Preach ye upon the	39	300	— 10. 27
Householder, Servants of the	32	247	— 13. 27
Humility taught	53	82	— 18.2-4
— Jesus exhorts to	87	357	Jno. 13. 12
Humiliation of Christ:—			
His coming down from heaven	43	329	Jno. 6. 38
Being born among the poor	4	24	Lu. 2. 24
Cradled in a manger	ib.	20	— 7
Forced to flee into Egypt	5	34	Mt. 2. 14
Brought up in a disreputable l	15	35	— . 23
(Compare Nathanael's remark	10	72)	Jno. 1. 46
Subject to Joseph and Mary	6	42	Lu. 2. 51
Cast out by his own townsmen	15	105	— 4. 29
Not believed in by his own br	54	87	Jno. 7. 5

XLV

ME—MI

Entry	Sect.	Page	Evang.
Meek, Blessed are the	19	120	Mt. 5. 5
— and lowly	29	229	— 11. 29
Meet that we should make merry	68	198	Lu. 15. 32
Memorial of her	81	257	Mt. 26. 13
Mercy, Tender	3	18	Lu. 1. 78
— and not sacrifice	36	276	Mt. 9. 13
— He that shewed	60	147	Lu. 10. 37
Merciful, Blessed are the	19	121	Mt. 5. 7
— God be m. to me a sinner	73	217	Lu. 18. 13
Merry, They began to be	88	193	— 15. 24
Messias, which is Christ	10	71	Jno. 1. 41
Messiahship of Jesus, Evidence	23	174	— 5.
Micah's prediction respecting Ch	5	82	Mt. 2. 6
— Book of	22	171	Addenda
Mile	ib.	127	Mt. 5. 41
Millstone § 52, p. 76,	70	206	Lu. 17. 2
Mind, Clothed and in his right	35	272	Mk. 5. 15
Mine, Not m. to give, but for	77	238	Mt. 20. 23
— are thine, and thine are m.	87	400	Jno. 17. 10
Ministered unto him	30	233	Lu. 8. 3
Ministry of John and Jesus comp	10	74	Addenda
— Conclusion of 2½ years	53	86	ib.
Minor prophets	19	171	ib.
Minstrels	39	283	Mt. 9. 23
Mint, anise, and cummin	85	317	— 23. 23
Miracle, John, did no	57	125	Jno. 10. 41
Miracles, Beginning of	11	78	— 2. 11
— On	ib.	80	Addenda
— The second in Galilee	14	101	Jno. 4. 54
— This man doeth many	58	132	— 11. 47
— On those at Jericho	79	244	Addenda
Miracles of Healing:—			
Blind, To many b. he gave sight	29	223	Lu. 7. 21
— Two b. men at Capern	36	283	Mt.9.27-31
— Many b. made to see	46	25	— 15.30,.1
— man at Bethsaida	49	34	Mk.8.22-6
— Man born b., Silcam	55	109	Jno. 9.
— On entering Jericho	78	240	Lu. 18. 35
— Two b on leaving	79	242	Mt. 20. 30
— came to him in the t	52	266	— 21. 14
Dead raised to life			
— Widow's son at Nain	29	221	Lu. 7.11-,6
— Jairus' daughter	36	282	Mk.5.35-43
— Lazarus	58	132	Jno. 11. 44
— Jesus' own resurrection	93	468	Lu. 24. 6
Deaf, Making the d. to hear was one of			
the signs to which John was re	29	223	— 7. 20-,9
— man healed nigh to Beths	46	24	Mk.7.32-,7
— When come down from m			
transfiguration	51	60	— 9. 25
Dropsy, In Pharisee's house	67	181	Lu. 14.
Dumb			
— A devil blind and	31	234	Mt. 12. 22
— man possessed with a	36	285	— 9. 32
— On a mountain in Deca	46	25	Mk.7.32-,7
— The lunatic met when coming			
from the mount of transfig	51	59	Mt. 17. 15
— A devil, and it was	62	153	Lu. 11. 14
Fever, Nobleman's son	14	100	Jno.4.46-54
— Peter's wife's mother	17	112	Mk.1.29-31
Halt or impotent thirty-eight years			
pool of Bethesda	23	175	Jno. 5. 1-9
Impediment in speech	46	24	Mk.7.32-,7
Infirmity of eighteen years'	65	175	Lu.13.10-,3
Issue of blood of twelve years	36	280	Mk.5.25-34
Lame, The l. walk (To John)	29	223	Mt. 11. 5
Leper, Probably near Chorazin	21	159	Mk.1.40-,4
Lepers, Ten in Galilee	70	208	Lu.17.12-,9
Lunatic	51	59	Mt. 17. 15
Maimed	46	25	— 15. 30
— High priest's servant	88	420	Lu. 22. 50
Palsy, He healed the	18	116	Mt. 4. 24
— Man borne of four	22	164	Mk. 2. 3
— Centurion's servant	28	218	Lu. 7. 1-10
Possessed (Unclean spirit)	17	110	Mt. 1. 23
— Legion	35	271	Lu. 8. 30
Sickness	17	112	— 4. 40
Withered hand	25	195	Mk. 3. 1-6
Other miracles	100	518	Jno. 21. 25
Miracles of Supply:—			
Water made wine	11	78	— 2. 3, 4
Feeding the multitudes			
— five thousand	40	311	— 6. 5-13
— four thousand	46	26	Mt.15.32-,8
Fish made to pay tribute	52	73	— 17. 27
— The draught at Peter's	20	153	Lu. 5. 1-11
— Again,			
after Jesus' resurrection	97	506	Jno. 21. 6
XLVIII			

MI—NE

Entry	Sect.	Page	Evang.
Miracles of Judgment:—			
Perishing of the swine	35	271	Mt. 8.30-,1
Withering of the fig tree	§83,,4 276-,81		Mk.11.12-,4
Miracles of Deliverance:—			
Quelling of the storm	34	266	— 4.37-40
Saving Peter from sinking	41	320	Mt.14.28-32
His restraining the power to			
apprehend him	88	417	Jno. 18.4-9
Mock, Shall m. and scourge him	77	236	Mk. 10. 34
Mocked Jesus,	91	456	— 15. 20
Moloch,	19	124	Mt. 5. 22
Money changers,	83	276	— 21. 12
Morning . . . sign of foul w	47	29	— 16. 3
— Early in the §55, p. 99,	86	357	Lu. 21. 38
Moriah	92	481	Geog. Not.
Moses,	7	48	Jno. 1. 17
— lifted up the serpent	12	85	— 3. 14
— wrote of Christ;	23	180	— 5. 46
— gave you not (The manna)	43	322	— 6. 32
— and Elias	51	53	Mt. 17. 3
— disciples	55	112	Jno. 9. 28
— and the prophets	69	202	Lu. 16. 29
— What did M. command	74	219	Mt. 10. 3
— Book of	84	308	Mk. 12. 26
— seat	85	312	Mt. 23. 2
Mote	19	138	— 7. 3
Mother	11	76	Jno. 2. 1
— Behold thy,	91	466	— 19. 27
— of Jesus, Her other ch	91	466	Addenda
Mount, Sermon on the	19	131	Mt. 5.-7.
— of Olives	82	260	— 21. 1
Mountain, High	9	65	— 4. 8
— of transfiguration	51	52	Note.
— Be thou removed	83	276	Mt. 21. 21
— This (Gerizim)	13	93	Jn. 4. 20
Mountains, Goeth unto the	53	89	Mt. 18. 12
— Flee into the	86	372	— 24. 15
Mourn, Blessed they that	19	129	— 5. 4
Mouth and wisdom	86	328	Lu. 21. 15
Multitudes	18	116	Mt. 4. 25
—	46	25	— 15. 30
Murders	44	10	— 19
Murderer from the beginning	55	106	Jno. 8. 44
— Barabbas	90	449	Mk. 11. 7
Murmured, The Jews then	43	330	Jno. 6. 41
Murmuring amongst the people	55	91	— 7. 12
Music and dancing	68	194	Lu. 15. 25
Mustard seed	34	249	Mt. 13, 31, ,2
— Grain of	65	176	Lu. 13. 19
Myriads	63	163	— 12. 1
Myrrh	5	33	Mt. 2. 11
— and aloes	92	475	Jno. 19. 39
Mysteries of the kingdom	32	244	Mt. 13. 11
—	33	254	Mk. 4. 11

N

Entry	Sect.	Page	Evang.
Nahum	22	171	Addenda
Nain, Raising of widow's son at	29	221	Lu. 7.11-,6
— Geographical	ib.	229	Geog. Not.
Naked, and ye clothed me	86	352	Mt. 25. 36
Name, In his	26	208	— 12. 21
— Gathered together in my	53	84	— 18. 20
— Ask in my	87	382	Jno. 14. 13
— I have manifested thy	ib.	400	— 17. 6
— Keep through thine own	ib.	401	— 11
— Have declared unto them	ib.	404	— 26
— In the n. of the Father,	96	503	Mt. 28. 19
Names, Meaning of Scripture	1	4	Lu. 1. 1
— Your n. are written in h	60	144	— 10. 20
Napkin, Found laid up in n	80	249	— 19. 20
— Face bound about with a	58	132	Jno. 11. 44
— that was about his head	93	490	— 20. 7
Napious, 'Shechem'	13	96	Geog. Not.
Narrative of mission to the Jews	42	323	Note
Nathanael (Probably John)	10	72	Jno. 1. 45
— of Cana	97	506	— 21. 2
Nation bringing forth the fruits	84	290	Mt. 21. 43
— shall rise against nation	86	325	— 24. 7
Nations, Shall be hated of all	ib.	327	— 9
— Published among all	ib.	ib.	Mk. 13. 10
— Go ye therefore and	96	503	Mt. 28. 19
Nazareth, On the return to	5	39	Addenda
— Jesus visits	15	102	Lu. 4. 16
— Jesus of	78	240	— 18. 37
— The title set up	91	460	Jno. 19. 19
Needful, One thing is	61	150	Lu. 10. 42
Needle's eye	75	227	— 18. 25

NE—PA	Sect.	Page.	Evang.
Neighbour love thy, as thyself	. 85	805	Mt. 22. 39
Nests	. 34	245	— . 8. 20
Net cast into the sea	. 33	262	— . 13. 47
Nevertheless, shall the Son of m	. 73	215	Lu. 18. 8
New and old	. 33	362	Mt. 13. 52
— Testament	. 87	378	— . 26. 28
Nicodemus comes to Jesus by n	. 12	63	Jno. 3. 1
— On our Lord's disc	. ib.	ib.	— . 1-21
— Art thou also of Gal.	. 55	97	— . 7. 52
— for Jesus' burial brought one hundred weight of a	. 92	475	— . 19. 39
Nine, Where are the?	. 70	209	Lu. 17. 17
Nineveh, The men of	. 31	238	Mt. 12. 41
Ninevites, Jonas a sign to	. 62	154	Lu. 11. 30
Noah, As it was in the days of	. 72	212	— . 17. 26
— As the days of N. were	. 86	341	Mt. 24. 37
Nobleman and his servants	. 80	248	Lu.19.11-27
Nobleman's son healed	. 14	100	Jno.4.46-54
Nothing, On Jesus answering	. 90	446	Mt. 27. 12
Notoriety not sought by Jesus	. 26	201	— . 12. 16
Nought, Herod, &c., set Jesus at	. 90	448	Lu. 23. 11
Now is my kingdom not from h	. ib.	441	Jno. 18. 36
Numbers, Book of	Ad . 19	143	(par. 5)
Numbered, Even the hairs are	. 39	301	Mt. 10. 30

O

Oath to Abraham	. 3	17	Lu. 1. 73
Oath's sake (Herod)	. 40	307	Mk. 6. 26
Obadiah	. 19	171	Addenda
Observation, The kingdom of God cometh not with	. 72	210	Lu. 17. 20
Occupy till I come	. 80	248	— . 19. 13
Odour of the ointment	. 81	254	Jno.12. 3
Offence, Thou art an o. to me	. 50	41	Mt. 16. 23
Offences, It must be that o. c	. 52	77	— . 18. 7
— Impossible but that	. 70	206	Lu. 17. 1
Offend, Least we should	. 52	73	Mt. 17. 27
— Whoso shall o. one of	. ib.	76	— . 18. 6
— If thy hand	. ib.	77	Mk. 9. 43
Offended	. 29	223	Mt. 11. 6
— at him	. 87	287	Mk. 6. 3
— The Pharisees were	. 44	8	Mt. 15. 12
— Then shall many be	. 86	328	— . 24. 10
Offending, How to treat an o. br	. 52	83	— .18.15-7
Officers sent to take Jesus	. 55	94	Jno. 7. 32
— Their report of him	. ib.	96	— . 45
Oil and wine, Pouring in	. 60	147	Lu. 10.34
— One hundred measures of	. 69	197	— . 16. 6
Olives, Mount of	. 55	97	Jno. 8. 1
— — Jesus at the descent	. 82	263	Lu. 19. 37
— — He departs to	. 87	405	— . 22. 39
— — His ascension from	. 98	516	— . 24. 51
Olivet, Return of disciples from	. 99	517	Ac. 1. 12
One, That they also may be o in us	87	403	Jno. 17. 21
Oneness of Christ with the Father in work, knowledge, power, judg, honour, life-giving power, will, &.	. 23	177	Jno.5,19-30
Oneness of Christ with his disciples	87	387	— . 15.
— — His prayer for	. ib.	403	— . 17. 21
Opened, Be	. 46	25	Mk. 7. 34
Ophel—see under 'Jerusalem'	. 92	481	Geog. Not.
Outer darkness	. 86	350	Mt. 25. 30
Outside of cup and the platter	. 62	156	Lu. 11. 39
Our Father, which art in heaven	. 19	132	Mt. 6. 9
— — —	. 62	151	Lu. 11. 2
Overcharged, Your hearts be	. 86	340	— . 21. 34
Overshadowed	. 51	55	Mk. 9. 7
Own, He came unto his	. 7	47	Jno. 1. 11
— Having loved his	. 87	365	13. 1
Ox fallen into a pit	. 67	181	Lu. 14. 5

P

Palace, The high priest's	. 89	426	Mt. 26. 58
Palm, emblematic of triumph	. 82	259	Jno. 12. 13
Palsy, Jesus healed those that had	. 18	116	Mt. 4. 24
Paralytic borne of four	. 22	164	Mk.2.3-12

Parables, Teaching—

I. *Faith and Practice:*—

1. Building on the rock	. 19	141	Mt.7.24-.7
— —	. 27	210	Lu. 6.47-.9

II. *Importance of possessing a sense of Forgiveness:*—

1. The two debtors	. 29	231	— . 7. 41-.7

III. *— — of not only being Outwardly Reformed, but possessed of Positive Holiness:*—

1. Unclean spirit seeking rest finding none, § 31, p. 239, M. 43-.5.	. 62	154	— 11.24-.6

PA—PA	Sect.	Page.	Evang.
IV. *Secret progress and ultimate development of Truth and Error:*—			
1. The sower	. 32	243	Mt. 13. 3-8
— explained	. 33	254	— . 19-23
2. Wheat and tares	. 32	246	— . 24-30
— explained	. 33	259	— . 37-43
3. Seed sown	. 32	247	Mk.4.26-.9
4. Grain of mustard seed	. ib.	248	Mt. 13.31,.2
5. Leaven hid in meal	. ib.	249	— . 33
V. *Paramount value of the Truth:*—			
1. Treasure hid in a field	. 33	261	— . 44
2. Merchant seeking	. ib.	ib.	— . 45
3. Net cast into the sea	. ib.	262	— . 47-50
VI. *Of exercising Forgiveness and Graces:*—			
1. The lost sheep	. 53	82	— . 18.12-.4
2. The king and his debtors	. ib.	84	— . 23-35
3. The good shepherd	. 55	114	Jno.10.1-18
4. The good Samaritan	. 60	145	Lu.10.29-37
5. The rich glutton	. 63	165	— 12.16-21
VII. *Faithfulness in Office:*—			
1. Servants waiting	. ib.	166	— . 35-40
— — and co	. 86	342	Mk.13.34-6
2. Faithful and wise steward	. 63	167	Lu. 12.41-8
3. Fig tree planted in a vin	. 64	174	— . 13. 6-9
VIII. *Improvement of Time and Opportunity:*—			
1. The door shut	. 66	177	— . 23-30
2. Taking the lowest place	. 67	182	— . 14. 7-11
3. The great supper	. ib.	183	— . 15-24
4. Of building a tower	. ib.	185	— . 28-30
5. A king going to war	. ib.	ib.	— . 31-3
IX. *Recovery of the Lost:*—			
1. The lost sheep, compare 52, Mt. 18. 12-.4 § 53, p. 82,	. 68	189	— 15. 3-7
2. The lost piece of money	. ib.	190	— . 8-10
3. The Prodigal son	. ib.	ib.	— . 11-32
X. *Prudent Forethought and Prayer:*—			
1. The unjust steward	. 69	196	— 16. 1-13
2. Rich man and Lazarus	. ib.	199	— . 19-31
3. Importunate widow	. 73	214	— . 18. 1-8
4. Pharisee and publican	. ib.	216	— . 9-14
XI. *On Merit and Reward:*—			
1. Servant come from the field	. 70	207	— . 17.7-10
2. The labourers hired	. 76	231	Mt. 20.1-16
3. Nobleman and his servants	. 80	247	Lu.19.11-27
XII. *Removal of the Kingdom from the Jews, and giving it to Another People:*—			
1. The two sons	. 84	285	Mt.21.28-32
2. Vineyard let out to husb	. ib.	286	— . 33-46
3. Marriage for the king's son	. ib.	291	— 22. 1-10
4. Wedding garment	. ib.	293	— . 11-.4
XIII. *Ending of Present Dispensation, and Judgment of the Nations:*—			
1. Faithful and wise servant	. 86	343	— 24.45-51
2. Wise and foolish virgins	. ib.	346	— 25. 1-13
3. Faithful and slothful serv	. ib.	347	— . 14-30
4. Sheep and goats	. ib.	351	— . 31-46
XIV. *Only in Christ can we bring forth Fruit unto God, and understand his Word and Workings:*—			
The true vine	. 87	387	Jno.15.1-16
A little while	. ib.	345	— 16.16-23

Parallelisms:—

1. Who is the greatest? Lu. 9. 46., 7-50 (p. 72),with Mt. 18.1-9; Mk.9. 33-50	52	79	
2. On following Christ, Lu. 9. 57-62, with Mt. 8. 19-22	. 59	137	
3. The twelve and the seventy, Lu. 10. 1-12, with Mt. 10. 1, 5-15; 9. 37, .8; Mk. 6. 7-11	. 60	143	
4. The woe on Chorazin, &c., Lu. 10. 13-.5, with Mt. 11. 21-.3	. ib.	149	
5. I thank thee, O Father, Lu.10.21-.4, with Mt. 11. 25-.7; 13. 16, .7	. ib.	ib.	
6. Form and efficacy of prayer, Lu. 11. 1-13, with Mt. 6. 7-13; 7. 7-11	. 62	158	
7. On blasphemy, Lu. 11. 14-.26, 29-32 with Mt. 12. 22-30, 38-45	. ib.	60	
8. Light not to be hid, Lu. 11. 33-.6, with Mt. 5. 15; 6. 22, .3	. ib.	160	

PA—PE	Sect.	Page.	Evang.
9. Reproof of Pharisees and Lawyers, Lu. 11. 37-54, with Mt. 23. 4, 6, 7, 13, 23-36		ib.	ib.
10. On trust in God while doing his will, Lu. 12, with parts of Mt. 5., 6., 10., 12., 16., 24		63	171
11. Mustard seed and leaven, Lu. 13. 18-21, with Mt. 13. 31-.3		64	176
12. Strive to enter in at the strait gate, Lu. 13. 22-30, .4, .5, with parts of Mt. 7., 8., 19., 28		66	180
13. Great supper and marriage feast, Lu. 14. 16-24, with Mt. 22. 1-10		67	186
14. Coming of the Son of man, Lu. 17. 25-.7, 30, with Mt. 24. 26, .7, 37-.9		72	213
15. The ten pounds and talents, Lu. 19. 12-27, with Mt. 25. 14-30		80	254
Parents of the man who was born	53	111	— 9. 20
Paraclete promised	57	583-.5	—14.16,26
Passed by on the other side	60	146	Lu.10.31,.2
Passion week, Sunday, first day	81	253	Mt.26.6-13
— — Monday, second	82	259-.69	Jn.12.12-36
— — Tuesday, third	83	275	Mk.11.12-.9
— — Wednesday, fourth	84	280-.99	M t.21.23-22.22
— — —		85	300-.21 — 22.23-23
— — —		86	322-.57 — 24.-.6.16
— — Thursday, fifth	87	365-406	Jno.13-.8.1
— Gethsemane	88	412	Mt.26.36-56
— Jesus before the Sanhe	89	424-.35	Jn.18.12-28
— — before Pilate	90	440-.53	—18.28-19.10
— — His crucifixion	91	454	Mt.27.27-50
— — put in the tom.	92	470	— .51-66
Passover—see on 'Time of Jesus' birth	4	29	Addenda
— Went every year at the	6	40	Lu. 2. 41
— One of the three great festivals		ib.	43 Addenda
— Ceremonies observed at		ib.	44 ib.
— Feeding of 5000 near the	40	311	Jno. 6. 4
— Approach of	86	355	Mt. 26. 2
— must be killed	87	362	Lu. 22. 7
Pastor, Character of a true	55	114	Jno. 10. 4
Patience	33	257	Lu. 8. 15
— In your p. possess ye	86	329	— 21. 19
Pavement	90	445	Jno. 19. 13
Peace on earth	4	21	Lu. 2. 14
— makers	19	121	Mt. 5. 9
— not immediate to the earth	30	301	— 10. 34
— Have p. one with another	52	79	Mk. 9. 50
— Desiring conditions of	67	185	Lu. 14. 32
— be unto you	95	498	— 24. 36
Pearl of great price	33	261	Mt. 13. 45
Pearls, Neither cast ye your	19	138	— 7. 6
— Goodly	33	261	— 13. 45
Pence, Three hundred	81	255	Mk. 14. 5
Peony a day	76	281	Mt. 20. 2
Pennyworth, 200 p. of bread	40	312	Mk. 6. 37
People, All	4	20	Lu. 2. 10
— My p. Israel	5	32	Mt. 2. 6
— Jesus called the	50	42	Mk. 8. 34
— Jesus accused of deceiving	55	91	Jno. 7. 12
Peræn, Jesus passes into	71	209	Mt. 19. 1
Perfect, Be ye therefore p. as your	19	128	— 5. 48
— as his master	27	209	Lu. 6. 40
— in one	87	404	Jno. 17. 23
Performance of oath to Abraham	2	11	Lu. 1. 73
Perish, They shall never	56	121	Jno.10.27,.8
Persecuted for righteousness' sake	19	122	Mt. 5. 10
Persecution, To flee from	29	300	— 10. 23
— predicted	86	326	Lu. 21. 12
— Why forewarned of	87	392	Jno. 16.1-.4
Perplexed, Herod was	40	304	Lu. 9. 7
Persuaded the multitude	90	451	Mt. 27. 20
Perverse generation	51	58	— 17. 17
Perverting the nation	90	445	Lu. 23. 2
Pestilences	86	326	Mt. 24. 7
Peter, His introduction to Jesus	10	71	Jno.1.40-.2
— and see on 'Simon'		ib.	75 Addenda
— His second call	16	108	Mt. 4. 18-.9
— Wife's mother healed	17	112	— 8. 14,.5
— His third call	20	153	Lu. 5. 1-11
— with Jas. & John, in Jairus'	36	283	— 8. 51
— I say unto thee, Thou art	50	37	Mt. 16. 19
— contradicts Jesus		ib.	41 — 22
— is rebuked by Jesus		ib.	42 — 23
— The keys in P's 2 epistles		ib.	47 Addenda
— on the holy mount	51	51	Lu. 9.23-36
— says his Master pays trib	52	73	Mt. 17. 26
— sent to prepare the Passove	87	362	Lu. 22. 8
— He boasteth		ib.	376 — 33
L			

PE—PR	Sect.	Page.	Evang.
Peter, His fall predicted	ib.	377	Lu. . 34
— — — third time	ib.	406	Mt.26.34,.5
— smites with the sword	88	419	Jno. 18. 10
— follows Jesus to the palace,	89	388	— . 15,.6
— denies Christ three times	ib.	390	—17,25-.7
— His repentance	ib.	453	Lu.22.61,.2
— The angel's message to	93	486	Mk. 16. 7
— His visit to the sepulchre	ib.	490	Jno.20.3-10
— Christ has appeared to him	93	497	Lu.24.33,.4
— goes a fishing	97	506	Jno. 21. 3
— is to feed Christ's lambs &c.	ib.	507	— 21.15-.3
— in his writings ministers to babes, young men, and fathers, as indicated by our Lord		ib.	— . 15-.7
— His manner of martyrdom	ib.	509	— . 18,-9
— The beloved disciple, John, not left under his supervision		ib.	— . 20-.2
Phanuel	4	27	Lu. 2. 36
Pharisee and publican	73	216	— 18. 10
Pharisees, Many came to John's bm	7	52	Mt. 3. 7
— Their name, tenets, &c		ib.	56 Addenda
— conspire with Herodians	25	197	Mk. 3. 6
— One of them invites Jesus	29	229	Lu. 7. 36
— murmur at his eating,	36	277	Mt. 9. 11
— Jesus tells them what	44	8	— 15. 12
— seek a sign from heaven	47	28	— 16. 1
— Beware of the leaven of	48	32	— 6
— Jesus at dinner with one	62	155	Lu. 11. 37
— — goes in to eat bread	67	181	— 14. 1
— Their quest'n concern. d	74	218	Mt. 19. 3
— take counsel with Herod.	84	295	— 22.15,.6
— Jesus questioned by one	85	304	— 35
— ask 'What think ye of C	85	306	— 42
Philip (brother of Herod)	p. 40	§ 7. 40	305 — 14. 3
— (of Bethsaida)	10	72	Jno. 1. 44
— fifth of twelve apostles	27	216	Addenda
Philosophers, Different sects of	33	263	ib.
Philippians, Epistle to	19	145	ib.
Physician, heal thyself	15	104	Lu. 4. 23
— Christ considered as a	36	277	Mt. 9. 12
Phylacteries	85	313	— 23. 5
Pinnacle of the temple	9	64	— 4. 5
Pilate, Had massacred Galileans	64	173	Lu. 13. 1
— Jesus formally arraigned	90	445	Mt. 27. 11
— says, 'I find no fault in	ib.	446	Lu. 23. 4
— sends Jesus to Herod	ib.	447	— 7
— His wife's message	ib.	450	Mt. 27. 19
— intercedes for Jesus	ib.	451	Lu. 23. 20
— washes his hands, saying,	ib.	452	Mt. 27. 24
— scourges Jesus, and delivers him to be crucified		ib.	453 — 26
— writes a title for the cross	91	460	Jno. 19. 19
— Which he refuses to alter	ib.	461	— 22
— permits Joseph to take Jesus	92	474	— 38
— comm. the sepulch. to be	ib.	478	Mt. 27. 65
— Proposal to deceive	93	487	— 28.13,.4
Piped unto you	29	298	— 11. 17
Plain, Jesus' sermon on a	27	207-.10	Lu. 6.17-49
Plant, Every	44	8	Mt. 15. 13
Pleased, In whom I am well	51	55	— 17. 5
Pleasures of this life	33	256	Lu. 8. 14
Plough, Having put his hand to the	50	137	— 9. 62
Pondered, Mary	4	22	— 2, 19
Pontius Pilate—and see 'Pilate'	7	55	Addenda
Pool of Bethesda	21	175	Jno. 5. 2
Poor, Jesus chose his associates fr	16	108	Mt.4.18-22
— Blessed are the p. in spirit	19	120	— 5. 3
— Blessed be ye	27	207	Lu. 6. 20
— invited to the great supper	67	184	— 14. 21
— Judas' pretended care for	81	255	Jno. 12. 5
— Jesus took the place of p.	90	443	—19.5,&c.
Popularity of Jesus	22	164	Mk. 2. 2
Porch	89	431	Mt. 26. 71
Porches, Having five	23	175	Jno. 5. 2
Portion that falleth to me	68	190	Lu. 15. 12
Possessed with devils	18	116	Mt. 4. 24
Possible, If it were	86	335	— 24. 24
Potter's field	89	436	— 27. 7
Poured it on his head	81	253	— 26. 7
Power of the Spirit	15	102	Lu. 4. 14
— of God	85	301	Mk. 12. 24
— over all flesh	87	398	Jno. 17. 2
— of darkness	88	421	Lu. 22. 53
Powers of the heavens	86	337	Mt. 24. 29
Praise, Perfected	55	111	Jno. 9. 24
— of men	85	311	— 12. 43
Pray, Jesus exhorts his disciples to	58	413	Lu. 18. 1
— went up into a moun.	40	318	Mt. 14. 23
— at transfig	51	52	Lu. 9. 28
— Men ought always to	73	214	— 18. 1
— Two men went into the tem	ib.	216	— 10

PR

	Sect.	Page.	Evang.
Prayed, Jesus, before first circuit	18	114	Mk. 1. 35
— — in Gethsemane	88	414-.6	Mt.26.39 45,4
— — on the cross	91	459	Lu. 23. 34
Praying without, 'he whole m	1	3	— 1. 10
— Jesus at his baptism	8	59	— 3. 21
— On p. to be seen of men	19	131	Mt. 6. 5
— in a certain place	62	151	Lu. 11. 1
Prayer, Vain repetitions in	19	131	Mt. 6. 7
— Jesus all night in	27	205	Lu. 6. 12
— and fasting	51	61	Mt. 17. 21
— The Lord's 192 Mt. 6. 9-13,	62	151	Lu. 11. 2-4
Preach, The twelve commanded to	39	296	Mt. 10. 7
Preached the word	22	164	Mk. 2. 2
— in all the world	86	330	Mt. 24. 14
— Gospel p. in all the world	ib.	359	Addenda
Preaching of the Baptist	7	50	— 3. 1
— of Jesus	16	108	— 4. 17
— of twelve apostles	39	303	Lu. 9. 6
Precedence, Dispute concerning	52	80	Addenda
— see again	87	375	— 22. 24
Preface to Luke's Gospel	1	1	— 1. 1-4
— Greswell on—'In order'	ib.	7	Addenda
Preferred before me	10	69	Jno. 1. 27
Premeditate, Neither do ye	86	328	Mk. 13. 11
— compare also	ib.	359	Addenda
Prepare ye the way of the Lord	39	299	Mt. 10. 19
— compare also	7	51	Lu. 3. 4
Preparation, Because it was the	92	473	Jno. 19. 31
— Day that followed the	ib.	477	Mt. 27. 62
Prepared of my Father	77	238	— 20. 23
Presence of the angels of God	68	190	Lu. 15. 10
Present him, to the Lord	4	24	— 2. 22
Presented unto him	5	33	Mt. 2. 11
Presumption, Temptation to	9	64	— 4. 6, 7
Prevail, Gates of hell shall not	50	37	— 16. 18
Pride	44	10	Mk. 7. 22
Priest's office	1	3	Lu. 1. 8
Priests and Levites p. 74, A	10	68	Jno. 1. 19
— profane sabbath and are bl	24	189	Mt. 12. 5
— Chief p. and scribes	50	40	— 16, 21
— agreed to procure Jesus' d	89	434	— 27. 1
Prince of the devils	31	235	— 12. 24
— of this world	82	268	Jno 12 31
Prisoner, How to be treated	59	426	— 18.19-23
Privilege, Apostles'	75	228	Mt. 19. 28
— Believers'	87	383	Jno.14.16,.7
Privileges, Outward p. insure not sal	60	142	Lu.10,13,.4
Proceeded forth and came from G	55	105	Jno. 8. 42
Procession to the temple, Time of	81	258	Addenda
Prodigal son, Case of Ephraim	68	190	Lu.15.11-32
Profited, What is a man	50	42	Mt. 16. 26
Proud, Scattered the	2	12	Lu. 1. 51
— to be brought low	67	152	— 14. 11

Prophecies CONNECTED WITH THE FIRST ADVENT OF CHRIST, AND IN CONFIRMATION OF THE PROMISES MADE UNTO THE FATHERS:—

Prophecy, Gabriel's, respecting the Baptist and his ministry—was to turn many of the children of Israel to the Lord	1	4	— 1. 16
—hearts of fathers to the children	ib.	ib.	— . 17
—respecting the birth and reign of Christ—was to sit on 'the throne of his father David' and 'reign over the house of Jacob for ever'	2	10	— .32,.3
The casting down of the proud, and elevation of the poor, 'Hath holpen Israel . . . as he spake to Abraham,' &c. Mary's song	ib.	11	— . 46-55
Zacharias' song, anticipating the fulfilment of God's covenant mercy to Israel	3	16	— . 67-79
Angel's song, Gospel to all people	4	20	— 2.10-.4
Simeon's, 'A light to lighten the Gentiles, and the glory of thy people Israel'		ib.	— . 29-32
— 'Christ to be for the fall rising again of many in Israel'.	ib.	ib.	— . 33-.5

THE SUFFERINGS OF CHRIST.—

Christ predicts his own death and resurrection	12	82	Jno. 2. 19
— His being three days and nights in the heart of the earth	31	233	Mt. 12. 40
Christ's rejection and suffering at Jerusalem	50	40	— 16, 21
— 'decease at Jerusalem' contemplated on the Holy	51	54	Lu. 9. 31
— rising from the dead	ib.	57.	Mt. 17. 9.

PR

	Sect.	Page.	Evang.
Prophecies—Continued.			
— rising from the dead	ib.	57	Mt. 17. 9
— see also descending the	52	70	— .22,.3
— foretold his sufferings,	72	211	Lu.17.25,6
Christ's, and yet again, 'Behold, we go up to Jerusalem'	77	235	Lu. 18.31-.3
Christ, purpose of his sufferings, 'Ransom of many'	ib.	239	Mt.20.26-.8
THE DISCIPLES:—			
Jesus' prediction respecting Na	10	73	Jno. 1. 51
Judas' betrayal, Jno. 6. 70, .1, § 43,	87	369	Lu. 22. 21
Peter's denials	ib.	406	Mt. 26. 34
—. ministry and martyrdom	97	507	Jno.21.15-.9
Persecution, Their	19	122	Mt. 5. 11
— —	27	207	Lu. 6. 22
— — by all	39	298	Mt.10.17-24
— — by nearest ki	ib.	301	— . 34-.9
— — by the Jews	62	157	Lu. 11. 49
— — co	85	319	Mt. 23. 34
— — and by the Ge	86	326	— 24. 9
Must be prepared to bear the cro	50	40	—16.21-.7
And see Discourse at last s	87	390	Jno.15.18-21
And again, Jno. 16. 1-4, § 87,	ib.	397	— 16. 32
The Holy Ghost to come previous to leaving Jerusalem	98	511	Ac. 1. 4
— to bring all to remembr	87	335	Jno. 14. 26
— to enable them to testify from the beginning	ib.	391	—15.26,.7
— to shew them things to c	ib.	394	— 16. 13
— to empower them to 'rivers of living water'	55	95	— 7.38

JEWS, JERUSALEM, &c.:—

Cities in which Christ's mighty works were done, Their destruction foretold	29	227	Mt.11.21-.4
And compare	60	142	Lu.10,13,.4
Destruction of Jerusalem, Lu. 19.,	85	320	Mt.23.37,.8
§ 84, p. 264	86	331	— 24.15-23
Its ceasing to be the place of w	13	93	Jno. 4. 21
Their house left unto the Jews de	66	179	Lu.13.34,.5
— 'Not one stone upon	86	324	Mt. 24. 2
Utter ruin to that generation	31	239	— 12. 45
Signs of their approaching destru	64	173	Lu. 13. 1-5
'Daughters of Jerusalem,' &c.	91	457	—23.28-31
'Beginning of sorrows described	86	324	Mt. 24. 4-8
The great and long tribulation	ib.	332	Lu.21.23,.4

THE GENTILES, &c.			
Christ a light to lighten the Gent.	4	25	— 2. 32
Calling of Gentiles—see Marriage	67	184	—14.23,.4
Gospel to 'be published among	86	327	Mk. 13. 10
— 'of the kingdom preached in all the world'	ib.	330	Mt. 24. 14
— throughout the whole w	81	257	Mk. 14. 9
Disciple all nations	96	503	Mt.28.19,20
Course of the preaching of the G indicated in the parable of The so	32	243	— 13. 3-9
Shall come from east, west, north, and south	66	178	Lu.13.28,.9
— Christians trampled upon, and despised, when they cease to diffuse the savour of salvation	19	122	Mt. 5. 13
Their fruitfulness depends upon a vital union with Christ; and losing the truth, they lose their standing	87	388	Jno. 15. 4-6
Divisions among Christians	86	328	Mt. 24. 10
Many deceiving and being dece	ib.	329	— . 11
Lukewarmness of many	ib.	ib.	— . 12
Righteous and wicked mixed	32	247	— 13. 30
till the harvest	33	260	— .40,.1
The Spirit to reprove the world of sin, of righteousness, and of judgme.	87	393	Jno.16.8-11

RESTORATION OF ISRAEL.			
The kingdom taken from the Jews, was to be given to a nation bringing forth the fruits thereof	84	290	Mt. 21. 43
See Parables on Recovery of the	68	188-.95	Lu. 15.
The other sheep, not of the Jewish fold, to be gathered into one	55	116	Jno. 10. 16
'The children of God that were scattered abroad' to be gathered into one	58	133	— 11. 52
Prayer for their oneness	87	403	— 17. 21
Christ to draw ALL unto him	82	268	— 12.32
The restoration of ALL, preparatory to Christ's appearing in glory	51	57	Mt. 17. 11
In the kingdom of Christ, the restoration of ALL (the twelve tribes of Israel) is recognized	87	376	Lu.22.29,30

L1

PR—QU

	Sect.	Page.	Evang.
Important stewardship of the chosen nation	86	343	Mt.24.45-51
God's faithfulness to them, & deficiency of faith in Him	73	215	Lu. 18. 7, 8
When they do put their trust in Him He will avenge them speedily	ib.	ib.	— . 7

SECOND COMING OF CHRIST

'The sign of the Son of man in h	86	338	Mt. 24. 30
Christ gone ' to receive for him a kingdom, and to return	80	248	Lu. 19. 12
— to prepare a place for his people, into which he will receive them at his coming	87	380	Jno.14.1-3
State of the world at the time	86	335	Mt.24.36,.7
Kind of danger to which Chr will be exposed	ib.	340	Lu.21.34-.6
Will give reward to his servants	ib.	341	Mt.24.37-.9
At the coming of the Son of m	50	43	16. 27
Shall come with power and g	86	333	— 24.30,.1
And on his throne judge the n	ib.	351	— 25. 31
Then all who have rejected him as king shall be cut off	80	250	Lu. 19. 27

RESURRECTION OF BELIEVERS

Those who shall be raised	23	178	Jno. 5, 25
'I am the resurrection,	43	329	— 6.39,30
Condition of the raised saints	58	129	— 11. 25
A sample of the kingdom given Mt. 16. 28, § 60, p. 44,	85	302	Lu.20.35,.6
and see The promise to the	51	51	Mt. 17. 1-8
	75	228	— 19. 28
Prophesy unto us, thou Christ.	89	430	— 26. 68
Prophet, That	10	68	Jno. 1. 25
— This is of a truth that	41	317	— 6. 14
— In his own country	15	104	Lu. 4. 24
— A great p. is risen up	29	222	— 7. 16
— Of a truth this is the	55	96	Jno. 7. 40
— not expected from Galil	ib.	97	— 52
— Jesus the p. of Nazareth	82	265	Mt. 21, 11
— Woman of Samaria said	13	93	Jno. 4. 19
— And man born blind said,	55	111	— 9. 17
— John Baptist was more	29	224	Mt. 11. 9
Prophets wrote of Christ	10	72	Jno. 1. 45
— His sufferings predicted	77	235	Lu. 18, 31
— Came not to destroy	19	123	Mt. 5, 17
— This is the law and the	ib.	139	— 7. 12
— and the law prophesied u	29	225	— 11. 13
— Reward to true and f	27	208	Lu.6.23,.6
— and righteous men	82	246	Mt. 13, 17
— The law and the p. until	69	199	Lu. 16, 16
— They have Moses and	ib.	202	— 29
— Beginning at Moses and	94	495	— 24. 27
— In .. Moses, the p., and	98	512	— 44
— wise men, and scribes.	85	319	Mt. 23. 34
— Many false p. warned	86	329	— 24. 11
Proselyte	85	315	— 23. 15
Proverbs, Book of	19	172	Addenda
— Jesus sometimes spoke	67	396	Jno. 16, 25
Psalms	19	172	Addend t
— David himself saith in the	85	307	Lu. 20. 42
— Moses, and the prophets,	98	512	— 24. 44
Public example	2	13	Mt. 1. 19
Publican standing afar off	83	217	Lu. 18. 13
Publicans	7	53	— 3. 12
— Mt. 9.10, § 36, p. 277,	68	198	— 15. 1
— the harlots	84	285	Mt. 21. 31
Punishment proportioned to priv'	68	168	Lu.12.47, 8
— Everlasting	86	354	Mt. 25. 46
Pure in heart	19	121	— 5. 8
Purge his floor	7	54	Lu. 3. 17
Purgeth the fruitful branch	87	387	Jno. 15. 2
Purify themselves	81	252	— 11. 55
Purifying	11	77	— 2. 6
— Dispute concerning	13	89	— 3. 25
Purple and fine linen	69	199	Lu. 16. 19
Purse, When I sent you without	87	377	— 22. 35
Purses	39	296	Mt. 10. 9
Put away his wife for every cause	74	213	— 19. 3

Q

Quake, The earth did	93	470	— 27. 51
Quarantania	9	65	— 4. 8
Quarrel, Herodias had with John	40	306	Mk. 6, 19
Quarter, Came to Jesus from ev	21	161	— 1. 45
Queen of the South shall rise up	31	239	Mt. 12. 42
Quenched, The fire that never sh	62	77	Mk. 9. 45
Queries on ' our origin ' Ad	16	Lu. 15.
Question about purifying	13	89	Jno. 3. 25
— I will ask of you	84	263	Mt. 11. 29
— Then a lawyer asked	85	304	Mt. 22. 35
— No man durst ask him	ib.	306	Mk. 12. 34
— Pharisees began to q.	47	23	8. 11

QU—QU

	Sect.	Page.	Evang
— What q. ye with them ?	51	58	— 9. 16
Questioned. Herod q. with him	90	448	Lu. 23, 9
Questioning. What rising from the	51	57	Mk. 9. 10
Questions, Both hearing and ask	6	41	Lu. 2. 46

Questions occurring in the G History:—

Angel to M. Magd., ' Woman,	93	491	Jno. 20. 13
Caiaphas—see ' High priest ;'			
Cleopas—Devils—see ' Jesus			
Damsel to Peter, ' Art not thou ?	89	431	— 18. 17
Disciples, ' Hath any man	13	95	— 4. 33
— ' What is this .. a little	87	395	Jno. 16. 17
— ' Did not our heart burn ?' &c.	94	496	Lu. 24. 32
Elisabeth, ' Whence is this to	2	11	— 1. 43
Herod, ' Who is this, of whom	40	305	— 9 9

— JESUS questioned by—

Caiaphas—see ' High priest '			
Cleopas, ' Art thou only a str	94	494	— 24. 18
Devil, ' What have we to do with	17	110	Mk. 1. 24
Disciples, ' Whence so much	46	26	Mt. 15. 33
— ' Why say the scribes Elias ?'	51	57	Mk. 9. 11
— ' Who is the greatest ?'	52	74	Mt. 18. 1
— ' Which among them	87	375	Lu. 22. 24
— ' How oft forgive a brother ?'	53	84	Mt. 18, 21
— ' When shall these things be ?'	86	324	— 24. 3
— ' What the sign of thy coming ?,	ib.	ib.	— 3
— ' And of the end of the age?'	ib.	ib.	— 3
— ' Lord, shall we smite with	88	419	Lu. 22. 49
— ' Lord, wilt thou at this time	98	513	Ac. 1. 6
Disciples of John, ' Why do .. disciples fast not ?'	36	278	Mt. 9. 14
Elders, ' By what authority ?'	84	282	— 21. 23
Herod, ' Questioned with him,'	90	448	Lu. 23. 9
Herodians, ' Is it lawful .. to	84	296	Mt. 22. 17
High priest, ' Asked Jesus of	89	426	Jno. 18. 19
— ' Answerest thou nothing ?'	ib.	428	Mt. 14. 60
— ' Art thou the Son of the Bl	ib.	ib.	— 61
— to the Sanhedrim, need we any further witn	ib.	429	— 63
— ' Ye have heard ... what th	ib.	ib.	— 64
Jews, ' Art thou gr. than .. A	55	107	Jno. 8. 53
— ' Whom makest thou thyself ?	ib.	ib.	ib.
John the Evangelist, ' Lord, who	87	372	— 13. 25
John, ' Comest thou to me ?'	8	58	Mt. 3. 14
John's disciples, ' Art thou he	29	223	Lu. 7. 20
Judas, ' Master, is it I ?'	87	372	Mt. 26. 25
Judas, not Iscariot, ' How thou wilt manifest thyself ?	87	384	Jno. 14. 22
Lawyer, ' What shall I do to	60	145	Lu. 10. 25
— ' Who is my neighbour ?'	ib.	146	— 29
Mary, ' Son, why hast thou	4	21	— 2. 48
Nathanael, ' Whence knowest ?'	10	72	Jno. 1. 48
Nicodemus, ' How can a man be	12	83	— 3. 4
— ' How can these things be ?'	ib.	84	— 9
Officer, ' Answerest thou the	89	426	— 18. 22
Jesus' ans, ' If I have spoken ev	ib.	ib.	— 23
People, ' Rabbi, when camest	43	325	— 6. 25
— ' What sign shewest thou What dost thou work ?'	ib.		— 30
— ' Are there few that be saved ?'	66	177	Lu. 13. 23
Peter, ' Lord, whither goest	87	374	Jno. 13. 36
— ' Lord, why cannot I follow	ib.	ib.	— 37
— ' Lord, and what shall this.	97	510	— 21. 21
Pharisees, ' Why do ye eat and drink with publicans and sinners ?'	22	168	Ln. 5. 30
— ' Why do .. thy disciples	ib.	169	Mk. 2.18,.9
— ' Why on the sabbath day do	24	108	— 24
— ' Why do thy disciples transg	44	5	Mt. 15. 2
— ' Where is thy Father ?'	ib.	89	Jno. 8. 19
— ' When the k. of God should c	72	210	Lu. 17. 20
— ' Is it lawful to divorce for every	74	218	Mt. 19. 3
— ' Which is the great command	85	304	— 22. 36
Pilate, ' Art thou the King of the	90	441	Jno. 18. 33
— ' Am I a Jew ?'	ib.	ib.	— 35
— ' Art thou a king then ?'	ib.	442	— 37
— ' What is truth ?'	ib.	ib.	— 38
— ' Whence art thou ?'	ib.	444	— 19. 9
— ' Speakest thou not unto me ?'	ib.	ib.	— 10
— ' Knowest . not that I have p	ib.	ib.	— 10
— ' Art thou the King of the J	ib.	446	Mt. 27. 11
— ' Hearest thou not how they witness against thee ?'	ib.	ib.	— 13
Ruler, ' What good thing shall	75	223	Mt. 19. 16
— answered, ' Why callest	ib.	224	— 17
Sadducees, ' In resurr., whose	85	301	— 22. 28
Woman of Samaria, ' How	13	92	Jno. 4. 9
— ' Art thou greater than ...	ib.	ib.	— 12

LII

QU			
	Sect.	Page.	Evang.
— JESUS *questions the*			
David, 'Whom seek ye?'	88	413	Jno. 18. 4. 7
'Be ye come out, as against a	ib.	421	Lu. 22. 52
Blind men, 'Believe ye that I	36	285	Mt. 9. 28
'What will ye that I should	79	243	— 20. 32
Caiaphas, 'Why askest thou	89	426	Jno. 18. 21
Disciples, 'Know ye not this pa			
and how then will ye know	33	254	Mk. 4. 13
'Whence shall we buy bread,	40	311	Jno. 6. 5
'How many loaves have ye?'	ib	312	Mk. 6. 38
'Do ye not yet understand, neither			
remember the 5 loaves of bread			
and how many baskets ye	48	33	Mt. 16. 9, 10
'Whom do men say that I..'	50	35	— . 13
'But whom say ye that I am?'	ib.	36	— . 15
'What is a man profited, if?'	ib.	42	— . 26
'See ye not all these things?'	86	324	— 24. 2
'Whether is greater, he that sitteth			
at meat, or he that serveth?'	87	375	Lu. 22. 27
'When I sent you without p	ib.	377	— . 35
'Do ye inquire among yourselves			
that I said, A little while,	ib.	385	Jno. 16. 19
'The cup which my Father,'	83	420	— 18. 11
'Thinkest thou I can not now pray			
to my Father, and he shall pre-			
sently give me more than?	ib.	45.	Mt. 26. 53
'What manner of communications			
are these that ye have one with			
another, as ye walk, and	94	494	Lu. 24. 17
'What things?' (*to Cleopas*)	94	494	— 24. 19
'O fools, and slow of heart to believe			
all that the prophets have spoken:			
ought not Christ to have suffered			
these things, and to enter into his			
glory?'	94	494	Lu. 24. 25
'Children, have ye any meat?'	97	500	Jno. 21. 5
And see 'The eleven'			
Daughters of Jerusalem, 'If they do			
these things in a green tree?'	11	458	Lu. 23. 31
Doctors, 'Whether is easier to say, Thy			
sins be forgiven thee; or?	22	166	— . 5. 23
Elders, 'The baptism of John,	84	293	Mt. 21. 25
Eleven, 'Why are ye troubled?	95	498	Lu. 24. 38
'Have ye here any meat?'	ib.	ib.	— 24. 41
Herodians, 'Whose is this im	84	297	Mt. 22. 20
Jews, 'Why do ye not underst	55	105	Jno. 6. 43
John's disciples, 'What seek ye?	10	70	— . 1. 33
Judas, 'Friend, wherefore art?'	88	419	Mt. 26. 50
'Betrayest thou the Son of m	ib.	ib.	Lu. 22. 48
Lawyer, 'What is written in the	60	145	— 10. 26
'Which was neighbour to h	ib.	147	— . 36
Mary his mother, 'How is it that	6	41	— 2. 49
'Wist ye not that I must be?'	ib.	42	— . 49
'What have I to do with thee?	11	76	Jno. 2. 4
Mary Magdalene, 'Why weepest	93	491	— 20. 15
Nicodemus, 'Art thou a ruler in Israel			
and knowest not these thi	12	84	— . 3. 10
People, 'What went ye out to	29	224	Lu. 7. 24, 5
'Who is my mother? and	31	240	Mt. 12. 48
'Who touched me?'	36	281	Lu. 8. 45
Peter, 'O thou of little faith,' &c.	41	320	Mt. 14. 31
'Wilt thou lay down thy life?'	87	375	Jno. 13. 38
'Simon, sleepest thou?'	88	415	Mk. 14. 37
'Couldest not thou watch one	ib.	ib.	— ib.
'Simon, son of Jonas, lovest	97	509	Jno. 21. 15-.7
— — more than	ib.	507	— . 15
'If I will that he tarry till I	ib.	510	— . 23
Pharisees, 'Is it lawful to do well on			
the sabbath days, or to do	25	196	Mk. 3. 4
'What man shall there be			
that shall have one sheep,	ib.	ib.	Mt. 12. 11
'If Satan cast out Satan, how?	31	235	— . 26
(and John's disciples,) 'Cau the			
children of the bride - chamber			
mourn, so long as?' p. 169, Mk.	36	278	Mt. 9. 15
'Why do ye also transgress the com-			
mandm't of God by your tradi	44	5	— 15. 3
'Can ye not discern the signs	47	29	— 16. 3
'Is it lawful to heal on the s	67	181	Lu. 14. 3
'Which of you shall have an	ib.	ib.	— . 5
'What think ye of Christ?'	85	306	Mt. 22. 42
'How then doth David in spi	ib.	ib	— . 43
Philip, 'Have I been so. with	87	381	Jno. 14. 9
'How sayest thou, shew us?	ib.	ib.	— . 9
'Believest thou not that I am	ib.	382	— . 10
Simon the Pharisee, 'Which			
will love him most?'	29	231	Lu. 7. 42
The twelve, 'Will ye also go	43	334	Jno. 6. 67
'Have not I chosen you	ib.	ib.	— . 70
'Are ye also yet without?' &c.	44	9	Mt. 15. 16

QU—RE			
	Sect.	Page.	Evang.
John ques. by the Jews, 'Who art	10	68	Jno. 1. 20, 1
— *by publicans,* solui	7	53	Lu. 3. 10-.4
Pagi, 'Where is he that is	5	31	Mt. 2. 2
Mary to the angel, 'How shall	2	10	Lu. 1. 34
Nathanael, 'Can any good thi	10	72	Jno. 1. 46
Nicodemus to Phar., 'Doth our	55	97	— 7. 51
People, 'Is not. Jesus. son of J	43	330	— 6. 42
'Is not this the Son of David?	31	234	Mt. 12. 23
'How can this man give us h	43	331	Jno. 6. 52
'How knoweth this man let	55	91	— 7. 15
Pharisees to Nicodemus, 'Art t	ib.	97	— . 52
Pilate to the Jews, 'What accus	90	440	— 18. 29
'Will ye that I release the K	ib.	442	— . 39
'Shall I crucify your King?'	ib.	448	— 19. 15
'Whom will ye tha: I rel	ib.	450	Mt. 27. 17
'What shall I do then with	ib.	451	— . 22
'Why, what evil hath he d	ib.	452	Lu. 23. 22
Priests to Judas, 'What is that	89	435	Mt. 27. 5
Servants to Peter, 'Art not thou	ib.	431	Jno. 18. 25
'Did not I see thee in the gar	ib.	432	— . 25
Thief on the cross, 'Dost not thou fear			
God, seeing thou art in?' &c.	91	464	Lu. 23. 40
Townsmen, 'Whence....this wis-			
dom, and these mighty works is			
not this the carpenter's son?	37	286	Mt. 13. 54
Woman of Samaria, 'Is not	13	95	Jno. 4. 29
Women going to the sepulchre, who			
shall roll us away the stone?	1	485	Mk. 16. 3
Zacharias, 'Whereby shall I?'	1	5	Lu. 1. 19
Quickeneth, The Son *q.* whom he	23	177	Jno. 5. 21
— It is the Spirit that	43	333	— 6 63
Quickly, Agree with thine advers	19	135	Mt. 5. 25
— into the streets and lanes	67	184	Lu. 14. 21
— Sit down *q.* and write	69	197	— 16. 6
— tell his disciples ... he	93	486	Mt. 28. 7
— That thou doest, do	87	372	Jno. 13. 27
Rabbi, Jesus so addressed	10	70	— 1. 33
Rabbi, Origin of title and office	12	87	*Addenda*
— Scribes loved to be called	85	314	Mt. 23. 7
Rabboni, Mary to Jesus	93	491	Jno. 20. 16
Raca	19	124	Mt. 5. 22
Rachel weeping for her children	5	34	— 2. 18
Raiment of camel's hair	7	51	— 3. 4
— And why take ye th	19	135	— 6. 28
Rain in Palestine	ib.	141	— 7. 25
Raise at the last day	43	329	Jno. 6. 39
Ramah	5		*Geog. Not.*
Ransom for many	77	279	Mt. 20. 28
Ravening, Inwardly they are r. w	19	140	— 7. 15
Ravens, God feedeth	63	165	Lu. 12. 24
Reach hither thy finger	95	501	Jno. 20. 27
Read, Jesus r. in the book of Isa	15	102	Lu. 4. 16, .7
Ready, Make r. a people for the L	1	4	— 1. 17
Reapeth, Both he that soweth,	13	95	Jno. 4. 36
Reapers, The angels	33	260	Mt. 13. 29
Reasoned, Jesus, when a child, r. with the			
Jewish doctors in the	6	41	Lu. 2. 46
— during his ministry	55		Jn.ch.5.7.8.9.10
— And at the close of it			Mt. 21.-.3.
— The disciples disputed who			
should be the greatest	74	220	Mk. 9. 34
— When two r. together, Jesus			
joined them on their way to			
Emmaus	94	493	Lu. 24. 15
Rebuked, Jesus r. the unclean sp	17	111	— 4. 35
— Peter, saying, Get thee			
me, Satan, &c.	50	41	Mk. 8. 33
— The disciples r. those who			
brought little childr	74	220	Mt. 19. 13
Receive one such little child, &c.,	52	75	Lu. 9. 48
— He that is able to	74	220	Mt. 19. 12
— for himself a kingdom, &c.	80	248	Lu. 19. 12
— ye the Holy Ghost	95	499	Jno. 20. 22
Received to hold (traditions)	44	4	Mk. 7. 4
— As many as r. him	7	47	Jno. 1. 12
— The Galileans r. him	14	100	— 4. 45
— That he should be r. up	59	135	Lu. 9. 51
Receiveth you, receiveth me	39	302	Mt. 10. 40
Reckoneth with them	86	348	— 25. 19
Reconciled, Be r. to thy brother	19	125	— 5. 24
Reconciliation to be instantly	63	170	Lu. 12. 59
Record of John	10	68	Jno. 1. 19
— Thou bearest r. of thyself	55	100	— 8. 13, .4
Recovering of sight to the blind	15	102	Lu. 4. 18
Redeemed, The Lord God of Israel	3	17	— 1. 68
— He which should have r.	94	494	— 24. 21
Redemption looked for in Jerusal	4	27	— 2. 38
— Your r. draweth nigh	86	339	— 21. 28

LIII

RE—RO

	Sect.	Page.	Evang.
Reed, A bruised	26	302	Mt. 12. 20
— shaken with the wind	29	224	— 11. 7
— given to Christ in mockery	91	455	— 27. 29
Regeneration, In the	75	228	— 19. 23
Region and shadow of death	16	103	— 4. 16
Reign over the house of Jacob	2	10	Lu. 1. 33
Reject, Full well ye r. the comm.	44	6	Mk. 7. 9
Rejected of the elders, chief pr.	50	40	— 8. 31
— of this generation	72	212	Lu. 17. 25
Rejoice with me	68	190	— 15. 9
— If ye loved me ye would	87	385	Jno. 14. 28
Rejoiced, The neighbours r with	3	15	Lu. 1. 58
— The wise men	5	33	Mt. 2. 10
Rejoiceth more over one	53	82	— 18. 13
Religion, The true r. described in 8 beatitudes	19	120	— 5. 2-12
— The counterfeit in 8 woes.	85	315	— 23. 13-32
Remember his holy covenant	3	17	Lu. 1. 72
— Do ye not.	48	33	Mk. 8. 18
— me when thou comest	91	465	Lu. 23. 42
Remembrance of me.	87	390	— 22. 19
— Bring all things to	ib.	385	Jno. 14. 26
Remission of sins	3	18	Lu. 1. 77
Remove hence to yonder place.	51	61	Mt. 17. 20
Render unto God, &c.	81	297	— 22. 21
Repent ye, Preaching of John.	7	50	— 3. 2
— Jesus	16	108	— 4. 17
— the apost	30	303	Mk. 6. 12
— Except ye	64	173	Lu. 13. 3-5
Repentance, Baptism of	7	50	— 3. 3
— Fruits worthy of	ib.	52	— 8
— Judas'	89	435	Mt. 27. 3-10
— Peter's	ib.	433	Lu.22.61,.2
Repented, Afterward he	84	285	Mt. 21.29,.9
Repetitions, Use not vain.	19	131	— 6. 7
Report, Who hath believed our?	85	309	Jn. 12.37,.8
Reproach, To take away my	1	6	Lu. 1. 25
Reprove the world of sin	87	393	Jno.16.7-11
Reproved, Lest his deeds be	12	87	— 3. 20
Required, Pilate ordered as the J.	89	439	Lu. 23.24 5
Resist not evil	19	127	Mt. 5. 39
Resorted, Jesus ofttimes	88	417	Jno. 18. 2
Rest unto your souls	29	228	Mt. 11. 29
Restoration of all Israel	51	67	Addenda
Restore all things, Elias shall	ib.	57	— 17. 11
Resurrection, I am the r. and the l.	58	129	Jno. 11. 25
— Whoso shall lose his l.	72	212	Lu. 17. 33
— denied by the Sadd.	80	300	— 20. 27
Reward, A prophet's and r. man's	39	302	Mt.10.41,.2
Rich he hath sent empty away	2	12	Lu. 1. 53
— man, Parable of	63	165	— 12. 16
— Not r. toward God	ib.	ib.	— 21
Riches the baggage of virtue *Notes*	ib.	ib.	— 17
Right hand and left in the k.	77	237	Mt. 20. 21
Righteous, God heareth not	55	112	Jno. 9. 31
— Trusted in themselves they were	73	216	Lu. 18. 9
Righteousness, in holiness and	3	17	— 1. 75
— Fulfil all	8	58	Mt. 3. 15
— Hunger, &c, after	19	121	— 5. 6
— of the scribes, &c.	ib.	124	— 20
— Seek first, &c.	ib.	136	— 33
— Way of	84	286	— 21. 32
Ring on his hand	68	193	Lu. 15. 22
Rise again	50	40	Mk. 8. 31
Risen, The Lord is	95	497	Lu. 24. 34
Rising from the dead should mean.	51	57	Mk. 9. 10
Robe	68	193	Lu. 15. 22
— Gorgeous	90	448	— 23. 11
— Scarlet	91	455	Mt. 27. 28
Robes, Long	85	308	Lu. 20. 46
Rock, built his house upon a	11	141	Mt. 7. 24
— as exhibited in N. T. scripture	ib.	149	Addenda
— Upon this r. will I build	50	38	— 16. 18
— Hewn out in the	93	476	— 27. 60
Rocks rent	ib.	471	— 51
Rod out .... stem of Jesse *Notes*	74	222	Mk. 10. 16

Romish Controversy, Some Passages relating to.*

Antichrist, &c. *Notes*	86	254	Jno. 12. 4
Apostles were not to exercise authority like the princes of this world	87	375	Lu 22.25,.6
Baptism of repentance, &c.	7	50	— 3. 3
Baptism of John and Christ	7	54	Mk. 1. 8
— contrasted	10	70	Jno. 1. 33

* See, on many of these topics, an excellent little book, well adapted for general circulation, 'The Root and Fruits of the Tree of Life, by Miss Jane Kennedy. Published by Binns and Goodwin, Bath.

LIV

RO

	Sect.	Page.	Evang.
Rom. Controversy—(*continued*).			
Jesus removes his disciples from the scene of their baptising with water	13	91	Jno. 4. 1-3
Speaks of the water which he gives—comp Jno. 3. 5, § 12, p. 83, 'born of water,' &c.	ib.	93	— 14
Vanity of putting outside washings for internal holiness—'cleanse first that which is within'	85	317	Mt. 23.25,.6
The disciples made clean through the word § 87, p. 387, Jno. 15.3	67	402	Jno. 17. 17
Binding and loosing	53	83	Mt. 18. 18
Celibacy, Not .... in Peter	17	112	Lu. 4,38,.9
Not commanded by our L.	74	220	Mt. 19.10-.2
Cephas, 'a stone,' the new name given to Simon, when first called to be a disciple	10	71	Jno. 1. 42
His second call	16	108	Mt. 4. 18,.9
His third call—and see 'Peter'	20	153	Lu. 5. 1-11
Church, 'Tell it unto the'	53	83	Mt. 18. 17
The dilemma in which those are placed who take Peter for the foundation of their church	50	41	Mk. 8. 33
Commandments, The relation which the keeping of them has to salvation. *Scrip. Illus.*	75	224	Mt.19.17-.9
Confession to the priests, Ill success of, in Judas	89	435	— 27. 3,.4
Eucharist, Jno. 6. 53, 'Except ye eat,' &c.	43	335	Addenda
'This is my body,' &c.	87	369	— 26. 26
The cup: 'Drink ye all of it'	ib.	378	— 27
Father, The disciples forbid to call any man pope	85	314	— 23. 9
Forgiveness, Jesus exercises forgiveness without any reference to either water baptism, or penance.... § 22, p. 165, Mk. 9 2	29	232	Lu.7. 48-50
Gifts to the house of God, to the neglect of our nearest relations, not approved	44	6	Mt. 15. 4-6
Inquisition, The servants forbid to root out the tares *until the harvest*	32	247	— 13. 30
Justified, The humble penitent, not the man boastful of his own good works	73	216	Lu. 18.9-14
Keys of the kingdom, what they are, and how Peter used them	50	39	Mt. 16. 19
— *and see Addenda*	ib.	47	
Liberty to do good—see on ' The disciples forbidding those who followed not with them'	52	76	Mk.9. 38,.9
Mary, Saluted by the angel	2	9	Lu 1. 28
— see 'On Mary the m. of Jesus'	91	469	Addenda
— Rejoices in God her Saviour	2	11	— 1. 47
— Joseph takes her to wife	ib.	14	Mt. 1. 24,.5
Jesus (not Mary) subject of angels' song	4	20	Lu. 2. 10-.4
And of the wise men's enquiry	5	31	Mt. 2 1,.2
— compare	ib.	33	— 11
Jesus' answer to Mary at Cana	11	77	Jno. 2. 4
Her blessedness came not by her relation to Christ according to the flesh, but was partaken of by her in common with all who '*hear the word of God, and keep it.*' So Jesus' reply to the woman who cried, '*Blessed is the womb that bare thee*' *	62	154	Lu.11.27,.8
Meats—see on what defileth	44	8	— 15. 11
Peter—see 'Cephas,' *supra*	27	213	Addenda
See on his three names	50	37,.8	Mt.16.17,.8
'*The first, Simon,*' &c.	37	296	— 10. 2
His supremacy over the beloved disciple not acknowledged by our Lord	97	500	Jno.21.20-.3
Prayer to saints, Only Scripture example of prayer to the saints, ineffectual	69	201	Lu.16.24,.5
Rock—see description of him who builds thereupon. § 19, p. 141, Mt. 7. 24, .5]	27	210	— 6. 47, .8
— *and see Addenda*	ib.	215	
Christ, not Peter, is the Rock upon which the church of God is built	50	38	Mt. 16. 18
Scriptures, Com. to search them	23	180	Jno. 5. 39

* Last mention of her in the Gospels, § 91, p. 466, John 19. 27.

RO—SA	Sect.	Page.	Evang.
Rom. Controversy—*(continued)*.			
Scriptures, Their sufficiency objected to by a man in hell	69	203	Lu.16.29,30
— Our Saviour teaches his disciples that they may receive light upon them from all who are able to give it, though it may be otherwise unknown to them	94	494	—24.25,.6
Sufferings of Christ, Scripture doctrine concerning them	50	46	*Addenda*
Teachers from God not to be known by their commission from man, but by their fruits.	19	140	Mt.7.15-20
'*Make the tree good, and his fruit good*'	31	237	—12.33
Tradition	44	4-12	—15.1.9
Works, None of supererogation	70	208	Lu. 17.10
Roof, On the uncovering the	22	170	*Addenda*
Root, The axe is laid to the	7	53	Mt. 3.10
— These have no	33	255	Lu. 8.13
Rubbing them in their hands	24	189	—6.1
Rufus and Alexander, Father of	91	457	Mk. 15.21
Rule A Governor that shall	5	32	Mt. 2.6
Ruler of the Jews (Nicodemus)	12	83	Jno. 3.1
— of the synagogue	36	296	*Addenda*
— over his household	63	167	Lu. 12.42
— — all that he hath	*ib.*	168	—44
— The young	75	223	—18.18
Rumours of wars	86	325	Mt. 24.6
Rust doth corrupt	19	134	—6.19
Ruth	22	172	*Addenda*

S.

	Sect.	Page.	Evang.
Sabbath at Nazareth	15	102	Lu. 4.16
— at Capernaum	17	110	Mk. 1.21
— at Bethesda	23	176	Jno. 5.9
— Second *s.* after the first	21	148	Lu. 6.1
	ro.	194	*Addenda*
— made for man	*ib.*	190	Mk. 2.27
— 'Son of man Lord of the'	*ib.*	—	—29
— Antiquity of the	*ib.*	191	*Addenda*
— Change at the Exodus	*ib.*	*ib.*	do.
— Resitution at resurrection	*ib.*	192	do.
— Jews' preparation for the	*ib.*	*ib.*	do.
— Remember the *s.* day	*ib.*	193	do.
— a day of rest	*ib.*	*ib.*	do.
— exercises of the Jews	*ib.*	194	do.
— Jesus heals withered hand	25	195	Lu. 6.6-10
— Lawful to do well on the	*ib.*	197	Mt. 12.12
— Eyes of man opened on	55	110	Jno 9.13,.4
— Heals woman on	65	175	Lu.13.10-.3
Sacrifice, Mary's	4	24	—2.24
— What is more than	85	305	Mk.12.32,.3
— Christ offered this	13	95	Jno. 4.34
— even to the death	88	415	Mt. 26.42
Sackcloth and ashes	29	227	—11.21
Sadducees came to John's baptism	7	52	—3.7
— Origin of doctrine of	*ib.*	56	*Addenda*
— Pharisees, at Magdala	47	26	Mt. 16.1
— Beware of leaven of	48	32	—6
— reduced to silence	85	300	Mt.20.27-40
Saida (*see* 'Sidon') *Geog. Not.*, p. 21	45	13	Mt. 15.21
Saints, Many bodies of *s.* arose	92	471	—27.52
Salim	13	69	Jno. 3.23
— Locality of	*ib.*	96	*Geog. Not.*
Salt of the earth, lost its savour	19	122	Mt. 5.13
— have *s.* in yourselves	52	79	Mk. 9.50
Salted with fire	*ib.*	78	—49
Salutation in the markets	85	309	—12.38
Salute no man by the way	60	143	Lu. 10.4
Saluted Elisabeth	2	11	—1.40
Salvation, Raised up an horn of	2	17	—69
— To give knowledge of	*ib.*	18	—77
— before the face of all	4	25	—2.31
— All flesh shall see	7	51	—3.6
— is of the Jews	13	91	Jno. 4.22
— come to this house?	80	217	Lu. 19.9
Samaria, Messengers sent to	59	135	—9.52
Samaritan, Say we .. Thou art	55	106	Jno. 8.48
— that shewed mercy	60	147	Lu. 10.37
— One of the ten was a	70	204	—17.16
Samaritans described	13	98	*Addenda*
Samuel, *see on* 'The prophets'	94	512	Lu. 24.44
Sanctified, Whom the Father	56	123	Jno. 10.36
Sanctify them through thy truth	87	402	—17.17
— For their sakes I	*ib.*	*ib.*	do.
Saphet, or Bethulia *Notes*	19	122	Mt. 5.14
Sarepta, Elisha sent to	15	101	Lu. 4.26
Sat, after reading in synagogue	*ib.*	*ib.*	—20
— The people .. in darkness	16	107	Mt. 4.16
Satan, Get thee behind me	50	41	—16.23

SA—SE	Sect.	Page.	Evang.
Satan as lightning fall from	60	143	Lu. 10.18
— hath bound 18 years	65	176	—13.16
— desired to have Peter	87	376	—22.31
Save his people from their sins	2	13	Mt. 1.21
— ine, Lord (Peter's cry)	41	320	—14.30
— Whosoever will *s.* his life	50	42	Mk. 8.35
Saved from our enemies	3	17	Lu. 1.71
— The world through him	12	86	Jno. 3.17
— Are there few that be	66	177	Lu. 13.23
— others, himself he	91	463	Mt. 27.42
Saviour, Christ the Lord	4	21	Lu. 2.11
— of the world	13	96	Jno. 4.42
— His bequest	87	385	—14.27
Savour, On salt losing its	19	122	Mt. 5.13
Saw, Jesus *s.* Nathanael	10	73	Jno. 1.48
— Abraham *s.* and was glad	55	107	—8.56
Saying, This is an hard	43	332	—6.60
Sayings noised abroad	3	16	Lu. 1.65
— of mine(Lu. vi.47, § 27, p. 210)	19	141	Mt. 7.26
— Jesus repeated his *Notes*	*ib.*	142	—25
Scattered the proud	2	12	Lu. 1.51
Scorpions	60	144	—10.19
Scourge of small cords	12	81	Jno. 2.15
— you in their synagogues	39	299	Mt. 10.17
Scourged Jesus	90	443	Jno. 19.1
Scribe proposed to follow	34	264	Mt. 8.19
Scribes, &c., gathered by Herod	5	32	—2.4
— their righteousness	19	124	—5.20
— Certain of the	22	165	—9.3
— watched Jesus	25	195	Lu. 6.7
— On	*ib.*	199	*Addenda*
— and Pharisees of Jerusalem	44	4	Mt. 15.1
— Chief priests and	50	40	—16.21
— Beware of the	85	308	Mk. 12.38
— sit in Moses' seat	*ib.*	312	Mt. 23.2
Scripture confirmed by Jesus' res.	12	82	Jno. 2.22
— fulfilled in your ears	15	104	Lu. 4.21
— Search the	23	180	Jno. 5.39
— As the *s.* hath said	55	95	—7.38
— Christ cometh of .. David	*ib.*	96	—42
— saith, He that eateth, &c.	87	370	—13.18
— How then shall the	88	421	Mt. 26.54
— saith, I thirst	91	467	Jno. 19.28
— that he must *r.* again	93	450	—20.9
— He expounded to them	94	495	Lu. 24.27
— While he opened the	*ib.*	495	—32
— That they might under.	96	512	—45
— *See Moses, Prophets,* &c.			
Sea and waves roaring	86	337	—21.25
— of Galilee, Jesus walks	16	108	Mt. 4.18
— Partial circuit (p. 204, *Ad*)	26	200	Mk. 3.7
— Seal, Hath set to his	13	90	Jno. 3.33
Sealed, Him hath God	43	326	—6.27
Sealing the stone	92	478	Mt. 27.66
Search diligently for	5	32	—2.8
Sea side	22	167	Mk. 2.13
— Jesus teaches again by	32	242	—4.1
Season, Satan departed for a	9	66	Lu. 4.13
Secret, Nothing is *s.* that shall n.	33	258	—8.17
— No man doeth anything in	54	87	Jno. 7.4
— In *s.* have I said nothing	89	426	—18.20
See greater things than these	10	73	—1.50
— heaven open	*ib.*	73	—51
— Having eyes, *s.* ye not	48	33	Mk. 8.18
— the Son of man coming	86	338	Mt. 24.30
— Abraham rejoiced to	55	107	Jno. 8.56
— the Son of man *s.* there	72	211	Lu. 17.23
Seed, We be Abraham's	55	104	Jno. 8.33
— I know .. ye are Abraham's	10	71	—1.38
Seek, What *s.* ye?	19	114	Mk. 1.37
— All men *s.* for thee	66	177	Lu. 13.24
— Many will *s.* to enter in	93	488	—24.5
— Why *s.* ye the living	13	90	Jno. 3.32
Seen, What he hath *s.* that he	14	100	—4.45
— The Galileans having	87	381	—15.9
— me, hath *s.* the Father	85	311	—12.44
Seeth him that sent me	33	261	Mt. 13.44
Selleth all that he hath	7	49	Mk. 1.2
Send my messenger before me	39	298	Mt. 10.16
— you forth as sheep in the	46	26	—15.24
— them away, I will not	87	391	Jno. 15.26
— unto you from the Father	5	—	Lu. 1.19
Sent, I am Gabriel, and am	18	115	—4.43
— Therefore am I	56	110	Jno. 9.3
— Siloam, by interpretation	84	292	Mt. 22.3
— forth his servants	85	311	Lu. 12.49
— Seeth Him that *s.* me	95	499	—20.21
— As my Father hath *s.* me	63	169	Lu.12.13
Separations by the truth	92	476	Jno.19.41,.2
Sepulchre, The body of Jesus in	*ib.*	478	Mt. 27.66
— made sure	93	481	Mk. 16.1,2
— Visit of Salome, &c.			

LV

SE—SI

	Sect.	Page.	Evang.
Sepulchre, The stone from the	93	485	Mk. 16. 3, 4
— The party of Joanna	ib.	488	Lu. 24. 1
— Peter and John	ib.	490	Jno. 20. 4
— Mary Magdalene to the s. sees Jesus	ib.	491	— . 14
Sepulchres, Whited	85	318	Mt. 23. 27
Sermon on the Mnt. *Introd. to* ch. vi.	19	119	— 5. 7.
— — Plain	27	207	Lu. 6. 17-49
Sermons, The two compared *Introd.*	ib	205..11	Addenda.
Serpent, As Moses lifted up the	12	85	Jno, 3. 14
— Will he give him a?	19	139	Mt. 7. 10
Serpents, Be wise as	39	298	— 10. 16
— I give you power	60	143	Lu. 10. 19
Servant, Behold my	26	201	Mt. 12. 18
— of centurion	28	216	Lu. 7 2
— The unfaithful	63	168	— 12. 45
— Faithful and wise	86	343	Mt. 24. 45
— who beat his fellows	ib.	344	— . 49
— Wicked and slothful	ib.	349	— 25. 26
— Unprofitable	ib.	350	— . 30
Servants, Hired	16	109	Mk. 1. 20
— Would take account of	53	84	Mt. 18. 23
— Peter sat with the	89	427	— 26. 58
Serveth, I am as he that	87	375	Lu. 22. 27
Service of Christ	34	265	Mt. 8. 21,.2
— Will think .... doeth God	87	392	Jno. 16 2
Set, When he was	19	120	Mt. 5. 1
Seven other spirits	31	239	— 12 45
— loaves	48	33	— 16 10
— baskets	ib.	ib.	Mk. 8. 20
— Found as Jesus had said in s. particulars *Note*	82	262	Lu. 19. 32
— times in a day	70	205	— 17. 4
— fold defence of Mary's anointing p. 252, *Introd.*	81	255	Mt. 26.10..3
Seventy times seven	53	84	— 18. 22
— Jesus appointed other	60	141	Lu. 10.1-12
— Their return	ib.	143	— . 17
Shadow of death	3	18	— . 1 79
Shechem, or Sichem	13	96	Geog *Not.*
— (*See on* 'City of the Samaritans')	39	235	Mt. 10. 5
Shechinah, or cloud of glory	51	55	Mk. 9. 7
Shed for many	87	379	Mt. 26. 28
Sheep having no shepherd	39	294	— 9. 36
— in the midst of wolves	ib.	298	— 10. 16
— Character of Christ's	55	114	Jno. 10. 4, 5
— Other s. not of	ib.	116	— . 16
Shepherd of the sheep	ib.	114	— . 11
— I am the good	ib.	115	— . 11
— divideth the sheep	86	351	Mt. 25. 32
Shepherds, at Christ's birth	4	20	Lu. 2. 8
Shewbread—*see Note on*	94	189	Mk. 2. 26
Shewing unto Israel (John's)	3	19	Lu. 1. 80
— *see* 'Made manifest to Israel'	10	70	Jno. 1. 31
Shine, Then shall the righteous	33	260	Mt. 13. 43
Ship, Jesus teaches out of a	20	153	Ln. 5. 3
— — in parables	32	243	Mk. 4. 2
— — to wait on him	26	201	— 3. 9
— Entering into the	48	31	— 8. 13
— Cast the net on	97	506	Jno. 21. 6
Shipping, Took, seeking for Jesus	42	322	— 6. 24
Shoes, I am not worthy	7	54	Mk. 1. 7
— latch. I am not	10	69	Jno. 1. 27
— Neither two coats	39	298	Mt. 10. 10
— on his feet	68	195	Lu. 15. 22
Shortened, Except those days	86	333	Mt. 24. 22
Shut up the kingdom of God	55	315	— 23. 13
Sick, Nobleman's son was	14	100	Jno. 4. 46
— I was	86	353	Mt. 25. 43
Sickness, This is not unto death	58	127	Jno. 11. 4
Shilon *Geog Notice*,	p. 21	43	Mk. 7. 24
Sift you as wheat	87	376	Lu. 22. 31
Sighed, And looking up to	46	.25	Mk. 7. 34
— deeply in his spirit	47	30	— 8. 12
Sight to the blind	15	103	Lu. 4. 18
Sign, This shall be a s. to you	4	21	— 2. 12
— spoken against	ib.	26	— . 34
— The Jews required a	{12	81	Jno. 2 18
	{31	228	Mt. 12. 38
	{43	327	Jno. 6. 30
— from heaven	47	28	Mt. 16. 1
— On the s. from heaven *Addenda*	62	159	*Note*
— of the prophet Jonas	31	238	Mt. 12 39
— No s. to this generation	47	30	Mk. 8. 12
— of the Son of man in heaven	86	338	Mt. 24. 30
— given by Judas	88	418	— 26. 48
Signs, Except ye see	14	100	Jno. 4. 48
— of the times	47	29	Mt. 16. 3
— Great s. and wonders	86	335	— 24. 24
Siloam, Go, wash in the pool	{55	110	Jno. 9. 7
	{ib.	118	Geog. *Not.*

L.VI

SI—SO

	Sect.	Page.	Evang.
Siloam, Village of	55	120	Geog *Not.*
Silver, Ten pieces of	68	190	Lu. 15. 8
Simeon, a just and devout man	4	24	— 2. 25
Simon brought by Andrew to Jesus	10	71	Jno. 1. 41
— *see* Peter § 27, pp. 213,.5	ib.	75	Addenda
— sleepest thou?	88	415	Mk. 14 37
— son of Jonas, lovest	97	507	Jno. 21. 15
— the leper	81	253	Mt. 26. 6
— Zelotes (6th par., col. 1)	27	214	Addenda
— — (last par., col. 1)	ib.	216	ib.
Sin of the world, taken away	10	69	Jno.1 29,35
— forgiven	22	165	Mt. 9. 2
— no more	23	176	Jno. 5. 14
— Who, this man or his parents?	55	109	9. 2
Sins, Shall save his people	2	13	Mt. 1. 21
— Remission of	3	18	Lu. 1. 77
— Confessing their	7	52	Mk. 1. 5
— Shall die in your	55	101	Jno.8.21, 4
Singleness of eye	19	134	Mt. 6. 22
	62	155	Lu. 11. 34
Sinners above all in Jerusalem	64	173	— 13. 4
— Betrayed into the hands of	86	416	Mt. 26. 45
— Christ came to call	22	168	Mk. 2. 17
— *see* washing of his feet	29	229	Lu.7.36-50
Sisters—*see* Martha and Mary	61	150	— 10.4 1,.2
— Their different characters	81	253	Jno. 12.2,3
Sion, which is Hermon(*see* 'Jerusalem')	6	42	Geog *Not*
— *see on* 'An high mountain'	51	52	Mt. 17. 1
— Tell ye the daughter of	82	261	— 21. 5
Sixth hour	13	92	Jno. 4. 6
— And about the	90	445	— 19. 14
Sky, Ye can discern the face	47	29	Mt. 16. 3
Sleep on now	88	416	— 26. 45
Slept, While men	32	246	— 13. 25
— Slumbered and	86	348	— 25. 5
Slothful servant	ib	349	— . 26
Smite thee on thy right cheek	19	127	— 5. 39
Smote upon his breast	73	217	Lu. 18. 13
Snare, As a s. shall it come	86	340	— 21. 35
Sodom, More tolerable for	{29	227	Mt. 11. 24
	{39	298	— 10. 15
— The day that Lot	72	212	Lu. ,7. 29
Solitary place and prayed	18	114	Mk. 1. 35
Soldiers not to do violence	7	53	Lu. 3. 14
Solomon in all his glory	19	135	Mt. 6. 29
— Greater than	31	239	— 12. 42
— Epitome of his prayer, &c.	62	151	Lu. 11. 2
Solomon's porch	56	120	Jno. 10. 23
Son of Abraham	4	23	Mt. 1. 1
— — Forasmuch as	80	247	Lu. 19. 9
— David, Jesus is called	4	23	Mt. 1. 1
— — Is not this the ?	31	234	— 12. 23
— — Have mercy on me	45	13	— 15. 22
— — have mercy on me	78	240	Lu 18. 38
— — O Lord, thou	79	243	Mt.20.30,.1
— — They say unto him	85	306	— 22. 42
— God, He shall be called	2	10	Lu. 1. 35
— — Jesus Christ, the	7	49	Mk. 1. 1
— — If thou be the	9	64	Mt. 4. 3
— — This is the	10	70	Jno. 1. 34
— — Nathanael's confession	10	73	— . 49
— — Jesus so called	41	321	Mt. 14. 33
— — Dost thou believe on ?	55	113	Jno. 9. 35
— — which should come	58	130	— 11. 27
— — Purpose of his coming	12	86	— 3. 17
— — Oneness with the F.	23	178	— 5. 30
— — called also Son of	89	428	Mk. 14. 61
— — The only begotten	7	48	Jno. 1. 18
— — My beloved	8	60	Mk. 1. 11
— — *see* 'Glorify', &c.	67	398	Jno. 17.
— man, Ascending, &c.	10	73	— 1. 51
— — must be lifted up	12	85	— 3. 14
— — When ye have lifted up	55	103	— 8. 26
— — Shall execute judgment	23	178	— 5. 27
— — not where to lay	34	265	Mt. 13. 20
— — If ye shall see the	43	328	Jno. 6. 62
— — Ashamed of the	49	40	Mk. 8. 38
— — come to save	53	82	Mt. 18. 11
— — One of the days of the	72	211	Lu. 17. 22
— — When the S cometh	73	216	— 18. 9
— — And to stand before	86	341	— 21. 36
— — in his glory	ib.	351	Mt. 25. 31
— — is betrayed	19	355	— 26. 2
Song of Mary (comp. with Hannah's)	2	11	Lu. 1. 46
— Zacharias	3	16	— . 67
— Solomon	22	172	Addenda
Sorrowful, He went away	75	226	Mt. 19. 22
Sought, How is it that ye s. me ?	6	41	Lu. 2. 49
— to slay him	23	176	Jno. 5. 16
— the more to kill him	ib.	177	— . 18
Soul, My s. doth magnify the Lord	2	11	Lu. 1. 46
— What profited, if he lose	50	42	Mt. 16. 26

SO—SY

	Sect.	Page.	Evang.
Soul, much goods laid up	. 63	165	Lu. 12. 19
Sower, Parable of the	. 32	213	Mt. 13. 3
— The s. soweth the word	. 33	254	Mk. 4. 14
Soweth, Both he that s and he.	. 13	95	Jno. 4. 36
Spake to our fathers, to Ab-. .	. 2	12	Lu. 1. 55
— by all his holy prophets .	. 3	17	— . 70
— Never man s. like this man	. 55	96	Jno. 7. 46
Speak, We s. that w do know .	. 12	84	— 3. 11
— On premeditat ng what to	. 39	299	Mt. 10. 19
— Neither do ye premeditate	. 86	299	Mk. 13. 11
Speaketh the words of God	. 13	91	Jno. 3. 34
Speechless. And he was .	. 81	294	Mt. 22. 12
Speedily, I tell you he will av.	. 73	215	Lu. 18. 8
Spices and ointments prepared	. 92	477	— 23. 56
Spirit, God is a .	. 13	94	Jno. 4. 24
— John waxed strong in	. 3	19	Lu. 1. 80
— Jesus ditto	. 6	40	— 2. 40
— of God descended on Jesus	. 8	59	Mt. 3. 16
— of the Lord was upon him	. 15	102	Lu. 4. 18
— Came in the power of the	. ib.	ib.	— . 14
— Groaned in .	. 58	130	Jno. 11. 33
— Rejoiced in .	. 60	144	Lu. 10. 21
— It is the s. that quickeneth	. 43	333	Jno. 6. 63
— This spake he of the	. 55	96	— 7. 39
— of your Father .	. 30	299	Mt. 10. 20
— Comforter to abide .	. 87	383	Jno. 14. 16
— of truth ; whom the world can-			
not receive .	. ib.	ib.	— 17
— sent from the Father	. ib.	301	— 15. 26
— to testify of Jesus .	. ib.	ib.	— . 26
— convinces of sin .	. ib.	393	— 16. 7, 8
— see ' Holy Ghost '			
— Baptism of the S. promised .	7	54	Mt. 3. 11
— — referred to by Jesus	98	513	Ac. 1. 5
— An unclean s. at Capernaum	17	110	Mk. 1. 23
Springing up into everlasting life	. 13	93	Jno. 4. 14
Stedfastly set his face, &c .	. 59	135	Lu. 9. 51
Steward, The faithful and wise	. 63	167	— 12. 42
— The unjust .	. 69	196	— 16. 1
— in parable of the labourers	76	232	Mt. 20. 8
Stone, to be built upon the rock	. 50	38	— 16. 18
— Whosoever shall fall on this	84	290	— 21. 44
— which the builders rejected	. ib.	ib.	— . 42
— The people will s. us	. ib.	284	Lu. 20. 6
Stoned, Such should be .	. 55	99	Jno. 8. 5
Stones, God is able of these	. 7	53	Lu. 3. 8
— What manner of .	. 86	323	Mk. 13. 1
— would immediately cry out .	82	264	Lu. 19. 40
— They took up s. to cast.	. 55	100	Jno. 8. 59
Stood up for to read .	. 15	102	Lu. 4. 16
Strait, Enter ye in at the s. gate	. 19	139	Mt. 7. 13
— the gate which leadeth unto			
life .	. ib.	ib.	— . 14
Stranger will they not follow	. 55	114	Jno. 10. 5
— I was a.	. 86	352	Mt. 25. 35
Strangers, Of their own children, or	52	73	— 17. 25
— To bury .	. 89	436	— 27. 7
Strength, Hath shewed s. with his a.	2	12	Lu. 1. 51
Strengthen thy brethren .	. 87	376	— 22. 32
Strife which should be the gr. .	. ib.	375	— . 24
Strong, Bind the s man .	. 31	206	Mt. 12. 29
Subject to Joseph and Mary .	. 6	43	Lu. 2. 51
Substance, Ministered of their .	. 30	233	— 8. 3
Substitution taught throughout the			
Old Testament—see ' Present him			
to .. Lord ' .	. 4	24	— 2. 22
Subtilty, Consulted to take Jesus by	88	356	Mt. 26. 4
Suffer many things p. 40, Mt. 16. 21	50	46	Addenda
— Jesus again foretells he shall	. 52	71	Mt.17. 22, 3
— And a third time .	. 77	235	— 20. 17, 9
Sufficient unto the day is the evil	. 19	136	— 6. 34
Sun, made to rise on the evil and g.	ib.	128	— 5. 45
— shall be darkened .	. 85	337	— 24. 29
Supplementary rel. of Jno. vii, &c.	54	83	Addenda
— Lu. ix. 51—Lxvii. 14.	59	139	—
Superscription on the cross	. 91	462	Mk. 15. 26
Supper, Parable of the great	. 67	183	Lu. 14. 16
— being ended .	. 87	365	Jno. 13. 2
— Discourse after .	. ib.	391	— 14.—6.
— On the time of celebrating.	. ib.	408	Addenda
Swear not at all .	. 19	128	Mt. 5. 34
Swearing by gold of the temple, On	85	316	— 23. 16, 7
Swine, Cast not pearls before	. 19	138	— 7. 6
Sword shall pierce through thy	. 4	26	Lu. 2. 35
— Shall fall by the edge .	. 86	9	Lu.
— He that hath no .	. 87	377	Lu. 22. 36
— Shall perish with the .	. 88	401	Mt. 26. 52
Sychar . . (Geog. Not., p. 96)	13	92	Jno. 4. 5
Synagogue, Jesus cast out of .	. 15	103	Lu. 4 28,.9
— described .	. ib.	106	Addenda
— at Capernaum .	. 17	110	Mk. 1. 21
— Ruler of the .	. 36	266	Addenda

SY—TE

	Sect.	Page	Evang.
Synagogues, Put out of the	{ 55	111	Jno. 9. 22
	{ 87	362	— 16. 2
— Chief seats in the .	. 85	314	Mt. 23. 6
Syria described .	. 18	117	Geog. Not.
Syro-Phœnician woman .	. 45	14	Mk. 7. 26

T.

Tabernacles, Let us make three	. 51	55	Lu. 9. 33
— The feast of .	{ 51	87	Jno. 7. 2
	{ ib.	89	
— Jesus goes up to .	ib.	91	— . 10
Table, A writing .	. 3	16	Lu. 1. 63
Tabor, Mount .	. 51	62	Geog. Not.
Tabular view of Sermon on Mount,			
and its Correspondences, &c.	. 19	152	Addenda
Talitha cumi .	. 36	284	Mk. 5. 41
Talents, Ten thousand .	. 53	85	Mt. 18. 24
— Parable of the .	. 86	347	— 25. 14-30
Talking, Moses and E. with Jesus	. 51	54	Mk. 9. 4
Tares, The enemy sowed .	. 32	246	Mt.13.24-30
Taught as having authority	. 19	142	— 7. 29
— All t. of God .	. 43	330	Jno. 6. 45
Taxed, A decree .. all should be	. 4	19	Lu. 2. 1
Teach, Whosoever shall do and	. 19	124	Mt. 5. 19
— Beginning to t. in parables	. 32	251	Addenda
— you all things .	. 87	385	Jno. 14. 26
Teacher—(see ' Christ ')			
— Jesus ackn. by the Jewish			
ruler to be a t. from God	12	83	— 3. 2
— Him hath God the Father s.	43	326	— 6. 27
— He had the words of e. life	ib.	334	— . 68
— The voice, ' Hear ye him ' .	51	56	Mt. 17. 5
— The officers said, ' Never ' .	55	96	Jno. 7. 46
— He knew and rev.the Father	29	228	Mt. 11. 26
— He knew what was in man	12	82	Jno. 2. 25
— Made known wh G. is to m.	ib.	84	— 3. 11.-7
— requires of man	13	94	— 4 23. 4
— Describes his disciples	. 19	120.-42	Mt. 5-7.
— Warns what to avoid .	. 85	312	— 23.
— He taught by formal disc.	. 27	207	Lu 6.17-49
— familiar conversation	13	92	Jno. 4.7-26
— questioning others	. 85	306	Mt.22.41-6
— replies to his disc. {	33	255	— 13.36-43
	53	82	— 18. 1-6
— and to strangers	. 75	223	— 19.16-22
— in the house .	. 67	182	Lu. 14 7-24
— and by the way .	. 50	36	Mk.8.27-38
— on the mountain .	. 19	120	Mt. 5.
— in the ship . .	. 20	153	Lu. 5. 1
— — synagogue	. 43	332	Jno. 6. 59
— — temple .	. 84	282	Mt. 21. 23
— the learned .	. 6	41	Lu. 2.46.-7
— unlearned .	. 29	228	Mt.11.25-30
— rich .	. 67	182	Lu.14.12.-4
— poor .	. 29	223	Mt. 11. 5
— late .	. 12	83	Jno. 3. 2
— early .	. 55	99	— 8. 2
— daily .	. 83	278	Lu. 19. 47
— standing in the t.	. 55	95	Jno. 7. 37.
— walking .	. 84	2'6	Mk. 11. 27
— sitting .	. 85	308	— 12.41. 4
— by applying Scripture	15	102	Lu.4 16.30
— improving events.	. 61	173	— 13. 1-5
— in plainness .	. 87	396	Jno.16.26.-9
— by parables .	. 32	243	Mt. 13. 3
— prophecy .	. 86	324	— 24.
— significant acts	. 87	368	Jno.13 4-17
— becom. all things .	85	300	Mt. 22. 23
— grad.unfold the tr.	32	249	Mk. 4. 33
— his disciples to bear it	87	394	Jno.16 19, 3
— see case of Samaritan	. 13	92	— 4. 7-26
— man born blind .	. 55	103	— 9. 5-38
— by discriminating cha.	61	150	Lu.10.41,-2
— detecting the secret			
springs of action			
— our duty to God	. 85	304	Mk.12 29,30
— to our neighbour	. 60	145	Lu.10.27-37
— from the highest mo.	87	382	Jno.14.13.-7
— after the best ex.	. 19	128	Mt. 5. 48
— for the noblest ends	. ib.	123	— . 16
— The three witnesses, see			
1 Jno. v. 6, to t hint as—			
1. The water—purity of life and			
doctrine. . 9.10 63-152 — 4.7.
2. The spirit—miracles, &c. . 21-46 159 — 8.15.
3. The blood—suffering all things			
for the truth's sake, even unto			
the death . . . 47.91 28-408 — 16-27.
Teaching, In vain do they worship			
me, t. for doctrines the command-			
ments of men . . . 41	7	— 15. 9

LVII

TE—TH

	Sect.	Page.	Evang.
Teaching, On Christ's manner of	17	113	*Addenda*
— in their synagogues, and preaching	18	115	Mt. 4. 23
— The elders came as he was	84	283	— 21. 23
— daily in the temple	88	421	— 26. 55
— them to observe all	96	501	— 28. 20
Tell whence it cometh	12	81	Jno. 3. 8
— He (Christ) will *t. us*	13	91	— 4. 25
— We cannot (whence John's b.)	84	284	Mt. 21. 27
— Neither do I *t.* you	*ib.*	*ib.*	— 27
Tempest on the lake	34	266	— 8. 24
Temple of the Lord	1	3	Lu. 1. 9
— Account of	*ib.*	8	*Addenda*
— Jesus presented in	4	25	Lu. 2.27, 8
— — found in it	6	41	— . 46
— — drives out	12	81	Jno.2.13-7
— The *t.* of his body	*ib.*	82	— 21
— at f. of Tabernacles	55	91	— 7. 10
— — Dedication	56	120	— 10. 22
— Adulteress brought	55	99	— 8. 2-11
— One greater than	24	190	Mt. 12. 6
— Triumphal entry into	82	262	Mk. 11. 7
— The blind and lame	*ib.*	266	Mt. 21. 14
— Description of the	*ib.*	270	*Addenda*
— The second	*ib.*	271	*do.*
— of Herod	*ib.*	*ib.*	*do.*
— Day of Procession to the	*ib.*	272	*do.*
— Second cleansing of the	83	276	Mt. 21. 12
— Jesus' authority quest. in	84	283	— 23
— Jesus departs from the	86	323	24. 1
— — foretells the destr.	*ib.*	324	— 2
— — accused of saying he would destroy it	89	427	Mk. 14. 58
Tempt, Thou shalt not	9	65	Mt. 4. 7
Temptations, Jesus'	*ib.*	63	Mk. 1. 12
— On the scene of the	*ib.*	67	*Addenda*
— — order of the	*ib.*	*ib.*	*do.*
— Lead us not into	{ 19	133	Mt. 6. 13
	62	152	Lu. 11. 4
— Pray that ye	88	413	— 22. 40
Tempting, Pharisees, &c.	47	28	Mt. 16. 1
— and Herodians	84	295	— 22.15,,6
— A lawyer came	65	301	— . 34–6
Ten, much displeased	77	238	Mk. 10. 41
— Rule over *t.* cities	80	249	Lu. 19. 17
— pieces of silver	63	190	— 15. 8
— virgins, The parable of	86	316	Mt. 25.1-13
Tender mercy of our God	3	18	Lu. 1. 78
Test of being disciples	55	103	Jno.8.31,,2
Testify, He needed none to	12	82	— 2. 25
— I *t.* of *t.* (the world)	54	88	— 7. 7
— The Spirit of truth	87	391	— 15. 26
Testimony, No man receiveth	13	90	— 3. 32
— He that hath rec.	*ib.*	*ib.*	— 33
— For a *t.* against them	39	299	Mt. 10. 18
— It shall turn to you	86	327	Lu. 21. 13
Tetrarch, Herod *t.* of Galilee	{ 7	49	— 3. 1
	40	304	Mt. 14. 1
Thanks, Anna gave	4	27	Lu. 2. 38
— for revealing to babes	29	227	Mt. 11. 25
— for the loaves	40	313	Jno. 6. 11
— bread	87	368	Lu. 22. 19
— wine at last supper	*ib.*	378	Mk. 14. 23
Theophilus	2	—	Lu. 1. 3
Thessalonians (1st and 2nd Epistles)	19	146	*Addenda*
Thief and robber	55	11.	Jno. 10. 1
— The penitent	91	464	Lu. 23. 40
Thieves and robbers	55	115	Jno. 10. 8
— Man that fell among	60	146	Lu. 10. 30
— The temple a den of	83	278	Mk. 11. 17
— Two *t.* crucified	91	462	Mt. 27. 38
Thine, Take that *t.* is	76	233	— 20. 14
Third day .. rise again	77	236	— 19
Thirst, Shall never	13	93	Jno. 4. 14
Thirty pieces of silver, Judas'	86	357	Mt. 26. 15
— They took the	89	437	— 27. 9
Thomas, eighth of 12 apostles	27	214	*Addenda*
— Meaning of name (2d col.)	*ib.*	218	*do.*
— Let us also go, that	58	124	Jno. 11. 16
— at sea of Galilee	97	505	— 21. 2
Thorns, Seed sown among	32	244	Mt. 13. 7
— Jesus crowned with	{ 90	443	Jno. 19. 2
	91	455	Mt. 27. 29
Thorny ground hearers	33	256	Mk. 4. 18
Thought, While he (Joseph)	2	13	Mt. 1. 20
Thoughts of many hearts revealed	4	26	Lu. 2. 35
— Jesus knew their	25	196	— 6. 8
Three measures of meal	{ 32	249	Mt. 13. 33
	65	176	Lu. 13. 21
— days, They continue	44	26	Mt. 15. 32
— After *three* d. I will r.	92	478	— 27. 63
— disc. & Andrew on M. Olivet.	86	324	Mk. 13. 3

J.VIII

TH—TR

	Sect.	Page.	Evang.
Three with Jesus' agony	88	413	Mt. 26. 37
— years and six months (Elijah)	15	104	Lu. 4. 25
— — seeking fruit, &c.	64	174	— 13. 7
Throat, Took him by the	53	85	Mt. 18. 28
Throne of his father David	2	10	Lu. 1. 32
Thrones, Apostles to sit on 12	75	229	Mt. 19. 28
Thunder, James and John sons of	27	206	Mk. 3. 17
Thundered, The people said it.	82	268	Jno. 12. 29
Tiberias, Lake of	32	250	*Geog. Not.*
Tiberius Cæsar	7	49	Lu. 3. 1
Tidings of great joy	4	20	— 2. 10
Tiling	22	165	— 5. 19
Time, From that *t.* Jesus began	50	40	Mt. 16. 21
— My *t.* is not yet come	54	87	Jno. 7. 6
— is fulfilled	16	105	Mk. 1. 15
— On *t.* of our Saviour's birth	4	29	*Addenda*
— The return to Naz., &c.	5	39	*do.*
— — residence in Egypt	*ib.*	*ib.*	*do.*
— — passover	6	43	*do.*
— — Baptist's ministry	7	56	*do.*
— Our Lord's min. in Judea	12	87	*do.*
— The 2nd sab. aft. the first	24	194	*do.*
— — first partial circuit	26	204	*do.*
— — begin. to teach in parables	32	251	*do.*
— — crossing to Gergesa	34	268	*do.*
— year of feeding the 5,000	40	316	*do.*
— feast of the Dedication	56	124	*do.*
— Lu. ix. 51—xviii. 14	59	138	*do.*
— Suggestions on place and *t.* of	*ib.*	139	*do.*
— of arrival in Bethany	81	258	*do.*
— unction in Bethany	*ib.*	*ib.*	*do.*
— procession to the temple	82	272	*do.*
— cleansing of the temple	83	279	*do.*
— fulfilment of Mt. xxiv.	86	338	*do.*
— the Last Supper	87	403	*do.*
Times of Peter's denials	89	439	*do.*
— the Gentiles	86	334	Lu. 21. 24
Timothy, Paul's first Epistle to	19	147	*Addenda*
Tiari, Particulars of the 22nd of	55	89	Jno. 8. &c.
Tithe, mint and rue	62	156	Lu. 11. 42
— anise and cummin	85	317	Mt. 23. 23
Title on the cross	91	460	Jno.19.19,20
Tittle, One *t.* shall in no wise	19	123	Mt. 5. 18
— One	*ib.*	*ib.*	— 18 *Addenda*
To-day and to-morrow, and third	66	178	Lu.13.32-5
Told you before	86	335	Mt. 24. 25
— If I have *t.* you earthly	12	85	Jno. 3. 12
— A man that hath *t.* you	55	105	— 8. 40
— if it were not so, I would have	87	380	— 14. 2
— you before it come to pass	8	385	— 29
— — that when the *t.* shall come	*ib.*	393	— 16. 4
— I have *t.* you that I am he	88	418	— 18. 8
Tolerable, More *t.* for the land of S.	29	237	Mt. 11. 24
Tomb, In his own new	92	476	— 27 60
Tombs, Demoniacs dwelt in the	35	269	Mk. 5. 3
— of the prophets	85	318	Mt. 23. 29
Tongue was loosed—*see* 'Touched'	3	16	Lu. 1. 61
Tooth for a tooth	19	127	Mt. 5. 38
Tophet	*Addenda* *ib.*	129	— 22
Tormentors, Delivered him to the	53	85	— 18. 34
Torn, When the unclean spirit had	17	111	Mk. 1. 26
Touch, A blind man besought him	49	31	— 8. 22
— Jesus heals a leper by	21	160	Lu. 5. 13
— Ye yourselves *t.* not &c.	62	157	— 44. 46
— Brought children, &c.	74	220	Mk. 10. 13
— me not, I am not yet asc.	94	492	Jno. 20. 17
Touched the tongue	46	34	Mk. 7. 33
Touching the resurrection	85	303	Mt. 22. 31
Towel, and girded himself	87	366	Jno. 13. 4
Tower, Which of you intending	67	185	Lu. 14. 28
— Built a	84	286	Mt. 21. 33
Towns, Let us go into the next	18	114	Mk. 1. 38
Truefoundity (*Geog. Not.*, p. 55)	7	49	Lu. 3. 1
Tradition of the elders	44	4	Mk. 7. 3
— Through your	*ib.*	7	— 9
Traitor, Judas Iscariot which was	27	207	Lu. 8. 16
Transfiguration on the Holy Mount.	51	51	Mt. 17. 1-8
Transgress, Why do ye also?	43	5	— 15. 3
Transgressors, Reckoned among	87	377	Lu. 22. 37
— Jesus numbered with	91	462	Mk. 15. 18
Travail, A woman when she is in	87	395	Jno. 16. 21
Travelling, As a man	86	317	Mt. 25. 14
Treasure is, there will your heart	19	134	— 6. 21
— hid in a field	33	261	— 13. 44
— Thou shalt have *t.* in h.	75	225	— 19. 21
Treasures, Lay up *t.* in heaven	19	134	— 6. 20
Treasury, These words spake Jesus	55	101	Jno. 8. 20
— Not lawful to put	89	436	Mt. 27. 6
Tree which bringeth not forth, &c.	19	128	Lu. 3. 9
— Every good *t.* bringeth	19	140	Mt. 7. 17
— known by his fruit	31	237	— 12. 33
— Mustard seed becometh a	32	248	— 13. 32

TR—VA

	Sect.	Page.	Evang.
Tree, Ye might say to this	70	207	Lu. 17. 6
— If they do these things in a gr.	91	458	— 23. 31
Trench, Thine enemies shall cast a.	82	265	— 19. 43
Trespass, If thy brother t ag. thee.	53	83	Mt. 18. 15
Tribulation, or persecution	33	255	— 13. 21
— Great	86	333	— 24. 21
Tribute, Doth not your master pay?	52	72	— 17. 24
— unto Cæsar	84	296	— 22. 17
— Forbidding to give	90	445	Lu. 23. 2
Trinity, On the doctrine of the	8	60	Note
Triumphal entry into Jerusalem	82	259	Jno. 12. 12
Trodden down, Jerusalem to be	86	331	Lu. 21. 31
Troubled, Mary was	2	9	— 1. 29
— Herod was	5	32	Mt. 2. 3
— Jesus .. in spirit	87	370	Jno. 13. 21
— Let not your heart be	ib.	380	— 14. 1
Troubling of the water	23	175	— 5. 4
True, Set to his seal that God is	13	90	— 3. 33
— worshippers	ib.	94	— 4. 23
— bread from heaven	43	328	— 6. 32
— He that sent me is	55	94	— 7. 28
— Who will commit .. the	69	198	Lu. 16. 11
Trumpet, Do not sound a	19	131	Mt. 6. 2
— Great sound of a	86	338	— 24. 31
Trust, Danger of putting t. in riches	75	227	Mk. 10. 24
Trusted in themselves	73	216	Lu. 18. 9
— He t. in God	91	464	Mt. 27. 43
— that it had been he	94	494	Lu. 24. 21
Truth, He that doeth	12	87	Jno. 3. 21
— Shall worship the Father in s.	13	94	— 4. 23
— Lord: yet the dogs eat of	45	15	Mt. 15. 27
— I am the way, the t.. &c.	87	381	Jno. 14. 6
— The Spirit of—(see 'Spirit').	ib.391	..4	—15.26-16.13
— I tell you the	ib.	393	— 16. 7
— Sanctify them through thy	ib.	402	— 17. 17
— Christ came to witness of the	90	442	— 18. 37
— Pilate asked, What is?	ib.	ib.	— 38
Turn the hearts of the fathers	1	5	Lu. 1. 17
Turtle doves offered in sacrifice	4	24	— 2. 24
Twelve, Jesus when t. years old	6	43	Addenda
— The—(see 'Apostles').	27	206	Lu. 6. 13
— sent out two and two	39	295	Mk. 6. 7
— Jesus sat down with the	87	364	Mt. 26. 20
— Judas, one of the	88	417	— 47
— Will ye also go away?	43	334	Jno. 6. 67
— taught lesson of humility	52	74	Mk. 9.35,6
— promised twelve thrones	75	229	Mt. 19. 28
	ib.	ib.	— 28
— tribes of Israel {	51	67	Addenda
— legions of angels	88	421	Mt. 26. 53
Two or three witnesses	53	83	— 18. 16
— women grinding at the mill {	72	213	Lu. 17. 35
	86	342	Mt. 24. 41
— went into the t. to pray	73	216	Lu. 18. 10
— sons, Parable of the	84	285	Mt.21 28 31
— great commandments	85	304	— 22.36-40

U.

Unbelief, Because of their	37	288	Mk. 6. 6
— On	ib.	292	Addenda
— Because of your	51	61	Mt. 17. 20
— Help thou min..	ib.	60	Mk. 9. 24
Unclean spirit, in the synagogue	17	110	— 1. 23
— spirits near sea of Galilee	26	201	— 3. 11
Uncovered the roof {	22	165	— 2. 4
	ib.	170	Addenda
Unction at Bethany	81	258	do.
Understand, Hearken and	44	8	Mk. 7. 14
Understanding and answers	6	41	Lu. 2. 47
— Having had perfect	1	1	— 1. 3
Understood not, Joseph and Mary	6	42	— 2. 50
— The disciples	52	71	Mk. 9. 32
— at the first	82	262	Jno. 12 16
Union of Christ with his people	87	384	—14.19-23
Unprofitable servants, We are	70	208	Lu. 17. 10
— Cast ye the u. servant	86	350	Mt. 25 30
Unwashen hands	44	7	Mk. 7. 2
— On the question of	ib.	11	Addenda
Unworthiness	39	297	Mt. 10. 13
Up to Jerusalem	77	235	Mk. 10. 32
Usury, or with its produce	80	250	Lu. 19. 23
— Mine own with	86	350	Mt. 25. 27
Uttermost farthing	19	125	— 5. 26
— parts of the earth	31	239	— 12. 42

V.

Vain almsgiving, praying, &c.	19	131	Mt. 6. 1-18
— repetitions	ib.	ib.	— 7
Valley, Every	7	51	Lu. 3. 5
— of the son of Hinnom	19	129	Addenda
Vanished out of their sight	94	496	Lu. 24. 31

VE—WE

	Sect.	Page.	Evang.
Vehemently, The stream did beat	27	210	Lu. 6. 49
— chief priests v. accus.	90	448	— 23. 10
Veil of temple rent in the midst	91	468	— 45
— from top to bottom	92	470	Mt. 27. 51
Vengeance. These be the days of	86	332	Lu. 21. 22
Verbal differences, On	8	62	Addenda
Verily	19	123	Mt. 5. 18
— verily, I say, Hereafter, &c.	10	73	Jno. 1. 51
Vespasian	86	332	Note
Vessels, Oil in their	ib.	346	Mt. 25. 4
Village, A certain	61	149	Lu. 10. 38
Villages, Jesus taught in v.	38	293	Mk. 9. 35
Vine, Jesus the true	87	387	Jno. 15. 1
Vinegar given Jesus to drink	91	459	Mt. 27. 34
Vineyard let out	84	287	— 21. 33
Violence, Do v. to no man	7	53	Lu. 3. 14
— Kingdom of heaven suff.	29	225	Mt. 11. 12
Vipers, Generation of	7	52	Lu. 3. 7
— How can ye speak good	31	237	Mt. 12. 34
— How can ye escape?	85	319	— 23. 33
Virgins, Parable of the ten	86	346	25. 1-13
Virtue went out of him, &c.	27	207	Lu. 6. 19
— is gone out of me	36	281	— 8. 46
Vision to Zacharias	1	3	1. 11
— of angels at sepulchre	94	494	— 24. 23
Visit of Mary to Elisabeth	2	11	— 1. 39
— of the Magi, On the	5	38	Addenda
Visited and redeemed his people	3	16	Lu. 1. 68
— The dayspring hath v. us	ib.	18	— 78
— That God hath v. his people	29	222	— 7. 16
— I was sick, and ye v. me	86	352	Mt. 25. 36
Voice of one crying in the wild. {	7	49	Mk. 1. 3
	10	69	Jno. 1. 23
— at Jesus' baptism	8	59	Mt. 3. 17
— transfiguration	51	55	— 17. 5
— upon his last vis. to Jerusalem	82	268	Jno. 12. 28
— Jesus cried with a loud v.	58	131	— 11. 43
— on the cross	91	468	Mt. 21. 50
Voices of them .. chief pr. prevailed	90	453	Lu. 23. 23

W.

Wages, He that reapeth receiveth	13	95	Jno. 4. 36
— see Para. of day labourers	76	231	Mt. 20.1-16
Wagging their heads	91	463	— 27. 39
Walled greatly	36	283	Mk. 5. 38
Waited, For Zacharias	1	6	Lu. 1. 21
Walk not in darkness	55	100	Jno. 8 12
Walked no more with him	43	334	— 6. 66
Walking in all the commandments.	1	3	Lu. 1. 6
— upon the sea	41	319	Mk. 6. 48
— Men as trees	49	34	8. 24
Warned, Who hath w. you to flee	7	52	Mt. 3. 7
Wars and rumours of	86	325	— 24. 6
Wash in the pool of Siloam	55	110	Jno. 9. 7
— If I w. thee not	87	306	— 13. 8
Washed before dinner	62	156	Lu. 11. 38
— Woman w. Jesus' feet	29	230	— 7. 38
— Pilate w., saying, I am	90	452	Mt. 27. 24
Washing of hands, On	44	4	Mk. 7. 3
— see 'On eating without'	ib.	11	Addenda
Wasted his goods	69	196	Lu. 16. 1
Watch, The fourth	41	319	Mt. 14. 25
—, therefore	86	342	— 21. 42
— and pray	88	415	— 26. 41
— Pilate said, Ye have a	92	478	— 27. 65
Watching, Blessed whom the Lord.	63	167	Lu. 12 37
Water, The best wine made of	11	77	Jno. 2. 8
— Must be born of	12	83	— 3. 5
— In Ænon, near to Salim	13	89	— 3. 23
— Samaritan w. came to draw	ib.	92	— 4. 7
— Shall flow rivers of living	55	96	— 7. 38
— Cup of	52	76	Mk. 9. 41
— Forthwith came thereout	92	473	Jno. 19. 34
Waxed strong in Spirit, John	3	19	Lu. 1. 80
— Jesus	6	40	— 2. 40
— gross, This people's heart	32	246	Mt. 13. 15
Way, Whiles thou art in the	19	125	— 5. 25
— Some fell by the w. side	32	243	Mk. 4. 4
— of the Gentiles	39	295	Mt. 10. 5
— By the w. he asked his	50	36	Mk. 8. 27
— Christ the w., and the truth	87	381	Jno. 14. 6
We forbad him, because he	52	76	Mk. 9. 38
Weapons	88	417	Jno. 18. 3
Wearied with his journey, sat	13	92	— 4. 6
Weather fair and foul, Signs of	47	29	Mt. 16. 2,3
Wedding, When he shall return	63	166	Lu. 12. 76
— garment	83	282	Mt. 22. 11
Weep for yourselves, & for your, ch.	91	457	Lu. 23. 28
Well, Jacob's, at Sychar	13	92	Jno. 4. 5
— On	ib.	96	Addenda
Well, He hath done all things	46	25	Mk. 7. 37

	Sect.	Page.	Evang.
Well done, good and faithful servant	86	348	Mt. 25.21..3
Want into Galilee	11	100	Jno. 4. 43
— about all the cities	38	293	Mt. 9. 35
— through .. preaching	39	303	Lu. 9. 6
— He also w. up unto the feast	55	91	Jno. 7. 10
— Hid himself, and w. out of the temple	ib.	108	— 8. 59
— Passing through the midst	15	105	Lu. 4. 30
— back, and walked no more	43	331	Jno. 6. 66
Wept, Jesus	58	130	— 11. 35
West, Cloud rise out of the	63	170	Lu. 12. 54
Whale's belly	31	234	Mt. 12. 40
Whatsoever he saith, do	11	77	Jno. 2. 5
Wheat, Will gather his	7	51	Mt. 3. 12
When shall these things be	86	321	— 24. 3
— ye therefore .. see the abomin.	ib.	359	Addenda
Whence is this to me?	2	11	Lu. 1. 43
— I know w. I came	55	100	Jno. 8. 14
Where is he that is born King, &c.	5	31	Mt. 2. 2
— David was (Bethlehem)	55	96	Jno. 7. 42
— is thy Father?	ib.	101	— 8. 19
Whereby shall I know?	1	5	Lu. 1. 18
While, A little w. am I with you	55	94	Jno. 7. 33
— the bridegroom tarried	86	346	Mt. 25. 5
— I was with them in the w.	87	401	Jno. 17. 12
Whit, A man every w. whole	55	93	— 7. 23
White as the light	51	53	Mt. 17. 2
— and glistering	ib.	ib.	Lu. 9. 29
Whited sepulchres	85	318	Mt. 23. 27
Whithersoever thou goest	31	264	— 8. 19
	59	136	Lu. 9. 57
Whole, They that be	36	278	Mt. 9. 12
— If I may touch but .. I, &c.	ib.	280	Mk. 5. 28
— As many as touched him	42	323	— 6. 56
— Daughter was made	45	16	Mt. 15. 28
Whom ye know not	10	69	Jno. 1. 26
— To w. shall we go?	43	334	— 6. 68
Whosoever believeth	12	85	— 3. 15
Wicked and adulterous generation	47	29	Mt. 16. 4
— and slothful servant	86	349	— 25. 26
Wickedness	44	10	Mk. 7. 22
Wide is the gate	19	139	Mt. 7. 13
Widow, Only son of his mother, a	28	221	Lu. 7. 12
— The importunate	73	215	— 18. 3
Widow's, The poor w.'s two mites	85	309	Mk. 12. 42
Widows in Israel in the d. of Elias	15	101	Lu. 4. 25
— houses devoured	85	315	Mt. 23. 14
Wife, The espousal	2	13	— 1. 23
— On putting away a	19	126	— 5. 31, .2
— Whosoever putteth away his	69	199	Lu. 16. 18
Wilde, on the village of Siloam	55	120	Geog. N.t.
Wilderness, John preaches in the	7	50	Mt. 3. 1
— Jesus led by the Spirit	9	63	Lu. 4. 1
— As Moses lifted up the	12	85	Jno. 3. 14
— Jesus withdraws into	21	101	Lu. 5. 16
Will of God, Born of the	7	47	Jno. 1. 13
— him that sent me	13	95	— 4. 34
— Prayer that the w. of God	19	132	Mt. 6. 10
— of the Father, Th. son seeketh	23	178	Jno. 5. 30
— If any man will do his	55	91	— 7. 17
— Not my w., but thine be done	88	414	Lu. 22. 42
— ye also go away?	43	334	Jno. 6. 67
— come after me	50	42	Mt. 16 24
— not believe	89	434	Lu. 22. 67
Willan's narrative quoted (3 par.)	87	407	Geog. Not.
Willing, Pilate was w. to release	90	451	Lu. 23. 20
— to content the people	ib.	453	Mk. 15. 15
Wilson on our origin	68	195	Addenda
Wind bloweth where it listeth	12	81	Jno. 3. 8
— obeyed Jesus' command	31	268	Mt. 8. 26
Wine, J drink no	1	4	Lu. 1. 15
— see ' Beginning of miracles'	11	73	Jno. 2. 11
— New w. into new bottles.	22	169	Lu. 5. 34
— Old, no man having drunk	ib.	ib.	— . 39
Wings, As a hen her brood under	60	179	— 13. 34
— of the Roman eagle	6	359	Addenda
Winter, And Jesus walked in the t.	56	120	Jno. 10 22
— Pray that your flight, &c.	86	332	Mt. 24. 20
Wipe with the hairs of her head	29	230	Lu. 7. 38
— towel wherewith he was girded	87	365	Jno. 13. 5
Wisdom of the just	1	5	Lu. 1. 17
— Jesus filled with	6	40	— 2. 40
— — increased in	ib.	42	— . 52
— What w. is given him?	37	2-7	Mk. 6. 2
— of God	62	157	Lu. 11. 49
Wise men from the East	5	31	Mt. 2. 1
— build upon the rock	19	141	— 7. 21
— and foolish virgins	86	346	— 25. 1-13
Wisely, He had done	69	197	Lu. 16. 8
Wiser in their generation	ib.	ib.	— . 8
Wist ye not that I must be about	6	42	— 2. 49

Wist not what to say			
With, The Lord is w. thee			
— Emmanuel, God w. us			
— Lo. I am w. you alway			
Within, From w. out of the h			
Without fear, Might serve hi			
Witness, John sent for			
— Ye receive not our			
— for Christ, Summar			
— The Gospel to be fo			
— Christ is w. to the tr			
— John bare			
Witness, Thou barest			
— Ye sent unto John,			
— The Father beareth			
— And ye (the apostl			
Witnesses, Those at Christ's			
— Those on the holy			
— Two or three			
— The Spirit and th			
— Eye-w. of the wo			
— Many false, again			
Woe unto you that are rich,			
— thee, Chorazin			
— th world, bec. of			
— — Pharisees, &c.			
— eight times repeat			
Wolf scattereth the sheep			
Wolves in sheep's clothing			
— Sheep in the midst o			
Woman, Mary thus addresse			
— And at the cross			
— of Samaria			
— of Canaan			
— Whoso looketh on			
— which was a sinner			
— taken in adultery			
Women followed Jesus from			
— of Jerusalem follow			
— earliest at the tomb			
— first heralds of the			
Wondered, While they			
Wont to release unto the pe			
Word, Eye-wit. and ministe			
— was with God, and w			
— The creator and sus			
— was made flesh			
— of God came to John			
— Not by bread alone,			
— of God, Pressed .. to			
— of none effec			
— Jesus preached the			
— abiding in you.			
— The sower soweth th			
— of the kingdom			
— Thy w. is truth			
— Shall believe on me			
— Men taken at their			
Words of God, Speaketh the			
— Gracious w. out of hi			
— of eternal life			
— My w. not pass awa			
— On keeping his			
— Have given them th			
— must be accounted f			
Work, My meat is to finish			
— For a good w.			
— I have finished the			
— This is the w. of Go			
— I have done on			
Works, Good			
— of Jesus witnessed			
— Mighty			
— That thy disciples			
— of Abraham, Ye wo			
— of God should be m			
— Many good w. have			
World (αιων)			
— Since the w. began			
— Neither in this w.,			
— The care of this			
— In the end of this			
— So shall it be at the			
— What .. and of the en			
— Gospel preached in a			
— Even unto the end o			
— (συντελεια)			
— That all the w. shou			
— All the kingdoms of			
— Shall be preach. in all			
— (κοσμος)			

WO—WR

Entry	Sect.	Page	Evang.
World, He (True Light) was in the	7	47	Jno. 1. 10
— Lighteth every man that cometh into the	.	ib.	— . 9
— Taketh away the sin of the	10	69	— . 29
— God so loved the	12	86	— 3. 16
— Giveth life unto the	43	328	— 6. 33
— Shew thyself to the	54	87	— 7. 4
— Ye are of this	55	102	— 8. 23
— cannot receive	87	383	— 14. 17
— Not as the w. giveth, give I	ib.	385	— . 27
— Christ's discl. nated by the	ib.	390	— 15. 18
— Will reprove the	ib.	393	—16. 8-11
— In w. ye shall have tribul.	ib.	397	— . 33
— Gavest me out of the	ib.	400	— 17. 6
— That the w. may believe	ib.	403	— . 21
— Lovedst me before the f.	ib.	404	— . 24
— Its ignorance	ib.	ib.	— . 25
— Go ye into all the	98	515	Mk. 16. 15
Worldly things, Be not careful of	19	135	Mt. 6. 25
— anxiety, Avoid	63	165	Lu. 12. 22
Worm dieth not	52	77	Mk.9.44,.6,.8
Worse thing, Sin no more, lest a	23	176	Jno. 5. 14
Worship given by wise m. to Jesus	5	33	Mt. 2. 11
— asked by Satan from Jesus	9	66	— 4. 9
— the Lord thy God.	ib.	ib.	— . 10
— On the place of	13	93	Jno. 4. 20
— Ye w. ye know not what	ib.	94	— . 22
— in spirit and in truth	ib.	ib.	— . 23
— The Father seeketh such to w. him	.	ib.	ib. — . 23
— by a leper, given to Jesus	21	159	Mt. 8. 2
— by woman of Canaan	45	14	— 15. 25
— by the disciples	96	502	— 28. 17
— At his ascension	99	517	Lu. 24. 52
— according to tradition vain	44	7	Mt. 15. 9
Worthy, The centurion was	28	218	Lu. 7. 4,
— But if it be not	39	297	Mt. 10. 13
— Not w. of me, &c.	ib.	302	— . 37,.8
— They which were bidden not	84	293	— 22. 8
— May be accounted	86	341	Lu. 21. 36
Wrapped him in swaddling clothes	4	20	— 2. 7
Wrath to come	7	52	— 3. 7
— of God abideth on unbelievers	13	91	Jno. 3. 36
— Jesus' townsmen filled with	15	105	Lu. 4 28
Written, He gave them bread from h.	43	327	Jno. 6. 31
— Is it not w. in your law	56	122	— 10. 34
— Your names are w. in heaven	60	144	Lu. 10. 20
— What is w. in the law	ib.	145	— . 26
— in their law	87	391	Jno. 15. 25
— in Hebrew, and Gr., & Lat.	91	460	— 19. 20

WR—ZE

Entry	Sect.	Page	Evang.
Written, What I have w. I have	91	461	Jno. 19. 22
— All things must be fulfl. in Moses, Prophets, and Psalms	98	512	Lu. 24. 41
— And said, Thus it is w. thus it behoved Christ to suffer, and to rise from the dead	ib.	ib.	— . 46
Wrong, Friend, I do thee no	76	233	Mt. 20. 13
Wrote, Moses w. of me	23	180	Jno. 5. 46
— on the ground	55	99	— 8. 6
— And again he	ib.	ib.	— . 8
Wroth, His lord was	53	85	Mt. 18. 34
Wrought in God	12	87	Jno. 3. 21

Y.

Entry	Sect.	Page	Evang.
Ye are the salt of the earth	19	122	Mt. 5. 13
— — light of the world	ib.	ib.	— . 14
— they which justify yourselves	69	198	Lu. 16. 15
Yea, yea, Let your communica.	19	127	Mt. 5. 37
Year, Acceptable y. of the Lord	15	103	Lu. 4. 19
— Let it alone this y. also	61	174	— 13. 8
Yesterday at the seventh hour	14	101	Jno. 4. 53
Yet, Do ye not y. understand?	48	33	Mt. 16. 9
— The Holy Ghost was not y. given	55	96	Jno. 7. 39
Yoke, Take my y. upon you	29	228	Mt. 11. 29
— My y. is easy	ib.	ib.	— . 30
Young man having a linen cloth	88	422	Mk. 14. 51
— When thou wast	97	509	Jno. 21. 18
Younger gathered all together	68	191	Lu. 15. 13
— Let him be as the	87	375	— 22. 26
Youth, All these have I kept	75	225	Mt. 19. 20

Z.

Entry	Sect.	Page	Evang.
Zabulon and Nephthalim	16	107	Mt. 4. 13
Zacchæus the publican	80	246	Lu. 19. 2, 5
— conversion, &c.	ib.	ib.	— . 8
Zacharias, f. of John (p.7, Addenda)	1	2	— 1. 5
— Angel's address to	ib.	4	— . 13
— His prophetic song	3	16	— . 67-79
— son of Barachias	85	320	Mt. 23. 35
Zeal of thine house	12	81	Jno. 2. 17
Zebedee's children	16	109	Mt. 4. 21
— Their request	77	237	Mk. 10. 37
Zechariah the prophet	19	152	Addenda
Zech. ix. 9	82	262	Jno. 12. 15
Zelotes, Simon (p. 272, Addenda)	27	207	Lu. 6. 15
Zephaniah	19	152	Addenda

PART FIRST.*

MATTHEW I., II. LUKE I., II., III. 23-33.

ARRANGED IN THE ORDER OF TIME.

Comprehending the Space of 31 Years; viz.,—from the Prediction of the Birth of John the Baptist, B. C. 6, to the Commencement of his Public Ministry, A. D. 26.†

SECTION 1.—PREFACE OF THE GOSPEL ACCORDING TO ST. LUKE.—THE BIRTH OF JOHN FORETOLD, AND HIS CONCEPTION. Luke i. 1—25.

(G. 1.) *The Preface according to St. Luke.‡ Luke i. 1—4. Jerusalem.‡‡*

1 FORASMUCH-as many have-taken-in-hand, to-set-forth-in-order αναταξασθαι a-declaration of those-things which-are-most-surely-believed° πεπληροφορημενων among us, 2 even-as they-delivered *them* unto-us, which from the-beginning were eye-witnesses, and 3 ministers of-the word; it-seemed-good to-me-also, havi g-had-'perfect'-understanding-of all-things from-the- very -first παρηκολουθηκοτι ανωθεν πασιν ακριβως to-write unto-thee

MARGINAL READINGS:—° Most fully borne (witness to).

SCRIPTURE ILLUSTRATIONS. ||

2. *eye-witnesses*—appointed, Lu. xxiv. 48, § 98; Jno. xv. 27, § 87; Ac. x. 39—41 — of the sufferings of Christ, 1 Pe. v. 1—His majesty, 2 Pe. 1. 16—His resurrection, Ac. 1. 3—8; 1 Jno. i. 1—3—their obligation to speak, Ac. iv. 19, 20—ours to hear, Heb. ii. 3. *ministers*—those who attend upon others for service:

Joshua, Ex. xxiv. 13—Elisha, 1 Ki. xix. 19—21—Christ the example, Mt. xx. 26—8, § 77—having washed the disciples' feet, Jno. xiii. 12—5, § 87; Ep. v. 26, .7—Paul a minister, Ac. xxvi. 16; Ro. xv. 15, .6—Christ a minister in heaven, He. viii. 6; the ministry on earth, Ep. iv. 11, .2; the twelve, Mk. iii. 14, § 27, p. 206,

NOTES.

1. *Many.* Matthew and Mark, the only Evangelists supposed to have written before Luke, cannot, with any propriety, be called ' many !' And the gospel by John was not yet written. It is probable that Luke refers to verbal statements of our Lord's life and ministry, which were now to be embodied in writing. The lack of living witnesses required to be supplied by the written word —See Addenda, p. 6, ' *Evangelists.*'

To set forth in order. Simply to give a narrative.

2. *From the beginning.* From the time John pointed to Jesus as ' the Lamb of God.'

Eye-witnesses. One of these, Matthew, wrote for the use of the Jewish converts. St. Mark did the same under the direction of St. Peter. Still there were many important things not inserted, and Luke wrote this history under the advice, it is commonly believed, of St. Paul.

Ministers. Those who serve in the gospel.

3. *Having had perf.* Having accurately followed out every thing; having accurately traced all.

From the very first. He not only searched diligently, but had divine guidance in his search into all things connected with our Lord's history, even from the first announcement of the birth of his forerunner John.

[It was by *tracing up* every account till he became satisfied of its truth. Here observe, 1st. That in religion God does not set aside our natural faculties. He calls us to look at evidence, to examine accounts, to make up our own minds. Nor will any man be convinced of the truth of religion who does not make investigation, and set himself seriously to the task. 2d. We see the nature of Luke's inspiration. It was consistent with his using his natural faculties; his own powers of mind, in investigating the truth. God, by his Holy Spirit, presided over his faculties; directed them; and kept them from error.]

PRACTICAL REFLECTIONS.

1 *ver.* We should seek to obtain for ourselves and present to others, a clear, consistent, and orderly view of the matters connected with our religious belief; especially as to the incarnation, life, teaching, death, and resurrection of our blessed Redeemer.

2 *ver.* We are to be thankful to our God, who, in the testimony of those that, from the beginning, were eye-witnesses and ministers of the word, hath provided abundant materials for our possessing this most profitable knowledge.

3 *ver.* The same help from above being offered unto us in the study of this history, which was granted unto the Evangelists in the writing thereof, we do well earnestly to look up for the divine teaching, at the same time that we use all diligence in the use of all the ordinary means with which we are favoured.

---

* The division of the Harmony into PARTS is according to Greswell's ' Harmonia Evangelica.

† See Chronological Table. p. xxvi ‡ ' Luke,' see Addenda, ' *Evangelists*,' p. 6.

‡‡ The Geography of the History may be introduced by a few leading particulars from the ' Introductory Sketch of a Journey from London to Jerusalem,' pp. v.–vii. For Geog. Notice of JERUSALEM, see Sect. v.

|| The Sections are continuous, and agree with the numbers as Geographically delineated in the Gospel Chart. The Section referred to, as, ' *eye-witnesses*,' Lu. xxiv. 48, § 98; Jno. xv. 27, § 87, will afford an agreeable opportunity to test the pupil's knowledge in the Chronology, or Order of Events.

PROVE ALL THINGS; HOLD FAST THAT WHICH IS GOOD.—1 Thess. v. 21.

| PART I. | A PRIEST NAMED ZACHARIAS. | SECT |

4 in-order *ᴋαθεξης, most-excellent Theophilus, that thou-mightest-know the certainty ασφαλειαν of those-things, wherein thou-hast-been-instructed.

(G. 2.) *John's Birth foretold. Luke i. 5—23. Jerusalem.*

5 There-was in the days of-Herod,* the king of Judea,* a-certain priest named Zacharias,⁵ of the-course of-Abia:ʰ and his wife *was* of the daughters of-Aaron,ⁱ and her

MARGINAL READINGS:—ᶜ According to succession. ᵈ Stability. ᵉ That hath the dominion,—*see* Ge. xxvii. 40. ᶠ Praise. ᵍ Memorial or remembrance of the Lord. ʰ My Father is the Lord. ⁱ Mountainous; teaching.

SCRIPTURE ILLUSTRATIONS.

3. *most excellent*—title of office. Ac. xxiii. 26; xxvi. 25.—those to whom it truly belongs, Ps. xvi. 3; Pr. xii. 26. *Theophilus*—'lover of God,' Ac. i. 1; appropriate name to a keeper of Christ's words, Jno. xiv. 23, .4, § 67; 1 Jno. v. 3.

4. *certainty*—should know the truth of what is commended to our religious belief. Pr. iv. 4, 5; viii. 6—12; Is. xxxiii. 6; Jno. xx. 31, § 100—Bereans, Ac. xvii. 11.

5. *Herod*—the king of Judea, Mt. ii. 1—15, 6, § 5—to be distinguished from Herod the tetrarch, Lu. iii. 1, 19, § 7—to whom Pilate sent Jesus, xxiii. 7—12, § 90.

Zacharias—' memorial of the Lord.' '*to perform the mercy promised to our fathers, and to remember his holy covenant,*' Lu. i. 72, § 3—the Lord's memorial, Ex. iii. 15—He will remember his covenant, his people, and the land, Le. xxvi. 42. .5—would be put in remembrance, Is. xliii. 26; lxii. 6, 7.

course of Abia—or Abijah, as 1 Ch. xxiv. 7, 10, .9; 2 Ch. viii. 14; xxxi. 2; Ezr. vi. 19.

Aaron—' teacher,' to be taught of God. what he should teach the people, Ex. iv. 14—.6; De. xxxiii. 10; Mal. ii. 6, 7.

NOTES.

In order. Chronologically; as the events occurred.—*See* Addenda, '*In order*,' p. 7.

Most excellent Theophilus. ' Theophilus,' *friend or lover of God.* ' Most excellent,' in Acts xxiii. 26; xxvi. 25, is given to men in office. Certain it is, that those who love God are the truly excellent in the earth.—*See* above.

[Mr. Greswell says:—' It appears to me a probable conjecture that Theophilus was one of the freedmen of Nero, or some other personage about the court of that Emperor, to whom, among others, St. Paul alludes in the Epistle to the Philippians, first. when he speaks of his bonds having become manifest, *εν ὅλῳ τῷ πραιτωριῳ,* as well as *τοις λοιποις ϖασι,* Phil. i. 13, " *So that my bonds in Christ are manifest in all the palace, and in all other places;*" which proves that some converts had been made in the imperial palace, as well as among the other inhabitants of Rome. This is corroborated by what he again says in ch. iv. 22, " *All the saints salute you, chiefly they that are of Cæsar's household.*"

' That Theophilus was a recent convert, or had been only just instructed in the facts and doctrines of Christianity, when the gospel was written, appears. I think, plainly from the language of the preface —*ινα επιγνῳς περι ὧν κατηχηθης λογων την ασφαλειαν:* That thou mayest be assured of the certainty of the things, concerning which thou hast received the first instruction.'—Dies. ii. vol. I. pp. 182, .3.]

4. *Been instructed.* In the early times of the Christian church, young believers were catechized upon the facts contained in the gospel history, and were called catechumens. Theophilus was here presented with that which he had already received as a catechumen.

5. *Herod.* Was commonly called the Great. He was the first king of Judea of that name; the son of Antipater, by extraction and birth an Idumean, but a Jewish proselyte. When a young man Antipater gave him the government of Galilee. With great prudence and valour he cleared the country of thievish banditti, who swarmed there. He was appointed king of Judea by the Romans. He was cruel and ambitious. To ingratiate himself with the Jews he rebuilt their temple, and rendered it exceedingly stately and glorious. He ornamented, likewise, with great magnificence, the cities of his kingdom. He had reigned 36 years at the time of Jesus' birth.—*See* Sect. v. pp. 31, .2, .3, .9.

Priest. The word *Cohen,* signifies one that intercedes, or deals familiarly with a sovereign. When it relates to civil things, it denotes such as are chief and intimate rulers under a king, 1 Ch. xvii. 18. When it relates to religion, *Cohen* signifies priest, or one who, by virtue of a divine appointment, offered sacrifices, and interceded for guilty men.— *See* Addenda, ' *Aaron,*' p. 8.

[Before the consecration of Aaron, fathers, elder brothers, princes, or every man for himself, offered his sacrifice, as is clear in the case of Abel, Cain, Noah, Abraham, Isaac, Jacob, & Job. When God a Sinai ratified his covenant with the Hebrews, young men, perhaps the eldest sons of their princes, officiated as priests, when Moses came down from the mount,—*see* Ex. xxiv. 5, 6. The whole Hebrew nation are called priests, because they were devoted to God, and much employed in his service. Ex. xix. 6, ' *and ye shall be unto me a kingdom of priests, and an holy nation.*' In the consecration of Aaron and of the tabernacle, Moses acted as priest, Ex. xl.; Lev. viii. After which, the priesthood, in ordinary cases, permitted solely to the family of Aaron; and Korah, *Uzza,* and king *Azariah,* were severely punished for interfering with their work.]

Zacharias. Every word of God is good. The very names of Scripture are most significant. Thus, Zacharias means ' memorial of the Lord,' and Elisabeth, ' oath of my God.'—*See* Addenda, ' *Zacharias,*' p. 7.

Of the course of Abia. When the priests became so numerous that they could not all at once minister at the altar, David divided the priests into 24 classes or courses, each one of which officiated for a week, 1 Ch. xxiv. These courses began each successively on the sabbath.—*See* 2 Ki. xi. 7; 2 Ch. xxiii. 4; and above.

Aaron. Of the tribe of Levi; which, under the law, was accepted for the first-born of all the tribes of Israel. Out of all the families of Levi, that of Aaron was taken to exercise the priesthood, until the coming of the Holy One of Israel, with regard to whom it was spoken by Moses, the brother of Aaron, Deut. xxxiii. 8, ' *And of Levi he said. Let thy Thummim and thy Urim be with thy Holy One, whom thou didst prove at Massah, and with whom thou didst strive at the waters of Meribah.*' It was with the Lord that the children of Israel there strove. Jesus is the Holy One, whose assumption of the priesthood was thus contemplated even from the beginning of the Levitical priesthood.—*Perfection* or ' Thummim ' was not by the law, but Christ hath brought life and immortality to *light,* ' Urim,' by the gospel.—*See* Addenda, ' *Aaron,*' p. 8.

PRACTICAL REFLECTIONS.

1 *ver.* It is not enough that we are instructed in the general, as to those things which God has been pleased to make known to us in his word; we should shew our gratitude for his kindness and condescension in instructing us, by diligently inquiring into the particulars of what he does reveal, that we may know the certainty of them.—Those who truly love God will prize the knowledge of Him, and will value that word whereby He is made known in his saving power and grace.

BE NOT IDLE IN THE MEANS, NOR MAKE AN IDOL OF THE MEANS.

SECT. I.   ZACHARIAS IN THE TEMPLE.   PART I.

6 name was Elisabeth.[k] And they - were both righteous before God, walking in all the 7 commandments and ordinances[l] δικαιωματι of-the Lord- blameless. And they had no child, because-that Elisabeth was barren, and they-'both'-were now well-stricken in years.
8 And it-came-to-pass, that-while he executed-the-priest's-office before God in the order 9 of-his course, according-to the custom of-the priest's-office, his-lot-was to-burn-incense 10 when-he-went into the temple of-the Lord. And the whole multitude of-the people were praying without at-the time of incense.
11 And there-appeared unto-him an-angel of-the-Lord standing on the-right-side of-the
MARGINAL READINGS:—*k* Oath of my God. *l* Righteousnesses; judgments.

SCRIPTURE ILLUSTRATIONS.

Elisabeth—'oath of my God,' Lu. i. 73, § 3—to Abraham, Ge. xxii. 16—.9; Mi. vii. 20; He. vi. 13—20.

6. *righteous*—examples: Noah, Ge. vi. 9; vii. 1; Job i 1–8 Simeon, Lu. ii. 25, § 4—how made righteous, Ro. iii. 24—.6; viii. 3, 4; 2 Co. v. 21; 1 Jno. ii. 1, 2—actually so, 1 Jno iii. 7—their prayers acceptable, Pr. xv. 29; Ja. v. 16—.8; 1 Pe. iii. 12.

walking—before God: Enoch, Ge. v. 24—Solomon called to do so, 1 Ki. ix. 4, 5; Paul, Ac. xxiv. 16; 2 Co. i. 12—contrasts, Ph. iii. 17, .8; 2 Pe. iii. 2–4.

blameless—as to the law, Ph. iii. 6—according to the gospel, Ph. ii. 15; 1 Th. ii. 10—in the judgment, Col. i. 21, .2.

7. *no child*—Abram's case, Ge. xv. 2, 3—Manoah's, Ju. xiii. 2, 3—Hannah's, 1 Sa. i. 10, .1.

well-stricken in years—so Abraham, Ge. xvii. 17.

8. *Priest's office*—Aaron and sons chosen thereto, Ex. xxviii. 1—transferring of the office to Christ anticipated, De. xxxiii. 8—confirmation, He. vii. 21; x. 19—22— his people, xiii. 15, .6—a royal priesthood, 1 Pe. ii. 9; Re. i. 6; v. 9, 10; xx. 6.

9. *lot*—how used, Pr. xvi. 33—purpose, xviii. 18—used in religious service, Le. xvi. 8—10; 1 Ch. xxiv. 5—as to possessions, Nu. xxxiii. 54; Jos. xiii. 6; Eze. xlvii. 22; xlviii. 29.

incense—compounded of four ingredients, Ex. xxx.

7, 8, 31—.8 — represents the prayers of saints, Ps. cxli. 2; Re. v. 8; viii. 3.

temple—built by Solomon, 1 Ki. vi.—ark received into it, 1 Ki. viii. 1—11—destroyed, 2 Ki. xxv. 8, 9—rebuilding foretold, Is. xliv. 2ᵈ—rebuilding ordered, Ezr. i. 1—4: iii. 5–13—Messiah to come to this latter house, Hag. ii. 9; Mal. iii. 1—Jesus entered the temple as his own house, Jno. ii. 13—.7, § 12, (*when he drove out the money-changers, &c., of the first passover*,)—Mt. xxi. 12, .3, § 83, (*when he cast out the buyers and sellers at the last passover*.)—He, the glory, departed therefrom, and foretold its destruction, Mt. xxiii. 37—.9, § 85; xxiv. 1, 2, § 86. The temple was destroyed by the Romans under Titus, about forty years after.—*See* Addenda, *' Temple*,' p. 8.

10. *praying*—the rule, Le. xvi. 17—belonged to the high priest in particular, but seems to have had a more general application, as well as that with regard to blessing, Nu. vi. 22—.6.

11. *angel*—the ministry of angels in behalf of the heirs of salvation: Lot, Ge. xix. 1—Jacob, xxviii. 12—Gideon, Ju. vi. 11—21—Elisha, 2 Ki. vi. 17—Daniel, vi. 22; viii. 16, &c.—serve those that truly serve the Lord, Ps. xxxiv. 7; He. i. 14; Ac. xii. 7—10—messengers of God's mercy: to Mary, Lu. i. 26—33, § 2—to the shepherds, ii. 8—15, § 4—testified of his *second* coming, Ac. i. 10, .1, § 98.

NOTES.

6. *Righteous*. Doing what is right. [Just or holy, it means more than outward conformity to the law. No man, by the deeds of the law given by Moses, can be justified before God, but only as possessing the faith of Abraham.]

Walking in all the commandm. The ten commandments, or moral precepts of the law, directing as to the general exercise of love to God and love to man.

Blameless. Speaking after the manner of men; 'blameless' in their public deportment; 'blameless' as far as man has a right to judge. ' Unreserved and unfeigned belief in every known duty, and unfeigned belief in every known truth of divine revelation.'

9. *His lot*. [Zacharias was not high priest: he was chosen by lot to burn incense; the high priest did it by right of succession, and burned it in the holy of holies, into which Zacharias entered not. Zacharias was priest of the course of Abia, whereas the high priest was of no course at all.] It was customary for the priests to divide their daily task by lot.

Incense. That which is ordinarily so called, is a precious and fragrant gum, issuing from the frankincense tree. The incense used in the Jewish offerings, at least that which was burnt on the altar of *incense* and before the ark, was a precious mixture of sweet spices, stacte, onycha, galbanum, and pure frankincense, beaten very small. None but priests were to burn it, nor was any, under pain of death, to make any like to it. This incense was burnt twice a day on the golden altar, Ex. xxx. 7, 8, 31—.8. Among the various offices distributed by lot, the most honourable was this of burning incense; so much so, that no priest was allowed to burn it more than once.

[There is something beautiful and poetical in that part of the Jewish ceremonial, which supposes the prayers of devout worshippers to be wafted to heaven in odoriferous wreaths of incense. David adopts the idea in Ps. cxli. 2, ' *Let my prayer be set forth before thee as incense; and the lifting up of my hands as the evening sacrifice*.']

10 *Praying without*. That is in the courts around. When the priest, whose lot it was to burn incense, entered the holy place, a small bell was rung to notify that the time of prayer was come. When this was heard, those priests and Levites who had not taken their stations, hastened to do so; the space between the altar and the sanctuary was cleared; and the whole multitude, in all the courts of the temple, commenced their prayers.

[These prayers were perfectly silent; and it is probably to the deep silence which prevailed throughout the temple during the time of offering incense and of prayers, that there is an allusion in Rev. viii. 1—3, ' *There was silence in heaven about the space of half an hour*.' When the priest came forth from the holy place, the sacrifice was laid upon the altar, and then the Levites commenced their psalmody, and their sounding of trumpets; to which, also, there seems to be an allusion in the sequel of the above cited passage from the Revelations.]

11. *An angel of the Lord*. The word 'angel' literally means a *messenger*.—*See* '*Angel*,' Sect. ii. This vision appeared to Zacharias about 400 years from the time of Malachi, the last of the prophets; during which period there is no divinely recorded prophecy nor angelic ministry.

Right side, &c. The altar of incense stood close by the vail which divided the holy place fr. the most holy.

PRACTICAL REFLECTIONS.

6 *ver*. Let us, like Zacharias and Elisabeth, seek to be righteous before God, which can only be through the priesthood of Him whom John declared unto the people.—Let us not be contented with performing a part of our duty, either as to the commandments or the ordinances of the Lord; let us walk in *all* the appointments of the Lord, and that *blameless*.

7 *ver*. The Lord's deferring a favour until the time he sees most fit to grant it, may rather be cause of thankfulness than of regret.

9 *ver*. Let us rejoice that we have a Priest on high, through whose intercession our prayers ascend up as the incense of the morning and evening sacrifice.— We are not out of the way of obtaining blessing for ourselves, when engaged in public service for others, as in the sight of God.

HE THAT WALKETH UPRIGHTLY WALKETH SURELY.—PROV. X. 9.

PART I. — THE BIRTH OF JOHN FORETOLD. — SECT. I.

12 altar of incense. And when Zacharias saw *him*, he was troubled, and fear fell upon him. 13 But the angel said unto him, Fear not, Zacharias: for thy prayer^m ἡ δεησις is-heard; and thy wife Elisabeth shall-bear thee a-son, and thou-shalt-call his name John.ⁿ 14 And thou shalt-have joy and gladness; and many shall-rejoice at his birth. 15 For he-shall-be great in-the-sight of-the Lord, and shall-drink neither wine nor strong-drink; 16 and he-shall-be-filled-with the-Holy Ghost, even from ετι εκ his mother's womb. And 17 many of-the children-of Israel^o shall-he-turn to the-Lord their God. And he shall-go

MARGINAL READINGS:— ^m Request. ⁿ Grace of the Lord. ^o Prince of God.

SCRIPTURE ILLUSTRATIONS.

11. *altar of incense*, Ex. xxx. 1—10; xxxvii. 25—.8—prayers of the saints, Re. viii. 3.

13. *fear not*—same to Abram, Ge. xv. 1—to Israel, Is. xli. 10, .3, .4; xliii. 1, 5—to Mary. Lu. i. 30, § 2—to the shepherds, ii. 10, § 4—to the women at the sepulchre, Mt. xxviii. 5, § 93—spoken by Jesus as our high priest, Re. i. 17.

prayer—for children: Isaac, Ge. xxv. 21—Hannah, 1 Sa. i. 9, 11, 26—Its power in removing curse and procuring blessing, Ja. v. 13—8.

son—promised to Abraham, Ge. xviii. 10, .4—the Shunammite, 2 Ki. iv. 14—.7.

call his name—importance attached to names: Adam, *likeness*, Ge. v. 1—3—Eve, iii. 20—Cain, *gotten or possession*, iv. 1—Seth, *placed or appointed*. iv. 25—Noah, *comfort or rest*, v. 29—Abram, *great father*, xii. 1—3—Abraham, *father of a multitude*, xvii. 5—Melchizedek, xiv. 18; compare with He. vii. 2—Isaac, *laughter*, Ge. xxi. 3, 6—Jacob, *heeler or supplanter*, xxv. 26; xxvii. 36—Israel, *prince*, xxxii. 28. Jacob's sons: Reuben, *see a son*, xxix. 32—Simeon, *hearing*, 33—Levi, *joined*, 34—Judah, *praise*, 35—Dan, *judg-

ment*, xxx. 6—Naphtali, *wrestling*, 8—Gad, *troop*, 11—Asher, *happy*, 13—Issachar, *hire or reward*, 18—Zebulun, *dwelling*, 20—Joseph, *adding or increase*, 24—Benjamin, *son of the right hand*, xxxv. 18.

John—'grace of the Lord,' sent to declare this, Lu. iii. 3, § 7—taught men to manifest the same in their conduct, 11, § 7—it is the character of the dispensation he came to introduce, Jno. i. 16, .7, 29, § 7, 10—the grace of the Lord as to the great promised salvation and blessing of his people, spoken of by his father, Lu. i. 68—79, § 3.

15. *great*—John acknowledged Jesus as mightier, Mk. i. 1—8, § 7—least in the kingdom of heaven greater than John, Lu. vii. 28, § 29—great nation promised to Abram, Ge. xii. 2.

neither wine—the Nazarite, Nu. vi. 2—4—Samson, Ju. xiii. 4—7—John lived a Nazarite Mt. iii. 4, § 7; xi. 18, § 29.

filled with the Holy Ghost—required in the Christian, Ep. v. 18—promised to Israel, Eze. xxxvii. 14.

from his mother's womb, Jer. i. 5—Paul, Ga. i. 15, .6.—See also Is. xlix. 1, 5.—See NOTES.

NOTES.

11. *Altar*. The altar of incense was a small table of Shittim-wood, overlaid with gold, about 22 inches in breadth and length, and 44 in height. Its top was surrounded with a cornice of gold; it had spires, or horns, at the four corners thereof; and was portable by staves of Shittim-wood, overlaid with gold,—see '*An horn of salvation,*' Sect. iii. The altar of incense stood in the sanctuary, just before the inner vail; and on it was sacred incense, and nothing else,—see 'Incense,' p. 3. The altar of incense and the altar of burnt offering were solemnly consecrated with sprinkling of blood, and unction of oil; and their horns yearly tipped with the blood of the general expiation. The altar of burnt offering stood in the open court, at a small distance from the east end of the tabernacle, or temple: on it were offered the morning and evening sacrifices, and a multitude of other oblations. To it criminals fled for protection.

13. *Thy prayer.* His prayers in general. We may rather suppose that his prayer was for the deliverance of Israel by the expected Messiah.

[It is not likely that himself and his wife, being so old, could have any expectation of a son.]

John. The grace or favour of the Lord.

14. *And thou shalt have joy and gladness*, και εσται χαρα σοι, 'he will be joy and gladness to thee.'

15. *Shall be great.* Herod, who beautified the temple, was called 'Great' among men; but the son of the poor priest serving in the temple, and to be brought up in obscurity, was to be called 'great in the sight of the Lord;' i. e. God shall regard him as truly great.—See Mt. xi. 7—15, § 29, our Lord's testimony to John—at Nain.

Drink neither wine. The kind of wine used in Judæa was a light wine, often not stronger than cider in this country. It was the common drink of all classes of the people. The use of wine was forbidden only to the Nazarite, Nu. vi. 3. As John was to preach repentance and self-denial, so he was to be a pattern of both.

Strong drink. Distilled spirits were not then known. The art of distilling was discovered by an Arabian chemist, in the ninth or tenth century. Europe and America have been the places where this *poison* has been the most extensively used; and there it has degraded and ruined millions, and is yearly sweeping tens of thousands, unprepared, into a wretched eternity. There is no scourge, whether pestilence or war, so fatally destructive of the best interests of man, nor any custom so paralysing to all benevolent exertions to train the young in the love and fear of the Lord, as the use of distilled and fermented liquors. Through their use, thousands of almost broken-hearted mothers, who would delight to send their children to the sabbath school, are compelled to keep them, clothed in rags, confined in their squalid homes. The strong drink among the Jews was probably fermented liquor obtained from dates, figs, and the juice of the palm, or the lees of wine, mingled with sugar, and having the property of producing intoxication.

Shall be filled with the Holy Ghost, &c. Shall be divinely designated or appointed to this office, and qualified for it by all needful communications of the Holy Spirit. To be filled with the Holy Spirit is to be illuminated, sanctified, and guided by his influence. [It refers to an actual fitting for the work from the birth, as was the case.—See Je. i. 5, '*Before I formed thee in the belly I knew thee; and before thou camest forth out of the womb I sanctified thee, and I ordained thee a prophet unto the nations.*']

16. *Children of Isr.* Descendants of Israel or Jacob.

PRACTICAL REFLECTIONS.

12 ver. If Zacharias, a righteous man, was troubled at the sight of the angel of the Lord, bringing a message of peace, how will the wicked tremble at the presence of the Lord, when he cometh in flaming fire to punish the despisers of his word!

13 ver. Those who, like Zacharias, are the Lord's remembrancers, need not fear. Their prayer shall be heard.—The answer of prayer, as in the case of this man of God, may sometimes be deferred only that it may be the more signally answered.—What we should most earnestly desire in the present time, is that which 'John,' the name of the child promised to Zacharias, represents, 'the grace of the Lord.'

14 ver. We should rejoice more especially in such favours as will be the occasion of rejoicing to others.

15 ver. Self-denial, and want of the wealth, and honours, and pleasures of the world, however looked upon by men, are not inconsistent with greatness in the sight of the Lord.

[Those who are employed in preparing others for the coming of the Lord, should seek to be themselves filled with the Holy Ghost.]

SECT. I.   ZACHARIAS STRUCK DUMB.   PART I.

before him in the-spirit and power of-Elias,^{p} to-turn the-hearts of-the-fathers to the-children, and the-disobedient to the-wisdom of-the-just;^{r} to-make-ready a-people prepared for-the-Lord.
18 And Zacharias said unto the angel, Whereby shall-I-know this? for I am an-old-19 man, and my wife well-stricken in years. And the angel answering said unto-him, I am Gabriel, that stand in-the-presence of God; and am-sent to-speak unto thee, and 20 to-shew-·thee these'·-glad-tidings.^{s} ευαγγελισασθαι σοι ταυτα. And, behold, thou-shalt-be dumb, and not able-to-speak, until the day *that* these-things shall-be-performed, because αιθ' ὡν thou-believest not my words, which shall-be-fulfilled in their season.^{t}
εις τον καιρον αυτων.

MARGINAL READINGS:—p My God is the Lord. r Righteous (plural). s To evangelize to thee these things. t Unto the time of them

SCRIPTURE ILLUSTRATIONS.

17. *go before*—predicted, Mal. iii. 1—as Elijah, iv. 5, 6—fulfilment, Jno. i. 19—34, § 10.
power of Elijah, 1 Ki. xvii. 1; xviii. 17—40, .6; xix. 2; 2 Ki. i. ii.; Lu. ix. 54, § 59; Ja. v. 17—John was not the very person Elias, Jno. i. 21, .5, § 10—yet was the Elias which was for to come, Mt. xi. 14, § 29.
to turn—directed multitudes to the God of Abraham, in simplicity of faith and practice, Mt. iii. 5—10; Lu. iii. 7—14, § 7—to Jesus as the Lamb of God, Jno. i. 29—36, § 10—as the bridegroom, Jno. iii. 29, § 13.
wisdom of the just, Ho. xiv. 9; 1 Co. i. 30; Ja. iii. 17; Ro. iv. 20—.6; He. xi. 13—.6.

ready—Hezekiah and people prepared, 2 Ch. xxix. 36—call to be ready, Lu. xii. 40, § 63; Mt. xxiv. 42—4, § 86; Re. xv. 15—the bride made ready, Re. xix. 7, 8; xxi. 2.
18. *whereby*—Abraham asked a sign, Ge. xv. 1—8; xvii. 17—Gideon, Ju. vi. 36—40.
Gabriel—'man of God,' or 'God is my strength,' appeared to Daniel, viii. 16; ix. 21—.3—to Mary, Lu. i. 26, § 2, p. 9.
20. *because thou believest not*—Moses and Aaron, Nu. xx. 12—a lord at Samaria, 2 Ki. vii. 1—20—God faithful notwithstanding, 2 Ti. ii. 13.

NOTES.

17. *Shall go before him.* Before the Messias, or the Lord Jesus—see Mat. xi. 11, § 29, p. 223.

In the spirit and power of Elias. As possessing the same prophetic spirit, and commissioned with similar authority.

To turn the heart, of the fathers to the children. The restoration of mutual affection uniformly accompanies true religion. It is part of the character of the irreligious to be without natural affection. -See Ro. i. 31, 'Without understanding, covenant-breakers, without natural affection, implacable, unmerciful.'

['*The disobedient.* The people who had, because of their disobedience to the law, been called ' Backsliding Israel ;' and who were given a bill of divorce and sent away out of the land, but who were to be espoused to the Lord, according to the gospel. Je. iii. 8—12. 8, '*And I saw, when for all the causes whereby backsliding Israel committed adultery I had put her away, and given her a bill of divorce ; yet her treacherous sister Judah feared not, but went and played the harlot also.* 9, *And it came to pass through the light-ness of her whoredom, that she defiled the land, and committed adultery with stones and with stocks.* 10. *And yet for all this her treacherous sister Judah hath not turned unto me with her whole heart, but feignedly, with the Lord.* 11, *And the Lord said unto me, The backsliding Israel hath justified herself more than treacherous Judah.* 12, *Go and proclaim these words toward the north, and say, Return, thou backsliding Israel, saith the Lord; and I will not cause mine anger to fall upon you: for I am merciful, saith the Lord, and I will not keep anger for ever.*' Ho. ii. 14—20, wherein Christ is shewn to be made of God unto us wisdom, righteousness, sanctification, and redemption. All that have been truly just before

God, such as Abraham and David, have delighted in this hidden wisdom, in Christ, who is the end of the law fοr righteousness to every one that believeth.]

To make ready a people. By shewing them what they were in the sight of God, and what they ought to become. Thus preparing them for his free offer of salvation, by proving their want of that mercy and divine grace, which might enable them to walk before God in righteousness and holiness.

The three persons in the Godhead seem to be referred to in ver. 14—7. John was to '*be filled with the Holy Ghost;*' he was to '*turn many of the children of Israel to the Lord their God,*' i. e. the Father; and with regard to the Son, in whose sight he was to '*be great,*' he was to '*go before him in the spirit,*' &c.

In the presence of God. An image borrowed from the customs of oriental courts, where he is said to stand before the king, who has always access to the royal presence; it may, therefore, be interpreted, 'a favourite minister.' So to stand before God, signifies that he was honoured or favoured by God; permitted —see 1 Ki. xvii. 1. Elijah said unto Ahab, ' *As the,*' &c.

And am sent, &c. The angels are *ministering spirits*, sent forth to those who shall be heirs of salvation. He. i. 7, 14. '*And of the angels he saith, Who maketh his angels spirits, and his ministers a flame of fire. Are they not all ministering spirits, sent forth to minister for them who shall be heirs of salvation?*'

Because thou believest not, &c. This was both a sign and a judgment: a sign that he had come from God, and that the thing would be fulfilled, and a judgment for not giving credit to what he had said; it was wisely ordained to fix the attention of the Jews on the promised child.

PRACTICAL REFLECTIONS.

17 *ver.* We should set before us the example of those who have been eminently serviceable in the cause of God.
[Few, like Elijah, have been willing to endure much for the truth's sake; for which we have now the example of a greater than Elias or John, even of Him who endured all things for us. The great preparation required is, the preparation of a people for the Lord. The reconciling of men, one to another, in the Lord, & the bringing them back to the simplicity, in faith and practice, of those who were truly just before God, are among the best preparations for the coming of the Lord.—Those who would sit down with Abraham, Isaac, and Jacob, in the kingdom of God, must walk in the steps of faithful Abraham.]
19 *ver.* The very appearance of the angel was a

sufficient sign that the word of promise would be fulfilled to Zacharias.
[The first appearance of Jesus, the angel of the covenant, to us a sufficient sign that all covenant mercy will be bestowed.]
[20 *ver.* However long delayed the things promised may have been, those that stand in the presence of God and know his mighty power can, with assurance, testify that the words of God will all be fulfilled in their season.]

God requires of us that we should not be unbelieving as to unfulfilled prophecy; we should know his revealed purposes, and look forward to their fulfilment. God punishes unbelief, even in those who are truly righteous in his sight.

PART I.   THE CONCEPTION OF JOHN THE BAPTIST.   SECT. I.

21 And the people waited-for Zacharias, and marvelled that he tarried-so-long in the 22 temple. And when-he-came-out, he-could not speak unto-them; and they-perceived that he-had-seen a-vision in the temple: for he beckoned unto-them, and remained 23 dumb speechless." And it-came-to-pass, *that*, as-soon-as the days of his ministration were-accomplished, he-departed to his-own house.

(G.L.) *The Conception of John the Baptist. Luke* i. 24, .5. *Hill Country of Judæa.*

24 And after those days his wife Elisabeth conceived, and hid herself five months, 25 saying, Thus hath-' the Lord'-dealt with-me in the-days wherein he-looked-on *me*, to-take-away my reproach among men.

MARGINAL READINGS:—" Deaf and dumb."

SCRIPTURE ILLUSTRATIONS.

22. *vision* — first vision recorded, Ge. xv. — God spake in them to Jacob, xlvi. 2—visions and dreams, Nu. xii. 6—Balaam, xxiv. 4—Daniel, ii. 19—Ananias, Ac. ix. 10—Cornelius, x. 3—Paul, xvi. 9; xviii. 9.

25. *thus hath the Lord dealt with me*—Naomi was dealt bitterly with whilst the Lord was leading her into great blessing, Ru. I. 20; iv. 15.—*See* He. xi.

NOTES.

21. *Waited.* For his coming out, to be blessed by him, as was the custom of the priest to do.—*See* Nu. vi. 23—6. 23, ' *Speak unto Aaron and unto his sons, saying, On this wise ye shall bless the children of Israel, saying unto them,*—24, The LORD *bless thee, and keep thee:*—25, *the* LORD *make his face shine upon thee, and be gracious unto thee:*—26, *the* LORD *lift up his countenance upon thee, & give thee peace.*'

Marvelled. Wondered. The priest, it is said, was not accustomed to remain in the temple more than half an hour.

22. *They perceived—for he beckoned.* He made signs, he nodded assent to what appeared to be their impression.

Had seen a vision. The word ' vision' means sight, appearance, or spectre, and is commonly applied to spirits, or to beings of another world.

23. *As soon as the days of his ministration, &c.* As soon as he had fulfilled the duties of the week.

[It might have been supposed that the extraordinary occurrence in the temple, together with his own calamity, might have induced him at once to leave his place, and return home. But his duty was in the temple. His piety—his strong sense of the imperative nature of obedience—prompted him to remain there in the service of God. He was not unfitted for burning incense by his dumbness, and it was not proper for him to leave his post.]

25. *Thus hath the Lord dealt with me.* Alluding to the painful dealing of God as to her husband's inability to speak, which sobered the joy she would naturally feel at being given a child. She felt that, although specially blessed, she was under the chastisement of the Lord, in Zacharias' punishment.

To take away my reproach. Among the Jews, a family of children was counted a signal blessing; an evidence of the favour of God.—*See* Le. xxvi. 9; Ps. cxiii. 9; cxxviii. 3; Is. iv. 1.

PRACTICAL REFLECTIONS.

24 *ver.* When under chastisement, we must patiently continue in the performance of duty. Perseverance in the service of God is the best way to have our afflictions removed, and to lighten them while they continue.

[Public worship is but a part of our duty; the domestic circle claims much of our time and care.]

[24, 5 *ver.* When God sees it meet to temper mercy with judgment, as in the case of Elisabeth, who was so dealt with, as to her husband, whilst she was being given a son, we should, like her, humble ourselves under the mighty hand of God, and be thankful for the grace bestowed.—Correction is no sign of the Lord's having forsaken his people; the time of His hiding may be the time of ripening mercy.]

GOD SHEWS MERCY TO THE FULL.; AND YET REMAINS FULL OF MERCY

ADDENDA.

EVANGELISTS, p. 1.

Evangelists. Matthew, Mark, Luke, and John are called ' The four Evangelists,' in a special sense, being the messengers, heralds or preachers, and the writers of the Narratives of our Lord's Life, &c.

MATTHEW, (sig. ' *The Gift*,') surnamed Levi, the son of Alpheus. He was a Jew, and a publican or tax gatherer. Jesus called him from the receipt of custom, 'and he left all, rose up, and followed him,'— *see* § 22. He was chosen to be an Apostle,—*see* Matt. x 3, § 27 ; and is supposed to have remained in Jerusalem, with the rest of the apostles, until after the council recorded in Acts. xv. ch., (A. D. 42,) about which time he wrote his gospel in Hebrew for the Jewish converts who remained in Judæa after the dispersion of the mother church, when all the apostles, except James, departed on their evangelizing mission. . . . .

. . . . . . It is supposed Matthew took Æthiopia for his lot, and there suffered martyrdom.

Matthew presents Christ to us as our *Prophet ;* as He who was *son* of the Father, to reveal to us a knowledge of the kingdom of heaven, which is ' the gift of God,' in Christ Jesus. He speaks much about the reward of the righteous in the world to come. He has the most frequent reference to Christ's fulfilling or confirming the words of the prophets; and our Lord's prophetic discourses are more fully given in this gospel.

MARK (sig. ' *Cleansing* '). He was converted by the instrumentality of Peter, who (1st Ep. v. 13) styles him his son. The internal evidence of this gospel proves him to have been a Jew, intimately acquainted with the language, idioms, and topography of Palestine. He is thought to be the young man alluded to, Mark xiv. 51, 2, § 86. He is supposed to have written his gospel at Rome as the interpreter of Peter. The frequency of Latin terms and phrases, clothed in Greek, prove it to have been designed not for Jews, but for Roman converts in particular. The *Mark* mentioned in the Acts, and at Col. iv. 10; 2 Tim. iv. 11 ; Philem. 24, Mr. Greswell thinks is not the same as the reputed convert of St. Peter. It is a character of Mark's gospel, that where Matthew is full, Mark is concise, and *vice versa*.

Mark dwells more on the miracles, or power, of Him who is our King and our *example* of service.

LUKE (sig. ' *Light-giving* '). He is the writer of this gospel and of the history of the Acts of the Apostles. The first intimation of his connexion with the propagation of the gospel is at Acts xvi. 9—18, in the account of St. Paul's second mission, and when he was arrived at Troas: where the use of the plural number plainly indicates that the writer of the ' Acts ' was in company with St. Paul. From Col. iv. 14, ' *Luke, the beloved physician, and Demas, greet you*,' we learn he was a surgeon or physician, be-

6]   DUTIES CANNOT HAVE TOO MUCH DILIGENCE, NOR TOO LITTLE CONFIDENCE.

EVANGELISTS.—(*continued.*)

tween whom and Paul it is clear there was reciprocal attachment.—See Philemon 24. '*Marcus, Aristarchus, Demas, Lucas, my fellowlabourers;*' and especially at a time when the 'Acts' history had ceased, and the close of St Paul's ministry itself, by his martyrdom, was at hand, from 2 Tim. iv. 11, '*Only Luke is with me.*' It is a natural inference from these proofs, that he was either his convert or a favourite disciple. If we may advance a conjecture where there is total absence of positive information to direct us, St. Luke, though he might first become acquainted with St. Paul, and might even be first converted at Troas, was a native or an inhabitant of Philippi, in Macedonia; which was a Roman colony.

Luke enlarges more upon those things which belong to the *priesthood* of Christ; his receiving sinners, and introducing them into the favour of God, through the forgiveness of sins, by his blood so that we are brought to enjoy the light of our Father's countenance.

JOHN (sig. '*Grace of Jehovah*') was the son of Zebedee and Salome. He was called by our Lord to be his disciple while he was following his ordinary calling of a fisherman,—*see* § 16. He was one of the twelve apostles,—*see* § 27; and, with James his brother, was surnamed '*Boanerges*'—'sons of thunder.'

These two apostles, with Peter, were peculiarly favoured on several occasions,—*see* § 36, 51, 86, 71; and John is called 'the disciple whom Jesus loved,- see § 91, .7. He was the youngest of the apostles when called; and is the only one who is supposed to have died a peaceful death. He suffered banishment, under *Domitian,* in the *Isle of Patmos,* where he wrote the *Apocalypse*. He probably resided in *Judæa* until the Roman war, A.D. 66 or 70, and died at Ephesus, when he was above 100 years old. During his later years he was accustomed to say nothing but—' Little children, love one another.' This gospel, while it sanctioned the rest, added what was necessary to their completion. The others recorded the *miracles* and the *external* evidence of Jesus' divine mission: John's gospel contains more about Christ, his person, design, and work. He aims to shew that Jesus was the Messiah, and from *Jesus' words* what the Messiah was. The great grace of the Lord that we enjoy, through the adoption that is in Jesus, the Son of God, the word made flesh, that came to give himself for the life of the world, is the subject of this sweetly simple, but truly sublime gospel. John's gospel is said to have been written at Ephesus at the close of his life. He wrote also the three Epistles which bear his name.—*See Greswell on the Times and Order of the Gospels,* vol. i. Diss. ii.

IN ORDER,' p. 2.

Mr. Greswell says:—' The possession of a preface, which is not the case with any other of the gospels; a model of conciseness, and yet of sufficiency; asserting, in the most compendious form, whatsoever an introductory admonition might be expected to assert —the motive which induced the author to undertake the work—his qualifications for its execution—the method which he proposed to observe in it—and the end which he had in view by it. Now prefaces are not commonly premised except to regular histories, and if St. Luke's gospel agrees with a formal and methodical history at the outset, this is some argument that it will be found to agree also with such an history in the subsequent arrangement and distribution of the work.

' His own declaration that he proposed to write in order, and, consequently, to observe the course of time and succession in the detail of events: for what other meaning can be put on the words in question,

"Έδοξε κάμοι παρηκολουθηκότι ἄνωθεν πᾶσιν ἀκριβῶς καθεξῆς σοι γράψαι, κράτιστε Θεόφιλε, I. 3.

' It hath seemed good to me also, having carefully attended to the course of all things from the beginning, to write *of them* in order for thy sake, most excellent Theophilus.

' The natural and obvious construction is clearly to convey the promise of a regular account.

' For an integral period of the Christian history, and through an integral portion of its contents, the gospel of St. Luke is regular, and consistent with the professions of its preface. For, *first,* proposing to deduce that history from its earliest point of time, he begins with the conception and the birth of the Baptist, and afterwards passes to the conception and the birth of Jesus Christ; that is, he begins with the private history of each, before he proceeds to the public. *Secondly,* as far as was practicable, without actually violating the order of events, he manifests a strict anxiety to separate the private history of the Baptist from the private history of Christ. There

were some circumstances connected with the conception, which preceded the birth of Christ, but followed upon the conception of John; these he has related, as historical precision required, between the two. But after the birth of John, when there was nothing in his private history any way connected with the private history of Christ, he despatches that history once for all—summing up in a single sentence—' The child grew, and waxed strong in spirit, and was in the deserts till the day of his shewing unto Israel,' i. 80—the substance of thirty years, before he proceeds to the account of the birth of Christ. Why was this done, except that the course of the history might be left free to begin, and to continue, in like manner, the account of the birth, the infancy, and the domestic privacy, of Christ? all which are next related, and in a strictly methodical order.

' Again, being arrived at the point of time when the public ministry of both the Baptist and Christ was about to commence, he begins with the ministry of John, and despatches, as before, the ministry of John, before he says a word upon the ministry of Christ: of this there cannot be a clearer proof than that, after a regular account of the preaching, the teaching, and the testimonies, of John, he concludes the whole by the history of his imprisonment, before he relates even the baptism of Christ. This was to introduce an anachronism of probably four months in extent; but it is manifestly an anachronism introduced on purpose, to keep the unity of his next and principal subject unbroken; that so the history of our Saviour's ministry might begin and be continued from his baptism forward, without any admixture of the history of John. In this case, then, this exception, instead of weakening, serves rather to confirm our assertion.

' From the time of the commencement of this ministry to the end of the gospel, there is no instance of a supposed transposition, which, upon a fair and dispassionate examination, will not turn out to be quite the contrary.'—*See Diss. i. vol. L pp. 6—12.*

' ZACHARIAS,' p. 2.

Zacharias. Every word of God is good. The very names of Scripture are most significant. Thus, Zacharias means ' memorial of the Lord,' and Elisabeth, ' oath of my God.'

The former name is pointed out, Ex. iii. 14, .5. 14, '*And God said unto Moses,* I AM THAT I AM: *and he said, Thus shalt thou say unto the children of Israel,* I AM *hath sent me unto you.* 15, *And God said moreover unto Moses, Thus shalt thou say unto the children of Israel, The* LORD *God of your fathers, the God of Abraham, the God of Isaac, and the God of Jacob, hath sent me unto you: this is my name for ever, and this is my memorial unto all generations.*'

And, as we learn from our Lord, Mk. xii. 21—6, § 85, It implies the resurrection of the Lord's people. That which is referred to in the name Elisabeth, 'the oath of my God,' is given Ge. xxii. 15—8, and it contains the same three things referred to in the three names mentioned in the memorial of the Lord. Thus, the promise of the seed, numerous as the stars of the heaven or as the sand on the sea-shore, is contained in the name Abraham; and their being made blessed and the cause of blessing to all the nations of the earth, is expressed in Isaac; and their supplanting power, so as to possess this gate of their enemies, we have in the name Jacob. Christ came to confirm the promises made to the fathers, and that confirmation seems to have been written in the very names of

BELIEVERS ON EARTH ARE SUPERIOR TO ANGELS IN HEAVEN.

ZACHARIAS—(continued.)

the parents of his forerunner, whose name also describes the peculiar character of the dispensation he came to introduce; the word John, meaning 'the grace of Jehovah,' at whose birth not only his father, but the prophets generally, began to speak according to the prediction of Hab. ii. 3, '*The vision is yet for an appointed time, but at the end it shall speak, and not lie!*' The name Gabriel means 'man of God,' a name whereby Elijah, that had been taken up into glory, was generally designated. The word which here expresses man, is more expressive of power or glory than that whereby Elijah was called before his translation, to stand more immediately in the presence of God, and execute more extensively his commands. There is no true power but of God.—*See* 'call his name,' p. 4, *Scripture Illustrations.*

'AARON,' p. 2.

Aaron. Was a Levite, the son of Amram, and brother of Moses and Miriam. He was born about a year before Pharaoh, king of Egypt, ordered the male infants of the Hebrews to be slain; appointed of God to be spokesman for his brother Moses to Pharaoh and the Hebrews, Ex. iv. 14—.6. Along with his brother, and in the name of God, he demanded of Pharaoh immediate permission for the Hebrews to go into the wilderness of Arabia, to serve the Lord their God.

Shortly after the departure of the children of Israel from Egypt, while the Hebrews fought with Amalek in Rephidim, Aaron and Hur attended Moses, and held up his hands, while he continued encouraging the struggling Hebrews, and praying for victory to their arms, Ex. xvii. 10, .3. At Sinai, he, with his two eldest sons, and seventy of the elders of Israel, accompanied Moses part of his way up to the mount: and had very near and distinct views of the glorious symbols of the divine presence, when the Lord talked with Moses, Ex. xxiv. 1—11.

Soon after, he fell into the most grievous crime. The Hebrews solicited him to make them gods, to be their directors, instead of Moses, who still tarried in the mount. He ordered them to bring him all their pendants and earrings; he caused them to be melted down into a golden calf, in imitation of the ox Apis, which the Egyptians adored. He appointed a solemn feast to be observed to its honour; and caused to proclaim before it, '*These be thy gods, O Israel, which brought thee up out of the land of Egypt.*' While he was thus occupied, Moses descended from mount Sinai, and sharply reproved him for his horrid offence, Ex. xxxii.

Aaron heartily repented of his scandalous crime; and, with his four sons, was, about two months after, solemnly invested with the sacred robes, and consecrated by solemn washing, unction, and sacrifices, to his office of priesthood, Le. viii. He immediately offered sacrifice for the congregation of Israel; and while he and his brother Moses blessed the people, the sacred fire descended from heaven, and consumed what lay on the brazen altar, Le. ix. His two eldest sons, instead of taking sacred fire from the *brazen* altar, took common fire, to burn the incense with, on the *golden* altar: and God immediately consumed them, with a flash of lightning; and ordered, that henceforth no priest should taste wine before officiating in holy things, Le. x.

It was perhaps scarcely a year after, when Aaron and Miriam, envying the authority of Moses, rudely upbraided him for his marriage with Zipporah the Midianitess; and for over-looking them in the constitution of the seventy elders. Aaron, whose priestly performances were daily necessary, was spared; but Miriam was smitten with a universal leprosy. Aaron immediately discerned his guilt, acknowledged his fault, begged forgiveness for himself and his sister, and that she might speedily be restored to health, Nu. xii. It was not long after, when *Korah* and his company, envying the honours of Aaron, thought to thrust themselves into the office of priests. These rebels being miraculously destroyed by God, the Hebrews reviled Moses and Aaron, as guilty of murdering them; the Lord, provoked herewith, sent a destructive plague among the people, which threatened to consume the whole congregation. Aaron, who had lately, by his prayers, prevented their being totally ruined along with Korah, ran in between the living and the dead, and by offering of incense, atoned for their trespass, and so the plague was stayed.—*See* Nu. xvi.

THE TEMPLE,' p. 3.

The temple. The temple of God, or the temple dedicated and devoted to the service of God, was built on mount Moriah, on the spot where Abraham offered up his son Isaac. The first temple was built by king Solomon about 1005 years B.C. David, with his princes, provided immense treasures for it, amounting, it is computed, to 939 millions sterling; and in weight to about 46,000 tons of gold and silver. About 183,600 men, Hebrews and Canaanites, were employed in its erection. Every thing was made ready ere it came to the spot; and no tool was heard lo its progress. Hiram, king of Tyre, supplied the cedar from Lebanon, which was floated to Joppa, and thence conveyed to Jerusalem. It was seven years in building, 1 Kl. vi. 38. David was not suffered to build it because he had been a man of war, 1 Ch. xxii. 1—19. About eleven months after the building was finished, and just before the feast of tabernacles, this temple was furnished with the ark, and other sacred utensils; and the Shechinah, or cloud of divine glory, entered it, to take up its rest over the ark, between the cherubims; and it was dedicated with a solemn prayer by Solomon, and by seven days of sacred feasting, and by a peace offering of 22,000 oxen and 120,000 sheep, 1 Kl. viii. 63; to consume which, the holy fire anew came down from heaven, 2 Ch. vii. 1—3. The temple service consisted in sacrifices, songs, prayer, &c., 1 Ch. xxv.—xxix. 1—9; 1 Kl. vi.—viii.; 2 Ch. iii.—vi. This temple remained but about thirty-four years in its glory, when Shishak, king of Egypt, carried off its treasures, 1 Kl. xiv. 25, 6. After repeated desecrations, its golden vessels were carried to Babylon, and the temple was demolished by Nebuchadnezzar, about 588 years B.C., 2 Ch. xxxvi. 6, 7, 17—20. After the Babylonish captivity it was rebuilt by command of Cyrus, but with vastly diminished beauty. The aged men wept when they compared it with the glory of the former temple, Ezr. iii. 8—12. This temple was often defiled in the wars, and before the time of Christ had become much decayed. Herod the Great, being exceedingly unpopular among the Jews on account of his cruelties, to gain their affections, and to gratify his own ambition, about B. C. 20, began to build it anew: this he did, not by taking it down entirely at once, but by removing one part after another until it became a new temple. He employed 18,000 men upon it, and completed it, so as to be fit for use, in nine years: but forty-six years after he began to repair it, when our Saviour had begun his public ministry, it was not quite finished; nay, till the beginning of their ruinous wars, the Jews added to its buildings. The temple itself was 60 cubits high, and as many broad. But in the front Herod added two wings or shoulders, each of which projecting 20 cubits, made the whole length of the front 100 cubits, and the breadth as many; and the gate was 70 cubits high, and 20 broad, but without any doors. The stones were white marble, 25 cubits in length, 12 in height, and 9 in breadth, all polished, and unspeakably beautiful. Instead of doors, the gate was closed with vails, flowered with gold, silver, purple, and every thing rich and curious. At each side of the gate were two stately pillars, from whence hung golden festoons, and vines with leaves and clusters of grapes, curiously wrought. The whole enclosure was about a furlong square, surrounded with a high wall of large stones, some of them above 40 cubits long, and all fastened to one another with lead or iron. The wall of the temple, and its roof, being covered with gold on the outside, made a most brilliant appearance in the sunshine. This vast, and splendid, and, apparently, imperishable pile, was destroyed, A.D. 70, by the Romans under Titus, after about only seventy years continuance from the time of its rebuilding by Herod.

SECTION 2.—THE BIRTH OF JESUS FORETOLD.—MARY VISITS ELISABETH, AND RETURNS HOME. Luke i. 26—56.
(G. 1.) *The Birth of Jesus foretold. Luke i. 26—38. At Nazareth.*

26 And in the sixth month the angel Gabriel was-sent from God unto a-city of Galilee,*a* 27 named Nazareth,*b* to a-virgin espoused to-a-man whose name *was* Joseph,*c* of the-28 house-of David;*d* and the virgin's name *was* Mary. And the angel came-in unto her, and-said, Hail, thou that art highly-favoured,*e* κεχαριτωμενη the Lord *is* with 29 thee: blessed *art* thou among women. And when-·she·-saw *him*, she-was-troubled at his saying, and cast-in-her-mind*f* διελογιζετο what-manner-of salutation this should-be.
30 And the angel said unto-her, Fear not, Mary: for thou-hast-found favour with God.
31 And, behold, thou-shalt-conceive in thy-womb, and bring-forth a-son, and shalt-call

MARGINAL READINGS:—*a* Circuit or revolution. *b* Branch or slip preserved. *c* He (the Lord) shall add, or give increase. *d* Beloved. *e* Given great cause of joy. *f* Reasoned or debated.

SCRIPTURE ILLUSTRATIONS.

26. *Galilee*—' revolution, circuit, or heap,' Jos. xx. 7; xxi. 32—Solomon gave to Hiram 20 cities in Galilee, 1 Ki. ix. 11—the king of Assyria took Galilee, 2 Ki. xv. 29—prediction respecting it, Is. ix. 1, 2—Jesus made several circuits around Galilee, in raising up that heap of witness, which is contained in the gospels, § 18, (*first circuit*); § 30, (*second circ.*); § 38, (*third circ.*)—the word began from Galilee, Ac. x. 37.

Nazareth—' kept or preserved.' The word signifies a valuable young stem or shoot; hedged around, or defended, from destroying animals. The place where the Rod out of the stem of Jesse (Is. xi. 1) was brought up, Lu. iv. 16, § 15—after having been preserved, as being taken into Egypt, Mt. ii. 13—23, § 5—remarkably preserved in Nazareth, Lu. iv. 28—30, § 15.—See *Nazarene*, § 5.

27. *Mary*—' bitterness,' or my myrrh, or of the sea'—Marah, Ex. xv. 23—.6—Mara, Ru. i. 20—enmity predicted between the seed of the woman and that of the serpent, Ge. iii. 15—Mary sorely tried, as to character, Mt. i. 18—20, § 2—privations, Lu. ii. 7, § 4—a fugitive, Mt. ii. 14—22, § 5—forewarned of affliction, Lu. ii. 34, .5, § 4—Jesus lightly esteemed as being her son, Mk. vi. 3, § 37—Jesus upon the cross said to her, 'Woman, behold thy son,' Jno. xix. 26, § 91.

28. *the Lord is with thee*—the true ground of confidence: *examples*, Gideon, Ju. vi. 12—Israel, as new created, and called by the Lord's name, Is. xliii. 1—Paul, Ac. xviii. 9, 10; xxiii. 11.

29. *troubled*—Nebuchadnezzar, Da. ii. 3; iv. 4—19—Belshazzar, v. 6—these had reason to be troubled; but the prophet himself was so, Da. vii. 15; x. 3—Cornelius, Ac. x. 3, 4.

31. *a son*—prediction, Is. vii. 14—fulfil. Mt. i. 22—.5, p. 14; Lu. ii. 7, § 4; Ga. iv. 4.

Jesus—' the Lord the Saviour,' Is. xliii. 11; Zep. iii. 17; Mt. i. 25, p. 14; Lu. ii. 11, 21, § 4—saves his people from their sins, Mt. i. 21, p. 13—from the present evil world, Ga. i. 4—from the wrath to come, 1 Th. i. 10—His salvation exemplified, Lu. vii. 47—50, § 29.

NOTES.

26. *Angel*, or messenger, is the common name given to those spiritual and intelligent beings, by whom God partly executeth his providential work, and who are most ready and active in his service. They were created with eminent wisdom, holiness, and purity, and placed in a most happy and honourable estate; but capable of change. Their knowledge is great, but not infinite: they *desire to look* into the mystery of our salvation, and *learn from the church* the manifold wisdom of God. Nor can they search the hearts of men, nor know future things, but as particularly instructed of God. Mt. xxiv. 36, § 86, '*But of that day and hour knoweth no man, no, not the angels of heaven, but my Father only.*' Nor do we understand their manner of knowing things corporeal and visible; nor the manner of their impressing bodies, or their method of communicating among themselves. Their power, too, is very extensive; but reaches to nothing strictly called miraculous. Their number is very great, amounting to a vast many millions: Ps. lxviii. 17, '*The chariots of God are twenty thousand, even thousands of angels.*' Mt. xxvi. 53, § 88, '*Thinkest thou that I cannot now pray to my Father, and he shall presently give me more than twelve legions of angels?*' Rev. v. 11, '*And I beheld, and I heard the voice of many angels round about the throne and the beasts and the elders: and the number of them was ten thousand times ten thousand, and thousands of thousands.*' And their names, of archangels, thrones, dominions, principalities, and powers, suggest an order among them, though of what kind we know not. Col. i. 16, '*For by him were all things created that are in heaven, and that are in earth, visible and invisible, whether they be thrones, or dominions, or principalities, or powers; all things were created by him, and for him.*'

Gabriel. see on ver. 11, p. 3.

26—.9 *ver.* It becomes us, not only with reverence to listen to the Lord's messenger, but, with Mary, earnestly to inquire into the import of the message which is brought unto us; those who so listen and inquire will find it a message of joy and peace, however it may at first excite alarm in the spirit.

[27 *ver.* The woman's own name, as having come under the curse, was Mary, *bitterness*, but, as the waters of Marah were sweetened by the tree cast into them, so was there sweetness to the troubled spirit of

[He forwarded the ruin of Persia, Da. x. 13, 20. He explained to Daniel his visions of the four beasts, of the ram and goat; he declared the time of our Saviour's appearance on earth, and his death, and the fearful consequents thereof to the Jewish nation. He informed him of the ruin of the Persian empire; of the wars between the Grecian kings of Egypt and Syria; of the distress of the Jews under Antiochus Epiphanes; of the rise and fall of Anti-Christ; and of the present adversity, and future restoration of Israel, Da. vii.—xii.]

27. *To a virgin espoused.*—See Mt. i. 18, p. 13. Matthew informs us of the subsequent appearance of the angel to Joseph; Luke, of the previous annunciation to Mary.

28. *Highly favoured.* As the mother of the long expected Messiah: the mother of the Redeemer of mankind. To be reckoned among his *ancestors*, was accounted sufficient honour for even Abraham and David. But now on Mary, a poor virgin of Nazareth, was to come this honour of giving birth to the world's Redeemer—the Son of God.

Blessed art thou. A form of salutation denoting kindness, but not necessarily implying reverence; the happiest, most fortunate, art thou of women.

30. *Found favour with God.* God hath chosen thee before all others.

31. *JESUS.* The Lord and Saviour of mankind. He is called *JESUS* because, by his righteousness, power, and Spirit, he is qualified to save, to the uttermost, them that come unto God through him, and appointed of God for that end, and freely given in the offer of the gospel. Isa. lxi. 1, 2, 3, '*The spirit of the Lord GOD is upon me,*' &c. Mt. i. 21, p. 13, He is the eternal Son of God, equal with his adored Father in every unbounded perfection.

PRACTICAL REFLECTIONS.

Mary, and so there is to that of every repentant sinner who receives the message respecting the Rod out of the stem of Jesse; to such are the words, '*Fear not, Mary, for thou hast found favour with God.*'—See Ex. xv. 22—7.]

[31 *ver.* How wonderful that Jesus, the Lord, the Saviour, should condescend to become the seed of the woman! And how marvellous the grace, that we should have the privilege of having Christ formed in us, '*the hope of glory!*' Ga. iv. 19; Col. i. 27.]

THE CLOTH OF HUMILITY SHOULD BE WORN ON THE BACK OF THE SAINTS. [9

32 his name Jesus.ᵃ He shall-be great, and shall-be-called the-Son of-the-Highest: and 33 the-Lord Godᵇ Κυριος ὁ Θεος shall-give unto-him the throne of-his father David; and he-shall-reign over επι the house of-Jacobᶜ for everᵈ εις τους αιωνας; and of-his 34 kingdom there-shall-be no end.ᵉ ουκ εσται τελος. Then said Mary unto the angel, 35 How shall-·this'-be, seeing I-know not a-man? And the angel answered and-said unto-her, The-Holy Ghost shall-come upon thee, and the-power of-the-Highest shall-overshadow thee: therefore also that holy-thing which-shall-be-born *of thee* shall-be-36 called the-Son of-God. And, behold, thy cousin Elisabeth, she hath-·also'-conceived a-son in her old-age: and this is the-sixth month with-her, who was-called barren./ 37 For with God nothing shall-be-impossible. 38 And Mary said, Behold the handmaid of-the-Lord; be-it unto-me according-to thy word. And the angel departed from her.

MARGINAL READINGS: ᵃ The Lord shall save. ᵇ Lord the God. ᶜ Healer or supplanter. ᵈ Unto the ages. ᵉ Shall not be an end. ƒ Sterile.

SCRIPTURE ILLUSTRATIONS.

32. *great, &c.*—predicted, Mi. v. 2, 4; Ps. lxxxix. 27; Is. ix. 6, 7; xii. 6—*confirmation*, Ph. ii. 9—11; He. i. 3—6; Mt. iii. 17, §8—confessed by devils, Mk. i. 24, §17; v. 7, §35.

throne of his father David — Jerusalem, 2 Sa. v. 6-10—prediction, vii. 12—16—shall call Jerusalem the throne of the LORD, Je. iii. 17, *see* Notes, *infra* —*confirm.*, Mt. xix. 28, §75; xxi. 5, §82—Christ is now on the throne of his Father in heaven, Rev. iii. 21.

father David — prediction, 2 Sa. vii. 11—29; Ps. lxxxix. 3, 6; cxxxii. 11; Je. xxiii. 5, 6—recognition, Mt. i. 1, §4; xxi. 9, §82—David's Lord, as well as David's son, Mt. xxii. 41—5, §85.

31. *reign* — prediction, 'my servant David their Prince for ever,' Eze. xxxvii. 25—the Lord, Ps. cxlvi. 10; Mi. iv. 2; v. 2—*confirm.*, 2 Ti. ii. 11, .2; Re. xi. 10; xx. 4, 6.

no end—prediction, Is. ix. 7; Da. ii. 44; vii. 13, .4, 27—*confirm.*, He. i. 8; Re. xi. 15; xxii. 5.

35. *Son of God*—His name, a subject of inquiry for the wise, Pr. xxx. 4—prediction, Ps. ii.; lxxxix. 26—confirmation, Ac. iv. 24—31; Col. i. 12—9—with his servants in the fire, Da. iii. 25—acknowledged of the Father, Mt. iii. 17, §8; xvii. 5, §51—questioned by the tempter, Mt. iv. 3, 6, §9—confessed by devils, Lu. iv. 41, §17; Mk. iii. 11, §26, *see* 'great,' above—Jesus declared himself to be the Son of God, Jno. iii. 16, .7, §12; v. 25, §28; ix. 35—.7, §55; x. 36, §56; xiv. 4, §58; xvii. 1, §87—His accusation, Jno. xix. 7, §90; Lu. xxii 70, §90; Mt. xxvii. 43, §91—witnessed by the Baptist, Jno. i. 34, §10—by Nathanael, ver. 49, §10—by the centurion, Mt. xxvii. 54, §92—the gospel of Jesus Christ, the Son of God, Mk. i. 1, §7—by the apostles, Ac. ix. 20; xiii. 32, .3; Ro. i. 4; v. 10; Ga. iv. 4, ; 1 Jno. L. 7; iv. 10. .5; v. 5, 20—*for what purpose*, Jno. iii. 16, .8, § 12; xx. 31, § 100—His manifestation in power, Ro. ii. 16, 27—*compare* Ps. ii, 7—9.

37. *with God nothing shall be impossible* — said to Abraham, Ge. xviii. 14—to Moses, Nu. xi. 23—by Job, xlii. 2—by Nebuchadnezzar, Da. iv. 35—by and to the prophet Jeremiah, xxxii. 17—27—by Jesus, Mt. xix. 26, §75—the power to be had in Christ, 2 Co. xii. 9, 10; Ph. iv. 13

NOTES.

32. *He shall be great.* Illustrious.—*See* Is. ix. 6, 7. '*For unto us a child is born, unto us a son is*,' *&c.*

['Great in power and authority, in glory and fame, in office and administration, when he shall reign.' 'Great in his person, as God and man united;' in his Prophetic office, 'mighty in word and deed,' doctrine and miracles; in his Priesthood, establishing upon its merits a constant and universal intercession.]

The Son of the Highest; that is, 'of God;' one of whose names is—'the Most High.' 'The Highest' often stands as a title of God. 'The Son of God,' in a sense in which no creature can be. 'The Son of God,' in his higher and Divine nature.

Throne of his father David. David is called his *father,* because Jesus was lineally descended from him. —————— The promise to David was, that there should *not fail a man to sit on his throne,* 1 K. viii. 25. David had reigned over all Israel—the Jews rejected his rightful heir when he appeared among men. But, by the foundation being laid in Zion, at the time of Christ's first coming to suffer, the purpose of God was not frustrated, but rather infallibly secured. To Christ not only belongs the kingdom, or throne of the house of *Judah;* he was appointed to reign over the house of '*all Israel*,' few belonging to which were then in the land, and in whose empty heritages the Jews, such as Joseph and Mary, were then dwelling. Until the kingdom shall come, when *Israel* will acknowledge their King, and submit to his righteous government, permanent peace cannot be expected.

33 *ver.* Not Herod, who had usurped the throne of David, was recognised as 'great' by God, but he whose right it is, although the child of a poor inhabitant of despised Nazareth. Let us patiently wait upon Him who, however we may be tried, forgetteth not the cause of the poor and needy.—Jesus was properly the Son of the Highest; but behold what manner of love the Father hath bestowed upon us poor sinners, that we, accepted in that Son, should be called the *sons* of God!

[Although, by men, Jesus was denied, with cruelty and scorn, '*the throne of his father David*;' yet was it given to him by the Lord God, as a place in which should be displayed his truth as a prophet, and his awful justice as a king, seeing it refused to come under the blessing of his priesthood.]

Of his kingdom there shall be no end. His is the kingdom predicted by the prophets, as by Da. ii. 44, ['*And in the days of these kings shall the God of heaven set up a kingdom, which shall never be destroyed: and the kingdom shall not be left to other people, but it shall break in pieces and consume all these kingdoms, and it shall stand for ever.*'—vii. 27, '*And the kingdom and dominion, and the greatness of the kingdom under the whole heaven, shall be given to the people of the saints of the Most High, whose kingdom is an everlasting kingdom, and all dominions shall serve and obey him.*']

35. *The power of the highest, &c.* This evidently means that the body of Jesus should be created by the direct power of God.

Shall be called the Son of God. Rom. i. 4, '*And declared to be the Son of God with power, according to the spirit of holiness, by the resurrection from the dead.*'—Ac. xiii. 33—*compare* with Ps. ii. 7.—*See* above, in ' Scrip. Illustra.;' and *see* 'Jesus,' p. 9.

38. *Behold the handmaid of the Lord.* This expresses prompt obedience.—*See* Ac. ix. 10; He. x. 7.

PRACTICAL REFLECTIONS.

33 *ver.* However we may refuse allegiance to the King of Israel, there is no time in which entire submission to him is not due: and the Father will vindicate the Son's right to reign throughout all ages, even unto the dispensation of the fulness of times: and thenceforth shall his dominion be for ever: '*of his kingdom there shall be no end.*'

34 *ver.* Whilst we avoid the unbelief of Zacharias, as asking, *whereby* we shall know that God will accomplish his word? let us, with Mary, exercise believing solicitude as to *how* the will of God is to be done.

37, 8 *ver.* God is omnipotent ; and we do well, like Mary, to resign ourselves willingly into his hands, who can do for his people marvellous things.

I DELIGHT TO DO THY WILL O MY GOD.—Psalm xl. 8.

(G. 5.) *Mary visits Elisabeth. Luke* i. 39—55. *In the Hill Country of Judea.*

39 And Mary arose in those days, and-went into the hill-country with haste, into a-city
40 of-Juda; and entered into the house of-Zacharias, and saluted Elisabeth.
41 And it-came-to-pass, *that*, when Elisabeth heard the salutation of Mary, the babe
42 leaped in her womb; and Elisabeth was-filled with-the-Holy Ghost: And she-spake-
out with-a-loud voice, and said, Blessed *art* thou among women, and blessed *is* the
43 fruit of-thy womb. And whence *is* this to-me, that the mother of-my Lord should-
44 come to me? For, lo, as-soon-as the voice of-thy salutation sounded in mine ears,
45 the babe leaped in my womb for joy. And blessed *is* she that-believed: for there-
shall-be a-performance^a of-those-things τελειωσις τοις which-were-told her from the-
46 Lord. And Mary said, My soul doth-magnify the Lord, 47 and my spirit hath-
48 rejoiced in God my Saviour επι τω Θεω τω σωτηρι μου. For he-hath-regarded the
low-estate^b ταπεινωσιν of-his handmaiden: for, behold, from henceforth all genera-
49 tions shall-call-me-blessed. For he that-is-mighty hath-done to-me great-things;^c

MARGINAL READINGS:—^a Completion or perfection to. ^b Littleness; insignificance. ^c Majestic things; magnificences.

SCRIPTURE ILLUSTRATIONS.

39. *hill country*—where the children of Aaron had portions, Jos. xxi. 4—19.

42. *blessed*—those that trust in the Son, Ps. ii. 12—they that hear the word of God and keep it, Lu. xi. 27, .8. § 62—John the Baptist, Mt. xi. 6, § 29—this truth declared to Thomas, Jno. xx. 29, § 95.

45. *performance*—of the oath to Abraham, Ge. xxii. 15—.8—performance promised to Isaac, xxvi. 3—confirmed to Jacob, xxviii. 13—.5—same in the prophets, Je. xxxiii. 14; Mi. vii. 20—God did not become the Son of man, that he should repent, Nu. xxiii. 19—but in order to confirm the promises made unto the fathers, Ro. xv. 8—performance continuous from its commencement at Philippi, Ph. i. 6; ii. 16—where the gospel began to be preached in Europe, Ac. xvi. 6—12.

46. *my soul*—Hannah so rejoiced in song, 1 Sa. ii. 1—10—David, Ps. xxxiv. 2, 3—so all the seed of Israel shall glory, Is. xlv. 25.

48. *all generations*—all families of the earth to be blessed, Ge. xii. 1—3—all nations, Ps. lxxii. 17—.9 —call you blessed, Mal. iii. 12—the word to a thousand generations, Ps. cv. 6—10—the blessing upon the nations, through Christ, Ga. iii. 13, .4.

49. *holy*—glorious in holiness, Ex. xv. 11—holy in all his works, Ps. cxlv. 17—Holy, holy, holy, Is. vi. 3; Re. iv. 8—His name Holy, Is. lvii. 15; Ps. xcix. 3 —the holy One of God: his coming disturbed the unclean spirits in the synagogue, Lu. iv. 34, § 17—the saints to reflect his holiness, Le. xix. 2; 1 Pe. i. 15, .6; 1 Co. vi. 19, 20.

NOTES.

39. *Arose, and went into the hill country of Juda*. The region south of Jerusalem, about eighteen miles distant. The principal city was Hebron, which, with other neighbouring cities, was given to the priests. It is now principally in ruins, and much venerated by Jews, Arabs, and Christians; because in it were buried Abraham, Sarah, Isaac, and Rebekah. Zacharias probably lived at Juttah, near to Hebron.—See 'Geography,' p. 14.

40. *Saluted Elisabeth*. Expressed great joy and gratification at seeing her, and used the customary tokens of affectionate salutation.

41. *Filled with the Holy Ghost*. By the Spirit she was enabled to speak the words that follow, verses 42—5; and in the same power Mary replies, verses 46—56.

43. *Whence is this to me?* An expression of humility. Why is it that the mother of my Lord should come to-me, as if to honour me?

46. *And Mary said, &c*. Most of these phrases are borrowed from the Old Testament, especially from the song of Hannah, 1 Sa. ii. 1—10. The Spirit of prophecy frequently uses expressions before given.

48. *All-gener*. The children of God in all after-ages.

Shall call me blessed. Highly favoured. This certainly does not warrant us to worship her, or to pray to her. Abraham was blessed in being the father of the faithful; Paul in being the apostle to the Gentiles; Peter in first preaching the gospel to them: but who would think of worshipping or praying to Abraham, Paul, or Peter? It is from the honour conferred on Mary, the Romanists have determined that it is right to worship the Virgin, and to offer prayers to her; which is idolatry. For, 1st. It is nowhere commanded in the Bible. 2nd. It is expressly forbidden to worship any being but God, Ex. xx. 4, 5; xxxiv. 14; De. vi. 13, .4; Is. xlv. 20. 3rd. It is idolatry to worship or pray to a creature. 4th. It is absurd to suppose that the Virgin Mary can be in all places at the same time, to hear the prayers of thousands at once, or that she can aid them.—*See* Ro. i. 25.

49. *Great things*. Wonderful benefits; distinguishing mercies:—God hath conferred unspeakable mercy in making me the mother of Messias.

Holy is his name. Holy and to be reverenced is his name. . . . . That name is holy, and to be regarded as holy; and to make a common or profane use of it, is solemnly forbidden in the third commandment, Ex. xx. 7.

PRACTICAL REFLECTIONS.

39 ver. It is good for us not to neglect the signs which God is pleased to point out for the confirmation of our faith. The long and difficult journey of Mary to Elisabeth was abundantly rewarded.

40 ver. It is blessed to have the communion of saints —especially of those who are older and have a similar experience with ourselves in the things of God. 'Then they that feared the LORD spoke often one to another: and the LORD hearkened, and heard it, and a book of remembrance was written before him for them that feared the LORD, and that thought upon his name,' Mal. iii. 16.

41—4 ver. The word of the Lord is, indeed, found to be truth, by such as believingly inquire into his faithfulness; Mary's own case, and that of Elisabeth, which was given as a sign, were at once witnessed to by the Spirit in Elisabeth, with increased confirmation to her who had believed the words of the heavenly messenger. However mighty the messenger, it is as from the Lord that the message should be received.

[15 ver. There is not only blessing in believing obedience now, but especially in the glorious triumph of Messiah's kingdom, chiefly concerning which were the things spoken of by the angel. That kingdom is equally the subject of promise to all that believe, as it was to the believing and obedient Mary. The blessing of being related to Christ in the flesh was great, but a greater may be ours, for thus said our Lord himself, 'Yea, rather, blessed are they that hear the word of God, and keep it,' Lu. xi. 28, § 62.]

46, .8 ver. However highly favoured, we should ever remember that it is all through Grace; that, along with the most vile, we require salvation through Him who had been promised to Mary, and of whom she sings, saying, 'My soul doth magnify the Lord, and my spirit hath rejoiced in God my Saviour.'

— Let us, with Mary, magnify the Lord for his most favourable regard to the poor.

[19 ver. The mighty One doth not only put forth power on behalf of his people, but in them, so as to sanctify them unto his service—'Holy is his name.']

THE DESIRE OF ALL NATIONS.—Haggai ii. 7.

MARY'S SONG OF PRAISE.

50 μεγαλεια and holy *is* his name. And his mercy *is* on-them that-fear him from-gene-
51 ration to generation.ᵃ εις γενεας γενεων. He-hath-shewed strength εποιησε κρατος with
52 his arm; he-hath-scattered the-proud in-the-imagination of-their hearts.ᵇ He-hath-put-
53 down the-mighty from *their* seats, and exalted them-of-low-degree. He-hath-filled the-
54 hungry with-good *things*; and the-rich he-hath-sent-'empty'-away. He-hath-holpen
55 αντελαβετο his servantᶜ Israel, in-remembranceᵈ μνησθηναι of-his-mercy, (as he-spake
to our fathers,) to Abraham, and to his seed for ever.ᵉ εις τον αιωνα. [56 *ver*., see p. 14.]

MARGINAL READINGS :—ᵃ Unto generations of generations. ᵇ Heart or inner part. ᶜ Child or son.
ᵈ To remember mercies. ᵉ Unto the age.

SCRIPTURE ILLUSTRATIONS.

51. *strength*—sung of by Moses at the Red Sea, Ex. xv. 1–19—by David, Ps. lxv. 6; xcviii. 1—arm of the Lord to put on strength, Is. li. 9, 11—Zion to put on strength, lii. 1—made bare his arm, lii. 9, 10—mine own arm, lxiii. 5, 6—strong to judge Babylon, Re. xviii. 8.

scattered the proud—same sung by Moses, Ex. xv. 1–10—and by Hannah, 1 Sa. ii. 1–10—and by David, Ps. ii.—to be fulfilled in great future deliverances,

Eze. xxxviii. 14–23; xxxix.; Ro. xix. 17–21; Zep. iii. 8–13; Joel iii. 11–.7.

55. *Abraham*—first promise to, Ge. xii. 1–7—vision, xv.—covenant, xvii. 1–8—confirmed with an oath, xxii. 16–.8—fulfilment anticipated, in the new song, Ps. xcviii. 3—to be fulfilled to her that was reckoned barren and desolate, Is. liv. 1, 9, 10—the promise secured, and only to be enjoyed in Christ, Ga. iii. 16, .7, 29—the promise immutable, He. vi. 13–.8.

NOTES.

50. *That fear him.* That *reverence* or honour him. One kind of fear is that which a servant has of a cruel master, or a man has of a precipice, the plague, or danger. This is not the *fear* which we ought to have of God. It is the fear which a dutiful child has of a kind and virtuous father: a fear of dishonouring him by our life; of doing anything which he would disapprove. It is on those who have *such* fear of God that his mercy descends. This is the fear of the Lord which is the beginning of wisdom, Ps. cxi. 10; Job xxviii. 28, '*And unto man he said, Behold, the fear of the Lord, that is wisdom; and to depart from evil is understanding.*'

From generation to generation. From one age to another; it continues; is unceasing; and abounds.

51. *He hath shewed strength with his arm.* A metaphor derived from putting to flight a defeated enemy. He utterly discomfits. The arm is the symbol of strength. The expression in this and the subsequent verses has no particular reference to this mercy to Mary. Having sung of her Saviour, the promised seed of the woman, she reaches forward, in the spirit of prophecy, to a contemplation of his ultimate triumph, in bruising the serpent's head.

Scattered the proud, &c. [We are to consider that Mary prophesied in this song, and thus spoke of the ultimate triumph as if already come. It was secured by the coming of the conqueror, the seed of the woman, which shall bruise the head of the serpent.]

52. *Put down the mighty.* Speaking prophetically of the destruction of Satan's kingdom, and the establishment of the kingdom of Messiah.

Exalted them, &c. In the first coming of Christ an assurance was given, that all the promises shall be fulfilled. The meek shall inherit the earth; the poor in spirit shall be given the kingdom of heaven.

53. *The hungry with good things.* This is a celebration of the general mercy of God: but more particularly for the abundance of blessing which our God hath designed for his chosen people.

The rich he hath sent, &c.—See Ps. xxxvii.

54. *He hath holpen.* Hath succoured.

[Whatever may threaten, he will defend his servant Israel in possession of the goodness he hath

prepared, and truly fulfil the mercy promised to Abraham and to his seed for ever.]

In rememb. of his mercy. Of his promised mercy. [The expression has here peculiar emphasis, meaning, to give a fresh proof of mercy and favour to Israel, in addition to the ancient mercies shewn to that people. The fulfilment of all the promises made to the fathers, as to the multitude, power, and blessedness of the chosen seed, was secured in God's giving his only begotten Son into the world.]

55. *As he spake to our fathers, &c.* That is, He hath dealt mercifully with the children of Israel, according as he promised Abraham, Isaac, and Jacob, &c. Seeing that God did not withhold his own Son, there could be now no doubt as to the full accomplishment of the promises made to the fathers, however difficult that accomplishment may at one time have appeared to be. As truly as the Prince hath come of Judah, his people Israel shall be found, and find in Him the blessing & the deliverance promised.

Abraham. First called Abram, or 'Great father.' It was promised that a great nation would proceed of him, Ge. xii. 2. Afterwards his name was changed to Abraham, sig. '*Father of a great multitude,*' Ge. xvii. 5, 6; and it was predicted that he should be the '*father of many nations.*' He was called to leave his father's country, and go into a land which the Lord would shew him, Ge. xii. 1. Being led into the land of Canaan, this was wholly promised to his seed, Ge. xii. 7. [He was, however, long in being given the son of whom the promised "one seed" (Christ) and the multitudinous seed were to come; and neither Isaac, nor his grandson Jacob, obtained possession of the promised land. Nor, when brought out of Egypt, were the children of Israel given possession, according to the free covenant made with Abraham. The possession then obtained was under the law. But the possession promised through the covenant of grace, remains to be given to Abraham's descendants, when they obey the call, '*Look unto Abraham your father,*' Is. li. 1–3. When, as possessing the same simplicity of faith, they exemplify the same willing obedience as Abraham, Is. lvii. 15, .4. Abraham is called the friend of God, Is. xli. 8 Believers, being all one in Christ Jesus, are in Christ, Abraham's seed, and heirs according to the promise, Ga. iii. 28, .9.]

PRACTICAL REFLECTIONS.

50–.5 ver. We may, with Mary, and as in the general language of prophecy, speak of that as done, which God hath begun to do. It should be to us as much a reality. Thus may we walk by faith.

51 ver. The counsels of the proud will produce their own discomfiture.

52 ver. The exaltation of the wicked will but prepare for their greater downfall.

53 ver. It is not the full and self-satisfied that may be expected to enjoy the promised good, but those who, knowing their own folly, weakness, and poverty, are willing to be guarded, upheld, and provided for simply as the Lord may choose.

[54 ver. As the high priest had the names of the children of Israel upon his shoulders and upon his

breastplate, for remembrance before God, so of God our Saviour it shall yet be said, '*He hath holpen,*' &c.]

[54, .5 ver. As truly as the Lord will give help to his servant Israel, in raising up the tribes of Jacob, so truly will he remember to perform the fulness of the mercy promised to Abraham, and to his seed for ever.—Let us prove that we are truly the children of Abraham, by our having the same faith, and manifesting it by the same patient waiting and ready doing the will of our God.—Let us see the grace of God as manifested in these, the very first instances of prophesying as recorded in the New Testament. They are both by woman, who was first in the transgression. And with the spirit of prophecy, which is the testimony of Jesus, he hath thus honoured both youth and old age.]

PART I.   JOSEPH IS COMMANDED TO TAKE MARY TO WIFE   SECT. II.

(G. 6.) *Mary returns home, and is taken into the house of Joseph as his espoused wife.*
Matt. i. 18—25. Luke i. 56. *At Nazareth.*

18 Now the birth of Jesus Christ was on-this-wise: when-as his mother Mary was-espoused to Joseph, before they came-together, she-was-found with-child of the-Holy
19 Ghost. Then [a] δὲ Joseph her husband, being a-just man, & not willing to make-her-
20 a-publick-example, παραδειγματίσαι was-minded to-put-·her·-away privily. But while-·he·-thought-on [b] αὐτοῦ ἐνθυμηθέντος these-things, behold, the-angel of-the-Lord appeared unto-him in a-dream, saying, Joseph, *thou* son of-David, fear not to-take-unto
21 *thee* Mary thy wife: for that which-is-conceived in her is of the-Holy Ghost. And she-shall-bring-forth a-son, and thou-shalt-call his name JESUS: for he shall-save his

MARGINAL READINGS:— [a] However or moreover. [b] While anxiously-meditating

SCRIPTURE ILLUSTRATIONS.

(Mt. 1.) 19. *just*—light ariseth to such, in the darkness, Ps. cxii. 4—walketh in his integrity, Pr. xx. 7—Simeon, a just man., waited for the consolation of Israel, Lu. ii. 25 § 4—God compassionates the ignorance of the sincere: Cornelius, Ac. x. 22—Paul, 1 Ti. i. 12, .3.

public example—Judah would have dealt severely with Tamar, Ge. xxxviii. 21—the law directed that the adulteress should be stoned, De. xxii. 21, .2; Jno. viii. 4, 5, § 85—Jesus allowed such to be put away, Mr. v. 32, § 19—the house of Israel had been so dealt with, Je. iii. 8, ' And I saw, when for all the causes whereby backsliding Israel committed adultery I had put her away, and given her a bill of divorce; yet her treacherous sister Judah feared not, but went,' &c.

20. *while he thought*—the Lord teaches the meek, Ps. xxv. 8—10; Pr. iii. 5, 6; Is. xxvi. 7.
dream -- Jacob's, Ge. xxviii. 12—Joseph's, xxxvii. 5—11—Solomon's, 1 Ki. iii. 5—15—use of them, Job xxxiii. 15—.7—promise with reward to, Joel ii. 28—Pilate's wife's, Mt. xxvii. 19, § 90.

fear not—to Jacob, Ge. xlvi. 3—See Lu. i. 13, p. 4.

21. *bring forth—see* promise to Sarah, Ge. xvii. 19, 21—the Shunammite, 2 Ki. iv. 16, .7.—See Lu. i. 31, p 9.
save his people, &c.—redeem Israel from all his iniquities, Ps. cxxx. 7, 8—all the ends of the earth to look to Jesus, Is. xlv. 22, .3—*confirm.*, Jno. xii. 32, § 82.—See ' Jesus,' Lu. i. 31, § 2, p. 10.

NOTES.

(Mt. 1. 18—25.) 18. *Was espoused to Joseph.* Espousing was a solemn engagement or contract of marriage, made before witnesses; after which the parties were accounted husband and wife, although they might live for some time after separate.

[No woman of Israel was married unless she had been first espoused. Generally six months or a year intervened between the espousals and nuptials, De. xx. 7.]

19. *A just man.* A lover of justice, and a man of uprightness and integrity. Strict in his obedience to all God's commandments; and so could not associate with Mary, were she guilty, as he supposed.

A public example. To expose her to public shame or infamy. Joseph was not only just, but merciful, and so was desirous that the separation he esteemed just, should be in a manner the least injurious to Mary. The infidelity of a *betrothed* woman was punished with death by stoning.

[To *put her away privily.* The law of Moses gave the husband the power of divorce, De. xxiv. 1. It was customary in a bill of divorce to specify the causes for which the divorce was made, and witnesses were also present to testify to the divorce. But in this case, it seems, Joseph resolved to put her away *without specifying the cause;* for he was not willing to make her a public example.]

[It was not necessary that it should be a public transaction. The man could give the woman a bill of divorce in private, delivering it into her hand or her bosom. Two witnesses only were necessary; it was not needful that any cause should be assigned.]

20. *But while he thought on these things.* He reflected, meditated, turned the matter in his mind. His not acting rashly, but listening thus to the voice of mercy, gave occasion for the voice of mercy to reach himself.

[In the patriarchal times, as well as in the earlier ages of Judaism, God often revealed his will by dreams or visions, not only to his own people, but to the nations at large. The ancients in general much regarded them; and rules for their interpretation were formed, both among Jews and Gentiles; the former of whom were, however, forbidden to seek their interpretation from any but the prophets of the Lord, or the high priest.]

Joseph, thou son of David. He was of the house and lineage of David: of whom the Messiah was promised.

Thy wife. The Hebrews called the betrothed of a man, his wife, De. xxii. 24.

JESUS.—See ' Reflections,' p. 9, and *infra*, 21 ver.
21. *He shall save.* This expresses the same as the name, and on this account the name was giver to him. He saves men by having died to redeem them; by giving the Spirit to renew them, Jno. xvi. 7, 8, § 87; by his power in enabling them to overcome their spiritual enemies; in defending them from danger; in guiding them in the path of duty; in sustaining them in trials & in death; & in rescuing them from the prison of the grave, & raising them up at the last day, to exalt them to be with him in his kingdom.

PRACTICAL REFLECTIONS.

(Mat. 1. 18—25.) 18 *ver.* In the bestowment of his best of blessings, God is not restrained by the distinctions of rank that take place among men; she who was favoured among women, was an obscure but pious virgin, espoused to a just man, who was a carpenter.

Virtue is sometimes tried, not only by temptations, but most painfully by unjust and cruel suspicions; and sometimes even by unmerited punishment and disgrace.

[We should not be rash in forming an uncharitable judgment of those with whom we have entered into friendly relations: those circumstances which at first appear the most suspicious, may arise from a cause the most opposite to that which was suspected.]

[19 *ver.* We should be careful lest our very sense of justice lead us, in our ignorance, to commit that which is most unjust, lest our very desire to shew mercy impel us to act with the greatest cruelty, as it would have been in Joseph to put away Mary without her being given an opportunity of explaining her innocence.]

[20 *ver.* It is best, in the spirit of ready obedience and humble submission, to leave our case in the hands of Him, who hath all wisdom & power to vindicate the cause of those who put their trust in Him.]

The ways of God are various in communicating his will unto men: it was by vision to Zacharias and Mary; by the spirit of prophecy to Mary and Elisabeth; and now in a dream to Joseph.

21 *ver.* Let us never forget why the child of Mary was to be called Jesus, and see that it be legibly written in our lives, in our being indeed saved from our sins, otherwise we have not the evidence of being truly his people. Our Lord hath his name Jesus, not merely because he delivers from the wrath to come, but especially because · he saves his people from their sins. He hath taken them away, *justifyingly*, by his blood; and he takes them away, *sanctifyingly*, by his Spirit, as applying to all who believe the good word of his grace.

SHEW ME THY WAYS, O LORD; TEACH ME THY PATHS.—Psalm xxv. 4.

SECT. II.   MARY RETURNS HOME.   PART I.

22 people from their sins. Now all this was done, that it-might-be-fulfilled which was-
23 spoken of the Lord by the prophet, saying, Behold, a virgin [a] ἡ παρθένος shall-be with-
child, and shall-bring-forth a-son, and they-shall-call his name Emmanuel, which
24 being-interpreted is, God ὁ Θεὸς with us. Then Joseph being-raised from sleep did as
25 the angel of-the-Lord had-bidden him, and took-unto *him* his wife: and knew her not
till she-had-brought-forth her first-born son.[b] [Matt. ii. 1, ‖ v., p. 31.]

Lu. i. 56   And Mary abode with her about three months, and returned to her-own house.

MARGINAL READINGS:—[a] The virgin.   [b] The son of her, the first-born.

SCRIPTURE ILLUSTRATIONS.

23. *Emmanuel* — prediction, Is. vii. 14—the virgin's son, Immanuel, must be distinguished from the
prophet's son, Shear-jashub, which means '*the remnant shall return*,' referred to ver. 3, 15, .6—the remnant, the Jews, did return from Babylon: but when
the fulness of the time came they did not believe in
the sign Emmanuel, which was then given: in consequence, they were not established, ver. 9—the consumption determined upon the whole land has come,
as predicted, ver. 17—25—*confirmation*, Jno. i. 14,
§ 7; viii. 24, § 55; Ro. ix. 5; 2 Co. v. 19; Col. ii. 9—
the fulness of the promise yet to be realized, Re. xxi. 3.

NOTES.

21. *His people.* Those whom the Father hath given
him. The children of Israel were called the people
of God, because he had chosen them to himself, and
regarded them as his peculiar and beloved people.
Christians are called the people of Christ, because it
was the purpose of the Father to give them to him.
[Is. liii. 11, ' *He shall see of the travail of his soul, and
shall be satisfied: by his knowledge shall my righteous
servant justify many; for he shall bear their iniquities.*' Jno. vi. 37, § 43. And because in due time he
came to redeem them to himself. Tit. ii. 14, '*Who
gave himself for us, that he might redeem us from all
iniquity, and purify unto himself a peculiar people,
zealous of good works.*' 1 Pe. i. 2, '*Elect according
to the foreknowledge of God the Father, through sanctification of the Spirit, unto obedience and sprinkling
of the blood of Jesus Christ: Grace unto you, and
peace, be multiplied.*']

From their sins. 1st. By dying to make an atonement, Tit. ii. 14; and, 2nd. By renewing the heart
and purifying the soul, and preparing his people for
his kingdom of glory.

22. *That it might be fulfilled, &c.* The prophecy
here quoted is recorded in Is. vii. 14. It was delivered
about 740 B.C., in the reign of Ahaz king of Judah.

23. *They shall call his name*, *i. e.* His name
shall be called, or be, for the fulfilment of the prophecy depends not upon Christ's literally having
borne the name Emmanuel, but upon his *being* such:
which he clearly was as GOD-MAN. Thus the Evangelist has interpreted both Emmanuel and Jesus, to
shew that the prophecy was fulfilled not in the names,
but in their *signification* or *application*.

Emmanuel. This is a Hebrew word, and means literally, *God with us*. Matthew doubtless understands
this word as denoting that the Messiah was really
' God with us,' or that the Divine nature was united
to the human.—See Ph. ii. 6—8.

PRACTICAL REFLECTIONS.

23. Christ, as born of a virgin, is the great sign
that all the promises of God shall be fulfilled. Christ
is the alone foundation, Is. vii. 9—14, upon which we
can be established.

24. Where we find we have unjustly condemned
any, we should be eager to make reparation. And,
in all cases, make haste to do God's holy will, when
it is clearly made known to us.

24, .5. Jesus submitted to be thought the son of
Joseph, although he was in truth the only-begotten
Son of God. ' *Beloved, now are we the sons of God;
and it doth not yet appear what we shall be,*' 1 Jno. iii. 2.

GEOGRAPHICAL NOTICES.

GALILEE.—See 'Historical Sketch of the Land of
Promise,' p. ix.

NAZARETH.—In Arabic, *En Nazirah*. Is a small
city in Galilee, about 70 miles north of Jerusalem,
and about six miles west from mount Tabor. The
town lies upon the lower slope of the western side of
an oblong basin extending about a mile from S.S.W.
to N.N.E., and about half a mile in breadth. The
valley has sometimes been compared to a cup: and
the hills have all a whitish appearance, from the limestone of which they are composed. The houses are
substantially built of white stone, and have only flat
terraced roofs, without the domes so common in Jerusalem and the south of the land. There are but
few ruins. The largest building is the Latin convent,
which monkish legends say is built over the house
where Mary, the mother of our Lord, lived. Under
the church is shewn the grotto in which it is pretended Mary received the salutation of the angel
Gabriel—' *Hail! thou that art highly favoured, the
Lord is with thee*,' &c. The buildings of the convent
are massy; and there is a mosque in the town adorned
with cypress trees. Fig trees and olives abound in
the gardens, hedged in with prickly pear. The pretended dwelling of Joseph, cut out of the rock, is
shewn, and the pillar curiously (the inhabitants say
miraculously) suspended from the roof. In another
part of the town is also shewn the stone table, off which,
according to a lying tradition of the monks, Christ
dined with his disciples, both before and after his resurrection; a visit to which procures seven years' indulgence to the deluded pilgrims of the church of
Rome. They have also a curious ancient picture,
which they say is a portrait of our blessed Lord, and
the very one sent by him to the king of Edessa, on
which is inscribed,

' *Hæc vera imago Domini.*'

A late traveller thus describes his visit to Nazareth:—

' We rode directly to the Latin convent, and were
civilly received, in a dirty cell set apart for pilgrims.
Two rude beds were allotted to us, and a suitable place
to stow away our baggage. I was unwell, and ill at
ease. Nazareth, of all places, seemed to me the most
outrageously clamorous. Every hour of the day and
night was broken by incessant yelling; scores of children were all crying and screaming at once, and at
the top of their voices; donkeys were braying, cocks
crowing, and camels grunting.

' Notwithstanding all that is wearisome at Nazareth,
one delightful train of thought is kept up: that there
the human nature of our adorable Redeemer expanded
to its full maturity; and that there, in humble obscurity, he trained his soul for those achievements which
have shed light and lustre and hope upon a blighted
world. It is delightful to gaze upon every rocky
height, and upon every silent valley around, and to
be assured that there He walked and meditated and
prayed, and yearned over the degraded posterity of
the fallen Adam.'—See '*A Pastor's Visit*,' &c.

' The greater part of the population of Nazareth is
professedly Christian: but it is the deformed and life-
less Christianity of the Roman and Greek churches.
Only a few attend vespers on the Lord's day.

' The extreme seclusion of the town, and the resort
of bad and doubtful characters of Galilee, gave rise to
the ancient proverb, "*Can any good thing come out of
Nazareth?*" It is not much better now, if any judgment
may be formed from the physiognomy of the idle and
wretched looking population. A great many bony-
featured Bedouins, with the rope of camel's hair
round their head, loiter in the streets.'—*See* Sect. vi.

HILL COUNTRY OF JUDEA.—By the ' hill country '
we may understand, generally, the whole hilly district
of Judæa, from the region around Hebron northward
to the plain of Sharon.

That part of it into which Mary went on a visit to
Elisabeth, was most probably the district south of
Hebron, where *Juttah* is situated; which city is sup-
posed by some to have been the birth-place of John

PART I: THE BIRTH OF JOHN THE BAPTIST.   SECT. III.

Baptist. It is now called *Yutta*; and from a little distance has the appearance of a large Muhammedan town, on a low eminence, with trees around. It was a city of the priests; and has been lost sight of since the days of Jerome.

Dr. Robinson says, 'The distance between Hebron and Jerusalem is definitely given by Eusebius and Jerome at twenty-two Roman miles, equivalent to about seventeen and a half geographical miles. Our time between the two cities was eight and a quarter hours with camels; affording a good coincidence.'

[In the division of the land, among other cities, (see Jos. xxi. 4, 11, 16,) ' *The children of Aaron the priest, which were of the Levites, had to lot. out of the tribe of Judah, and out of the tribe of Simeon, and out of the tribe of Benjamin, thirteen cities... And they gave them the city of Arba the father of Anak, which city is Hebron, in the hill country of Judah, with the suburbs thereof round about it. ... And Ain with her suburbs, and Juttah with her suburbs, and Bethshemesh with her suburbs*.' Indeed this whole region of Hebron is what is expressly called in the book of Joshua the *hill country*. Of the district south of Wady-el-Musurr, Dr. Robinson observes, ' the precipitous western wall of the higher mountainous tract towards Hebron lies further back, nearly in a line with the spot on which we stood, *viz*. a high point, *west of Wady Bittir, about one hour and a half from Jerusalem going to Gaza*; while a broad region of lower hills and open valleys is spread out between it and the western plain. This higher tract of mountains ... rises to the height of nearly 2,800 feet; the region of hills reaches apparently about one-third of the same elevation above the sea and plain.' Of this hilly region the same writer elsewhere observes, ' This may be called the "*hill country*," in distinction from the higher mountains on the east. It is the middle region between the mountains and the plain, stretching, as we have seen, far to the north and south. ... This region is for the most part a beautiful open country, consisting of low hills, usually rocky, separated by broad arable valleys mostly sown with grain, as are also many of the swelling hills. The whole tract is full of villages and deserted sites and ruins; and many olive-groves appear around the former.'—ROBINSON's *Researches*. vol. ii. pp. 327, 341.

' As we approached the hills,' (writes Mr. Paxton, when travelling towards them from Ramleh,) ' the face of the plain became more uneven; the points of the ridges ran out irregularly, and more rocks began to appear on the surface. The line of hills is, however, more regular than is usual, and the transition from the plain to the hills is more gradual than is usually found on the borders of large plains. ... The hills are not continuous ridges, but knobs, not very high, nor very steep: the top rounded over. Many of them are separated from each other, almost to the base; but a greater number join at one or more sides, at various heights from their bases. Taking the hollows, and the passages between the hills, (and, in some places, there are little level spots,) as the level of the country, I should say that the general level, as we pass east, rises; and the height of the hills above this general level continues about the same for a great part of the way from the commencement of the hills, to near Jerusalem. This district is well called the "*Hill country of Judea*;" nothing could better express it. They are usually, in books, called mountains, but their size—that is, their height above the general level of the country—hardly entitles them to that appellation; they are rather hills than mountains. As we rode among the hills, we began to see a few small shrubs and bushes of oak. Most of them, however, were small; few as high as a man on horseback. ... As we passed farther in among the hills, the vegetation increased, both as to size and quantity; it, however, never amounted to much. As we approached the higher part of the hilly district, we saw some hills that were, to some extent, covered with the olives. A ride of between two and three hours, from the time we entered the hill country, brought us to the higher part of the district. Our road still lay along what may be called a hollow, and on each side of us the hills rose to a considerable size. We passed on this high district one or two villages. In one of them were some pretty good houses. ... The country around was in a better state of cultivation.']

SECTION 3.—THE BIRTH AND CIRCUMCISION OF JOHN THE BAPTIST, AND HIS PRIVATE HISTORY. Luke i. 57—80.

(G. 7.) *The Birth of John, &c. Luke i. 57—79. In the Hill Country of Judæa.*

57 Now Elisabeth's full-time-came that-she-should-be-delivered; and she-brought-forth
58 a-son. And her neighbours and her cousins heard how the-Lord had-shewed-great mercy εμεγαλυνε το ελεος upon her; and they-rejoiced-with her.
59 And it-came-to-pass, *that* on the eighth day they-came to-circumcise the child; and

SCRIPTURE ILLUSTRATIONS.

58. *rejoiced with her*—foretold, Lu. i. 14, § 1, p. 4—compare birth of Isaac, Ge. xxi. 6—rejoicing at the birth of Zion's children, Is. lxvi. 8—13—compare with Ro. vii. 9, 10.

59. *eighth day*—commanded Abraham, Ge. xvii. 12—children of Israel, Le. xii. 3—Jews' strictness in observing the letter of the law, Jno. vii. 22, 3, § 55—neglected the spirit of it, Ac. vii. 51—done away in Christ, Ga. vi. 12—7.

NOTES.

[59. *Circumcise*. To distinguish Abraham's family from others; to seal the new covenant to them, and their obligation to keep the laws thereof; and to represent the removal of their natural corruption, by the blood and Spirit of Jesus Christ, in virtue of his resurrection,—on the eighth day, God appointed that all the males in Abraham's family should be circumcised, and that his posterity should afterwards be circumcised on the eighth day of their life.—*See* Ge. xvii. 10—27; xxi. 4.

The uncircumcised child was to be *cut off* from his people; but that threatening seems not to have affected the child, till he was grown up, and wilfully neglected that ordinance of God for himself, Ge. xvii. 14. For the last 38 years of their abode in the desert, the Hebrew children were not circumcised. Just after the Hebrews passed the Jordan, their males were all circumcised; this is called a circumcision of them the *second time*, as, on this occasion, the institution was again revived, after it had long gone into disuse: and it was a *rolling away of the reproach of Egypt*; God hereby declared they were his free people, and heirs of the promised land, and removed from them what they reckoned the shame of the Egyptians, Jos. v. 1—10. No man is a whit more readily accepted of God, or saved by him, that is either a Jew or a Gentile, 1 Co. vii. 19; Ga. v. 6; vi. 15.

Beside the outward *circumcision of the flesh*, we find an inward one mentioned, which is what was signified by the other. It consists in God's changing of our state and natures, through the application of the blood and Spirit of his Son. By this we are made God's peculiar people, have our corruptions mortified, and our souls disposed to his service; and, for this reason, the saints are called the *circumcision*, while the Jews, with their outward circumcision, are, in contempt, called the *concision*, Ph. iii. 2, 3.]

PRACTICAL REFLECTIONS.

57 ver. Let us rest assured that, at the full time, the word of God will be truly accomplished.

58 ver. We should rejoice at seeing the good which our God is pleased to bestow upon others.

SECT. III. ZACHARIAS PROPHESIES. PART I.

60 they-called him Zacharias, after the name of his father. And his mother answered
61 and-said, Not so; but he-shall-be-called John. And they-said unto her, There-is none
62 of thy kindred that is-called by-this name. And they-made-signs to his father, how
63 he-would have-'him'-called. And he-asked-for a-writing-table, and wrote, saying, His
64 name is John. And they-marvelled all. And his mouth was-opened immediately, and
65 his tongue *loosed*, and he-spake, and-praised God. And fear came on all that dwelt-
round-about them: and all these sayings were-noised-abroad throughout all the hill-
66 country of Judea. And all they that-heard *them* laid-*them*-up in their hearts, saying,
What-manner-of child shall-'this'-be! And the-hand of-the-Lord was with him.
67 And his father Zacharias was-filled with-the-Holy Ghost, and prophesied, saying,
68 Blessed be the-Lord God^a of Israel; for he-hath-visited and redeemed^b εποιησε λυτρωσιν

MARGINAL READINGS:—^a Jehovah the God. ^b Wrought redemption.

SCRIPTURE ILLUSTRATIONS.

64. *mouth was opened*—as foretold, Lu. i. 20, § 1, p. 5—promise of opening of the mouth, to Ezekiel, Ch. xxix. 21—the *fulfilment*, xxxiii, 22—vision sealed up, Is. xxix. 10–2—at length shall speak, Hab. ii. 2, 3 —the new song then to be sung, Is. xlii. 9–12—compore with Re. v. 10–4.

66. *hand of the Lord*—was with Joseph, Ge. xxxix.

2, 3—with disciples in preaching to the Gentiles, Ac. xi. 21—see farther as to, Lu. i. 80, § 3, p. 19.

68. *blessed the Lord God of Israel*—same, 1 Ki. i. 48; Ps. xli. 13—new covenant blessing promised to Israel, Je. xxxi. 31–4; Eze. xxxiv. 30—only to be enjoyed in Christ, Ga. iii. 13–29—sure to Israel, Is. xli. 8–10— their rejoicing when the vision is opened, Is. xlii.9–16.

NOTES.

59. *And they called him Zacharias.* The *name of* the child was commonly given at the time of circumcision, Ge. xxi. 3, 4. We find no instance in the ancient scriptures of any person in Israel who was called after the name of his father; but it seems to have become customary, as in the case of Herod.

60. *John.* Means '*Grace of Jehovah*'—the peculiar character of that dispensation John came to introduce, wherein God's grace shines more bright than ever.

63. *A writing table,* π. *τabλίον,* 'a tablet;' a diminutive of π. *τabλα,* 'a table.' 'A little table,' such as they used to write not only upon, but in, using a stylus or pen. The ancients frequently wrote on a thin board or lead smeared over with wax.

64. *His mouth, &c.* That is, he was enabled to speak. With true gratitude, he offered praise to God; for the birth of a son, a pledge of the speedy coming of the Messiah.

65. *And fear came, &c.* The word fear often denotes *religious reverence.* The remarkable circumstances attending the birth of John, and the fact that Zacharias was suddenly restored to speech, convinced them that GOD was there, and filled their minds with awe and veneration.

[*Sayings.* Rather 'things,' comprehending both what was said and done; ρημα, having here, as in ver. 37, and other places, the sense of 'matter,' 'affair,' 'transaction.']

66. *The hand of the Lord was with him.* Denoting

God's special favour to John, watching over and protecting him.

67. *Prophesied.* The word is to be taken here in its proper acceptation as predicting future events, for Zacharias speaks by inspiration both of what God had done and what he was about to do.

68. *Hath visited.* ' Ruth visited with his mercy or favour.' The metaphor is derived either, as is commonly supposed, from the custom of princes to visit the provinces of their kingdom to redress grievances and to confer benefits; or rather from the visiting of the distressed by the benevolent, to afford them relief. God looked upon the world—He saw it miserable—He came to relieve it, and brought salvation.—*See* 78 ver.

And redeemed. That is, was *about to redeem,* or had given the pledge that He *would redeem.* This was spoken under the belief that the Messiah, *the Redeemer,* was about to appear, and would certainly accomplish his work. [The literal translation of this passage is, ' He hath made redemption, or *ransom,* for his people.' A ransom was the price paid to deliver a captive taken in war. God gave his Son a ransom, to shew his love; his justice; and his willingness to save men; and his Son in his death was a ransom. Jesus is often so called in the New Testament.—*See* Mt. xx. 28, § 77; Mk. x. 45, *ib.* '*Who gave himself for us, that he might redeem us from all iniquity, and purify unto himself a peculiar people, zealous of good works,*' Tit. ii. 14. '*Neither by the blood of goats and calves, but by his own blood he entered in once into the holy place, having obtained eternal redemption for us,*' He. ix. 12.]

PRACTICAL REFLECTIONS.

[60, 1 *ver.* Let us, with Elisabeth, regard the Lord's favours rather as tokens of his grace, than as remembrancers of the creature, however near and dear; she would not call her child Zacharias, after his father, but John, 'grace of the Lord.']

63, 4 *ver.* Those who are thankful for the favour received, will have that for which to be thankful to God. To them he giveth more grace, as he did to Elisabeth; who not only had the promised son, but also her husband restored to intelligent communion with her in the deep and delightful things of God.

Blessing is to be found in the way of obedience. Zacharias had suffered through not believing the promises which had been delivered to him by Gabriel; teaching us that it is not enough for us to believe in prophecies after they have been fulfilled, but simply as being announced of God. [Nor may we limit the power of God, so as to question his ability to do that which he hath said. This unbelief it is which hath made many of the servants of God comparatively dumb.—Let us pray that soon may be brought forth, according to the oath of our God, the children of promise; and soon may the mouths of the Lord's remembrancers be opened, as in the case of Zacharias, to declare the high praises of the Lord.]

[66 *ver.* Let us not merely talk of the wonderful workings of God with his people, but also lay them up in our hearts, and look forward to the farther results.]

67 *ver.* The word of prophecy is not to be regarded as the word of man, but as dictated by the Holy Ghost, and so may be expected to go beyond the ordinary conceptions or understanding of the individual who uttered it.

68–79 *ver.* Zacharias is no more doubtful as to the fulfilment of the prophecies; but sings of their accomplishment as if it had already come. He looks forward to the time when the vision shall indeed speak, and to the times of restitution, which have been spoken of by all the holy prophets since the world began; and especially to the promises written in the names of himself and his wife Elisabeth, '*To remember his holy covenant; the oath which he sware to our father Abraham.*' [He also alludes to the deliverance he will yet effect for Israel, from the hand of their enemies, when he will grant unto them to serve him, without fear, in holiness and righteousness before him, all the days of their life,— the salvation and the grace spoken of in the names of Jesus and John, are the beginning and ending of the song.]

68 *ver.* God in his prophetic word speaks of those things that are not yet, as though they already were; as here when Zacharias gives thanks for God's having visited and redeemed his people, although Jesus was not yet born, and the day of redemption was yet future.

HE THAT HANDLETH A MATTER WISELY SHALL FIND GOOD.—Prov. xvi. 20.

PART I.   ZACHARIAS PROPHESIES.   SECT. III.

69 his people. And hath-raised-up un-horn of-salvation for-us in the house of-his ser-
70 vant⁵ David ; as he-spake by the-mouth of his holy prophets, which *have-been-since-*
71 the-world '-began αn' αιωνος: that-we-should-be-saved from ʰ σωτηριαν εξ our enemies,
72 and from the-hand of-all that hate us ; to-perform ⁱ the-mercy *promised to ποιησαι*
73 ελεος μετα our fathers, and to-remember his holy covenant ; the-oath which he-sware
74 to our father Abraham, that-he-would-grant ᵏ του δουναι unto-us, that-we-being-delivered
75 out-of the-hand of-our enemies might-serve him without-fear, in holiness and righteous-

MARGINAL READINGS:—ᵍ Child. ʰ Salvation from, &c. ⁱ To effect mercy with. ᵏ Of which to give us.

SCRIPTURE ILLUSTRATIONS.

68. *visited*—Israel in Egypt, Ex. iii. 16—God visiting man, Ps. viii. 4—visited his flock, the house of
Judah, but Jerusalem knew not the time of her
visitation, Lu. xix. 44, §82—compare Je. xiv. 8—shall
see him again when prepared to receive him, Zep. iii.
12—7.

Redeemed—sent redemption unto his people, Ps.
cxi 9—their redemption contemplated, Is. lxiii. 1—13
—joy of the redeemed people, Is. xxxv. 10 ; li. 11—
their Redeemer, liv. 5, 8—their redemption consummated in the resurrection, Ho. xiii. 14 ; 1 Co. xv. 54, 5.

69. *horn*, Ps. lxxxix. 3, 4, 23, 4 ; cxxxii. 17.

70. *as he spake*—Israel spake of the people who
should enjoy the blessing of redemption, Ge. xlviii.
14—22—of their Redeemer to come of Judah, xlix.
8—10—Moses spake of the promised salvation, De.
xxxiii. 26—9—David spake, 2 Sa. xxiii. 2—5—words

of the prophets confirmed by Christ, Lu. xxiv. 25, 7,
§ 94—by Peter, Ac. iii. 11—21 ; 2 Pe. i. 21—by the angel
of Jesus, Re. xix. 10.

71. *saved from*—prediction, Is. xlv. 22 ; Je. xxiii. 6 ;
xxx. 8 ; Eze. xxxiv. 25—the salvation was to be by
him who first came lowly and riding upon an ass,
Zec. ix. 9.

72. *remember—see* Sect. 1. pp. 2, 7, ' *Zacharias*'—
promise to remember his covenant to Jacob, &c., Le.
xxvi. 42—5—with Jerusalem, Eze. xvi. 60—3—the
Lord's remembrance of his covenant rejoiced in, Ps.
xcviii 3 ; cv. 8—11—*see* ver. 54, 5—*confirmation*, Ac.
iii. 25, 6 ; Ga. iii. 15—7.

73. *the oath—see* Scripture Illustrations, p. 3, '*Elisabeth,*' Ge. xxii. 16—8—*see* Notes—*confirm*., He. vi. 13.

74. *without fear*—nothing to hurt or destroy, Is.
lxv. 25—not learn war any more, Is. ii. 4 ; Mi. iv. 3—
confirmation, Ro. viii. 19—21.

NOTES.

69. *An horn of salvation.* The metaphor may be
derived from *horned animals*, whose strength is in
their horns: hence ' horn ' was a term commonly
used to denote strength, and thus became an emblem
of power and principality.

[On each of the four corners of the altar there
was an eminence, or small projection, called a *horn*.
To this, persons might flee for safety, when in danger, and were safe, 1 Ki. i. 50 ; ii. 28. So the Redeemer may be called the ' horn of salvation,' because
those who flee to him are safe.]

In the house. In the *family*, or among the descendants of David.

70. *Since the world began.* All true prophets, from
the beginning of the world, bare witness to the coming Messiah. ' The testimony of Jesus is the spirit
of prophecy.'

72. *To perform the mercy.* To shew the mercy
promised. The expression in the original is, ' to
make mercy with our fathers.' Which seems to
point forward to the great result of the work of
redemption, through Christ, when all true believers
shall sit down with Abraham, Isaac, and Jacob, in
the kingdom of God.

His holy covenant. The word covenant means
compact, or agreement. When the word *covenant*
is used in the Bible, it means sometimes *a command*,
sometimes a *promise*, sometimes a *regular law*, as
the covenant of the day and night, and sometimes the
way in which God dispenses mercy, or the old and
new covenants. In the place before us it means *the
promise* made to Abraham.

73. *The oath.* This oath is recorded, Ge. xxii. 16—8.
16, ' *By myself have I sworn, saith the LORD, for because thou hast done this thing, and hast not withheld
thy son, thine only son ;* 17. *That in blessing I will
bless thee, and in multiplying I will multiply thy seed
as the stars of the heaven, and as the sand which is
upon the sea shore ; and thy seed shall possess the gate
of his enemies ;* 18. *And in thy seed shall all the nations
of the earth be blessed ; because thou hast obeyed my
voice.*' That oath was fully confirmed by the coming

of Messias, through whom the promised mercy will
be fully bestowed.

[The *oath* and the *memorial* of the Lord do both
express the same three things, as may be seen by
comparing them thus :—The *first* name, Abraham,
corresponds with the *first* part of the oath : the *third*
name, Jacob, with the *second* part, which respects
the supplanting of the enemy ; and the *second* name,
Isaac, is expressive of the *third* and concluding part
of the oath, which speaks of universal happiness as
administered through the promised seed.

Zacharias, | Elisabeth,
Memorial of the Lord, | *Oath of my God*, Ge. xxii.
Ex. iii. 14, 5. | 16—8.
' I AM THAT I AM.' | ' By myself have I sworn,
' The LORD God of your | saith the LORD, for be-
fathers.' | cause thou hast done
  | this thing, and hast not
  | withheld thy son, thine
  | only son :
' *The God of Abraham*,' | That in blessing I will
The father of a great | bless thee, and in mul-
multitude. | tiplying I will multiply
  | thy seed as the stars of
  | the heaven, and as the
  | sand which *is* upon the
  | sea shore ;
' *And of Jacob*,' | And thy seed shall pos-
The supplanter. | sess the gate of his
  | enemies.
' *Of Isaac*,' | And in thy seed shall all
Laughter, or great re- | the nations of the earth
joicing. | be blessed ; because
' This *is* my name for | thou hast obeyed my
ever, and this *is* my | voice.'
memorial unto all ge-
nerations.'

74. *Without fear.* In the sure hope of God's eternal
favour ; fully confiding in his Almighty protection.
God must be served with a filial, but not a slavish,
fear — without the spirit of bondage. Ro. viii. 15,
' *For ye have not received the spirit of bondage again
to fear ;* but we have received the Spirit of adoption,
whereby we cry, Abba, Father.'

PRACTICAL REFLECTIONS.

[69 *ver.* When Israel's redemption shall take place,
an horn of salvation upon which the shedder of
blood may lay hold, will be recognised by the Jew, in
Him, who by wicked hands was crucified and slain.]

70 *ver.* Let us never neglect to recognise the unity
of the prophetic word as testifying of Jesus.

[71 *ver.* When Jesus hath saved his people from
their sins and brought Judah to the cross, he will
also be their salvation from their enemies ; and he

will remove from off them the band that hath afflicted them.]

72 *ver.* The promised redemption to Israel reaches
not only to the soul but to the body ; not only to the
children but the fathers.

[73 *ver.* Our Lord having visited his people was
not to break, but to remember, his holy covenant,
the oath which he sware to our father Abraham ;
of the promises made in which oath, we should be
the Lord's remembrancers.]

REJOICE THE SOUL OF THY SERVANT.—Psalm lxxxvi. 4.   [17

SECT. III.   ZACHARIAS PROPHESIES.   PART I.

76 ness before him, all the days of our life.* And thou, child, shalt-be-called the prophet of-the-Highest: for thou-shalt-go before the-face of-the-Lord^m to-prepare his
77 ways ; to give knowledge of-salvation unto his people by the-remissionⁿ *en aphesei* of-
78 their sins, through the-tender mercy^o *dia splanchna eleous* of our God; whereby^p *en ois*
79 the-day-spring^q *anatolē* from on-high hath-visited us, to-give-light *epiphanai* to-them that-sit in darkness and in the-shadow of-death, to-guide our feet into the-way of-peace.

MARGINAL READINGS:—*l* All our days.   ^m (Without the article of Jehovah).   ⁿ In forgiveness.
^o Bowels of compassion.   ^p In which.   ^q Sun-rising.

SCRIPTURE ILLUSTRATIONS.

75. *holiness and righteousness*—law to be written in the hearts of his united people, Je. xxxi. 31–3—he that remaineth in Jerusalem to be holy, Is. iv. 3—the people to be all righteous, Ix. 21—*confirmation*, Ep. i. 4; iv. 21; 2 Ti. i. 9.

76. *go before the face of the Lord*—as predicted, Is. xl. 3; Mal. iii. 1—*confirmation*, Mt. iii. 1–12, Mk. i. 1–8; Lu. iii. 3–6, § 7; vii. 27, 8, Mt. xi. 10, .1, § 29.

77. *remission of sins*—to be proclaimed, Je. iii. 12, 3 —promised, xxxi. 34—to many, Is. liii. 11—*confirmation*, Jno. i. 29, § 10—Jesus exalted to give repentance to Israel, and forgiveness of sins, Ac. v. 31—preached to Cornelius, x. 43—proclaimed by Paul in Pisidia, xiii. 23–39—before Agrippa, xxvi. 18—through the shedding of blood, He. ix. 22—by faith, Ro. iii. 21, 5—according to grace, Ep. i. 7.

78. *tender mercy* — the Lord's relentings over Ephraim, Je. xxxi. 20; Ho. xiii. 11—prayer for t. m., xiv. 8—*confirmation*: the reception of the prodigal,

Lu. xv. 20, § 68—God commendeth his love toward us, Ro v 7, 8—gave his only-begotten Son, Jno. iii. 16, § 12; 1 Jno. iv. 9—rich in mercy, Ep. ii. 4, 5.

day-spring—prediction, Mal. iv. 2—*confirmation*, Jno. viii. 12, § 55; Re. xxii. 16.

79. *to give light!*—prediction: the light, Is. ix. 2— the darkness, to become light, xiii. 16—thy light is come, lx. 1–3—*confirmation*: Simeon's, Lu. ii. 26–32, § 4, p. 24—John Baptist's, Jno. i. 9, § 7—Paul's, Ac. xxvi. 23; 2 Co. iv. 4–6; Ep. v. 8, 14.

shadow of death, Ps. cvii. 10. 4; Is. ix 2-valley of dry bones, Eze. xxxvii. 1–14; Am. v. 8.

guide—promised, Is. xlviii. 17–22; xlix. 10—they shall ask this guidance with true repentance, and their faces Zionward, Je. l. 4, 5—and, asking, they shall obtain, xxxi. 9—taking heed according to the word, Ps. cxix. 1—*confirm.*: the good Shepherd, Jno. x. 4–16, § 55; 1 Pe. ii. 21—5; Re. vii. 17; xiv. 1–5.

NOTES.

75. *In holiness and righteousness.* In holy devotedness of heart and life towards God, and in all uprightness of conduct towards man.

Before him. Performed as in his presence, and with the full consciousness that God sees the heart. Such as God would approve.

All the days, &c. Not for a day or two, or only on festivals and sabbath days, as under the Jewish dispensation, but every day we live.

76. *And thou, child, &c.* Zacharias predicts in this and the following verses, the dignity and the employment of John; the subject and success of his preaching.

Face of the Lord. ' The Lord Jesus Christ,' whose prophet, harbinger, and forerunner, John was; and so is a proof of Christ being the Supreme, or Most High God.

[In this verse, and following verses, we have a remarkable prophecy respecting the dignity, office, and success of John; also describing the nature, privileges, and effects of the gospel, and foretelling its salvation both among Jews and Gentiles]

To prepare his ways. This is taken from Is. xl. 3, ' The voice of him that crieth in the wilderness, Prepare ye the way of the Lord, make straight in the desert a highway for our God.'

77. *Knowledge of salvation.* Knowledge of Jesus, who is the *way of salvation*; and of that manner of life unto which men are saved, who in truth are led unto the Author of salvation, who was then about to appear.

By the remission of their sins. The word remission means *pardon.* This implies that the *salvation* about to be offered, was that which was connected with the pardon of sin.

[78. *Whereby the day-spring, &c.* The word *dayspring* means the morning light, the aurora, the

rising of the sun. God is its author, and through his mercy it shines on men. Christ is the morning light, the rising sun, Mal. iv. 2, ' But unto you that fear my name shall the Sun of righteousness arise with healing in his wings; and ye shall go forth, and grow up as calves of the stall.' As the dawn or day-spring is the pledge of the coming glory of the natural sun, so is the birth of the Lord Jesus a sure pledge of the coming of the Sun of Righteousness—even the same blessed Lord, to reign in great power and glory.—See 2 Ti. i. 10, ' But is now made manifest by the appearing of our Saviour Jesus Christ, who hath abolished death, and hath brought life and immortality to light through the gospel.']

79. *In darkness and in the shadow of death.* Terms expressive of a sad and miserable condition. [: Sa. xxii. 29, ' For thou . . . my lamp, O Lord: and the Lord will lighten my darkness.' Is. viii. 22; Ps. xliv. 19, ' Though thou hast sore broken us in the place of dragons, and covered us with the shadow of death.' Job iii. 5; Ps. cvii. 10, 4. 10, ' Such as sit in darkness and in the shadow of death, . . . bound in affliction and iron; 14, He brought them out of darkness and the shadow of death, and brake their bands in sunder.' And Is. ix. 1.]

To guide our feet, &c. The figure in these verses is taken from travellers, who being overtaken by night know not what to do, and who wait patiently for the morning light, the rising of the sun, that they may know which way to go.—See Is. xlix. 9–12.

[This song of Zacharias is exceedingly beautiful. It expresses with elegance the great points of the plan of redemption, the doings of John, and the mercy of God in providing that plan. That mercy was great. It is worthy of praise; of our highest, loftiest songs of thanksgiving; for we were in the shadow of death—sinful, wretched, wandering—and the light arose, the gospel came, and men may rejoice in hope of eternal life.]

PRACTICAL REFLECTIONS.

[73. *4 ver.* How kind is our God in assisting our remembrance, by writing his promises, not only in words, but in the names of himself and his people! Zacharias having paraphrased the name Jesus, the Saviour, now refers to his own name, 'memorial, or remembrance of the Lord,' and Elisabeth, 'oath of my God,' and then dwells upon that of his child John, that is, 'grace, or what is granted or given of Jehovah.']

74. *5 ver.* Let us earnestly seek to be favoured with the deliverance which is yet to be granted unto

Israel, even that we may serve our God without dread of the enemy, in holiness and righteousness, before the Lord, all the days of our Life.

76 *ver.* If the ways were to be prepared for the Lord as coming in humiliation, how much more should we desire their preparation for his appearing in glory?—That which John preached, the gracious manifestation of practical charity, is one of the best preparations for the coming of Him who gloried in this characteristic of his ministry. ' To the poor the gospel is preached,' Lu. vii 22, § 20.

THERE IS NO RESPECT OF PERSONS WITH GOD.—Rom. ii. 11.

PART I.   JOSEPH AND MARY GO TO BE TAXED.   SECT. IV.

(G. 8.) *The residue of the private history of John the Baptist.* Luke i. 80.
In the Wilderness of Judæa, East of Jordan.

80 And the child grew, and waxed-strong in-spirit, and was in the deserts till the day of-his-shewing αναδείξεως unto Israel.

SCRIPTURE ILLUSTRATIONS.

80. *grew*—see the same of Samson, Ju. xiii 24, 5—of Samuel, 1 Sa. iii. 19–21—Jesus, Lu. ii. 40–52, § 6. *deserts*—the call to repentance, and comforting promised to be given in the wilderness, Ho. ii. 14; Eze. xx. 35–7; Is. xl. 1, 3—*confirmation*, Mt. iii. 1, &c., § 7; xl. 7, § 29.

NOTES.

80. *Strong in spirit.* Has been supposed to mean, 'remarkable for strength of intellect and boldness of resolution, and his attainments in religious knowledge:' but we are to recollect that John was to be filled with the Holy Ghost even from his mother's womb; and it is not unlikely that the truth of this prediction became more and more manifest. *In the deserts.* The period of his retirement was probably when he would have strength of body and mind to bear that solitude, which for him was so necessary. In that seclusion he would not be warped by the prejudices of the Jewish teachers; and would moreover approach unto God, and seek that guidance of the Holy Spirit, which was indispensable to enable him to be the herald of the gospel.

His shewing, &c. [αναδείξεως The word αναδείξις is used for the entering upon an office to which any one has been previously appointed.] Until his manifestation unto Israel, Lu. viii. 33—5. Until he entered on his public ministry, as recorded in Matt. iii., § 7. That is, probably, until he was about thirty years of age.—*See* Luke iii. 23, § 9, *of Jesus' age at baptism.*

GEOGRAPHICAL NOTICES.

HILL COUNTRY OF JUDEA.—*See* Sect. ii., p. 14. | DESERTS.—*See* '*Wilderness of Judea,*' Sect. vii. § 50.

SECTION 4.—MESSIAH IS BORN AT BETHLEHEM; HIS BIRTH IS ANNOUNCED BY AN ANGEL TO THE SHEPHERDS; THE SHEPHERDS GO TO BETHLEHEM; HE IS CIRCUMCISED AND CALLED JESUS; THE GENEALOGIES OF CHRIST; HE IS PRESENTED IN THE TEMPLE; SIMEON AND ANNA BEAR WITNESS TO HIM. Matt. i. 1–18, 25; Luke ii. 1–38; iii. 23–38.

(G. 9.) *The Messiah born.* Luke ii. 1–7. *At Bethlehem.*

1 And it-came-to-pass in those days, *that* there-went-out a-decree from Cæsar Augustus,
2 that all-the world οἰκουμενην-should-be-taxed.   (*And* this taxing was-*first*-made
3 when-*Cyrenius* was-governor of-Syria.)   And all went to-be-taxed, every-one into
4 his-own city.   And Joseph also went-up from Galilee, out-of-the-city of-Nazareth, into
Judæa, unto the-city of-David, which is-called Bethlehem; (because he was of-the-house

SCRIPTURE ILLUSTRATIONS.

1. *Joseph*, Mt. i. 18—the name means 'adding' or 'increase,' Ge. xxx. 24—' The LORD shall add to me another son.' *Bethlehem*—Rachel died in the way to Ephrath, 'fruit bearing,' which is Bethlehem, 'house of bread'—there he who is the bread of life, Jno. vi. 48–51, § 43, was brought forth. It appears to have been also the birth-place of David, who was chosen to feed Jacob his people, and Israel his inheritance, 1 Sa. xvi. 1, 13; Ps. lxxviii. 70–2—David's appearance in the camp of Israel was as conveying bread to his brethren there, 1 Sa. xvii. 17—*see* as to Boaz, Ru. ii. 4; iv. 11—prediction, Mi. v. 2—*confirmation*, Mt. ii. 1–6, § 5; Jno. vii. 42, § 55.

NOTES.

1. *In those days.* About the time of the birth of John and of Christ. *A decree.* A law, commanding a thing to be done. *Cæsar Augustus.* [This was Caius Cæsar Octavianus Augustus. (*Augustus*—i. e., *august*, or honourable—as a compliment to his own greatness, and from him the month *August*, which was before called *Sextilis*, received its name.) he was proclaimed Emperor of Rome B.C. 29, died A D 14.   He had received the name of Cæsar from Julius Cæsar by adoption; and by that name were called, first, all those of the family of Augustus, afterwards the heirs of the empire, and finally the emperors themselves.]
All the world. The whole commonwealth. The Jews called Judæa the world *of all the earth.* *Should be taxed.* Our word *tax* means to levy and raise money for the use of the government. This is not the meaning of the original word here. It means rather to *enrol*, or take a *list* of the citizens, with their employments, equivalent to what was meant by *census.* (An enrolment *per capita* would necessarily require the Jews to repair to the places where their genealogical records were kept; a valuation of property would have been made only where they were residing and had possessions.)

[' To decide upon its nature, or its object, regarded as a state measure of the reigning emperor, may be extremely difficult; but its use, in a providential point of view, is too obvious to be mistaken. The safest course is to understand the words of St. Luke, as a parenthetic admonition not to confound this ἀπογραφη at the birth of Christ, with the much later, and much more memorable, ἀπογραφη in the time of Cyrenius. Such an admonition was both necessary in itself, and justly to be expected from the accuracy of this Evangelist. In this case, the text must be rendered, *This enrolment took place before Cyrenius was governor of Syria.*'—*See* Greswell, vol. I. Diss. xiv. pp. 531–546.]

3. *His own city.* The city which formerly belonged to his family.

4. *The city of David.* Bethlehem, called the city of David because it was the place of his birth.—*See* Nt. ii. 1, § 5, p. 31.

Bethlehem. 'The House of Bread;' and he who was born there is called the 'Bread of Life.'

PRACTICAL REFLECTIONS.

(Lu. ii.) The movements of the mightiest empires are overruled so as that the words of God shall be fulfilled in their season. On account of the decree of the Roman Emperor, Joseph and Mary were brought to Bethlehem, where Jesus should be born. 1 *ser.* That which seems to be grievous oppression, as, in the circumstances— Mary's being compelled to make such a serious journey, God is able to overrule for the more effectual securing of our right, and procuring our deliverance.

BLESSED IS THE MAN WHOM THOU CHOOSEST &c.—Ps. lxv. 4.   [19

THIS IS THE LORD'S DOING; IT IS MARVELLOUS IN OUR EYES.—Psalm cxviii. 23.

5 and lineage of David:) to-be-taxed with Mary his espoused wife, being great-with-child.
6 And so-it-was, *that*, while they were there, the days were-accomplished that-'she'-
7 should-be-delivered. And she-brought-forth her first-born son, and wrapped-·him·-in-
swaddling-clothes, and laid him in a manger;ᵃ because there-was no room for-them in
the inn.

Jesus' birth is announced by an angel to the shepherds. Luke ii. 8—15.
In the fields of Bethlehem.

8 And there-were in the same country shepherds abiding-in-the-field, keeping watch
9 over their flock by-night. And, lo, the-angel of-the-Lord came-upon them, and the
10 glory of-the-Lord shone-round-about them: and they-were-·sore·-afraid. And the angel
said unto-them, Fear not: for, behold, I-bring-·you·-good-tidings of-great joy, which

MARGINAL READINGS:—ᵃ Shed or stable.

SCRIPTURE ILLUSTRATIONS.

7. *brought forth*—prediction, Is. vii. 14—the fulfilment, 'made of a woman,' Ga. iv. 4—became poor, that his people might be enriched, 2 Co. viii. 9—the word, who is God, was made flesh, (God with us,) Jno. i. 1, 14, § 7.

8. *shepherds*—Jacob was so occupied, Ge. xxxi. 39, 40—Moses, Ex. iii. 1—David, 1 Sa. xvi. 11—careless shepherds reproved, Is. lvi. 9, 10; Eze. xxxiv. 1—10—the good shepherd, Jno. x. 1—18, § 55.

9. *glory of the Lord*—its appearing to the children of Israel, Ex. xvi. 7, 10—its filling the temple, 1 Ki.

viii. 11—predict.: 'I will fill this house with glory,' Hag. ii. 7—*confirm.* Jno. ii. 13, § 12; Mt. xxi. 12, 3, § 83; xxv. 31, § 86—the brightness that appeared to Saul in the way, Ac. ix. 3; xxvi. 12—8—glory of God, 2 Co. iv. 6.

10. *you*—Jews: the gospel was first to be preached unto Jews, and of them were made the first heralds of salvation, Zec. x. 3; xii. 7; Ac. ii.; xi. 19· xiii. 46, 7.

tidings of great joy—good tidings predicted, Is. xl. 9; xli. 27; lii. 7; lxi. 1—*confirmation,* Lu. iv. 17—21, § 15; Re. xiv. 1—6; xxi. 3—7.

NOTES.

4. *Of the house and lineage.* The *lineage* denotes that he was descended from David as his father, or ancestor.

[In taking a *Jewish* census, families were kept distinct. Hence all went into the *tribe* to which they belonged, and to the *place* where their family had resided. Joseph was of the *tribe* of Judah, and of the particular family of David. Hence he went up to the city of David. Thus an overruling providence fulfilled the prophecy, Mi. v. 2.—*See* 'Reflections,' p. 19.

5. *With Mary.* This also would be an additional proof that Mary was of the same tribe, since she could not marry out of it.]

Espoused wife.—See 'Espoused,' p. 13.

7. *First-born.* The eldest son, or he that by the law had the privilege of the birthright.

[Whether Mary had any other children or not has been a matter of controversy. The obvious meaning of the Bible is that she had; and if this be the case, the word *first-born* is here to be taken in its common acceptation.]

Wrapped him, &c. When a child among the Hebrews was born, it was washed in water, rubbed with salt, and then wrapped in swaddling clothes; that is, not garments regularly made, as with us, but bands or blankets that confined the limbs closely, Eze. xvi. 4. There was nothing peculiar in the way in which the infant Jesus was treated.

Laid him in a manger. The word *manger*, in the English language, means 'the box or trough in which provender is placed for horses or cattle.' This is not the meaning of the word here. It means simply the *stable*, or the place where the *cattle* and *camels* lodged. The Easterns have no mangers, for they have no hay, but lay their fodder in stone troughs. There was no room in the *inn*, and they were obliged to lie in the

stable, and it was there that the child was laid. It might be either an enclosed court, or a collection of caves or stables in the rock, according to tradition. Their being there was no *proof* of poverty. It was a simple matter of necessity: there was *no room* in the inn. It may be added, that in eastern countries, in the *caravansary*, it is common for the whole caravan of camels, horses, and people, to lodge in the same place. Indeed, the only *pillow* which children often have is the side of a horse, with which the whole family lie down. Horses are trained to remarkable gentleness and docility.

In the inn. 'In the house of strangers.'

6. *The same country.* Round about. Bethlehem was a place of pasture. Here David kept his father's sheep, 1 Sa. xvii. 15.

Shepherds abiding in the fields, &c. Remaining out of doors, under the open sky, with their flocks. This was commonly done. The climate was mild; and, to keep their flocks from straying, they spent the night with them. It is also a fact that the Jews sent out their flocks into the mountainous and desert regions during the summer months, and took them up in the latter part of October or the first of November, when the cold weather commenced.

Keeping watch. Tending their flocks by turns through the night watches; each three hours in turn, to preserve the sheep from beasts of prey, and from banditti.

9. *Angel of the Lord.* Probably Gabriel, who stands in the presence of God.—*See* ver. 19, § i., p. 5; § ii., p. 9.

The glory of the Lord. The extreme splendour in which the Deity is represented as appearing unto men; and sometimes called the Shechinah, an appearance frequently attended, as in this case, by a company of angels.—*See* 'Scrip. Illus.,' above.

PRACTICAL REFLECTIONS.

7 *ver.* The condition of the poor is not to be despised, therein 'the Son of the Highest' was born. Privations are not always the sign of the Lord's displeasure; for amid these, at the birth of her firstborn, was found Mary, the highly-favoured of the Lord.—Let us be content with such things as we have; and make the best use of the circumstances in which we are placed.—Let us not be forgetful to entertain strangers, and assist them in their necessities: it would have been an honour to any in Bethlehem who had kindly received the neglected family from Nazareth! Christ, who is the Bread of Life, was to be born in Bethlehem, which name means '*the house of bread.*' This had been predicted, Mi. v. 2. Out of thence was to come forth, as being man, He whose goings orth, as being God, are from everlasting.

[8 *ver.* It is good to be watchful even in worldly duty. It was thus the shepherds enjoyed the sight of the glory of the Lord, when, after long absence, it returned to the earth, now, that He who previously dwelt in the cloud of glory, was to tabernacle with man in human flesh.]

8, 9 *ver.* It is good to be found diligent in business, and faithful to our charge, as were the shepherds, when called to a higher service and a rich participation in the joys of heaven.

The children of God are often, like the shepherds, sore afraid when they have the least occasion to be so.

[10 *ver.* How gracious is the command 'Fear not;' and true ground have they for obeying the command, who repose their confidence in the incarnate Son of God.]

PRAISE YE THE LORD.

PART I.   THE ANGELS GO AWAY INTO HEAVEN.   SECT. IV.

11 shall-be to-all people.*a* For unto-you is-born this-day in the-city of-David a-Saviour, 12 which is Christ*b* the-Lord. And this *shall be* a sign*c* το σημειον unto-you; Ye-shall-13 find the-babe wrapped-in-swaddling-clothes, lying in a manger. And suddenly there-14 was with the angel a-multitude of-the-heavenly host praising God, and saying, Glory to-God in the-highest,*d* and on earth peace, good-will toward men.

15 And it-came-to-pass, as the angels were-gone-away from them into heaven, the shepherds said one-'to-'another, Let-us-'now'-go even-unto Bethlehem, and see this thing which is-come-to-pass, which the Lord hath-made-known unto-us.

MARGINAL READINGS:—*a* All the people.   *b* Messiah, or Anointed.   *c* The sign.   *d* Highest (places).

SCRIPTURE ILLUSTRATIONS.

10. *all people,* Ge. xii. 3; Ps. lxvii. 3; xcviii.; Is. xlix.—specially all the house of Israel, who, by the word and Spirit of God, were to be raised up and quickened, Eze. xxxvii. 11—.4 — 'in the countries where they shall come,' xi. 15, .6—the glad tidings sent after them toward the north, Je. iii. 11, .2—all the nations, &c., ver. 17—*confirmation:* 'Go, teach all nations,' Mt. xxviii. 18—20, § 96—preach the gospel to every creature,' Mk. xvi. 15, § 98—'whosoever,' Jno. iii. 16, § 12—reconcile all to himself, Col. i. 20—chief of sinners, 1 Ti. i. 15, .6—Christ Jesus, a ransom for all, a testimony in due time, 1 Ti. ii. 6—*see also* 2 Ti. ii. 11; 1 Jno. ii. 2; Re. vii. 1—4; xiv. 6.

11. *Christ the Lord,* Ge. xlix. 8—10; Ps. ii.; lxxxix. 15—37; ex. 1, 2, 4—*confirmation,* Mt. xvi. 16, § 50; Jno. i. 41, § 10; vi. 69, § 43—both Lord and Christ, Ac. ii. 36—Jesus is Christ, xvii. 3—'Christ, who is over all, God blessed for ever,' Ro. ix. 5—'every tongue should confess Jesus Christ to be the glory of God the Father,' Ph. ii. 4—11—thou art worthy, &c., Re. v. 8—10.

13. *multitude*—of the heavenly hosts: Jacob, the angels of God met him, and he said, 'This is God's host,' Ge. xxxii. 1, 2—'thousands of angels,' Ps. lxvii. 17—'Bless the Lord, ye, his angels,' Ps. ciii. 20, .1—'Praise ye him, all his angels, his hosts,' Ps. cxlviii. 2; Da. vii. 10—'worship him, all God's,' Ps. xcvii. 7—*confirmation:* 'when he bringeth again the first-begotten,' &c.; 'let all the angels of God worship him,' He. i. 6—voice of many angels, Worthy is the Lamb, &c., Re. v. 11, .2.

14. *glory to God in the highest*—'Sing, O ye heavens; for the Lord hath done ... hath redeemed Jacob, glorified himself in Israel,' Is. xliv. 23—'my servant, O Israel, in whom I will be glorified,' xlix. 3—'will place salvation in Zion for Israel my glory,' xlvi. 13—*confirm.:* 'he shall come to be glorified in his saints,' 2 Th. i. 10—*see also* Ro. viii. 17, .8—raised in glory, 1 Co. xv. 43—'hath raised ... up together, and made ... sit together in heavenly places in Christ Jesus,' Ep. ii. 6; Mt. xxv. 34, § 86; Re. iv. 6—8.

on *earth peace*—predicted, Ps. lxxii., cxlvii.—'the Lord hath sworn it,' Is. lxii. 8, 9—will prove a God of truth in this, lxv. 16—'unto us a son is given ... the Prince of Peace,' ix. 6—will extend peace, lxvi. 12—'will watch over them to build and to plant,' Je. xxxi. 27, .8—'a covenant of peace with them,' Eze. xxxvii. 26—*same,* Ho. ii. 18—23—*see also* Joel iii. 17, 8; Am. ix. 11—.5—shall speak peace to the nations, and his domin., &c., Zec. ix. 12—.7—*confirm.:* 'my peace I give unto you,' Jno. xiv. 27, § 87—'peace with God,' Rom. v. 1—'Christ 'is our peace', Ep. ii. 14, .5, .7—'made peace through the blood of his cross,' Col. i. 20—'the God of peace shall bruise Satan under your feet shortly,' Ro. xvi. 20—'will return and build again the tabernacle of David,' Ac. xv. 14—.8—'great multitude rejoicing in peace,' Ro. vii. 9—17—the creature delivered, Ro. viii. 19—22—every creature, Re. v. 13—the destroyers destroyed, xi. 18.

good will toward men—What is man, &c.? Ps. viii. 3—9—'O taste, and see that the Lord is good,' &c., Ps. xxxiv. 8—Bless the Lord, who forgiveth, redeemeth, satisfieth, vindicateth, hath made known and accomplisheth, forbeareth, removeth transgression, pitieth, considereth our weakness and mortality, bestows everlasting mercy, introduces to glory, Ps. ciii. —*confirm,* Jno. iii. 14, § 12—'rich in mercy,' Ep. ii. 4—7—reconciling the world unto himself, 2 Co. v. 19—'Herein is love,' 1 Jno. iv. 10—will take up men to be with him on his throne, Rev. iii. 21—will bring his dwelling place down to be with men, xxi. 3, 4.

15 *let us*—should invite one another to contemplate the Lord's fulfilment of his word, both as to judgment and mercy, Ps. xlvi. 8—10; Is. ii. 3—5; xlv. 21, .2—so Andrew brought his brother to Jesus, Jno. i. 41, .2, § 10—and Philip said to Nathanael, 'Come and see,' ver. 45, .6, § 10—so the Samaritan woman, ch. iv. 29, § 13—'let him that heareth say, Come,' Re. xxii. 17.

now go—so, many cities are yet to invite each other, saying, 'Let us go speedily;' 'I will go also,' &c., Zec. viii. 20—.2—the danger of delay exemplified in the foolish virgins, Mt. xxv. 10—.3, § 86.

NOTES.

11. *Christ the Lord.* The anointed One of God, chosen to be King in Zion.

12. *And this shall be a sign, &c.* The birth of Jesus, in the circumstances predicted, was an assured sign that God will fulfil all his promises as to the great salvation. It was the sign long before pointed out, as in Is. vii. 14, 'Therefore the Lord himself shall,' *&c.*

13. *Suddenly, &c.* As representing that which is to be the unexpected appearing in glory of Him, whose coming in humiliation was now made known. —*See* 1 Th. v. 2—9.

Heavenly host. Angels, who are ministering spirits, doing the will of God in heaven and earth.

14. *Glory to God.* That is, the praise for the redemption of man is due to God. The plan of redemption expresses his power and glory. It is the highest expression of His love and mercy.

In the highest. 'In the highest heaven.'—*See* Job xvi. 19. As the Jews reckoned three heavens, the highest was considered as the place of the throne of God.—*See* Mt. xxi. 9, § 82. The plural number is used in the original, because the Hebrew word for heaven is never in the singular.

On earth peace. That is, the gospel shall bring peace. The Saviour was predicted as the Prince of Peace, Is. ix. 6, 7. 'For unto us a child is,' *&c.*

[The world is at war with God: sinners are at enmity against their Maker, and against each other. But Jesus came to make peace. And this he did,

1st. By reconciling the world to God by his atonement. 2nd. By bringing the sinner to a state of peace with his Maker, inducing him to submit himself to God, and thus giving him the peace which passeth all understanding. 3rd. By diffusing in the heart universal good will to men. In the days of the long promised reign of Messiah, who is styled 'the Prince of Peace,' and under whose feet all things are to be placed, there will be universal peace; all the *causes* of war will have ceased; men will love each other, and do justly; and *notions* be brought under the influence of the royal law of LOVE.]

Good will toward men. The gift of the Saviour is an expression of good will or love to men, and therefore God is to be praised. [The work of redemption is uniformly represented as the fruit of the love of God, Jno. iii. 16, § 12; 1 Jno. iv. 10, 'Herein is love, not that we loved God, but that he loved us, and sent his Son to be a ... propitiation for our sins.' Ro. v. 5, 6. 5, 'And from Jesus Christ, ... the faithful witness, ... the first begotten of the dead, and the prince of the kings of the earth. Unto him that loved us, and washed us from our sins in his own blood, 6. And hath made us kings and priests unto God and his Father; to him ... glory and dominion for ever and ever. Amen.' No words can express the greatness of that love. It can only be measured by the condescension, sufferings, and death of Jesus; and by the eternal honour and happiness to which he will raise his people. Jesus is the full expression of the Father's good will.]

WHERE SIN ABOUNDED, GRACE DID MUCH MORE ABOUND.—Rom. v. 20.   [21

SECT. IV.   JESUS IS CIRCUMCISED AND NAMED.   PART I.

The shepherds go to Bethlehem. Luke ii. 16—20.

16 And they came with-haste, and found Mary, and Joseph, and the babe lying in a manger. And when-they-had-seen-it, they-made-known-abroad the saying which was-
18 told them concerning this child. And all they that-heard-it wondered at those-things which-were-told them by the shepherds.
19 But Mary kept all these things, and-pondered *-them συμβαλλουσα in her heart.
20 And the shepherds returned, glorifying and praising God for all-the-things that they-had-heard and seen, as it-was-told unto them.

Jesus is circumcised and named. (Matt. i. 25.) Luke ii. 21. At Bethlehem.

21 And when eight days were-accomplished for-the-circumcising-of the child, his name was-called JESUS, which was-so-named of the angel before he was-conceived in the womb. [For ch. ii. 22, see p. 24.]

MARGINAL READINGS:—*a* Cast together; weighed.

SCRIPTURE ILLUSTRATIONS.

16. *They came with haste*—they not only believed the word, but acted according thereto: so Abraham went forth, Ge. xii. 1, 4—to Moriah, xxii. 2, 3, 9—Israel actually went forth out of Egypt, and that in haste, Ex. xii. 11, 31—,9, 42—punished for not immediately and cheerfully going into the land, Nu. xiv. 29—31— Paul actually and immediately went, as called, into Macedonia, Ac. xvi. 10—see also Ga. i. 15, .6.

lying in a manger—(where cattle are fed). Jesus, as becoming the babe of Bethlehem, as being made flesh, is the food of his people, Jno. vi. 48—58, § 43— the words of eternal life, ver. 68, *ib.*—must be more than wondered at, as by the people, ver. 18—comp. Ac. xiii. 40, .1—must be kept and pondered, as by Mary, ver. 19—comp. Is. lv. 2, 3.

19. *kept*—so Jacob, Ge. xxxvii. 11—see Lu. ii. 51 § 6.

21. *which was so called*—to Mary, Lu. i. 31, § 2, p. 9 —and afterwards to Joseph, Mt. i. 21, § 2, p. 13—his great manifestation, Is. xlv. 21—.5.

NOTES.

[19. *Mary kept all these things.* All that happened, and all that was said respecting her child. Here is a delicate and beautiful expression of the feelings of a mother.]

Pondered. She revolved them; weighed. This is the original meaning of the word *weighed.* She kept them; she *weighed* them in her mind, giving to each circumstance its just importance, and anxiously seeking that it might indicate respecting her child.

In her heart. She remembered and thought of these things often and anxiously.

20. *Glorifying* ... *God, &c.* Giving honour to God, and celebrating his praises.

21. *Eight days, &c.* This was the regular time for performing the rite of circumcision. Ge. xvii. 12.—*See* Sect. III.—[If the birth of our Lord took place on the first day of the week, his circumcision would take place eight days after, on the first day of the week also; which is not only a striking coincidence, if we consider the spiritual import of the rite of circumcision itself, and the connexion of this import with the final end of both the birth, the death, and the rising again, of our Saviour, but saves the further difficulty whether, in administering this necessary rite upon the body of our Lord, it would be requisite to dispense with the sabbath.' — *Greswell*, vol. I. Diss. xii. p. 309.]

His name ... JESUS. This was given by divine appointment.—*See* Mt. i. 21, p. 13.

PRACTICAL REFLECTIONS.

[11 ver. Although the gospel was first preached to, and by Jews, yet was it especially designed for all the people. It is not selfish, exclusive joy, but is increased as it becomes diffused. The fulfilment of the prophecy is to be looked for in the very place predicted; God gave not only the type, David, but the antitype, the true Beloved, to be born in Bethlehem. As truly as Jesus was born to be a Saviour, so truly was He to be Christ, the Anointed, from whom the anointing upon his several people descends, and so truly is he to be submitted to as their Lord, by whom they are fed, led, protected, and ruled over.]

12 ver. The sign that Christ is indeed the Saviour of the literally poor and needy, is most strikingly given in the circumstances of his humble birth—in his being laid in a manger.

[13, 4 ver. As truly as the sign was given of Christ's appearing in the weakness of infancy, and the depth of humiliation, so truly will that glorious consummation be, of which this was the sign.—Now is the time for the manifestation of God's great will, in the preaching of the gospel; then follows peace to the individual, and our God will yet command peace to the ends of the earth; and then, and thereafter, shall the whole result in songs of eternal gladness, from the church, which shall be to Him for a glory in heavenly places.]

14 rer. From the conduct of the angels who sang thus together when the Foundation-stone was brought forth, in anticipation of man's full redemption, let us learn to look forward to the coming glory, and rejoice in the display of God's goodness to others.

15 rer. Like the shepherds, who said, 'Let us now go even unto Bethlehem,' let us make no delay to make ourselves acquainted with whatever evidence our God is pleased to give, that his great salvation will be completed; and surely if God hath not withheld his own Son, he will, with Him, give all he hath promised.

Let us not merely acquiesce in that which God makes known to us, but let us show that we have faith, by doing what we know to be the divine will.

16 rer. Those who take God at his word will find his promise true, as did the shepherds, upon going to see the sign that God will accomplish all that he hath promised.

17 rer. Let us be faithful to the great Shepherd of the sheep; and, like the shepherds, make known to others what the Lord hath revealed unto us respecting Jesus. Let us speak of the coming glory of Him who appeared as the babe of Bethlehem.

[19 ,9 rer. Let our lot not be with the despisers who wonder and perish, but with Mary who kept all these things and pondered them in her heart.]

20 rer. Let us, with the shepherds, when we return to our ordinary callings, continue to give thanks unto the Lord, and acknowledge his truth. Let us, with the shepherds, praise God, and not the creature, whether heavenly or earthly, for what we have heard and seen respecting his grace or his glory.

[21 rer. Jesus was made a servant—a minister of the circumcision — to confirm the promise made unto the fathers; at the same time that He is, as he was named, Jesus, the Lord, the Saviour.]

[Every word of God shall stand, as here did that which seals them all, the incarnation of Messiah; of Him whose name was called JESUS.]

The Genealogy of Jesus Christ, according to St. Matthew, being that of his supposed father, Joseph;—the Genealogy, according to St. Luke, shewing his descent through Mary.

(G. 10.) Matt. i. 1—17.

1 The book * of the generation of Jesus Christ, the son of David, the son of Abraham.
2 Abraham begat Isaac; and Isaac begat Jacob; and Jacob begat Judas and his brethren;
3 and Judas begat Phares and Zara of Thamar; and Phares begat Esrom; and Esrom begat Aram; and Aram begat Aminadab; and Aminadab begat Naasson; and Naasson begat
5 Salmon; and Salmon begat Booz of Rachab; and Booz begat Obed of Ruth; and Obed begat Jesse;
6 and Jesse begat David the king;. And David the king begat Solomon of her *that had been the*
7 *wife* of Urias; and Solomon begat Roboam; and Roboam begat Abia;
8 and Abia begat Asa; and Asa begat Josaphat; and Josaphat begat Joram; and Joram begat Ozias;
9 and Ozias begat Joatham; and Joatham begat Achaz; and Achaz
10 begat Ezekias; and Ezekias begat Manasses; and Manasses begat Amon; and Amon begat Josias;
11 and Josias begat Jechonias and his brethren, about the time they were carried away to Babylon:
12 And after they were brought to Babylon, Jechonias begat Salathiel;
13 and Salathiel begat Zorobabel; and Zorobabel begat Abiud; and Abiud begat Eliakim; and Eliakim begat
14 Azor; and Azor begat Sadoc; and Sadoc begat Achim; and Achim
15 begat Eliud; and Eliud begat Eleazar; and Eleazar begat Matthan; and Matthan begat Jacob;
16 and Jacob begat Joseph the husband of Mary, of whom was born Jesus, who is called Christ.

Luke iii. 23—38.

———— Jesus being (as was supposed 23 ἐνομίζετο) the son of Joseph, which was the son of Heli, which was *the* son of Matthat, 24 which was *the son* of Levi, which was *the son* of Melchi, which was *the son* of Janna, which was *the son* of Joseph, which was *the son* 25 of Mattathias, which was *the son* of Amos, which was *the son* of Naum, which was *the son* of Esli, which was *the son* of Nagge, which was *the son* of Maath, which was *the* 26 *son* of Mattathias, which was *the son* of Semei, which was *the son* of Joseph, which was *the son* of Juda, which was *the son* of Joanna, 27 which was *the son* of Rhesa, which was *the son* of Zorobabel, which was *the son* of Salathiel. Which was *the son* of Neri, which was *the* 28 *son* of Melchi, which was *the son* of Addi, which was *the son* of Cosam, which was *the son* of Elmodam, which was *the son* of Er, which was *the son* of Jose, which was *the son* 29 of Eliezer, which was *the son* of Jorim, which was *the son* of Matthat, which was *the son* of Levi, which was *the son* of Simeon, which 30 was *the son* of Juda, which was *the son* of Joseph, which was *the son* of Jonan, which was *the son* of Eliakim, which was *the son* of 31 Melea, which was *the son* of Menan, which was *the son* of Mattatha, which was *the son* of Nathan, which was *the son* of David, Which was *the son* of Jesse, which was *the* 32 *son* of Obed, which was *the son* of Booz, which was *the son* of Salmon, which was *the son* of Naasson, which was *the son* of Ami- 33 nadab, which was *the son* of Aram, which was *the son* of Esrom, which was *the son* of Phares, which was *the son* of Juda, which was *the son* 34 of Jacob, which was *the son* of Isaac, which was *the son* of Abraham, which was *the son* of Thara, which was *the son* of Nachor, Which was *the son* of Saruch, which was 35 *the son* of Ragau, which was *the son* of Phalec, which was *the son* of Heber, which was *the son* of Sala, which was *the son* of Cainan, 36

[Jesus Christ, the Anointed Saviour, is called the son of David, 'the Beloved,' to whose son was promised the throne of universal sovereignty; and the son of Abraham, 'the father of a great multitude,' unto whose 'one seed' was given the promise of the land. The names in the genealogy between Abraham and David are all expressive of promises respecting the kingdom and inheritance promised unto the fathers. The names between David and Jechonias describe the history of the church until the captivity in the mystical Babylon. The names between Jechonias and Jesus describe the church of Christ as coming out of Babylon, into the light and glory of the latter day, so much the subject of Scripture promise, and of which assurance is given in the birth of Emmanuel.

The genealogy in Matthew, whose gospel has most frequent reference to prophecy, is, thus, not to be regarded merely as a historical document, in which view it would seem to be somewhat defective; but it is on this account the more complete in reference to prophecy, of which it is a most beautiful summary.

This genealogy in Matthew is most expressive of grace to the Gentile, as well as full of promise to Israel: the first two of the four women mentioned in the genealogy being Tamar, the Canaanitess, who, by the third from Abraham, was the mother of the Jews; and Ruth, the Moabitess, from whom, in the third descent, was David.

Jeremiah (xxii. 29, 30) had prophesied of Coniah, or Jehoiakim, or, as here, Jechonias, that no man of his seed should prosper sitting upon the throne of his father David, and ruling any more in Judah; how then should come of him Jesus, the Messiah, the King of the Jews? The answer is, that Christ was the seed of the woman, and not literally the seed of Joseph, who was only the reputed father of Jesus, and thus in Matthew is the genealogy of Joseph; whilst that in Luke is the genealogy of Mary: as being born of whom, Jesus was literally the son of David according to the flesh, as, by his reputed father, he had a legal claim to the throne of David.

Luke, who dwells more upon the priesthood of Christ, gives the genealogy of Jesus according to the flesh; tracing him up not merely to the great receivers of the promises, but to the first Adam, upon whose head was placed the crown of sovereignty, which hath fallen from our head, because of sin; and which is regained by our kinsman Redeemer, the second Adam, the Lord from heaven. The relation to Adam, who was made possessor of the earth and the son of God, is here traced, of Him, who is emphatically the Son of God; and the Heir of all things; and who shall yet claim the dominion, for which the redemption price hath been paid.— *See* ADDENDA, '*Genealogies*,' p. 30.

* See ADDENDA, 'Book.'

SECT. IV. JESUS PRESENTED IN THE TEMPLE. PART 7.

17 So all the generations from Abraham to David *are* fourteen generations; and from David until the carrying-away-into Babylon *are* fourteen generations; and from the carrying-away-into Babylon unto Christ *are* fourteen generations.

[For Matt. i. 18, sec § 2, p. 13.]

which-was *the son* of-Arphaxad, which-was *the son* of-Sem, which-was *the son* of-Noe, which-was *the son* of-Lamech, which-was 37 *the son* of-Mathusala, which-was *the son* of-Enoch, which-was *the son* of-Jared, which-was *the son* of-Maleleel, which-was *the son* of-Cainan, which-was *the son* of-Enos, which-38 was *the son* of-Seth, which-was *the son* of-Adam, which-was *the son* of-God. [iv. 1, § 9.]

(G.11.) *Jesus is presented in the temple; Simeon and Anna bear witness. Luke* ii. 22—38. [ch. ii. 21, p. 22.] *At Jerusalem.*

22 And when the days of-her purification [a] according-to the law of-Moses were-accom- 23 plished, they-brought him to Jerusalem, to-present *him* παραστησαι to-the Lord; (as it-is-written in the-law of-the-Lord, Every male that-openeth the-womb shall-be-called 24 holy to-the Lord;) and to offer a-sacrifice according-to that which-is-said in the-law of-the-Lord, A-pair of-turtle-doves, or two young pigeons.

25 And, behold, there-was a-man in Jerusalem, whose name *was* Simeon; [b] and the same man *was* just and devout ευλαβης, waiting-for the-consolation of Israel: and 26 the-Holy Ghost was upon him. And it-was revealed [c] κεχρηματισμενον unto-him by the Holy Ghost, that-he-should-'not'-see death, before he-had-seen the Lord's Christ. [d]

MARGINAL READINGS:—[a] Cleansing; expiation.   [b] Hearing.   [c] Communicated.   [d] The Anointed of Jehovah.

SCRIPTURE ILLUSTRATIONS.

22. *purification*—prescribed, Le. xii.

present him to the Lord—'Every male that,' &c. Of Israel, (the Lord's first-born, Ex. iv. 22) the first-born males were to be redeemed, as xiii. 11—6; xxii. 29—the Levites accepted in place of the first-born of Israel, Nu. iii. 12, .3; viii. 5–22—redemption of the remnant, iii. 40–51—Aaron, chosen to represent the first-born, bare all Israel upon his shoulders, and upon his heart, for a memorial before the Lord, Ex. xxviii. 1, 9–12, 29—his consecration by blood, &c., Le. viii. 22, .3, 30—*confirm.*: Jesus is ' the first-born among many brethren,' Ro. viii. 29—' redeemed with the precious blood of Christ,' 1 Pe. i. 18–21—who hath entered into heaven itself, now to appear in the presence of God for us, He. ix. 21; Col. i. 14—.9—*see* Hebrews throughout.

24. *a pair of turtledoves*—offering of the poor, Le. xii. 8—the dove is the emblem of simplicity, love, and peace, Ca. i. 15; Jl. 14; v. 2; vi. 9—*see* Christ's baptism, Lu. iii. 22, § 8—and ' be ... wise as serpents, and harmless as doves,' Mt. x. 10, § 39—the wisdom from above, Ja. iii. 17, .8.

25. *Jerusalem*—' the seeing of peace.' *Simeon—*

'Hearing,' Ge. xxix. 33—*see* Simeon's recognition of Christ, as our Peace, and ' The Light,' in whom we are given to see peace: ' Lord, now lettest thou thy servant depart in peace, according to thy word: for mine eyes have seen thy salvation, which thou hast prepared,' &c., ver .29—32, p. 25—The Lord will hear the cry of a people waiting to see the Lord Himself provide peace for his people, Is. xxx. 18, .9—The people that truly and obediently hear the word of the Lord will be given to *see* the promised peace, xxxii. 13—22—*see also* ii. and iii.

26. *Lord's Christ*—' Messiah,' or ' anointed.' Aaron, chosen to represent the Lord's first-born, and typifying the first-born of every creature, was anointed with most precious ointment, Ex. xxx. 30—.8—described, Le. viii. 12, 30—referred to, Ps. cxxxiii.—David, *i.e.* ' *beloved,*' anointed to be king of Israel, 1 Sa. xvi. 13—a type of the true Beloved, Ps. lxxxix. 20—whose anointing is foretold, Da. ix. 24—' Messiah the Prince,' ver. 25—to be cut off, but not for himself, ver. 26—for *confirmation.* see the New Testament throughout. Upon the Pentecostal anointing, Jesus was declared to be ' *both Lord and Christ,*' Ac. ii. 36.

NOTES.

[22. *Days.* Among the Hebrews, a mother was required to remain at home for about forty days after the birth of a male child, and eighty for a female; during that time, she was not permitted to go to the temple, or to engage in religious services with the congregation, Le. xii. 2–5.]

To Jerusalem. The place where the temple was, and the ordinances of religion were celebrated; and also the seat of the civil government among the Jews. It had been established as such by David. Its name means *sight* or *vision of peace*, which it partly was during the reign of Solomon, but he was only a type of the greater Son of David, the true Prince of Peace, of whose government and peace ... no end.—*See* GEOGRAPHICAL NOTICE.

To present him to the Lord. Every first-born male child, in Israel, was regarded as *holy* to the Lord, Ex. xlii. 2. The first-born were presented to the priest, as God's representative, at the eastern gate.

[* If the day of our Saviour's birth coincided with the first day of the week, the fortieth day, reckoned from the day of his birth, according to the usage of the Jews, *inclusive*, coincided with the fifth, or fell on the Thursday. The forty-first, therefore, which was

the day after the purification of the Virgin Mary would be complete, (Le. xii. 2–6,) and of the presentation of our Lord in the temple, when he was manifested to Simeon and to Anna, coincided with the sixth, or fell on the Friday; that is, our Lord's presentation in the temple after his birth at first, coincided with the same day of the week on which he suffered at last.'—*Greswell,* vol. I. Diss. xii. p. 410.]

[23. *As it is written.* In Ex. xiii. 2; Nu. iii. 13. When God smote the first-born of Egypt, he saved the first-born of Israel; hence this claim of redemption. See Nu. iii. 12, 13, 46, .7, and xviii. 15, .6.]

24. *And to offer a sacrifice, &c.* Those who were able, on such an occasion were required to offer a lamb for a burnt-offering, and a pigeon or a turtle-dove for a sin-offering. If not able to bring a *lamb,* then they were permitted to bring two turtle-doves or two young pigeons.—*See* Le. xii. 8; xiv. 21, .2.

Just. Righteous before God and man; approved by God as a righteous man, and discharging faithfully his duty to man: and pious and devout, scrupulously performing his duty towards GOD.—*See* Ac. x.

PRACTICAL REFLECTIONS.

[22 *ver.* May all those who seek to present others to the Lord, seek to be first themselves pure.]

[Let us seek that both ourselves and all that may be placed under our care, be not only called holy to the Lord, but be actually made so, through a union with Jesus, in whom alone we can be accepted before God.]

25 *ver.* Let our ears be opened to the word of God,

so as, with Simeon, to know both what he hath promised, and what he would have us to do: and, in the spirit of humble and loving obedience, look and long for the accomplishment of his promise.

[26, .7 *ver.* Let us earnestly desire that the anointing from our great exalted Head, may descend upon all the members of the body of Christ, so that both our minds may be enlightened, and our feet may be led, like those of Simeon, by the Holy Ghost.]

PART I. JESUS IS PRESENTED IN THE TEMPLE. SECT. IV

Luke ii. 27 And he came by* εν the Spirit into the temple: and when και εν τῳ the parents
28 brought-in the child Jesus, to do for him after the custom of-the law, then took-
29 he him·-up in his arms, and blessed God, and said, Lord now lettest-thou*·-thy
30 servant·-depart in peace, according-to thy word: for mine eyes have-seen thy salvation
31 το σωτηριον σου, which thou-hast-prepared before the-face of-all people;* 32 a-light
33 to lighten εις αποκαλυψιν the-Gentiles,* and the-glory of-thy people Israel. And Joseph

MARGINAL READINGS:—*In. *b* Now enfranchise thy slave, O master. *c* The peoples.
d For an unveiling of the nations.

SCRIPTURE ILLUSTRATIONS.

28. *blessed God—see* Ps. ciii.—'bless the Lord who redeemeth,' &c., ver. 4—*compare* with Ep. i. 3–7—'blessed be the God and Father;' hath chosen us in him, ver. 6, 7.

29, 30. *depart in peace . . . for mine eyes have seen thy salvation—see* above, 25 ver., p. 24, 'Scripture Illustrations,' *Jerusalem*—so Paul, 2 Ti. iv. 6–8.

31. *all people,* Is. xlv. 22, .3—'look unto me, and be ye saved, all the ends of the earth,' ver. 22—a ransom for all, to be testified in due time, 1 Ti. ii. 6; Rev. xiv.

32. *a light to lighten*—for an apocalypse, or revealing, or uncovering, the nations: for taking away the great darkness—*see* Ge. xv. 5, 12, .7—' the vail spread over all nations,' Is. xxv. 7, 8—*see* also xxix. 17–24;

Ho. i. 10, .1—*see*, for our High Priest proceeding to unveil, Rev. i. 12–20—*comp.* with 2 Co. iii. 16—the unveiling, Ro. v., and thereafter—*see,* as to the glory, ch. iv., xxi., ..ii.—*Israel*, Rev. vii., xxi. 12, .3—*comp.* with Is. lx. 'Arise, shine; for thy light is come, and the glory of the LORD is risen upon thee. 2, For, behold, the darkness shall cover the earth, and gross darkness the people,' &c.—*see* on ver. 25, p. 24.

the glory—all redemption, blessing, and sanctification is by Christ. He says, by his holy prophet, Is. xlv. 22, .5. 22, 'Look unto me, and be ye saved, all the ends of the earth: for I am God, and there is none else.' 25, ' In the Lord shall all the seed of Israel be *justified,* and shall glory.'—*See* the glory described, Eze. i., x.; *comp. with* Rev. iv., &c.

NOTES.

Waiting for the consolation of Israel. That is, waiting for the Messiah, who is called ' The consolation of Israel' because he would give comfort to them by his appearing. This name was often applied to the Messiah before he actually appeared. It was common to swear, also, by '*the Consolation of Israel*'—that is, by the Messiah about to come.

26. *It was revealed.* 'He was divinely informed,' he had an express communication from God, by the Holy Ghost, concerning the subject.

Not see death. Should not die. To *see* death, and to *taste* of death, was a common way among the Hebrews of expressing death.—*Comp.* Ps. lxxxix. 48, ' What man is he that liveth, and shall not see death? shall he deliver his soul from the hand of the grave? Selah.'

The Lord's Christ. Rather, *the Lord's Anointed.* The word *Christ* means *anointed.*—*See* ' Christ the Lord,' ver. 11, p. 21.

27. *Temple.* Place of prayer for *all* people, where sacrifices were offered for the whole nation, by the sons of Levi, as types of Him who hath offered the atonement for us, and is gone within the most holy place, ' now to appear in the presence of God for us.'—*See* He. ix. 24, and ADDENDA, Sect. i. p. 8, '*Temple.*'

The custom of the law. That is, to make an offering for purification, and to present the child to God.

29. *Now lettest.* Now thou dost let, or permit. This word is in the indicative mood, and signifies that God *was permitting* him to die in peace, by having relieved his anxieties, as having given us his dear Son, the assured pledge that all would be fulfilled which God had promised.

Depart, &c. ἀπολυεις.] 'Ἀπολυειν sig. properly ' to let go from any place,' or fig. from any state which implies coercion.—*See* MARGINAL READINGS, ' Now enfranchise,' &c.

According to thy word. He seems to have understood, by the revelation made to him, that, as he should not die before he saw the Messiah, so, when he had seen him, he should speedily be removed by death.

30. *Thy salvation.* The Saviour; or He who is to procure salvation for his people.

31. *Before the face of all people.* Whom thou hast provided *for* all people, or whom thou dost design to *reveal* to all people.

32. *A light to lighten the Gentiles.* This is in accordance with the prophecies in the Old Testament, [Ps. xcviii. 3; Is. xlix 6; Mal. iv. 2.] The Gentiles are represented as sitting in darkness, *i. e.,* in ignorance and sin. Christ is *a light* to them, as by him they will be made acquainted with the character of the true God, his law, and the plan of redemption and salvation.

Glory. The manifestation of excellency, 2 Co. iii. 7; and is applied in Scripture variously.

The *glory* is eminently considered as the emblem of the divine presence, or rather the divine presence itself. [The church expresses her hope, Ps. lxxxv. 9, '*that glory may dwell in our land*;' and John bears witness, that this glory was displayed tabernacling in flesh, and they beheld it, the glory as of the only begotten of the Father, &c., Jno. i. The ark of the covenant was called the glory of the Lord, because it represented *God manifest in flesh*; therefore said the mother of Ichabod, when the ark was taken, ' *The glory is departed,*' 1 Sa. iv. 21. The ark seems also to be *the glory* referred to in Rom. ix. 4. Therefore, when the tabernacle was completed, the *Shechinah,* or visible display of divine glory, filled the tent, and took up its residence upon the ark, between the cherubims, signifying that the divine glory should rest upon the man Christ Jesus; and hence, the worship of the Old Testament church was addressed to him who dwelt between the cherubims, Ex. xxix. 43. When Solomon had dedicated the temple, the cloud of divine glory so filled the house, that the priests could not stand to minister in it, 1 Ki. viii. 11. We find the prophets who prophesied after the glory was indeed departed, promising that the glory of the second house should be greater than the glory of the first, Hag. ii. 3, 7, 9; and God promises in the latter day blessedness, in Jerusalem to be, a wall of fire round about, and the glory in the midst, Zec. ii. 5. Moses requested to see this glory, Ex. xxxiii. 18, but the time had not then come when it could be displayed, so as guilty man could see and live. Isaiah foretold the days when the glory of the Lord should be revealed, Is. xl. 5; and in Jesus Christ ' *the brightness of the divine glory,* and the express image *of his person,*' shone, He. i. 3. When Simeon took up his infant Lord in his arms, he called him ' a *light to lighten the Gentiles,* and the glory *of thy people Israel.*'—See ver. 32.]

PRACTICAL REFLECTIONS.

28 ver. Let us bless God for the gift of his Son, in whom all new covenant mercy is secured; through faith in him he hath made us accepted in the Beloved; in whom we have redemption through his blood.

29 ver. Let our only desire of living be, that we may serve God and witness the development of his great salvation.

31 ver. Let us not only seek salvation for ourselves,

but that the manifestation of the prepared salvation may be made before the face of all people on the face of the whole earth.

[32 ver. Let us not forget that it is only by their looking unto Jesus, ' the light of life,' that the true unveiling of the nations can take place; and let us earnestly desire that soon, by the bright reflection of his image, his people Israel may indeed be to him for a glory.]

GOD IS LOVE.—1 John iv. 8.

Luke ii. 34 and his mother marvelled at those *things* which-were-spoken of him. And Simeon blessed them, and said unto Mary his mother, Behold, this *child* is-set for the-fall and rising-again of-many in Israel; and for a-sign which-shall-be-spoken- 35 against; (yea, a-sword shall-pierce-through thy-own soul also,) that the-thoughts διαλογισμοι of many hearts may-be-revealed.

SCRIPTURE ILLUSTRATIONS.

31. *fall and rising again*—Christ predicted to be 'a rock of offence to both houses of Israel,' Is. viii. 14—.7—' to raise up the tribes of Israel,' xlix. 6, 8—13 all Israel made to stand upon their feet, 'an exceeding great army,' Eze. xxxvii. 10, .1—an ensign upon his hand, Ze. ix. 16—*confirm.*, Mt. xv. 24, § 15; Rom. xi. 12, 25, .6—*comp* Rev. vii. with xlv. 1—5.
sign spoken against, Is. liii. 14. .5; liii. 1—3; Ps. xxii. 6—8, 12, .3—*fulfilm.*, Mt. xxvii. 89—44, § 91—the people, ver. 89, 40. § 91—the chief priests, scribes, and elders, ver. 41—.3—the soldiers, Lu. xxiii. 36, .7, § 91

—the crucified with him, ver. 39—both Jews and Greeks, 1 Co. i. 18—31.
35. *thoughts of many hearts . . . revealed,* Ps. 1. 19—21; Is. li. 7, 8; xli. 21, .2; iii. 15; Eccl. xii. 14—*confirm.*: when Jesus healed the sick of the palsy, the Pharisees reasoned within themselves, Mt. ix. 4, § 22—when he cast out the blind and dumb devils, the Pharisees blasphemed, xii. 36, .7, § 31— when the disciples disputed who should be chief, Lu. ix. 47, § 52—when God shall judge the secrets of men by Jesus Christ, Rom. ii. 12, .6.

NOTES.

[*Thy people Israel.* This is spoken of the multitudinous 'seed' that was to come of Abraham—*See* Ge. xiii. 16; xv. 5; xxxii. 12: and De. xvi. 18, 9. Simeon recognises the promise, (*see* Ge. xxii. 18,) that in the 'one seed,' Christ, all the nations of the earth should be blessed; and the time is fast approaching when the literal and spiritual Israel shall 'sing unto the LORD a new song.'—*See* Ps. xcviii. 1—3.]

The *glory of thy people Israel.* The Glory is Jesus, rejoiced in by his people, as their Prophet, Priest, and King. The children of Israel and the children of Judah are to be gathered together, and make to themselves one head, and to come out of the land of the North into the land that he gave for an inheritance to their fathers.—*See* Ho. i., ii.; Je. xxx. 3; xxxi. 8, 9.

[For a description of the glory upon the heads of the living creatures, *see* Eze. i. and x. The four living creatures are supposed to represent the hosts of Israel, whose four leading standards, the *Man* for Reuben, the *Lion* for Judah, the *Ox* for Ephraim, and the *Eagle* for Dan, were correspondent to those mentioned in Ezekiel's vision. The ox of Ephraim was more particularly characteristic of the cherub. —*Compare* ch. i. 10 with x. 14. Over the heads of the living creatures was the glory, consisting of a bright firmament or platform, having placed on it a sapphire throne, and the appearance of a man above upon it. It is Christ, our High Priest, occupying his kingly throne, borne aloft on the body of glorious light supplied by Himself as our Prophet. It is Jesus rejoiced in as their Prophet, Priest, and King. Then shall be the great predicted return from the north country.—*Comp.* Je. xxiii. 7, 9, with Eze. i. 4. Then shall it be said, as in Ps. xlvii. 8, 9. '8, *God reigneth over the heathen; God sitteth upon the throne of his holiness.* 9, *The princes of the people are gathered together, even the people of the God of Abraham; for the shields of the earth belong unto God: he is greatly exalted.*']

34. *For the fall, &c.* Simeon implies that Christ would be the occasion of sin and offence to those who look for a temporal Messiah, and of reformation and forgiveness to those who are less prejudiced against him. 'Fall,' through infidelity; 'rising,' through faith. He will be the means of bringing aggravated ruin upon some, as well as salvation and recovery to others.

[There is a plain reference here to the passage where it is said that he should be a *stone of stumbling, and a rock of offence.* Is. viii. 14, .5. The nation rejected him, and put him to death, and, as a judgment, fell into the hands of the Romans; thousands were led into captivity, and thousands perished. The nation rushed into ruin; the temple was destroyed, and the people were scattered into all the nations.—*See* Rom. ix. 32, .3. '32. *Wherefore? Because they sought it not by faith, but as it were by the works of the law. For they stumbled at that stumbling-stone ; 33, as it is written, Behold, I lay in Sion a stumbling-stone and rock of offence : and whosoever believeth on him shall not be ashamed.* 1 Pe. ii. 8, '*And a stone of stumbling, and a rock of offence, even to them which stumble at the word, being disobedient : whereunto also they were appointed.*'—See also 1 Co. i. 23, .4.]

For *a sign.* A butt or mark to shoot at; which finely intimates the deliberate malice of Christ's persecutors. That he should be for 'a monument,' and 'a remarkable example of rejection and contempt.' He was despised and rejected, and his religion has been the common mark or sign for all the wicked and the profligate to ridicule and oppose.
[Compare Is. viii. 18, '*Behold, I and the children whom the LORD hath given me are for signs and for wonders in Israel from the LORD of hosts, which dwelleth in mount Zion.*' Lam. iii. 12—.4. '12, *He hath bent his bow, and set me as a mark for the arrow.* 13, *He hath caused the arrows of his quiver to enter into my reins.* 14, *I was a derision to all my people ;* and *their song all the day.*' Ac. xxviii. 22, '*But we desire to hear of thee what thou thinkest : for as concerning this sect, we know that every where it is spoken against.*'—See also He. xii. 3.]

35. *Yea, a sword, &c.* 'A javelin or dart.' 'She must expect to witness such things, from the cruelty and enmity of the people and rulers against her son, as would, like a sword, pierce her soul with the most exquisite anguish.' And Mary herself has not been free from cruel suspicion and reproach—*See* Pr. xii. 18, '*There is that speaketh like the piercings of a sword : but the tongue of the wise is health.*'

That the thoughts, &c. 'So that the thoughts,' &c. The ministry, miracles, and death of Jesus, will discover, or bring to light, the thoughts, designs, and dispositions of all characters. Nothing so brings out the feelings of sinners, as to tell them of Jesus Christ; many treat him with silent contempt; many are ready to gnash their teeth; many curse him;—all shew how much by nature the heart is opposed to religion, and there are really, in spite of themselves, fulfilling the prophecies of the Holy Scriptures. So true it is, that *none can say that Jesus is Lord, but by the Holy Ghost,* 1 Co. xii. 3.

PRACTICAL REFLECTIONS.

[33 ver. Let us marvel at our own stupidity, who have inquired so little into the meaning of Simeon's words, at which even Joseph and Mary marvelled— they who had already heard and seen such marvellous things concerning Jesus.]

[34 ver. As truly as Jesus, the one Foundation-stone laid in Zion, hath proved to be for the fall of many in Israel, so truly will he prove to be for the rising again of the people of promise, and only through him, and to him, can their lifting up be.]

Let us be careful in our judgments! He, who appeared as a poor and despised man, and who was put to death as one of the vilest malefactors—is the only true foundation of the world's peace and blessing— was a sign that God would prove most faithful to all his promises.

35 ver. Even Mary, the highly-favoured of the Lord, the mother of our blessed Redeemer, was not exempt from trial. Let us not expect that we can entirely escape.

Let us be careful as to what thoughts we have, or express about Christ, as, according to this rule, we must be judged; and let us seek to be clean in heart if we would have right views respecting him. Let us in Him see God.

PART I. BETHLEHEM. SECT. IV.

Luke ii. 36 And there was one Anna, a prophetess, the daughter of Phanuel, of the tribe
of Aser:[a] she was of a great age, and had lived with an husband seven years from her
37 virginity; and she was a widow of about fourscore and four years, which departed
38 not[b] from the temple, but served God with fastings and prayers night and day. And
she coming in that instant αυτη τη ωρα gave thanks likewise ανθωμολογειτο unto the
Lord, and spake of him to all them that looked for redemption in Jerusalem.

MARGINAL READINGS:— [a] Happy, or prosperous. [b] Absented not herself.

SCRIPTURE ILLUSTRATIONS.

36. *Anna*—'grace.' *Phanuel*—'face of God'—same as Ge. xxxii. 30—Jacob called the name of the place *Peniel*: for 'I have seen God face to face, and my life is preserved.'

Asher—'happy or blessed.' Ge. xxx. 13—salvation, through the redeeming blood, is of grace, Ep. ii. 7, 8—obtained in answer to earnest, persevering prayer, like that of Jacob when he obtained the name of Israel, Ge. xxxii. 24—8; Is. xliii. 22, 5, 6; Ho. xii. 3—6—those who, sensible of their poverty, thus seek and obtain, are the truly blessed or happy, Mt. v. 3—12, § 10; 2 Co. iv. 6.

38. *looked for redemption in Jerusalem*—'waited for him,' Is. xxv. 9—'blessed all they,' xxx. 18—'ye shall be comforted in Jerusalem,' lxvi. 13; Ps. cxviii.—*confirm*, 1 Th. i. 10; He. ix. 28; Tit. ii. 13, 4—'O Jerusalem, Jerusalem, . . . ye shall not see me henceforth till ye shall say, Blessed is he that cometh in the name of the Lord,' Mt. xxiii. 37, 9, § 85.

NOTES.

36. *Anna*. The same with Hannah, signifying 'Grace, or gracious.' The daughter of Phanuel, of the tribe of Asher: she had been early married, and lived seven years with her husband. After his death, she devoted herself to the service of God, and at every morning and evening sacrifice attended to pour forth her prayers.

Phanuel. 'Face of God.'—See Ge. xxxii. 29, 30.

A prophetess. One endued with the χαρισμα, or spiritual grace of uttering divine revelations; or, in a general way, one to whom God reveals himself by his Spirit. As there were prophetesses before Christ —as Miriam, Deborah, and Huldah—so this 'Anna' after; and afterwards four of Philip's daughters.

Of the tribe of Aser. The tribe of Aser, or Asher, dwelt in the northern part of the land of Canaan.

37. *Fastings and prayers*. Constant religious service. Spending her time in prayer, and in all the ordinances of religion.

Night and day. Continually, i. e., at the usual times of public worship, and in private. When it is said that she departed not from the temple, it is meant that she was constant and regular in all the public services at the temple. There were occasionally bright services of sacred music.

38. *Coming in*. At the time Simeon uttered the above words.

Gave thanks, &c. Returned praises to the Lord.

PRACTICAL REFLECTIONS.

36, 7 *ver.* Let us, with Anna, seek in self-denial and prayer the face of God, that we may be happy ourselves in the heart-possession of his grace, and so be able to exhibit to others the light of the knowledge of the glory of God in the face of Jesus Christ.

38 *ver.* Let us, with Anna, both give thanks unto the Lord for the gift of his Son, and before men confess Him, through whom alone redemption can be looked for. And let us not forget that the mouth of the Lord's handmaiden was more especially opened to those 'who looked for redemption in Jerusalem.'

GEOGRAPHICAL NOTICE.

BETHLEHEM —(Sig. 'House of Bread,') anciently Ephrath. In Arabic, *Beit Lahm*, 'House of Flesh.' Is called 'Bethlehem of Judæa,' to distinguish it from a city of the same name in the tribe of Zebulun. Is perhaps the earliest Scripture town with which tho rightly trained infant mind is acquainted. The babe of Bethlehem is ever contemplated, in infancy, with delight. The first beam of hope for future bliss is ever associated with Bethlehem of Judæa. Its earliest notice by the sacred historian is Ge. xxxv. 16—20, when Jacob was bereaved of his beloved Rachel. 'And Rachel died, and was buried in the way to Ephrath, which is Bethlehem. And Jacob set a pillar upon her grave: that is the pillar of Rachel's grave unto this day.' This history is plaintively touched again by Jacob, when preparing to be gathered to his fathers, Ge. xlviii. 7, 'And as for me, when I came from Padan, Rachel died by me in the land of Canaan in the way, when yet there was but a little way to come unto Ephrath; and I buried her there in the way of Ephrath; the same is Bethlehem.' This spot, in the way from Jerusalem to Bethlehem, about one mile from the latter place, on the right, at a little distance from the road, is still an object of much Muslim veneration: the small square building of stone with a dome, and within it a tomb in the ordinary Muhammedan form, the whole plastered over with mortar, is kept in order by the Muhammedans: and those of Bethlehem were formerly accustomed to bury around it. The touching story of the devoted Ruth to her widowed and childless mother, and the tender sympathy of the benevolent Boaz, the progenitor of king David, have Bethlehem for their locality.—*See Ruth*. In the fields of Bethlehem David kept his father's sheep.—*See* 1 Sa. xvi. 11—3.

There too, in a deep valley on the east of Bethlehem, still exists the refreshing well, so ardently longed for by Israel's king, as he lay concealed, with 400 faithful followers, in Adullam's cave.—See (2 Sa. xxiii. 13—7;) 1 Ch. xi. 15—9. '*Now three of the thirty captains went down to the rock to David, into the cave of Adullam; and the host of the Philistines encamped in the valley of Rephaim. And David was then in the hold, and the Philistines' garrison was then at Bethlehem. And David longed, and said, Oh that one would give me drink of the water of the well of Bethlehem, that is at the gate! And the three brake through the host of the Philistines, and drew water out of the well of Bethlehem, that was by the gate, and took it, and brought it to David: but David would not drink of it, but poured it out to the Lord, and said, My God forbid it me, that I should do this thing: shall I drink the blood of these men that have put their lives in jeopardy? for with the jeopardy of their lives they brought it. Therefore he would not drink it. These things did these three mightiest.*'

Bethlehem is called '*the city of David*,' Lu. ii. 4, because it was the place of his birth. God put special honour upon it, in bringing to pass there his ancient prophecy, (see Mi. v. 2;) and making it the birthplace of his own dear Son, whom he gave for the sin of the world. From this circumstance, pilgrims and tourists to the Holy Land, of every creed and from every clime, look upon their visit to Bethlehem among the most interesting incidents of Eastern travel. The road to Bethlehem, from 'Solom 's pools,' which are about 6 miles to the south, is extremely rugged, shut in on both sides by hills, sometimes quite bare, and at others covered with low prickly shrubs and slender herbage: an abrupt bending of the pass gives the first glimpse of the town, which soon again disappears in the winding of the path. At length, crossing a somewhat level plain, the ascent of the rocky path is begun, by which the elevated site of Bethlehem is approached; and looking back and around, naturally and mentally are vividly repre-

• Dr. Clarke describes it as containing pure and delicious water. Dr. Robinson says, 'That to which the monks give the name of the "Well of David," is about half or three quarters of a mile N. by E. of Bethlehem, beyond the deep valley which the village overlooks: which was dry when we saw it.'

WE LOVE HIM, BECAUSE HE FIRST LOVED US.—1 John iv. 19.   [27

Side margins: EVERY SPIRIT THAT CONFESSETH NOT THAT JESUS CHRIST IS COME — IN THE FLESH IS NOT OF GOD.—1 John iv. 3.

sented the hills, the plains, and the birth-place, where the royal shepherd boy and sweet psalmist of Israel, the princely David, had wandered with his flocks, and with every peak and slope of which his eye had been familiar. The hills in the vicinity are terraced, and vines and figs abound. The towers in the vineyards are numerous, and remind one of Ca. ii. 15, 'Take us the foxes, the little foxes, that spoil the vines: for our vines have tender grapes.' Near the top of the hill, it is said, you come upon ' the well of Bethlehem, that is at the gate. It is protected by a piazza of four small arches, under which the water is drawn up through two apertures.'* 'And to this well may be seen the women of the city coming out to draw water, bearing their earthen vessels upon their heads: their figures easy and graceful, as their flowing drapery casts its long folds about them.' 'Delicate complexions, united to the ever-brilliant Eastern eye, distinguish them from all other Arab women; while the finely cut lips, thin, but vermillion bright, and a Grecian profile, distinguish them from the Jewish race.'

The city occupies a commanding position, on the E. and N.E. slope of a long ridge, looking over towards the region of Moab. The substance of the hill is limestone, which, like white marble, reflects the sun's rays, and makes it very painful to the eyes. The winding path of ascent is, in several places, slippery, toilsome, and difficult. The hill on which the city stands is terraced in all directions, and planted with fine healthy olive and fig trees. On the south side it is very steep. The fig trees, olives, and pomegranates, and the ripe barley fields which cover the north side, shew that it is still capable of being made what its name imports, 'The House of Bread.' The aspect of the town itself is poor. Its buildings are in the usual style, square and rude, and finished with small domes. It is a saddening thought, while entering within the walls of Bethlehem, that the crescent of Mahomet gleams over the spot where the wondrous star guided to the humbled presence of the incarnate God; and that Christianity is there but a tolerated, a permitted, a despised thing. The present population is about 3,000, and nominally Christian, which arises from the circumstance of Ibrahim Pacha, a Mussulman, driving out the Arab population, who defended the place for the sultan, in the rebellion of 1834, against his attacks; and spared the Christians, as he said, because they had been guilty of no offence. The inhabitants chiefly subsist by agriculture, and by making crucifixes, beads, models of the Holy Sepulchre, &c., in olive wood, palm, and mother-of-pearl, which are highly valued and eagerly purchased by the devout visiters. The monks of Bethlehem claim the exclusive privilege of marking the limbs and bodies of pilgrims who choose to submit to the operation, with crosses, stars, and monograms, by means of gunpowder. This is a very ancient practice, and. like other superstitions, may be traced to the religious customs of the heathen nations. The town has gates at the entrance of some of the streets. The main street is steep, narrow, gloomy, and dirty.

To the east of Bethlehem, not much more than a mile and a half distant, is the village traditionally said to be that to which the shepherds dwelt, to whom was made the supernatural announcement of Messiah's birth. It is approached by a steep descending road, with fig and olive trees scattered on every side. The soil is very white and chalky. It is inhabited by Greek and Latin Christians. Is miserably dilapidated, in poverty and wretchedness. Many of the inhabitants were engaged in thrashing and winnowing corn. Passing downwards from the village, a view presents itself of the spot, where it is said the shepherds heard that heavenly minstrelsy, which still sounds forth sweetly from the pages of Inspiration. It is carefully enclosed with a rough stone wall, and covered with numerous olive trees of vigorous growth and considerable age. In the midst of the enclosure is a small grotto-chapel. It contains a rude altar, and the usual pictorial appendages.

Of the road from Jerusalem to Bethlehem, a modern traveller writes, 'Across the plain of Rephaim to Bethlehem is about five miles; and the way lies, for the most part, over arid and dreary hills, with here and there a scanty crop of wheat in the intervening valleys; and an occasional herd of goats browsing invisible herbage, under the guardianship of a herdsman as shaggy as his flock, and as brown and almost as bare as the rocks around him.'

'Occasionally we catch glimpses of the wild mountain scenery that wraps the Dead sea in its barren bosom. No other landscape in the world is like this. It resembles rather some visionary sketch roughly done in raw sienna, than anything in nature: distorted piles of cinderous hills, with that Dead sea lying among them like melted lead, unlighted,† even by the sunshine that is pouring so vertically down as to cast no shadow. After passing the convent of Mar Elyas upon the left, and the tomb of Rachel in a valley on the right, the scenery becomes more attractive: some olive groves, intermingled with small vineyards, clothe the hills; rich corn-fields are in the valleys: and, lo! as we round a rugged projection in the path, BETHLEHEM stands before us. This little city, as it is called by courtesy, has an imposing appearance; walled round, and commanding a fertile valley from a rugged eminence.'—(Continued, Sect. v.)

ADDENDA.

'Book,' p. 23.

Book. In Latin Liber, in Hebrew Sepher, in Greek Biblos. Several sorts of materials were used formerly in making books. Plates of lead and copper, the barks of trees, bricks, stone, and wood, were the first matters employed to engrave such things and monuments upon as men were willing to have transmitted to posterity. The letters which Rabshakeh delivered from Sennacherib to Hezekiah, are called a book. The contract which Jeremiah confirmed for the purchase of a field, is called by the same name. Ahasuerus' edict in favour of the Jews is likewise called a book. Job wishes, that his judge or his adversary would himself write his sentence. The writing likewise which a man gave to his wife when he divorced her, was called a book of divorce.

Book, a written register of events, or declaration of doctrines and laws, Ge. v. 1; Est. vi. 1. The books of Moses are the most ancient in being; nor does it appear that any were written before them. Josephus says, the children of Seth, before the flood, wrote their discoveries in arts, and in astronomy and other sciences, upon two pillars; the one of stone, to withstand a deluge; and the other of brick, to endure a conflagration: but the obscurity of his narrative, and the want of concurring evidence, render his account very suspicious Moses' books are called the book of the law; and a copy of Deuteronomy, if not the whole of them, was laid up in some repository of the ark, De. xxxi. 26. Hesiod's works were written on tables of lead; the Roman laws on twelve tables of brass; Solon's on wood; and those of God on stone, probably marble. In very ancient times the Persians and Ionians wrote on skins. When Attalus formed his library, about A.M. 3770, he either invented or improved parchment. This, when written on, was either sewed together in long rolls, and written only on one side, in the manner of the copy of the law now used in the Jewish synagogues; or, it was formed in the manner of our books. Some Indian books are extant, written on leaves of the Malabar palm-tree. Books now, and for about five hundred years backward, have been generally written on linen paper.

The book of the Lord is either the scriptures, Is. xxxiv. 16; or his purpose, wherein every thing is regulated and fixed. Ps. cxxxix. 16; Rev. v. 1, and x. 2; or his providential care and support of men's natural life, Ex. xxxii. 32; Ps. lxix. 28; or his omniscient observation and fixed remembrance of things, Ps. lvi. 8; Mal. iii. 16. Men's conscience is like to a book; it records whatever they have done....... The opening of the books at the last day denotes the manifestation of the purposes and words of God, and the exact procedure in judgment, according to divine purposes, laws, and real facts, Rev. xx. 12. Christ's opening the sealed book, imports his pre-declaration and exact fulfilment of the purposes of God, relative to the New Testament church, Rev. v. 5, 6, and viii. 1.

* Dr. Robinson thinks these to be only openings over an aqueduct, which here passes through a sort of deep vault or reservoir, from which the water is drawn up about twenty feet.

† Paxton calls it 'that black sea.'

ADDENDA—(continued).

ON THE TIME OF OUR SAVIOUR'S BIRTH.

'The year of our Saviour's birth, was U.C. 750, B.C. 4; and the passover was celebrated in that year, on April 10: that is to say, the fourteenth *τεσσαρεσ* of Nisan, on which the passover was always slain, coincided with the interval between sunset April 9, and sunset April 10. If so, the tenth *τεσσαρεσ* of Nisan, which began and expired four days before the fourteenth, began at sunset April 5, and expired at sunset April 6. The tenth of Nisan, then, U.C. 750, coincided partly with April 5, and partly with April 6. April 5, therefore, or April 6, must express the day of our Saviour's birth; the former, if he was born on the evening of the tenth of Nisan; the latter, if he was born on the morning.

'From the narrative of St. Luke, who only of the Evangelists has given any account of the circumstances of our Saviour's birth, especially from ii. 8, 9, 11, though the fact is not expressly asserted, yet it is plainly to be inferred, that the Nativity took place on the evening of some Jewish day: either in the night time as such, or after sunset at least. Sunset, on April 5 or 6, U.C. 750, thirteen or fourteen days later than the vernal equinox, would not take place earlier than 6, 30, in the evening; and the tenth of Nisan, which would begin with sunset, would begin with 6, 30, in the evening also. If our Saviour, then, was born in the evening of a Jewish day, and born on the tenth of Nisan, he was born on the night of April 5, or on the morning of April 6: if he had been born in the evening, and born on the sixth of April, he would have been born on the eleventh of the Jewish Nisan. It may be difficult to decide between these two days, each of which, apparently, possesses an equal right to be pronounced the true birthday of Christ; for the evening of the same Jewish day coincided in part with both. I assume, however, for the present, that the date of our Saviour's birth, if it was Nisan the tenth, in a lunar Jewish year answering to U.C. 750, was April 5 in the solar or Julian, answering to the same year, on which the tenth of Nisan at that time began. For subsequent years, therefore, the tenth of Nisan will express the nominal, and the fifth of April the actual, birthday of Christ; but the tenth of Nisan will never express the actual date of the Nativity, unless it coincides with the fifth of April also.

'Let us now consider on what days in subsequent years, more especially in the three years of our Lord's personal ministry, this tenth of Nisan would fall. These days may be immediately obtained from the Table of passovers, vol. II. Diss. vii. p. 531.

'I. U.C. 780, A.D. 27, the fourteenth *τεσσαρεσ* of Nisan began at sunset April 8, and expired at sunset April 9; and, consequently, the tenth *τεσσαρεσ* of Nisan began at sunset April 4, and expired at sunset April 5.

'II. U.C. 781, A.D. 28, the fourteenth of Nisan began at sunset March 28, and expired at sunset March 29; and, consequently, the tenth of Nisan began at sunset March 24, and expired at sunset March 25.

'III. U.C. 782, A.D. 29, the fourteenth of Nisan began at sunset April 15, and expired at sunset April 16; and, consequently, the tenth of Nisan began at sunset April 11, and expired at sunset April 12.

'IV. U.C. 783, A.D. 30, the fourteenth of Nisan began at sunset April 4, and expired at sunset April 5; and, consequently, the tenth of Nisan began at sunset March 31, and expired at sunset April 1.

'It appears, then, that U.C. 780, the year when our Lord began his ministry, the tenth of Nisan and the fifth of April, that is, his nominal and his real birthday, coincided together, as they had done in the year of his birth: but in no other year of his ministry besides.

'It appears, also, that U.C. 783, the year when he concluded his ministry, the fourteenth of Nisan, the day on which our Saviour suffered, coincided with April 5, the day upon which he was born.—(See Sect. 87.)—*Greswell*, vol. I. Diss. xii. pp. 401—4.

'All the cardinal points, in the transaction of our Lord's part in the Christian scheme, are determined to the vernal, and not to the autumnal, quarter of the year; or, what is the same thing, to the passover, and not to the feast of Tabernacles. No special distinction is conferred, during his lifetime, on any feast but the passover; nor, after his resurrection, on any but the feast of Pentecost. The feast of Tabernacles, in particular, has nothing to render it memorable either before or after. He began his ministry at one passover, and he ended it at another; and if he ever visited Jerusalem at stated times, it was at the passovers between. It is just as probable that he would be born at one passover, as that he would suffer at another; and if the paschal lamb was the most expressive type (furnished by the symbolical sacrifices of the Law) of the great Christian sacrifice, it was not less agreeable to the analogy of the type, that the true Paschal Victim should have been born at one passover, than that he should have suffered at another.'—*Ibid.*, p. 386.

'The two sacrifices under the Law, the daily sacrifice of morning and evening, and the sacrifice of the fourteenth of Nisan, which are unquestionably the liveliest emblems of the sacrifice of Christ—the one of its *perpetual*, the other of its *universal*, efficacy,—were both required to be made with a lamb, or at least, in the case of the latter, with a kid instead of a lamb. Concerning this requisition, *see* Maimonides, De Rat. Sacrif. i. 14. This requisition was not peculiar to other sacrifices, numerous as they were: nor would it be easy to assign a reason why it should have been peculiar to the two most Evangelical of the legal ordinances, except by supposing that Christ, as soon as, in the integrity of our nature and substance, he came into the world, was virtually the true *ὁλοκαυτον θυσια* of morning and evening prayer, and the true spiritual antitype designed by the paschal victim. And Christ, when he came into the world, came as a child: and, though he suffered as a man, yet in all those qualities, which rendered his sacrifice of himself acceptable to God, and which especially were adumbrated by the properties of the typical victim—in meekness, simplicity, and innocence—he continued ever a child.'—*Ibid.*, p. 386.

'At the original institution of the passover, it was commanded, the lamb, to be offered on the *fourteenth*, should be taken up and set apart for that purpose, on the *tenth* of the same month; 4 days before its sacrifice. The reason of this provision does not appear: but, if we were to conjecture that, in the fulness of time, the birth of our Saviour was to happen on the tenth of Nisan, as it is certain that his death was to happen on the fourteenth, we should assign a reason which would explain it at once, and be entirely in unison with what has been proved respecting the period of the nativity in general.'—*Ibid.*, p. 389.—*See* § 82, *On Jesus presenting himself in the temple.*

'I advance it, therefore, as a conjecture which to pious minds may not appear improbable, (though it must still be received as a conjecture,) that the true day of our Saviour's birth, and, consequently, the true date of the nativity, is the tenth of the Jewish Nisan. The Paschal Chronicon assigns this date to the fact of the Annunciation; and tradition may so far have blended, in this instance, as well as in others, error with truth, as to have confounded the day of the birth with the day of the supposed conception of Christ. It would follow that the Baptist, who was born six months before Christ, might be born on the tenth of Tisri, or about the feast of Tabernacles; which, however, must be received as even a more conjectural date than the other. Yet there would be occasion, from this coincidence also, to admire the economy of the Divine Providence in causing one, designed by his office not merely to be the precursor of the Messias, but a preacher of repentance and righteousness—one who by coming and acting, *ἐν ὁδῳ δικαιοσυνης*, was not only to preach, but also to practise the lessons of his preaching—to be born at this season of the year in general, if not on this day in particular.'—*Ibid.*, p. 390.

'There is no fact in the subsequent history of our Saviour, whether more or less remote, which is not altogether consistent with this first and cardinal point in the whole—that he was born about the vernal equinox. I have proved thus much of the time of the commencement, and of the time of the close of his ministry; and of his age at the first of those points, and the duration of his ministry previously, at the other.'—*Ibid.*, p. 391.

ADDENDA—(continued).

'Genealogies,' p. 23.

The necessity of some genealogy of our Lord in general must be evident: for if he was the predicted Messias of the Jews, whose birth and descent had been fixed long before to a certain line, the fulfilment of the prophecy in his person could not be made apparent but by exhibiting his descent accordingly. That their genealogical records were still preserved, among the Jews, after, as well as before, the Babylonish captivity is too notorious a fact to require proof. (Jos. Vit. i. Contra Ap. i. 7.) The numerous family notices, which occur in the books of Chronicles, Ezra, and Nehemiah, (1 Ch. ix. 1–22; 2 Ch. xxxi. 16–.9; Ne. vii. 5,) *passim*, were doubtless extracted from such records; and so late even as the reign of Domitian, when Josephus composed his own Memoirs, (Ant. Jud. xx. xi. 2), he may still be found appealing, in proof of his extraction, to the δημόσιαι δέλτοι, as yet in existence, and yet open to inspection.

'Again; As our Saviour's parents, whether both really, or both nominally, such—or the one really, the other only reputed so—were necessarily distinct individuals, his descent might be exhibited through either; and, as traced through the one, must necessarily differ from the same descent as traced through the other. Yet the one would be truly an account of his descent, as much as the other

Again; If Joseph was really the father of our Lord, the genealogy of Joseph, according to the flesh, would be the genealogy of our Lord, in the same respect—and it would be superfluous to search for any other. But if Joseph was not really the father of our Lord, that is, if the Christian doctrine of the Incarnation be scriptural and true—a doctrine, which St. Matthew confirms as plainly as St. Luke the genealogy of Joseph, according to the flesh, could in nowise be the similar genealogy of Christ. Now the genealogy, which is given by St. Matthew, is obviously the genealogy of Joseph, according to the flesh: the use of the assertion ἐγέννησε, between its several links, from first to last, admits of no other conclusion. If so, it could not be the genealogy of Christ in the natural sense. But it might still be his genealogy in some other sense—as reputed, for instance, the son of Joseph—that is, as naturally the son of the wife of Joseph. It might be, therefore, his genealogy in a civil or political sense. Accordingly, the same Evangelist, who so clearly propounds it as the natural genealogy of Joseph, does by no means propound it as the natural genealogy of Christ; for, when he is arrived at the name of Joseph, instead of continuing, as he had begun, and had proceeded all along until now—᾽Ιωσὴφ δὲ ἐγέννησε τὸν ᾽Ιησοῦ—he changes his language in a striking manner —᾽Ιακὼβ δὲ ἐγέννησε τὸν ᾽Ιωσὴφ, ΤΟΝ ΑΝΔΡΑ ΜΑΡΙΑΣ ΕΞ ΗΣ ἐγεννήθη ᾽Ιησοῦς ὁ λεγόμενος Χριστός—It is evident, then, that he intended the previous line to stop short with Joseph—or not to pass on to Christ, except as the son of Mary, whose husband was Joseph. Nor is this all; but, if the words be rightly translated, it is further implied by them, that Joseph did not become the husband of Mary until after the birth, or at least the conception, of Christ: that Jacob begat Joseph, the husband of Mary, of whom had been born, or, had been conceived, Jesus who is called Christ. That this is a possible meaning of ἐγεννήθη I have no hesitation in affirming.

'Again: The genealogy of St. Matthew not being the genealogy of Christ, according to the flesh, the general reason, alluded to already, would require some other to be left on record, which should be his genealogy according to the flesh. But any genealogy, distinct from that of his reputed father, must be the genealogy of his real mother. St. Luke has exhibited such a genealogy. St. Luke's genealogy, therefore, may be the natural genealogy of Mary, but cannot be the natural genealogy of Joseph.

'It ought to excite no surprise, if the genealogy of Mary, regarded as the genealogy of our Lord, were exhibited nominally as the genealogy of Joseph. It follows only that, as the *natural* genealogy of Joseph, distinct from Mary's, is exhibited by St. Matthew as the *legal* genealogy of Jesus; so the *natural* genealogy of Jesus, distinct from Joseph's, is exhibited by St. Luke, as the *legal* genealogy of Joseph.

'Again: We have but to suppose that Mary, the mother of our Lord, was the daughter of Eli, and the wife of Joseph, and we assign a reason why the descent of our Lord, though in reality *through Mary*, might yet be set forth as apparently *through Joseph*. Tradition seems to have perpetuated thus much—that the names of the Virgin's parents were Joachim (which is but another form for Eliachim, or for Eli) and Anna—which so far agrees with the supposition. And though, if the fact of their marriage be admitted, we may not in strictness be concerned with the further question, how Joseph, the son of Jacob, might come to be contracted to Mary, the daughter of Eli, yet if we may also suppose, what I think is very probable, that Mary was the only child of Eli, and Joseph was the next of kin to her, then the Law of Moses would require their union.

'It is certain that, as both descended from David, Joseph and Mary were of kin; and as each standing at analogous points in the lines of this descent, it is probable they were the next of kin. It is probable, also, that Mary was an orphan at the time of the annunciation; or that her parents were then dead; and, though she was already espoused to Joseph, it is almost presumptively certain that she was much younger than he; ... which disparity of age, if it be rightly assumed, must be among the strongest presumptive arguments that they were espoused as the next of kin.

'If, then, it be asked why St. Matthew should have given the genealogy of Joseph, as the genealogy of Christ, knowing it to be merely his civil, but not his natural, it may be answered, first, that if the Jewish records did not recognise Mary, though the daughter of Eli, except as the wife of Joseph, her son, who would appear to be his son, must be described accordingly. Secondly, the final end of any genealogical account of Christ being merely to demonstrate his lineal descent from David, if the Virgin Mary was really ἐπίκληρος ὠφάνερος and married to Joseph, as the next of kin, this end would be answered by the line of Joseph, as well as by the line of Mary. The wife of Joseph, under such circumstances, must have been descended from David, as well as he. Thirdly, what is, perhaps, the true reason, St. Matthew, writing exclusively for the Jews, proposes our Saviour as *their* Messiah—and confines his line to David and Abraham accordingly, with a view more particularly to establish his title, as the βασιλεὺς τοῦ ᾽Ισραήλ, and, in that capacity, his right to the temporal kingdom of Israel. This temporal kingdom, at first, was undoubtedly assured to Solomon, and to his posterity according to the flesh, (2 Sa. vii. 12–6; 1 Ki. i. 13, 30; ix. 5; 1 Ch. xvii. 11–4; xxii. 7–10; xxviii. 5); and though this promise may seem to have been revoked in the person of Coniah, or Jeconiah, the grandson of Josiah, and even before that in the person of Jehoiakim, the father of Coniah. (Je. xxii. 10, 2, 24–7, 28–30; xxii. 13–9; xxxvi. 30), yet a contemporary prophecy, relating to the last king Zedekiah, (Eze. xxi. 25—7), and another prophecy of Jeremiah himself (xxxiii. 17–end), will shew it was never absolutely revoked, but merely for a time suspended. It was taken away from the present possessor, Shallum, Jeholakim, Coniah, or Zedekiah, but only to be reserved until *he* should come whose right it was—and to him it should be restored. This person was doubtless Christ—and his right, as entitled to the crown of Israel, must be as derived from David. For this reason St. Matthew has traced up his descent through the line of Solomon, because the promise of the temporal kingdom was originally assured to David, in the person of Solomon. The right conveyed by that promise, and transmitted through the descendants of Solomon, was now centred in Joseph—and through Joseph became vested in Christ—a result which would be the same, in whatever sense our Saviour were considered the son, provided he was only the ἐπικληρόνομος of Joseph. Nor is it any objection that the temporal kingdom has not yet been actually restored to the descendants of David, in the person of Christ. It may be restored hereafter—and that is sufficient for the end in view. But the genealogy of St. Luke, which, beginning with Jesus, proceeds up to Adam, can have no object except to represent Christ as the promised seed of the woman, in whom all the nations of the earth were interested alike. It is such a genealogy, therefore, as was to be expected from a gospel, written expressly for Gentiles, and not for Jews.'—*Greswell*. vol. II. Diss. xvi. pp. 83–107.

PART I.   WISE MEN FROM THE EAST.   SECT. V.

SECTION 5.—MAGI, OR WISE MEN, FROM THE EAST, BEING WARNED BY THE APPEARANCE OF A STAR OF THE INCARNATION AND BIRTH OF THE MESSIAH, ARRIVE AT JERUSALEM; THEY ARE SENT TO BETHLEHEM; AND BEING CONDUCTED, BY THE SAME STAR, TO THE HOUSE OF JOSEPH, THEY WORSHIP THE INFANT CHRIST; AND RETURN HOME. JOSEPH IS WARNED OF GOD TO FLEE, WITH THE INFANT JESUS AND MARY, INTO EGYPT. THE CHILDREN AT BETHLEHEM, FROM TWO YEARS OLD AND UNDER, BY COMMAND OF HEROD, ARE PUT TO DEATH. AFTER THE DEATH OF HEROD, JOSEPH IS AGAIN WARNED OF GOD TO RETURN FROM EGYPT. HE SETTLES WITH THE HOLY FAMILY AT NAZARETH. Matt. ii. 1—23; Luke ii. 39.

(G. 12.) No. 5. *The Magi from the East inquire for the Messiah, and are sent to Bethlehem.* [Ch. i. ver. 25, § 4, p. 22.] *Matt.* ii. 1—8. *At Jerusalem.*

1 Now when-'Jesus'*a*-was-born in Bethlehem of Judæa in the-days of-Herod's the 2 king, behold, there-came wise-men *c* from the-east to Jerusalem, saying, Where is he that-is-born King of-the Jews? for we-have-seen his star in the east, and are-come to-worship him.

MARGINAL READINGS:—*a* The Lord the Saviour.   *b* Who hath dominion.   *c* Or magi.

SCRIPTURE ILLUSTRATIONS.

1. *Herod*—this name, considered as from the Greek, is supposed to mean 'glory of the skin;' for which, as to Esau or Edom, his ancestor, see Ge. xxv. 25; xxvii. 21, 2—in the Hebrew, Herod means 'the reigning or dominating one;' and *Herod the king*, an Edomite, who, by the favour of the Romans, had attained to the kingdom, as well as his successor of the same name, justified the prediction, ' When thou shalt have the dominion, thou shalt break his yoke,' Ge. xxvii. 40—comp. Ps. ii. 2, 3. with Ac. iv. 25—8; Lu. xxiii. 6—12, § 90—see § 1, p. 2. *Herod*.

Solomon the king had been renowned for wisdom over all the East, 1 Ki. x. 6—afterwards Daniel, (Eze. xxviii. 3.) and he who had been over the wise men in the East, was made acquainted with the time of Christ's appearing, as One to be cut off, Da. ix. 26.—It is to be observed that these wise men had come to a knowledge of the promises, as to the Messiah, through the medium of the Jews, such as Daniel, and not through the outcasts of Israel; else they would have called him, 'King of Israel,' not 'King of the Jews'—see Is. xliv. 6; Zep. iii. 15; Ho xiii. 9, 10.

1, 2. *wise men*—there were those in Egypt who were so called, Ex. vii. 11—so also in Babylon, Da. ii. 18—Daniel interceded for them, ver. 24—declared their incompetence, ver. 27—and was made chief of the governors over all the *wise men* of Babylon, ver. 48—

King of the Jews—so questioned by Pilate, Jno. xviii. 33, § 90—mocked by the soldiers, xix. 3, ib.—presented as such by Pilate, ver. 14, ib.—mocked by the soldiers after condemnation, Mt. xxvii. 29, § 91—his superscription, ver. 37, ib.

NOTES.

Wise men. Or *magi.* These probably came from Persia, or beyond the Euphrates, a country east of Judæa, 1 Ki. iv. 30. Daniel was placed over this class of men in Babylon, Da. v. 11. These magi might have been Jews, as many were mixed with the people of the East. The word is of Persian origin, *Mogh*, and designated throughout the East, (and especially Persia, the original seat of this class of persons,) the *priests, philosophers,* and *men of letters* in general; who devoted themselves to the study of human science, especially medicine and astrology.

[Their doctrines are said to have been derived from *Abraham,* or at least purified by him from Zabian idolatry. They again became corrupted, and were again purified by *Zoroaster,* who is supposed to have been a descendant of the prophet Daniel; deriving from him that intimate knowledge of the Mosaic writings, which his religion evinces.]—See ADDENDA, ' *On the Visit of the Magi,*' p. 39.

2. *Where is he, &c.* There was, at this time, a prevalent expectation that some remarkable personage was about to appear in Judæa. The Jews were anxiously looking for the coming of the Messiah.

[By computing the time mentioned by Daniel (ch.

ix. 25—.7), they knew that the period was approaching when the Messiah should appear. This personage, they supposed, would be a temporal prince, and they were expecting that he would deliver them from Roman bondage. It was natural that this expectation should spread into other countries. Many Jews, at that time, dwelt in Egypt, in Rome, and in Greece; many, also, had gone to eastern countries, and in every place they carried their scriptures, and diffused the expectation that some remarkable person was about to appear. He whom the nation was looking for.]

His star. Which seems to have moved in the middle region of the air, somewhat in the manner of the cloudy pillar before the Hebrews in the wilderness, Ex. xlii. 21.

In the East. Being in the East, they saw the star in the West, and were guided by it to Jerusalem.

To worship him. προσκυνησαι αυτω, 'To prostrate ourselves before him.' ' To do him homage.' It signifies a complete prostration of the body (especially the head) to the ground, a form of reverential salutation which has ever prevailed in the East.

PRACTICAL REFLECTIONS.

(Mt. ii. 1—12.) 1 *ver.* Let us beware of mistaking worldly dignity, outward prosperity, or even intimate connexion with the cause of God, as sure indications of the divine favour. They only gave to Herod the power of bringing upon himself the greater condemnation. He rebuilt with remarkable splendour the house of the Lord, yet refused Him, the Lord of glory, a place where to lay his head. He even, with sweeping fury, sought to put to death the infant Prince of Life.

2 *ver.* Let us learn from the example of our great Teacher, to address men according to their condition in life, previous pursuits, and means of ascertaining evidence. Zacharias, a priest, was met in the exercise of his priestly office, Lu. i. 8—11; Mary was given a sign in domestic life, correspondent to her own predicted condition, Lu. i. 36; the shepherds were with their flocks, when they were pointed to the sign of the babe in the manger, Lu. ii. 8—12; whilst the wise men were led to Jesus by his star. These last, however, had to be assisted in this by the chief

priests and scribes, who had information, according to their peculiar vocation, from the written word, Mt. ii. 4—6.

[From the case of the wise men, who appear to have profited by instruction, derived from the dispersed of Judah, so long after the time that they had Daniel for their teacher, let us learn to attend to the precept, ' *Cast thy bread upon the waters: for thou shalt find it after many days.*' ' *In the morning sow thy seed, and in the evening withhold not thy hand,*' &c., Eccl. xi. 1, 6]

5 *ver.* Those who had the written word were privileged to direct others to Jesus; yet, is does not appear that they went themselves. Let us hereby be warned, for those who are nearest to the greatest means of grace may be the farthest from the right use of them. The same investigation may be made from very different motives, as by the wise men for the King of the Jews, that they might worship him; and by Herod, that he might destroy the heir to the throne of David, which throne he had himself usurped.]

SALVATION IS OF THE JEWS.—John iv. 22.

Matt. ii. 3 When·'Herod the king'·had-heard *these things*, he-was-troubled, and all
4 Jerusalem with him. And when-he-had-gathered·'all the chief-priests and scribes
5 of-the people'·together, he-demanded of them where Christ should-be-born. And they
6 said unto-him, In Bethlehem of Judæa: for thus it-is-written by the prophet, and
thou Bethlehem, *in the* land of-Juda, art not the-least among the princes *a* of-Juda: for
7 out-of thee shall-come a-Governor, that shall-rule ποιμανεῖ my people Israel. *b* Then
Herod, when-he-had·'privily'·called the wise-men, enquired·'of' them'·diligently
8 ηκριβωσε παρ' what time the star appeared. And he-sent them to Bethlehem, and-
said, Go and-search diligently for the young-child; and when ye-have-found *him*,
bring·'me'·word-again, that I-'may-come and-worship him'·also.

MARGINAL READINGS:—*a* Or leaderships; thousands.   *b* The prince of God.

SCRIPTURE ILLUSTRATIONS.

3. *he was troubled*—so Zacharias, Lu. i. 12, § 1, p. 4; —so Mary, i. 29, § 2, p. 9—so the shepherds, Lu. ii. 9, § 4, p. 20—so Pilate, Jno. xix. 8, § 90—the guard at his resurrection, Mt. xxviii. 4, § 93—*see* 'troubled,' Lu. i. 29, § 2, p. 9.

4. *gathered all the chief priests and scribes*—they gathered to condemn him, Lu. xxii. 66, § 89.

scribes—called doctors of the law, Lu. v. 17, § 22—also lawyers, Mt. xxii. 35, § 85.

5. *Bethlehem of Judæa*—Joseph went to his own city, &c., Lu. ii. 4, § 4, p. 19—*see* also ver. 6.

6. *Governor that shall rule*—Mi. v. 1–3, this prophecy invites to the future gathering of Israel—'now gather thyself in troops,' ver. 1—it recognises the past desolation of Jerusalem, 'he hath laid siege against us,' ver. 1—intimates the cause of the Jews being given up to the terrors of the Roman siege, 'they shall smite the Judge of Israel,' &c.—the prophecy then goes back to his birth, and the purpose for which he came into the world, 'But thou, Bethlehem, &c., of Judah, out of thee ... unto me ... ruler in Israel,' ver. 2—such was his origin as man; but he is also God, 'whose goings forth have been from of old,' ver. 2—having stated the cause of the Jews being given up, it is intimated, that so they would be left, until the people of promise had been gathered unto their King, when the remnant of his brethren, the Jews, shall return to the children of Israel, ver. 3.

rule—or 'feed,' Ps. lxxviii. 71, .2; Is. xl. 11; Je. xxiii.; Eze. xxxiv. 23–.5; xxxvii. 24–.6; Ps. c.—Christ, the good Shepherd, who gave his life for the sheep, Jno. x. 11, § 55—other sheep than the Jews, ver. 16, *ib.*; ver. 26, § 56.

my people Israel—the name of 'Ammi,' *my people*, had been taken from the house of Israel, as under the old covenant—*see* Ho. i. 6–9—but it was to be restored under the *new*, ver. 10, .1; ii. 19, 20, .3—*see* also Je. iii., as to the being re-married, as under the gospel, ver. 11—.4—and of the Lord subsequently ruling his people, ver. 15–.7—and of Judah then being added unto them, ver. 18, .9.

8. *go and search diligently*—see such as Herod described, his pride, cruelty, and deceit, Ps. x. 4–10—his words, Ps. lv. 21—the folly of such wisdom, 1 Co. iii. 19, 20—overruled, Ps. lxxvi.

NOTES.

3. *When Herod the king heard these things, he was troubled.* Lest he should lose his kingdom by the birth of the rightful heir; he himself being a foreigner and usurper.

And all Jerusalem, &c. Lest it might occasion a renewal of some of those tyrannical actions of which Herod was continually capable. There were many '*waiting for the consolation of Israel*,' and to whom the coming of the Messiah would be a matter of joy; but Herod's friends would be alarmed.

4. *The chief priests.* By the *chief priests* here are meant not only the high priest and his deputy, but all those who had passed the office, and who still, by courtesy, enjoyed the title, and probably wore an Archieratical robe; also the heads or chiefs of the twenty-four classes into which David had divided the sacerdotal families, 1 Ch. xxiii. 6; xxiv.; 2 Ch. viii. 14; Ezr. viii. 24. All the members of the Sanhedrim or great Ecclesiastical Council.

[*And scribes.*—*See* ADDENDA, p. 199.

5. *In Bethlehem of Judæa.* The word *Bethlehem* denotes 'house of bread'—perhaps given to the place on account of its great fertility. [It was also called *Ephrata*, Mi. v. 2, a word supposed likewise to signify fertility, Ru. iv. 11; Ephrath, Ge. xlviii. 7.]

Bethlehem.—*See* 'GEOGRAPHICAL NOTICE,' p. 27. It was called the city of David, Lu. ii. 4, because it was the city of his nativity, 1 Sa. xvi. 1, 11–3, .8. It was called Bethlehem *of Judæa*, to distinguish it from a town of the same name in Galilee, in the tribe of Zebulun, Jos. xix. 15.

By the prophet. The Sanhedrim answered without hesitation. It was settled by prophecy. This prophecy is found in Mi. v. 2—*See* above, '*Governor*.' The scope of the prophet and of the Evangelist is the same—namely, to state, that though Bethlehem be one of the smallest cities of Judah, yet it will not be the smallest (*i.e.* will be the greatest) in celebrity—since out of it shall come forth, &c.

[The passage in Micah, which was referred to by the Jews themselves, as denoting the place of Jesus' birth, clearly intimates, that although he was to be born in Judah, his dominion should be Israel; in order to which he had first to ascend unto the Father. ' *But thou, Bethlehem Ephratah, though thou be little among the thousands of Judah, yet out of thee shall he come forth unto ME, that is to be* RULER IN ISRAEL,' Mi. v. 2.—*See* Nathanael's confession, Jno. i. 49, and the taunt of the chief priests, Mt. xxvii. 42.]

[6. *In the land of Judah.* The word γῆ without the article, joined to the name of a tribe also without the article, denotes the *canton* or territory assigned to that tribe. In this sense, γῆ Ζαβουλὼν and γῆ Νεφθαλὶμ, occur in chap. iv. 15. Therefore, γῆ Ἰούδα, does not signify the country of JUDÆA, but the canton or district of the tribe of Judah.]

The princes of Judah. In Mi. v. 2, it is, '*the thousands of Judah*.' There is much reason to believe, that each tribe was divided into small portions called *thousands, i.e.* companies of 1,000 families; so the term was sometimes taken to denote the district where they resided; as in England certain small divisions are called *hundreds*. [*See* Ju. vi. 15, where, instead of *my FAMILY is the poor in Manasseh*, the Hebrew is, *my THOUSAND is the meanest in Manasseh*.—See 1 Sa. x. 19; 1 Ch. xii. 20; Ex. xviii. 25, '*And Moses chose able men out of all Israel, and made them heads over the people, rulers of thousands, rulers of hundreds, rulers of fifties, and rulers of tens*.' These THOUSANDS being petty governments, the apostle renders the word *princes* or *governors*, as more intelligible in the Greek tongue than thousands, though in this case both may signify the same.]

A Governor. A ruler. This is one of the characters of the Messiah, who is the King of his people, Jno. xviii. 37, § 90. [The word *rule* here means to rule as a shepherd does his flock, in faithfulness and tenderness.—*Comp.* Jno. x. 11; Is. xl. 10, .1, 10, ' *Behold, the Lord* GOD *will come with strong hand, and his arm shall rule for him : behold, his reward is with him, and his work before him.* 11. *He shall feed his flock like a shepherd;*' &c.—*See* also ix. 7.]

7. *Privily.* To ascertain the *time* when Jesus was born.

8. *Diligently.* Accurately; exactly. He took pains to learn the exact time that the star appeared; for he wished to know precisely how old the child was.

PRACTICAL REFLECTIONS.

6 *ver.* That may be little in men's esteem, which, in the eye of God, may be far from being the least, as was the case with the small political division of Bethlehem of Judah, out of which the king, not only of the Jews, but of all Israel, was to proceed.

PART I.   THE MAGI WORSHIP CHRIST.   SECT. V.

The Magi worship Christ, and return home. Matt. ii. 9—12. At Bethlehem.

9 When they had heard the king, they departed; and, lo, the star, which they saw in the east, went before them, till it came and stood over where the young child was.
10 When they saw the star, they rejoiced with exceeding great joy.
11 And when they were come into the house, they saw the young child with Mary his mother, and fell down, and worshipped him: and when they had opened their treasures, they presented[a]
12 unto him gifts; gold, and frankincense, and myrrh.[b] And being warned of God in a dream that they should not return to Herod, they departed into their own country another way.

MARGINAL READINGS:—*a* Or offered.   *b* Gr. Myra.

SCRIPTURE ILLUSTRATIONS.

10. *they rejoiced*—so Elisabeth's cousin, &c., Lu. i. 58, § 3, p. 15.

11. *worshipped*—see Ps. lxxii. 10, 1, 5, ...—' All should honour the Son, even as they honour the F.,' Jno. v. 23, § 23—had been predicted, 'Thy father's children shall bow down before thee,' Ge. xlix. 8—fulfilment anticipated, Ps. i.—*confirm.*, Ph. ii. 9—11; He. i. 6—*examples:* by the apostles in the ship, Mt. xiv. 33, § 41—by the women after his resurrection, xxviii. 9, § 95—by the disciples, ver 16, 7—not only his brethren, but all creation, will yet harmoniously join in the worship of our blessed Redeemer, Rev. v. 8—14.

presented unto him gifts, &c.—gifts were especially presented to prophets, 1 Sa. ix. 6—9; 2 Ki. viii. 8—these lived more immediately upon the providence of God; so the apostles of our Lord were sent forth.

11. *Fell down.* This was the usual way of shewing respect or homage among the Jews.—See Est. viii. 3; Job i. 20; 1s. xlvi. 6; Da. iii. 7.—See also Ps. lxxii. 11.
Worshipped him.—See NOTE, p. 31, ' To worship him.'
Opened their treasures. θησαυρους, 'Caskets,' 'chests,' or other receptacles.—See Mt. xii. 35, 'A good man out of the good treasure of the heart,' &c: —See § 31.
They presented unto him gifts. Agreeable to the Oriental custom, (still existing,) of never appearing before a king, or any great personage, without offering him gifts; usually the choicest productions of the country of the giver: It was customary, at the birth of a prince, to shew respect for him by making him presents, or offerings of this kind, and to approach a great personage with gifts.—See Ge. xxxii. 13, 4; 1 Sam ix. 7, 8; x. 27; 1 Ki. x. 2, the queen of Sheba, *' came to Jerusalem with a very great train; with camels that bare spices, and very much gold, and precious stones,' &c.* The gifts; gold, and frankincense, and myrrh, might be not mere ceremonial offering, but to Joseph and Mary a most seasonable provision for them in their long journey which was so soon to follow.

Gold, frankincense, and myrrh. It is evident from the gifts which the wise men presented, that they considered the infant as a royal child. If they had judged from appearance only, a citron, a rose, or even the least gift, would have been sufficient for the infant of the poor Mary. But, mean as his appearance was, they treated him as a royal child; and even after they discovered the poverty of his parents, they presented him with presents of the richest kind; gold, frankincense, and myrrh.—See above, 1 Ki. x. 2.

Frankincense. This was a production of Arabia.

PRACTICAL REFLECTIONS.

8, 9 ver. The greatest tyrants have frequently to submit to the meanest actions; as was the case with Herod, who used such cowardly concealment and falsehood in order to make the wise men the unsuspecting instruments of his tyranny.

[9 ver. Those who rightly are the light they have, may expect its continuance and increase, as shewn in the case of the wise men coming to Jerusalem. They had there the teaching of the prophets, and thereafter the renewal of the star to guide to the young child.]

10, 11 ver. We should neither despise former assistance because new is given, nor reject the light which more peculiarly belongs to others; had the wise men neglected either the written word, or the star they had previously seen, it is not likely they would have been led so directly, and without being

Mt. x. 9—14, § 39—and required assistance in temporal things from those to whom they ministered, ver. 40—2, *ib.*—Jesus himself, as being a prophet, was thus provided for, Lu. viii. 3, § 30—Paul vindicates his claim in this respect, 1 Co. ix. 11—yet would not receive from the Corinthians, 2 Co. xi. 8—12—although he did from the Philippians, iv. 15—8.

gold—may have more respected the kingly office, and *frankincense and myrrh* the priesthood of Christ. Such offerings are yet to be brought from the East, Ps. lxxii. 10, 5—Jesus is ' The Christ;' the anointed Prophet, King, and Priest.

12. *in a dream*—dream of Abimelech, Ge. xx. 3, 6 —of the butler and baker of Pharaoh, xl. 5, 8, 12, 3—also of Pharaoh, xli. 15, 25.—The Lord expressly declares that he would sometimes thus reveal himself, Nu. xii. 6.—See ' Scr. Ill.,' § 2, p. 13, & NOTES, *infra*.

NOTES.

It was a yellowish white resin or gum, of a bitter taste. It was obtained from a tree by making incisions in the bark, and suffering the gum to flow out. It was highly odoriferous or fragrant when burned, and was therefore used in worship, where it was burned as a pleasant offering to God.—See Ex. xxx. 7, 8, ' Aaron shall burn thereon sweet incense every morning : when he dresseth the lamps, he shall burn incense upon it. And when Aaron lighteth the lamps at even, he shall burn incense upon it, a perpetual incense before the Lord throughout your generations.' It is produced in the East Indies and Arabia.

Myrrh. A precious kind of gum, procured, in the same manner as frankincense, from a tree growing in Egypt, Arabia, and Abyssinia. Its name denotes bitterness; but its smell, though strong, is not disagreeable. Among the ancients it entered into the composition of the most costly ointments, and as a perfume, it appears to have been used to give a pleasant fragrance to vestments; and was much used to embalm the dead. Jno. xix. 39, § 92, *' And there came also Nicodemus,' &c.*

12. *A dream.* By this word are to be understood those images which are formed in the imagination while we are asleep: they are—(1.) Natural, Ec. v. 7.—(2.) Divine: God shewed Jacob the mysterious ladder, Ge. xxviii. 12—4; Joseph was early forewarned, xxxvii. 4, 5, 6; Nebuchadnezzar was warned of the destruction of his empire, Da. ii., and of his own abasement, ch. iv.—see ' Script. Illus.,' § 2, p. 13.—And (3.) Diabolical and sinful, as De. xiii. 1, 3, 5; such dreamers were to be put to death, and the prophet. Jeremiah exclaims against the false prophets, who pretended to have dreams, ch. xxiii. 32.

Another way. ' A more direct way.'   ' They bent back their course.'

involved in trouble, to pay their homage to the infant Redeemer.]

Jesus, who hath a right to reign, who is appointed to rule over Israel, we should, as did the wise men, serve with our best; worshipping him as God, and acknowledging him as our Prophet, Priest, and King.

12 ver. Those who, in simplicity, follow the direction of heavenly wisdom, will be likely to find their guide fully a match for the most crafty.

2—12 ver. The wise men were led in such a way as to teach them their dependance upon intelligence and wisdom greater than their own: first, their attention was arrested by the star; then they were taught from the written word; and last of all, in their slumberings upon the bed, God himself opened their ears and sealed instruction. Thus did he at the same time reward their diligence and integrity.

WHOM WILL YE LOVE IF NOT THE KING OF SAINTS?   [33

THE MASSACRE OF THE CHILDREN.

(G. 13.) *Joseph is warned to flee with the infant Jesus and Mary into Egypt; they depart by night. Matt. ii. 13—.5. From Bethlehem.*

13 And when·˙they·˙were-departed, behold, the-angel of-the-Lord appeareth to Joseph in a-dream, saying, Arise, and-take the young-child and his mother, and flee into Egypt,*" and be-thou there until I-bring·˙thee·˙-word: for Herod will seek the young-
14 child to destroy him. When-˙he˙-arose, he-took the young-child and his mother by-
15 night, and departed into Egypt: and was there until the death of-Herod: that it-might-be-fulfilled which was-spoken of the Lord by the prophet, saying, Out-of Egypt have-I-called my son.

The massacre of the children. Matt. ii. 16—.8. At Bethlehem and Rama.

16 Then Herod, when-he-saw that he-was-mocked of the wise-men, was·˙exceeding·˙-wroth, and sent-forth, and-slew all the children that *were* in Bethlehem, and in all the coasts thereof, from two-years-old and under, according-to the time which he-had-
17 diligently-enquired of the wise-men. Then was-fulfilled that which-was-spoken by
18 Jeremy *b* the prophet, saying, In Rama *c* was-there·˙a-voice·˙-heard, lamentation, and weeping, and great mourning, Rachel weeping-*for* her children, and would not be-comforted, because they-are not.

MARGINAL READINGS:—*a* Gn. Dark coloured, like a vulture. *b* Who exalts the Lord, or, the Lord shall lift up. *c* Lifted up; elevation.

SCRIPTURE ILLUSTRATIONS.

12, .3. *in a dream*—so Joseph, to take Mary to wife, Mt. i. 20, § 2, p. 13—to return to the land of Israel, ver. 19, 20.

15. *out of Egypt*, Ho. xi. 1—the Lord, in visions of the night, encouraged Jacob to go down to Egypt, Ge. xlvi. 3, 4—ho thence brought out Israel as his first-born, Ex. xii. 51; xiii. 2, 3—Jesus, the true First-born, fulfilled the case of the people he represented, 'In all their affliction he was afflicted,' Is. lxiii. 9—this is particularly noticed in connection with the bringing out of Egypt, ver. 10—.4.

16. *wroth*—see this case described, Pr. xxvii. 3, 4; xxviii. 15—Nebuchadnezzar, Da. iii. 13, .9, 20.

18. *Rachel weeping for her children*, Je. xxxi. 15—this is another instance of the identification of the case of Christ with that of his people; the merit of his work is given unto them, ver. 16, even as their sorrows were laid upon Him, Is. liii. 4—Rachel was the mother of Joseph, in the portion of whose children was SAMARIA; she was also the mother of Benjamin, in whose portion was JERUSALEM. Both these capitals, first Samaria, Am. v., viii., and then Jerusalem, Je. iv. 31; ix. 17, 21, were appointed to Lamentation and bitter weeping. The restoration of the redeemed people to Zion, as described, Is. li. 11; lii., is through their being made one with the Redeemer, whose suffering for them is expressed, ch. liii.—The seed of promise, however apparently destroyed or lost sight of by man, hath still been preserved, as was Jesus, upon the slaughter of the young children of *Bethlehem*, Is. lxv. 8, 9; Jo. xxxi. 36; Ho. i. 6, 9, 10.

NOTES.

13. *Flee into Egypt*. Egypt is situated to the south-west of Judæa, and is distant from Bethlehem perhaps about sixty or seventy miles. It was at this time a Roman province. The Greek language was spoken there. There were many Jews there, a temple at HELIOPOLIS, and synagogues; and Joseph, therefore, would be among his own countrymen. The jurisdiction of Herod extended only to the river Sihon, or river of Egypt, and of course, beyond that, Joseph was safe from his designs.

[The *Babylonian Gemara* states, that provision was made, by the Jews then resident in Egypt, for the wants of poor strangers who took refuge in that country. ... Joseph and Mary had, however, just before been provided with gold, &c.—*see* ver. 12, p. 31.]—*See* ADDENDA, '*Of the residence in Egypt,*' p. 39.

[15. *Out of Egypt have I called my son.* These words out of Ho. xi. 1, are not cited merely by way of accommodation, but, referring primarily to the deliverance of the children of Israel out of Egypt, they were, secondarily, fulfilled in the person of Christ. That Israel was a type of Christ appears from Ex. iv. 22, where he is called by God, *his son*; his *first-born*; whence also *Israel* is put for *Christ*, Is. xlix. 3.—*See* ADDENDA, '*Out of Egypt,*' &c., p. 39. It is in Christ that a right is given to become the sons of God—it is as being made one with the Son of God; who, in all his people's afflictions, was afflicted; in him was fulfilled the case of his people.]

16. *Mocked of the wise men.* When he saw that he had been deceived by them—that is, that they did not return, as he had expected. Literally, was trifled with; imposed upon.—*See* Je.·*x*. 14.

Exceeding wroth. Very angry. He had been disappointed and deceived. He expected to send an executioner, and kill Jesus alone. But since he was disappointed in this, he thought he would accomplish the same thing, and be sure to destroy him, if he sent forth and put *all the children in the place* to death.

Slew all the children. That is, all the *male* children. The design of Herod was to cut off him that had been born *king* of the Jews. According to the Jewish reckoning, a child that had entered its second year would be called two years old.

In all the coasts thereof. The adjacent places; the settlements or hamlets around Bethlehem.

18. *Lamentation and weeping.* A most pathetic accumulation of terms expressing bitter grief.

[*Rachel weeping*, &c. A fine figure, whereby Rachel is personified and supposed to be bewailing the slaughter of her children, as Ephraim is, in the same ch., represented as lamenting for himself. Rachel's children appeared to be hopelessly cut off by the Assyrian captivity; but as in the case of the destruction of the infants at Bethlehem, so to the children of promise, who are to be brought into blessing in him, the Lord will be found to have fulfilled his words.—*See* Is. lxv. 8–10.]

PRACTICAL REFLECTIONS.

13, *.4 ver.* Like Joseph, who, being warned by a dream, stayed not till the morning, but left by night for Egypt, let us make haste to obey the word of the Lord.

[13—.5 ver. The word of the Lord must be viewed in relation to circumstances, times, and seasons. The same place, Egypt, out of which Israel had been commanded to hasten, under Moses, and into which they were forbidden to return, at the time of their captivity, was yet that place of refuge into which Joseph was now directed to flee with the infant Redeemer.]

16 *ver.* Let us learn, from the case of Herod, the folly of cunning and cruelty, and the wisdom of avoiding an evil course before it is entered upon.

[16—.8 *ver.* If some unworthy feeling had not prevailed, so as to stop the mouths of the people of Bethlehem from uttering the words of praise, sent them from heaven, when the shepherds were led to look at their inhospitable reception of the Redeemer, there would not have been that obscurity about who was born King of the Jews, which led to the destruction of their infants. Let us learn from this to beware of envy, and of being slow to acknowledge the just claims of others.]

(G. 14.) *After the death of Herod, Joseph is again warned of God to return from Egypt; he settles at Nazareth. Matt. ii. 19—23; Luke ii. 39. At Nazareth.*

19 But when Herod*-was-dead, behold, an-angel of-the-Lord ap-
20 peareth in a-dream to Joseph in Egypt, saying, Arise, and-take the young-child and his mother, and go into the-land of-Israel: for they
21 are-dead which sought the young-child's life. And he arose, and took the young-child and his mother, and came into the-land of-
22 Israel. But when-he-heard that Archelaus did-reign in Judæa in-the-room of his father Herod, he-was-afraid to-go thither: not-withstanding, being-warned-of-God in a-dream, he-turned-aside into
23 the parts of Galilee: and he-came and-dwelt in a-city called Nazareth: that it-might-be-fulfilled which was-spoken by the prophets, He-shall-be-called a-Nazarene. [For Matt. iii. 1, see § vii.]

And when 39 they-had-performed all-things according-to the law of-the-Lord, they-returned into Galilee, to their-own city Nazareth.* [ch. ii.38,p.27.]

On the return to Nazareth, Lu. ii. 39—see ADDENDA, p. 39.

SCRIPTURE ILLUSTRATIONS.

19. *angel of the Lord—see* § 1, p. 3—so was Joseph encouraged to take Mary to wife, Mt. i. 20, p. 13, § 2.
in a dream—see § 2, p. 13.; and pp. 33, .4.
23. *Nazareth*—sig. 'a branch'—*see* Note—Jesus called 'of Nazareth,' Mk. i. 24: Lu. iv. 34, § 17—so named to Peter, Mk. xlv. 67, § 89—to the women at his resurrection, Mk. xvi. 6, § 93—by the two disciples, going to Emmaus, Lu. xxiv. 19, § 94—title on the cross, Jno. xix. 19, § 91—also Ac. ii. 22; iv. 10;

NOTES.

19. *When Herod was dead.* Herod died of a most painful and loathsome disease about March, at Jericho, in the 37th year of his reign, U.C. 751, B.C. 3, and in his seventieth year. At his funeral 500 slaves or freedmen are said to have been employed in carrying the spices merely.—*See* ADDENDA, p. 39.
An angel of the Lord.—See Lu. i. 11, § 1, p. 3, and ver. 26, § 2, p. 9.
20. *Land of Israel.* The land given to Abraham and his seed for ever. It was called 'THE LAND OF CANAAN,' from CANAAN, the eldest son of HAM: 'PALESTINE,' from the Philistines; they occupied the sea coast; their ancestors were the PHILISTIM, who anciently came from Egypt: 'THE PROMISED LAND,' from God's covenant with Abraham, that his seed should possess it: 'THE LAND OF JUDAH,' from the two tribes, 'Judah' and 'Benjamin,' who remained with king Rehoboam at the revolt of the ten tribes. 'JUDÆA' was properly the *south* part of the land, but the term was applied to the whole land after the restoration of the Jews from the Babylonian captivity. It is called the 'HOLY LAND,' because Jesus was born and crucified there. Herod the Great was king over all that land; but at his death, the land was divided among his three sons.—*See* 22 ver., '*But when he heard,' &c.*
They are dead, &c. Both Herod and Antipater his son; though some think that the plural is here used for the singular, and that the death of Herod alone is here intended. Mr. Manne conjectures that Antipater, the son of Herod, who at the time when Christ was born was heir-apparent to the throne, and had cruelly procured the death of his two elder brothers to clear his way to the succession, would very probably be an active instrument in seeking the destruction of the new-born Jesus, and in advising to the *slaughter of the infants.* And as Antipater *died* but five days before his father, both might be referred to in these words of the angel.
22. *But when he heard that Archelaus did reign.* Herod having put Antipater to death in consequence of a conspiracy formed against him, of which he (Antipater) was the author, altered his will, and disposed of his dominions in the following manner. The tetrarchy of *Galilee* and *Perea* to his son Antipas; the tetrarchy of *Gaulonitis, Trachonitis, Batanea,*

Paneadis, to his son Philip; and left Judæa to his eldest remaining son, Archelaus. This son inherited the bloodthirsty disposition of his father, and is properly styled the 'heir of Herod's cruelty.' In the very beginning of his reign he massacred three thousand Jews who had behaved themselves tumultuously in the temple. Joseph's fears might well be excited, when he heard that Archelaus swayed the sceptre in Judæa; for it was a common Jewish proverb; '*It were better for us to be without a king, than that Archelaus should reign over us.*' In the tenth year of his reign he was banished by Augustus to Vienne in Gaul, (on a complaint alleged against him by the chief of the Jews for his various cruelties), where he died.
Into the parts of Galilee. Galilee was not within the government of Archelaus, but of his brother Herod Antipas.
23. *Nazareth.—See* § 2, p. 9, 'Scrip. Illus.'
[*That it might be fulfilled by the prophets, &c.* The words here are not found in any of the books of the Old Testament; and there has been much difficulty in ascertaining the meaning of this passage. No particular prophet is meant, but the *substance* of what occurs in all those passages of the Old Testament, which were supposed to refer to the contempt with which Messiah should be treated. 1st. Matthew does not say, 'by the *prophet*,' as in ch. i. 22, § 2, p. 14; ii. 5, 15—*see* pp. 32, .4; but, '*by the prophets,*' meaning no one particularly, but the general character of the prophecies. 2nd. The leading and most prominent prophecies respecting him were, that he was to be of humble life; to be despised, and rejected.—*See* Is. liii. 2, 3, 7—9, 12, Ps. xxii.]
A Nazarene. The character of the people of Nazareth was such, that they were proverbially despised and contemned.—*See* Jno. i. 46, § 10, '*And Nathanael said unto him, Can there any good thing come out of Nazareth?*' To come from Nazareth, therefore, or to be a *Nazarene*, was the same as to be despised, and esteemed of low birth; *to be a root out of a dry ground, having no form or comeliness*: hence Jesus and his disciples were called Nazarenes in contempt. Most of the prophets spoke of Christ as a person reputed vile and despised, so that the meaning is, 'that it might be fulfilled which was spoken in effect by many of the prophets.'—*See* Is. xi. 1, Appendix A, p. [336, 'NAZARENE.'

PRACTICAL REFLECTIONS.

1—22 ver. The visit of the wise men was one of the most favourable opportunities for making known to the Jews the birth of Jesus. Even the malicious design of Herod was overruled for giving a knowledge of this to the great body of the teachers of the people. Let us be warned to improve our advantages by the ease of those teachers, who seem to have so little profited, by that whereby those that were far off were brought nigh unto Jesus.

19—21 ver. Although the child of promise was taken into Egypt, he was not to remain there. He was to be brought up where his people had been, in the land of Israel.

22, 3 ver. Though under the especial protection of God, we are to use all prudence in escaping from needless danger, and in seeking to be free from the oppression of the wicked.

GEOGRAPHICAL NOTICES.

JERUSALEM, Jebus, or Salem.—The most noted city of Canaan, about 25 miles westward of Jordan, and forty east of the Mediterranean sea. First named Salem, which is by interpretation 'Peace.' Afterwards it was compounded of both Jebus and Salem, probably to denote that the city consisted of two parts, of which one was the old city, where . . . . the Jebusites dwelt; and the other the new city, built by David and his successors, which, for its extent, might be regarded as a new city, or new Jerusalem. All this is doubtful, but—

If so, it was founded nearly 2,000 years before the b. of Christ. It is certain that it constituted one of the more powerful kingdoms of Canaan in the days of Joshua, who routed Adonizedek the king of it: but it does not appear that he reduced the city; for the Jebusites long retained possession of the fortress. It was partly given to the tribe of Judah, and partly to the Benjamites, Jos. xv. 63, '*As for the Jebusites the inhabitants of Jerusalem, the children of Judah could not drive them out: but the Jebusites dwell with the children of Judah at Jerusalem unto this day.*'—xviii. 28, '*And Zelah, Eleph, and Jebusi, which is Jerusalem, Gibeath, and Kirjath; fourteen cities with their villages. This is the inheritance of the children of Benjamin according to their families.*' Not long after Joshua's death, the tribe of Judah took and burnt it, Ju. i. 8, '*Now the children of Judah had fought against Jerusalem, and had taken it, and smitten it with the edge of the sword, and set the city on fire.*' The Jebusites rebuilt and fortified it to such a degree, that they thought their blind and lame sufficient to defend it against all David's forces. David, however, by means of Joab, made himself master of it, and changed its name to 'The city of David,' to signify the importance of the conquest, and to perpetuate the memory of the event.—See 1 Ch. xi. 4—8; 2 Sa. v. 6—9. He built a new city on the N.W. of the former; and a valley ran from W. to E., between the two hills of Zion on the S. and Acra on the N. Under David and Solomon this city was exceedingly enlarged. Ps. xlviii. 12, 3. 12, '*Walk about Zion, and go round about her: tell the towers thereof. 13, Mark ye well her bulwarks, consider her palaces; that ye may tell it to the generation following.*' For beauty and splendour it was the admiration of the world. Its magnificence was chiefly owing to the works of Solomon, who adorned it with sumptuous edifices; and over against the N.E. end of Zion, on M. Moriah, *i. e.,* 'The mount of Vision,' he built the temple for the worship of the true God, which has in no age been excelled in splendour.—See Sect. i. p. 8. In the height of its glory, the city was spread over four hills; viz., *Moriah* on the E., *Acra* on the N.W., *Zion* on the S.W., and *Bezetha* on the N.E. Josephus (who nowhere mentions Zion) says, 'The city is built upon two hills, which are opposite to each other, and a valley divides them. Of these hills, that on which is the upper city is the higher, and was called "the Citadel" by king David; but is is by us called the "Upper Market-place."'—*De Bell.* B. v. ch. iv.

Acra, on the N.W., contained the lower city; over against this was another hill, *Bezetha,* and parted from it by a valley, but which was afterwards filled up by the Asmoneans. On the outsides, these hills are surrounded by deep valleys, and, by reason of the precipices belonging to them on both sides, are every where impassable.' We find ten or eleven gates of it mentioned, which we suppose situated in the following manner: the *sheep-gate*, near to which was the *sheep-market*, on the north-east and northward of the temple; the *Ash-gate*, at some considerable distance to the westward; the *old gate*, or gate of Damascus, still farther westward, and which is perhaps the same as the *high gate of Benjamin;* the gate of *Ephraim*, on the north-west; the *valley-gate,* at the west end; the *dung-gate*, on the south-west; east from it the *fountain-gate;* and at the east end, south of the temple, the *horse-gate*, and the Miphkad or prison-*gate.* The walls round Jerusalem never seem to have been above four miles and a half, if they were anciently so much. On these walls towers were built; 2 Ch. xxvi. 9, '*Moreover Uzziah built towers in Jerusalem at the corner-gate, and at the valley-gate, and at the turning of the wall, and fortified them;*' the tower of Meah on the east, of Hananeel on the north-east, Ne. xii. 39, (and in the future renoration of Jerusalem, Hananeel is referred to, Zec.

xiv. 10.) of Hattauoarim or the furnaces on the west, and of Ophel on the south. The city had but a moderate supply of water, and what they had was brackish. Nor was the country around it proper for digging wells. Solomon brought water, by an aqueduct, from the country south of Bethlehem; the remains of which pools are the wonder and admiration of all modern travellers. In order to prevent Sennacherib's army having plenty of water in the siege, Hezekiah brought the stream of Gihon, which used to run along the south of the city, into it, and caused it to run straight eastward, 2 Ch. xxxii. 3, 4; (2 Ki. xx. 20). Pilate brought water from Etam, by an aqueduct, into the city. It is said that no trees except rose-bushes grew there; that fire being not much used in it, except of charcoal, there were no chimneys in it, any more than latticed windows. Having become the residence of the symbols of the divine presence, or the holy city, Jerusalem became as it were common to all the tribes of Israel; they visited it thrice a year at the solemn feasts; at the feast of the passover nearly 3,000,000 of people have lodged in it; and it was every whit as capable to lodge them all in houses or tents, as Mecca, which contains but about 1,000 families, is able to lodge 70,000 when the caravans go thither. Under Rehoboam, it was taken and pillaged by Shishak, 2 Ch. xii. 2—9. Under Amaziah, it was taken by Joash, king of Israel, 2 Ki. xiv.; 2 Ch. xxv. No doubt the Assyrians took it in the time of Manasseh, 2 Ch. xxxiii. 11, '*Wherefore the LORD brought upon them the captains of the host of the king of Assyria, which took Manasseh among the thorns, and bound him with fetters, and carried him to Babylon.*' Pharaoh-necho entered it; but we do not find that he plundered it when he made Jehoiakim king, 2 Ch. xxxvi. Nebuchadnezzar ravaged it oftener than once. After a siege of about two years, he committed terrible ravages, in the 11th of Zedekiah's reign, razing the fortifications, setting flames to the temple, and carrying away the inhabitants to add to the population of Babylon; 2 Ki. xxiv., xxv.; 2 Ch. xxxvi.; Je. lii. Seventy years afterward they were restored, and Zorobabel began to rebuild the sacred structure. After it had lain almost in ruins about 130 years, Nehemiah, together with Eliashib the high-priest, and a great number of others, repaired its walls, and it became populous, as in former times. Alexander the Great became master of it by the voluntary submission of the people, and offered sacrifices in the temple. Long after, Ptolemy took it by stratagem, and carried off 100,000 of the inhabitants to Egypt, whom he settled in Alexandria and Cyrene. Antiochus Epiphanes ravaged it, and murdered about 40,000, and sold as many more to be slaves; and profaned the temple by sacrificing a swine on the altar, and making broth of its flesh, sprinkled it all about the Holy place, and set up the image of Jupiter in the temple. Two years after, Apollonius took it, and murdered multitudes of the inhabitants. Many of the survivors held it to the Heathen and their idolatries. Judas Maccabeus re-took it, and built a third part on the north side, which was chiefly inhabited by artificers. Pompey the Roman took it about sixty-three years before our Saviour's birth. About twenty-four years after, it was taken by Sosius the Roman, and Herod, surnamed the Great.—See '*Herod,*' p. 39. At the time of our Lord, the city and temple existed in great magnificence, having been richly beautified and extended by Herod; nevertheless it was doomed to destruction. Of the temple, our Lord declared that not one stone should be left upon another.—See Sect. lxxxvi. At that time it was governed by the Romans.

Judæa revolting from the Roman yoke, Jerusalem was besieged by Titus, captured, and totally destroyed A.D. 70, when 97,000 persons were taken prisoners, and 110,000 perished. Reflecting on its former beauty, riches, and glory, Titus could not forbear weeping, and cursing the obstinacy of the seditious Jews, who forced him, against his inclination, to destroy so magnificent a city, and such a glorious temple as was not to be paralleled in the whole world.—See Sect. lxxxvi. About A.D. 130, or a little later, Adrian began a new city on the ruins of the old, (which is supposed to be the present one,) and expelled every Hebrew: he made it death for any of them to enter it; and erected a temple to Jupiter on the site of the true temple; and the name of the city was changed to

I WILL MAKE JERUSALEM HEAPS, AND A DEN OF DRAGONS; AND

I WILL MAKE THE CITIES OF JUDAH DESOLATE, WITHOUT AN INHABITANT.—Jer. ix. 11.

PRAY FOR THE PEACE OF JERUSALEM.—Psalm cxxii. 6.

PART I.   BETHLEHEM.   SECT. V.

Ælia, so that its ancient name was entirely forgotten, until the days of Constantine, in whose reign the Jews were again permitted to enter the Holy city once a year to wail over the ruins of their ancient sanctuary. Constantine, and his mother Helena, had the honour of restoring here the worship of the one living and true God, about A. D. 326. About A. D. 363. Julian, the apostate emperor, to falsify our Saviour's prediction, encouraged the rebuilding of the city and temple; but fiery earthquakes stopped them. About A. D. 614, Cosrhoes II., king of Persia, took Jerusalem, and 90,000 of the Christian inhabitants were sacrificed to the malice of the Jews, when every thing venerated by the Christians was demolished; but it was quickly retaken by Heraclius the Roman emperor, who returned the Jewish malice upon their own heads. In A.D. 637, the Arabic Saracens, under the Caliph Omar, the third in succession from Mahomet, seized on it. In 1077, the Seljukian Turks took it from them. In 1099, Godfrey of Boulogne, with his European croisades, wrested it from these, and the standard of the cross was triumphantly displayed upon its walls. In 1187, Saladin, the sultan of Egypt, took it from the Christian croisades. In 1517, the Ottoman Turks took it from the Egyptians, and it still continues under the Turkish dominion, ' trodden down of the Gentiles,' (Lu xxi. 24, '*And they shall fall by the edge of the sword, and shall be led away captive into all nations; and Jerusalem shalt be trodden down of the Gentiles, until the times of the Gentiles be fulfilled.*') In literal fulfilment of our Lord's predictions.—*See* Sect. lxxxvi. The JERUSALEM of sacred history is, in fact, no more. Not a vestige remains of the capital of David and Solomon; not a monument of Jewish times is standing. The very course of the walls is changed, and the boundaries of this ancient city are become very doubtful. The monks impose on the credulous, and make a gain of pretended sites for every thing that superstitious minds make a merit, to weigh with their good works as a right to salvation.—(*Continued* Sect. xxiii.)

BETHLEHEM.

BETHLEHEM—(*continued from* p. 28.)—At the eastern extremity of the town, like a citadel, stands the convent of Saint Giovanni, which contains 'the church of the Nativity.' This convent is divided among the Greek, Roman, and Armenian Christians, to each of whom are assigned separate portions, as well for lodging as for places of worship; and who, on certain days, all perform their devotions at the altars which are erected over the most memorable spots within these sacred walls. The monastery is said to have been built by the Empress Helena, over the spot on which our blessed Saviour was born; she having previously swept away a heathen temple built in the time of Adrian in contempt of Christianity. Externally, it has less the appearance of an ecclesiastical, than a defensive edifice. Its bold buttresses, and small grated windows, betoken a great regard to inward security; while its low and iron-bound portal, too narrow to allow more than one person to pass at a time, seems intended to prevent the once daring custom of the Arabs, of riding into the interior of religious houses, for the purpose of violence and spoliation. The whole structure is of extreme solidity, and appears capable of resisting all modes of assault short of a vigorous cannonade. From the roof of the monastery is an extensive view of spots endeared to the heart of the Christian. In the distance, eastward, are the mountains of Moab, and the plains of Jordan; while southward is the hill of Tekoah, from which the surrounding wilderness takes its name, familiar as the scene of the pastoral life of the prophet Amos.—*See* i. ch. 1 ver., '*The words of Amos, who was among the herdmen of* TEKOA, *which he saw concerning Israel in the days of Uzziah king of Judah, and in the days of Jeroboam the son of Joash king of Israel, two years before the earthquake.*' (B.C. 786.) And vii. ch. 14 ver., '*Then answered Amos, and said to Amaziah, I was no prophet, neither was I a prophet's son; but I was an herdman, and a gatherer of sycamore fruit.*'—Beyond, and rather more towards the east, lies the wilderness of Engedi, to which David retreated for concealment from the pursuit of Saul.—*See* 1 Sa. xxiii. 29, '*And David went up from thence, and dwelt in strong holds at En-gedi;*' and where the allied armies of the Amorites, Moabites, and others encamped, when they came forth against Jehoshaphat king of Judah. — See 2 Ch. xx. 1, 2, '*It came to pass after this also, that the children of Moab, and the children of Ammon, and with them other beside the Ammonites, came against Jehoshaphat to battle. Then there came some that told Jehoshaphat, saying, There cometh a great multitude against thee from beyond the sea on this side Syria; and, behold, they be in Hazazon-tamar, which is En-gedi;*' and nearer at hand, a little more to the south, is seen the spot (*see* p. 28) which tradition assigns as that wherein there were '*shepherds abiding in the field, keeping watch over their flock by night.*' Many of the surrounding hills are thinly clothed with fig and olive trees, and here and there are traces of scanty corn growth. At the more distant parts of the picture, a brown and sterile appearance pervades the surface both of hill and plain, betokening that the hand of God is withdrawn for a season from the once luxuriantly productive soil. Among these hills, and in these valleys, the sweet Psalmist of Israel once tended his father's flock; and amid these scenes did the Almighty nerve the arm of his youthful servant, who said unto Saul, *see* 1 Sa. xvii. 34, .5, '*Thy servant kept his father's sheep, and there came a lion, and a bear, and took a lamb out of the flock: and I went out after him, and smote him, and delivered it out of his mouth: and when he arose against me, I caught him by his beard, and smote him, and slew him.*'

The church of the Nativity is a fine spacious building, and the rows of Corinthian columns are substantial masses of granite. This is called the upper church, and is in the form of a Latin cross; it contains nothing worthy of particular notice, except some paintings of Scripture subjects, rude, and apparently ancient; and a star in the floor, immediately under that part of the heavens where the star of Bethlehem, it is said, became visible to the *Wise Men*, and is directly above the *grotto*, or place of the Nativity, in the church below. It is the church underground which absorbs all interest, especially in minds possessing credulity enough to find the actual place of the nativity, amidst the paintings and gildings and lamps, in which the church of Rome has disguised the humble realities which she professes to venerate. The entrance to this grotto (as all such places are called) is by a flight of narrow steps cut in the rock; the grotto is of small dimensions, about 30 feet long and 12 feet broad, not very lofty, and the roof is supported by a single column. It receives no light from without, being also cut in the rock; but is illuminated by a great number of suspended lamps, presented by various princes of Christendom; and there are several good paintings by the first artists. The alleged scene of the nativity of the Redeemer is designated by a tawdry altar, above which massive silver lamps are kept continually burning. The precise spot where Immanuel, having laid aside his glory, first appeared in human nature, is indicated by a circle of agate and jasper, surrounded with a silver glory, with the following inscription:—

'*Hic de Virgine Maria Jesus Christus natus est.*'

In a crypt on one side, into which there is a descent of one or two steps, is exhibited a manger, entirely composed of *white marble*, retaining its supposed original form, upon which stand large silver candlesticks, with wax tapers constantly lighted. Immediately opposite is another altar, illuminated with lamps like the former, where, it is said, the wise men of the East sat, when they came to worship; and in another is an altar representing the table on which they offered their gifts. Descending still further, by a winding passage of some length, (cut in the rock,) are two similar grottoes: one said to be that in which Herod caused the children of Bethlehem to be massacred; and the other, the cave in which St. Jerome is said to have made his Latin translation of the Bible. All this is only a miserable profanation, calculated to call up, in the truly devout Christian, mingled feelings of pity and indignation. A ceremony connected with the midnight mass of the Romish church at Christmas, as performed in the grotto of the nativity, is thus described by a member of that church:—' At midnight, at the hour of salvation, when, in all the Catholic churches in the world, the infant Jesus receives the homage of all faithful Christians, the reverend father warden opens the procession, and advances with slow step, his head bowed, and reverentially carrying in his arms the " infant Jesus" (or, as we should say, the idolatrous representation of him). On reaching the very spot of the nativity,

PUT JERUSALEM SHALL BE SAFELY INHABITED.—Zech. xiv 11   [37

the deacon, with deep devotion, chants the gospel. When he comes to the words, "and wrapped him in swaddling clothes," he receives the infant from the hands of the father warden, wraps him in swaddling clothes, lays him in a manger, falls on his knees and worships.'—(*What?* we ask.) * 'At that moment,' continues Baron Geramb, the Romish narrator, 'there flashes into the soul something supernatural, I may venture to call it, judging from what I have witnessed—from what I myself have felt. Piety ceases to find a voice to express its gratitude, its love: it speaks only in the melting language of the eyes, in sighs and tears.' Those who know what it is to live in the habitual exercise of faith by the power of the Holy Ghost, will smile with pitying concern, at that morbid piety which displays itself in sighs and tears, amidst the childish stage-play of such a scene as this. The tendency of man's natural heart, is to walk by sight and not by faith; and to this corrupt tendency, the church of Rome ministers in all her externals. All these things suggest an idea of littleness utterly beneath the regard of simple christian faith, which absorbs the soul on the sacred site of BETHLEHEM. What a mighty influence for good has gone forth from this little spot upon the human race, both for time and for eternity! It is impossible to approach the place without a feeling of deep emotion, springing out of those high and holy associations. The legends and puerilities of monastic tradition may safely be disregarded: it is enough to know that this is BETHLEHEM, the city of David, and where David's greater Son, Jesus the Redeemer, Christ the Saviour of the world, was born. For eighteen hundred seasons the earth has now renewed her carpet of verdure, and seen it again decay. Yet the skies and fields, the rocks and the hills, and the valleys around, remain unchanged; and are still the same as when the glory of the Lord shone round about, and the song of the multitude of the heavenly host resounded among the hills, proclaiming 'Glory to God in the highest, and on earth peace, good will toward men.' This once highly privileged city now presents a sad picture of filth, poverty, and ruinous desolation; thus to remain while under the grasp of Muhammedan dominion. But there is a day coming —and we think not far distant—when the glory so long departed from the land shall return with renewed lustre, and gathered Israel, with the now dispersed of Judah, shall chant forth the promised anthem, 'Blessed be he that cometh in the name of the Lord.'—'*A Pastor's Visit,*' pp. 225—36.

GALILEE.—See '*An Historical Sketch,*' &c., p. ix.

NAZARETH.—See Sect 2, p. 14.

ADDENDA.

'ON THE VISIT OF THE MAGI,' p. 31.

'When the Magi were come to Jerusalem, Herod, having privately sent for them, ἠκρίβωσεν παρ᾽ αὐτῶν τὸν χρόνον τοῦ φαινομένου ἀστέρος (Mt. ii. 7); the answer to which inquiry would ascertain this time, or shew how long before their arrival the star had first been seen. Upon this information he proceeded in limiting the age of the children: it was, κατὰ τὸν χρόνον ὃν ἠκρίβωσε παρὰ τῶν Μάγων (*ibid.* 16). The age of the children, therefore, had a certain relation to what we may call the age of the star; and, if the former could once be determined in either of its extreme limits, the latter would so far be determined also.

'St. Matthew has defined this age by ἀπὸ διετοῦς καὶ κατωτέρω (ii. 16). The order was limited to children of two years old and under; that is, it was limited at one extreme, but not at the other; a child above two years old would be exempted from it, a child of two years old, or of any age less than that, would be included in it. Now it was a maxim among the Jews, that the son of a day was the son of a year: Unus dies in anno habetur pro anno integro. A ram, or any other animal, was considered *bimus*, or two years old, which was one year and thirty days old, or thirteen months old in all. (De Rat. Sacrif. i. 14.) On this principle, a child of thirteen months old would answer to the limit ἀπὸ διετοῦς as well as a child of full two years.

'From the time of Zoroaster downwards to the age of christianity itself, the parts beyond the Euphrates —Persia, Bactria, or Parthia—had always been the chief seats of the Magian philosophy.

'That the Magi in the present instance came, accordingly, from these regions, which are as much to the east of Judæa as Arabia, has been uniformly the tradition of the church.

'If the Magi, then, came from this part of the East, they would be four months on the road; and, therefore, if the star had appeared thirteen months before they arrived at Jerusalem, it had appeared nine months before they set out. Hence, if they set out at the time of the birth of Christ, the star must have appeared at his incarnation.

'From *their* part in the transaction, it seems clear that they acted throughout as instruments. They knew, from some assurance or other, before their arrival, that the Christ had actually been born, but they did not know where; they came to Jerusalem, in the expectation of finding, or of hearing of him there; but they did not go to Bethlehem, until they were sent. It is most reasonable to conclude, that they were directed throughout by an express command from God; nor is a special revelation more incompatible with the beginning, than with the end of the same transaction. They were super- naturally assisted in their researches after the Christ, and they were supernaturally admonished what to do when they had found him: it is not less credible that they were supernaturally instructed in the meaning of the star at first In this case, though it had appeared at the incarnation, they would not set out until the birth.

'But the truth appears to be this: The star, which had first been seen at the incarnation, was seen again at the birth of Christ; in the former instance to announce the beginning of this great mystery, in the latter to announce its consummation; the one, consequently, thirteen months, the other, four, before the time of their arrival at Jerusalem. No supposition is better adapted to explain the peculiarity of Herod's order, why the age of the children was not to exceed thirteen months, but might be any thing below that. He inquired about the age of the star solely with a view to the age of the Christ; and if the star had appeared once thirteen months, and a second time four months, before the arrival of the Magi, he would not be able to determine which intimated the real age of the Christ; and, therefore, by way of precaution, and little solicitous how many more innocent victims might be sacrificed to his cruel policy, he would naturally so frame his order as to take in children of every age, beginning from thirteen months old, indiscriminately.

'Every special dispensation of Providence must have a special purpose in view, and that, an adequate and satisfactory purpose. In this visit and adoration of the Magi, the unanimous concurrence of the christian world has long since discovered the first distinct intimation of that great mystery or secret, the communication of gospel privileges to the Gentiles. Regarded in this point of view, the advent of these strangers from the East becomes wonderfully ennobled; they are no longer simple individuals, but the first fruits of the Gentile church; the manifestation of Christ to them is the manifestation of a Redeemer; the adoration which they pay him is not mere homage, but religious worship. Nor is it less observable, that in all their leading steps, the economy of Divine grace with respect to the Gentiles, and the economy of the same grace with respect to the Jews, run parallel together. An angel announces the incarnation to the Virgin, and a star, whose message is as intelligible as that of an angel, announces it to the Gentiles: a similar angelic vision apprizes the shepherds, and a second appearance of the star apprizes the Magi, of the birth of the Christ: he is presented in the temple, and so far manifested to the Jews first; but he is made known to the Magi, and so far revealed to the Gentiles also, directly after: he is preached to the Jews, for a certain time, by his

* A sculptured image, in silver or gold, mother-of-pearl, palm or olive wood.—*Comp.* this idolatry with the second commandment, Ex. xx. 3–6: but which is not found in the catechisms of the Romish church.

ON THE VISIT OF THE MAGI—(continued)

apostles, exclusively; at the end of this time he is preached also to the Gentiles; until at last, when every distinction had been levelled, both the Jew and the Gentile are made one, in the unity of a common faith in Christ.

'The case of Ezra proves it to have been possible that a person, setting out from the parts beyond the Euphrates, on a certain day in the *first* month, might arrive at Jerusalem exactly on the same day in the *fifth* month, of the Jewish year. Hence, if the Magi set out on the tenth of Nisan, U.C. 750, they might arrive in Jerusalem on the tenth of Lous, or Ab, the fifth month afterwards. The tenth of Nisan, in that year, coincided with April 6; and, consequently, the tenth of Ab would coincide with August 2. April 6, in that year, was a Sunday, and August 2 was a Saturday. We may consider it probable, that in one week's time after this, consequently about August 9 or 10, the holy family would set out for Egypt; where they would, perhaps, arrive at the place of their abode, August 25 or 26. From this time to March 31, the date of the next Passover, the included term of days is as nearly as possible 215 in all.'—*Greswell*, vol. 1I. Diss. xviii. p. 13;—147.

ON THE RETURN TO NAZARETH, Lu. ii. 39, p. 35.

This return to Nazareth, mentioned by Luke, although by both Greswell and Robinson placed alongside of that recorded by Matthew, may have taken place at a different time, and previous to the flight into Egypt, and immediately after the visit to Jerusalem, mentioned, Lu. ii. 22—38, § 4, p. 27. Joseph and Mary at first left Nazareth without, as it would appear, any idea of permanently removing therefrom. They may have thought that a change of residence would be well-pleasing to the Lord, who had so pointed out Bethlehem, as the place out of-which the Governor of Israel was to come. Not having made any preparation for a permanent removal, when they left Nazareth on account of the taxing, it may have been requisite that they should now return at the earliest opportunity for that purpose. If they had not resolved upon a removal previously, still, it may be, that after they had returned to Nazareth they would see such a change to be desirable. It is not likely that Mary would be adverse to such a change: she had before made a still farther journey in the same direction, to have the fellowship, for a time, of her cousin Elizabeth—*see* Lu. i. 39—55, § 2, p. 11; and this she would again the more readily enjoy, as removing to Bethlehem, than as remaining at Nazareth. It is likely that they had but just returned to Bethlehem, when they were visited by the wise men from the East. They were now, not in a shed for cattle, where, on a previous occasion, they were found by the shepherds. They were in a house οικια, not καταλυμα; and now, when they may have supposed themselves to be permanently settled in the place of Divine appointment, they receive orders to remove again, and that in such haste, as that the departure is by night. Such frequent removal of the child Jesus to and fre would greatly tend to bewilder those to whom an inquisition into the matter may have been appointed by Herod, after his being disappointed by the wise men; and may have tended to exasperate him under the idea that the whole neighbourhood was in a conspiracy to deceive him, and save from his power the infant 'King of this Jews.'

'OF THE RESIDENCE IN EGYPT,' pp. 34, 5.

'If the birth of our Lord took place at the beginning of April, U.C. 750, then it may be rendered presumptively certain that the Magi arrived in Jerusalem at the beginning of the following August; and, consequently, in all probability, that the flight into Egypt could not have been delayed much beyond the middle of the same month, and would thus happen in the mildest season of the year, when both the facilities of travel, and the means of subsistence in a strange land, were likely to be the greatest.

'It is a singular fact, that in the year after his birth, when Christ the true Passover was absent in Egypt, there was, strictly speaking, no passover celebrated as usual in Judæa: a circumstance almost unexampled in the previous history of the Jews. The cause of this anomaly was the disturbances which ensued upon the death of Herod, and which, by the time of the arrival of the paschal day, had reached to such a height, that Archelaus was obliged to disperse the people, by force of arms, in the very midst of the sacrifices themselves.

'Now we may collect, I think, from Mt. ii. 22, 3, that it was not long after this occurrence, and, consequently, when the offensiveness and odium of the late severity were likely to be greatest, that Joseph received the command to return into his own country. No reason is so likely as this to have produced his hesitation about taking up his abode again at Bethlehem, in the immediate neighbourhood of Archelaus, which seems to have been his first intention before he was admonished to retire to Nazareth. We may infer, then, that the return from Egypt, U.C. 751, was not earlier than March 31 in that year at least; to which time *inclusive*, from the end of August *exclusive*, are seven months, or two hundred and twelve days, a residence in duration, like that of the ark among the Philistines in the days of Samuel, (1 Sa. vi. 1); which is a much more probable period than a residence either of less than six months on the one hand, or of more than a year on the other.

'St. Matthew, by applying to this residence the text of Hosea, 'Out of Egypt have I called my son,' (ii. 15,) has shewn that the sojourning of the children of Israel there was in some respect or other typical of this of Christ. Now the Israelites came up from Egypt at the passover; and so it is manifest did the holy family, if they returned shortly after the death of Herod. The descent of the holy family into Egypt took place about the close of the summer; and so, I think, it may be proved, did the descent of the Israelites also.'—*Greswell*, vol. I. Diss. xii. p. 392—4.

'HEROD,' p. 35.

Herod the king. Judæa, where our Saviour was born, was a province of the Roman empire. It was taken about 63 years B.C., by Pompey, and placed under tribute. Herod received his appointment from the Romans, and had reigned at the time of the birth of Jesus 36 years. Though he was permitted to be called *king*, yet he was in all respects dependant on the Roman emperor.—He was commonly called Herod the Great, because he had distinguished himself in the wars with Antigonus, and his other enemies, and because he had evinced great talents, as well as great cruelties and crimes, in governing and defending his country; in repairing the temple; and in building and ornamenting the cities of his kingdom. —At this time Augustus was emperor of Rome. The world was at peace.

HEROD was notorious for cruelty. Josephus calls him 'a man of great barbarity, and a slave to his passions.' The facts of his reign prove that he was abundantly capable of this wickedness. The following will shew that this slaying of the infants was perfectly in accordance with his odious character. Aristobulus, brother of his wife Mariamne, was murdered by his directions at eighteen years of age, because the people of Jerusalem had evinced affection towards him. In the seventh year of his reign he put to death Hyrcanus, grandfather of Mariamne, then eighty years of age, and who had formerly saved Herod's life; a man of a mild and peaceable disposition. His beloved and beautiful wife Mariamne, whom he professed to idolize, had a public execution, and her mother Alexandra followed soon after. Alexander and Aristobulus, his two sons by Mariamne, were strangled in prison by his orders, upon groundless suspicion, as it seems, when they were at man's estate, were married, and had children. He also caused his son Antipater to be slain about five days before his death; and gave orders, when dying, to shut up the chief persons among the Jews, whom he commanded to be slain at his death, that every family of the Jews might mourn; which happily was not executed. Herod would think the massacre of the infants but a small affair; and although Josephus does not particularly mention it, he seems to hint at it when he says 'many slaughters followed the prediction of the new king.'—*Ant.* 1—17. c. 3.

THE WICKED IS RESERVED TO THE DAY OF DESTRUCTION.—Job xxi. 30.

SECTION 6.—The Residue of the History of Jesus, before his Appearance in Public; from the Close of the First Year of his Age to the Middle of his Thirteenth.

(G. 15.) *Luke* ii. 40—52. *At Jerusalem and Nazareth.*

40 And the child grew, and waxed strong in spirit, filled with wisdom: and the grace of
41 God was upon him. Now his parents went to Jerusalem every year at the feast of
42 the passover. And when he was twelve years old, they went up to Jerusalem after the
43 custom of the feast. And when they had fulfilled the days, as they returned, the child

SCRIPTURE ILLUSTRATIONS.

40. *strong in spirit*—'a wise man is strong,' Pr. xxiv. 5—the Spirit of the Lord was upon Samson, Ju. xiii.—xvi.—'not by might, nor by power, but by my spirit, saith the Lord,' Zec. iv. 6—given to John, Lu. i. 15—7, § 1, p. 4—spirit of counsel and might to rest upon Christ, Is. xi. 2—5—out of whose fulness we all receive, and grace for grace, Jno. i. 16, § 7—the disciples to receive *power*, after that the Holy Ghost was come upon them, Ac. i. 8—were made strong, accordingly, Iv. 33—prayer for the being strengthened with might by the Spirit in the inner man, Ep. iii. 16;

wisdom—given to Bezaleel for the work of the tabernacle, Ex. xxxi. 2—6; xxxv. 30—5 — shewn in keeping God's commandments, De. iv 6—possessed by David, 2 Sa. xiv. 20—by Solomon, 1 Ki. iii. 28; iv. 29—34—granted in answer to his prayer, 2 Ch. i. 10—.2—his description of wisdom, Pr. viii.—the principal thing, ch. iv. 5—9—wisdom of Christ foretold, Is. xi. 2—4; lii. 13—5—*confirm.*, Luke ii. 47, 52; Mt. xiii. 54, § 37—in whom are hid all the treasures of wisdom and knowledge, Col. ii. 3. Wisdom from above, even of Christ crucified, contrasted with worldly wisdom, 1 Co. i. 17—31; Ja. iii. 15—7—the first of spiritual gifts, 1 Co. xii. 8—*comp.* with Is. xi. 2; see also '*astonished*, 'p. 41; and *comp.* Prov. iv. 5—9.

grace of God was upon him—represented by the anointing of Aaron and his sons, Ex. xxx. 30; Le. viii. 12—*comp.* with Ps. cxxxiii. 1, 2; Is. xlii. 1—*it*. lxi. 1—3—his people to be found as having his grace upon them, ver. 9, 10—and manifesting the same in their conduct, Is. lviii. 7—9—this, after the example of the grace of our Lord, 2 Co. viii. 9 — 'a sweet

smelling savour,' Ep. v. 1, 2—'whatsoever things are lovely,' Ph. iv. 8.

41. *went to Jerusalem*—this rejoiced in, Ps. cxxii.—predicated as to both Israel and Judah, when to be joined to the Lord in an everlasting covenant, Je. l. 4, 5—'let us go speedily ... many people and strong nations,' Zec. viii. 19—22—true worship of God at Jerusalem was for a time to cease, Jno. iv. 21, § 13—Paul went thither bound in the spirit, knowing that bonds and imprisonments awaited him there, Ac. xx. 22—4.

passover—instituted upon the escape of Israel, the Lord's firstborn, out of Egypt, Ex. xii.—the paschal lamb, ver. 3—6—the blood to be sprinkled upon the door-posts, ver. 7, 13, 22—the lamb to be eaten roast, and with unleavened bread and bitter herbs, ver. 8, 9—and by Israel, as equipped for a journey, ver. 11—why called the Lord's passover, ver. 11—3—see also xxiii. 15; De. xvi. 1—8, 16—kept in the wilderness, Nu. ix. 5—in Canaan, Jos. v. 10—by Hezekiah, 2 Ch. xxx. 13—27—Josiah, xxxv. 1—9—our Lord's observance of it; *first*, Jno. ii. 13, § 12; *second*, v. 1, § 23; the next passover, about the time of the feeding of the 5,000, Jno. vi. 4, 30, § 40, *in the desert of Bethsaida*, Jesus does not appear to have attended; *fourth*, xi. 55, § 81; Mt. xxvi. 17—30, § 87—Christ our Passover, 1 Co. v. 7, 8—besides these Jesus attended the feast of Tabernacles, Jno. vii. 10—x. 21, § 55—and the feast of Dedication, Jno. x. 22—39, § 56, both in the last year of his ministry.

NOTES

40. *Waxed strong in spirit*. More and more manifested spiritual perception and power.

Filled with wisdom. Acquaintance with the word and works of God, *see* '*Nazarene*,' p. 35.

And the grace of God, &c. Great kindness; tenderness; love; the favour of God. It is remarkable that this is all that is recorded of the infancy of Jesus. And this, with the short account that follows of his going to Jerusalem, is all that we know of him for thirty years of his life. The design of the Evangelists was to give an account of his *public ministry*, and not his *private* life. Hence they say little of him in regard to his first years. What they do say, however, corresponds entirely with what we might expect. He was wise, pure, and deeply skilled in the knowledge of the divine law. He set a lovely example for all children; was subject to his parents, and increased in favour with God and man.

41. *Every year*. Men went three times a year to Jerusalem, viz., at the feasts of the passover, pentecost, and tabernacles, De. xvi. 16; but women were not obliged to go to the passover; this was quite a voluntary thing in Mary, which discovers her piety.

At the feast of the passover. It was instituted to be observed every year, to preserve the memory among the children of Israel, of their deliverance from Egyptian bondage, where they had sojourned, according to God's word, 400 years.—*See* Ge. xv. 13, .4. The name *passover* was given to the feast, because the Lord *passed* over the houses of the Israelites without slaying their first-born, while those of the Egyptians were cut off, Ex. xii. 21—30.—*See* Addenda, '*Passover*,' p. 43.

42. *Twelve years old*. It is probable that this was the age at which males at first went up to Jerusalem. They were commanded to appear three times a year before God, to attend on the ordinances of religion, in the temple; which they commenced to do at the age of twelve years, Ex. xxiii. 14—7; De. xvi. 16.—*See* Addenda, '*Twelve years old*,' p. 43.

To Jerusalem. Where the feasts of the Jews were all held. This was a journey from Nazareth of about seventy miles.

After the custom of the feast. According to the usual manner of the feast. The way in which it was properly observed.

PRACTICAL REFLECTIONS.

[40 ver. We should not only seek to cultivate, enlarge, and strengthen the natural powers of our minds, but, ever remembering the word, 'Not by might, nor by power, but by my Spirit, saith the Lord,' Zec. iv. 6; we should especially seek to be strong in the Spirit.]

We should not only endeavour to be acquainted with the deep things of God, so as to be able to speak of them, but we should seek to be so filled with the wisdom that cometh from above, as to be ever led by the Spirit in all the ways of wisdom, deriving practical instruction from all God is pleased to say to us, or do with us.

Whilst we seek to be strong and wise, let us at the same time earnestly desire that the grace of God may be upon us. Let us *be kind, tender-hearted, forgiving one another, even as God, for Christ's sake hath forgiven us,* Eph. iv. 32.

[41 ver. However individually favoured of God, as to communion with Him in knowledge and grace, let us not forsake the assembling of ourselves together, for the more public observance of religious ordinances.]

42 ver. Children should be early accustomed to the public as well as family worship of God with their parents.

THE WISE SHALL UNDERSTAND THESE THINGS.—Hos. xiv. 9.

PART I.   JESUS IN THE MIDST OF THE DOCTORS.   SECT. VI.

Lu. ii. Jesus tarried-behind in Jerusalem; and Joseph and his mother knew not *of it*.
44 But they,-supposing him to-have-been in the company, went a-day's journey; and
45 they-sought him among *their* kinsfolk and acquaintance. And when-they-found him
46 not, they-turned-back-again to Jerusalem, seeking him. And it-came-to-pass, *that* after
three days they-found him in the temple, sitting in the-midst of-the doctors, both
47 hearing them, and asking them *questions*. And all that heard him were-astonished at
48 his understanding and answers. And when-they-saw him, they-were-amazed: and
his mother said unto him, Son, why hast-thou-' thus '-dealt with-us? behold, thy father
49 and-I have-sought thee sorrowing. And he-said unto them, How *is it* that ye-sought

SCRIPTURE ILLUSTRATIONS.

42. *custom*—so Paul went up to worship at Jerusalem, Ac. xviii. 21; xxiv. 11—the apostles were daily in the temple. ii. 46—went up together into the temple at the hour of prayer, iii. 1.

45. *turned back*—there is yet to be a turning back to Jerusalem, as Je. iii. 12, .4–.7—unto the Lord, iv. 1.

seeking him—the promised return is to be of a people seeking the Lord, Is. li. 1; Zec. viii. 22—the character of the generation who shall seek him successfully, is described Ps. xxiv. 3–6—the earnest manner in which he is to be sought, Joel ii. 12—.7—the success of this seeking, ver. 18–27; Is. xxx. 18.

46. *after three days*—so in Ho. vi. 2, 3—with regard to his seeking people: ' In the third day he will raise us up, and we shall live in his sight. Then shall we know, . . . we follow on to know the Lord,' ver. 1–3—*comp.* with 2 Pe. iii. 8—as to the commencement of the time, *see* Is. viii. 8—Jesus spake of his resurrection, Jno. ii. 19, § 12—to the Pharisees, Mt. xii. 39, 40, § 31; xvi. 21, § 50; Mk. ix. 31, § 52; Mt. xx. 19, § 77.

midst of the doctors—' He that walketh with wise men shall be wise,' Pr. xiii. 20; Ps. cxix. 63.

hearing them, Pr. xviii. 13—*see* Elihu's conduct, Job xxxii. 6.

and asking them questions—so, upon their return, the Lord will, by catechizing, instruct his people, and all the nations around—as in Is. xli., ' Produce your cause,' &c., ver. 21, .2–.6; xliii. 8–12, 26; xlv. 19–21—so also one of the twenty four elders excited attention to the subject, upon which he afterwards gave the required information, Rev. vii. 13–.7.

47. *astonished at his understanding and answers*—how the scholar may become wiser than his teachers, Ps. cxix. 99, 100—*see* also Ps. viii. 2: Is. xxix. 14, .7–24—as to Jesus, Mt. vii. 28, § 19; Jno. vii. 15, 46, § 55—*see* also 1 Co. i. 20–.4.

49. *how . . . that ye sought me?*—Christ to be found in the sanctuary, Ps. lxviii. 24; Rev. i. 12, .3.

Father's business—this had been foretold, Ps. xl. 7–10—' my meat is to do the will of him that sent me,' Jno. iv. 34, § 13—*see* also vi. 38, § 43—' finished the work' the Father appointed, xvii. 4, § 87.

NOTES.

[43. *Had fulfilled the days*. The days of the passover. Eight days in all—one day for killing the paschal lamb, viz. the *fourteenth* of the month Abib, or Nisan (April), Ex. xii. 1, 3–6; and seven days for the observance of the feast of unleavened bread, viz. from the fifteenth to the twenty-first, xii. 15; Le. xxiii. 5, 6. 5, ' *In the fourteenth* day *of the first month at even is the* LORD'S *passover*. 6. *And on the fifteenth day of the same month is the feast of unleavened bread unto the* LORD: *seven days ye must eat unleavened bread*.']

44. *Supposing him to have been in the company*. εν τη συνοδια, means, properly, ' a company of travellers.' Those who came from a distance to attend the festivals at Jerusalem, usually travelled in large companies, for greater safety against the attacks of robbers. They carried tents for their lodging at night. In the daytime, as circumstances might lead them, the travellers would probably mingle with their friends and acquaintance; but in the evening, when they were about to encamp, every one would join the family to which he belonged. As Jesus did not appear, his parents first sought him where they supposed he would most probably be, among his relations and acquaintance.

46. *After three days*. The first day spent in their journey homeward; the second, in their return to Jerusalem; and the third, in searching after Christ there.

PRACTICAL REFLECTIONS.

[43 ver. We should not be unnecessarily singular in the public worship of God, but observe the custom of the feast, so far as is allowed of God, whilst at the same time our trust is only in Him who hath fulfilled for us all righteousness.]

44 ver. Had the parents of Jesus sought for him at the proper time, they would have been saved much trouble and anxiety; let us hence learn to do every thing at the right season, taking nothing for granted that may be easily ascertained.

45 ver. As soon as we perceive our error, let us instantly seek to remedy it; grudging no necessary labour for the purpose.

We should not expect our godly relations to love us and our company, more than they love God, and his more immediate service.

We should, with Jesus, choose the society of those who make it their business to obtain and communicate the knowledge of God's holy will.

46 ver. We should speak and act with becoming modesty, according to our station in life, as did Jesus, who, although the Teacher sent from God,

In the temple. In the court of the temple. For Jesus, not being a Levitical priest, could not enter into the temple itself.

In the midst. The doctors, teachers, and rabbis; they were the instructors of the people in matters of religion. They sat on benches of a semi-circular form, raised above their auditors and disciples, the learners sitting at their feet.—*See* Ac. xxii. 3.

Asking them questions. Proposing questions to them respecting the law and the prophets. The questions were doubtless proposed in a respectful manner, and the answers listened to with proper deference to their age and rank. Jesus was a child; and religion does not teach a child to be rude or uncivil, even though he may really know much more than more aged persons. Religion teaches all—and especially the young—to treat others with respect; to shew them the honour that is their due; to venerate age; and to speak kindly of and to all.

48. *Why hast thou thus dealt with us?* Why hast thou given us all this trouble and anxiety, in going so far, and returning with so much solicitude?

[*Thy father.* Joseph was *legally* so; and as the secret of Jesus' birth was not commonly known, Joseph was called his father. Mary, in accordance with that usage, also called him so.]

Sorrowing. Anxious, lest in the multitude he might not be found; or lest some accident might have happened to him.

was, when a child, among the doctors, ' both hearing them, and asking them questions.'

[Our first duty is to hear, and then clearly to elicit the truth of what has been spoken, so as to ascertain whether we, and those with whom we converse, understand the terms of discourse: otherwise we can scarcely expect to attain to a satisfactory conclusion.
—When we have excited the spirit of inquiry in others, we should endeavour to gratify it, by the communication of knowledge to them, according as they are able to bear it.—We should especially encourage the young in their searching after truth; thus may we expect to be ourselves the more taught, as doubtless were the doctors in their conversing with Jesus.]

48 ver. Let us not be rash or severe in our judgments or reproofs:—the fault we condemn may be occasioned by our own mistake or negligence.

May our conduct ever be such, as that, when we are missing from our families, it may be taken for granted that we are about our heavenly Father's business.

SECT. VI. JESUS IS SUBJECT TO HIS PARENTS. PART I.

Lu. ii. me? wist-ye not that I must be about my Father's *business?* εν τοις του Πατρος
50 μου. And they understood not the saying which he-spake unto-them.
51 And he-went-down with them, and came to Nazareth, and was subject-unto them:
52 but his mother kept all these sayings in her heart. And Jesus increased in-wisdom
and stature,[a] and in-favour with God and man.

MARGINAL READING:—[a] Age.

SCRIPTURE ILLUSTRATIONS.

50. *understood not*—so, afterwards, the Jews, when he spake of his Father, Jno. viii. 20, .7, § 55—and his disciples, when he spake to them of his death, the 2nd time, Lu. ix. 44, .5, § 52; and the *third*, xviii. 31, § 77—the commandment he had received of the Father, Jno. x. 17, 20, § 55.

51. *subject unto them*—according to the fifth commandment, Ex. xx. 12—' the first commandment with promise,' Ep. vi. 1, 2—' well pleasing unto the Lord,' Col. iii. 20.

kept all these sayings—' cast in her mind,' Lu. i. 29, § 2, p. 9—' kept all these things, and pondered them,' &c., Lu. ii. 19, § 4, p. 22—' marvelled at those things which were spoken of him,' ver. 33, § 4, p. 26—*see* us to another Mary, the sister of Martha and Lazarus, Lu. x. 39, 42, § 61—' Thy word have I hid in mine heart,' Ps. cxix. 11—so the exhortation, Pr. iv. 4—10, 20—.2.

52. *increased in wisdom—comp.* with ver. 40, p. 40—and pray for the same in Christ's mystical body, as described Ep. iv. 13—.6.

in favour with God—witnessed to at his baptism, Mt. iii. 17, § 8—at his transfiguration, xvii. 5, § 51—at the last passover, Jno. xii. 28, § 82.

NOTES.

49. *Wist ye not. Know ye not.* [You knew my design in coming into the world; and that design was *superior* to the duty of obeying earthly parents, who should ever be willing to give me up to the proper business for which I live.]

[*My Father's business.* Some think that this should be translated ' in my Father's house,' that is, in the temple.]

50. *They understood not, &c.* It is remarkable that they did not understand Jesus in this; but it shews how slow persons are to believe.

51. *Was subject unto them.* Performed the duty of a faithful and obedient child; and not improbably was engaged in the trade of Joseph—that of a carpenter. Every Jew was required to learn some trade; and there is good reason to think that our Saviour followed that of his reputed father.

52. *In favour with God.* That is, in proportion to his advance in wisdom. This does not imply that he ever *lacked* the favour of God, but that God regarded him with favour *in proportion* as he shewed an understanding and spirit like his own. In obeying his parents he fulfilled the fifth commandment, and God loved him; and men probably took notice of him. Happy are those children who imitate the example of Jesus—who are obedient to parents—who increase in wisdom—are sober, temperate, and industrious; and who thus increase in favour with God and man.

PRACTICAL REFLECTIONS.

49 *ver.* Let the work of God be the delightful business of our lives, and not merely our occasional occupation.

[Mary had spoken of his supposed earthly father, but Jesus gently corrected her, by referring to Him who was really his Father—his Father in heaven. Men miss the meaning of the sayings of Christ by regarding that which merely *seems* to be, in place of apprehending that which is spiritual and true.]

51 *ver.* Although Jesus recognised his high relationship, yet did he not neglect the humblest duties belonging to his meaner relationships. Let us learn obedience from Him who was Lord of all.

[Let us not suppose that our natural relationship to those who are highly favoured with divine wisdom or grace, will be any substitute for personal application to study; even the mother of Jesus had to ponder over his sayings.]

51 *ver.* Let us, after the example of Mary, observe, remember, and reflect upon the sayings of our dear Lord, keeping them in our hearts.

[52 *ver.* May we grow up unto the stature of a full man in Christ Jesus, increasing in wisdom and in grace: so as to have greater access to God for blessing; and to men, for the distribution thereof among them.]

GEOGRAPHICAL NOTICES.

JERUSALEM.—*See* § v. p. 36. The antiquity of the Holy City some have traced to Melchisedek king of Salem, who brought forth bread and wine to entertain the patriarch Abraham, Ge. xiv. 18. It is not, however, clear that this was the '*Salem*' of which '*the priest of the most high God*' was king. With regard to David, it is said, 2 Sa. v. 5, '*In Hebron he reigned over Judah seven years and six months: and in Jerusalem he reigned thirty and three years over all Israel and Judah.*' He brought the ark of God into it—*see* 1 Ch. xv. 1, '*And David made him houses in the city of David, and prepared a place for the ark of God, and pitched for it a tent.*' And of Solomon, 2 Ch. iii. 1, '*Then Solomon began to build the house of the LORD at Jerusalem in mount Moriah, where the LORD appeared unto David his father, in the place that David had prepared in the threshingfloor of Ornan the Jebusite.*' This was on the east of Jerusalem, north of the stronghold of Zion, ' the city of David,' and which, as well as the Temple mount, appears to have been devoted to sacred purposes—*see* 2 Ch. viii. 11, '*And Solomon brought up the daughter of Pharaoh out of the city of David unto the house that he had built for her: for he said, My wife shall not dwell in the house of David king of Israel, because the places are holy, whereunto the ark of the LORD hath come.*' From this passage, and ch. v. 2, it would appear that Zion was not the higher part of the city, as is now by many supposed; it was lower than the Temple mount, so that the ark had to be brought up out of it, into its place. It was lower also than the less sacred part of the city, for Pharaoh's daughter was ' *brought up* ' *out of the city of David,*' otherwise called Zion, into the house that Solomon had built for her. The reason assigned for this change of the queen's residence seems to intimate that Zion, up out of which she was brought, was henceforth to be devoted to religious uses, it having in a manner been consecrated by the presence of the ark. It would thus most likely be given to the priests to dwell in; and it is worthy of observation, that the part of the city which they did inhabit exactly answers to the description, and was called Ophel, or the *stronghold*. It lay directly south of the temple, and between the highest portion of the city, and the mount of Corruption. It lay between the Tyropœan valley and the valley of Jehoshaphat, and where these meet with the valley of the son of Hinnom.

Ophel, or the stronghold of Zion, was at Jerusalem, and given to the priests; but it does not very clearly appear that this was called ' the mount Sion.' Mount Sion, which is Hermon, lay at the northern extremity of the land as promised under the law, De. iv. 48, and very nearly in the centre of the land as promised to Abraham, and to be possessed by his posterity according to the gospel covenant, Ge. xv. 18.—*Comp. with* Eze. xlvii., .viii., pp. (43, 111), where it may be seen that the house and city of the Lord are to occupy a central portion, and not to be placed in one of the most inaccessible corners of the land, as before.

Multitudes of passages in the Old Testament foretold the ruin of the old Jerusalem. The Lord said by his servant Isaiah, ch. iii. 8, '*For Jerusalem is ruined, and Judah is fallen: because their tongue and their doings are against the LORD, to provoke the eyes of his glory.*' And by Jeremiah, ch. xix. 8, 9, '*And I will make this city desolate, and an hissing; every one that passeth thereby shall be astonished and*

42] TAKE FAST HOLD OF INSTRUCTION; LET HER NOT GO.—PROV. iv. 13.

PART I.   OF THE PASSOVER.   SECT. VI.

JERUSALEM—(continued).

hiss because of all the plagues thereof. 9. And I will cause them to eat the flesh of their sons and the flesh of their daughters, and they shall eat every one the flesh of his friend in the siege and straitness, wherewith their enemies, and they that seek their lives, shall straiten them.' And in Lam. ii. 15, 'All that pass by clap their hands at thee; they hiss and wag their head at the daughter of Jerusalem, saying, Is this the city that men call The perfection of beauty, The joy of the whole earth?' And in Mi. iii. 12, 'Therefore shall Zion for your sake be ploured as a field, and Jerusalem shall become heaps, and the mountain of the house as the high places of the forest'—see Lu. xxi. 24, § 86. Jerusalem is to change her position. The call is yet to be heard, Mi. iv. 1, 2, 'It shall come to pass in the last days, that the mountain of the house of the LORD shall be established [Marg. prepared] in the top of the mountains, and shall be exalted above the hills; and all nations shall flow unto it. 2, And many nations shall come, and say, Come, and let us go up to the mountain of the LORD, and to the house of the God of Jacob; and he will teach us of his ways, and we will walk in his paths: for the law shall go forth of Zion, and the word of the LORD from Jerusalem.' Is. ii. 2, 3. So also the call is to be obeyed, and that in preparation for the coming of the Lord God with strong hand, and as bringing his reward, Isa. xl. 9, 10. ' O Zion, that bringest good tidings, get thee up into the high mountain; O Jerusalem, that bringest good tidings, lift up thy voice with strength; lift it up, be not afraid; say unto the cities of Judah, Behold your God! 10, Behold, the Lord GOD will come with strong hand, and his arm shall rule for him: behold, his reward is with him, and his work before him.' And again, lii. 1, 2. 'Awake, awake; put on thy strength, O Zion; put on thy beautiful garments, O Jerusalem, the holy city: for henceforth there shall no more come into thee the uncircumcised and the unclean 2, Shake thyself from the dust; arise, and sit down, O Jerusalem: loose thyself from the bands of thy neck, O captive daughter of Zion.' And lxvi. 10, .1, &c. 'Rejoice ye with Jerusalem, and be glad with her, all ye that love her: rejoice for joy with her, all ye that mourn for her: 11, that ye may suck, and be satisfied with the breasts of her consolations; that ye may milk out, and be delighted with the abundance of her glory.' Also xxiv. 23, ' Then the moon shall be confounded, and the sun ashamed, when the LORD of hosts shall reign in mount Zion, and in Jerusalem, and before his ancients gloriously.'

NAZARETH.

NAZARETH—See § ii. p. 14. The situation of Nazareth, as a frontier town, conduced much to its iniquity. By degrees it became a nest of evil doers, and was proverbially used to signify vileness and infamy. At this day, the name for Christians in Arabic is en Nusara; i. e., Nazarene, and given to the first followers of the Lamb in scorn.—Continued at Section xxxvii., p. 276.

ADDENDA

'OUR LORD TAKEN UP TO JERUSALEM AT TWELVE YEARS OLD,' see p. 40.

' That the purpose for which our Lord was now taken up, was not to celebrate the passover, but to appear, as one of the male Israelites, at a stated time of such appearing, before the Lord—to be made in short a disciple of the Law, and to undergo a ceremony something like to our confirmation—is presumptively certain even from what is recorded of his mode of employment in the temple, when he was found, 'sitting in the midst of the doctors, both hearing them, and asking them questions;' and astonishing those who heard him by 'his understanding and answers.' I think that Josephus had his eye upon this ceremony, and on the age of the party when it was usually undergone, to have made him tell us that Samuel, an eminent type of Christ, began to prophesy—πυπληρωκως έτος ήδη ὀυδέκατον, (Ant. v. x. 4). He cannot mean the age of puberty, for that would have required έτος ήδη τρισκαιδέκατον; and though it is certain from 1 Sa. iii. 1, 19, that Samuel was comparatively still young when the word of the Lord was first revealed to him, we are not told he was only twelve years old.

' It follows, then, and this is what we are bound chiefly to attend to, that our Saviour was twelve at the passover; or that the passover was the first feast, after he became twelve years old, to which he could have been so taken up. If Maimonides is to be relied on, it must be demonstratively certain that, had he been of the same age at the feast of Tabernacles, he would have been taken up first to that in particular, above any other, (De Sucr. Soll. iii. Vide also Ant. Jud. iv. viii. 13). No feast was, otherwise, better calculated for such a ceremony, and such a purpose, than the feast of Tabernacles. It appears to me, then, a certain inference that Jesus was not twelve at the feast of Tabernacles, before he was taken up, and was twelve at the feast of the Passover, when he was taken up—and, if so, that he was born after a feast of Tabernacles, and before a feast of the Passover, at least.

' Moses instituted three Annual Festivals, viz. the Passover, the Feast of Pentecost, and the Feast of Tabernacles, (see Sect. liv.): these were denominated the Great Festivals, during which the Israelites were expected to rejoice before the Lord for all their deliverances and mercies, De. xvi. 11–.7. All the males, at a certain age (see above), of the twelve tribes were commanded to be present; and for their encouragement the Lord promised that no man should desire their land in their absence, Ex. xxxiv. 24. The first and most eminent of these festivals was the Passover. The etymology of the name is

' If our Lord was born U.C. 750, the twelfth year of his age complete was the same time U.C. 762. In that year the passover was celebrated on March 29: the fourteenth of Nisan, therefore, coincided with March 29: and if our Lord was born on any day prior to the fourteenth of Nisan according to the Jewish reckoning, though posterior to the 29th of March according to the Julian, it might still be said with truth, according to the Jewish mode of reckoning, that he was already twelve years old by the 29th of March, because he was actually so before the fourteenth of Nisan.

' According, however, to the same mode of reckoning, a person would be said to be twelve years old, who had just completed his eleventh year, and was barely entered on his twelfth. It is not improbable that this is what St. Luke means here; and, consequently, that the passover of U.C. 761, is the passover in question, not that of U.C. 762. This passover was celebrated on April 8: the superior advantages of which date will appear more fully by and by.

' The knowledge of the actual day, on which the nativity took place, may justly be ranked among the mysteries or secrets which are known, for certain, to God alone. Nevertheless I have advanced a conjecture that it might possibly be the TENTH of the Jewish Nisan.'— Greswell, vol. I. Diss. xii. pp. 397–400.

' St. Mark has omitted the private history of Christ before the commencement of his public, and St. Matthew has related no more of it, than what may be proved to have been subsequent to the third or fourth month after the conception, and not later than the return from Egypt, that is, no more than was comprehended within six months before, and twelve months after, the nativity. Each of these omissions, as far as they are supplied by any gospel, are entirely supplied by St. Luke's.'—Greswell, vol. I. Diss. i. p. 20.

' PASSOVER,' p. 40.

expressly given in Ex. xii. 27, ' It is the sacrifice of the Lord's passover, who passed (by, or leaped) over the houses of the children of Israel in Egypt,' &c.
' The time when this feast was to be celebrated, is very particularly expressed in Leviticus, ' In the fourteenth day of the first month at even is the Lord's passover,' Le. xxiii. 5: wherein is remarked the month, the day, and the time of the day.
' The month.—It is called the first month, that is, of the ecclesiastical year, which commenced with the Israelites' flight out of Egypt, Ex. xii. 2. This month had two names; Abib, Ex. xiii. 4, and Nisan,

TRULY GOD IS GOOD TO ISRAEL.—Psalm lxxiii. 1.   [43

Ne. ii. 1; Est. iii. 7. It is called Abib, that is, the earing month, or the month of new corn; for Abib signifies a green or new ear of corn, such as was grown to maturity, but not dried or fit for grinding. In Le. ii. the offering of the first fruits is called Abib, and it is ordered to be dried by the fire, in order to its being beaten or ground into flour, Le. ii. 14; and in Ex. ix. 31, the barley is said to be smitten with hail, because it was Abib, that is, in the ear.

'The other name, *Nisan*, is derived by some from *nus, fugere;* and so it signifies the mouth of flight, namely, of the Israelites out of Egypt.

'As to the day of the month when this feast was to begin, it was ordered to be on the *fourteenth* at even, at which time the paschal lamb was to be killed and eaten, and from thence the feast was to be kept seven days, till the twenty-first, Ex. xii. 6, 8, 15; Le. xxiii. 5, 6. The day preceding its commencement was called '*the preparation of the passover*,' Jno. xix. 14, § 90. Sacrifices, peculiar to this festival, were to be offered on each of the seven days; but the first and last, namely, the fifteenth and the twenty-first, were to be sanctified above all the rest, as Sabbaths, by abstaining from all servile labour, and holding a holy convocation, Ex. xii. 16; Le. xxiii. 7, 8; especially the seventh, or last day, was called '*a feast to the LORD*,' Ex. xiii. 6, and '*a solemn assembly*,' De. xvi. 8.

'The reason of the first and seventh day being thus peculiarly consecrated above the rest, is, by Dochart, supposed to be, because the *first* was the day of the Israelites' escape out of Egypt, and the *seventh* that on which Pharaoh and his army were destroyed in the Red Sea. But the special holiness of the first and the last day being a circumstance common to the feast of tabernacles, as well as the passover, Le. xxiii. 39; Jno. vii. 37, § 55; for this reason others think it was intended to signify in general, that we should persevere in the diligent prosecution of the work unto which we are called; and, instead of growing more remiss, should be the more active and vigorous, the nearer we arrive to the end of our race, to our heavenly rest and reward.—See 2 Pe. iii. 14; also Re. x. 25.

'Although the whole time of the continuance of this feast is, in a more lax sense, styled the passover, Jno. xviii. 39, § 90; Lu. xxii. 1, § 86; yet, strictly speaking, the passover was kept only on the evening of the *fourteenth* day of the month, and the ensuing seven days were the feast of unleavened bread; so called, because during their continuance the Jews were to eat unleavened bread, and to have no other in their houses. '*The children of Israel . . . kept the passover, . . . and the feast of unleavened bread seven days,*' 2 Ch. xxxv. 17; and in Ezr. vi. 19, 22. '19, *The children of the captivity kept the passover upon the fourteenth day of the first month. 22, And kept the feast of unleavened bread seven days with joy.*'

'*Of the Ceremonies with which the Passover was to be celebrated.*—The paschal sacrifice was to be a male without blemish, of the first year, either from the sheep or the goats, * Ex. xii. 5: it was to be taken from the flocks four days before it was killed; and one lamb was to be offered for each family; and if its members were too few to eat a whole lamb, two families were to join together. In the time of Josephus a paschal society consisted at least of ten persons to one lamb, and not more than twenty, (De Bell. Jud. lib. vi. c. 9, § 3). Our Saviour's society was composed of himself and the twelve disciples, Mt. xxvi. 20; Lu. xxii. 14, § 87. Next followed the killing of the passover: before the *exode* of the Israelites from Egypt, this was done in their private dwellings; but after their settlement in Canaan, it was ordered to be performed '*in the place which the LORD shall choose to place his name there*,' De. xvi. 2. This appears to have been at first wherever the ark was deposited, and ultimately at Jerusalem in the courts of the temple. † Every particular person (or rather a delegate from every paschal society) slew his own victim, according to Josephus, between the *ninth* hour, or *three* in the afternoon, and the *eleventh*, that is, about sunset; and within that space of time it was, that Jesus Christ, our true paschal lamb, was killed,— Mt. xxvii. 46, § 91. The victim being killed, one of

the priests received the blood into a vessel, which was handed from one priest to another, until it came to him who stood next the altar, and by whom it was sprinkled at the bottom of the altar. After the blood was sprinkled, the lamb was hung up and flayed: this being done, the victim was opened, the fat was taken out and consumed on the altar, after which the owner took it to his own house. The paschal lamb was to be roasted *whole*; no part of it was to be eaten either in a *raw* state, or boiled, Ex. xii. 9.

'The propriety of the prohibition of eating any portion of the paschal lamb in a *raw* state will readily appear, when it is known that raw flesh and palpitating limbs were used in some of the old heathen sacrifices and festivals, particularly in honour of the Egyptian deity Osiris, and the Grecian Bacchus, who were the same idol under different names. That no resemblance or memorial of so barbarous a superstition might ever debase the worship of Jehovah, He made this early and express provision against it. On the same ground, probably, He required the paschal lamb to be eaten privately and entire, in opposition to the bacchanalian feasts, in which the victim was publicly torn in pieces, carried about in pomp, and then devoured. Further, the prohibition of boiling the paschal lamb was levelled against a superstitious practice of the Egyptians and Syrians, who were accustomed to boil their victims, and especially to seethe a kid or lamb in the milk of its dam; as the command to roast and eat the *whole* of the lamb—not excepting its inwards—without leaving any portion until the following morning, was directed against another superstition of the ancient heathens, whose priests carefully preserved and religiously searched the entrails of their victims, whence they gathered their pretended knowledge of futurity. Those, likewise, who frequented pagan temples, were eager to carry away and devote to superstitious uses some sacred relics or fragments of the sacrifices. In short, the whole ceremonial of the passover appears to have been so adjusted as to wage an open and destructive war against the gods and idolatrous ceremonies of Egypt, and thus to form an early and powerful barrier around the true worship and servants of Jehovah.

'After the lamb was thus dressed, it was eaten by each family or paschal society. The FIRST passover was to be eaten standing, in the posture of travellers, who had no time to lose; and with unleavened bread and bitter herbs, and no bone of it was to be broken, Ex. xii. 8, 11, 46. The posture of travellers was enjoined them, both to enliven their faith in the promise of their then speedy deliverance from Egypt; and also, that they might be ready to begin their march presently after supper. They were ordered, therefore, to eat it with their loins girded; for as they were accustomed to wear long and loose garments, such as are generally used by the eastern nations to this day, it was necessary to tie them up with a girdle about their loins, when they either travelled or engaged in any laborious employment. Thus when Elisha sent his servant Gehazi on a message in haste, he bade him '*gird up his loins*,' 2 Ki. iv. 29; and when our Saviour set about washing his disciples' feet, '*he took a towel, and girded himself*,' Jno. xiii. 4, § 87. Further, 'they were to eat the passover *with shoes on their feet*, for in those hot countries they ordinarily wore sandals, which were a sort of clogs, or went barefoot; but in travelling they used shoes, which were a kind of short boots reaching a little way up the legs. Hence, when our Saviour sent his twelve disciples to preach in the neighbouring towns, designing to convince them by their own experience of the extraordinary care of Divine Providence over them, that they might not be discouraged by the length and danger of the journeys they would be called to undertake;—on this account he ordered them to make no provision for their present journey, particularly, not to take shoes on their feet, but to be shod with sandals, Mt. x. 10, compared with Mk. vi. 9, § 39. Again, they were to eat the passover with *staves in their hands*, as were always used by travellers in those rocky countries, both to support them in slippery places, and defend them against assaults,' Ge. xxxii. 10; see Mk. vi. 8; Lu. ix. 3, § 39.—*Horne's Introd.*, vol. III. pp. 306–8.—(*Continued*, Sect. xii.)

---

* The Hebrew word שֶׂה (SEH) means either a lamb or a kid: either was equally proper. The Hebrews, however, in general preferred a lamb.

† The area of the three courts of the temple, besides the rooms and other places in it, where the paschal victim might be offered, contained upwards of 435,000 square cubits: so that there was ample room for more than 500,000 men to be in the temple at the same time.—Lamy, De Tabernaculo, lib. vii. c. 9, §§ 4, 5.

PART SECOND.

MATT CHAP. III.—VIII. 1—4, 14—.7; IX. 2—9. MARK CHAP. I., II 1—22
LUKE CHAP. III 1—23; IV., V. JOHN CHAP. I.—IV.

ARRANGED IN THE ORDER OF TIME.

COMPREHENDING THE SPACE OF ONE YEAR AND SIX MONTHS; VIZ.,—FROM THE COMMENCEMENT OF THE PREACHING OF JOHN THE BAPTIST, U.C. 779, A.D. 26 (MEDIO), TO THE END OF THE FIRST YEAR OF THE MINISTRY OF JESUS CHRIST, U.C 781, A.D. 28 (INEUNTEM).

SECTION 7.—THE INTRODUCTION OF THE GOSPEL ACCORDING TO ST. JOHN. JOHN THE BAPTIST BEGINS TO PREACH IN THE WILDERNESS OF JUDÆA. MULTITUDES RESORT TO HIM, AND ARE BAPTIZED IN THE RIVER JORDAN, AND INSTRUCTED IN THEIR PROPER DUTY. JOHN BEARS TESTIMONY TO THE MESSIAH. THE RESIDUE OF JOHN'S PUBLIC MINISTRY, ACCORDING TO ST. LUKE. Matt. iii. 1—12. Mark i. 1—8. Luke iii. 1—20. John i. 1—18.

(G. 1,) No. 7. *Introduction of the Gospel according to St. John.* John* i. 1—18.

1 IN the-beginning was the Word, and the Word was with God, and the Word was
2 God. The-same was in the-beginning with God. 3 All-things were-made by him;
4 and without him was-'not any thing'-made that was-made. In him was life; and the
5 life was the light of men. And the light shineth in darkness; and the darkness comprehended κατελαβεν it not.

SCRIPTURE ILLUSTRATIONS.

1. *in the beginning was the Word*—see Ge. 1. 1—comp. with He. i. 2, 10; also Ep. iii. 9; Col. i. 17.

and the Word was with God—the same called 'the voice of the Lord,' Ge. iii. 8—'nine angel,' Ex. xxiii. 20—3—'the angel of his presence,' who saved and redeemed, Is. lxiii. 9—'the messenger of the covenant,' Mal. iii. 1—the sent of the Lord, who is the Lord, Zec. ii. 8, 9, 11—described, 'made flesh,' Jno. i. 14, p. 48; 1 Jno. i. 1, 2.

and the Word was God—'I and my Father are one,' Jno. x. 30, § 56—' Christ, who is over all, God blessed for ever,' Rom. ix. 5—'thought it not robbery to be equal with God,' Ph. ii. 6—see also Jno. xx. 28, § 95; He. i. 8; 1 Jno. v. 7.

3. *all things were made by him*—'My Father worketh hitherto, and I work,' Jno. v. 17, § 23—'by him were all things created,' &c., Col. i. 16—see also 1 Co. viii. 6; Ep. iii. 9; He. i. 2, 10.

4. *in him was life*—this Jesus himself witnessed, Jno. v. 21, .2, § 23; vi. 48, 51, § 43; x. 27, .8, § 56; xi. 25, § 58; xiv. 6, § 87—so Peter, vi. 67—.9, § 43; Ac. iii. 15—and Paul, Rom. v. 21; vi. 23; 1 Co. xv. 45; Col. iii. 3, 4; 2 Ti. i. 1; and 1 Jno. i. 2; v. 11, .2.

the life was the light of men—'a sun and shield . . . will give grace and glory,' Ps. lxxxiv. 11—'the light of the world . . . the light of life,' Jno. viii. 12, § 55—'arise from the dead, and Christ shall give thee light,' Ep. v. 14—see also Jno. ix. 4, 5, § 55.

5. *the light shineth in darkness, &c.*—'light is come into the world, and men loved darkness rather,' &c., Jno. iii. 19, § 12—'Walk while ye have the light, lest darkness come upon you,' xii. 35, § 82—'the natural man receiveth not the things of the Spirit of God,' 1 Co. ii. 14—'their minds were blinded; for until this day remaineth the vail untaken away in the reading of the old testament;' 2 Co. iii. 14.

NOTES.

1. *In the beginning.* This expression is used also in Ge. i. 1. To that place John evidently has allusion here, and means to apply here to 'the Word,' an expression which is there applied to God. In both places it clearly means 'before creation,' 'before the world was made.' This is not spoken of the *man* Jesus, but of that which *became* a man, or was incarnate, ver. 14, p. 48. The Hebrews, by expressions like this, commonly denoted eternity. Thus the *eternity* of God is described Ps. xc. 2, ' *Before the mountains were brought forth,' &c.*

[That this is not said of the written word, but of the essential Word of God, the Lord Jesus Christ, is clear from all that is said from hence to ver. 14; and likewise from what this Evangelist elsewhere says of him, when he calls him 'the Word of Life,' and places him between the Father and the Holy Ghost; and speaks of the record of the Word of God, and the testimony of Jesus, as the same thing, and represents him as a warrior and conqueror, 1 Jno. i. 1, 2; and v. 7; Rev. i. 2, 9; and xix. 11—6. Moreover, this appears to have been spoken of Christ, from what other inspired writers have said of him under the same character.—See Lu. i. 2, § 1, p. 1; Ac. xx. 32; He. iv. 12; 2 Pe. iii. 5.]

And the Word was with God. 'The term ' God' is here plainly meant of God the Father, though he is not here so called, because the Evangelist had not yet spoken of Christ under the title of the Son; and this Word, who, in the close of the verse, is called God, was with God; not as one God with another God, but as one divine person (subsistence) with another in the same Godhead.'—*Guyse.* [The fair interpretation of being with God, in the time and circumstances pointed out by the connexion, is, that the Word existed in the eternal period before all creation, naturally and essentially ONE BEING with the Deity, yet possessing some species of relative distinction from the Father.........—*See* Jno. xvii. 5, § 87, 'And now, O Father,' &c. Jno. i. 18, p. 48, 'No man,

&c.—See also Jno. iii. 13, § 12. Comp. Ph. ii. 6, 7, ' *Who, being in the form of God, thought it,' &c.*

[*And the Word was God.* Not made a God, as he is said hereafter to be ' *made* flesh.' As to the personality of Jesus, there is distinctness from the Father's, 'The Word was with God;' as to his essence, there is oneness with the Father's, ' He was God.' The name *God* is elsewhere given to Christ, shewing that he is the supreme God.—See Rom. ix. 5; He. i. 8—12; 1 Jno. v. 20, ' *And we know that,' &c.*]

It may here be remarked, that the other Evangelists leave us to collect the Deity of Christ from his miracles and doctrine, and from the various declarations and displays of his glory and perfections which they record; but John opens his gospel with an express avowal & statement of this fundamental truth.

2. *The same.* An emphatical repetition.—The Logos, or the Word.

3. *All things.* The expression cannot be limited to any part of the universe.—See Col. i. 16, ' *For by him were all things created, that are,' &c.* And He. i. 2, ' *By whom also he made the worlds.*'

4. *In him was life.* The life which is here spoken of appears to be the Holy Spirit, which can be had only in Christ, and whereby those who know him as the Light, are enabled to live unto God. ' *The Spirit is Life because of righteousness,'* Rom. viii. 10.

And the life was the light of men. The Messiah was predicted by the prophets, and described by himself as the light of Israel; the light to illuminate all nations; the light of men; the light of the world, Is. viii. 20; ix. 2.—Comp. Mt. iv. 15, .6, § xvi.; Is. lx. 1, 2. ' *Arise, shine; for thy light is come, and the glory of the Lord is risen upon thee;'* Rev. xxi. 23. Light is in all languages put for *knowledge.* ' *Whatsoever doth make manifest is light,'* Ep. v. 13—see Jno. viii. 12, § 55, ' *I am the light of the world'*—and xii. 46, § 85, ' *I am come a light into the world.*'

PRACTICAL REFLECTIONS.

[1, 2 *ver.* He was co-existent with the Father; one with him in counsel and in works; so that we are not to look upon God's previous working, in creation and providence, as inconsistent with, or isolated from, the subsequent work of redemption.]

3, 4 *ver.* Jesus hath a natural right to the headship over all creation, and He only, of all Teachers, can lead into the true knowledge of the nature and uses of the things that are made.

4 *ver.* No life, nor power to act aright, can be had but in Jesus; and the living in him, by the power of his Spirit, (for the Spirit is life), unto the glory of God the Father, is the only true knowledge—the light to be desired by men.

* See Gresswell, vol. II. Diss. xxi. p. 197, on the supplemental relation of John, I.—iv.

IN HIM WAS NO DARKNESS AT ALL.

PART II. THE INTRODUCTION OF JOHN'S GOSPEL. SECT. VII.

Jno. i. 6 There-was a-man sent from God, whose name *was* John.*a* 7 The-same came for a-witness, to *ἵνα* bear-witness of *περὶ* the Light, that all *men* through him might-believe. 8 He was not that Light, *τὸ φῶς* but *was sent* to bear-witness of that Light. 9 That 10 was the true Light, which lighteth every man that-cometh into the world. He-was in 11 the world, and the world was-made by him, and the world knew him not. He-came 12 unto his-own,*c* *εἰς τὰ ἴδια* and his-own*d* *οἱ ἴδιοι* received him not. But as-many-as received him, to-them gave-he power*e* *ἐξουσίαν* to-become the-sons of-God, *even* to-them 13 that-believe on his name: which were-born, not of blood, nor of the-will of-the-flesh, nor of the-will of-man, but of God.

MARGINAL READINGS:—*a* Grace of the Lord. *b* So that '*he might*' is understood in the verb 'bear witness.' *c* His own .hings. *d* Own people. *e* Right; privilege; liberty.

SCRIPTURE ILLUSTRATIONS.

6. *sent from God*—the same messenger predicted, Mal. iii. 1—*comp.* here with Mt. iii. 1—1; Mk. i. 2, § 7, p. 49; Jno. i. 33, § 10; iii. 26—.8, § 13.

7. *that all through him might believe*—' In the Lord shall all the seed of Israel be justified, and shall glory.' Is. xlv. 25—' behold, see, we beseech thee, we are all thy people,' lxiv. 9—*see* Lu. ii. 10, § 4, p. 20— through him, 1 Pe. i. 21—' For through him we both have access by One Spirit unto the Father,' Ep. ii. 18.

8. *was not that light*—John ' was a burning and a shining light,' Jno. v. 35, § 23—but Christ is ' the Light of the world,' viii. 12, § 55—as the Lamb, of whom John testified, Jno. i. 29, § 10—he is the light of the glory of the heavenly city; in which light 'the nations of them which are saved shall walk,' Rev. xxi. 23, .4—he gives light through his people, as brought into oneness with him, Mt. v. 14, § 19.

9. *which lighteth every man, &c.*—or which, coming into the world, lighteth every man, as ' All flesh shall see together,' Is. xl. 5—' all the ends of the earth shall see the salvation of our God,' lii. 10—' when the eyes of man, as of all the tribes of Israel, . . . toward the Lord,' Zec. ix. 1—' every eye shall see him,' Rev. i. 7.

10. *was in the world, &c.*—predicted, Is. vii. 14; Ix. 6, 7; liii. 1, 2—fulfilled, Lu. ii. 1—6, § 4, p. 19—*comp.* ver. 8—14, with He. i. 6—' made the worlds,' He. i. 2 —' the world knew him not,' 1 Jno. iii. 1.

11. *he came unto his own*—his own land, Is. viii. 8 —born at Bethlehem, Lu. ii. 1—7, § 4, p. 19; where

he was sought to be slain, Mt. ii. 13—.6, § 5, p. 34— brought up at Nazareth, Lu. iv. 16, § 15, p. 102—from which he was thrust out, ver. 29, § 16, p. 105—his own house; his temple, Mal. iii. 1—*comp.* Jno. ii. 13—7, § 12—' mine house,' Is. lvi. 7—his authority questioned therein, Mt. xxi 23, § *3.

his own received him not—his own brethren: predicted, Mi. v. 1, 3; Is. liii. 3—S—*fulfilment:* neither did his brethren believe in him, Jno. vii. 3-5, § 51— his townsmen, Lu. iv. 28, .9, § 15—his nation, Mk. xv. 9—13, § 90; Ac. iii. 13—.5.

12. *sons of God*—the adoption 'by faith in Christ Jesus,' Ep. i. 5; Ga. iii. 26—given the spirit of his Son, Ga. iv. 6—are led by the Spirit, Rom. viii. 14—they separate from evil, 2 Co. vi. 16—.8—are unknown to the world, 1 Jno. iii. 1—their future manifestation, ver. 2 —heirs of God, Ga. iv. 7—shall inherit all things, Rev. xxi. 7.

13. *not of blood, nor, &c.*—not as being, by nature, descended from Abraham, Mt. iii. 9, § 7, p. 55—children by adoption, Jno. viii. 33—.6, § 55; Rom. ii. 28, .9; ix. 7—14; Ga. vi. 12—5.

nor of the will of man—the new birth, Jno. iii. 3, 5, 7, § 12—' not of him that willeth, . . . but of God that sheweth mercy,' Rom. ix. 16—' For it is God which worketh in you,' &c., Ph. ii. 13—his workmanship, created in Christ Jesus unto good works,' Ep. ii. 10— ' of his own will begat he us, by the word of truth,' Ja. i. 18—' begotten us again unto a lively hope,' 1 Pe. i. 3—of incorruptible seed, ' by the word of God '—*see also* 1 Jno. iii. 9; v. 1.

NOTES.

7. *Of the light*; *i.e.* of Messiah.—*See* Is. lx. 1.

That all men through him might believe. Jesus was to be regarded by all men as the author of salvation.

9. *That was the true light.* Not John, but the Messiah. A true light is one that does not deceive us, as the true beacon may guide us into port, or warn us of danger. John shone by reflection; Christ, in himself, and by his life and doctrine, was the 'true light.'

10. *He was in the world*—*See* ver. 11.

And the world was made by him.—*See* ver. 3, p. 46.

[11. *He came unto his own.* These words affirm the appearance and existence of the Logos on earth in a human form; *i.e.* that he became incarnate. In this and the preceding verse, there is a kind of climax in the *four* particulars now presented concerning the True Light; q.d. ' The only and true Saviour came to, and abode in, the world—a world created by him, but which recognised him not as such.']

12. *As many as received him.* As the Messiah and Son of God, Mt. x. 40, § 30; Jno. xiii. 20; xiv. 23, § 87.

To them gave he power, &c. To all these he gave the power, privilege, or divine right, by adoption, of becoming the children of God.

Sons of God. Children of God by adoption. Christians are called sons of God, 1st. Because they are adopted by him, 1 Jno. iii. 1, ' *Behold*,' &c. 2d. Because they are *like him*; they resemble him, and have his Spirit. 3d. They are united to the Lord Jesus, the Son of God—are regarded by *him* as his brethren, Mt. xxv. 40, § 86; and are, therefore, regarded as the children of the Most High.

On his name. Name is frequently put for power.— See Ac. iii. 16; iv. 7, 10—.2.

13. *Which were born.* This doubtless refers to the *new birth*, or to the great change in the sinner's mind, called regeneration, or conversion. The term, ' to be born,' is often used to denote this change.— *Comp.* Jno. iii. 3—8, § 12; 1 Jno. ii. 29. *see* 'Pr. Refl.'

Nor of the will of the flesh. Not by the individual's own will.

Nor of man. Not by the power or will of friends, teacher, or parents.

But of God. Meaning, 'who obtained that privilege of sons, not by virtue of ancestry, nor by any affinity or connexion of human descent, but by the free grace of God.'

PRACTICAL REFLECTIONS.

7 *ver.* John, who proclaimed the grace of the Lord, and who so directed that it should influence the lives of all, had this written in his very name. Let us hence learn to look for light in every word of God.

8, 9 *ver.* There is but one light to be looked to by all; and that light is for all, who will open their eyes to receive it—even Jesus Christ.

10 *ver.* Let us be warned not to neglect the opportunities afforded us of enjoying the light, however they may be slighted by others, as Jesus was both by Gentiles and Jews.'

[11 *ver.* The secret cause of blindness is unrighteousness, as evidenced in the case of the Jews. He came

unto his own—his own land, his own house, his own throne; but his own, who might have been expected to acknowledge his claim, received him not—fearing man rather than God.]

12 *ver.* Men are made the sons of God, not by what is done for them of man, but by their receiving Christ, who was despised and rejected of men: as having no trust in the flesh, but as believing in him.

13 *ver.* No natural relationship, as being of Abraham; nor human rite, such as according to the law; nor any human device, nor exercise of authority, can give us to be heirs with Christ; but only the being born of God, of incorruptible seed, by the Word.

KEEP YOURSELVES IN THE LOVE OF GOD.—Jude, 21 ver. [47

SECT. VII. THE INTRODUCTION OF JOHN'S GOSPEL. PART II.

Jno. i. 14 And the Word was made flesh, and dwelt ^a εσκηνωσεν among εν us, (and we-
beheld εθεασαμεθα his glory, the glory as of-the-only-begotten of the Father,) full of
15 grace and truth. John bare witness of him, and cried, saying, This was-he of whom I-
spake, He that cometh after me, is preferred before me: for he-was before me. πρωτος
16 μου ην. And of his fulness have-'all we'-received, and grace for αντι grace. 17 For the
law was given by Moses, but grace and truth ^b η χαρις και η αληθεια came by Jesus
18 Christ. No man hath seen God at any time; the only-begotten Son, which is in εις the
bosom of the Father, he hath declared him. εξηγησατο. [For John i. 19, see ¶ 10.]

MARGINAL READINGS:—^a Tabernacled. ^b The grace and the truth.

SCRIPTURE ILLUSTRATIONS.

14. *made flesh*—of the seed of David, Rom. i. 3—
'in the likeness of sinful flesh,' viii. 3—'God was
manifest in the flesh,' 1 Ti. iii. 16—*see also* Ga. iv. 4;
Ph. ii. 6–8; He. ii. 14, 8; x. 5; 1 Jno. iv. 2, 3.

we beheld his glory—as on the mount of Transfiguration, Mt. xvii. 1–3, § 51—referred to, 2 Pe. i. 16, 7
—*see also* Jno. ii. 11; He. i. 3; iii. 1–6.

Only-begotten. This term is never applied by John
to any but Jesus Christ. It is by John five times
applied to Christ, ch. i. 14, 8, *supra*; iii. 16, 8, § 12;
1 Jno. iv. 9.—*Comp.* Ge. xxii. 2, 12, 16.

full of grace and truth—(in his tabernacling among
men) 'went about doing good,' Ac. x. 38—the truth
of Scripture, Lu. xxiv. 25–7, § 94.

15. *John bare witness*—as Mt. iii. 11, § 7, p. 51—referred to, Jno. iii. 25, 6, § 13–and by Jesus, v. 33, § 23.

and the Word was made flesh. 'And (accordingly) the Logos was clothed with a human body,
and sojourned among us *men*.' This addition of the
human nature to the Divine, implies that conjunc-
tion by which the same person is both Son of God
and Son of man.

The glory as of the only-begotten of the Father.
This glory was seen eminently on the Mt. of Transfiguration, § 51, and to this John had doubtless
special reference. It was also seen in his miracles,
his doctrine, his resurrection, and his ascension.

[*Grace and truth, &c.* χαριτος και αληθειας, denotes
the largeness of the possession, and the profuseness
of infinite liberality of communication.—*See* Ep. iii.
8, 18, 9. As the moral law pointed out the disease
which Christ cures, and the ceremonial law shadowed
forth that which Christ indeed performed, therefore
grace answers, by way of contrast, to the moral law,
and truth to the ceremonial.]

He was before me. 'Or, This is He of whom I said,
He who cometh into the world [or entereth on his
office] after me, is become of greater dignity than
myself, inasmuch as by his own divine nature, he was
[always] before me: *i.e.*, more honourable than I.'—
Bloomfield.—*See* Sect. X. ver. 27–30.

[16. *Of his fulness have all we received, and grace
for grace.* In the 14th verse the Evangelist had said
that Christ was *full of grace and truth*. Of that fulness he now says that all the disciples received grace
answering or correspondent to that which is in Christ
Jesus: that is, they derive from Christ, from his
abundant truth and mercy, grace to understand the
plan of salvation, to preach the gospel, and to live
lives of holiness. The declaration had not exclusive
reference probably to the apostles, but it is to be extended to *all* Christians, for all believers have received
of the *fulness of grace and truth* that is in Christ.—
Comp. Ep. i. 23; iii. 19; Col. i. 19; ii. 9. In all these
places our Saviour is represented as the fulness of
God, as *abounding* in mercy, as exhibiting the divine
attributes, and possessing to himself all that is necessary to fill his people with truth, and grace, and love.
—'Yea of his fulness (*i.e.*, his exuberant abundance)
have we all received [grace], even grace upon grace,
blessings superlatively great.'—*Bloomfield.*]

Grace for grace. Correspondent to his grace of
'wisdom,' he, as our Prophet, gives us 'understand-

16. *his fulness*—'riches of his grace ... abounded
toward us,' Ep. i. 6–8—'all fulness,' Col. i. 19—'all
the treasures of wisdom and knowledge,' ii. 3—fulness of the Godhead bodily,' ver. 9, 10—*see also* Ep. i.
22, 3; ii. 4–7; iv. 7, 13—*comp.* also Jno. xv. 4, 5,
§ 67; Col. ii. 9.

17. *grace and truth came,* Ro. vi. 22, 3; viii. 2–4—

18. *no man hath seen God at any time*—that is,
apart from his only-begotten Son, who hath declared
him: as, to Adam, Ge. iii. 8–11—to Abraham, Ge.
xviii.—the Lord who appeared as a man, ver. 2—and
with whom Abram pleaded for Sodom, ver. 23—5—
the man with whom Jacob wrestled at Peniel, where
he saw God 'face to face,' Ge. xxxii. 24–30—the angel
who was with Moses in the wilderness, Ex. iii. 2–10.

NOTES.

ing;' correspondent to his 'counsel,' he, as our King,
bestows upon us 'might,' or power to do his will;
and, correspondent to his 'knowledge,' or the acquaintance with God, into which he, as a Priest,
introduces us, he imparts 'the fear of the Lord,' a
holy reverential confidence in him; Is. xi. 2, '*And
the spirit of the* LORD *shall rest upon him,' &c.*

By Moses. By Moses, as the servant of God. He
was 'the great legislator of the Jews, by whom, under
God, their polity was formed. The *law* worketh
wrath, Rom. iv. 15, '*Because the law worketh wrath:
for where no law is,* there is no transgression.' It
was attended with many burdensome rites and ceremonies, Ac. xv. 10, '*Now therefore why tempt ye God,
to put a yoke upon the neck of the disciples, which
neither our fathers nor we were able to bear?*' It was
preparatory to another state of things.

Grace and truth came by Jesus Christ. A system
of religion full of favours. The old system was one
of *law,* and *shadows,* and burdensome rites. This was
full of mercy to mankind, and was true in all things.
This excludes proud boasting, by shewing that we
have nothing but what *we have received*; and si-
lenceth perplexing fears, for whatever we want, *we
may receive it.*

[18. *No man hath seen God at any time.*—*See* Jno.
v. 37, § 23; vi. 46, § 43; 1 Jno. iv. 12; Ex. xxxiii. 20.
The prophets delivered what they heard God speak;
Jesus what he knew of God as his equal, and as
understanding fully his nature.]

In the bosom of the Father. 'This expression is
taken from the custom among the Orientals of reclining at their meals.—*See* Note John. xiii. 25. It
denotes an intimacy of communion, not merely that
of saints with angels, but of one who is his Son, in a
sense absolutely *unique*; intimates that the acquaintance the Messiah has with the Divine nature,
will, and purposes, is peculiar to him, and such as
could be affirmed of no other being: and corresponds
with ver. 2, '*the Word was with God.*'—*I'ye Smith.*

Declared him. 'Made him known.' Fully declared
his nature, perfections, purposes, promises, counsels,
covenant, word, and works—his thoughts and schemes
of grace—his love and favour to the sons of men—his
mind and will concerning the salvation of his people.
—*See* 'Scrip. Illus.' above, *No man hath, &c.*

PRACTICAL REFLECTIONS.

[14 *ver.* Although Jesus leads many sons into glory,
he is himself the only-begotten of the Father; and in
him alone can they be found complete. In tabernacling among men, Jesus hath left us an example
of the fulness of truth and grace which becomes the
sons of God.]

Those who behold and follow Jesus in humiliation,
have the assurance that they will be with him in
glory; for which, *see* Sect. 51, Jesus' Transfiguration.

15 *ver.* Jesus, although following John, as to his

personal ministry, was before him as to office—his
goings forth having been from everlasting.

16 *ver.* The fulness which is in Christ, is that out
of which all must be supplied, with grace answering
to the grace which shone forth in the only-begotten
Son of God.

17 *ver.* The law ministered by Moses was but the
shadow of better things to come: the grace and the
truth to which he pointed, are truly found in Jesus
Christ.

WE LOVE HIM, BECAUSE HE FIRST LOVED US.—1 John iv. 19.

(G. 2,) No. 7. *John the Baptist enters upon his public ministry.—In the Wilderness of Judæa, East of Jordan*

MATT. iii. 1—4.
[For Matt. iii. 23, see § 5, p. 35.]

MARK i. 1—4, 6.
1 "* The beginning of the gospel of Jesus Christ, the Son of God;

LUKE iii. 1—6.
[For Luke ii. 52, see § 6, p. 42.]

2 As it is written in the prophets, Behold, I send ἀποστελλω my messenger τον αγγελον before thy face, which shall prepare thy way before thee.

3 The voice of one crying in the wilderness, Prepare ye the way of the Lord, make his paths straight.*

b Now in the fifteenth year of the reign of Tiberius Cæsar, 1 Pontius Pilate being governor of Judæa, and Herod being tetrarch of Galilee, and his brother Philip tetrarch of Ituræa and of the region of Trachonitis, and Lysanias the tetrarch of Abilene, Annas & Caiaphas being the high-priests, the word of 2 God came unto John the son of Zacharias in the wilderness.*c*

SCRIPTURE ILLUSTRATIONS.

Mk. i. 1 *beginning of the gospel—*'good tidings of great joy.' Lu. ii. 10, § 4. p. 20—had been promised afore by the prophets, Rom. i. 2—concerning Jesus Christ our Lord; made flesh; declared the Son of God with power, according to the Spirit of holiness, by the resurrection from the dead, ver. 3, 4—'When John had first preached,' Ac. xiii. 24—the fellowship of the gospel, 1 Jno. i. 1—4.

*Son of God.—*see Lu. i. 35, § 2, p. 10, and Rom. viii. 3—for a paraphrase on this first sentence in Mark's Gospel, see the Gospel of John, ch. i. p. 48—Jesus' testimony of himself, vi. 46, § 43; Mt. xi. 27, § 29—the attributes of God are often ascribed to him as the *Son—see* John's last testimony, Jno. iii. 31, .4, .5. § 13 —testimony of the centurion, Mt. xxvii. 54, § 92 —his character as Son is often plainly distinguished from his office as CHRIST—*see* Jno. i. 49, § 10—so Peter, Jno. vi. 68, .9, § 43, and Mt. xvi. 15, .6, § 50 —Jesus' testimony, Jno. vii. 29, § 55—and often by his silence he granted to his enemies that his claim to be the Son of God imported his asserting himself equal with God, Jno. v. 17—9, § 23; Jno. x. 30—§, § 56—*see* Scripture Illustrations, Lu. i. 35, § 2, p. 10.

2, 3. *behold, I send,* Mal. iii. 1—the voice, Is. xl. 3— *confirm.,* Jno. i. 15—.8, p. 48; ver. 19, 27, § 10—John's last testimony, iii. 25—36, § 13.

NOTES.

Mk. i. 1. *The beginning of the gospel.* The word *gospel* literally signifies good tidings, and particularly the good tidings respecting the way of salvation by the Lord Jesus Christ. Good tidings of the coming kingdom.

Jesus Christ. The name of Jesus so often added to the name of Christ in the New Testament is, not only that Christ might be thereby pointed out as the *Saviour,* but also that Jesus might be pointed out as the true *Christ,* or *Messiah,* against the unbelief of the Jews. This observation will be of great use in many places of the New Testament.—*See* Ac. ii. 36, *'Therefore let all the house of Israel know assuredly, that God hath made that same Jesus, whom ye have crucified, both Lord and Christ.'—See* Jno. v. 31, § 23; . . . 1 Jno. ii. 22; iv. 15.

Prepare thy way, &c. When a man of rank has to pass through a town or village, a messenger is despatched to tell the people to *prepare* the way, and to await his orders. Some then sweep the road, others spread garments, others form arches and festoons on the way.

3. *The voice of.—See* 'Came,' p. 50, also p. 51

Tiberius. He was a most infamous character—a scourge to the Roman people. He reigned twenty-three years, and was succeeded by *Caius Caligula,* whom he appointed his successor on account of his notorious wickedness; and that he might be, as he expressed it, a *serpent* to the Romans. And yet it is said that Tiberius, hearing of the miracles of our Saviour, was earnest to have him enrolled among the Roman deities, but was hindered by the senate. He so favoured the Christians, as to threaten death to such as molested them on account of their religion.

[Lu. iii. 1. *Now in the fifteenth year.* This was the thirteenth year of his being sole emperor. He was two years joint emperor with Augustus; and Luke reckons from the time when he was admitted to share the empire with Augustus Cæsar

*Pontius Pilate.—*See ADDENDA, p. 55.

Herod being tetrarch of Galilee. This was *Herod Antipas,* son of Herod the Great, to whom Galilee had been left as his part of his father's kingdom. The word *tetrarch* properly denotes one who presides over a *fourth* part of a country or province; but it also came to be a general title, denoting one who reigned over any part, a third, a half, &c. It was this Herod who imprisoned John the Baptist, Lu. iii. 18—20, p. 36; and to whom our Saviour, when arraigned, was sent by Pilate, Lu. xxiii. 8—11, § 90.

Philip. Another son of Herod, said to be of a mild disposition. He raised Bethsaida, in Decapolis, from a poor village to be a beautiful city, and named it *Julia,* after a daughter of the emperor Augustus.— *See* Sect. 48, GEOGRAPHICAL NOTICE.

2. *Annas and Caiaphas, &c.* The law of Moses appointed one high priest, therefore in strict propriety there could be but one. But after the subjection of Judæa to the Roman yoke, great changes were made; and the occupants of an office, in which had been vested almost regal authority, were removed at the will of the conquerors. Annas had held the office eleven years, when he was deposed by the Roman governor, and succeeded by his son-in-law, Caiaphas. Probably the authority of Annas was still respected by the people, and he is on that account mentioned here conjointly with Caiaphas. Some imagine that the title is given to Annas, as being the chief of Aaron's family then alive, and regarded as the rightful high priest of the Jews, though *Caiaphas* held the *office* by appointment of the Roman governor

*The word of God.—*See in Jeremiah, Ezekiel, &c., for many examples of the word of the Lord coming to the prophets.

Came John the Baptist. So named, because he baptized those who professed to be contrite on

---

* This, and other superior letters, are introduced to direct to the commencement of the history; and a letter as at the end of ver. 3, signifies that the reader is to find the succeeding or supplemental portion in another gospel: so that, taking up in proper sequence each part, a continuous history may be obtained: *as,* Mk. i. 1, *a The beginning of, &c.,* going on to the end of ver. 3, indicated by *b after straight.—*The second portion is in Lu. iii. 1, *b Now in the, &c.,* ending at ver. 2, *wilderness. c—*The succeeding portion is at Mt. iii. 1, *c In those days, &c.,* concluding at *Judæa. d—*Continued at Lu. iii. 3, *d And he came into, &c.,* to the end of the ver., *the remission of sins. e—*And is taken up at Mt. iii. 2, *e saying. Repent ye. &c.*

I AND MY FATHER ARE ONE.—John x. 30.

| SECT. VII. | JOHN CALLS TO REPENTANCE. | PART II. |

MATT. iii. 1, 2.	MARK i. 4.	LUKE iii. 3
1 ᶜ In those days came John the Baptist, preaching in the wilderness of Judæa,ᵈ and 2 ᵉ saying, Repent-ye: for the kingdom of heaven is-at-hand.	4 John did baptize in the wilderness, and preach the-baptism of-repentance for the-remission of-sins. [For 5 ver. see p. 52.]	ᵈ And he- 3 came into all the country- about Jordan, preaching the-baptism of-repentance for the-remission of-sins;ᵉ

SCRIPTURE ILLUSTRATIONS.

3. *Jordan*—('river of judgment')—*see* Section viii., Mt. iii. 13. p. 58.
4. *baptism of repentance for the, &c.*—'not the putting away of the filth of the flesh, but the answer of a good conscience toward God,' 1 Pe. iii. 21; Mi. vi. 8 —the goodness of God should lead to repentance, Rom. ii. 4; Tit. ii. 11—.4—' we love him, because he first loved us,' 1 Jno. iv. 19.

Mt. iii. 2. *repent ye*—'let the wicked forsake his way, and the unrighteous man his thoughts,' Is. lv. 7 —' turn ye, turn ye from your evil ways; for why will ye die, O house of Israel?' Eze. xxxiii. 11—Jesus preached, Mk. i. 15, § 16—preached by the twelve, vi. 12, § 39—joy in heaven over such as repent, Lu. xv. 7, 10, § 68—repentance to be preached to all nations, xxiv. 47, § 98; Ac. ii. 38; iii. 19; xvii. 30; xxvi. 20.

NOTES.

account of their sins. Baptism, or the application of water, was a rite well known to the Jews, and practised when they admitted proselytes to their religion from heathenism. It was believed, that the administration of this rite would form part of the office of the Messiah. John's parents were Zacharias and Elisabeth, and he was born about six months before our blessed Lord. Of his almost miraculous conception and birth, we have a circumstantial account in the gospel of St. Luke, ch. i.—*See* pp. 2–6, 15–.9. For his fidelity in reproving Herod, he was cast into prison, no doubt on the suggestion of Herodias, the wife of Herod's brother. He was at last beheaded at her instigation, and his head given as a present to *Salome*, her daughter, who by her dancing had greatly pleased Herod.—*See* Sect. 40. His ministry was about six months' duration.

Mt. iii. 1. *In those days.* This phrase is here used with great propriety, as John did indeed appear under his public character, while Christ continued to dwell at Nazareth; which was the event that Matthew last mentioned.

Preaching signifies, to proclaim as a *herald* and common crier; κηρυσσω, *vivâ voce, i. e.* to preach. And is applied to those, who in the *streets*, *fields*, and *open air*, lift up their voice, that they may be heard by many, while they proclaim what has been committed to them by *regal* or *public authority*: as the KERUKES among the *Greeks*, and PRÆCONES among the *Romans*. John made proclamation of the speedy coming of the Messiah.

In the wilderness. Ερημος, Hebrew מדבר: means any uncultivated and generally mountainous country: sometimes, totally dry and barren; often, flourishing and fruitful in wood and herbage; better fitted for pasture than for tilling, like the *steppes* of Asia, the *llanos* of South America, the sheep walks of Spain, and the extensive commons lately existing in our own country.—*Comp.* Ps. lxv. 13; Je. ix. 10; Joel i. 20. It is probable that John first began to preach, or proclaim, the baptism of repentance in the towns as well as in the rural districts belonging to the city of *Hebron*, and then toward Jordan near Jericho. This tract was sufficiently desert, yet had a great resort of people, and was near large cities; for Jericho had ten thousand men of the courses

of the priests in it; and the road from Jerusalem to that city and to Peræa, especially near the time of the passover, was frequented by multitudes. The wildernesses of Canaan were not without towns, nor cities, so called, but they were districts little cultivated and thinly inhabited. In the time of Joshua, there were six cities, in what was called the wilderness. '*In the wilderness, Beth-arabah, Middin, and Secacah, and Nibshan, and the city of Salt, and En-gedi; six cities with their villages,*' Jos. xv. 61, .2.—*See* ADDENDA, p. 56, ' *On the Ministry of John the Baptist.*'

[Lu. iii. 3. *The baptism of repentance.* Repentance, or change of mind—so to see all our unprofitableness towards God, the ingratitude of idolizing the world, and folly of seeking our portion among the things that perish, as that our minds and purposes are changed: ashamed of ourselves, and grieved for our sins, we place all our dependence for forgiveness upon God, through the merits of Christ, and seek to live altogether unto the praise of the glory of his grace, having a good hope, through grace, of the coming and kingdom of our Lord Jesus Christ. Baptism denotes washing in general, Mk. vii. 8; but the washing of persons in token of dedication to God, is peculiarly so called. Possibly this rite commenced immediately after the flood. Jacob and his family washed themselves before they approached to God at Bethel, Ge. xxxv. 2. The Hebrews washed themselves before they entered into covenant with God at Sinai, Ex. xix. 14. Aaron and his sons washed their clothes before their consecration to the priesthood, Ex. xxix. 4.]

Mt. iii. 2. *Repent ye*—*See* ' Baptism of Repentance,' above. In the time of John, the nation had become extremely wicked and corrupt, perhaps more so than at any preceding period. Hence, both he and Christ began their ministry by calling to repentance.

Kingdom of heaven. [An expression peculiar to St. Matthew; the other evangelists calling the same glorious object of our hope, the kingdom of God. This latter expression seems to refer to the strength or power of our Lord's coming kingdom, which shall break in pieces every opposing power, and itself stand for ever. Whereas the expression used by St. Matthew may refer more to the light and glory of the same blessed reign of righteousness and peace; which shall be over all the earth, under the whole heaven.]

PRACTICAL REFLECTIONS.

Mk. i. 1. The message which God was pleased to send respecting his Son Jesus Christ is to be regarded as good news.

3 *ver.* Let us take warning from the case of the highly-favoured Jews, so as rightly to employ the far more abundant means we possess for preparing the way of the Lord.

Lu. iii. 1, 2. There were abundance of rulers and high priests in the days when John commenced his ministry; but it is not said that he received his commission from any of them; he had a higher authority, ' the Word of God came to him.'

[Mk. i. 1–3. Seeing God has been pleased to declare the free remission of sins through the Lamb of God who hath taken them away, it becomes us to repent—to have no longer hard thoughts of God, but

to seek to be cleansed from our sins, and to obtain the gift of the Holy Ghost through faith.]

Mt. iii. 2. We should repent, not only because of that which is presented to our faith—The Lamb of God; but because of that which is presented to our hope—The kingdom of heaven.

[The kingdom of heaven, although it was distant as to its fulness of outward development upon earth, has been at hand as to every individual saint. That which had a beginning in John's preaching is not terminated; but let us hope that it may soon be consummated, now that such means are provided for the literally making of the crooked straight, and the rough ways plain, that a rapid intercommunion of all nations may take place, and all flesh see the salvation of God.]

HEAR, AND YOUR SOUL SHALL LIVE.—Isaiah lv. 3.

JOHN CLOTHED IN CAMEL'S HAIR, ETC.

MATT. iii. 3, 4.	MARK i. 6.	LUKE iii. 4—6.
3 For this is he-that was-spoken-of by the prophet Esaias, saying, The-voice of-one-crying in the wilderness, Prepare-ye the way of-the-Lord, make his paths straight.		As it-is-written in the-book 4 of-the-words of-Esaias the prophet, saying, The-voice of-one-crying in the wilderness, Prepare-ye the way of-the-Lord, make his paths straight.
		f Every valley shall-be-filled, and 5 every mountain and hill shall-be-brought-low ταπεινωθησεται; and the crooked shall-be-made εσται εις ευθειαν straight, and the rough ways shall be-made-smooth;
		And all flesh shall-see the salva- 6
	[Ver. 5, p. 52.]	tion σωτηριον of God. *g*
4 *e* And the-same John had his raiment of camel's hair and a-leathern girdle about his loins; and his meat was locusts and wild honey.	6 And John was clothed-with camel's hair, and *with* a-girdle of-a-skin about his loins; and he-did-eat locusts and wild honey. [For i. 7, see p. 54.]	

SCRIPTURE ILLUSTRATIONS.

3. *by the prophet,* Is. xl. 3–5—promised to his father, Lu. i. 16, .7, § 1, p. 4—and spoken of by him, ver. 76, § 3, p. 19—the Baptist, Jno. i. 23—the mission not completed until the restoration; spoken by Jesus at the transfiguration, Mt. xvii. 11, § 51—*comp.* with Is. i. 25—.7—*see* also ch. lvii. 14.

Lu. iii. 5. *every valley, &c.*—literally, as Is. xlix. 11—figuratively, as Is. ii. 11; xlii. 16; He. xii. 13.

6. *all flesh shall see,* Is. xl. 5—'all the ends of the earth,' Ps. 10—'I will pour out my Spirit upon all flesh,' Joel ii. 28—*see* also Mal. i. 11.

Mt. iii. 4. *raiment of camel's hair, &c.*—so Elijah, 2 Ki. i. 8—referred to by our Lord, Mt. xi. 8, § 29—*see* as to the two witnesses, Rev. xi. 3.

locusts, &c.—allowed by the law, Le. xi. 22.
wild honey, 1 Sa. xiv. 25, .7.

NOTES.

It is the object of hope presented to us; not merely in the prophets and the gospels, but also in the Acts, epistles, and the Apocalypse. The promised kingdom of God, in which the saints shall reign with Christ, is one of the grand motives to godliness. 'Whereby are given unto us exceeding great and precious promises: that by these ye might be partakers of the divine nature,' 2 Pe. i. 4. 'He are saved,' or delivered from the influence of the present evil world, 'by hope: but hope that is seen is not hope,' Rom. viii. 24. It is still matter of promise, and is a motive to repentance, as in the days of John, and the ministry of our Lord and his apostles: all of whom preached the same good news or glad tidings, 'The kingdom of heaven is at hand.'

3. *Spoken of by the prophet.* The ministry of John fulfilled the prophecy, Is. xl. 3–5. John was 'a voice,' which conveys the mind of the speaker, and then vanishes: he declared the mind of God concerning his Son, and then was seen no more; for his ministry was of short continuance.

Of one crying. Or, 'of a crier;' one proclaiming.—See 'Note,' p. 50, . . *preaching.*

Prepare ye the way of the Lord. The office of John the Baptist was to prepare the way for the Redeemer by removing difficulties, & counteracting prejudices.

Lu. iii. 6. *All flesh, &c.* Persons of all nations should know and enjoy that great and glorious salvation which God was then bringing into the world by Jesus Christ.

Mt. iii. 4. *His raiment of camel's hair.* A sort of coarse or rough covering, which it appears was common to the prophets, 2 Ki. i. 8; and was made of the long and shaggy hair of camels. In the East there is a coarse kind of stuff manufactured, which was anciently worn by monks and anchorets. Such garments are still worn in the *East* by the poor, and such as affect austerity of life. Camel's hair is also made into fine and luxurious clothing for the rich.

Leathern girdles. The austerity consisted in the materials: for otherwise these *girdles* formed a regular part of the dress, and were of linen, silk, or even of silver, and sometimes gold. Such the Orientals now wear. Its uses are to keep the lower garments fast to the loins, to strengthen the body, and to command respect. Chiefs have numerous folds of muslin round their loins, and they march along with great pomp, thus enlarged in their size.—*See* Sect. 63, 'Let your loins be girded about.'—Lu. xii. 35.

His meat was locusts. His food. These were the food of the common people among the Greeks; the vilest of the people used to eat them; and the fact that John made his food of them is significant of his great poverty and humble life. Israel was allowed to eat them, Le. xi. 22. They are at this day eaten in many parts of Asia. When sprinkled with salt and fried, they are not unlike our fresh water craw fish in taste. The Arabs salt them, and eat them as a delicacy. The Hottentots look for their arrival among them with anticipations of a great feast. Locusts are flying insects, and are of various kinds. The green locusts are about two inches in length, and about the thickness of a man's finger. The common brown locust is about three inches long. The general form and appearance of the locust is not unlike the grasshopper. They were one of the plagues of Egypt, Ex. x. 12. In eastern countries they are very numerous. They appear in such quantities as to darken the sky, and devour in a short time every green thing. The whole earth is sometimes covered with them for many leagues. . . . . . . They are sometimes dried and salted, or ground into a kind of cake, &c.

Wild honey. This was probably the honey that is found in the rocks of the wilderness. Palestine was often called 'a land flowing with milk and honey,' Ex. iii. 8, 17; xiii. 5. Bees were kept with great care; and great numbers of them abounded in the fissures of trees and the clefts of rocks.—*See* also Ju. xiv. 8. There is also a species of honey called wild honey, or *wood-honey,* . . . . or honey-dew, produced by certain little insects, and deposited on the leaves of trees, which frequently flows from them in great quantities to the ground.—*See* 1 Sa. xiv. 24—.7. This is said to be produced still in Arabia. In Arabia, the honey of bees is drunk with water, and forms a common beverage among the Arabs.

PRACTICAL REFLECTIONS.

3 *ver.* Soon also may every obstruction be removed from the minds of men, and all be made willing to spread abroad the message of salvation.

4 *ver.* Those who give themselves more immediately to the service of God for the good of man should not seek great things for themselves; but, like John, be examples of the self-denial and benevolence they require in others.

SECT. VII.   MULTITUDES RESORT TO JOHN'S BAPTISM.   PART II.

(G. 3.) *The multitudes resort to the baptism of John; the Pharisees and Sadducees are reproved by him; the common people, the publicans, the soldiers, are each instructed by him in their proper duty.—At Bethabara, East of Jericho.*

MATT. iii. 5—10.	MARK i. 5.	LUKE iii. 7—14.
5 Then went-out to him Jerusalem, and all Judæa, *b* & all the region-round-about Jordan,*c* 6 and were-baptized of him in Jordan, confessing εξομολογουμενοι their sins. 7 *d* But when-he-saw many of-the Pharisees and Sadducees come to his baptism, he-said unto-them,*e* O-generation Γεννηματα of-vipers, who hath-warned υπεδειξεν you to-flee from the wrath to-come μελλουσης? 8 Bring-forth ποιησατε therefore fruits ‖ meet-for repentance:	5 *a* And there-went-out unto him all the land of-Judæa, and they of-Jerusalem, *b* *c* & were -all -baptized of him in the river of-Jordan, confessing their sins.*d* [For i. 6, see p. 51, and i. 7, p. 54]	Then said-he *f* to-the multitude that-came-forth to-be-baptized of him, O-generation of-vipers, who hath-warned you to-flee from the wrath to-come? Bring-forth therefore fruits + worthy of repentance

MARGINAL READINGS:—‖ Answerable to amendment of life. + Meet for.

SCRIPTURE ILLUSTRATIONS.

Mk. i. 5. *conf. their sins*—he that confesseth and forsaketh shall have mercy, Pr. xxviii. 13—so Job, xxxiii. 27, 8; Ps. xxxii. 5; 1 Jno. i. 8, 9—spoken of Israel, Le. xxvi. 40—2; Is. lxiv. 5—9; Ho. v. 15—call thereto, Joel ii. 12—8—exemplified, Da. ix. 9—23—and in the returning prodigal, Lu. xv. 18—23, § 68.

Mt. iii. 7. *Pharisees*—self-righteous, Lu. xviii. 10—2, § 73—formalists, vi. 6—11, § 25; xi. 39—44, § 62—hypocrites, xii. 1, § 63—covetous, xvi. 14, § 69—did their works to be seen of men, Mt. xxiii. 1—7, § 85.

Sadducees—said there is no resurrection, Mt. xxii. 23, § 85—neither angel nor spirit, Ac. xxiii. 8—they and the Pharisees were unbelievers in the signs given of God, Mt. xvi. .—4, § 47—the disciples of Jesus to beware of their doctrine, ver. 5—12, § 48.

Lu. iii. 7. *generation of vipers*, Mt. xii. 34, § 31; xxiii. 32, § 85—seed of the serpent, predicted, Ge. iii. 15—children of the wicked one, Mt. xiii. 38, § 33—of the devil, 1 Jno. iii. 8, 10.

8. *fruits worthy of repentance*—represented by washing, as in baptism, 'wash you, make you clean,' &c., Is. i. 16—clearing of yourselves, 2 Co. vii. 10, .1—amend your ways, Je. vii. 3—works meet for repentance, Ac. xxvi. 20—exemplified in the first son, Mt. xxi. 28, 29, § 84.

NOTES.

Mk. i. 5. *There went out to him.* The novelty of a prophet's appearance in Israel, *the family of John,* the circumstances of his birth, his prophetical habit and mode of life, the extraordinary character he had no doubt maintained for strict and undissembled piety, together with the general expectation which prevailed, that the Messiah would immediately appear, to liberate them from the Roman yoke, which then bore hard upon them, all concurred to draw great multitudes after him.

All the land of Judea. It does not mean that literally every individual went, but that vast multitudes from all the cities, towns, and villages of Judea, and from *Jerusalem* itself, went out.

[*Were all baptized, &c.* Baptismal ablutions or lustrations had been, even among the heathens, thought necessary for admission to religious ceremonies, and for the expiation of offences. That they were in use, too, among the *Jews,* we find alike from the Old Testament, the rabbinical writers, and Josephus.—See J. B. ii. 8, 7. But the baptism here meant is one solemn rite, founded partly on the ceremony which (as the Jewish theologians inform us) took place immediately previous to the promulgation of the law, at Mount Sinai, and partly on the Jewish baptism of proselytes; though essentially differing from it: the one involving an obligation to perform the whole law; the other, an obligation to reformation, and faith in the Messiah about to appear—the one founded on a system of justification by works, the other on faith in Christ. The custom, however, is believed not to have been introduced until after the return from the Babylonish captivity; and that to provide a less revolting mode of initiation into the Jewish church than circumcision.—See 'Baptism of Repentance,' NOTE, p. 50.]

Confessing their sins. A general confession of sins, and renunciation of all hope of justification by works.

Many of the Pharisees, &c. They were called Perushim, which signifies persons who are separated from others. They pretended to more sanctity and strictness in religious observances, Ac. xxvi. 5. They held the traditions of the elders in equal, if not greater, veneration than the word of God. Their religion was a system of consummate hypocrisy; and at the bottom, they were the slaves of every vicious appetite; proud, arrogant, and avaricious; consulting only the gratification of their lusts. They devoted themselves, with insatiable greediness, to the acquisition of honours & riches.—See ADDENDA, p. 56.

Sadducees.—See ADDENDA, p. 56. They are commonly represented as the most wicked and profligate of all the Jews. They rejected the traditions of the Pharisees, and did not, like them, boast of their own righteousness. They acknowledged the world to have been created by God, and that it was upheld by him. They denied that there was any resurrection, or angel, or spirit; and, it is said, rejected all the Scriptures but the five books of Moses. Caiaphas, the high priest, who condemned our Saviour, was a Sadducee. They were generally the richest men among the Jews.

Lu. iii. 7. *Generation of vipers.* 'Ye brood of vipers.' By this was meant to be designated their deadly malignity and wickedness. Vipers are a species of serpents. They are from two to five feet in length, and about an inch thick, with a flat head. They are of an ash or yellowish colour, speckled with long brown spots. Whereas other serpents have two rows of teeth, vipers have but one, consisting of sixteen small ones in each jaw; and at least the male vipers have two large teeth, which being raised when they are angry, their bite distils poison into the wound. There is no serpent's bite more poisonous than theirs. The person bitten swells up almost immediately, and falls down dead.—See Ac. xxviii. 3—6.

Who hath warned. τις υπεδειξεν ὑμιν, &c. 'Who hath shewn or taught?'

Wrath to come. απο της μελλουσης οργης, 'from the impending vengeance.' The passage might possibly glance at the destruction of Jerusalem; but, doubtless, John looked forward to the final revelation of the wrath of Jehovah. John expresses his astonishment that sinners so hardened and so hypocritical as they were, should have been induced to flee from coming wrath. The wrath to come means the divine indignation, or the punishment that will come on the guilty.—See 1 Th. i. 10; v. 9.

9. *Bring forth therefore fruits, &c.* That is, the proper fruits of reformation; the proper evidence that you are sincere; humility, meekness, patience, faith, love, equity, mercy, and every good work, worthy, consistent with expressive of repentance.

HE THAT COMMITTETH SIN IS OF THE DEVIL.— John iii. 8.

PART II.   JOHN INSTRUCTS THE PEOPLE.   SECT. VII.

MATT. iii. 9, 10.	LUKE iii. 8—14.
9 and think not to-say within yourselves, We-have Abraham τον Αβρααμ to-our-father for I-say unto-you, that God is-able of these stones to-raise-up children unto Abraham.	and begin* not to-say within yourselves, We-have Abraham to-our-father: for I-say unto-you, that God is-able of these stones to-raise-up children unto Abraham.
10 And now also the axe is-laid unto the root of-the trees: therefore every tree which-bringeth ·-not·-forth good fruit is-hewn-down, and cast into the-fire. [ch. iii. 11, see p. 54.]	And now also the axe is-laid unto the 9 root of-the trees: every tree therefore which-bringeth ·-not·-forth good fruit, is-hewn-down, and cast into the-fire.

And the people asked him, saying, What shall- 10 we-do then? He-answereth and-saith unto-them, He that- 11 hath two coats, let-him-impart to-him that-hath none; and he that-hath meat, let-him-do likewise.
Then came also publicans to-be-baptized, and said unto 12 him, Master, what shall-we-do? And he said unto them, 13 Exact πρασσετε no more than that which-is-appointed you.
And the-soldiers likewise demanded-of him, saying, And 14 what shall·-we·-do? And he-said unto them, Do-violence-to διασεισητε no-man, neither accuse-any-falsely συκοφαντησητε; and be-content-with your wages οψωνιοις.

SCRIPTURE ILLUSTRATIONS.

these stones—twelve stones, representing the twelve tribes, were taken out of Jordan by Joshua, and left for a sign at their encampment at Gilgal, Jos. iv. 19–24; and twelve were set up in the river, ver. 9.

9. *the root of the trees*—Christ the root, Rev. xxii. 16—it had been for his sake that Judah had been preserved, Is. i. 27—while Israel was cut down by the Assyrian, ver. 15, 33, 4.

every tree, Is. v. 1–7; xxvii. 11—the unfruitful fig tree to be cut down, Lu. xiii. 6–9. § 64—every branch that beareth not fruit in Christ, Jno. xv. 2. § 87.

11. *he that hath two coats*—love, practical charity, called for under the law, De. xv. 7–10, open thine hand wide unto thy poor brother—by the prophets, Zec. vii. 9–11—the same under the gospel, Mt. xxv. 36, § 86; Lu. vi. 30–.6, § 27; 2 Co. viii. 14; 1 Ti. vi. 17, .8; Ja. ii. 15, .6; 1 Jno. iii. 17—Christ the example, Rom. v. 7, 8; 2 Co. viii. 9.

13. *exact no more*—justice required, under the law, just judgment, De. xvi. 18–20—landmarks, xix. 14—as to servants' wages, xxiv. 14–.7—as to weights, xxv. 13–.6—by the prophets, Is. i. 17; Zec. vii. 9, 10; Am. ii. 6—under the gospel, Mt. vii. 12, § 79; 1 Co. vi. 7–11—Christ the example, Rom. viii. 3, 4; Ga. i. 4.

14. *Do violence to no man*,— Ex. xxi. 12–27; Mi. ii. 2, 8; Mt. v. 38–42, § 19.

neither accuse any falsely—truth, Ex. xx. 16; De. xix. 16–.9—comp. Is. xxxiii. 15–.7; 1 Pe. ii. 1, 2.

NOTES.

Think not to say, &c., μη δοξητε λεγειν, 'presume not to say.' Think not the Messiah will advance you for being the carnal seed of Abraham, without his faith and holiness.

These stones. The words, however, are meant to shew the omnipotence of God, who can raise up instruments to effect his own wise and benevolent purposes from the meanest subjects.

[9. *The axe is laid*, i.e. 'the axe of judgment and punishment is now being directed at;' directing the axe at the *root* of a tree denotes that it is to be *cut down*, not merely *lopped*. It was customary with the prophets to represent the *kingdoms*, *nations*, and *individuals*, whose ruin they predicted, under the notion of *forests* and *trees* doomed to be cut down.—See Je. xlvi. 22, .3, of Pharaoh's overthrow. The Baptist follows the same metaphor, representing the *Jewish nation* as the *tree*, and the *Romans* as the *axe*.]

The root of the trees. In all the calamities that had befallen the Jewish nation, the line of Jesse could never be rooted out or extinguished, because the promised Messiah was to proceed from it. But now Messiah was come, and about to be cut off. When such was the case, the Jewish nation, which until this time had been preserved—might well stand in fear.

Bringeth not forth, &c. This is a beautiful and very striking figure of speech, and a very direct threatening of future wrath. John regarded them as making a fair and promising profession, as trees do in *blossom*. But he told them, also, that they must bear *fruit* as well as *flowers*.

He that hath two coats, &c. It is remarkable that one of the *first* demands of religion is to do good; and in *this* way it is that it may be shewn that the repentance is not feigned. For, 1st. The *nature* of religion is to do good. 2d. This requires self-denial, and few will in truth deny themselves who are not assisted by divine grace. And, 3d. This is to imitate Jesus Christ, who, though he was rich, yet, &c.

12. *Publicans.* Collectors of the public monies or taxes belonging to the Roman government, an office generally undertaken, among the Jews, by those who had not much regard for the esteem in which they were held by their fellow countrymen, who felt it degrading to be under a foreign yoke. There is reason to think that the *publicans* or *tax-gatherers* were peculiarly oppressive, and hard in their dealings with the people; and that, as they had every opportunity of exacting more than they ought, so they often did it, and thus enriched themselves. The evidence of repentance in them would be to break off their sins, and to deal justly.

13. *Exact no more, &c.* That is, by the government. Though it was hated by the people—though often abused, and therefore unpopular—yet *the office itself* was not dishonourable.—See Rom. xiii. 1, 6.

14. *Do violence*, διασσειητε, signifies, ' to take a man by the collar and shake him.'. This forbids bullying conduct. ' Neither extort any man's goods or money by threats of violence.' The Romans governed chiefly by military force.

Neither accuse any falsely, συκοφαντειν, signifies, ' to circumvent' and ' oppress.'

PRACTICAL REFLECTIONS.

[7 ver. Those who are the most familiar with the forms and doctrines of religion, such as the Pharisees, are in the greatest danger of remaining unwarned; such are particularly called to self-examination.]

[9 ver. We are not to trust in what our ancestors were, nor in what they may have done for us, any more than in our own Pharisaic observances or Sadducean philosophy. Those may be manifested as the children of Abraham, you, as the sons of God, who have been the least expected to be found as such.]

10 ver. The repentance which John required was a real change of heart and life, from selfishness to justice and benevolence.

Lu. iii. 12–.4. It becomes us to inquire into what is our own more especial duty in our particular station or occupation, that we may therein adorn the gospel of the grace of God. The repentance which John taught is that which is taught us in the gospel, see 11–.3 ver., mercy and righteousness; 14 ver., peace and truth.

* On verbal differences, &c., ADDENDA, p. 62.

LOVE THE TRUTH AND PEACE.—Zech. viii. 19

(G. 4.) *The people beginning to doubt whether John were not the Christ, he foretells the coming of another and a greater person, after him; which is the first of his testimonies to the Messiah or Christ.*—*At Bethabara, East of Jericho.*

MATT. iii. 11, 12.	MARK i. 7, 8	LUKE iii. 15—.7.
		And as-the people were-in- 15 *expectation,* Προσδοκωντος *and all-men mused* διαλογιζομενων *in their hearts of John, whether he were*
	[Ch. i. 6, see p. 51.] 7 And preached, saying,	*the Christ, or not;* John answered, 16 *saying unto-them-*all,
11 I indeed baptize you with εν water *unto repentance: but* he that-cometh after me is mightier than-I,	*There-cometh one mightier than-I after me, the latchet of-whose shoes I-am not worthy to-stoop-down and-unloose.*	I indeed baptize you with-water; but one might-ier than-I cometh, the latchet of- whose shoes I-am not worthy to unloose:
whose shoes I-am not worthy ικανος to bear:	8 I indeed have-baptized you with εν water: but	
he shall-baptize you with εν the-Holy Ghost, *and with-fire:*	he shall-baptize you with εν the Holy Ghost *d*	he shall-baptize you with εν the-Holy Ghost and *with-*fire:
12 whose fan *is* in his hand, and he-will-throughly-purge his floor, and gather his wheat into the garner; but he-will-burn-up the chaff with-*unquenchable*-fire.		whose fan *is* in his hand, and 17 he-will-throughly-purge his floor, and will-gather the wheat into his garner; but the chaff he-will-burn with-fire unquenchable.

SCRIPTURE ILLUSTRATIONS.

16. *baptize with water, &c.*—as to the contrast between John's baptizing and that by Jesus—*see* their testimony, Jno. i. 26–33, § 10; Ac. i. 5; xi. 16.

he shall baptize with the Holy Ghost —' pour my Spirit upon thy seed,' Is. xliv. 3 — predicted, Eze.

xxxvi. 25—' pour out my Spirit upon all flesh,' Joel ii. 28—*confirm.*, Ac. ii. 2—4; 1 Co. xii. 3.

17. *throughly purge his floor*—same figure used, Job xxi. 17, .8; Ps. i. 4; xxxv. 5—prediction, Mal. iii. 2, 3; iv. l—*confirm.*, whent and tares, Mt. xiii. 30, § 32 —*see* also xxv, 31, § 56; also ver. 41, .6, § 86.

NOTES.

15. *In expectation.* In suspense, and looking for the full evidence of his being the Messias.

Mused in their hearts. Thought of his character, his preaching, and success, and anxiously inquired whether he did not do the things which were expected of the Messias.

I baptize, &c.—See 'Baptism of repentance,' p. 50.

One mightier, &c.—See ' He was before me,' p. 48.

Mk. i. 7. *Whose shoes I am not worthy, &c.* At first, in order to keep the feet from the sharp stones, or the burning sand, small pieces of wood were fastened to the soles of the feet, called *sandals.* Leather, or skins of beasts dressed, afterwards were used. The foot was not covered at all; but the sandal, or piece of leather or wood, was bound by thongs. The people put off these when they entered a house, and put them on when they left it. To loose and bind on sandals, on such occasions, was the business of the lowest servants; and their office was, to loose and carry about their masters' sandals. The general sense is, ' I am not worthy to perform to him the humblest offices.'

Mt. iii. 11. *The Holy Ghost.* The third person of the adorable Trinity, whose office it is to renew, enlighten, change, and comfort the soul.

[*With the Holy Ghost and with fire.* Flames appeared on the heads of the apostles and first converts on the memorable day of Pentecost, when they received the miraculous effusion of the Spirit, of which these flames were the symbols. It is also to be remarked, that accompanying the Holy Spirit's cleansing of the soul by the application of the word, there are fiery trials, (1 Pe. iv. 12,' *Beloved, think it not strange concerning the fiery trial which is to try you, as though some strange thing happened unto you.*') There are painful providences, which not only give occasion to the exercise of newly-acquired

grace, but which are intended to consume all impure desires and unprofitable habits of thought and action.]

12. *Whose fan.* ' Winnowing shovel,' mentioned Is. xxx. 24. It seems, they had two kinds of them; one with teeth, wherewith they turned up the corn to the wind, that the chaff might be blown away; another that made wind, if the air was calm.

[God's judgments are likened to a *fan;* he there-by turns up persons and nations, and scatters and disperses them for their wickedness; and his thus scattering and overturning them are called his *fanning* of them, Je. xv. 7,' *I will fan them with a fan in the gates of the land; I will bereave them of children, of whatsoever is dear,* Mano.) *I will destroy my people, since they return not from their ways.*']

Purge. Shall cleanse, or purify.

His floor. The threshing-floor was an open space, or area, in the field, usually on an elevated part of the land, Ge. l. 10; Ju. vi. 37; Ho. ix. 1. It had no covering or walls. It was a space of ground thirty or forty paces in diameter, and made smooth by rolling it, or treading it hard. A high place was selected, for the purpose of keeping it dry, and for the convenience of winnowing the grain by the wind. It is said they were formed of clay and lees of oil beaten together; which, when once dried, no water could enter it, no weed grow on it, nor any mice, rats, or ants, penetrate into it. The grain was usually trodden out by oxen. Sometimes it was beaten with flails, as with us; and sometimes with a sharp threshing instrument, made to roll over the grain, and to cut the straw at the same time, Is. xli. 15. After being threshed it was winnowed. The grain was then separated from the dirt and coarse chaff by a sieve, and then still further cleansed by a fan, an instrument to produce an artificial wind. This method is still practised in eastern nations.—*See Chaff,* next page, ' Notes.'

* On this *first* testimony of the Baptist, *see* Greswell, Vol. II. Diss. xix. p. 175.

PART II.   HEROD IMPRISONS JOHN.   SECT. VII.

(G. 5.) *The residue of the history of the public ministry of John the Baptist, according to St. Luke.* Luke iii. 18—20.

18 And μεν ουν και many other things in his exhortation preached he unto the people.
19 But Herod the tetrarch, being reproved by him for Herodias his brother Philip's
20 wife, and for περι all the evils πονηρων which Herod had done, added yet this above all, that he shut up John in prison.

SCRIPTURE ILLUSTRATIONS.

19. *Herod the tetrarch*—surnamed Antipas—*see* Lu. iii. 1, p. 49—killed John the Baptist—*see* § 40—mocked Jesus, &c., Lu. xxiii. 8—11, § 90.

NOTES.

Garner. A repository where thrashed corn is laid up or preserved. In the East, the garner is generally subterraneous, or partly so, but covered down, and thatched over. Spiritually, it is the store-house into which Jesus Christ, as the true husbandman, collects his precious harvest.

Lu. iii. 17. *But he will burn up the chaff.* These words evidently allude to the Jewish practice of burning the chaff, or coarse and broken straw. The Jews themselves describe it thus; ' Then comes the threshing: the straw they throw into the fire, the chaff into the wind; the wheat they keep on the floor. So the nations shall be burnt; but Israel alone shall be preserved.' Isa. i. 28, 31. 28, ' *And the destruction of the transgressors and of the sinners shall be together, and they that forsake the Lord shall be consumed.*' 31, '*And the strong shall be as tow, and the maker of it as a spark, and they shall both burn together, and none shall quench them.*'—Comp. Mt. xiii. 40—2. § 33, p. 260. Wicked men, particularly hypocrites, are likened to chaff; Ps. l. 4, ' *The ungodly are not so: but are like the chaff which the wind driveth away.*'

The following is extracted from a recent publication:—' A large threshing-floor was near, (*see* p. 54,

His floor,) and we put many questions to the peasants in regard to their farming operations. A flat board, which is drawn over the corn to bruise it, is called *loah.* It is made of two or three boards firmly united, and the bottom is spiked with stones, arranged at regular distances, not unlike the nails in a ploughman's shoe. It is drawn by two horses or oxen, a boy sitting upon it, and driving them round and round. This instrument is universally used. The wooden fork, used for throwing the corn up in the air, is called *midra;* and the flat, hollow, wooden shovel next used for a similar purpose, is called *raha.* The latter is evidently the *fan* of the New Testament. When this implement is used, the wheat falls down in a heap on the threshing-floor, while the chaff is carried away by the wind, and forms another large heap at a little distance. The peasants do not burn it, but give it to their cattle, *see* Is. xxx. 24; and it is so perfectly dry, that were it set on fire, it would be impossible to quench it. These simple customs strikingly illustrate the words of David.'—*See* also the last Note, p. 51, *Chaff.—Narrative of a Mission of Inquiry to the Jews,* pp. 64, 116.

18. *Preached he, &c.* ' He evangelized the people;' proclaimed to them the gospel.—*See* Ac. viii. 25.

19. *Herod the tetrarch.*—*See* above, & ' Note,' p. 49.

PRACTICAL REFLECTIONS.

15, .6 *ver.* Let us take example from John, not to put our own performances in place of Christ, nor to put the sign in the place of the thing signified.

[16 *ver.* John acknowledged that it was only with water he baptized, and that the baptism of the Holy Ghost was yet to be ministered by Jesus; this was the principal thing to be desired. We are to be washed from all our filthiness as with pure water; and to this purifying, let every trial, however painful, conduce. Let us willingly submit ourselves to the

cleansing power of the truth, as in the light of Him ' whose eyes are as a flame of fire.']

19, 20 *ver.* It is dangerous to be in a position of worldly authority. Whilst the people could bear to be reproved, and whilst the publicans and soldiers even asked to be directed by John, Herod could not allow his sin to be pointed out.

20 *ver.* It is better to be a sufferer in the cause of truth and righteousness, as was John, than to have, like Herod, the power of adding to our guilt.

GEOGRAPHICAL NOTICES.

JUDÆA. — *See* ' Historical Sketch,' p. ix. — *See* ADDENDA, *Pontius Pilate.*

GALILEE.—*See* ' Historical Sketch,' p. ix.

ITUREA.—So called from *Jetur,* one of the sons of Ishmael, Ge. xxv. 15; 1 Ch. i. 31. It was situated on the east side of Jordan; and was taken from the descendants of Jetur by the tribes of Reuben and Gad, and the half tribe of Manasseh.

TRACHONITIS.—Has Damascus on the north, Iturea

on the south, Arabia Deserta on the east, and Batanea on the west. It derived its name from the Trachones mountains *Khiara.* Philip obtained these regions from the Romans, on condition that he would extirpate the robbers.

ABILENE.—It was to the south of *Baalbec;* formed part of Cœlo-Syria, between Libanus and Anti-Libanus, and north-west of Damascus.

THE RIVER JORDAN.—*See* Sect. 8, p. 60.

ADDENDA.

'PONTIUS PILATE,' p. 49.

Pontius Pilate. Herod the Great left his kingdom to three sons.—*See* § 5, p. 35. He left Judea to Archelaus, who reigned *nine* years; when, on account of his crimes, he was deposed by Augustus, and banished into Vienne, and Judea was made a Roman province, and placed entirely under Roman governors, or *procurators,* and became completely tributary to Rome. Pontius Pilate was the *fifth* governor that had been sent. He was probably an Italian, & was the successor of Gratus, in the government of Judea, A.D. 26 or 27. He was a most obstinate, passionate, covetous, cruel, and bloody wretch, tormenting even the innocent, and putting people to death without so much as a form of trial. Taking offence at some Galileans, he murdered them in the court of the temple as they offered their sacrifices, when they assembled to eat the passover, Lu. xiii. 1, 2. This, as our Saviour hint-

ed, was a prelude of the Jews being shut up in their city, and murdered. Wicked as he was, his conviction of our Saviour's innocence caused him to try several methods to preserve his life. His wife too sent him word to have nothing to do in condemning Jesus, as she had a terrible dream about him. When the Jews accused our Saviour of calling himself the Son of God, Pilate was the more afraid, as he suspected he might be so. They then cried out, he would be a traitor to Cæsar if he dismissed Jesus. Dreading a charge of this nature, he washed his hands, and protested that he was innocent of Jesus' death, and then condemned him to be crucified. Guided by Providence, he, instead of an abstract of the causes of condemnation, caused to be written on our Saviour's cross, *This is Jesus of Nazareth, the King of the Jews,* which at once declared his innocence, royalty, and

THE FOOLISH SHALL NOT STAND IN THY SIGHT.—Psalm v. 5.   [65

SECT. VII.   THE MINISTRY OF JOHN THE BAPTIST.   PART II.

ADDENDA—(continued).

Messiahship: nor could all the intreaties of the Jews cause him in the least to alter the inscription. He readily allowed Joseph the dead body to give it a decent interment. He as readily allowed the Jews to seal and guard the sacred tomb; and so our Saviour's resurrection became the more notorious. About three years after the crucifixion of our Saviour, Pilate, for his cruelty and oppression, was deposed by Vitellius, governor of Syria, and sent to Rome, to give an account of his conduct. Caligula, the emperor, soon after banished him to Vienne, in Gaul, where extreme poverty and distress influenced him to put a wretched end to his own life.

'PHARISEES,' p. 52.

The Pharisees were the most numerous and wealthy sect of the Jews, supposed to have originated about 150 years B.C. They derived their name from the Hebrew word *Pharash*, which signifies to set apart, or to separate, because they *separated* themselves from the rest of their countrymen, to peculiar strictness in religion. Their leading tenets were the following: that the world was governed by fate, or by a fixed decree of God; that the souls of men were immortal, and were either eternally happy or miserable beyond the grave; that the dead would be raised; that there were angels, good and bad; that God was under obligation to bestow peculiar favour on the Jews; and that they were justified by the merits of Abraham. They were proud, haughty, self-righteous, and held the common people in great disrespect, Jno. vii. 49, '*But this people who know not the law are cursed*.' They sought the offices of the state, and affected great dignity. They were superstitiously exact in paying tithe of the most trifling articles, while in general they neglected the weightier matters of the law. They were of opinion that good works might claim reward from God, and ascribed an extraordinary degree of merit to the observance of rules, which they had themselves established as works of supererogation. Of this sort were their frequent washings and fastings, their nice avoidance of reputed sinners, their rigorous observance of the sabbath, and the long prayers which they ostentatiously made in the synagogues and in the corners of the streets. Trusting in themselves that they were righteous, they not only despised the rest of mankind, but were entirely destitute of humility toward God; yet their hypocritical display of zeal for religion gave them great influence over the common people, and consequently great authority in the Jewish state. Some of the laws of Moses they maintained very strictly. In addition to the written laws, they held to a multitude which they maintained had come down from Moses by tradition. These they felt themselves as much bound to observe as the written law. Under the influence of these laws, they washed themselves before meals with great scrupulousness; they fasted twice a week—on Thursday, when they supposed Moses ascended mount Sinai, and on Monday, when he descended; they wore broad phylacteries, see Mt. xxiii. 5, § 85, and enlarged the fringe or borders of their garments; and loved the uppermost rooms at feasts, and the chief seats in the synagogues. They were in general a corrupt, hypocritical, office-seeking, haughty class of men. There are, however, some honourable exceptions recorded, &c. v. 34.

'SADDUCEES,' p. 52.

The Sadducees are supposed to have taken their name from Sadok, who flourished about 260 years before the Christian era. He was a pupil of Antigonus Sochœus, president of the sanhedrim, or great council of the nation. He had taught the duty of serving God *disinterestedly*, without the hope of reward, or the fear of punishment. Sadok, not properly understanding the doctrine of his master, drew the inference that there was no future state of rewards or punishments; and on this belief he founded the sect. The other tenets they held were: 1st. That there is no resurrection, neither angel nor spirit, Mt. xxii. 23, § 85; Ac. xxiii. 8; and that the soul of man perishes with the body. 2d. They rejected the doctrine of fate. 3d. They rejected all traditions. They carried their ideas of human freedom so far as to assert, that men were absolutely masters of their own actions, and at full liberty to do either good or evil. Some of these tenets led, as might be expected, to great profligacy of life; hence we find the licentious wickedness of the Sadducees frequently condemned in the New Testament. It is commonly alleged, that the Sadducees denied the authority of all the sacred writings, except the Pentateuch. They considered Messias as a great temporal prince, who was to erect a vast monarchy, wherein all nations were to be subjected to the Jews. This appears from their flocking to John's baptism along with the Pharisees, desiring to be prepared for his coming. Confining all their hopes to this world, enjoying its riches, and devoting themselves to its pleasures, they might well be anxious that their lot of life should be cast in the splendid reign of this expected temporal king, with the hope of sharing in his conquest and glory; but this expectation was so contrary to the lowly appearance of our Saviour, that they joined their inveterate enemies, the Pharisees, in persecuting him and his religion.

In point of numbers, Josephus says, the Sadducees were an inconsiderable sect; but their numerical deficiency was amply compensated by the dignity and eminence of those who embraced their tenets, and who were persons of the first distinction; and several of them were advanced to the high-priesthood. The great and the rich are apt to prefer the pleasure and grandeur of this life, to any expectancy in a future state.

'ON THE MINISTRY OF JOHN THE BAPTIST, p. 49.

'John began his ministry probably Oct. 5, U.C. 779, the assumed date of his nativity when he completed his thirtieth year, about the feast of Tabernacles, which began this year on Sept. 15, and expired Sept. 22. We may conjecture that it would begin after, not before the 10th of Tisri, and the expiration of the feast itself. If it began at this time, it might last until the day of his imprisonment, as nearly as possible, seven months; but until April 5th, the day of the commencement of our Saviour's ministry, at the Passover,—Jno. ii. 13, U.C. 780; exactly six months.' —*Greswell*, Vol. II. Diss. xix. p. 183.

'Those who maintain the longer duration of the ministry of John are too apt to regard him as a simple Levite; than which there cannot be a more gross mistake. The son of Zacharias was a priest, and the son of a priest; by each of his parents lineally descended from the founder of the priesthood; and capable to have represented the Levitical high priest himself. It can hardly be necessary to observe, that the *sacerdotal* order, among the Jews, was entirely distinct from the *Levitical*: their origin was different; their duties and privileges were altogether of a superior rank; and, what is more, were incommunicable to others: so that to degrade a priest to the level of a Levite, would be as great a presumption as to raise a Levite to the degree of a priest. The priests were the lineal progeny of Aaron: the twenty-four courses, which embodied them all, were entirely derived from Eleazar and from Ithamar, the only two sons of Aaron who survived after the death of Nadab and Abihu. The Levites were descended from the rest of the family of Levi; Merari, Gershon, and (excepting only the particular family of Aaron) Kohath. The strictness of the law for the preservation of the line of the priesthood is well described by Josephus. —*Contr. Ap.* i. 7, ii. 5; *vide* also 2 Ch. xxxi. 16—9; Ezr. ii. 62.—*Ibid.*, Vol. I. Diss. xi. p. 374.

'The scene of this ministry is laid by St. Matthew, and by St. Mark, at its commencement, in the wilderness of Judæa; which does not mean an absolute desert, but a plain and champaign country, devoted to pasturage, and, though comparatively remote from the more populous parts, yet not unoccupied by villages. Thus Josephus mentions Βηθαλαγαν ... κωμην οὐσαν ἐν τῇ ἐρήμῳ *a village in the desert*.—Ant. Jud. xiii. i. 5. The principal scene of his ministry, we learn from St. Luke, was the Perichorus of Jordan;

SHALL ANY TEACH GOD KNOWLEDGE?—Job xxi. 22.

ADDENDA—(continued).

the proper name of which was the Aulon,—Hieron. Oper. ii. 393, ad calcem, De Situ et Nominibus: described by Josephus,—B. iv. viii. 2; Ant. xvi. v. 2,—as two hundred and thirty stades in length, one hundred and twenty in breadth—intersected by the Jordan, enclosed on either side by mountains; desert and barren, and reaching from the southern extremity of the lake of Tiberias, to the northern extremity of the lake Asphaltites. The locality of this Perichorus appears to have been chosen as the fittest scene for the ministerial labours of John, because when overflowed by the Jordan, and laid under water, without being too deep, it would afford the greatest facilities for baptism, or immersion. The scene, thus chosen, seems to have been ever after the same; Bethabara or Bethany, Ænon or Salem; all contiguous places, or not very remote from each other: the former in Peræa, on the eastern side of the Jordan, the latter in Galilee, on the western. The locality of Bethabara continued to be still pointed out by tradition, even in the time of Origen—Oper. iv. 140. A—142. A. in Joan. tom. vi. 24; but whether correctly or not, may be doubted. The preponderance of critical reasons makes rather in favour of *Bethany beyond Jordan*, than of *Bethabara*. Such a country was well adapted for the supply of John's peculiar food, ἀκρίδες καὶ μέλι ἄγριον, *locusts and wild honey*, as the desert had been previously for the materials of his dress. Clothes made of hair, in general, are alluded to by Josephus as characteristic of poverty, or a mean state of life, B. i. xxiv. 3, Ant. xvi. vii. 3.

' The Perichorus of Jordan, for a great part of its extent, bordered upon Judæa; hence, among those who resorted to the baptism of John, the inhabitants of Jerusalem and of Judæa are specified among the first. It is, however, a circumstance of resemblance between John's ministry and our Saviour's also, that both appear to have been almost confined to Galilee, or to the dominions of Herod Antipas, beyond the jurisdiction of the Jewish sanhedrim.'—*Gresswell*, Vol. II. Diss. xix. pp. 183—.5.

' The first character in which John is represented, upon the public assumption of his ministerial office, is that of an herald, or proclaimer, of the tidings of the kingdom, accompanied by the conditions of faith —that is, belief in the tidings, and of repentance, or reformation of life, as a consequence of the belief, Mt. iii. 1, 2, § 7, p. 50.

' His next character is the character of a baptiser, Mt. iii. 5, 6. Another, and a third character, is that of a teacher of morals, as well as of a preacher of the kingdom, Lu. iii. 10—4, § 7, p. 53.

' A fourth, and the last character, is that of an harbinger of the Messiah, or of one commissioned to bear express testimony to the approaching advent of the Christ, Mk. i. 7, 8, § 7, p. 54.

' Besides these characters, we meet with no more: and of these the first and the last alone are really distinct; the intermediate two are not so much different from, as natural consequences of the first. The character of a preacher of repentance could not fail to include the character of a moral teacher: and the doctrine of the kingdom, as preached by John, being accompanied by the requisition of repentance, grounded upon faith in the approach of the kingdom, baptism was administered as the sign and seal of both.

' The administration of baptism, without any regard to the use of that rite among the Jews in the admission of proselytes, was a necessary part of the office of John; whether as a prophet of t e kingdom, or as a teacher of morality: in which might be supposed to be comprehended the sum and effect of his ministry as both. The reception of baptism at his hands was the last and most decisive step, to declare the faith of the recipient in both the message and the authority of John. Hence it is that the final end of his mission, so far as these objects are contemplated by it, may be fitly described as simply and solely *to baptize*; that his ministry, regarded in the complex, might be called *his baptism*; that his personal denomination, both in the Gospels and out of them, is John *ὁ βαπτιστής*—John *the baptiser*; that St. Mark and St. Luke do each concisely, express both his first and his second office in this one description, that John came preaching or proclaiming the *baptism* of repentance, unto remission of sins; and that St. Paul, in the synagogue of Pisidian Antioch, employs the same language: John having proclaimed, before the face of his entrance, *baptism* of repentance to all the people.—*See* Ac. xiii. 24.'—*Ibid.*, pp. 150—.2.

' The Baptist wrought no miracles; but in other respects, whether as a preacher of the kingdom, or as a teacher of moral duties, he was absolutely the counterpart, and merely the forerunner of Christ.'— *Ibid.*, p. 155.

' The mission and ministry of John, as far as they were subservient to the future gospel dispensation, were the same in kind with the mission and ministry of our Lord himself, of the twelve and of the seventy, respectively, during the lifetime of Christ.'—*Ibid.*, p. 157.

' The personal ministry of John is not to be regarded as distinct from the personal ministry of our Saviour, except in the order of succession: both were continuous, though individual parts of the same scheme or dispensation in general, which may be called indifferently either the ministration of the kingdom, or the ministration of the Messiah, as discriminated from the propagation of formal Christianity, or the ministration of the apostles. It may be said, however, that prophecy, both ancient and recent, had represented the ministry of John in a different light, viz., as the ministry of an herald, harbinger, or precursor specially in reference to the coming of Christ; and therefore as distinct from the ministry of Christ. *The voice of one crying in the wilderness, Prepare ye the way of the Lord; make straight his paths*, Is. xl. 3-5. *Behold I do send my messenger before thy face, who shall get ready thy way before thee*, Mal. iii. 1. *He shall be mighty before the Lord, . . . and many of the children of Israel shall he turn to the Lord their God. And he himself shall go before him in the spirit and power of Elias, to turn the hearts of the fathers to the children, and the disobedient to the wisdom of the righteous; to prepare for the Lord a duly provided people*, Lu. i. 15—7. *And thou, child, shalt be called the Prophet of the Highest: for thou shalt go before the face of the Lord to prepare his ways; for the sake of giving knowledge of salvation to his people, by the remission of their sins through the tender mercies of our God; wherewith the dayspring from on high hath visited us, to shine unto those who were sitting in the darkness and shadow of death, whereby to direct our feet safely into the way of peace*, 76—9.'—*Ibid.*, pp. 176, ..1.

' If such had not been the original design of the ministry of John, would the prophet Isaiah have specified *this*, as the final result of that preparation which he attributes to the spiritual harbinger, that all flesh should see the *salvation* of God? For what is *the salvation* of God, but God *the Saviour*? and what is God *the Saviour*, but a *crucified Saviour*? and when was a crucified Saviour revealed, or seen, before the day of Pentecost, when the first Christian sermon was preached? Would the angel Gabriel have said that John should get ready for the Lord, λαὸς κατεσκευασμένον? For what is this *duly prepared* or *befitting* people, but the members of his future church, his *peculium* among the Jews, the ἐκλογὴ in short, of Israel? Would his father Zacharias have said, that he should go before the face of the Lord to give knowledge of salvation to his people? For when was the knowledge of *salvation*, that is, the knowledge of a *Saviour*, communicated in the lifetime of John? Or when were the tender mercies of God fully developed in the remission of sins; before the great forfeit had been paid in the sacrifice for sins, and human redemption was complete? Or when could the dayspring from on high be said to have alone forth on the darkness of the Gentile world, before the gospel was preached to that world? Or when were the feet of sinners, whether Jews or Gentiles, safely guided into the way of peace, before Christ, the Way, the Truth, and the Life, the Captain of salvation, and the Prince of peace, had been distinctly proposed in all these capacities, to the Jew first, and afterwards to the Gentile?'—*Ibid.*..pp. 179, ..1, .181, ..2

HEAR INSTRUCTION, AND BE WISE, AND REFUSE IT NOT.—Prov. viii. 33.

SECTION VIII.—THE BAPTISM OF JESUS.

SECTION VIII.—ABOUT THE MIDDLE OF THE MINISTRY OF JOHN THE BAPTIST, JESUS COMES TO HIS BAPTISM: THE HOLY GHOST DESCENDS UPON HIM; A VOICE FROM HEAVEN BEARS WITNESS TO HIM.

(G. 6,) No. 8.   *Line from Nazareth to Jordan.*

MATT. iii. 13—17.   MARK i. 9—11.   LUKE iii. 21—.3.

13   Then cometh Jesus from Galilee *to Jordan unto John, to-be-baptized of him.
14   But John forbad διεκωλυεν him, saying, I have need to-be-baptized of thee, and comest thou to me?
15   And Jesus answering said unto him, Suffer *it to be so* now: for thus it-becometh πρεπον εστιν us to fulfil all righteousness.

9 ᵃAnd it-came-to-pass in those days, *that* Jesus came from Nazareth of Galilee,*ᵇ*

SCRIPTURE ILLUSTRATIONS.

Mk. i. 9. *Nazareth*—the city where Mary the mother of Jesus lived, Lu. i. 26, J. 1, § 2, p. 9—Mary returned to her own house at, 56, § 2, p. 14—Joseph and Mary went from, ii. 4, § 4, p. 19—returned from Egypt to, 39, § 5, p. 35—Philip said to Nathanael, '*We have found ... Jesus of Nazareth,' &c.,* Jno. i. 45, § 10—his superscription, Jno. xix. 19, § 91—by the disciples going to Emmaus, Lu. xxiv. 19, § 94.

Mt. iii. 13. *Jordan*—to the plain of which, Lot departed, eastward, from Abram, Ge. xiii. 11—where the judgment of God was signally manifested on the cities of the plain, xix. 23—9—east border of the land of Canaan, Nu. xxxiv. 12—between the two and a half and uine and a half tribes, Jos. xxii. 25—its waters divided for Israel to pass through, Jos. iii. 17—see iv. 22, .3; for Elijah, 2 Ki. ii. 6; for Elisha, 13, .4—Naaman to wash in Jordan seven times for the leprosy, 2 Ki. v. 10—for which disease there was to be a sprinkling seven times, Le. xlv. 7.

Jordan means, 'River of Judgment.' The waters of judgment were to be brought up over Israel, Is. viii. 7, 8; xvii. 12; xviii. 2, 7; Ps. xliii. 7—their sins to be left in the depths, Mi. vii. 19—the waters of judgment went over Jesus, as having taken upon him the case of his people, Ps. lxix. 1, 2, 14, .5; lxxxviii. 6, 7—twelve stones, representing the twelve tribes, taken out of Jordan by Joshua, and set up for a sign at Gilgal, Jos. iv. 8, 20—.4—multitudes baptized in, Mk. i. 5, § 7, p. 52—after the feast of dedication, Jesus went beyond Jordan, Jno. x. 40, § 57.

11. *baptized of thee*—the Lord was to baptize with the Holy Ghost—see Mt. iii. 11, § 7, p. 54.

15. *suffer it to be so now, for thus it becometh, &c.*—that is, not as having need of it for himself, but as one doing service for others, who through him should receive the better baptism. It was thus he washed his disciples' feet, Jno. xiii. 4–17, § 87—thus he gave himself for the church, ' that he might sanctify and cleanse it with the washing of water by the word,' Ep. v. 25—7—thus, though Lord of all, and needing not to be a servant, 'he became obedient unto death, even the death of the cross,' Ph. ii. 6–8—so it had been written of him, Ps. xl. 7, 8—and the Lord is well pleased for his righteousness' sake,' Is. xlii. 21—he esteemed it his meat to do his Father's will, Jno. iv. 34, § 13—he did always those things that pleased the Father, viii. 29, § 55—he kept his Father's commandments, and abode in his love, xv. 10, § 87—' such an High Priest,' &c., He. vii. 26—he 'offered himself without spot,' &c., ix. 14—' by one offering he hath perfected for ever them that are sanctified,' x. 14.

NOTES.

Mt. iii. 14. *Forbad him.* 'Was hindering; would have hindered.'—See ADDENDA, p. 62.

I have need. ' I am very far inferior to thee, so as rather to need *thy* baptism—the Holy Ghost; than thou mine—in water; and yet dost thou come to *me*, as to a superior?' I am a sinner, and unworthy to administer this to the Messiah.

15. *Suffer it to be so now.* 'For the present.' The meaning is, that John must suffer him, for the *present*, to be baptized with the baptism of *water*, for that baptism of His with the *Spirit* was yet to be.

It becometh us. Jesus was about to procure for his people that of which John's baptism was a sign.

To fulfil. To complete or make perfect the law ordained of God. Christ was the fulfiller of the law.

All righteousness. Some think here is an allusion to the priests washing previously to inauguration; Ex. xxix. 4, '*And Aaron and his sons thou shalt bring unto the door of the tabernacle of the congregation, and shalt wash them with water.*' To fulfil the law as the great High Priest, he must needs be washed. Jesus had no sin. But he was about to enter on his work. It was proper that he should be set apart by his forerunner, and shew his connection with him, and give his approbation to what John had done. Also, he was baptized, that occasion might be taken, at the commencement of his work, for God publicly to declare his approbation of him, and his solemn appointment as the Messiah.

PRACTICAL REFLECTIONS.

Mk. i. 9. We should be willing to go far, like Him whose steps we are to follow, for the purpose of witnessing to the truth, and strengthening the Lord's servants in their work.

[Mt. iii. 14. The condescension of Christ in seeking out his people may well have to us, as it was to John, the subject of admiring gratitude—as when he said, ' Comest thou to me?']

John's baptism could not be for the washing away of sin, seeing it was performed upon Jesus, who was himself ' the Lamb of God that taketh away the sin of the world;' and he was to be done by Him years afterwards, when he bare our sins in his own body on the tree.

[John's baptism could not be for the giving of the new birth, for Jesus, upon whom that baptism was performed, did not require regeneration—He was the Holy One, the only-begotten of the Father.]

After the example of Christ, let Christians learn to submit to the ministry of their less qualified or less honourable brethren, submitting in all things unto God.

The most eminent saints are, like John, ready to feel and to express their unworthiness of the honour put upon them, as being employed in the service of God.

15 ver. The defective views of our brethren should be met, as Jesus met those of John, with kindness and persuasion.

Jesus, in the time then present, submitted to his sign, as looking forward to his fulfilling all righteousness, when also he was to give the thing signified in the baptism of the Holy Ghost.

We ought, like John, to give up our former opinions or prejudices when they are shewn to be wrong.

[John allowed Jesus to be baptized of him, not as being less worthy than himself, but as being the fulfiller of all righteousness—who, in procuring the baptism of his mystical body, accomplishes the filling up of all ceremonial observances.]

We must not allow the private opinions of even those we recognise in office under God to prevent us from doing what we know to be his will.

| PART I | THE BAPTISM OF JESUS. | SECT. VIII. |

| MATT. iii. 16, .7. | MARK i. 10, .1. | LUKE iii. 21, .2. |

Then he-suffered him,*
16 And Jesus, when-he-was-baptized, *d* went-up straightway out-of απο the water:*
and,
f lo, the heavens were-*opened ανεωχθησαν unto-him,*g*
and he-saw the Spirit of God descending like a-dove, and lighting upon him:
17 and lo a-voice from heaven,

and was baptized of John in εις Jordan.

10 And straightway coming-up out-of the water,
he-saw the heavens opened, σχιζομενους
and the Spirit like a dove descending upon him:
11 *k* And there-came a-voice from heaven,

c Now when- all the 21 people -were-baptized, it-came-to-pass, *that* Jesus also being-baptized, *d*
e and praying,*f*
the heaven was-opened, ανεωχθηναι
g and the Holy Ghost 22 descended in-a-bodily shape σωματικω ειδει like a-dove upon him,*k*
and a-voice came from heaven,

MARGINAL READING:—*k* Or, cloven, or rent

SCRIPTURE ILLUSTRATIONS.

Lu. iii. 21. *and praying*—Jesus was a man of prayer. He prayed early, Mk. i. 35, § 18—late, Mt. xiv. 23, § 41—all night, Lu. vi. 12, § 27—when about to be transfigured, Lu. ix. 28, .9, § 51—for his disciples, Lu. xxii. 32, § 87; Jno. xvii. § 67—in the garden of Gethsemane, Mt. xxvi. 39-44, § 88—for his murderers, Lu. xxiii. 34, § 91—before sending forth the twelve, he directed them to pray for the sending forth, Mt. ix. 38, § 39—in the spirit of united prayer they were found when the baptism of the Spirit was given, Ac. i. 14; ii. 1, 2—in the same unity of the Spirit are they, who believe on him through their word, to be found, preparatory to the great and universal witnessing, Jno. xvii. 21, § 87—in the same earnest supplication, Is. lxii. 6, 7; Je. xxxi. 7; Eze. xxxvi. 37; Ho. xiv. 2, 3; Joel ii. 15-32, &c.

Mt. iii. 16. *the heavens were opened unto him*—so unto Stephen, Ac. vii. 56—there he saw Him who for

us fulfilled all righteousness; let us be found 'looking unto Jesus, the author,' &c., He. xii. 2—thence he shall come to receive up his redeemed into that glorious reward. Is. lxiv. 1, 4; Jno. xiv. 2, 3, § 87—*see* also ch. i. 51, § 10.

Lu. iii. 21. *and the Holy Ghost descended*—this as predicted, Ps. xlv. 7; Is. xi. 2; xlii. 1; lxi. 1—received by him as the Head of his people, Ge. xlix. 26; De. xxxiii. 16—he is the Head of his body, which is united to him by faith, Col. i. 18—29.

Mk. i. 11. *voice, &c.*—contrast with the voice to Nebuchadnezzar, announcing his degradation, Da. iv. 31—this voice of the Father was again heard on the mount of Transfiguration, Mt. xvii. 5, § 51—this voice from the excellent glory referred to, 2 Pe. i. 17—it was also heard just before his death, and was then supposed by many to be thunder, Jno. xii. 28—30, § 62.

NOTES.

Lu. iii. 21. *Now when all the people were baptized, &c.* ['A difference is to be noted between εν τω βαπτισθηναι τον λαον and εν τω βαπτιζεσθαι τον λαον, of which the latter means, "*while the people were being baptized,*" and the former, "*after they were baptized.*" Accordingly, in order to render the peculiar meaning of the Greek more distinct, the whole may be rendered thus: *And it came to pass, after all the people had been baptized, that when Jesus also had been baptized, and was praying, the heaven was opened, &c.*'—*Bloomfield.*

And praying. We may reasonably suppose that there was an intimate connection between the '*praying*' that accompanied the baptism, and the anointing of '*the Holy Ghost*' that immediately followed.—*Comp.* '*If ye then being evil,*' &c., Lu. xi. 13, § 62.

Mk. i. 10. *The heavens opened.* There is every reason to believe the light was *preternatural,* and to have accompanied the DIVINE SPIRIT; such a light as accompanied Jesus, on being visibly revealed to St. Paul at his conversion. The heavens were opened unto him—that is, to John the Baptist—as a testimony to John of the Messiahship of Jesus. And *he,* John, saw the Spirit of God ... lighting upon him, *i.e.* Jesus. The same appearance took place at Stephen's death, Ac. vii. 56, '*Behold, I see the heavens opened, and the Son of man,*' &c.

Mt. iii. 16. *The Spirit of God—see* ver. 11. This was the third Person of the Trinity, descending upon him in the form of a dove, Lu. iii. 22. The *dove,* among the Jews, was the symbol of purity or harm-

lessness; Mt. x. 16, § 39, '*Behold, I send you forth as sheep in the midst of wolves; be ye therefore wise as serpents, and harmless as doves.*' The form chosen here was doubtless an emblem of the innocence, meekness, and tenderness of the Saviour. The gift of the Holy Spirit, in this manner, was the public approbation of Jesus,—Jno. i. 33, § 10, '*And I knew him not: but he that sent me,*' &c.; and a sign of his being set apart to the office of the Messiah.

Lu. iii. 22. *The Holy Ghost.* So Luke: Matthew says, '*The Spirit of God:*' Mark says, '*The Spirit.*' This is the third Person in the Trinity.

In a bodily shape. This was a real visible appearance. The dove is an emblem of purity and harmlessness, and was early used to signify acceptance and reconciliation: and plainly indicated that Jesus should personify those very graces of which the dove is an emblem. '*For in him dwelleth all the fulness of the Godhead bodily,*' Col. ii. 9. [The *Holy Spirit,* when he assumes a visible form, assumes that which shall be emblematic of the thing intended. Thus he assumed the form of *tongues,* to signify the miraculous powers of language with which the apostles would be endowed; the appearance of fire, to denote their power, &c.; Ac. ii. 3, '*And there appeared,*' &c.]

Mk. i. 11. *A voice from heaven.* At his birth angels sung of his glory; and now, thirty years afterward, God the Father from heaven declared his acceptance of the Son in the work of our redemption. It was a public declaration that Jesus was the Messiah.—*See* '*Scripture Illustrations,*' Mk. i. 11.

PRACTICAL REFLECTIONS.

Lu. iii. 21. Religious observances should be attended to with prayer, after the example, and in the name of Jesus.

22 ver. The baptism of John was for witness: and it was accompanied with the witness of the Father, as acknowledging him from heaven, and of the Holy Ghost, as descending upon him like a dove.

[As the Holy Ghost descended upon Jesus in a bodily shape like a dove, so may the spirit of peace

and of love rest upon his mystical body and still bear witness of Jesus.]

Let us acknowledge the grace of the Father in the gift of his beloved Son, with whom he is well pleased, as the fulfiller of all righteousness in behalf of his people.

Let us acknowledge Jesus in his wondrous grace, in becoming a servant as under the law for us, and with whose service the Father is well pleased.

HE IS THE HEAD OF THE BODY, THE CHURCH.—Col. i. 18.

SECT. VIII.   THE BAPTISM OF JESUS.   PART II.

MATT. iii. 17.	MARK i. 11.	LUKE iii. 22, 3.
saying, This is my beloved Son, in whom I-am-well-pleased.	saying, Thou art my beloved Son, in whom I-am-well-pleased.	which-said, Thou art my beloved Son; in thee I-am-well-pleased.

'And Jesus himself began to-be about thirty 23 years-of-age. ην ωσει ετων ... τριακοντα αρχομενος. [For Luke iii. 24—38, see § 4.]

SCRIPTURE ILLUSTRATIONS.

my beloved Son—the true David or Beloved, chosen to stand in the room of the people, and to approach the Father for them, Je. xxx. 9, 21; Ps. lxxxix. 19, 20; as Mt. xii. 18, § 26; Jno. iii. 35, § 13; v. 20, § 23—hath made us accepted in the Beloved, Ep. i. 6—translated into the kingdom of his dear Son, Col. i. 13—of which kingdom the law is 'LOVE,' Ja. ii. 8—of obedience to which law, the Christ, the Beloved, the King, is himself the great example, Ep. v. 2.

in whom I am well pleased—the Father accepted him as fulfilling all righteousness substitutionally for his people, Jno. iii. 13—.6, § 12; He. x. 14—22.

Lu. iii. 23. *thirty years*—the age at which the priests entered upon their office, Nu. iv., where it is mentioned seven times, ver. 3, 23, 30, .5, .9, 43, .7—*see*, as to the priesthood of Christ, He. ix.

NOTES.

My beloved Son. This is the title which God himself gave to Jesus. It denotes the nearness of his relation to the Father, and the love of God for him; He. i. 1, 2, ' God, who at sundry times and in divers manners spake in time past unto the fathers by the prophets, hath in these last days spoken unto us by his Son, whom he hath appointed heir of all things, by whom also he made the worlds.' It implies that he was equal with God; He. i. 5–8, 'For unto which of the angels said he at any time, Thou art my Son, this day have I begotten thee? And again, I will be to him a Father, and he shall be to me a Son? And again, when he bringeth in the first-begotten into the world, he saith, And let all the angels of God worship him. And of the angels he saith, Who maketh his angels spirits, and his ministers a flame of fire. But unto the Son he saith, Thy throne, O God, is for ever and ever: a sceptre of righteousness is the sceptre of thy kingdom.'—Jno. x. 29–33, § 56, 'My Father, which gave them me, is greater than all; and no man is able to pluck,' &c.—xix. 7, § 90, ' The Jews answered him, We have a law, and by our law he ought to die, because he made himself the Son of God.'

In whom I am well pleased. By this voice and overshadowing of the Spirit, the mission of Christ was publicly and solemnly accredited: God intimating that he had before delighted in him; the law, in all its ordinances, having pointed him out; for they

could not be pleasing to God, but as they were fulfilled in, and shewed forth the Son of man, till he came.

Lu. iii. 23. *And Jesus himself, &c., i.e.,* he had nearly completed his thirtieth year.

The baptism of Jesus has usually been considered a striking manifestation of the doctrine of the Trinity, or the doctrine that there are three persons in the Divine nature.—1. There is the Person of Jesus Christ, the Son of God, baptized in the Jordan, elsewhere declared to be equal with God; Jno. x. 30, § 56, ' I and my Father are one.'—2. The Holy Spirit, descended in a bodily form upon the Saviour. The Holy Spirit is also equal with the Father, or is also God; Ac. v. 3, 4, ' But Peter said, Ananias, why hath Satan filled thine heart to lie to the Holy Ghost, and to keep back part of the price of the land? Whiles it remained, was it not thine own ? and after it was sold, was it not in thine own power? why hast thou conceived this thing in thine heart? thou hast not lied unto men, but unto God.'—3. The Father, addressing the Son, and declaring that he was well pleased with him. It is impossible to explain this transaction consistently in any other way than by supposing that there are three equal Persons in the Divine nature, or essence, and that each of these sustain important parts in the work of redeeming man.

PRACTICAL REFLECTIONS.

22 ver. (Mt. iii. 17.) Let us acknowledge Him, of whom the Father said emphatically, ' This is,' &c., ' Thou art,' &c. We were dead in trespasses and sins, and were worthy of eternal death, but Jesus ever liveth to make intercession for us.

Let us acknowledge Christ as our true David, the Beloved—who is not only David's son, but David's Lord, the Son of the Highest, unto whom his Father in heaven will give the throne of his father David.

[In John we have an example of humility. Blessed with great success; attended by the great and noble, and with nothing but *principle* to keep him from turning it to his advantage; he still kept himself out of view, and pointed to a far greater personage at hand.]

Everything about the work of Jesus was wonderful. No person had before come into the world under such circumstances. God would not have attended the commencement of his life with such wonderful events, if it had not been of the greatest moment to our race, and if he had not possessed a dignity above all prophets, kings, and priests. He was the Redeemer of men, the mighty God, the Prince of Peace.—*see* Is. ix. 6, ' For unto us a child is born, unto us a man is given: and the government shall be upon his shoulder: and his name shall be called Wonderful, Counsellor, The mighty God, The everlasting Father, The Prince of Peace.' And it was proper that a voice from heaven should declare it, that the angels should attend him, and the Holy Spirit signalize his baptism by his personal presence.

GEOGRAPHICAL NOTICES.

JORDAN.—There is no river of any magnitude in the Holy Land besides the Jordan. The historical notices respecting this river are extremely interesting. Moses mentions it, De. iii. 25, ' I pray thee, let me go over, and see the good land that is beyond Jordan, that goodly mountain, and Lebanon.' He continues,—*see* 26, .7 verse, ' But the LORD was wroth with me for your sakes, and would not hear me; and the LORD said unto me, Let it suffice thee; speak no more unto me of this matter. Get thee up unto the top of Pisgah, and lift up thine eyes westward, and northward, and southward, and eastward, and behold it with thine eyes: for thou shalt not go over this Jordan.' In Joshua, iii. ch., is a beautiful description of the Israelites passing over on dry ground,' ' clean over Jordan.' When David fled before his rebellious son Absalom, 2 Sa. xvii. 22, ' Then David arose, and all the people that were with him, and they passed over

Jordan: by the morning light there lacked not one of them that was not gone over Jordan.' The man of God smote the waters—*see* 2 Ki. ii. 8, 13, ' And Elijah took his mantle, and wrapped it together, and smote the waters, and they were divided hither and thither, so that they two went over on dry ground.' Elisha ' took up also the mantle of Elijah that fell from him, and went back, and stood by the bank of Jordan; and he took the mantle of Elijah that fell from him, and smote the waters, and said, Where is the LORD God of Elijah? and when he also had smitten the waters, they parted hither and thither: and Elisha went over.' In JORDAN the Syrian captain was cleansed, 2 Ki. v. 14, ' Then went he down, and dipped himself seven times in Jordan, according to the saying of the man of God; and his flesh came again like unto the flesh of a little child, and he was clean.'

THE RIVER JORDAN

GEOGRAPHICAL NOTICES—(continued).

'But the most interesting of all the associations with this river is, that Jesus came from Nazareth of Galilee, and was baptized of John in Jordan. It has two sources. The one at Banias, the ancient Paneas, afterwards called *Cæsarea Philippi.—See* § 50.

'Just on the north-east side of this village is the source of the river, (here called Banias,) issuing from a spacious cavern under a wall of rock, at the base of the eastern mountain. In the face of the perpendicular rock, directly over the cavern, and in other parts, several niches have been cut, apparently to receive statues. Each of these niches had once an inscription. The stream flows off on the north and west of the village, and joins another in the plain below.

'The fountains at *Tell el-Kady* directly correspond to the source, which Josephus speaks of as the "other source" of the Jordan, called also Dan; where stood the city Dan, anciently *Laish*. The same city *Dan*, placed by Eusebius and Jerome at four Roman miles from Paneas, towards *Tyre*, corresponds well to the present distance of the sources.

'Thus we find, at Banias and *Tell el-Kady*, the two sources of the greater and lesser Jordan, precisely as described by the ancients at Paneas, and the site of Dan.

'These streams unite about one hour from the *Tell*, and flow for about five miles, keeping along near the eastern hills, quite down to the lake or marsh *El-Huleh*, (the waters of Merom, of the Old Testament, Jos. xi. 5, 7).

'From lake *Huleh* it continues eight or ten miles south, and enters lake Tiberias, where it is from twenty to twenty-five yards across. The Jordan, at its entrance into the lake of Tiberias, runs near the foot of the western hills, which next its valley are steep, but not high; while on the other side of the stream, a fine fertile plain stretches off along the end of the lake, for an hour or more, quite to the mountains which skirt the eastern shore.—*See* Sect. 40, *Bethsaida in Decapolis*.

'The present Arabic name for the Jordan is *esh-Sheriah*, "the watering-place," to which the epithet *el-Kebir*, "the great," is sometimes annexed. The common name of the great valley through which it flows below the lake Tiberias, is *el-Ghor*, signifying a depressed tract or plain, usually between two mountains; and the same name continues to be applied to the valley quite across the whole length of the Dead Sea, and for some distance beyond.

'The Jordan issues from the lake of Tiberias, near its south-west corner, where are still traces of the site and walls of the ancient *Tarichæa*. The river at first winds very much, and flows, for three hours, near the western hills; then turns to the eastern, on which side it continues its course, for several hours, to the district called *Kurn el-Hemar*, " *Ass'* Horn," two hours below *Beisan*, where it again returns to the western side of the valley. Lower down, the Jordan follows more the middle of the great valley; though opposite Jericho, and towards the Dead sea, its course is nearer to the eastern mountains; about two-thirds or three-quarters of the valley lying here upon its western side.

'A few hundred yards below the point where the Jordan issues from the lake of Tiberias is a ford, close by the ruins of a Roman bridge of ten arches. About two hours further down is another old bridge, called *Jisr el-Mejamia*, consisting of one arch in the centre, with small arches upon arches at the sides; and also a khan upon the western bank. Somewhat higher up, but in sight of this bridge, is another ford. Thut near Beisan lies in a direction S.S.E. from the town. Indeed, the river is fordable in many places during summer; but the few spots where it may be crossed in the rainy season are known only to the Arabs.

'The banks of the Jordan appear to preserve everywhere a tolerably uniform character. The river flows in a valley of about a quarter of an hour (or one-third of a mile) in breadth, which is considerably lower than the rest of the valley of the Ghor,—in the northern part about forty feet. This lower valley, when Burckhardt saw it, was covered with high trees and a luxuriant verdure, affording a striking contrast with the sand slopes that border it on both sides. Further down, the verdure occupies in some parts a still lower strip along the river's brink. The channel of the river varies in different places; being in some wider and more shallow, and in others narrower and deeper. At the ford, near *Beisan*, on the 12th of March, Irby and Mangles found the breadth to be about 140 feet by measure; the stream was swift, and reached above the bellies of the horses. When Burckhardt passed there in July, it was about three feet deep. On the return of the former travellers, twelve days later (March 25th), they found the river, at a lower ford, extremely rapid, and were obliged to swim their horses. On the 29th of January, in the same year, as Mr. Bankes crossed at or near the same lower ford, the stream is described as flowing rapidly over a bed of pebbles, but as easily fordable for the horses. Near the convent of St. John, the stream, at the annual visit of the pilgrims at Easter, is sometimes said to be narrow, and flowing six feet below the banks of its channel. At the Greek bathing-place, lower down, it is described, in 1815, on the 3rd of May, as rather more than fifty feet wide and five feet deep, running with a violent current; in some other parts it was very deep.

'The Upper Jordan is less broad, less deep, and less rapid, than near the Dead Sea.'

Of the river near the Dead Sea, (the Lower Jordan,) Dr. Robinson observes: 'The upper or outer banks of the Jordan, where we came upon it, (at the ford *el-Helu*, which is the lowest point where the river is ordinarily crossed,) are not more than one hundred rods apart, with a descent of fifty or sixty feet to the level of the lower valley in which the river flows. There was here no sign of vegetation along the upper banks, and little, if any, in the valley below; except a narrow strip of canes, here occupying a still lower tract along the brink of the channel on each side. With these were intermingled occasionally the tamarisks, and the species of willow from which the pilgrims usually carry away branches for staves, after dipping them in the Jordan. Looking down upon the river from the high upper bank, it seemed a deep, sluggish, discoloured stream, winding its way slowly. Further up the river we could see that the high upper banks were wider apart, and the border of vegetation much broader, with many trees. There was a still though very rapid current; the water was of a clayey colour, but sweet and delightfully refreshing.

'In the Book of Joshua, the river Jordan is said "to overflow its banks" in the first month, or all the time of harvest. The original Hebrew expresses in these passages nothing more than that the Jordan "was full (or filled) up to all its banks," meaning the banks of its channel; it ran with full banks, or was brim-full. The phrase "swelling of Jordan," Eng. vers., Je. xii. 5; xlix. 19; l. 44, should be rendered "pride of Jordan," as in Zec. xi. 3, where the original word is the same. It refers to the verdure and thickets along the banks, but has no allusion to a rise of the waters.

'Thus understood, the biblical account corresponds entirely to what we find to be the case at the present day. The Israelites crossed the Jordan four days before the Passover (Easter), which they afterwards celebrated at Gilgal on the fourteenth day of the first month, Jos. iv. 19; v. 10. Then, as now, the harvest occurred during April and early in May, the barley preceding the wheat harvest by two or three weeks. Then, as now, there was a slight annual rise of the river, which caused it to flow at this season with full banks, and sometimes to spread its waters even over the immediate banks of its channel, where they are lowest, so as in some places to fill the low tract covered with trees and vegetation along its sides. Farther than this, there is no evidence that its inundations have ever extended.

'The low bed of the river, the absence of inundation and tributary streams, combine to leave the greater portion of the *Ghor* a solitary desert. Such it is described in antiquity, and such we find it at the present day. Josephus speaks of the Jordan as flowing "through a desert;" and of this plain as in summer scorched by heat, insalubrious, and watered by no stream except the Jordan. Near the ford, five or six miles above Jericho, the plain is described as "generally unfertile; the soil being in many places encrusted with salt, and having small heaps of a white powder, like sulphur, scattered at short intervals over its surface;" here, too, the bottom of the lower valley is generally barren. In the northern

LET US COME BEFORE HIS PRESENCE WITH THANKSGIVING ETC.—Psalm xcv. 2. [61

GEOGRAPHICAL NOTICES—(continued).

part of the *Ghor*, according to Burckhardt, "the great number of rivulets which descend from the mountains on both sides, and form numerous pools of stagnant water, produce in many places a pleasing verdure, and a luxuriant growth of wild herbage and grass; but the greater part of the ground is a parched desert, of which a few spots only are cultivated by the Bedawin. So, too, in the southern part, where similar rivulets or fountains exist, as around Jericho, there is an exuberant fertility; but these seldom reach the Jordan, and have no effect upon the middle of the Ghor. Nor are the mountains on each side less rugged and desolate than they have been described along the Dead Sea. The western cliffs overhang the valley at an elevation of a thousand or twelve hundred feet; while the eastern mountains are, indeed, at first less lofty and precipitous, but rise, further back, into ranges from two thousand to twenty-five hundred feet in height.' After a course of about 160 miles, inclusive of windings, it discharges itself at the rate of 250,000 tons an hour into the Dead Sea, being at this part a deep, discoloured stream, of about 100 feet wide. —*Dr. Robinson's Researches*, Vol. II. pp. 257-.67.

NAZARETH.—See Sect. II. p. 14, and Sect. vi. p. 43.

ADDENDA.

ON THE BAPTISM OF OUR LORD.

'The conduct of the Baptist, when he would have declined the administration of his own baptism on our Lord, was founded in a genuine humility, and a sincere conviction of the superior dignity of Christ, such as this knowledge of his person either conveyed or implied; and our Lord's answer, by which he impressed on him the necessity of performing his part in that ceremony, rightly understood, may instruct us in the final end of his baptism itself. Our Lord would not have said, Suffer it to be *so now*, could it have been as well suffered at any other time, before or after it, as at that—nor, For thus it behoveth us to fulfil all righteousness, had the same fulfilment, in that one respect, been equally incumbent on others, as on them in particular. The obligation in question was to no moral duty, binding upon moral agents in general; but to some legal requisition, incumbent on those two more especially: the nature of which we must needs collect from the instance of its observance, which was our Lord's receiving from John, and John's administering on our Lord, one and the same rite of baptism; but each, as part of a further, and much more important, ceremonial—the consecration of our Lord to his ministerial office, preparatory to his entering upon it.

'That the Levitical high priest was always a type of the Christian, may be taken for granted; and that John, as the son of Zacharias and Elisabeth, was competent to have sustained even the character of the Levitical high priest, is not less obvious. That there existed also, under the law, a high priest, and one only not the high priest, but, in other respects, superior in dignity, and in the sacreduess of his character, to all besides, is proved by various authorities. Καὶ ἄρα τίς που, οὐ λέγω τῶν ἄλλων Ἰουδαίων, ἀλλὰ καὶ τῶν ἱερέων, οὐχὶ τῶν ὑστάτων, ἀλλὰ τῶν, τὴν εὐθὺς μετὰ τὸν πρῶτον, τάξιν εἰληχότων, (Philo De Virtutibus, li. 591, l. 10—.4). Constituebatur autem sacerdos, qui dignitate proximus esset a summo sacerdote, sic tanquam in administratione regni est secundus a rege. is vicarius appellabatur; idem etiam dicebatur antistes. is igitur ad dextram summi sacerdotis semper adstabat (Maimon. De Apparatu Templi, iv. 16). Aud even this vicar had two sub-vicars (*Ibid.* 17). *Vide* also 2 Sa. viii. 17; xx. 25; 2 Ki. xxv. 18. Jos. Ant. Jud. viii. i. 4; x. viii. 5; xviii. iv. 3; xviii. i. 1, *comp.* with xvii. xiii. 1. Vit. 38, B. ii. xii. 6; iv. lii. 9.

'In this relation may the Levitical high priest be considered to have stood to the Christian, in general; and certainly, John, the representative of the Levitical high priesthood, the forerunner of the Messiah, the paranymph of the spiritual bridegroom, and the greatest prophet among all who had been born of women, to our Saviour, in particular. Now the consecration of the Levitical high priest was a necessary ceremony before he could enter on his ministry: much more, then, the consecration of the Christian.

'We may look upon this baptism, therefore, with all its circumstances and its effects, as constituting his true and his proper consecration; such as was naturally to be expected for the spiritual antitype of the legal prototype. Nor is there any particular, requisite to the integrity of the legal form, (Ex. xxix. 1—7; xl. 12—.5,) which may not be seen, *mutatis mutandis*, to have held good in what now took place. The previous ablution of the body of the priest was supplied by the baptism itself; and the agency, which performed that part of the ceremony, was a competent agency; for it was the agency of John. The absence of the sacred chrism (Ex. xxx. 22—33) was compensated by its antitype, the gifts and graces of the spiritual unction (Ps. xlv. 7, "*Thou lovest righteousness, and hatest wickedness: therefore God, thy God, hath anointed thee with the oil of gladness above thy fellows*"); and the medium by which these were effused was the medium of the Holy Ghost. The robes of beauty and of holiness, which adorned the person of the priest, (Ex. xxviii. 2, "*And thou shalt make holy garments for Aaron thy brother for glory and for beauty,*") were the essential innocence, and spotless purity, of the nature of Christ; a much more glorious garb, and more becoming for the Christian high priest, than the Aaronical vesture, and always typified by that, (Ps. xlv. 8, "*All thy garments smell of myrrh, and aloes, and cassia, out of the ivory palaces, whereby they have made thee glad.*") More than this I do not know to have been requisite to the inauguration even of the legal high priest; and, if it answered to all this, the baptism of our Lord, regarded as his inauguration also, would be complete.' —See Greswell, Vol. II. Diss. xix. pp. 189–191.

'From the time of this baptism, the sequel of the ministry of John is to be collected entirely from the last Gospel; shewing that the baptism of our Saviour, which, from the importance of the event itself, and from the nature of the testimony which John was, henceforward, enabled to bear to the Christ, compared with what he had been restricted to before it, was evidently qualified to become a cardinal point in the course of his ministry, actually was such; happening about the same time from its commencement, as before its termination. The first public testimony after his baptism borne to our Lord, was probably by the voice from heaven; and as he was immediately impelled into the wilderness, the first opportunity after the same event, which John could have of bearing witness to him, would be the opportunity afforded by the deputation and the question of the sanhedrim: and his answer to this question, as far as it conveys any such testimony, is no longer general and indefinite—speaking of some one, merely as to come—but particular and definite, so far as to speak of some one, who was already standing in the midst of them, and already known to the Baptist, though still unknown to them (Jno. i. 19–28, Sect. x.) This, then, is that instance of his testimony, to which, as understood to have been given to himself, though without any mention of himself, our Saviour referred (Jno. v. 33, Sect. xxiii.")—*Ibid.*, p. 187.

ON VERBAL DIFFERENCES, p. 53.

[Among the examples of occasional verbal differences amidst remarkable verbal agreements, it is easy to discover that, while the sense remains the same, some new beauty, some force or propriety, is introduced by the change. Thus, in the address of John the Baptist to the multitude, including scribes and Pharisees, it was indifferent whether he had said, according to St. Matt. lii. 9, καὶ μὴ δόξητε, or according to St. Luke iii. 8, καὶ μὴ ἄρξησθε; yet the latter is the more appropriate of the two; for it is implied that they were not to *think*, that is, to *begin*, to say so and so, in answer to this very address of John; and in vindication of themselves under his stern rebuke.' —Greswell, Vol. I. Diss. i. p. 53.

SECTION IX.—JESUS, BEING BAPTIZED, IS DRIVEN OF THE SPIRIT INTO THE WILDERNESS: HE FASTS FORTY DAYS AND FORTY NIGHTS: HE IS TEMPTED BY THE DEVIL;* ANGELS MINISTER UNTO HIM. Matt. iv. 1—11. Mark i. 12, .3 Luke iv. 1—13.

(G 7.) *Jesus is driven into the Wilderness; and fasts forty days and forty nights. Line from Jordan, going South and East.*

MATT. iv. 1, 2.	MARK i. 12, .3.	LUKE iv. 1, 2.
1 Then was-·Jesus·- led-up αυηχθη of the Spirit into the wilderness *to be-tempted of the devil.*	12 And immediately the Spirit driveth εκβαλλει him into the wilderness.	*And Jesus being-full of- 1 the Holy Ghost returned from Jordan, and was-led by ηγετο εν the Spirit into the wilderness,*
2 *And when-he-had-fasted forty days and forty nights, he-was-·afterward·-an-hungered.	13 *And he-was there in the wilderness forty days, tempted of Satan; & was with the wild-beasts;*	being·- 2 · tempted of the devil. *And in those days he-did-eat nothing: and when-·they·-were-ended, he-·afterward·-hungered.

SCRIPTURE ILLUSTRATIONS.

Mt. iv. 1. *tempted*—Abraham was tried as to the promised seed,(Ge. xii. 7)—first by long waiting, xvii. 17; xviii. 10—and then by his being directed to offer up his son, xxii. 1—18—so was Joseph, as being hated and sold by his brethren, Ge. xxxvii. 18—28—and as being, among strangers, long and unjustly imprisoned, xxxix. 20; xl. 23—so was Moses, as rejected by the people whom he was appointed to deliver, Ex. ii. 14—and when, after forty years' delay, he returned to Egypt, he was still long unsuccessful, v. 19—23; x. 3 —so was David tried, 1 Sa. xxvii. 1; 2 Sa. iii. 1. 'Blessed ... the man that endureth temptation,' Ja.

i. 12—advantage of the temptations of Jesus, He. ii. 17, .8; iv. 15, .6—use of the trials of his ministers, 2 Co. i. 3—7.

Mk. I. 13. *forty days*—Moses, at the receiving of the law, was in the mount forty days and forty nights, Ex. xxiv.—and again, at the renewal of the tables, he fasted there forty days, xxxiv. 28; De. ix. 9, 18—so also Elijah, 1 Ki. xix. 8—Christ, the fulfiller of the law, and the ratifier of the new covenant, in temptation, as well as in his obedience and suffering, left us an example, He. iv. 15.

NOTES.

Mt. iv. 1. *Wilderness.*—See GEOGR. NOTICE.
To be tempted. The word *to tempt*, in the original, means to try, to endeavour, to attempt to do a thing; then, to try the nature of a thing, as metals by fire; then, to test moral qualities by *trying* them, to see how they will endure; then, to endeavour to draw men away from virtue by suggesting motives to evil; the devil.—Comp. Ge. iii. 15, '*And I will put enmity between thee and the woman, and between thy seed and her seed; it shall bruise thy head, and thou shalt bruise his heel;*' and 1 Jno. iii. 8, '*He that committeth sin is of the devil; for the devil sinneth from the beginning.* For this purpose the Son of God was manifested, that he might destroy the works of the devil.' Christ was thus tempted, to shew his perfect holiness, to make him a sympathetic High Priest, and to give his people assurance of everlasting victory over the power of Satan.

Devil. A fallen *angel*, especially the chief of them: so called, because he is a malicious accuser of God and his people. The great enemy of God and man. [This word originally means an adversary, or an

accuser; thence any one opposed; thence an enemy of any kind. He is characterized as full of subtlety, envy, art, and hatred of mankind. He is known, also, by the name *Satan*, Job i. 6—12; Mt. xii. 26. *Beelzebub*, Mt. xii. 24, § 31. The *old Serpent*, Rev. xii. 9, '*And the great dragon was cast out, that old serpent, called the Devil, and Satan, which deceiveth the whole world: he was cast out into the earth, and his angels were cast out with him.*' He is also called the '*Prince of the power of the air*,' Ep. ii. 2.]

Mk. i. 13. *And was with the wild beasts.* In this place, surrounded by such dangers, the temptations offered by Satan were the stronger.

forty days tempted, &c. That is, through forty days he was *tried* in various ways by the devil. The temptations, however, which are recorded by Matthew and Luke, seem not to have taken place until the forty days were *finished*.

Lu. iv. 2. *In those days he did eat nothing.* He was sustained in the power of God during this season of extraordinary fasting. There are other instances of persons fasting forty days, recorded in the Scriptures.—*See* 'Scripture Illustrations,' Mk. i. 12

PRACTICAL REFLECTIONS.

Lu. iv. 1. When God has a great purpose to fulfil, he usually begins with proving the patience of the instruments he had otherwise fitted for the work.

[The proper preparation for trial, as well as for active service in the cause of God, is the being filled with the Spirit. After seasons of great spiritual enjoyment, and of being remarkably acknowledged of God, as was Jesus at his baptism, let us be prepared for privation and temptation.]

Although we should not needlessly involve ourselves in trouble, yet when led thereinto by the hand of God, we should patiently resign ourselves to his will, relying upon his wisdom to direct, and his power to sustain.

2 *ver.* We may thus the more confidently rely upon our Guide, seeing he was himself in all points tempted like as we are; not only as God, but even as man, he knows how to succour them that are tempted. Let us not think that we may escape the attacks of Satan, seeing that he spared no efforts even with regard to him, who could not be overcome.

* On the locality of this wilderness, *see* Vol. II. Diss. xxi. pp. 202—.4; and
On the order, proximate cause, and strength of the temptations, *see* ADDENDA.

SECT. IX.   JESUS IS TEMPTED BY THE DEVIL.   PART II.

Jesus is tempted to turn stones into bread.—Wilderness of Judea, E. of the River Jordan.

MATT. iv. 3—6.	LUKE iv. 3, 4, 9.
3 *ª And when-'the tempter'-came to-him, he-said, If thou-be the-Son of God, command that these stones be-made bread.*ᵇ	And the devil said unto-him, If thou-be the-Son of God, command this stone that it-be-made bread.
4 But he answered *ᶜ and-said,* It-is-written, Man shall-'not'-live by bread alone, but by every word that-proceedeth out-of the-mouth of-God.	*ᵇ And Jesus answered him,*ᶜ saying, It-is-written, That man shall-'not'-live by bread alone, but by every word of-God.

Jesus is tempted to throw himself from the pinnacle of the temple. At Jerusalem.

| 5   *ª Then the devil taketh-'him'-up* παραλαμβανει into the holy city, and | And he brought ηγαγεν him to Jerusalem, and 9 |
| 6   setteth him on a pinnacle of-the temple, and saith unto-him, If thou-be the-Son of God, cast thyself down ;ᵇ | set him on a pinnacle of-the temple, and said unto-him, If thou-be the Son of God, cast thyself down ᵇ from-hence : ᶜ |

SCRIPTURE ILLUSTRATIONS.

Mt. iv. 3. *If thou be the Son of God*—as at the commencement of his public ministry, so with these words was he taunted, at the end of his sufferings— see Mt. xxvii. 39—44, § 91.

command these stones—with similar taunting speech did the tempter address the woman, Ge. iii. 1—she was overcome, ver. 6—so was Israel, by the lust of the flesh, in the wilderness, Ex. xvi. 2, 3; Nu. xi.

4. *man shall not live by bread alone;* De. viii. 3, ' Humbled thee, and suffered thee to hunger, and fed thee with manna ... that he might make thee know that man doth not live by bread only, but by every *word* that proceedeth out of the mouth of the LORD doth man live.' The manna, as representing the word of life, was intended to feed the soul, as well as that it nourished the body—*see* Jno. vi. 27, 32, 3, § 43; also Job xxiii. 12; Je. xv. 16.

5 *on a pinnacle of the temple*—this appears to have been correspondent to the third inducement to eat the forbidden fruit: pride, presumption, 'as gods;' the having angels at command, for the display of power, not for the glory of God, according to God's appointment, Ge. iii. 4, 5—'a tree to be desired to make *one* wise,' ver. 6—'the pride of life,' 1 Jno. ii. 16—the temptation with which Israel was tried, as under the wise king, Solomon, when the kingdom was placed as on the pinnacle not only of earthly glory, but of religious privilege, as to the temple worship, and which even he could not bear, 1 Ki. xi. 6—11—and from which Israel was precipitated into destruction and death, 1 Ki. xix. 17—*comp.* with Hos. vi. 5; vii. 12, 3—' Wherefore say my people, We are lords; we will come no more unto thee?' Je. ii. 31—against the sin of presumption, to which those who are highly favoured of God, even as to the knowledge of his works and word, are particularly exposed, the psalmist prays, Ps. xix. 13.

NOTES.

Mt. iv. 3. *The tempter,* ὁ πειραζων, 'the trier,' from ναρω, 'to pierce through.' This is very emphatic, and explains Ep. vi. 16, '*Above all, taking the shield of faith, wherewith ye shall be able to quench all the fiery darts of the wicked.*'

If thou be the Son of God. Correspondent to this taunt of the enemy, was the first temptation presented to Eve in the garden; when suggesting hard thoughts of God, as putting restraint upon the enjoyment of his creatures.—See Ge. iii. 1, ' *Now the serpent was more subtil than any beast of the field which the Lord God had made. And he said unto the woman, Yea, hath God said, Ye shall not eat of every tree of the garden ?* ' also 'Reflections,' ver. 3.

Command that these stones. He had just been declared to be the Son of God, ch. iii. 17, § 8, p. 60. Satan here taunted him with the *destitution* in which He was left; and thus frequently the children of God are sorely tempted to question the truth of their high relationship, seeing the *destitution* in which they are left as to the things of this life.

4. *It is written.—See* De. viii. 3.—*See* ' Scrip. Illus.' God can feed and sustain by other means.

Man shall not live by bread alone, &c. The life of man depends on God, and not on food; which was abundantly proved in the case of Moses and Elijah, (see ' Scrip. Illus.' Mk. i. 13, p. 63,) and in our blessed Lord. The temptation is repelled by reference to the time when the children of Israel were in the like perilous situation in the wilderness, without the ordinary means of subsistence. God supplied them with food, by which their lives were preserved, which teaches us that no strait, however pressing, ought to shake our confidence in him.

By every word, &c. Jesus, whose meat and drink was to do his Father's will, is himself the 'living bread,' the word of life. The soul ought to feed upon the whole word of God.

5. *Then the devil taketh him up; i.e.,* ' prevailed upon him to make his station.'—*See* ' Scrip. Illus.'

The holy city. So Jerusalem was called, Da. ix. 16; Mt. xxvii. 53, § 92; and there God spake with the high priest on the great day of atonement once a year. The inscription on their coin; the shekel, was *Jerusalem the holy;* because the temple was there. Jerusalem is the appointed throne of the Lord Je. iii. 16, 7.

[*A pinnacle.* It is very likely this is what was called the στοα βασιλικη, 'the king's gallery,' at the S.E. corner of the temple, which, *Josephus* says, Herod erected over the stupendous depth of the valley, scarcely to be fathomed by the eye of him that stood above:—*Ant.,* lib. xv., c. 14. This was probably the porch called Solomon's, which was 150 feet high, on a wall of 400 cubits, built from the bottom of the valley.—See ADDENDA, Sect. 1, p. 8, *The temple.*]

PRACTICAL REFLECTIONS.

[Mt. iv. 3—13. Let us contemplate the second Adam, who overcame, as contrasted with the first, who was overcome. Our first parents were in the garden of God; Jesus was in the wilderness. They had abundance, with all under them in peaceable dominion; Jesus was an hungered amid the ruins of the fall, 'and was with the wild beasts.' They were tempted with 'the lust of the flesh,' that which appeared good for food; 'the lust of the eye,' 'it was pleasant to the eyes;' 'and the pride of life,' it was a tree to be desired to make *one* wise, 'knowing good and evil;' they were overcome in circumstances the most favourable to their virtue. He was tempted in all these respects, and did overcome, in circumstances the most discouraging and trying.]

3 *ver.* The grand attack of Satan is against our faith, and for insinuating hard thoughts of God; as when he said to Jesus tauntingly, ' If thou be the Son of God, command that these stones be made bread.' Look at the provision He hath made for thee, his child! He hath provided but stones in place of bread for thee, his son!

JESUS IS TEMPTED OF THE DEVIL.　　　　　SECT. IX.

. iv. 6—8.	LUKE iv. 10—12, 5.
ι, He-shall-give-·'his oncerning περι thee ːᵈ	for it-is-written, He-shall-give-·'his angels'-charge over thee, ᵈto-keep του διαφυλαξαι thee: 10
ιds they-shall-bear-· ː-any-time thou-dash gainst a-stone.	and in *their* hands they-shall-bear-· thee·-up, lest-at-any-time thou-dash thy foot against a-stone. 11
id unto-him, in, Thou-shalt-·not·· Lord thy God.	And Jesus answering said unto-him,ₑ It-is-said, Thou-shalt-·not·- tempt the-Lord thy God. 12

l to fall down and worship Satan.   *Supposed North of Jericho.*

iv. 8—11.	LUKE iv. 5—8, 13.
ril taketh-·'him·-up ι-exceeding high mountain, m all the kingdoms μου and the glory of-them ;ᵇ	And the devil, taking-·'him·-up αναγαγων into an-high mountain, shewed unto-him all the kingdoms of-the world της οικουμενης ᵇ in a-moment στιγμη χρονου of-time. 5

SCRIPTURE ILLUSTRATIONS.

gels charge, Ps. xci. 11, .2— *ways!*' in all the ways proper h, of course, does not imply tion, as plunging needlessly then the call of duty is into 2—the burning furnace, iii. ɜp, Ex. xiv.—the children of ow, Is. xliii. 1, 2. Whilst we his will, firmly laying hold i. 4, let us beware of wrest- own destruction, iii. 16, .7. *the Lord thy God*, De. vi. 16 iptuous chiding of the chil-

dren of Israel at Massah, (*temptation*,) when they demanded water of Moses in the wilderness; as if past deliverance had given them a claim to that as a right, which God would, in his own good time, have bestowed of his own free mercy, Ex. xvii. 1–7.

8. *and the glory of them*—the land of Israel is de- signated, 'the glory of all lands,' Eze. xx. 6, 15—unto which all lands are to contribute their glory, Is. lx. 3–16—the seat of a kingdom widely extended over all kingdoms, Ps. lxviii. 16—comp. with lxxii. 8—11—it is Immanuel's land, Is. viii. 8, who is appointed to reign over the predicted kingdom, Is. ix. 6, 7.

NOTES.

The former temptation was nce, this to presume upon it.

the former temptation the pture; but having been re- ΄ the sword of the Spirit, he 'eapon. The passage is, Ps. *gire his angels charge over thy ways.* *They shall bear ɪt thou dash thy foot against*

ː. In De. vi. 16,' *Ye shall not l, as ye tempted* him in Mas- e had produced Scripture to ould not contradict itself.

&c. That is, thou shalt not ιot, by throwing thyself into d' dangers, appeal to God for the promises made to those ger *by his providence.* The *parents,* who, in travelling p, and carry their children path, lest they should trip Thus Satan, artfully using e, was met and repelled by

ιountain. It seems that this 'not the very highest moun- t was one very nearly in the romised to Abraham. The north of Jericho, is fixed it is a commanding prospect ιbia, the country of Gilead, ιonites, the plains of Moab,

the plains of Jericho, the river Jordan, and the whole extent of the Dead sea. Others think it likely to have been *Nebo*, whence Moses was given a sight of the promised land, which is Immanuel's land, and shall be the glory of all lands. Contrast Moses in the mount with God, and Christ being in a mount with Satan: and the Lord's shewing to Moses from a high mountain (De. xxxiv. 1–4) all the kingdoms of Canaan, saying,' *This is the land which I sware unto Abraham, unto Isaac, and unto Jacob, saying, I will give it unto thy seed'* Israel; and the devil shewing to Christ all the kingdoms of the earth, and saying, ' *All these things will I give thee.*'

All the kingdoms of the world. Satan appears to have pointed to all the kingdoms of the world, as recognising the beautifully relative position which all other parts of the world bear to the HOLY LAND, which is appointed to be '*the glory of all lands,*' when Jerusalem shall be ' *holy, and there shall no strangers pass through her any more,*' Joel iii. 17.

[See the ancient kingdoms, as if in a circle around it. Africa, Asia, and Europe have it as their common centre; whilst bodies of water stretch out from it to America on the one hand, and to Australia on the other. By thus far acknowledging the truth of na- ture, of providence, and of revelation, with regard to the appointed seat of Messiah's empire, Satan may have intended both to throw our Lord off his guard, with respect to his insidious design, and to awaken an impatient desire to possess that which was in it- self so desirable; and which, through much tribula- tion both as to himself and people, he is appointed to possess; but which he might at once obtain on terms so apparently easy.]

PRACTICAL REFLECTIONS.

tempted by privation as to the ample provision for our

have raised the *faith* of the Son of God into *presump- tion*, and by trust in God's promising word he would

HE THAT DOETH RIGHTEOUSNESS IS RIGHTEOUS, EVEN AS HE IS RIGHTEOUS.—1 John iii. 7.

SECT. IX. JESUS IS TEMPTED OF THE DEVIL. PART II.

MATT. iv. 9—11.	MARK i. 13.	LUKE iv. 6—8, 13.
9 and saith unto-him, All these-things will-I-give thee, if thou-^c wilt-fall-down and-worship me.^d		6 And the devil said unto-him, All this power will-I-give thee, and the glory of-them: for that-is-delivered unto-me; and to-whomsoever I-will I-give it. 7 If thou therefore^e ‖ wilt-worship me, προσκυνησης ενωπιον μου ^d all shall-be thine.
10 Then saith Jesus unto-him, Get-thee-hence, Satan: for it-is-written, Thou-shalt-worship the-Lord thy God, and him only shalt-thou-serve.		8 And Jesus answered and-said unto-him, Get-thee behind me, Satan: for it-is-written, Thou-shalt-worship the-Lord thy God, and him only shalt-thou-serve λατρευσεις.
11 Then the devil leaveth him,		13 And when-^e the devil - had-ended all the-temptation, he-departed from him for a-season αχρι καιρου.^e
^e and, behold, angels came and ministered unto-him. [Ch. iv. 12, ₤ 16.]	MARK i. 13. and the angels ministered unto-him. [Ch. i. 14, ₤ 10.]	[Ch. iv. 14; ₤ 15.]

MARGINAL READINGS:—‖ Or, *fall down before me.*

SCRIPTURE ILLUSTRATIONS.

Lu. iv. 6. *delivered unto me*—Israel had been given the Land as under the law, Je. ii. 7—9—but Elijah had to testify to the king of Israel, ' Thou hast sold thyself to work evil in the sight of the LORD,' 1 Ki. xxi. 20—the same is said of the nation, 2 Ki. xvii. 17—' Ye have sold yourselves for nought,' Is. lii. 3—He whose is the right of redemption is shadowed forth, Je. xxxii. 7—14—the redemption acknowledged, Rev. v. 7—10—the Lord, the Redeemer, will vindicate his claim, Ps. xxiv. 1—when those who have resisted the temptation to serve Satan will be given possession with their Redeemer, ver. 3—6; Is. xxxiii. 15—22.

Mt. iv. 9. *fall down and worship me*—covetousness is Idolatry, Col. iii. 5—' they that will be rich fall,' &c., 1 Ti. vi. 9, 10—' ye cannot serve God and mammon,' Mt. vi. 24, § 19—by this temptation—an impatience to possess the outward pomp of a kingdom, Israel were tempted, as in the days of Samuel, and were overcome, 1 Sa. viii. 19, 20.

Lu. iv. 8. *get thee behind me*—so our Lord addressed Peter, who had acknowledged him as being ' the

Christ, the Son of the living God,' Mt. xvi. 16, § 50, but was for refusing his paying the price of our redemption, ver. 21, 2—' Get thee behind me, Satan: thou art an offence unto me: for thou,' &c., ver. 23—corresponding to this is the exhortation afterwards given by Peter, 1 Pe. v. 8, 9; as also in Ja. iv. 7—10.

thou shalt worship—it is written, ' Thou shalt fear the LORD thy God; him shalt thou serve, and to him thou shalt cleave, and swear by his name,' De. x. 20; vi. 13. *A*—the correspondent direction of our Lord is, ' Seek ye first the kingdom of God, and his righteousness; and all these things shall be added unto you,' Mt. vi. 33, § 19.

Mt. iv. 11. *angels came and ministered unto him*—so after all their trials will those that overcome in Christ be favoured, Mt. xxv. 31—40, § 86—even now, in the midst of trial, ' are they not all ministering spirits, sent forth to minister for them who shall be heirs of salvation?' He. i. 14—ministered to Jesus in his extreme suffering, Lu. xxii. 43, § 88.—*See on Lu.* i. 11, § 1, p. 3.

NOTES.

Lu. iv. 6. *And the glory of them.* This He will have when He comes, whose right it is to reign.

[*If thou wilt fall down & worship me, &c.* προσκυνησης. The word implies not merely *homage*, but *adoration*. The temptation here seems to be this, that Jesus should acknowledge Satan's right and power to bestow; and that he should now take the kingdom at Satan's hand, and not wait until, having satisfied Divine justice, and until, having been long a suitor in heaven for his kingdom, all things should be put under his feet by his Father.]

Here was a higher attempt, a more deadly thrust at the piety of the Saviour. It was a proposition that the Son of God should *worship* the devil, instead of honouring and adoring Him who made heaven and earth; that he should bow down before the prince of wickedness, and give him homage.

It is written. Satan asked him to worship him.

Shall worship God, the Creator of the world and our Saviour, is alone to be worshipped, as the supreme disposer of all things.

Departed for a season. αχρισν αιρσν, Mt. iv. 11. ' Let him alone for a time.' Our Saviour was afterwards subjected to temptations by Satan. Satan did much to excite the Pharisees and Sadducees to endeavour to *entangle him*, and the priests and rulers to oppose him. He assaulted him in the garden of Gethsemane, Lu. xxii. 53, § 58; Jesus saith to the Jews, ' This is your hour, and the power of darkness.'

And ministered, διηκονουν. The word often signifies, ' to wait at table.'—*See* Mt. viii. 15, § 17; Lu. xvii. 8, § 70; xxii. 27, § 87; and Jno. xii. 2, § 81. They furnished him with proper supplies for his hunger.

PRACTICAL REFLECTIONS.

8, 9 *ver.* Even that which is our own, and which we know God intends to bestow upon us, we should wait to obtain in his own appointed way and time. Thus Jesus, although all things are his, would not receive them at the hand of Satan, who had usurped the dominion, but would wait the will of his Father to have all things put under his feet.

That which seems the easiest and shortest way of obtaining the end may not be the best; nor does the end sanctify the means. Let us not seek to obtain wealth or power, even for the good of man or the service of God, as doing homage to Satan.

10 *ver.* Let us beware of entering into confederacy

with Satan, even for objects apparently the most desirable, but leave ourselves free for an entire devotedness to God.

Lu. iv. 13. When Satan is foiled for the present, we may not think he is departed for ever, but only ' for a season:' we should be still on our guard, and prepared for new conflicts.

Mt. iv. 11. Those who refuse the service of Satan, being faithful to their God, shall, like Jesus, have the angels of God to minister unto them: and surely it is better to be waited upon by the angels of light, than to become the slaves of the powers of darkness.

RESIST THE DEVIL, AND HE WILL FLEE FROM YOU.—James iv. 7.

| PART II. | ON THE ORDER OF THE TEMPTATIONS. | SECT. IX. |

GEOGRAPHICAL NOTICES.

JORDAN.—*See* Sect. viii. pp. 60—.2.
WILDERNESS.—*See* ADDENDA, '*The scene of the temptations of Jesus,*' *infra.*

ADDENDA.

ON THE WILDERNESS, THE SCENE OF THE TEMPTATIONS OF JESUS, p. 63.

' Whatever be supposed the locality of this wilderness—the appointed scene of each of these events, it must have been some wilderness, to arrive at which would carry him either to the east or to the south of Bethabara; and consequently away from Galilee, not towards it. The Talmudic writers acknowledge no more than two deserts as such, one of which would be the scene of the fasting and the temptation—the desert of Judah, which lay to the south, and the desert of Sihon and Og, which lay to the east, of Galilee. There was no desert to the north, except the great desert of Syria; to which it would be absurd to suppose our Saviour was carried.'—*See Gresswell,* Vol. II. Diss. xxi. p. 203.

' The temptation must have been transacted in less than one day after the close of the fast, if not on the last day of the fast itself: and though the scene of the fast had been the great wilderness to the S. and S.E. of Judæa, as I should be disposed to believe it was, even this would not be more than one or two days' journey from Bethabara.

' Beersheba, on the verge of that desert, was only twenty Roman miles distant from Hebron. Tekoah, only six miles from Bethlehem, stood upon its borders. Maimonides confirms Jerome, by making the distance of the wilderness, into which it was usual to carry the scape-goat on the day of expiation, only twelve miles from Jerusalem. Peræa, in which Bethabara was situated, approached still nearer to that wilderness. Strabo reckons it only three or four days' journey from Jericho to Petra, in Arabia Deserta. And this is confirmed by Diodorus Siculus, xix. 95, who mentions an instance of a march performed in three days and nights, from the parts about Gaza to Petra; a distance of 1,200 stades, or 150 Roman miles: at the rate of twenty-five such miles to the *day*. The same passage informs us that Petra was situated in the wilderness, two days' journey distant from the inhabited country: in which case, from the banks of the Jordan near Jericho, into the desert, could be merely one day's journey. Jerome (Oper. ii. 525, ..6) also makes it only a three days' journey from Gerara (which he places contiguous to Beersheba, and, consequently, on the verge of the same desert in general,) to Jerusalem. I am persuaded therefore that one day's journey must have sufficed to bring our Saviour to the borders of the scene of his fasting and temptation, if that was the wilderness of Arabia, and one day's journey to bring him back, from the locality of the last temptation again, to where John was baptizing, when he pointed to Jesus as the Lamb of God, Jno. i. 29, § 10, p. 69; and that a period of forty-one days might account for the transaction of everything between.'—*Ibid.*, p. 206.

ON THE ORDER OF THE TEMPTATIONS, pp. 63—.6.

' The order of the temptations in St. Matthew appears, from the notes of sequence which he employs, to be the real; the arrangement in St. Luke, who nowhere affirms his order, does not militate against this conclusion.

' Not one of the temptations is to be contemplated by itself, as what it is *in specie,* but as what it is *in genere,* that is, each of them *familiam ducit,* or is the representative of a class. St. Luke himself has intimated this, when he observes at the end of the account, iv. 13, συντελέσας πάντα πειρασμὸν ὁ διάβολος, not, πάντα ΤΟΝ πειρασμόν: every kind of temptation, not, *the* whole temptation.

' The first temptation, according to the order of St. Matthew, is addressed to a natural appetite; and is a specimen of such as may be addressed to the purely sensual principle. The second is addressed to the ostentatious display of superior worth, goodness, or estimation in the sight of God; that is, to the principle of pride; and consequently it is a specimen of temptations directed against the purely intellectual principle. The third is addressed to the love of honour, wealth, or power; and, therefore, is a specimen of temptations addressed to a mixed principle; or a principle partly intellectual and partly moral.

' The order of the temptations is the order of their strength; that is, they begin with the weakest, and proceed to the strongest; for any other order would manifestly have been preposterous: and the end of the whole transaction is to represent our Lord tempted at all points, like unto ourselves, yet without sin; as attacked in each vulnerable part of his human nature, yet superior to every art, and to all the subtlety, of the devil.

' The proximate cause of the first temptation was our Lord's being an hungred at the time: the proximate cause of the second, we may reasonably conjecture, was the voice from heaven at his baptism: and the proximate cause of the third, it is equally reasonable to conclude, was the expectation of a temporal Messiah.

' The immediate purpose of each temptation is purely tentative: but the object of the first two is to discover whether Christ was the Son of God; the object of the last is to discover whether he was the true, or a false Christ. If so, the last temptation in St. Matthew, besides being actually the last in the order of succession, would appear the strongest also in the eyes of a Jew; because it was directly a temptation that our Saviour should avow himself the Messiah, which the Jews expected. For, that to fall down and worship Satan, in the hope of worldly pomp and grandeur, was to renounce the character of the true Christ, and to assume the character of the false, is too obvious to require any proof. If St. Matthew then wrote for the Jews, his account of this temptation, besides being more agreeable to the order of the event, would make it appear the strongest also: for the last temptation was one which the true Christ only could withstand, and which the false Christs, who came successively after the true, never were able to withstand.

' This presumption, however, in favour of the last temptation, is ultimately reducible to the national prejudice in behalf of a temporal Messiah; and, consequently, must have been confined to the Jews. The Gentiles, who partook in no such prejudice, could not be prepared (on those grounds at least) to appreciate its force accordingly. To them it would appear in the light of a temptation, simply addressed to the desire of honour, wealth, or power; and therefore one of inferior strength to the second. For the history of their own philosophers could furnish instances of persons, whom their natural strength had enabled to surmount the last of these temptations; but few or none of such as, unassisted by the grace of God, had not fallen victims to the latter. Hence, if St. Luke wrote for Gentile Christians, as St. Matthew had written for Jewish, he would as naturally place the second temptation last, as St. Matthew, on the other supposition, had placed the third.

' The temptation, regarded in any point of view, was unquestionably one of the most mysterious transactions in our Saviour's personal history: and without pretending to unravel the mystery, or to be wise beyond what is written, I am content to profess my belief in the reality of the transaction itself, and in the reality of the parties concerned in it; of that being, who is together, the devil, or Satan, as much as of our Lord himself, whose personal existence no one will think of disputing.'—*See Gresswell,* Vol. II. Diss. xx. pp. 192—.6.

CLEANSE THOU ME FROM SECRET FAULTS.—Psalm xix. 12.   [67]

SECT. X.   JOHN'S SECOND TESTIMONY TO JESUS.   PART II.

SECTION X.—DEPUTIES ARE SENT BY THE COUNCIL OF THE JEWS TO QUESTION JOHN THE BAPTIST; JOHN RENDERS HIS SECOND TESTIMONY TO THE MESSIAH OR CHRIST. PARTICULARS OF TWO DAYS SPENT AT BETHABARA; DURING WHICH JOHN RENDERS A DOUBLE TESTIMONY TO JESUS, AND JESUS CONVERSES WITH CERTAIN OF THE DISCIPLES OF JOHN. THE NEXT DAY JESUS RETURNS INTO GALILEE. John i. 19–51.*

(G. 8.) *John renders his second testimony to Jesus.* John i. 19—28. *Bethabara or Bethany, opposite Scythopolis.* [Ch. i. 18, see § vii. p. 48.]

19 And this is the record μαρτυρια of John, when the Jews sent απεστειλαν priests and
20 Levites from Jerusalem to ask him, Who art thou? And he-confessed, and denied not;
21 but confessed, I am not the Christ. And they-asked him, What then? Art thou Elias?
22 And he-saith, I-am not. Art thou that prophet? And he-answered, No. Then said-they unto-him, Who art-thou? that we-may-give an-answer to-them that-sent us. What
23 sayest-thou of-thyself? He-said, I am the-voice of-one-crying in the wilderness, Make-
24 straight the way of-the-Lord, as said the prophet Esaias. And they which-were-sent
25 were of the Pharisees. And they-asked him, and said unto-him, Why baptizest-thou

SCRIPTURE ILLUSTRATIONS.

19. *record*—usually rendered witness, as in ver. 7, and given Mt. iii. 11, .2; Lu. iii. 15—.8, § 7, (by *John*)—referred to by our Lord, Jno. v. 33, § 23—and by Paul, Ac. xiii. 25.

priests and Levites—see ADDENDA, p. 74.

20. *I am not the Christ*—this witness referred to, Jno. iii. 28–36, § 13—believers are members of the body of Christ, 1 Co. vi. 15; Ep. v. 30.

21. *art thou Elias?*—he was not the very person Elijah, who was taken up into heaven, 2 Ki. ii. 11, .2—was the completeness of that witness to come

• *before the great and dreadful day of the Lord,' predicted Mal. iv. 5 — Elias was; to restore all,' Mt. xvii. 11, § 51; but John came in the spirit and power of Elias, Lu. i. 17, § 1, p. 5, and was, in his measure, of the Elias which was for to come, Mt. xi. 14, § 29.

23. *I ... the voice of one crying*—predicted, Is. xl. 3—*see* Mt. iii. 3, § 7, p. 51.

24. *Pharisees*—see on Mt. iii. 7, § 7, p. 52—opposed to the spirit of John, who made nothing of himself, and everything of Jesus, and whom his modesty in speaking of himself was well fitted to reprove—*see ib.*

NOTES.

19. *The record of John.* The testimony or witness of John.

The Jews sent. ' The Jews of Jerusalem.' The sanhedrim, or council of seventy, who had the authority of making inquiry into the pretensions of prophets.

[John's fame was great—*see* Mt. iii. 5, § 7, p. 52. It spread to Jerusalem, and the nation seemed to suppose, from the character of his preaching, that he was the Messiah, Lu. iii. 15, § 7, p. 54. The great council of the nation, or the sanhedrim, had, among other things, the charge of religion—see Eze. xliv. 15, 24. They felt it to be their duty, therefore, to inquire into the character and claims of John, and to learn whether he was the Messiah.]

Priests.—See Sect. I. p. 2. One of the chief employments of the priests, next to attending upon the sacrifices and the service of the temple, was the instruction of the people, the distinguishing the several sorts of leprosy, the causes of divorce, the waters of jealousy, vows, the uncleannesses that were contracted several ways; all these were brought before the priests.—*See* ADDENDA, '*Priests,*' p. 74.

Levites. They were chosen for the service of the tabernacle, Nu. iii., viii.; they were subordinate to the priests, and sung and played on instruments in the daily services, &c., 1 Ch. xxiii. 5, 30.—See ADDENDA, '*Levites,*' p. 75.

[20. *He confessed, and denied not.* A mode of expression not uncommon, and the strongest asseveration possible, since the two methods, assertion by affirmation and by negation of the contrary, together with a repetition of the affirmation, are here united. —See Is. xxxviii. 1, 13.]

I am not the Christ. The nation was expecting that the Messiah was about to come, and multitudes were ready to believe that John was the long-expected Messiah, Lu. iii. 15, § 7, p. 54.

21. *Art thou Elias?* The people expected that Elijah would appear before the Messiah came. [*They* supposed that it would be Elijah returned from heaven. In this sense, John denied that he *was* Elijah; but he did not deny that he was the Elias which the prophet intended (Mal. iv. 5), for he immediately proceeds to state (ver. 23) that he was sent to prepare the way of the Lord. So that while he corrected their expectations about Elijah, he stated to them his true character, as coming in the spirit and power of Elijah.]

That prophet. Jesus Christ is called *that Prophet*; he was infinitely superior to all the rest in dignity of person, in extent of knowledge, in high authority, and efficacious instruction, Jno. vi. 14, § 41. He was a *Prophet like unto Moses.* How noted his meekness, his intimacy with the Father, and his faithful discharge of his work! In him is to be found the truth of what was typified under the law, and promised by the prophets. It was by the Spirit of Christ that the prophets of old prophesied, 1 Pe. i. 11; and it is he who now '*speaketh* to us from heaven,' He. xii. 25; De. xviii. 15—.9; Ac. iii. 22.

22. *Who art thou?* i.e. ' What sort of a person art thou'—whether a prophet or not?

23. *I am the voice.* It is an humble mode of speaking of himself: ' Far from being the Messiah, or Elias, or one of the old prophets, I am nothing but a voice, a sound, that, as soon as it has expressed the thought, of which it is the sign, dies into air, and is known no more.'—*Fenelon.*

24. *Were of the Pharisees.* For account of this sect—see ADDENDA, § 7, p. 56. This makes the answer appear the more pointed. The Pharisees, by their ostentatious observances, wished to make themselves great in the eyes of the people. John made nothing of himself. He only wanted to draw attention to 'the voice;' to the words of the Holy Spirit, through him, calling for a preparation for the kingdom of heaven.

PRACTICAL REFLECTIONS.

23 *ver.* Let us, with John, confess our own unworthiness, and be content to spend, and be spent, in sending forth the word of God, that men may thereby be prepared for the coming of our Lord.

23—.5 *ver.* Let us endeavour to avoid the spirit and conduct of the Pharisees, who, unlike John, sought to magnify themselves before the people, in place of magnifying the words of God's grace, and pointing men's attention to Jesus as the Christ.

* On the hiatus in the first three Gospels, between the time of the baptism of our Saviour, and the commencement of his ministry in Galilee, and on its supplement by the Gospel of St. John,—*see Greswell*, Vol. II. Diss. xxi. p. 197.

PART II.   JOHN POINTS TO THE LAMB OF GOD.   SECT. X.

JOHN i. 26—30.

26 then, if thou be not that ὁ Christ, nor Elias, neither that ὁ prophet? John answered them, saying, I baptize with ἐν water. but there-standeth one among you, μεσος ὑμων 27 whom ye know not; he it-is, who coming after me is-preferred before me, ὁς ἐμπροσθεν 28 μου γεγονεν whose shoe's latchet I am not worthy to unloose. These-things were done in Bethabara beyond Jordan, where John was baptizing.

(G. 9.) *Particulars of two days spent at Bethabara; during which John renders a double testimony to Jesus. John* i. 29—36.—*Bethabara or Bethany, opposite Scythopolis.*

29 The next-day John seeth Jesus coming unto him, and saith, Behold the Lamb of God, 30 which *taketh-away ὁ αιρων the sin of-the world κοσμου. This is-he of whom I said,

MARGINAL READING:—*Or, beareth.*

SCRIPTURE ILLUSTRATIONS.

25. *that prophet*—spoken of by Moses, De. xviii. 15—8—Johu was a prophet, Mt. xi. 9, § 29—but Jesus was '*that prophet,*' Jno. vi. 14, § 41; vii. 40, § 55; Ac. iii. 22, .3.

26. *whom ye know not*—so Jesus himself testified, Jno. viii. 19, § 55; xvi. 3, § 87—and Paul, 1 Co. ii. 8—as it had been predicted, Is. liii. 3.

27. *who coming after me*—predicted, Mal. iii. 1—*confirm.*, Lu. i. 17, § 1. p. 5—*see* also Jno. i. 15, § 7, p. 48; Ac. xix. 4.

preferred before me—being the bridegroom, Jno. iii. 29, § 13—above all, ver. 31. *ib.*—had the Spirit above measure, ver. 34. *ib.*—*see* also Is. liii. 13; Ac. ii. 32, .3; Ep. i. 19—23; Ph. ii. 9; Col. i. 18; He. vii. 26.

whose shoe's latchet—John was unworthy to prepare the feet of Jesus for washing, yet our Lord condescended to wash his disciples' feet, Jno. xiii. 5,

NOTES.

25. *Why baptizest thou?* The Jews never used baptism, but by an order from the sanhedrim, or at least before three magistrates, or three graduates, who authorized it by their presence; besides, they never baptized Jews, nor those born of proselytes, because all those were born in the covenant, and they were not considered as needing baptism like those who were strangers before they entered into the covenant,

[Some have said, baptism had hitherto been confined to *Gentiles*, on their becoming proselytes to Judaism; that the Pharisees supposed that the power of baptizing *Jews*, and thereby establishing a new religion, was confined to the Messias and his precursors the prophets; who, they thought, would return to life for that purpose. Hence, they were desirous of knowing on what authority John had introduced such an innovation; and they presumed from this circumstance, that he claimed, in some way or other, a Divine mission, either as the Messiah, or as a prophet.]

26. *I baptize with water, &c.* John here speaks with his accustomed humility. He performed a ceremonial rite; but this was only important as pointing to the far greater change to be effected by Jesus, as baptizing with the Holy Ghost.

Among you. In the midst of you. The Messiah had already come, and was about to be manifested to the people.

27. *Is preferred before me.* He it is who was to come after me, but to be before me in dignity, even as much as the master is superior to the lowest menial. —*See* ADDENDA, '*On John* i. 15, 27,' p. 74

Whose shoe's latchet.—*See* Mk. i. 7, § 7. p. 54. The *latchet* of sandals was the string or thong by which they were fastened to the feet.

28. *In Bethabara beyond Jordan.* On the east side

§ 87—nay, 'washed us from our sins in his own blood,' Rev. i. 5—which washing is by the word, Ep. v. 25, .6.

28. *Bethabara*—*see* GEOGRAPHICAL NOTICE, p. 74—'house of passage'—referred to Ju. vii. 24.

29. *the Lamb of God*—'God will provide himself a lamb,' Ge. xxii. 8—the paschal lamb, Ex. xii. 3—the lamb for a continual burnt offering, xxix. 38—42—upon whom is laid the iniquity of us all, Is. liii. 6, 7 —*confirm.*, Ac. viii. 32; He. ix. 25, .6; x. 11, .2; 1 Pe. i. 19; Rev. v. 6, 12; vii. 9, 10, .4; xii. 11; xiii. 8; xiv. 1—marriage of the Lamb, xix. 7, 9—light of the glory, xxi. 23.

taketh away the sin of the world—the scape 'goat shall bear unto them all their iniquities unto a land not inhabited,' Le. xvi. 21, .2—predicted of Jesus, Is. liii. 11—*confirm.*, Lu. i. 77, § 3, p. 18; He. ix. 28; x. 14; Ga. iii. 13; 1 Pe. ii. 24; 1 Jno. ii. 2; iii. 5.

of the river Jordan. The true reading is *Bethany*. The common reading is supposed to have proceeded from a mere conjecture of Origen, who, because the situation here does not correspond with that of Bethany where Lazarus and his sisters lived, made the change; forgetting that there are in all countries several places of the same name. Bethany and Bethabara were different names for the same place, both of them denoting a *ford* or *ferry*.—*See* GEOGRAPHICAL NOTICE, p. 74.

29. *Behold the Lamb of Goa.* * A lamb, among the Jews, was killed and eaten at the passover, to commemorate their deliverance from Egypt, Ex. xii.—*See* Sect. vi., ADDENDA, '*Passover,*' p. 43.

[A lamb was offered in the temple every morning and evening, as a part of the daily worship, Ex. xxix. 38, .9. The Messiah was predicted as a lamb led to the slaughter, to show his patience in his sufferings, and readiness to die for man; Is. liii. 7, '*He was oppressed, but was afflicted, yet he opened not his mouth: he is brought as a lamb to the slaughter, and as a sheep before her shearers is dumb, so he openeth not his mouth.*' A lamb, among the Jews, was also an emblem of patience, meekness, gentleness. On all these accounts, rather than on any one of them alone, Jesus was called *the Lamb.* He was innocent; 1 Pe. ii. 23, .4, '*Who, when he was reviled, reviled not again; when he suffered, he threatened not; but committed himself to him that judgeth righteously: who his own self bare our sins in his own body on the tree, that we, being dead to sins, should live unto righteousness: by whose stripes ye were healed.*' He was a sacrifice for sin, the substance represented by the daily offering of the lamb, and slain at the usual time of the evening sacrifice, Lu. xxiii. 44—.6, § 91. And he was what was represented by the passover, satisfying the demands of God's justice, and saving us by his blood from vengeance and eternal death, 1 Co. v. 7.]

PRACTICAL REFLECTIONS.

[26 *ver.* Let us not be contented with mere outward baptism, but seek to have a sanctified knowledge of Jesus, who saves his people from their sins.]

27 *ver.* Let us, like John, be ready to confess our unworthiness, and be glad of the opportunity of performing the most menial service for Christ.

[29 *ver.* May Christian teachers, like John, be careful to magnify Christ before their disciples, that these

may become disciples of Jesus.—The Lamb, of God's own choosing, unto which John pointed, is also the most worthy to be our choice; and as he hath been acceptable to the Father as the sacrifice for sin, so should he be accepted by us, as saving from sin.— Jesus is not only now manifested in mercy as the Lamb of God who redeemed us, but is the purifier, to be manifested in judgment, when he will reign in glory over a renewed world.]

* On this act of the Baptist, *see* Greswell, Vol. II. Diss. xxiii. p. 283.

HE IS THE PROPITIATION FOR OUR SINS, ETC.—1 John ii. 2.

JOHN i. 30—.7.

After me cometh a-man which is-preferred before me ἔμπροσθέν μου γέγονεν: for he-was 31 before me πρῶτός μου. And-I knew him not: but that he-should-be-made-manifest to 32 Israel, therefore am-'I'-come baptizing with ἐν water. And John bare-record, saying, I-saw τεθέαμαι the Spirit descending from heaven like a-dove, and it-abode upon him. 33 And I knew him not: but he that-sent me to-baptize with ἐν water, the-same ἐκεῖνος said unto-me, Upon whom thou-shalt-see the Spirit descending, and remaining on him, 34 the-same is he which-baptizeth with ἐν the-Holy Ghost. And-I saw, and bare-record that this is the Son of God.

35 Again the next-day-after John stood, and two of his disciples; 36 and looking-upon Jesus as-he-walked, he-saith, Behold the Lamb of God!

Andrew and Simon follow Jesus. John i. 37—42.

37 And the two disciples heard him speak, and they-followed Jesus. 38 Then Jesus

SCRIPTURE ILLUSTRATIONS.

30. *for he was before me*—'from everlasting,' Mi. v. 2—before all things, Col. i. 17—see on Jno. i. 1—3, p. 46—see on ver. 27, p. 69.

31. *and I knew him not*—Jesus had come up to Jerusalem, as Lu. ii. 40–52, § 6, p. 40—where they might have met at the feasts, had not John been kept 'in the deserts till the day of his shewing unto Israel,' Lu. i. 80, § 3, p. 19.

32. *and it abode upon him*—that is, during his baptism; after which it is especially noticed, Mt. iii. 16; Lu. iii. 22, § 8, p. 59.

33. The Spirit was to point out Jesus as he who should baptize with the Holy Ghost, which was not known to John before he baptized him: the Spirit was yet to testify of Jesus, Jno. xv. 26, § 87.

34. *the Son of God*—so testified of by the Father, Mt. iii. 17, § 8, p. 59—so also at the transfig., Mt. xvii. 5, § 51—he who had been represented by the high priest, see 'Purification,' Sect. iv., p. 24.

NOTES.

29. *Of God.* Appointed by God, approved by God, and most dear to him, and provided by him. The sacrifice which he *chose*, and which he *approves* to save men from death.—See 'Scrip. Illus.,' '*Lamb of God*,' p. 69.

[The gift of God, ch. iii. 16, § 12; Rom. viii. 32; comp. Ge. xxii. 13; and the truly excellent and worthy sacrifice, He. x. 5; 1 Pe. i. 19.]

Which taketh away. Or 'beareth,'—amounting to the same thing,—because Christ has only taken away our sins by taking them upon himself in a representative character, and bearing them as a victim, loaded with the sins of him for whom it was sacrificed.

[In order to rightly understand these words, we must observe, that as often as in Scripture the name *Lamb* is applied to Christ, so often the subject of what is spoken is his suffering unto death, inasmuch as he underwent it for men. And in this view John the Baptist considered Jesus, when he called him a *lamb*, namely, as suffering and dying *like a victim*; and thus he represented our Lord as one *dying*, and that *in the place of others*. There is a manifest allusion to, and comparison with, a *piacular victim*. For such a victim was solemnly brought to the altar, and then the priest put his hands over the head; which was a symbolical action, signifying that the sins committed by the person expiated were laid upon the victim; and when it was slaughtered, it was then said to bear away, or carry, the sins of the expiated.—See 'Reflections.']

[*Of the world.* Jews and Gentiles; 1 Jno. ii. 2, '*And he is the propitiation for our sins: and not for our's only, but also for the sins of the whole world.*' The Saviour 'taketh away the sin of the world,' by removing every hindrance to the forgiveness of sin, original and actual, of all men throughout the world, who rely on him by humble faith. Through his atoning sacrifice it consists with the glory of God to pardon all persons who thus trust in him. And out of his kingdom, which shall ultimately extend itself over the whole world, he will root all things that offend and them that work iniquity. Not only has he meritoriously, but he will actually, take away the sin of the world.]

[31. *I knew him not.* 'It would seem impossible to doubt that John asserted a matter of fact, when he asserted that he knew not the Christ—33 ver.—before, at least, his baptism: and, if it is implied by St. Matthew's account of what passed between them at the time of his baptism—iii. 14, § 8, that he must have known him *then*, we have only to suppose that the knowledge in question was communicated to him, on the appearance of Christ—as the knowledge of Saul, and afterwards of David, was communicated to Samuel, 1 Sa. ix. 16, .7; xvi. 12; and the knowledge of the wife of Jeroboam to Ahijah, 1 Ki. xiv. 6—by a direct inspiration from above; and both facts become consistent. For as to the recognition implied by the descent of the Holy Ghost, and, consequently, not until the baptism was over, however much commentators may have overlooked this truth, nothing is clearer than that this descent was intended to mark out not the person, but the office, of Christ, Jno. ii. 33.'—*Greswell*, Vol. II. Diss. xix. pp. 187, ..3.]

Should be made manifest. That the Messiah should be *exhibited* or made known to Israel, as the High Priest of God's appointment.—See the ordinance to be observed with regard to Aaron and his sons, Ex. xxix. and Le. viii. The priest, at the time of his consecration, was to be shewn unto Israel, abiding at the door of the tabernacle of the congregation, day and night, seven days, keeping the charge of the Lord, Le. viii. 33—.6. John himself was a priest of the order of Aaron, Lu. i. 5, 13, § 1, pp. 2, 4. '*His shewing unto Israel*' had already taken place, Lu. i. 80, § 3, p. 19.

36. *Looking upon Jesus.* Contemplating him as the long-expected Messiah, and Deliverer of the world, he fixed his eyes intently upon him.

Behold the Lamb of God. Jesus is not only, in a proper sense, the Son of God, typified by the high priest: he is also the atoning Lamb represented by the sacrifice offered under the law.—See on ver. 29, p. 69.

PRACTICAL REFLECTIONS.

36 *ver.* Jesus was before John, not as to the time of his birth, or entrance upon his ministry on earth, but as being 'the Lord from heaven,' who was before all things, and by whom all things consist.

[31 *ver.* Those who know the witness of God respecting his Son should, like John, testify of Jesus to others.—John's baptism did not save from sin; it was for witness respecting Him who is now exalted to give repentance to Israel, and the forgiveness of sins, Ac. v. 31.—See 'Practical Reflections,' § 8, pp. 58, .9.]

32 *ver.* Let us pray that the Spirit which abode upon Christ may abide with us as the Spirit of peace and of love, which blessing can only be enjoyed by our abiding in Christ.

Let us never fail, while attending to the sign, to look, as God directed John, to the thing signified.—Let us be observant of the signs which God hath been pleased to give in testimony of his Son.

[31 *ver.* As John's baptizing would have been valueless without the coming to him of Jesus, of whom he was to testify, so let us remember that all outward ordinances are nothing without the life of Jesus being manifested, by his Spirit, in his people.]

36 *ver.* Let us, whilst we contemplate Jesus as the Lamb of God, and our atoning sacrifice, seek to be made partakers of his meek and lowly spirit.

JOHN i. 38—42.

turned, and saw θεασαμενος them following, and saith unto them, What seek-ye? They said unto-him, Rabbi, (which is-to-say, being-interpreted, Master,) where *a* dwellest- 39 thou? He-saith unto-them, Come and see. They-came and saw where he-dwelt, and abode with him that day: for it-was about *b* the-tenth hour.
40 One of the two which-heard ακουσαντων παρα John *speak*, and followed him, was 41 Andrew, Simon Peter's brother. He first findeth his-own brother Simon, and saith 42 unto-him, We-have-found the Messias, which is, being-interpreted, the Christ. And he brought him to Jesus. And when Jesus beheld him, he-said, Thou art Simon the son of-Jona: thou shalt-be-called Cephas, which is-by-interpretation, A-stone.

MARGINAL READINGS:—*a* Or, *abidest.* *b* That was, two hours before night.

SCRIPTURE ILLUSTRATIONS.

37. *they followed Jesus*—as the Lamb of God; so the election of Israel are represented as doing, Rev. xiv. 4.

38. *Rabbi,* Jno. i. 49, § 10, p. 73; iii. 2, § 12; 26, § 13 —see xiii. 13, .4, § 87—commanded his disciples not to be as the Pharisees, Mt. xxiii. 7, 8, § 85.

39. *come and see*—the invitation given to Nathanael, ver. 46—and by the Samaritan woman to her towns men, Jno. iv. 29, § 13—and by each of the four living creatures, Rev. vi. 1, 3, 5, 7—'in the midst ... stood a Lamb as it had been slain,' Rev. v. 6.

40. *Andrew*—(a strong man)—such should the follower of Christ be; 'strengthened with might by his Spirit in the inner man,' Ep. iii. 16—bearing 'the infirmities of the weak,' Rom. xv. 1.

41. *Simon*—(hearing, or one that hears or obeys)— 'hearken diligently unto me;' 'hear, and your soul shall live,' Is. lv. 2, 3—acknowledged the importance of hearing Jesus, Jno. vi. 68, § 43—contrast with ver. 60—see as to diligently searching into and carefully remembering what is heard, 1 Pe. i. 10–.2; 2 Pe. iii. 1, 2, 15–.8—the voice to be heard, i. 18.—See ADDENDA, *Simon*, p. 75.

Messias, which is the Christ, or Anointed—see Lu. ii. 11, 26, § 4, pp. 21, .4; and 1 Sa. ii. 10; Ps. ii. 2; xlv. 7; Da. ix. 25, .6.

42. *Jona*—(a dove)—hearing aright comes by the power of that anointing which was given under the appearance of a dove at Jesus' baptism—see ver. 32, p. 70; Lu. iii. 22, § 8, p. 59

a stone—meaning of the word 'Cephas,' or 'Peter;' and to which our Lord refers, Mt. xvi. 18, § 50—and Peter himself, 1 Pe. ii. 4–8—those who hear Christ aright are by the power of his Spirit built up as lively stones in Him who is the living stone—see Peter's confession, Mt. xvi. 16, .7, § 50.

NOTES.

38. *What seek ye?* 'What is your business with me?' It was a kind inquiry respecting their desires; an invitation to them to lay open their mind, to state their wishes, and to express all their feelings respecting the Messiah and their own *salvation.*

Rabbi. This was a Jewish title, conferred somewhat as the title of Doctor of Divinity now is, and meaning Master. Our Saviour solemnly forbade his disciples to bear that title, Mt. xxiii. 8, § 85. By calling him Rabbi, they shewed that they sought instruction.

Where dwellest thou? που μενεις. 'Where abidest thou?' Is used either of a fixed habitation or a lodging.—See Lu. xix. 5, § 80; xxiv. 29, § 94.

[By this question they probably requested a *private* conversation on the great doctrine which then occupied the minds of all serious and reflecting Jews. His usual home was Nazareth.]

39. *Come and see.* Our Lord graciously bade them follow him, to inspire them with confidence to ask what they wished to know.

The tenth hour. According to the Jewish reckoning, four in the afternoon, when there were but two hours to night. This was shortly after the time when the lamb of the daily sacrifice of the evening was offered up: very seasonably, then, did John point to Christ, the Lamb of God, the antitype of that sacrifice.

40. *Andrew.* The brother of Simon Peter, a native of Bethsaida, and apostle of Jesus Christ. He was originally a fisherman. When John Baptist commenced preacher, Andrew became one of his followers.

41. *We have found the Messias.* They had learned from the testimony of John, and now had been more fully convinced from conversation with Jesus, that he was the Messiah. The word Messiah, or Messias, is Hebrew, and means the same as the Greek word Christ, '*anointed.*' The Jews speak of *Messiah;* Christians speak of him as 'the Christ.' The word Christ *sig.* 'the anointed' one.

42. *Called Cephas.* Meaning the same as the Greek, *Peter,* 'a stone.' John wrote his Gospel in Greek, and in a Grecian city of Asia Minor, and therefore was the more careful to translate into Greek the Hebrew, Chaldee, or Syriac names, given for a special purpose, whereof they were expressive.

['St. John's allusion to this name is entirely prospective. Our Lord's address to Peter at that time contained a *prophecy,* which was designed to have both a *literal* and a *typical* fulfilment. In St. John it is, Thou *art* Simon: Thou *shall be called* Peter—in St. Matthew it is, Blessed art thou, Simon; ... Thou *art* Peter, Mt. xvi. 17, .8, § 50.'—*Greswell,* Vol. II, p. 415.]

[The three names, Simon, Bar-jona, Peter, appear to point very expressively to the great relations into which we, as the disciples of Jesus, are brought to the triune Jehovah. 'Simon,' *hearing,* intimates the necessity of our *hearing* the Father, or receiving instruction from God, and said Jesus, 'Every man therefore that hath *heard,* and hath learned of the Father, cometh unto me,' Jno. vi. 45, § 43. As a *stone,* which is the meaning of 'Cephas,' or, 'Peter,' the disciple is built on Christ the Rock; and this is as being born of the Spirit, expressed in Simon's other name, 'Bar-jona,' *son of a dove,*—under the form of a dove, the Holy Ghost appeared at our Saviour's baptism, Mt. iii. 16, .7, § 8, p. 59.]

PRACTICAL REFLECTIONS.

39 *ver.* Let us not only be hearers of the word; let us also follow Jesus, and take up our abode with him.

40–.2 *ver.* Let us, when we have found Jesus as the Christ, speak of him every man to his brother; and not rest contented until we have brought our relations to Him, in whom alone we can be established in truth and blessing.

[42 *ver.* In ourselves we are, like Peter, loose rolling stones; liable to sink under trial, or to be tossed to and fro by temptation. That Peter was in this respect a true sample of the professed followers of Christ, see his repeated defections at the commencement of his discipleship—at the trial of Jesus—and afterward, when Paul 'withstood him to the face, because he was to be blamed,' Ga. ii. 11.]

[Although we be, like Peter, loose rolling stones; yet, let us seek to attain stability, as being built upon the Rock, the one foundation, pointed out by Peter, as well as by all the apostles: and that stability in Christ we can attain only as *hearing* the Father, and *being born of the Spirit*—as being in *Christ,* given of the Father, his own blessed Spirit of peace and love.]

43–.5 *ver.* Let us also seek to bring our neighbours to Christ, as Philip did Nathanael, and increase our testimony of Jesus, according to our increase of knowledge, and the preparedness of mind in our hearers.

45 *ver.* We may not despise the testimony of the Father, by Moses and the prophets, on account of our having found the substance of their prophesying. Neither, although we have the words of the Father and the Son, should we despise the witness of the Spirit.

SECT. X. — JESUS' TESTIMONY TO NATHANAEL. — PART II.

(G. 10.) *The next day Jesus returns into Galilee. Jesus findeth Philip; Philip bringeth Nathanael to Jesus; Jesus' testimony to Nathanael. John i. 43—51.—Ibid.*

43 The day-following Jesus would go-forth into Galilee, and findeth Philip, and saith unto-him, Follow me.
44 Now Philip was of Bethsaida, the city of-Andrew and Peter. 45 Philip findeth Nathanael, and saith unto-him, We-have-found-him, of-whom Moses in the law, and the prophets, did-write, Jesus of Nazareth, the son of Joseph. And Nathanael said unto-
46 him, Can *there* any good-thing come out-of Nazareth? Philip saith unto-him, Come
47 and see. Jesus saw Nathanael coming to him, and saith of him, Behold an-Israelite
48 indeed αληθως, in whom is no guile! Nathanael saith unto-him, Whence knowest-thou

SCRIPTURE ILLUSTRATIONS.

43. *Galilee*—(circuit)—the north part of the land, around which Jesus made so many circuits, in the ministrations of the word—*see* Lu. i. 26, § 2, p. 9.

Philip—' lover of the horse '—(a native of Bethsaida in Galilee)—*see* as to the messengers on different coloured horses, Rev. vi. 2, 4, 5, 8—and the armies upon white horses that obey the command here given to Philip, ' Follow me,' Rev. xix. 11, .4—chosen an apostle, Mt. x. 3, § 27—informed Jesus that Greeks wished to see him, Jno. xii. 21, .2, § 82— . . . —
a speedy messenger of this name, Ac. viii. 26—40.

44. *Bethsaida*—' house of fishing '—the name of their native town, as well as their occupation. It probably was referred to, when Jesus promised to make Peter and Andrew *fishers of men*, Mt. iv. 19, § 16.

45. *Nathanael*—' God gives, or gift of God: ' ' if thou knewest the gift of God,' Jno. iv. 10, § 13—Nathanael, probably the same as John, 'the beloved disciple.'—*See* ' Note,' *infra*.

of whom the prophets did write—as Moses wrote of the seed of the woman, Ge. iii. 15—of the Shiloh, xlix. 10—of the prophet, De. xviii. 15—.9, &c.—David, who describes the sufferings of Christ, Ps. xxii. 1—21—and the glory that shall follow, ver. 22—31; lxxxix. 19—37—also Isaiah vii. 14; ix. 6, 7; xxviii. 16; liii.; iv. Mi. v. 1—4; Mal. iii. 1—*see* on Mt. ii. 5 ,8, § 4, p. 32.

Jesus of Nazareth—' branch carefully preserved '—

45. *Nathanael*. Is to be distinguished from ' Nathanael of Cana in Galilee,' mentioned at the close of this Gospel. The present Nathanael is introduced among other disciples ' *of Bethsaida, the city of Andrew and Peter;* ' along with whom, John, and his brother James, are always found in all lists of the apostles. John, *grace of the Lord*, means much the same as Nathanael, *gift of God*. The probability is that ' *the beloved disciple* ' here calls himself ' Nathanael; ' and afterwards, in reference to the favour with which he was from the first received, ' *the disciple whom Jesus loved*.' The character of Nathanael, as given by Him who knew all men, is the character of John. The promise to Nathanael, Jno. i. 50, .1, was eminently fulfilled to John in ' *The Revelation of Jesus Christ, which God gave unto him, to shew unto his servants things which must shortly come to pass;* *and he sent and signified it by his angel unto his servant John*.' The overwhelming impression which was made upon the mind of Nathanael, as to the omniscience of Jesus, ver. 49, is conspicuous throughout the whole of John's Gospel; which was written with the special design of exhibiting the truth of the first part of Nathanael's testimony, ' *Thou art the Son of God*.' The ' Israelite indeed' is described in his epistles; and for what concerns ' *the King of Israel*,' ' *the Prince of the kings of the earth*,' *see* the Apocalypse.—*See* this subject on JOHN, Sect. 27, ADDENDA, p. 216, and SCRIP. ILLUS. on Jno. xxi. 2, § 97, p. 508.

Moses in the law. Moses, in that part of the Old Testament which he wrote, called by the Jews ' the

see Lu. i. 26, § 2, p. 9; iv. 16, § 15; Mt. ii. 23, § 5, p. 35.

46. *can there any good thing, &c*.—the Jews thought meanly of his supposed origin, Jno. vi. 41, .2, § 43; Ac. ii. 7—Nathanael himself was of *Galilee*.—*See* ' Note.' § 97—Jesus was called a Nazarite, Mt. ii. 23, § 5, p. 35—but his birthplace was *Bethlehem*, Lu. ii. 4—10, § 4, pp. 19, 20—he was despised, Ac. iv. 10, .1—as also had been the people, Eze. xi. 15—who are to be found in him, ver. 16.

Philip saith, Come and see—so Jesus, ver. 39, p. 71 —and each of the living creatures, Rev. vi.

47. *Israelite indeed*—Israel, the name given to Jacob, as prevailing with the angel of the covenant at *Peniel*, Ge. xxxii. 24—32; Ho. xii. 4—*see* Phanuel, Lu. ii. 36, § 4, p. 27—the wrestling which will prevail, Joel ii. 15—21—the blessing upon him that overcometh (the Israelite indeed), Rev. ii. 7, 11, .7, 26—.9; iii. 5, 12, 21; xxi. 7

no guile—although an Israelite, yet it was as one, in the moral sense of the word, that he is here spoken of. Not by acting as a Jacob, supplanter, in a bad sense, Ge. xxvii. 35, .6—but as putting away all guile, is Israel to be exalted, Is. xxxiii. 15—.7; Rev. xiv. 5 —thus being made conformable to their Leader, 1 Pe. ii. 22—' blessed the man . . . in whose spirit . . . no guile,' Ps. xxxii. 2—' wherefore laying aside all malice, and all guile, and hypocrisies, and envies,' &c., 1 Pe. ii. 1, 2.

law.'—*See* De. xviii. 15, .8, ' *The Lord thy God will raise up*,' &c. Ge. iii. 15, ' *And I will put enmity*,' &c. xlix. 10, ' *The sceptre shall not depart from Judah, nor a lawgiver from between his feet, until Shiloh come; and unto him shall the gathering of the people be*.'

And the prophets.—*See* ' Scrip. Illus.,' p. 71.

Jesus of Nazareth. They spake of him as the son of Joseph, because he was commonly supposed so to be. They spoke of him as dwelling at Nazareth.

46. *Come out of Nazareth*. The whole country of Galilee was had in contempt with the Jews; but Nazareth was so mean a place, that it seems it was even despised by its neighbours, the Galilæans themselves.

Come and see. ' Judge for yourself; seeing is believing.'—*Bloomfield*. This was the best answer to Nathanael. He asked him to go and examine for himself, to see the Lord Jesus, to hear him converse, to lay aside his prejudice, and to judge from a fair and candid examination.

47. *An Israelite indeed*. Jacob received the name of Israel from his wrestling and prevailing in prayer. It is here used to designate a man of undoubted integrity towards men, and unfeigned piety towards God.'—*See* Ps. xxxii. 2.

No guile. Nathanael, although like Israel as to prayer, was unlike him as to guile. Jacob submitted to deceitful means of obtaining the birth-right blessing.—*See* ' Scripture Illustrations.'

PRACTICAL REFLECTIONS.

The obstacles to men receiving the testimony respecting Jesus may be more in appearance than in reality. Jesus had neither Nazareth as his birthplace, nor Joseph for his father, yet, as being supposed to have that lowly origin, Nathanael was in danger of rejecting Jesus as the Christ.

46 *ver*. Let us not be offended by the imperfect representations of even the advocates for the truth; but, with true simplicity of purpose, to know that which is testified of, let us, with Nathanael, ' come and see.

47 *ver*. Let us, like Jesus, deal in tenderness and kindness with the sincere in soul, whatever prejudices they may have been led to entertain respecting us.—Let us eschew the guile which Jacob was induced to use towards his father and brother; whilst, like him, we wrestle with the angel of the covenant, as when he received the name of Israel, and by which he truly obtained the blessing.

A SEED SHALL SERVE HIM.—Psalm xxii. 30.

PART II. NATHANAEL'S TESTIMONY TO JESUS. SECT. X.

JOHN i. 49—51.

me? Jesus answered and said unto-him, Before that-Philip called thee, when-thou-wast 49 under the fig-tree, I-saw thee. Nathanael answered and saith unto-him, Rabbi, thou art 50 the Son of God; thou art the King of Israel. Jesus answered and said unto-him, Because I-said unto-thee, I-saw thee under the fig-tree, believest-thou? thou-shalt-see 51 greater-things than-these. And he-saith unto-him, Verily, verily, I-say unto-you, Hereafter απ' αρτι ye-shall-see heaven open, and the angels of God ascending and descending upon επι the Son of man.

SCRIPTURE ILLUSTRATIONS.

48. *under the fig tree*—it reminds of man's fall, Ge. iii. 7—and of future peace and blessing, Zec. iii. 10—a pledge of which was given in the reign of Solomon, 1 Ki. iv. 25.

49. *Son of God*—see Lu. i. 35, § 2, p. 10; Jno. i. 1—18, § 7, p. 46—Philip had called Nathanael to see the *Son of Joseph*, ver. 45; Nathanael recognizes him as the *Son of God*: Jesus humbled himself to become *the Son of man*, ver. 51.

King of Israel—the Son was so appointed, Ps. ii. 6—12—the Holy One of Israel our King, lxxxix. 18—the Lord, Is. xxxiii. 22; xliv. 6; Zep. iii. 15; Zec. xiv. 9—'the Lord our Righteousness,' Je. xxiii. 5, 6—'just, and having salvation; lowly, and riding upon an ass,' Zec. ix. 8, 9; Mt. xxi. 5, § 82—Jesus hailed as such, Jno. xii. 12—6, § ib.—Jesus taunted with the title, Mt. xxvii. 42, § 91—'he is Lord of lords, and King of kings,' Rev. xvii. 14.

50. *thou shalt see greater things than these*—believing prayer is answered by being shewn greater things than were looked for, Je. xxxiii. 2, 3; so Da. ix. 20—7—none can imagine '*what* he hath prepared for him that waiteth for him,' Is. lxiv. 4—except by the teaching of the Spirit, 1 Co. ii. 9, 10—'things which must be hereafter,' Rev. iv. 1—great signs and wonders were shewn to the beloved disciple, Rev. xi. 1; xii. 1; xiv. 1; xv. 1, &c.

51. *angels of God ascending and descending*—referring to the vision with which Jacob was favoured at Bethel, in which the angels were seen ascending and descending, as if in attendance upon him who had but a stone for his pillow, Ge. xxviii. 11, .2—angels shall attend Christ in his glorious appearing, Da. vii. 10; Mt. xxv. 31, § 86; 2 Th. i. 7; He. xii. 22, .3—of which a pledge was given to the shepherds, Lu. ii. 9, 13, § 4, pp. 20, .1—examples of their ministering to Jesus: after his temptations, Mt. iv. 11, § 9; in the garden, Lu. xxii. 43, § 83; and at his ascension, Ac. i. 10, .1, § 98—so Peter, xii. 7—11 —all sent forth to minister, He. i. 14.—See on Lu. i. 11, § 1, p. 3; ver. 26, § 2, p. 9.

the Son of man—Jesus, as having become the Son of man, had not where to lay his head, Mt. viii. 20, § 31—yet is his kingdom appointed to be universal, Da. vii. 13, .4; Col. i. 12—.7—he did not become the Son of man that he should repent, Nu. xxiii. 19—but by his death, all is made sure that God hath promised, Rom. viii. 32—the Son of man hath power to forgive sins, Mt. ix. 6, § 22—is Lord of the sabbath day, xii. 8, § 24—soweth the good seed, xiii. 37, § 33—the angels and the kingdom are his, ver. 41—to be betrayed into the hands of men, xvii. 22, § 52—put to death, as was written of him, xxvii. 24, § 87—and remained in the grave until the third day, xii. 40, § 31 —but having risen from the dead, xvii. 9, § 51—he shall come as the lightning, xxiv. 27, § 86—and all the holy angels with him—'then shall he sit upon the throne of his glory,' xxv. 31, § ib.

NOTES.

48. *Whence knowest thou me?* πόθεν με γινώσκεις *Knowest my disposition and character.*—*Bloomf.* Nathanael was not yet acquainted with the Divinity of Christ.

Before that Philip called thee, &c. Philip had probably found Nathanael under a particular fig tree, and had then, as often before, conversed with him about Christ; and now our Lord mentions this in order to evince his omniscience.

When thou wast under the fig tree. The Jews were much in the habit of selecting such places for private devotion; and in such scenes of stillness and retirement there is something peculiarly favourable for meditation and prayer. So our Saviour also worshipped.—Comp. Jno. xviii. 2, § 88; Lu. vi. 12, § 27.

I saw thee. It is clear from the narrative that Jesus does not mean to say that he was bodily present with Nathanael, and saw him; but he knew his thoughts, his desires, his secret feelings, and wishes.

49. *Rabbi. Master:* applied appropriately to Jesus, and to no one else; Mt. xxiii. 10, § 85, '*Neither be ye called master: for one is your Master, even Christ.*'

The Son of God. By this title he doubtless meant that Jesus was the Messiah.

Thou art the King of Israel. Two characters combined throughout the chapter, because the Messiah could not be the King of Israel, in the sense which the oracles pointed out, if he had not been really the Son of God.—See Mk. i. 1, § 7; He. i. 8, '*But unto the Son* he saith, *Thy throne, O God, is for ever and ever: a sceptre of righteousness is the sceptre of thy kingdom.*'

[This case of Nathanael, John adduces as another evidence that Jesus was the Christ. The great object he had in view in writing this Gospel was, to collect the evidence that he was the Messiah, ch. xx. 31, § 100. A case, therefore, where Jesus searched the heart, and where his knowledge of the heart convinced a pious Jew that he was the Christ, is very properly adduced as important testimony.]

[This testimony of Nathanael is very similar to that by Peter; Mt. xvi. 16, § 50, '*Thou art the Christ, the Son of the living God.*' To the usual expression, to denote the Messiah, he adds, that of '*King of Israel*;' one of the titles designating the expected Saviour, and which is applied to Christ in various parts of the Gospels. This, from the circumstance that under the theocracy God was '*King of Israel,*' denotes the expectation of an earthly kingdom of righteousness.]

51. *Verily, verily.* [αμην, in the Greek; a solemn asseveration, intimating that the saying is true, and that we must regard it as proceeding from the 'Amen,' the true and faithful Witness.]

The word *Amen* is from a verb to confirm, to establish, to be true. It is often used in this Gospel. When repeated, it expresses the speaker's sense of the *importance* of what he is about to say, and the *certainty* that it is as he affirms.

Ye shall see. In prophetic vision, and in the pledge of full accomplishment, as well as afterwards in their glorious consummation.

Shall see heaven open, &c. 'See the frame of nature subject to my commands, and such a train of events, miracles, and providences, as shall leave no doubt of my mission: it will appear as the vision of Jacob.'—See Ge. xxviii. 12 and the Apocalypse throughout.

PRACTICAL REFLECTIONS.

48 ver. In prayerful retirement, let us search the Scriptures, to know Him of whom Moses and the prophets did write—see 45 ver. Jesus reveals himself unto those that seek him thus. He is the omniscient Jehovah, who seeth in secret.

48, .9 ver. The acknowledgment of what is good in others is one of the best means of removing their misconceptions respecting ourselves.

49 ver. He who has sought Christ in earnest prayer and diligent study of the Scriptures, may soon be expected to surpass his teachers, as Nathanael seems to have done Philip, who had testified of Jesus of Nazareth as the son of Joseph, but Nathanael confessed him to be 'the Son of God, the King of Israel.'

When we find that we have been misled, we are to allow neither the mistakes of others, nor our own previous prejudices, to prevent us from fully acknowledging the truth.

HE THAT OVERCOMETH SHALL INHERIT ALL THINGS.—Rev. xxi. 7.

SECT. X. OF THE PRIESTS. PART II.

PRACTICAL REFLECTIONS—(continued).

49 ver. Those who are made willing to acknowledge Christ in the day of small things have, with Nathanael, the promise of seeing greater things.

[51 ver. Let us never fail to connect the crown with the cross; to contemplate both the sufferings of Jesus as the Son of man, with the glory that will be when the vision of Jacob at Bethel shall be realized in our house which is from heaven—the house of God not made with hands, eternal in the heavens—when, as was seen upon the ladder reaching from earth to heaven, the angels of God shall be seen 'ascending and descending upon the Son of man.']

Let us not lose sight of one truth by attending to another. Nathanael acknowledged Jesus as being the Son of God; Jesus reminded him of his being the Son of man; and as he, as the Son of man, was to descend to a depth of humiliation which Nathanael may not have thought of; so also was he, as the Son of God, to ascend to a height of glory, and extent of dominion, which Nathanael may not have anticipated when he called him the King of Israel.

GEOGRAPHICAL NOTICE.

BETHABARA BEYOND JORDAN.—Bethabara signifies a place of passage: of which there were, and are, several in the course of the river Jordan. 'Bethabara' was a common name for such. The place of this history is supposed to have been near lake Tiberias, and in the region under the jurisdiction of Herod, who afterwards imprisoned John. Scythopolis, or the ancient Bethshan, in the south-east corner of Galilee, agrees very well with a known ford, frequently crossed by modern travellers, about eight or ten miles south of the sea of Galilee.—See ADDENDA, Sect. vii. p. 56, 'On the Ministry of John the Baptist.'

ADDENDA.

ON JOHN i. 15, 27—30, pp. 48, 69.

It is evidently necessary that Christ should be understood to have come after, in the same way, and in the same sense, in which John himself had gone before; in other words, that the personal ministry of each respectively was to be the same, differing only in the order of succession. The successor of the Baptist, even in a common work, was such as by the superior lustre of his person, and by the corresponding authority of his teaching, could not fail to eclipse and to supersede his predecessor. For He, who was from eternity; He, who was before the Baptist, by virtue of his essential pre-existence, his sublime and mysterious Divinity, could not possibly rank, or long continue to rank, after or beneath him; but must be preferred before him. The same assertion, therefore, of his own subordination to his successor, and the same reason for that subordination; viz., that John was from the earth, Christ was from heaven; John was from below, Christ was from above; are not more piously than naturally repeated in that other testimony of the Baptist's, which holds out the torch to the meaning of this, Jno. iii. 30—.2, § 13.

'The only difference between the personal ministry of John, and the personal ministry of Jesus Christ, was, that John baptized, and with water, because he was not to baptize with the Holy Ghost; Christ did not baptize with water, because he was to baptize with the Holy Ghost. The water-baptism, then, of John was typical of the Spirit-baptism of Christ; and water, as the medium of the baptism of John, was analogous to the Holy Ghost, the medium of the baptism of Christ. So far, therefore, from introducing a real difference into the office of John, compared with the office of Christ, this distinction brings them nearer to a resemblance than before: making the Baptist so exactly the counterpart of Christ, that even that most important particular in the functions of the latter, the mission and effusion of the Holy Ghost, is not without its significant prototype in the functions of the former. And this may be one reason why the baptism of John, though, as conveyed by the same external medium, but destitute of the same inward grace, it might so far appear the appropriate emblem of Christian baptism in general, should be considered in reality no type, or similitude, of that sacrament, but only of the one baptism, once for all administered, at the day of Pentecost, by Christ himself, upon the first Christian converts, in the communication of the extraordinary graces of the Spirit—and afterwards, as often as those graces were repeated, upon all converts subsequently.'—Greswell, Vol. II. Diss. xix. pp. 159, .60, ..7.

PRIESTS, p. 68.

'These were superior to the Levites in dignity, and chosen from the family of Aaron exclusively. They served immediately at the altar, prepared the victims, and offered the sacrifices. They kept up a perpetual fire on the altar of the burnt sacrifices, and also in the lamps of the golden candlesticks in the sanctuary; they kneaded the loaves of shew bread, which they baked, and offered on the golden altar in the sanctuary; and changed them every sabbath day. Every day, morning and evening, a priest (who was appointed at the beginning of the week by lot) brought into the sanctuary a smoking censer of incense, which he set upon the golden table, and which on no account was to be kindled with strange fire; that is, with any fire but that which was taken from the altar of burnt sacrifice, Ex. xxx. 9; Le. x. 1, 2. And as the number and variety of their functions required them to be well read in their law, in order that they might be able to judge of the various legal uncleannesses, &c., this circumstance caused them to be consulted as interpreters of the law, Ho. iv. 6; Mal. ii. 7, &c.; Le. xiii. 2; Nu. v. 14, .5; as well as judges of controversies, De. xxi. 5; xvii. 8—13. To them it belonged publicly to bless the people in the name of the Lord.

'The priests were divided by David into twenty-four classes, 1 Ch. xxiv. 7—18; which order was retained by Solomon, 2 Ch. viii. 14; and at the revivals of the Jewish religion by the kings Hezekiah, xxxi. 2, and Josiah, xxxv. 4, 5. As, however, only four classes returned from the Babylonish captivity, Ezr. ii. 36—9; Ne. vii. 39—42; xii. 1, these were again divided into twenty-four classes, each of which was distinguished by its original appellation. This accounts for the introduction of the class or order of Abia, mentioned in Lu. i. 5, § 1, p. 2, which we do not find noticed among those who returned from the captivity. One of these classes went up to Jerusalem every week to discharge the sacerdotal office, and succeeded one another on the sabbath day, till they had all attended.

'To each order was assigned a president, 1 Ch. xxiv. 6, 31; 2 Ch. xxxvi. 14, whom some critics suppose to be the same as the chief priests, so often mentioned in the New Testament, Mt. xxvii. 1; Ac. iv. 23; v. 24; ix. 14, 21; xxii. 30; xxiii. 14; xxv. 15; xxvi. 10. The prince or prefect of each class appointed an entire family to offer the daily sacrifices; and at the close of the week, they all joined together in sacrificing. And as each family consisted of a great number of priests, they drew lots for the different offices which they were to perform. It was by virtue of such lot that the office of burning incense was assigned to Zacharias, Lu. i. 9, § 1, p. 3; and the most honourable in the whole service. This office could be held but once by the same person.

'In order that the priests, as well as the Levites, might be wholly at liberty to follow their sacred profession, they were exempted from all secular burthens or labours. Of the Levitical cities already mentioned, thirteen were assigned for the residence of the priests, with their respective suburbs, Nu. xxxv. ; the limits of which were confined to 1,000 cubits beyond the walls of the city, which served for out-houses—as stables, barns, and perhaps for gardens of herbs and flowers. Beyond this they had 2,000 cubits more for their pasture, called properly, the fields of the suburbs, Le. xxv. 31. In all 3,000 cubits.—See Nu. xxxv. 4, 5.

'Their maintenance was derived from the tithes offered by the Levites out of the tithes by them received, from the first fruits, from the first clip of wool when the sheep were shorn, from the offerings made in the temple, and from their share of the sin-offerings and thanksgiving offerings sacrificed in the temple, of which certain parts were appropriated to the priests, Le. vii. 33, .4, .6, .8; De. xviii. 3; see also Nu. xviii. 13, .5, .6; Le. xix. 23, .4; Nu. xxxi. 28—41.'—Horne's Introduction, Vol. III. pp. 275—.7.

PART II.   ADDENDA:—LEVITES—SIMON.   SECT. X.

LEVITES, p. 68.

'The Levites were the posterity of Levi, the third son of Jacob by Leah, and one of the twelve tribes of Israel. Levi assisted Simeon in murdering the Shechemites, for which his father Jacob denounced his family to be scattered among the Hebrew tribes in Canaan, Ge. xxxiv. 25—30; xlix. 5—7. They were appointed by God to the service of the sanctuary, Nu. iii. 12, .3; viii. 18, in lieu of the '*first-born*' males, iii. 14—.6; viii. 17. They were, originally, distinguished into three classes, or families, (from the three sons of Levi,—Kohath, Gershon, and Merari). To them was committed the removal and setting up of the tabernacle in the wilderness. In David's time, the whole body of the Levites amounted to thirty-eight thousand, 1 Ch. xxiii. 3, of which number he appointed four and twenty thousand to attend the constant duty and work of the temple; and these being divided into twenty-four courses, 1 Ch. xxiii. 4; 2 Ch. xxxi. 17, there were one thousand for each week. Each class had its distinct service.

'The first class "*was to wait on the sons of Aaron, for the service of the house of the* LORD," i.e., to assist the priests in the exercise of their ministry, "to purify the holy things, to prepare the shew-bread, and flour, and wine, and oil for the sacrifice; and sometimes to kill the sacrifice," 1 Ch. xxiii. 28, 29; 2 Ch. xxix. 34; xxxv. 10—.4. Some of the chief amongst them had the charge of the sacred treasures, 1 Ch. xxvi. 20.

'The second class consisted of four thousand, 1 Ch. xxiii. 5. David divided them into twenty-four courses, and formed the temple choir, who thanked and praised the Lord every morning and evening, 1 Ch. xxiii. 30 —xxv. The music was both vocal and instrumental : "*As well the singers as the players on instruments shall be there*," Ps. lxxxvii. 7. In David's time, there were appointed three masters of the band of music, Heman, Asaph, and Ethan, 1 Ch. xv. 17, whose names are prefixed to some of the Psalms, probably because they set them to music. Asaph's name is inscribed to the fiftieth, seventy-third, and ten following Psalms; Heman's to the eighty-eighth; and Ethan's to the eighty-ninth. There was, also, over all the rest, one chief musician, or head master of the choir, to whom several of the Psalms are inscribed. At the time of writing the xxxix. lxii. lxxvii. Jeduthun was master.

'In the temple choir were both wind and stringed instruments, 2 Ch. vii. 6; xxix. 26. In both these passages the priests are said to sound the trumpets, see 1 Ch. xv. 16, 24, as it was prescribed in the law of Moses, "*The sons of Aaron, the priests, shall blow with the trumpets*," Nu. x. 8; this was done "*for the calling of the assembly, and for the journeying of the camps*," ver. 1, 2.

'The third class was the porters, consisting of four thousand, 1 Ch. xxiii. 5, to whose charge the several gates of the sanctuary were appointed by lot, 1 Ch. xxvi. 1—13, .9; 2 Ch. xxxv. 15; and they attended by turns in their courses, as the other Levites did, 2 Ch. viii. 14. Their proper business was to open and shut the gates, and to attend at them by day, as a sort of peace officers, in order to prevent any tumult among the people; to keep strangers and the excommunicated and unclean persons from entering into the holy court; and in short to watch over the safety, peace, and purity of the holy place and service, 2 Ch. xxiii. 19.

Notwithstanding the meanness of their employment, yet the pious king David said, Ps. lxxxiv. 10, "*I had rather be a doorkeeper in the house of my God, than to dwell in the tents of wickedness*." They also kept guard by night about the temple and its courts. They are said to have been twenty-four, including three priests, who stood sentry at so many different places. There was a superior officer over the whole guard, called by Maimonides, "the man of the mountain of the house." He walked the round, and when he passed a sentinel that was standing, he said, "Peace be unto you." But if he found one asleep, he struck him; and he had liberty to set fire to his garment. This custom may be alluded to in Rev. xvi. 15, "*Behold, I come as a thief. Blessed is he that watcheth, and keepeth his garments.*" Thus were the Levites employed in the work "*day and night*," 1 Ch. ix. 33. The consecration of the Levites in Moses' time was at the twenty-fifth year of their age, and they continued until fifty; but in David's time, when the labour was less, young men were eligible at twenty.

'None of the Levites, of what degree or order soever, had any right to sacrifice, for that was the proper duty of the priests only: the Levites, indeed, were to assist the priests in killing and flaying the sacrifices; and during the time they were offered up, to sing praises unto God. Neither had they any title to burn incense to the Lord. It was on account of their aspiring to the priest's office in this particular of burning incense, that Korah and his company (who were Levites) were destroyed, Nu. xvi. 1—36.

'The Levites, as well as the priests, were precluded by law from sharing the promised inheritance of Canaan with the other tribes, De. xviii. 1, 2; Jos. xxi. In lieu thereof they had forty-eight cities, with their suburbs, assigned them out of the other tribes; thirteen of which belonged to the priests, and thirty-five to the rest of the tribe of Levi, Nu. xxxv. 1—8. The cities of the priests were mostly in the tribes of Judah and Benjamin, and consequently nearer to Jerusalem, which stood in the confines of the two tribes; whereas those of the Levites were divided to them by lot, out of the other tribes on either side Jordan. And so God converted Jacob's curse on Levi, Ge. xlix. 5—7, into a national blessing; by dispersing the priests and Levites, whose office it was to instruct the people where they resided in the Mosaic law, throughout the whole land. They also kept the public records and genealogies. David made six thousand of them officers and judges, 1 Ch. xxiii. 4. Dr. Lightfoot makes these forty-eight cities to be so many universities, where the ministerial tribe studied the law, and diffused the knowledge of it through the nation. Of these, six were appointed cities of refuge, for protecting persons from the severity of the law in case of involuntary homicide. The Levitical cities had suburbs and fields surrounding them, to the extent of 3,000 cubits on every side, Nu. xxxv. 4, 5. From these suburbs they were maintained when not ministering in the temple, at which time they were supported by the dues arising from the sacrifices. The priests and Levites received likewise a tithe of a tenth of all the inheritance in Israel for their services, Nu. xviii. 21. This was done that they might give themselves wholly to the service of the Lord.'*

SIMON, p. 71.

Simon was a son of Jonas, and brother to Andrew; was a fisherman, and native of *Bethsaida* in Galilee— see 44 ver. Jesus called him ' Cephas, which is, by interpretation, A stone,' 42 ver. Simon was called to be a disciple, Mt. iv. 18—22, § 16—to be an apostle, ' Simon he surnamed Peter,' Mk. iii. 16, § 27—walked on the sea to J., Mt. xiv. 28, § 41—blessed by Jesus as having revealed to him from God that Jesus was the Christ, xvi. 17—20, § 50—chosen to be a witness of Jesus' glory, xvii. 1—8, § 51—*comp.* 2 Pe. i. 16, .7—appointed by Jesus to pay the tribute, Mt. xvii. 24—.7, § 52, (*Capern.*)—chosen with James and John and Andrew to be instructed concerning the destruction of Jerusalem, and the *second* coming of Christ, Mk. xiii. 3, § 85, (*on Mt. Olivet*)—appointed with John to prepare the passover, Lu. xxii. 8, § 87, (*at Jerusalem*)—refused to suffer Jesus to wash his feet, &c., Jno. xiii. 6—11, § 87, (*supper chamber*)—boasted of his attachment to Christ, ver. 36, .7; Lu. xxii. 33, .4; Mt. xxvi. 33, .4, § 87—chosen with James and John to witness Jesus' agony, Mt. xxvi. 37, § 88, (*in the garden*)—he smote off the ear of the high priest's servant, Jno. xviii. 10, § 88—with the rest of the disciples he forsook Jesus and fled, Mt. xxvi. 56, § 88—he denied Jesus three times; the last time with an oath; and afterwards wept bitterly, Mt. xxvi. 69—75, § 89—he was the first of the apostles to enter the tomb after Jesus' resurrection, Jno. xx. 3—10, § 93—he had a special manifestation of the Lord Jesus, Lu. xxiv. 34, § 93—he threw himself into the

* The Levites had under them others, called NETHINIMS, chiefly of the posterity of the Gibeonites, whose business it was to carry the water and wood that were wanted in the temple for the use of the sacrifices, and to perform other laborious services there. They had a particular place in Jerusalem where they dwelt, called Ophel, being near their place of service—the temple, Ne. iii. 26.

ALL NEED THE SAVIOUR.

SECT. XI.   THE MARRIAGE AT CANA.   PART II.

water to go to the Lord, as he appeared to the disciples, Jno. xxi. 7, § 97, (at the sea of Tiberias,) and received a special commission from Jesus to feed his lambs, &c., ver. 15–.9—was reproved, ver. 20–.2. After our Lord's ascension, Peter was the chief speaker in the church at Jerusalem, Ac. i. 15–22—on the day of Pentecost he defended the brethren, ii. 14, .5, and preached a sermon to the people, when 3,000 were converted, ver. 16–41, (in Jerusalem)—he healed a lame man at the Beautiful gate of the temple, iii. 1–11, and again preached Jesus, ver. 12–26—was imprisoned, &c., iv. 1–22—at his word Ananias and Sapphira fell down dead, v. 1–11—the sick laid in the streets, that the shadow of Peter, &c., ver. 15—with the other apostles he was again imprisoned, ver. 17, .8, and released by an angel, ver. 19; and as they taught in the temple, were taken and set before the council, and being beaten were let go, ver. 21–40—he rejoiced in suffering, and ceased not to teach and to preach Jesus Christ, ver. 41, .2—appointed by the church to go to Samaria, viii. 1–25—he raised Eneas, ix. 32–.5, (at Lydda)—restored Tabitha to life, ver.

36–43, (at Joppa)—was warned by a vision to go to Cæsarea, x. 9–17, (at Joppa)—baptized Cornelius, ver. 18–48. (at Cæsarea)—was imprisoned by Herod, the tetrarch of Galilee, &c., and delivered by an angel, xii. 3–17—was in Jerusalem at Paul's first visit after his conversion, Ga. i. 18—the gospel of the circumcision was committed to him, ii. 7—Peter and Paul met at Antioch, ver. 11—Paul withstood him to the face, ver. 11–.6. At the time Paul set out on his evangelical circuit from Antioch through Phrygia and Galatia, Ac. xviii. 23, A.D. 52, Peter is also supposed to have departed thence through Pontus, Galatia, &c., and passing by Corinth, to have arrived at Rome, accompanied by Mark, A.D. 54—during his stay there Mark's Gospel was written, A.D. 55—and from Babylon in Egypt, Peter wrote his first epistle, A.D. 59—he arrived in Rome a second time, A.D. 64, having ordained Mark bishop of Alexandria; and wrote his second epistle, A.D. 65—and in the same year suffered martyrdom; being, it is said, crucified with his head downwards, deeming it too great an honour even to die as his Lord.

SECTION II.—JESUS IS PRESENT AT A MARRIAGE-FEAST IN CANA: HE TURNS WATER INTO WINE, WHICH IS THE BEGINNING OF HIS MIRACLES. HE GOES DOWN TO CAPERNAUM, AND STAYS THERE SOME TIME. John ii. 1–12.

(G. 10.) *Jesus changes water into wine. John* ii. 1–11.—*At Cana.*

1 And the third day there was a marriage in Cana of Galilee; and the mother of Jesus
2 was there: and both Jesus was called, and his disciples, to the marriage. 3 And when
4 they wanted wine, the mother of Jesus saith unto him, They have no wine. Jesus

SCRIPTURE ILLUSTRATIONS.

1. *third day*—Jesus had been once and again proclaimed as the 'Lamb of God.' This was at length effectual in inducing two disciples to attach themselves to him, Jno. i. 35–.9, § 10—the day following Jesus would go forth into Galilee,' ver. 43—the day after this was the third, reckoning that as the first, near the close of which Jesus began to gather disciples, Jno. i. 39, § 10, p. 71—much regard is had to the third day in Scripture—*see* Sect. l., '*Jesus' first prediction of his death and resurrection.*'

a marriage—represents the union which shall have taken place between Christ the Bridegroom and his chosen people, previous to their restoration—*see* Je. iii. 14—a betrothment in faithfulness, Ho. ii. 14–20—upon which the word shall be fulfilled to Zion: ' For *as* a young man marrieth a virgin, *so* shall thy sons marry thee; and *as* the bridegroom rejoiceth over the bride, *so* shall thy God rejoice over thee,' Is. lxii. 5—*see* as to what the Lord hath done to accomplish the marriage, Ep. v. 25–33—and the importance of obeying the call to the marriage, Mt. xxii. 1–14, § 84; xxv. 1–13, § 86.

Cana—there was a Kanah in the north of Asher, as well as this, Cana the lesser in Galilee, Jos. xix. 28.

2. *disciples*—those already mentioned as followers of Jesus were Andrew, ch. i. 40, § 10, p. 71, and another disciple, probably James; *also* Simon Peter, ver. 41, p. 71—Philip, ver. 43, p. 72—and Nathanael, ver. 45—they had heard of Jesus as being 'the Lamb of God,' ver. 36, p. 70—acknowledged him, of whom Moses and the prophets did write, ver. 45, p. 72, to be the Christ, ver. 41, p. 71—and were, as living stones, to be built upon that one Foundation, ver. 42, p. 71—they were engaged in bringing others unto Jesus, ver. 41, .5, p. 71; and, submitting themselves to him as King of Israel, ver. 49, p. 73, they were taught to look forward to the glorious consummation of his kingdom, when he shall be obeyed both on earth and in heaven, ver. 51, p. 73.

3. *they have no wine*—wine had been promised in connection with the Lord's espousing a people to himself, Ho. ii. 19–22. 19, ' And I will betroth thee unto me for ever; yea, I will betroth thee unto me in righteousness, and in judgment, and in lovingkindness, and in mercies. 20, I will even betroth thee unto me in faithfulness: and thou shalt know the LORD. 21, And it shall come to pass in that day, I will hear, saith the LORD, I will hear the heavens and they shall hear the earth; 22, and the earth shall hear the corn, and the wine, and the oil; and they shall hear Jezreel.'—Je. xxxi. 12—' Ye shall be satisfied therewith,' Joel ii. 18, .9—' the mountains shall drop sweet wine,' Am. ix. 13.

NOTES.

1. *Marriage.* A solemn contract, whereby a man and woman engage to live together in a kind and affectionate manner. Anciently the Hebrews wore crowns on their marriage-day; and it seems, the bridegroom's was put on by his mother, Song of Sol. iii. 11). The ceremonies of marriage continued three days for a widow, and seven for a virgin, Gen. xxix. 27. During this time, the young men and young women attended the bridegroom and bride in different apartments, and the former puzzled one another with riddles, Song v. 1; Ps. xlv. 9, 14, .5; Ju. xiv. A friend of the bridegroom's governed the feast, that no drunkenness or disorder might be committed, ver. 9. At the end of the feast, the parties were, with lighted lamps, conducted to the bridegroom's house. The bridegroom, leaving his apartment, called forth the bride and her attendants, who, it seems, were generally about ten, Mt. xxv. 1–10, § 86. The modern Jews retain the most of these ceremonies: only since the ruin of their city

and temple, the bridegrooms wear no crowns on the marriage-day.

The mother of Jesus was there. Not invited, but as a relation. This may be inferred from her being present at the feast, and concerned about the wine.

As Joseph is not mentioned, we may suppose that he died before our Lord entered on his public ministry. It is conjectured this feast was at the house of Cleopas, or Alpheus, whose wife was sister to the mother of our Lord, *see* ch. xix. 25, § 91, and one of whose sons was Simon the Canaanite, whom some have thought to be so called from his being an inhabitant of this Cana, Mk. iii. 18, § 27.

3. *They have no wine.* Or, the wine is falling short. This might very well happen, without supposing an excess on the part of the guests, probably in consequence of the arrival of Jesus and many with him, beyond the number originally expected, and attracted by his presence.

PRACTICAL REFLECTIONS.

1, 2 *ver.* Jesus, although a man of sorrows and acquainted with grief, did not turn away morosely from witnessing the enjoyments of others. Let us ' rejoice with them that do rejoice, and weep with them that weep.'

2 *ver.* Let us indulge in no feasts to which we cannot invite Jesus as a guest, and rejoice in a sense of his being present

MANY ARE CALLED, BUT FEW ARE CHOSEN.—Matt. xxii. 14.

PART II.   WATER CHANGED INTO WINE.   SECT. XI.

JOHN ii. 5—9.

saith unto-her, Woman, what *have* I *to do with* thee? τι εμοι και σοι. mine hour
5 is-'not-yet'-come. His mother saith unto-the servants, Whatsoever he-saith unto-you,
6 do *it*. And there-were set there six water-pots of-stone, after the manner-of-the-
7 purifying of-the Jews, containing two or three firkins apiece. Jesus saith unto-them,
8 Fill the water-pots with-water. And they-filled-'them'-up to the-brim. And he-saith
   unto-them, Draw-out now, and bear unto-the governor-of-the-feast. And they-bare *it*.
9 When the ruler-of-the-feast had-tasted the water that-was-made γεγενημενον wine, and
   knew not whence it-was: (but the servants which drew the water knew;) the governor-

SCRIPTURE ILLUSTRATIONS.

4. *woman*—see 'Note' below.

what have I to do with thee?—an expression betokening a dislike at interference; used by David to the sons of Zeruiah, 2 Sa. xvi. 10; xix. 22—and to Jesus himself by two possessed with devils, Mt. viii. 29, § 35 —also by a man with an unclean spirit in the synagogue, Mk. i. 24, § 17—Jesus taught in the place where he had been brought up, that the exercise of spiritual power was not under the direction of natural relationships, Lu. iv. 23—.9, § 15.

mine hour is not yet come—frequently in language like this is the time of his being delivered up unto death referred to: 'the hour is at hand,' Mt. xxvi. 45, § 88—' your hour,' Lu. xxii. 53, § 59—' his hour was not yet come,' Jno. vii. 30; viii. 20, § 55—' the hour is come,' xii. 23, § 82—' save me from this hour,' ver. 27, § *ib*.—' Jesus knew that his hour was come,' xiii. 1, § 87—' being put to death in the flesh, but quickened by the Spirit,' 1 Pe. iii. 18, he thereby procured the means of cleansing his people from their sins, so that his church might be espoused to him in holiness, Ep. v. 25–.7—not until which is the hour for his providing the promised abundance of joy and rejoicing, of which he will himself partake, as is implied in his saying, 'I will not drink henceforth of this fruit of the vine, until that day when I drink it new with you in my Father's kingdom,' Mt. xxvi. 29, § 87.

5. *whatsoever he saith unto you, do*—' why call ye me, Lord, Lord, and do not the things which I say?' Lu. vi. 46–.9, § 27—' Lord, what wilt thou have me to do?' Ac. ix. 6—' bring every thought to the obedience of Christ,' 2 Co. x. 5—' the author of eternal salvation unto all them that obey him,' He. v. 9—' as obedient children, not fashioning yourselves according to the former lusts in your ignorance,' 1 Pe. i. 14.

6. *purifying*—the Jews were very particular as to ceremonial cleansing, Mk. vii. 2–5, § 44—it was the subject of dispute between them and John's disciples, Jno. iii. 25, § 13—' divers washings' . . . had been 'imposed on *them* until the time of reformation,' He. ix. 10.

9. *which drew the water knew*—' if any man will do his will, he shall know of the doctrine, whether it be of God,' Jno. vii. 17, § 55—*como*. with ver. 5.

NOTES.

4. *Woman*. This was a mild reproof of Mary for attempting to direct him in his power of working miracles. But it is evident that no disrespect was intended by the use of the term *woman* instead of *mother*. It is the same term by which he tenderly addressed Mary Magdalene after his resurrection, ' *Woman, why weepest thou?*' ch. xx. 15, § 93, and his mother, when he was on the cross, xix. 26, § 91; *comp*. also Mt. xv. 28, § 45; Jn. iv. 21, § 13.

Mine hour is not yet come. Ερα here *signifies* 'the accountable time,' or, 'the time for doing what you suggest is not yet come,' implying that he alone was the proper judge of that season, and would seize it, thus mixing comfort with mild reproof. The time would be when the wine was *quite* exhausted, whereby the reality of the miracle would be undoubted.

6. *Waterpots*. ὑδριαι. These were large vats or urns, from which the water was poured or drawn into lesser vessels for washing the hands and feet, see Lu. xi. 38, § 62. The guests washed their hands before they made their meal, which is still the constant practice of the Jews. The Jews had always in their houses vessels in which they kept water constantly ready for the ceremonial washings prescribed by the law; and also for the observance of the purifications enjoined by the traditions of the elders.

Of the purifying. Of the *washings* or ablutions of the Jews. They were placed there after the usual manner of the Jews, for the various washings and minute rites of purifying themselves at their feasts, Mt. xv. 2, § 44, and for the formal washing of vessels and even articles of furniture, Lu. xi. 39, § 62; Mk. vii. 3, 4, § 44.

Containing two or three firkins, &c. μετρητας, 'baths,' rendered by the same word in the *Septuagint*, 2 Ch. iv. 5. The firkin is about seven and a half gallons. We are not obliged to suppose that all the wine was drunk up; what was left would be acceptable to the new-married couple.

7. *With water*. It was done by the servants, so that there might be no opportunity of saying that the disciples of Jesus had filled them with wine to produce the *appearance* of a miracle.

To the brim. To the top; full; so that no *wine* could be *poured in* to give the *appearance* of a mixture. Further, vessels were used for this miracle in which wine had not been kept. These pots were never used to put wine in, but simply to hold *water* for the various purposes of ablution. And again, if any wine had been left in the waterpots, the mixture of water therewith would have deteriorated it, and it would have been *worse* than at the beginning.

8. *Draw out now*. This command was given to the servants. It shewed that the miracle had been *immediately* wrought. He willed it, and it was done.

Unto the governor of the feast. Or, 'the director of the feast;' namely, the person appointed to superintend the preparations for, and management of a feast; to examine the provisions and liquors brought forward, and pass among the guests to see that they were in want of nothing, and to give the necessary orders to the servants. He usually tasted the wine, to see if it were worthy of being set before the company.

PRACTICAL REFLECTIONS.

3 *ver*. Let us not rejoice in the embarrassments of others, but, having a sympathy with them, endeavour to procure the supply of their wants.

[4 *ver*. Let us beware of thinking that our natural relationships give us any claim to direct spiritual persons, in the exercise of supernatural gifts.]

Let us learn to ask God for things according to his will, patiently waiting his appointed time, which we shall always find the best.

5 *ver*. Whilst waiting his bestowment of the needful supply, let us at the same time be diligent in the use of whatsoever means he may appoint.

[6 *ver*. Let us cultivate both cleanliness of body, and purity of mind, whilst we eschew mere ceremonial washings, according to the traditions of the elders.]

[7 *ver*. May we, by the washing of water, by the word, be speedily prepared for sitting down as acceptable guests at the marriage supper of the Lamb, where the same truth which was for cleansing, we shall find to be cheering and invigorating—where we shall find that which was water changed into wine.]

7, 8 *ver*. What we do, let us do it faithfully as unto the Lord, in whatsoever station of life we are, and we shall find a correspondent reward through grace.

9 *ver*. Those who are lowest in station, and have most to do under the direction of Christ, are likely to become the greatest witnesses of the power of Jesus.

CONSIDER YOUR WAYS.—Haggai i. 5—7.

SECT. XI.   JESUS GOES TO CAPERNAUM.   PART II.

JOHN ii. 10—.2.

10 of-the-feast called the bridegroom, and saith unto-him, Every man at-the-beginning doth-set-forth good wine; and when men have-well-drunk μεθυσθωσι, then that which
11 is worse ελασσω: but thou hast-kept the good wine until now. This beginning of-miracles την αρχην των σημειων did Jesus in Cana of Galilee, and manifested-forth his glory; and his disciples believed on him.
Jesus goes down to Capernaum. John ii. 12.—[See Line from Cana to Capernaum.]
12 After this he-went-down to Capernaum, he, and his mother, and his brethren, and his disciples: and they-continued there not many days.

SCRIPTURE ILLUSTRATIONS.

10. *kept the good wine*—'we will remember thy love more than wine,' Ca. i. 4—'drink, yea, drink abundantly, O beloved,' v. 1—'the best wine for my beloved,' vii. 9—'wines on the lees well refined,' Is. xxv. 6.

11. *miracles*—the power of performing works out of the ordinary course of nature was given to Moses, to attest the truth of his mission; first to Israel, Ex. iv. 1—9; and afterwards to Pharaoh, vii. 19—21—miracles also attested the truth of Jesus' mission, Jno. ii. 23; iii. 2, § 12; v. 36, § 23—but the greater witness remains to be given in the promised witness of the Spirit, when shall be the great joy already referred to, Jno. xvii. 20—3, § 87—'according to the days of thy coming out of the land of Egypt will I shew unto him marvellous *things*,' Mi. vii. 15.

manifested forth his glory—'And ye said, Behold, the LORD our God hath shewed us his glory and his greatness, and we have heard his voice out of the midst of the fire: we have seen this day that God doth talk with man, and he liveth,' De. v. 24—the glory of the Lord Jesus was manifested on the Holy mount, Mt. xvii. 1—5, § 51—we have not followed cunningly devised fables, when we made known unto you the power and coming of our Lord Jesus Christ, but were eye-witnesses of his majesty. For he received from God the Father honour and glory, when there came such a voice to him from the excellent glory, This is my beloved Son, in whom I am well pleased. And this voice which came from heaven we heard, when we were with him in the holy mount,' 2 Pe. i. 16—.8—future, 'and the glory of the LORD shall be revealed, and all flesh shall see it together: for the mouth of the LORD hath spoken *it*,' Is. xl. 5.

his disciples believed on him—see Jno. vii. 31, § 55; viii. 30, § ib.; xi. 45, § 58; xiv. 11, § 87; xx. 30, .1, § 100—his being glorified in his people is to be accompanied with increase of faith, greater submission to the Divine teaching, Is. xxix. 18—24, and with the universal proclamation of the everlasting gospel, Rev. xiv. 1—7.

12. *his brethren*—Jesus had brethren who did not believe in him, Jno. vii. 5, § 54—his disciples were more dear to him than his mother or his brethren after the flesh, Mt. xii. 46—9, § 31; Lu. viii. 21, § 33—'his brethren, James, and Joses, and Simon, and Judas,' Mt. xiii. 55, .6, § 37—he sent to apprise the disciples, his brethren, of his resurrection, Jno. xx. 17, § 93, and appointed to meet them in Galilee, Mt. xxviii. 10, § 95—*fulfilm.*, 1 Co. xv. 6.

NOTES.

10. *And when men have well drunk, &c.* This is a general observation of what is customary when men have drunk freely, and the hilarity consequent incapacitates them for the nice discernment of the quality; and then they more easily take up with bad wine. Although the word usually denotes *intoxication*, it would be unjust and absurd to suppose that these guests had transgressed the rules of temperance.

Good wine. This is a proof that no wine could have been in the water pots.

11. *This beginning of miracles.* This his first public miracle. This is declared by the sacred writer to be a *miracle*; that is, an exertion of Divine power, producing a change of the substance of water into wine, which no human power could do.

[*Miracle.* A miracle may bring forth certain phenomena, not at variance with the laws of nature, but operating in a new way; and it may, by a direct agency or omnipotence, produce phenomena which the common laws of nature never could produce. A miracle may be defined 'Every sensible deviation from, and every *seeming* contradiction to the laws of nature, *so far as they are known to us.*'—See ADDENDA, '*Miracle*,' p. 80.]

Manifested forth his glory. Exhibited, shewed his power, and proper character as the Messiah; shewed that he had Divine power, and that God had certainly commissioned him. This is shewn to be a *real* miracle, by the following considerations: 1st. Real water was placed in the vessels. This the servants believed, and there was no possibility of deception. 2nd. The water was placed where it was not customary to keep wine. It could not be *pretended* that it was merely a *mixture* of water and wine. 3rd. It was judged to be wine without knowing whence it came. 4th. It was a change which nothing but a Divine power could effect. He that can change water into a substance like the juice of the grape must be clothed with Divine power.

His disciples. These were Peter, Andrew, Philip, and Nathanael. They were not yet called to be apostles. Probably James was among them.

Believed on him. This does not mean that they did not *before* believe on him, but thus their faith was *confirmed* or strengthened. They saw a miracle; and it satisfied them that he was the Messiah. They believed on the testimony of John and from conversation with Jesus, ch. i. 35—51, § 10, pp. 70—3. Now, they saw that he was invested with almighty power, and their faith was established.

'There is no evidence that any who were present on that occasion drank too freely. Nor can an argument be drawn from this case in favour even of drinking wine, such as we have. The wine of Judæa was the pure juice of the grape, without any mixture of alcohol, and commonly weak and harmless. It was the common drink of the people, and did not tend to produce intoxication, commonly. Our wines are a *mixture* of the juice of the grape and of brandy, and often of infusions of various substances to give it colour and taste, and the appearance of wine. Those wines are often little less injurious than brandy: and the habit of drinking them should be classed with the drinking of all other liquid fires. Yet to the pure juice of the grape, in moderate quantities, the Scriptures make no objection. But after all, the experience of the world has shewn that water, pure water, is the most wholesome, and safe, and invigorating drink for man.'—*Barnes*.

12. On the brethren of our Lord, *see* § 37, 'ADDENDA.'

Not many days. The reason why he remained there no longer was that the passover was near.

PRACTICAL REFLECTIONS.

10 *ver.* Jesus gives increase of blessing.

They lose nothing who bid Jesus and his disciples to the feast. When he comes, he may come with trial and difficulty, but he will leave behind an abundant evidence of his goodness and power.

[Let us look forward to that anticipated hour of happiness and glory when the marriage supper for the King's Son being come, his power to do wondrous things will indeed be made to appear, and the poor of his people will be abundantly fed and made joyful in the Lord.]

If the Lord wrought so wondrously for an ordinary marriage in Galilee, how much more when his glory shall be revealed, and all flesh see together, when he shall provide on his mount in a feast for all people: Then shall there be wine on the lees well refined, and it will in truth be said, '*Thou hast kept the good wine until now.*'

11 *ver.* Let us learn, as the disciples of Jesus, to trust in him that he knows his own set time best; and let us manifest our trust in him by our being ready, in preparation for that joyous solemnity, to do all his whole will.

LO, THIS IS OUR GOD.—Isaiah xxv. 9.

GEOGRAPHICAL NOTICES.

CANA OF GALILEE.—'Cana of Galilee is not mentioned in the Old Testament. In the New Testament it is celebrated as being the scene of our Lord's first miracle, and the place where he early shewed his omniscience, omnipresence, and omnipotence, in the cure of the nobleman's son, who was sick at Capernaum, Jno. iv. 46—54, § 14. One of the Nathanaels was a native of CANA, Jno. xxi. 2, § 97. The O. T. has only Kanah in Asher, S. E. of Tyre, Jos. xix. 28.

'The monks of the present day, and all recent travellers, find the CANA of the New Testament, where Jesus converted the water into wine, at *Kefr Kenna*, a small village an hour and a half N.E. from Nazareth, on one of the roads to Tiberias. This village lies on an eminence connected with the hills of Nazareth, on the south side of a branch of the plain, *el-Buttauf*, which runs up towards the village *el-Lubieh*. Here are shewn the remains of a Greek church, and of a house reputed to have been that of St. Bartholomew. Dr. Clarke saw in the church only fragments of water-pots; but a whole one has since been set up, and is shewn as one of the original six.' (Dr. Richardson, ii. p. 434). The distance of *Kefr Kenna* from Nazareth is given variously by travellers, from one hour up to three hours and a half. Burckhardt, by some error, has the latter.

'So fixed indeed has the impression now become, that this was the true Cana, that most travellers probably are not aware of its ever being questioned.

'From the Wely above Nazareth, (we had) pointed out to us a ruin called *Kana el-Jelil*, on the northern side of the plain, *el-Buttauf*, about north half-east from Nazareth, and not far from three hours distant. It lay at the foot of the northern hills beyond the plain, apparently on the slope of an eminence, not far on the east of *Kefr Menda*. In the days of Quaresmius it contained a few houses. This spot, we were told, was known both among Christians and Muslims only by this name, *Kana el-Jelil*; while the same name was sometimes applied by Christians alone to the village *Kefr Kenna*. Now as far as the prevalence of an ancient name among the common people is any evidence for the identity of an ancient site,—and I hold it to be the strongest of all testimony, when, as here, not subject to extraneous influences, but rather in opposition to them,—so far is the weight of evidence in favour of this northern *Kana el-Jelil*, as the true site of the ancient CANA of Galilee. The name is identical, and stands the same in the Arabic version of the New Testament; while the form *Kefr Kenna* can only be twisted by force into a like shape. On this single ground, therefore, we should be authorized to reject the present monastic position of Cana, and fix the site at *Kana el-Jelil*; which, likewise, is sufficiently near to Nazareth to accord with all the circumstances of the history.

'We can trace back the matter in history so that an earlier tradition actually regarded the present *Kana el-Jelil* as the ancient Cana; and that it is only since the sixteenth century that monastic convenience has definitely assigned *Kefr Kenna* as the site. Quaresmius relates, that, in his day, two Canas were spoken of among the inhabitants of Nazareth and the vicinity; one called simply Cana of Galilee, *Kana el-Jelil*, and the other Sepher Cana, *Kefr Kenna*; and he describes their position as above. He decides, however, very distinctly for the latter place, because of its being nearer to Nazareth and having some ruins; without, however, as he says, venturing to reject the other tradition. Quaresmius was in Palestine from A.D. 1616—1625; and again as guardian of the Holy Sepulchre from 1627—1629. From his time the true *Kana el-Jelil* was thrown into the shade and rarely noticed.

'Near the close of the sixteenth century, we find Cana placed three miles north of *Sepphoris*, and described as having a mountain on the north, and a broad, fertile, and beautiful plain towards the south; all which corresponds to the position of *Kana el-Jelil*, and not to *Kefr Kenna*. Several other notices might be brought forward, which, together with the strong evidence of the name, shew conclusively that the site of the Cana of the New Testament is to be sought at *Kana el-Jelil*, north of *Sefurieah*, about six miles north half-east of Nazareth; and that there is no good ground whatever for regarding *Kefr Kenna* as having any relation to that ancient place.'— *See Robinson's Researches*, Vol. III. pp. 204—.8.

CAPERNAUM

CAPERNAUM.—On the western shore of the lake of Tiberias is a beautiful plain, at the northern extremity of which lie the ruins regarded by Dr. Robinson as occupying the site of ancient CAPERNAUM, and at the south-east corner, the little village *El-Mejdel*, the MAGDALA of the New Testament. 'This plain,' writes Dr. Robinson, 'is exceedingly fertile and well-watered; the soil, on the southern part at least, is a rich black mould, which in the vicinity of *Mejdel* is almost a marsh. Its fertility, indeed, can hardly be exceeded; all kinds of grain and vegetables are produced in abundance, including rice in the moister parts; while the natural productions, as at Tiberias and Jericho, are those of a more southern latitude.' This plain is at first called *Ardel-Mejdel*, but further on takes the name of *El-Ghu-weir*, 'Little Ghor,' which strictly perhaps includes the whole. It is unquestionably the GENNESARET of Josephus.—*See Sect. xx.*

Dr. Robinson continues, 'Our attention and inquiries were now directed, I may say, with the most absorbing and exciting interest, to a search after some trace of the long-lost CAPERNAUM, so celebrated in the New Testament as our Lord's residence and the scene of several of his miracles; a city in that day "exalted unto heaven," but now thrust down so low that its very name and place are utterly forgotten. We had, indeed, begun our inquiries among the people of Nazareth, and pursued them systematically ever since; but as yet with no success. We now, however, were approaching the spot where the city must have stood; for there was every reason to suppose that it lay in or near the plain of Gennesareth; or at least must have been situated not very far beyond...

'We reached *Khan Minyeh*, not far from the shore, at the northern extremity of the plain. One hour and a half from *Mejdel*, around the inner side of the plain, while the distance along the shore is reckoned at one hour. Josephus gives its length at thirty stadia, and the breadth at twenty; which is not far from the truth. The Khan is now in ruins; it was once a large and well-built structure. The place is mentioned under its present name by Bohaeddin in 1189. Between the Khan and the shore, a large fountain gushes out from beneath the rocks, and forms a brook flowing into the lake a few rods distant. Over this source stands a very large fig-tree, from which the fountain takes its name, *'Ain et-Tin*. Near by are several other springs ... Along the lake is a tract of luxuriant herbage, occasioned by the springs; and on the shore are high reeds. Large flocks and herds were at pasture in this part of the plain. A few rods south of the Khan and fountain is a low mound with ruins, occupying a considerable circumference. The few remains seemed to be mostly dwellings of no very remote date; but there was not enough to make out anything with certainty. We could not learn that the spot has any other name than that of *Khan Minyeh*. Close on the north of the Khan and fountain, rocky hills of considerable elevation come down again quite to the lake.

'*Khan Minyeh*, or rather the mound with ruins, is one of the various places which, in the absence of all certainty, have been regarded as the site of the ancient Capernaum ... After long inquiry and investigation, my own mind inclines also to the opinion that we are here to seek for the probable position of the ancient Capernaum ... Often as Capernaum is mentioned in the New Testament, as the residence of our Lord, and the scene of his teaching and miracles, there yet occurs no specification of its local situation, except the notice that it lay "*upon the sea-coast, in the borders of Zebulon and Nephthalim.*" This only implies, that it lay on the sea within the territory of those adjacent tribes; which we have extended along the western coast of the lake of Tiberias. Some other incidental notices in the Gospels serve to point out more nearly the part of this western coast where Capernaum was situated. After the miraculous feeding of the five thousand on the eastern side of the lake, three of the evangelists relate that the disciples took ship to return to the other side; and it was on this passage that Jesus came to them during the storm, walking

TO EVERYTHING THERE IS A SEASON.—Eccles. iii. 1.

SECT. XI. BETHSAIDA.—A MIRACLE. PART II.

GEOGRAPHICAL NOTICES—(continued).

on the water, Mt. xiv. 13–34; Mk. vi. 32–53; Lu. ix. 10–.7; Jn. vi. 1–22; §§ 40–.2. According to Matthew, xiv. 34, and Mark, vi. 53. "*when they were gone over, they came into the land of Gennesaret.*" But John, vi. 17, re ates more definitely, that the disciples, in setting off from the eastern shore, "*went over the sea toward Capernaum;*" and after Jesus had stilled the tempest, ver. 21, "*immediately the ship was at the land whither they went;*" he further relates, ver. 24, that the multitudes also "*took shipping, and came to Capernaum seeking for Jesus,*" and found him there, or at least not far distant. From all these notices it follows conclusively, that Capernaum lay on that part of the western shore known as the region of Gennesareth. The evangelist Mark likewise says, that the disciples set off to go over the lake to Bethsaida; *comp.* vi. 45, 53, from which, in connexion with the preceding notices, it further follows, that the Bethsaida of Galilee lay near to Capernaum, and probably in the same tract of Gennesareth. This land of Gennesareth on the western side of the lake, as we learn from Josephus, was no other than the fertile plain we had just traversed, extending along the shore from *El-Mejdel*, MAGDALA, on the south, to *Khan Minyeh*, CAPERNAUM, cn the north. He describes in glowing terms its fertility and the excellence of its climate, which enabled it to produce the fruits of different climes all the year round. It was well watered, and particularly by a fertilizing fountain . . . . called by the inhabitants Capharnaum. Josephus here mentions no town of this name; but the conclusion is irresistible, that the name as applied to the fountain could have come only from the town; which, of course, must have been situated at no great distance.

* The language of Josephus may well apply to the fountain '*Ain el-Tin*, * near the Khan, which "creates a most luxuriant herbage and rich pastures in this quarter of the plain." Dr. Robinson concludes, taking into account all these circumstances, 'I am disposed to rest in the conclusion, that the source, '*Ain el-Tin*, is the fountain mentioned by Josephus as Capharnaum; and that the ancient site near by is the CAPERNAUM of the New Testament.'—*Robinson's Researches*, Vol. III. pp. 277–.92.

BETHSAIDA, p. 72.

' The BETHSAIDA OF GALILEE, the city of Andrew and Peter and Philip, must have lain very near to Capernaum, and probably in the same tract of Gennesareth. The same is true of Chorazin, which is mentioned only in immediate connexion with Bethsaida and Capernaum; and which, according to Jerome, lay on the shore of the lake, two Roman miles distant from the latter place. In all probability Bethsaida and Chorazin were smaller villages, on the shore of the plain Gennesareth, between Capernaum and Magdala. The very names of Capernaum, Bethsaida, and Chorazin, have perished . . . Such was the result of our minute and persevering inquiry among the Arab population, Fellahin and Bedawin, or Ghewarineh, along all the western shore of the lake, and around its northern extremity. No Muslim knew of any such names, nor of anything which could be so moulded as to resemble them.'—291, *ibid.*

'This scene,' writes Mr. Stephens, ' was not always so desolate. The shores of this lake were once covered with cities, in which Christ preached on the sabbath day; healed the sick, gave sight to the blind, cleansed the lepers, and raised the dead. In the city of Capernaum, Christ first raised his warning voice, saying, "*Repent: for the kingdom of heaven is at hand,*" Mt. iv. 17, § 16. And I could feel the fulfilment of his prophetic words, "*Woe unto thee, Chorazin! woe unto thee, Bethsaida! . . . it shall be more tolerable for Tyre and Sidon at the day of judgment, than for you. And thou, Capernaum, which art exalted unto heaven, shalt be brought down to hell: for if the mighty works, which have been done in thee, had been done in Sodom, it would have remained until this day,*" Mt. xi. 21–.3, § 29. Where are those cities now?'—See Sect. xvi.

ADDENDA.

MIRACLE, p. 78.

'Miracle, a wonderful effect, superior to the laws of nature. To pretend that there can be no miracles, as the laws of nature are fixed by the Divine will, and so very good, is stupidly and blasphemously to chain down the Almighty to the order of second causes. To pretend that no miracles ought to be credited, because they are contrary to the common observation of mankind, is idiotic in a superlative degree. If miracles were not contrary to the common observation of mankind, they could be no miracles at all, nor have any effect as such. The negative testimony of millions unnumbered, as to an event which they are not allowed to witness, is of no force at all. Miracles are never a whit more real discoveries of the power of God, than the common preservation and government of things; but are an exertion of his power in an uncommon manner, to alarm the world, and answer some important end. As we are not able to understand how far the power of second causes may go, or the power of evil angels may extend, God has not allowed us to rest the proof of a revelation upon miracles alone, but to examine also the doctrine confirmed thereby, whether it be worthy of God. Nor are the miracles, whereby he has confirmed the mission of the principal publishers of his revelation, a few, or any way doubtful, but multitudes, all of the uncontrolled kind, neither wrought to confirm anything trifling or base, nor contradicted by a superior power; and most of them in the openest manner, before friends and foes. Many of them were often repeated: they concurred to establish a system of religion, honourable to God, and unspeakably useful to men, calculated to render them happy in this, and in a future state. Nor did the workers thereof make any proud boasting of these wondrous exploits. The miracles pretended by the Papists either relate to trifles, unworthy of the Divine interposal, or they have been wrought before persons drowned in gross ignorance, and incapable to try them; or before persons resolved at any rate to believe them. Nothing of the delusive kind ever exceeded the exploits of the Egyptian magicians, but the miracles of Moses controlled them. Aaron's rod, when turned into a serpent, swallowed up their rods, which were transformed in like manner. Moses produced many miraculous plagues, which they could not. Our Saviour's miracles were so transcendant in their nature, so benevolent in their tendency, so Divine in the manner, by a touch or a word, so full in their evidence, before thousands of friends and foes, and so correspondent to the ancient prophecies concerning the Messiah, and so directed to confirm the most exalted and benevolent system of doctrines and laws, and the history thereof so plain and simple, and exposed to the trial of his worst enemies, that nothing but want of capacity to examine and perceive them, or hearty hatred of him and his way, can hinder us to believe them, and the gospel confirmed thereby. When the form of true religion is once established in the world, there is no need of the continuance of miracles for its confirmation; as men have been already sufficiently alarmed to consider it, and the mission of its publishers sufficiently attested; and the prevalence of the true religion in opposition to the inclinations and endeavours of men, with fulfilment of prophecies, succeed in their room. The miracles of Moses were similar to his fiery law, mostly ruinous and destructive; the miracles of Jesus, like his gospel, were wholly of the benevolent kind.'—*Gurney's Dictionary of the Bible.—See Notes* on ch. ii. 1, *Bloomfield's Greek Testament.*

* There is another fountain in the plain of Gennesareth, called the *Round Fountain*, which forms so striking a feature, that Pococke regarded it as the Capharnaum of Josephus, and Dr. Robinson at first was of the same opinion; but for various reasons he altered it on more minute examination. One of these reasons was, that no traces of an ancient site can be found in the vicinity.

PART II.   JESUS ATTENDS THE FEAST OF PASSOVER.   SECT. XII.

SECTION 12.—UPON THE APPROACH OF THE FIRST PASSOVER, JESUS GOES UP TO JERUSALEM: HE CASTS THE TRADERS OUT OF THE TEMPLE: AND WHEN THE JEWS DEMAND OF HIM A SIGN, HE FORETELLS THE RESURRECTION OF HIS BODY IN THREE DAYS' TIME. MIRACLES ARE WROUGHT, AND MANY BELIEVE UPON JESUS. NICODEMUS VISITS HIM BY NIGHT. John ii. 13—iii. 21.

(G. 11.) *Jesus attends the passover at the commencement of his public ministry; he casts the buyers and sellers out of the temple.* John ii. 13—22.—*At Jerusalem.*

13, .4 And the Jews' passover was at-hand, and Jesus went-up to Jerusalem, and found in the temple those that-sold oxen and sheep and doves, and the changers-of-money
15 κερματιστας sitting: and when-he-had-made a-scourge of small-cords, he-drove them-all out-of the temple, and the sheep, and the oxen; and poured-out the changers' money
16 των κολλυβιστων-το κερμα, and overthrew the tables; and said unto-them that-sold doves, Take these-things hence; make not my Father's house an-house of-merchandise.
17 And his disciples remembered that it-was written, The zeal of thine house hath-eaten - 'me'-up.
18 Then answered the Jews and said unto-him, What sign shewest-thou unto-us, *seeing*

SCRIPTURE ILLUSTRATIONS.

13. *Jews' passover*—for its institution, see Ex. xii. 1–28—the first of the three great feasts, De. xvi. 1–8—at which all the males were to appear, ver. 16—as to subsequent passovers, during the ministry of Christ, see 'Notes,' *infra*.

14. *found in the temple*—the people from a great distance had to purchase in Jerusalem the things necessary for the feast, De. xiv. 25—the sellers made it an occasion of scandalous abuse, Je. vii. 11.

doves—required to be offered, Le. xiv. 22—offered by Mary, Lu. ii. 24, § 4, p. 24.

15. *drove*—so Nehemiah turned out Tobiah, Ne. xiii. 4—9–it had been predicted of the Lord, Mal. iii. 1–5—the cleansing of the sanctuary foretold, Da. viii. 14—like a house smitten with a fretting leprosy, it was thereafter to be removed, *comp.* Mt. xxiv. 2, § 86, with Le. xiv. 41, .5—another preparatory cleansing, Mt. xxi. 12, .3, § 83.

16. *my Father's house*—not for a particular nation, but for the children of God, of all people, Is. lvi. 3–8 —its desirableness, when properly appropriated, Ps. lxxxiv. 10; cxxii. ; Is. ii. 3.

house of merchandise—'In that day there shall be no more the Canaanite (merchantman) in the house of the Lord of hosts,' Zec. xiv. 21.

17. *written*—'the zeal of thine house,' &c., Ps. lxix. 9—' the house of God, which is the church of the living God,' 1 Ti. iii. 15, .6—' which he hath purchased with his own blood,' Ac. xx. 28—' for even Christ our passover is sacrificed (or, *slain*) for us,' 1 Co. v. 7.

18. *sign*—see '*Miracle,*' Sect. xi. p. 80—signs referred to, Ex. iv. 17; De. vi. 22; 1 Sa. ii. 34; 1 Ki. xiii. 3–5; Is. vii. 11, .4—a sign asked, Mt. xii. 38, § 31; xvi. 1, § 47; Lu. xi. 16, § 62.

NOTES.

13. *Jews' passover.*—See ADDENDA, '*Passover,*' p. 88. The best commentators, ancient and modern, are generally agreed that John mentions *four* passovers, as occurring during Christ's ministry, of which this is reckoned the *first*: that mentioned at ch. v. 1, § 23, as the *second*: that at ch. vi. 4, § 40, as the *third*: and that at which Christ suffered, the *fourth*, §§ 81–92. Thus the united ministry of John and Jesus will extend to three years and a half.—See ADDENDA, '*Jesus' Ministry in Judæa,*' p. 87.

Jesus went up to Jerusalem. Every male among the Jews was required to appear at this feast.

14. *Found in the temple.*—See ADDENDA, '*Temple,*' Sect. i., p. 8. The transaction here recorded is in almost all respects similar to Mt. xxi. 12, .3, § 83.

Sold oxen, &c. βοας, i.e. 'cattle.' There must have been a grand market, for 256,500 victims are mentioned by Josephus as being offered at the passover. And it is certain, from the rabbinical writers, that immense traffic was carried on in beasts and birds for victims, and much extortion was practised, and a great part of the profit thence arising came into the hands of the priests.

Changers of money. The current coin was Roman. Yet the law required that every man should pay a yearly tribute to the service of the sanctuary of *half a shekel,* Ex. xxx. 11–.6. This was a Jewish coin. Of course the money-changers would demand a small sum for the exchange; and among so many thousands at came up to the great feasts, it would be a very profitable employment, and one which no doubt soon gave rise to much fraud and oppression.

15. *A scourge of small cords.* The original word implies that these *cords* were made of twisted *rushes* or *reeds*: probably the ancient material for making ropes, such as were used for tying up the cattle.

[14 *ver.* In the church of God, we should fear a self-seeking rest, which the Lord will certainly disturb and pour contempt upon, as he did in the temple where the changers of money were sitting.]

15 *ver.* The Lord may be pleased to make use of means small and despised for the effecting of great and salutary changes.

He drove, εξεβαλε, may be understood not of forcible ejection by stripes, but of strict and authoritative injunction, driving out the oxen and beasts only with the whip.

Poured out the changers' money, το κερμα, ' the small money.' Nobody resisted: for, by a law of the Jews, profaners of the temple might be killed or scourged by any person.

[If it be asked how it was that those engaged in this traffic so readily yielded to Jesus of Nazareth, that they left their gains and property, and fled from the temple at the command of one so obscure as he was, it may be replied: 1st. That their *consciences* reproved them for their impiety, and they could not set up the *appearance* of self-defence. 2nd. It was customary to cherish a profound regard for the authority of a prophet. There was something in his *manner,* as well as in his doctrine, that awed men, and made them tremble at his presence.]

17. *Zeal of thine house.* The *zeal of thine house* means extraordinary concern for the temple of God; intense solicitude that the worship should be pure.

Hath eaten me up. Hath surpassed all other feelings, so that it may be said to be the one great absorbing affection and desire of the mind.

18. *What sign, &c.* What *miracle* dost thou work? [He was reforming, by his authority, the temple. It was natural to ask by what *authority* this was done; and as they had been accustomed to miracles in the times of Moses, and Elijah, and other prophets; so they demanded evidence that *he* had authority thus to cleanse the house of God. Our Lord, in the next verse, enigmatically adverts to this question, intimating that, by his resurrection from the dead, they should have abundant proof of his Divine mission.]

PRACTICAL REFLECTIONS.

16 *ver.* God is to be worshipped by all people, as our Father in heaven—as the God and Father of our Lord Jesus Christ.

[17 *ver.* The honour of God's house does not consist in the costliness of its worship, or the crowding thereunto of worldly men; but in the worshipping of God 'in spirit and in truth.']

WHY IS THE HOUSE OF GOD FORSAKEN?—Neh. xiii. 11.

SECT. XII.   MIRACLES WROUGHT IN JERUSALEM.   PART II.

JOHN ii. 19—25.

19 that thou-doest these-things? Jesus answered and said unto-them, Destroy Λυσατε this
20 temple, and in three days I-will-raise-'εγερω it'-up. Then said the Jews, Forty and
six years was-'this temple'-in-building, and wilt-'thou-rear-'it'-up εγερεις in three
21 days? But he spake of the temple (his body. 22 When therefore he-was-risen from
ηγερθη εκ the-dead, his disciples remembered that he-had-said this unto-them; and
they-believed the scripture, and the word which Jesus had-said.

*(G. 12.) Miracles are wrought during the passover; many believe upon Jesus.
John ii. 23—5.—At Jerusalem.*

23 Now when he-was in Jerusalem at the passover, in the feast-day, many believed in
24 his name, when-they-saw θεωρουντες the miracles which he-did. But Jesus did-'not'-
25 commit επιστευεν himself unto-them, because he knew all *men*, and needed not that
any should-testify of man: for he knew what was in man.

SCRIPTURE ILLUSTRATIONS.

19. *destroy this temple*—his accusation, Mt. xxvi. 60, .1; Mk. xiv. 58, § 89—taunted on the cross, Mt. xxvii. 40, § 91.

this temple—his body; as of old in the temple, so in Christ 'dwelleth all the fulness,' &c., Col. ii. 9—believers in him are the temple of God, I Co. iii. 16; vi. 19; 2 Co. vi. 16—this body, like that of Jesus, the Jews sought to destroy, Ac. viii. 1; ix. 1, 2.

in three days—on the third day he arose, Mt. xxviii. 1—8, § 93—so also his people Israel are to be raised up on the third day: 'after two days he will revive us. In the third he will raise us up, and we shall live in his sight. Then shall we know,' &c., Ho. vi. 2, 3—comp. with Is. xxvi. 19—Jesus' first prediction of his death and resurrection—see § 50, and § 52

21. *temple of his body—see* above, on 'This *temple*.'

22. *believed the scripture*—Jesus' resurrection from the dead was the grand confirmation of what had been written respecting the raising up of his people, see above, '*In three days.*'

24. *did not commit himself*—when they would make him a king, Jno. vi. 15, § 41.

25. *knew what was in man*, Jno. i. 45—8, § 10; iv. 29, § 13; v. 42, § 23; vi. 64. § 43—'he knoweth our frame,' Ps. ciii. 11—'O Lord, thou hast searched,' &c., cxxxix. —' I the Lord search the heart,' Je. xvii. 10—Jesus knew the thoughts of men, Mt. ix. 4, § 22; Lu vi. 8, § 25; Jno. xvi. 30, § 87—'neither is there any creature that is not manifest in his sight,' He. iv. 13—*see* also Rev. ii. 23.

NOTES.

19. *Destroy this temple.* [τον ναον τουτον, 'this very temple,' perhaps pointing to his body at the same time. This was a somewhat obscure sentence, but of that sort which is not unfrequently used by the best teachers, for the purpose of exciting the attention and sharpening the perception of their auditors. He spoke obscurely of his death, that he might not discourage his disciples; and, to vindicate his authority and dignity, appealed to his resurrection.]

The word *temple*, or *dwelling*, was not unfrequently used by the Jews to denote the *body*, as being the residence of the spirit. Christians are not unfrequently called the temple of God, as being those in whom the Holy Spirit dwells on earth.—*See* 'Scrip. Illus.,' *supra*.

[*In three days I will raise it up.—See* ver. 18. A full and irrefragable proof of Divinity, since such language would be unsuitable to any created being.]

20. *Then said the Jews, &c.* They understood him as speaking of the temple at Jerusalem. What he said here was all the evidence adduced on his trial.

[The language which he used was often that of parables, or metaphor; and as they *sought* to misunderstand him, and pervert his language, so he often left them to their own delusions, as he himself says.—*See* Mt. xiii. 13, § 32.]

Forty and six years, &c. The temple in which they then were was that which was commonly called *the second temple*, built after the return of the Jews from Babylon.—*See* ADDENDA, '*Temple*,' § 1, p. 8.

As Herod began to repair the temple sixteen years before the birth of Jesus, and as this conversation took place in the thirtieth year of his age, so the time occupied in the rebuilding of the temple was *forty and six years*.

[22. *They believed the scripture.* επιστευσαν τη γραφη, *i. e.*, by a comparison of those parts of the Old Testament, including Ps. xvi. 10, '*For thou wilt not*

leave my soul in hell; neither wilt thou suffer thine Holy One to see corruption,' which predict the Messiah's rising from the dead, with the *words* of Jesus, treasured up in their minds, and the fact of his resurrection, they thoroughly believed what the scriptures declared, and were convinced of the Divine mission of Jesus. Πιστευω here simply signifies to *believe*, though in the next verse it is used, as generally in the New Test., of faith in Jesus as the Messiah.]

23. *Feast day.* During the celebration of the passover feast, which lasted eight days.—See § 6, p. 43.

Many believed. Their faith, however, as appears from what follows, was but external and historical; not an internal and vital one. The understanding was convinced, but the will was not subdued to obedience.

The miracles.—See ADDENDA, ' *Miracle*,' § 11, p. 80. What these were, we know not. But from this passage, and ch. iv. 45, § 14, and vi. 2, § 40, it is certain Christ worked many miracles not recorded by the sacred writers.—*See* ch. xxi. 25, § 100.

24. *Did not commit himself.* The word here translated *commit* is the same as in ver. 23 is translated *believed.* It means to put *trust* or *confidence* in. Jesus did not put *trust* or *reliance* on them. They were not yet in a fit state to receive their king, and to act worthy of his kingdom.

25. *Should testify of man.* Should give him the character of any man.

He knew what was, &c. ' He knew the heart of man.' This passage supplies one of the strongest proofs of Christ's Divinity; omniscience being the attribute alone of Deity.—*See* 1 Ki. viii. 39, '*Then hear thou in heaven thy dwelling-place, and forgive, and do, and give to every man according to his ways, whose heart thou knowest; (for thou, even thou only, knowest the hearts of all the children of men.*')

PRACTICAL REFLECTIONS.

[18 ver. We should sincerely use the means we already have of ascertaining the truth; else increase of evidence may only be to our greater condemnation, as it was to the unbelieving Jews.]

[19 ver. As it was in the temple that God more especially met with man, so was it a type of ' Immanuel, God with us,' as well as ' of his body the church.' ' Now ye are the body of Christ,' 1 Co. xii. 27—Let us contemplate in   as the example of these living temples, whose worship is acceptable to God; and who shall he brought together into one holy temple in the Lord. — Let us see in our

great Exemplar the assured pledge that all scripture will be fulfilled.]

22 ver. Let us, by the abundant confirmation which hath been given of the truth of God, see the great occasion there is for believing both what God hath caused to be written in the Old Testament prophets, and the words which Jesus spake as recorded in the New Testament.

25 ver. If we would know the secret of the Lord, and have intimate fellowship with him, let us regard him as the searcher of hearts, and seek to be holy in heart as well as fair in profession.

JESUS' INTERVIEW WITH NICODEMUS.

Nicodemus visits Jesus by night. John iii. 1—21.—Jerusalem.

1, 2 There-was a-man of the Pharisees, named Nicodemus, a-ruler of-the Jews: the-same came to Jesus by-night, and said unto-him, Rabbi, we-know that thou-art-·a-teacher ·-come from God: for no-man can do these miracles that thou doest, except God be with
3 him. Jesus answered and said unto-him, Verily, verily, I-say unto-thee, Except a-man
4 be-born again, γεννηθῇ ἄνωθεν he-can not see the kingdom of God. Nicodemus saith unto him, How can a-man be-born when-he-is old? can-he enter the-second-time into
5 his mother's womb, and be-born? Jesus answered, Verily, verily, I-say unto-thee, Except a-man be-born of water and of-the-Spirit, he-can not enter into the kingdom of

SCRIPTURE ILLUSTRATIONS.

1. *Nicodemus*—(innocent blood) He. ix. 22—.8; 1 Pe. i. 19, 20—through Jesus is that new birth, ver. 2, 3, concerning which is the ensuing discourse, ver. 3—21.

2. *by night*—some of the chief rulers believed in him, yet feared the Jews, Jno. xii. 42, § 85.

these miracles that thou doest—referred to, Jno. ii. 23, p. 82—his miracles are also referred to by Jesus, Jno. v. 30, § 23; x. 25, § 56; xv. 24, § 87—by the people, vii. 31, § 55; x. 21, ib.—by the Pharisees, ix. 16, § ib.; xi. 47, § 58—by Peter, Ac. ii. 22.

3. *born again*—or from above; born, not of blood, but of God, Jno. i. 13, § 7—'a new creature,' Ga. vi. 15—'cometh down from the Father of lights;' 'begat he us with the word of truth,' Ja. i. 17, .8—'quickened us together with Christ,' Ep. ii. 4, 5— born again, of

incorruptible seed, 1 Pe. i. 23—'and I will put my Spirit within you;' 'and ye shall be my people, and I will be your God,' Eze. xxxvi. 27, .8—after which will come the promised blessing in that kingdom which is righteousness and peace, ver. 28—39.

5. *water and Spirit*—'sprinkle clean water upon you;' 'and a new spirit will I put within you,' Eze. xxxvi. 25, .6—'pour water upon him that is thirsty;' 'my spirit upon thy seed;' 'and they shall spring up,' Is. xliv. 3, 4—'washing of regeneration, and renewing,' &c., Tit. iii. 5—'it is the spirit that quickeneth; the flesh profiteth nothing: the words that I speak unto you, *they* are spirit, and *they* are life,' Jno. vi. 63, § 43—'if any man have not the Spirit of Christ,' &c., Rom. viii. 9.—*See* as to water and spirit, Jno. iv. 14, 23, .4, § 13, pp. 93, .4; vii. 38, .9. § 55.

NOTES.

1. *Nicodemus.* Means 'the innocent blood.'

A ruler of the Jews. A professor of laws, and one of the *sanhedrim*, or great council of the nation. In the rabbinical writings he is described as a man of unbounded wealth, of magnificent liberality, and of piety the most ardent; insomuch that they ascribe to him the working of miracles. His splendid fortunes were attended, they say, with almost as great a reverse as Job's. He is twice mentioned after this as being friendly to our Saviour; in the first instance as advocating his cause, and defending him against the unjust suspicions of the Jews, ch. vii. 50, .1, § 55, and in the second instance as one who came to aid in embalming his body, ch. xix. 39, § 92.

2. *We know, &c.* Nicodemus seems here to intimate, that others beside himself, among the rulers, believed that Jesus was 'a teacher come from God,' was vested with extraordinary authority, as being commissioned to deliver some important message relative to the long-promised kingdom of Messiah, which was now expected speedily to appear. Our Lord, who knew what was in man, immediately proceeds to point out the preparation necessary to the enjoyment of the kingdom of God. He tells Nicodemus that he must be born again, must become like a little child, in order to be given at all an entrance into the kingdom. By a similar allusion did he afterwards bring down the high looks of his disciples when there was a strife among them which should be greatest, Mt. xviii. 1—4, § 53.

3. *Except a man.* This is a universal form of expression designed to include all mankind. Of *every* man it may be said, unless he is born again he cannot see the kingdom of God. It includes, therefore, men of every character, and rank, and nation, moral and immoral, rich and poor, in office and out of office, old and young, bond and free, the slave and his master, Jew and Gentile.

Be born again. γεννηθῇ ἄνωθεν, 'be born from above.'—*See* on ver. 4.

* [By the phrase, our Lord signifies that no man, either as a man, or as a son of Abraham, or as a proselyte to the Jewish religion, can have any true knowledge of, or right unto, the enjoyment of the

kingdom of God, unless he is born again, or regenerated, and quickened by the Spirit of God; renewed in the spirit of his mind; has Christ formed in his heart; becomes a partaker of the Divine nature; and in all respects a new creature,—another in heart, principle, practice, and conversation; or, unless he be born from above, as the word is rendered in ver. 31; that is, by a supernatural power, having the heavenly image instamped on him, and being called with an heavenly calling.]

The kingdom of God. Either in this world, or in that which is to come. The meaning is, that the kingdom which Jesus was come to set up can only be enjoyed by building on him as the one foundation. It is only by emptying ourselves, and being filled with the Spirit of God, that we can attain to the kingdom of glory.

4. *How can a man be born when he is old, &c.* It is said, the expression *be born again* was in common use among the Jews. The word with *them* meant a change from the *state* of a heathen to that of *a Jew*. But they never used it as applicable to a Jew, because they supposed that by his birth he was entitled to all the privileges of the people of God. Nicodemus may have had no difficulty in admitting the necessity of a new birth in the case of the Gentiles, so that they might become the children of Abraham; but as for those who were the children of Abraham by natural descent, he could not conceive of their being given anything better than what they already possessed.

[5. *Be born of water, &c.* Cleansing is particularly spoken of by the prophets as a necessary preparation for reception into blessing, as in Eze. xxxvi. 25—33, 'Then will I sprinkle clean water upon you, and ye shall be clean: from all your filthiness, and from all your idols, will I cleanse you.' So also was it promised, ver. 27, 'And I will put my Spirit within you, and cause you to walk in my statutes, and ye shall keep my judgments, and do them.' Then after the people so spoken of are recognized as born again, as made the Lord's people anew, ver. 28, '*And ye shall dwell in the land that I gave to your fathers; and ye shall be my people, and I will be your God.*']

PRACTICAL REFLECTIONS.

iii. 2. Although we may have been laboriously engaged through the day, let us not refuse to be at night employed in assisting others, or being ourselves assisted, in inquiries after the kingdom of God.

It is not enough that we acknowledge Jesus to be a teacher come from God; we must know what he does teach, and experience the power of his doctrine.

[God deals with men as rational beings. He gives us evidence upon which to believe. Thus, as appealing to Divine evidence, we ought to be able to give, like Nicodemus, a reason of the faith that is in us.]

[4 *ver.* Those high in rank and learning are often,

like Nicodemus, found very ignorant of the plainest matters in religion, and start difficulties to Divine truth which arise from their own absurd views of what has been spoken.—Let us, if we desire to reign with Christ in his kingdom, be sure that we are indeed born from above, that we are no longer selfish and worldly; but that, from the love of God, we act after the example of Him who came down from heaven.]

5 *ver.* It is not enough that we cease to do evil, we must also learn to do well, if we would indeed prove that we have the washing of regeneration and renewing of the Holy Ghost. May this be shed on us abundantly through Jesus Christ our Saviour.

THE LORD IS GRACIOUS.—1 Peter ii. 3.

JOHN iii. 6—11.

6 God. That which-is-born τὸ γεγεννημενον of the flesh is flesh; and that which-is-born 7 of the Spirit is spirit. Marvel not that I-said unto-thee, Ye must δει be-born again 8 ανωθεν. The wind bloweth where it-listeth, θελει and thou-hearest the sound thereof, but canst-'not'-tell whence it-cometh, and whither it-goeth: so is every-one that is-born 9 of the Spirit. Nicodemus answered and said unto-him, How can these-things be? 10 Jesus answered and said unto-him, Art thou a master of Israel, and knowest not these-11 things? Verily, verily, I-say unto-thee, We-speak that we-do-know, and testify that we-

SCRIPTURE ILLUSTRATIONS.

6. *born of the flesh*—'Adam begat *a son* in his own likeness,' Ge. v. 3—'all flesh had corrupted his way,' vi. 5, 12—'who can bring a clean *thing* out of an unclean? not one,' Job xiv. 4—'what is man . . . born of a woman, that he should be righteous?' xv. 14—6 —'in my flesh dwelleth no good thing,' Rom. vii. 5, 18—'the natural man receiveth not the things of the Spirit of God,' 1 Co. ii. 14—'as *is* the earthy, such *are* they also that are earthy,' &c., xv. 47—9—'the flesh lusteth against the Spirit,' Ga. v. 17—'the works of the flesh,' ver. 19—21—'by nature the children of wrath,' Ep. ii. 3—'for all that *is* in the world, the lust of the flesh, and the lust of the eyes, and the pride of life, is not of the Father, but is of the world,' 1 Jno. ii. 16.

8. *the wind bloweth*—as on the day of Pentecost, Ac. ii. 2, 4—'as thou knowest not what *is* the way of the spirit, nor how the bones *do grow*,' &c., Ec. xi. 5.

but canst not tell, &c.—this ignorance exemplified on the day of Pentecost, Ac. ii. 6—13—'even so the things of God knoweth no man, but the Spirit of God,' 1 Co. ii. 11—'they think it strange that ye run not with *them* to the same excess,' &c., 1 Pe. iv. 4.

10. *master of Israel*—wise men made rulers, De. i.

13—'gather unto me all the elders of your tribes,' xxxi. 28—30—*see* ch. xxxii., which contains the song rehearsed in their hearing, wherein is so strongly declared the need there would be in the latter days for Israel's being born again of the Spirit, ver. 1, 2— as making known the name of *Him* whose work is perfect, ver. 3, 4—so as to know *Him* to be their Father, who hath bought them, made them, established them, ver. 5, 6—They should have known what God had thus testified respecting the regeneration of his people: and afterwards by the prophets, as in Eze. xxxvi. 25—7; xxxvii. 3—10—but the spirit of deep sleep had fallen upon them, Is. xxix. 10—,2—'his watchmen are blind,' lvi. 10—'have rejected the word of the Lord; and what wisdom is in them?' Je. viii. 8, 9—so our Lord afterward testified: 'hid these things from the wise,' &c., Mt. xi. 25, § 29—'they be blind leaders,' &c., xv. 14, § 44—'ye do err, not knowing,' &c., xxii. 29, § 85—yet not conscious of their ignorance, Jno. ix. 39—41, § 55.

11. *we speak that we do know*—'no man hath seen God,' &c., Jno. i. 18, § 7—'I speak that which I have seen with my Father,' viii. 38, § 55—*see* xii. 49, § 85; and Mt. xi. 27, § 29; Rev. i. 5—men are to testify that which they know, Is. xliii. 8—12; xlv. 19—22.

NOTES.

[6. *That which is born of the flesh.* To shew the necessity of this change our Saviour directs the attention of Nicodemus to the natural condition of man. By *that which is born of the flesh* he evidently intends man as he is by *nature*, in the circumstances of his natural birth. As the parents are corrupt and sinful, so will be their descendants, Job xiv. 4. And as the parents are *wholly* corrupt by nature, so their children will be the same. The word *flesh*, here, is used to denote, *corrupt, defiled, sinful*.]

The *flesh* in the Scriptures is often used to denote the sinful propensities and passions of our nature, as those propensities have for their end the gratification of the animal nature alone.—*See* 'Scripture Illustrations,' *supra*.

8. *The wind bloweth where it listeth.* The work of the Spirit is felt, but his way of working is a mystery.

[The Holy Ghost is likened to *wind* or *winds*; incomprehensible in his nature; self-moved, powerful, convincing, quickening, comforting, and purifying in his influences. May not the *north-wind* figure out his convincing, and the *south-wind* his cherishing and comforting efficacy? In ἐνουθελει there seems an allusion to the freedom of Divine grace, both as to nations and to individuals.]

[*So is every one that is born of the Spirit.* These words are intended to apply the comparison; meaning that there are points of resemblance between the effects of the wind in nature and those of the Spirit in him who is born of the Spirit; and that they are of a kind which every one must ascribe to the Author of all good. He cannot indeed trace the exact *process* by which that heavenly agency is employed for this effect; but he does not the less believe it.]

10. *Art thou a master of Israel?* 'The teacher of Israel.' Nicodemus was so called as compared with

others. As such he ought to have understood this doctrine. It was clearly taught in the Old Testament.—*See* 'Scrip. Illus.,' *supra*; and 'Notes,' p. 83.

And knowest not these things? The things which Jesus had been teaching, having been previously taught by the prophets, ought to have been known by Nicodemus.

[Nicodemus having expressed his ignorance of what Jesus had said, our Lord refers to the words of the prophets, *see* Eze. xxxvi. 22—8, who had prophesied that before God would receive Israel into the promised kingdom, he would sprinkle *clean water* upon them; and also that a new heart he would give them, and a *right spirit* he would put within them. He would put his Spirit within them: so they, being born again, shall be his people, and he will be their God. Nicodemus, who, as being 'a master of Israel,' ought to have known these things, still, in amazement, asks, 'How can these things be?' And our Lord proceeds to shew him how these things can be, by pointing to his being the Divine Saviour, the antitype of the brazen serpent, lifted up by Moses, for the healing of the people in the wilderness; by believing in whom, as given of the Father out of pure love to the world, we are renewed in his image, who was made after our likeness, the likeness of sinful flesh.]

11. *We speak.* Jesus, agreeable to the usage of persons in authority, *see* Mk. iv. 30, § 32, here speaks in the plural number. Nicodemus had said, (ver. 2,) '*We know that thou art*,' &c., including himself and those with whom he acted.

We speak that we do know, and testify that we have seen. Both are expressive of that *complete knowledge* which the Son, as united with God the Father, could not but possess. There is also implied knowledge by *a virtue of his own*, and not by revelation.

PRACTICAL REFLECTIONS.

6 *ver.* Men are by nature carnally-minded, and can only become spiritually-minded by being born of the Spirit.

[7 *ver.* Man must have it deeply impressed upon him, that his being born into the kingdom of God must be from above: 'Not of blood, nor of the will of the flesh, nor of the will,' &c.—*See* Jno. i. 13, § 7.]

8 *ver.* Regeneration must be known by its effects. The Spirit of God operates freely as the wind. Its coming and issue are not otherwise visible.

9 *ver.* Men will often admit facts on other subjects, and be greatly perplexed by similar facts in religion.

Let us, whatever may be our standing, candidly acknowledge our difficulties, not to puzzle the weak, but that we may have the help of the strong.

[10 *ver.* Let the strong not be offended at the inquiries of the weak; but, like Jesus, persevere in presenting the truth to inquiring minds, according as they are able to bear it. Jesus, in teaching regeneration by the word and Spirit of God, taught no new doctrine, but that which had been taught by the prophets: which it should have been the business of Nicodemus, as a master of Israel, to make plain to the people.—*See* as to 'water and spirit,' Eze. xxxvi. 25—7; as to 'word and spirit,' xxxvii. 1—10.]

PART II. AS MOSES LIFTED UP THE SERPENT. SECT. XII.

JOHN iii. 12—.5

12 have-seen; and ye-receive not our witness. If I-have-told you earthly-things, τα επιγεια and ye-believe not, how shall-ye-believe, if I-tell you *of* heavenly-things? τα επουρανια.
13 And no-man hath-ascended-up to heaven, but he that-came-down from heaven, *even* the
14 Son of man which is in heaven. And as Moses lifted-up ὑψωσε the serpent in the
15 wilderness, even-so must the Son of man be-lifted-up ὑψωθηναι: that whosoever be-

SCRIPTURE ILLUSTRATIONS.

11. *receive not our witness*—so had they been forewarned—'none to answer,' Is. l. 2—'who hath believed our report?' liii. 1—'yea, thou heardest not,' xlviii. 8—'a rebellious people,' lxv. 2—'when I called, none did answer; when I spake, they did not hear,' lxvi. 4—so Jesus afterward testified, 'Ye will not come to me,' &c., Jno. v. 40, .3, § 23—'Ye would not,' Mt. xxiii. 37, § 85.

12. *earthly things*—things which are to take place upon earth, in preparation for the heavenly glory, which shall come to the people as waiting for the King—*see* as before, Eze. xxxvi. 25—38—*comp.* with Is. xxx. 18—25; xlix. 18—23; and Joel ii. 16—32.

heavenly things—'neither hath the eye seen, O God, beside thee, *what* he hath prepared for him that waiteth for him,' Is. lxiv. 4—'but God hath revealed *them* unto us by his Spirit,' 1 Co. ii. 9, 10—'our Saviour Jesus Christ . . . hath brought life and,' &c., 2 Ti. i. 10—'I go to prepare a place for you, I will come,' &c., Jno. xiv. 2, 3, § 67—'we shall be caught up together,' &c., 1 Th. iv. 16, .7—'he hath prepared for them a city,' He. xi. 16—'that great city, the holy Jerusalem, descending out of heaven from God,' Rev. xxi. 10—27—'they shall reign for ever and ever,' Rev. xxii. 5.

13. *no man*—'who hath ascended up into heaven?' Pr. xxx. 4—*see* also Jno. i. 18, § 7; vi. 46, § 43—'Jesus saith unto him, I am the way, & the truth, & the life: no man cometh unto the Father,' &c., Jno. xiv. 6, § 87.

but he that came down from heaven—'the bread of God is he which cometh down from heaven,' &c., Jno. vi. 33, .8, 51, § 43—'where he was before,' ver. 62, § *ib.* —'from above,' viii. 23, § 55—'from God,' ver. 42, § *ib.*; xiii. 3, § 87—'came forth from the Father,' xvi. 3—8, § *ib.*—'with thee before the world was,' xvii. 5, § *ib.* —'the Lord from heaven,' 1 Co. xv. 47—'when the fulness of the time was come, God sent forth his Son,' &c., Ga. iv. 4—'descended,' Ep. iv. 8—10.

14. *as Moses lifted up the serpent*—described, Nu. xxi. 7—9—this sign abused, like that of the cross among many professing Christians— Hezekiah destroyed it, 2 Ki. xviii. 4—Jesus again referred to his being lifted up, Jno. viii. 28, § 55; xii. 32—.4, § 82—'cursed is every one that,' &c., Ga. iii. 13—'made him *to be* sin for us, who,' &c., 2 Co. v. 21.

15. *whosoever believeth*—thus Abraham, Ge. xv. 6; Rom. iv.—thus all the ends of the earth are invited, Is. xlv. 22—'they shall look,' &c., Zec. xii. 10—'he that believeth on the Son,' &c., Jno. iii. 36, § 13—'though he were dead, yet,' &c., xi. 25, § 58—'justified from all things,' Ac. xiii. 39—'believe in thine heart that God hath,' &c., Rom. x. 9—'am persuaded that he is able to keep,' &c., 2 Ti. i. 12.

eternal life—'I give unto them eternal life,' Jno. x. 28—30, § 56—'and this is life eternal, that,' &c., xvii. 2, 3, § 87—'this is the record, that God hath given to us eternal life, and this life is in his Son,' &c., 1 Jno. v. 11.

NOTES.

Our witness. Our testimony. The *evidence* which is furnished by miracle, and the saving power of the gospel.

12. *If I have told you earthly things, &c.* 'If I have told you of that preparation which must be made upon earth, as introductory to the possession of the earthly portion of the inheritance, and yet you believe not things so evident, how shall you believe if I tell you of the unseen things of heaven?'

Heavenly things. The things belonging to the heavenly portion of the kingdom, to be enjoyed by the saints in resurrection glory.

13. *And no man hath ascended up to heaven.* To one alone, even the Son of man, belongs the knowledge of these heavenly things. He alone knoweth, and can declare the counsels of God.

[The expression must be taken *figuratively* to denote the investigation of hidden things, for which Christ, who came down *from heaven*, was peculiarly qualified. The phrase αναβαινειν εις τον ουρανον is here used agreeably to the language commonly employed of one who *announced any revelation*; *q. d.* that he had ascended into heaven, and fetched his knowledge from thence. 'No one knoweth the counsels of God, but he who came down from God.' De. xxx. 11, .2, *comp.* with Rom. x. 6. Christ, then, who *literally* was in heaven, is *figuratively* said to have ascended thither, because, being in the bosom of his Father, he had the fulness of knowledge in heavenly things.]

14. *And as Moses.* Jesus proceeds in this and the following verses to state the reason why he came into the world, and illustrates his design by a reference to the case recorded in Nu. xxi. 8, 9. The people were bitten by flying, fiery serpents. There was no cure for the bite. Moses was directed to make an *image* of the serpent, and place it in sight of the people, that they might look on it and be healed.

In the wilderness. Near the land of Edom. A desert and desolate country to the south of mount Hor, Nu. xxi. 4.

Even so. He here refers doubtless to his death—*comp.* Jno. viii. 28, § 55; xii. 32, § 82.

The points of resemblance between *his* being lifted up, and that of the brazen serpent, seem to be these: 1st. In both cases, those who are to be benefited can be aided in no other way. The bite of the serpent was deadly; and there is no cure for sin in any other manner. 2nd. The mode of their being lifted up. The brazen serpent was set on a pole in the sight of the people. So Jesus was exalted from the earth; raised on a tree, or cross. 3rd. The *design* was similar. The one was to save the life: the other the soul. The one to save from temporal, the other from eternal death. 4th. The manner of the cure was similar. The people of Israel were to *look* on the serpent, and be healed. And so sinners are to look, or believe, on the Lord Jesus, that they may be saved.

Must. It is proper, necessary, indispensable, if men are to be saved.—*Comp.* Lu. xxii. 42, § 68; xxiv. 26, § 94.

The Son of man. The Messiah.

15. Here consider—1st. The universality of the invitation, '*whosoever*;' all need, and all may have salvation.—2nd. The medium of salvation, '*faith*;' 'whosoever *believeth.*'—3rd. The object of faith, in whom is salvation, Jesus Christ the Son of God, as made sin for us, that we might be made the righteousness of God in him; 'whosoever believeth in *him.*'—4th. The danger of neglecting this great salvation: there is no other way of escape from perdition; 'should not perish.'—5th. That which is to be obtained through faith in the Saviour, '*life*;' it is the joy of the Holy Ghost now; it is '*eternal life*,' Jno. iv. 14, § 13. It is an ever-blessed abiding in the presence of God.

PRACTICAL REFLECTIONS.

[11 *ver.* He who hath Jesus for his teacher hath a teacher unlike many masters of Israel, who know not the things, nor the evidence of the things which they teach. He has a full knowledge of what he teaches; he testifies not by hearsay, but of what he hath seen.]

The disciples of Jesus should, like their Master, speak according to their knowledge, having for themselves full evidence of what they call upon others to believe.

12 *ver.* The change which Jesus had declared to Nicodemus, and the kingdom for which it is appointed a preparation, take place upon earth: but they are connected with still more wondrous things in the heavens.

[13 *ver.* That we be born again, it is necessary to see Jesus, as God, who both came down from heaven, and who yet was in heaven, at the same time that he was the Son of man talking with Nicodemus upon earth.]

14 *ver.* As it was in the wilderness that the lifting up of the serpent took place, for the healing of the people who would otherwise have perished, so it is in the wilderness of this world now that the Son of man must be lifted up; that by him, through faith, the people may receive healing.

ASCRIBE YE GREATNESS UNTO OUR GOD.—Deut. xxxii. 3. [85

SECT. XII.   HE THAT BELIEVETH IS NOT CONDEMNED.   PART II.

JOHN iii. 16—.9.

16 lieveth in him should-'not'-perish, but have eternal life. For God so loved the world, that he-gave his only-begotten Son, that whosoever believeth in him should-'not'-
17 perish, but have everlasting life. For God sent ἀπέστειλεν not his Son into the world
18 to condemn the world; but that the world through him might-be-saved. He that-believeth on him is-'not'-condemned: but he that-believeth not is-condemned already,
19 because he-hath-'not'-believed in the name of-the only-begotten Son of God. And this is the condemnation, that light is-come into the world, and men loved darkness rather

SCRIPTURE ILLUSTRATIONS.

16. *so loved*—' God commendeth his love toward us,' &c., Rom. v. 8—' great love.' Ep. ii. 4, 5—' hereby perceive we the love of God,' 1 Jno. iii. 16—' herein is love, not that we loved God,' &c., iv. 10—see ver. 7—21.

he gave his only begotten Son—' his well-beloved, he sent him,' Mk. xii. 6, § 84—' spared not his own Son,' Rom. viii. 32.

sh not perish—' the wages of sin,' &c., Rom. vi. 23.

17. *sent not to condemn*—' is come to save that which was lost,' Mt. xviii. 11, § 53—' not to destroy men's lives, but to save,' Lu. ix. 56, § 59—' came not to judge the world, but to save,' Jno. xii. 47, § 85—but he will come to judge, Mt. xxv. 31—46, § 86.

but that the world—as before, on ver. 15—' the Christ, the Saviour of the world,' Jno. iv. 42, § 13; 1 Jno. iv. 14—' the propitiation . . . for the sins of the whole world,' ii. 2—' for us all,' Rom. viii. 32—' died for all . . . reconciling the world unto himself,' 2 Co. v. 14, .5, .9—' will have all men,' &c., 1 Ti. ii. 3—6.

16. *For God so loved*. This does not mean that God approved the conduct of men, but was *desirous* of their happiness. A parent may love his child, and desire his welfare, and yet be strongly *opposed* to the conduct of that child.

The world. All mankind, the race, who had rebelled, and deserved to die, Jno. vi. 33, § 43; xvii. § 98.

That he gave. It was a free gift, unmerited. Man had no claim; and when there was no eye to pity, or arm to save, it pleased God to *give* his Son into the hands of man to die in their stead, Ga. i. 4; Rom. viii. 32; Lu. xxii. 19, § 67.

His only begotten Son. This is the highest expression of love of which we can conceive. A parent who should give up his only son to die—if this could, or might, be done, would shew higher love than could be manifested in any other way. From the 17—21 ver. seems to be levelled against the Jewish notion, that Messiah would come for the benefit of the Jews only; nay, would rather destroy the Gentiles.

17. Not to condemn the world. Not to *judge*, or pronounce sentence on mankind. Man deserved condemnation; but God was willing that there should be an offer of pardon, and the sentence of condemnation was delayed; and God was willing to put forth in mercy his arm of power, to rescue sinners from death. Though Jesus did not come *then* to condemn mankind, yet the time is coming when he will return to judge the quick and dead, Ac. xvii. 31; 2 Co. v. 10.

18. He that believeth. He that trusts to his merits and promises for salvation. To believe on him, is to go as lost sinners, and, relying on him, look to him *only* for salvation.

Is not condemned. Because believing on him, we are pardoned and delivered from deserved punishment. Jesus died in our stead. And by his sufferings God is satisfied, and our sins are expiated. 'There is therefore now no condemnation to them *which are in Christ Jesus, who walk not after the flesh, but after the Spirit*,' Rom. viii. 1.

18. *he that believeth is not condemned*—' that believing, ye might have life through his name,' Jno. xx. 31, § 100—' being justified by faith,' &c., Rom. v. 1—' no condemnation to them,' &c., viii. 1—' he that hath the Son hath life,' &c., 1 Jno. v. 12.

believeth not—death to unbelieving Israel in the wilderness, Nu. xxxii. 11—a warning to those that should come after, Ps. xcv. 7—11—*comp*. with He. iii. 7—12; iv. 5—11—' how shall we escape,' &c, He. ii. 3.

19. *light is come into the world*—' in him was life; and the life was,' &c., Jno. i. 4, § 7—' he that followeth me shall not walk in darkness, but shall have the light of life,' viii. 12, § 55.

men loved darkness—' say to the seers. See not,' Is. xxx. 10—' did not like to retain God in their knowledge,' Rom. i. 28—' received not the love of the truth, that,' &c., 2 Th. ii. 9, 10—' if we say that we have fellowship with him, and walk in darkness, we lie,' &c., 1 Jno. i. 5—8.

NOTES.

He is condemned already. So certain is his destruction. He is condemned by law, and in the judgment of God; and not unfrequently he is condemned even of his own conscience.

Because he hath not believed. All men are by nature condemned. There is but one way of being free from this state; and that is by believing on Jesus. Those to whom the gospel comes greatly heighten their guilt and condemnation by rejecting the offers of mercy, and trampling under foot the blood of the Son of God, Mt. xi. 23, § 29; Lu. xii. 47, § 63; He. x. 29; Pr. i. 24—30.

19. This is the condemnation, that light, &c. [It is here intimated that unbelief is not a speculative mistake, into which any honest mind may be led, but originates in the enmity of the heart to God. This is the ground of the sinner's condemnation—that light is come into the world, but men refuse to receive the truth, though coming with the fullest evidence, and spurn the gracious offer of salvation. '*In whom the god of this world hath blinded the minds of them which believe not, lest the light of the glorious gospel of Christ, who is the image of God, should shine unto them*,' 2 Co. iv. 4.]

[*That light is come*. Light often denotes instruction, teaching, doctrine, as that by which we see clearly the path of duty. *All* the instruction that God gives us by conscience, reason, or revelation, may thus be called light. But this word is used peculiarly to denote the Messiah, or the Christ, who is often spoken of as *the light—see* Is. ix. 2; lx. 1—*comp*. Mt. iv. 16, § 16; also Note on Jno. i. 4, § 7, p. 46. It was doubtless this light to which Jesus here makes particular reference.]

Men loved darkness. Darkness is the emblem of iniquity, error, superstition: whatever is opposite to truth and piety. Men are said to love darkness more than they do light, when they are better pleased with error than truth; with sin than holiness; with Belial than Christ.

PRACTICAL REFLECTIONS.

[16 *ver*. Regeneration is of the free love of God the Father, who gave the dearest object he had, ' his only begotten Son,' that men might not have the reward of their own evil doings, but the recompense of His perfect work in their behalf—have the Spirit given them, which is life—life eternal. Salvation is free to all who will have it, as confiding in Him who is God-man, given of the Father, lifted up for our redemption, that we might be regenerated through the power of his Spirit.]

17 *ver*. The mission of Jesus had not as its object that which might have been expected, the condemning of the world, but the enduring the curse of the law, that the world through him might be saved;

teaching us to deal with men, not according to the severity of justice, but according to the law of the kingdom, which is LOVE.

18 *ver*. Jesus gave the clearest evidence of his being the truth itself, and was the purest exemplification of LOVE; and his mission was abundantly attested of God: those therefore who reject him, condemn themselves in so doing.—He that refuses to be saved through the merits of Jesus Christ, must remain in condemnation.

19 *ver*. Condemnation is aggravated by the abuse of privilege.—The great cause of unbelief is the love of that which the principles of the gospel condemn, *viz*., the love of this world and its riches.

JOHN iii. 20, .1.

20 than light, because their deeds were evil. For every one that-doeth evil hateth the
21 light, neither cometh to the light, lest his deeds should-be-reproved. But he that-doeth truth cometh to the light, that his deeds may-be-made-manifest, that they-are wrought in God.

SCRIPTURE ILLUSTRATIONS.

20. *hateth the light*—' they hated knowledge, and did not choose the fear of the Lord,' Pr. i. 29—' a scorner loveth not one that reproveth him,' xv. 12—*comp.* 1 Ki. xxii. 8; so Am. v. 10—' ye are of your father the devil, and the lusts,' &c., Jno. viii. 44, .5. § 55.

21. *he that doeth truth*—' his delight is in the law of the Lord,' Ps. i. 1—3—' he that walketh uprightly, and worketh righteousness, and speaketh the truth in his heart,' xv.—*comp.* 2 Ch. xxxi. 20—' thy law is the truth,' Ps. cxix. 142—' grace and truth came,' &c., Jno. i. 17, § 7—' I am the way,' &c., xiv. 6, § 87—' when he, the Spirit of truth, is come,' &c., xvi. 13, § *ib.*—' let us draw near with a true heart,' He. x. 22—' a door of the work,' Ja. i. 25.

cometh to the light—' thy word is a lamp unto my feet,' &c., Ps. cxix. 105—' search me, O God, . . . and

lead,' &c.. cxxxix. 23, .4—' give to a wise man, and he will be yet wiser,' Pr. ix. 8—10—' every man . . . that hath heard, and hath learned of the Father, cometh unto me,' Jno. vi. 45, § 43.

that his deeds may be made manifest—' let your light so,' &c., Mt. v. 16, § 18—' by this shall all men know that,' &c., Jno. xiii. 35, § 87—' manifestly declared to be the epistle of Christ,' 2 Co. iii. 3—in the primitive church the Spirit revealed the true character and real condition of many individuals: ' the Spirit itself beareth witness with our spirit, that we are the children of God,' Rom. viii. 16—*see* 1 Co. xiv. 25.

wrought in God—' thou . . . hast wrought all our works in us,' Is. xxvi. 12—' for it is God which worketh in you,' &c., Ph. ii. 13.

NOTES.

20. *His deeds should be reproved*. To *reprove* here means not only to *detect*, or make manifest, but also includes the idea of *condemnation* when they are detected. The gospel would make his wickedness manifest, and his conscience would condemn him.

The sentiment at the last clause of ver. 19 is here illustrated, and the discourse concludes with a sentiment of general application, shewing the evil effects of a corrupt life on all inquiries after truth, and evincing, that ' when truth is against a man, a man is against truth.'

21. *He that doeth truth*. The sinner acts from falsehood and error, the good man acts according to truth. The sinner believes a lie—that God will not punish; or that there is no God; or that there is no eternity, or no hell; the Christian believes all these, and acts, knowing them to be true.

Cometh to the light. By prayer, and searching the Scriptures, he endeavours to ascertain the truth, and yield his mind to it.

May be made manifest. May be made clear or plain. He searches for truth and light, that he may have evidence that his actions are right.

Wrought in God. That they are performed according to the will of God; by the influence and aid of God. ' For it is God which worketh in you both to *will and to do of his good pleasure*,' Ph. ii. 13. Here is the character of a sincere Christian: 1st. He does truth. He loves it; seeks it; follows it. 2nd. He comes to the light. He does not attempt to deceive himself or others. 3rd. He desires to know the true state of his heart before God. 4th. An especial object of his efforts is that his deeds may be *wrought in God*. He *desires* to be a good man; to receive continual aid from God, and to perform such actions as God will approve.

This is the close of our Lord's discourse with Nicodemus—a discourse condensing the gospel; giving the most striking exhibition and illustration of truth; and presenting especially the fundamental doctrine of regeneration, and the evidence of the change. It is clear that the Saviour regarded this as lying at the foundation of religion. Without it we cannot possibly be saved.

PRACTICAL REFLECTION.

20, .1 *ver*. Men may be known to be in the truth by their walking in the light, and rejoicing to have their case fully investigated according to the truth of God, as revealed in his Holy Scriptures.

ADDENDA.

RABBI, p. 83.

' *Rabbi, rab, rabban, rabbon;* a title signifying *master.* It seems to have come originally from Assyria. In Sennacherib's army, we find Rab-shakeh, the *master of the drinking*, or butler, and Rab-saris, the *master of the eunuchs*. In Nebuchadnezzar's, we find also Rab-mag, the *chief of the magi*; and Nebuzaradan is called Rab-tebachim, the *master of the butchers, cooks, or guards*. We find also at Babylon, Rab-saganim, the *master of the governors*; and Rab-chartumim, the *master of the interpreters of dreams*, Je. xxxix. 3; 2 Ki. xxv. 8; Da. i. 3; ii. 48; v. 11. To keep order, Ahasuerus set a *rab*, or governor, at every table of his splendid feast, Est. i. 8. *Rab* is now with the Jews reckoned a more dignified title than *rabbi*; and rabbin, or rabbim, greater than either; and to become such, one must ascend by several degrees. The rector of their school is called *rab-chacham*, the *wise master*. He that attends it in order to obtain a doctorship is called *bachur*, the *candidate*. After that he is called *chabarierab*, the *master's companion*. At his next degree, he is called *rab, rabbi*, and *morenu, our teacher*. The *rab-chacham* decides in religious, and frequently in civil affairs. He celebrates marriages, and declares divorcements. He is head of the collegians, and preaches, if he has a talent for it. He reproves the unruly, and excommunicates offenders. Both in the school and synagogue he sits in the chief seat; and in the school his scholars sit at his feet. Where the synagogue is small, he is both preacher and judge; but where the Jews are numerous, they have ordinarily a council for their civil matters; but if the rabbin be called to it, he usually takes the chief seat. Our Saviour inveighs against the rabbins, whether scribes or Pharisees, of his time, as extremely proud, ambitious of honorary titles and honorary seats, and as given to impose on others vast numbers of traditions not warranted in the word of God, Mt. xv., § 44; xxiii., § 85. Since that time, God has given up the Jewish rabbins to the most astonishing folly and trifling; they chiefly deal in idle and stupid traditions, and whimsical decisions, on points of no consequence, except to render the observers ridiculous. In geography and history they make wretched work. Inconsistencies of timing things, absurdities, and dry rehearsals, crowd their page. In their commentaries on the Scripture, they are commonly blind to what an ordinary reader might perceive, and retail multitudes of silly fancies, fit to move our pity or contempt. The judicious Onkelos, laborious Nathan-mordecai, the famed Maimonides, the two Kimchis, Aben-ezra, Solomon Jarchi, Jachiades, Sephorno, and some others, however, deserve a better character.'—*Gurney's Dict.*

OUR LORD'S MINISTRY IN JUDÆA.—John ii. 13, p. 81.

' The entire history of our Lord's public ministry is divisible into that part of it which was discharged in Judæa, and that part of it which was confined to Galilee; and is recorded in distinct and independent gospels. The ministry in Judæa is confined almost totally to St. John; the history of the ministry in Galilee almost as exclusively to the other three evangelists.

THE LIPS OF THE RIGHTEOUS FEED MANY.—PROV. X. 21. [87

'The times and occasions of the ministry in Judæa are likewise twofold; the times and occasions when our Saviour was visiting Jerusalem, and the times and occasions when he was residing elsewhere in Judæa. The first instance on record of any attendance at Jerusalem is the attendance at the passover, Jno. ii. 13; and the first instance of any residence in Judæa, apart from Jerusalem, is that which begins to be recorded, Jno. iii. 22, § 13, p. 89; and is supposed to continue, or go on, to the time of the return into Galilee, iv. 1—3. Of any residence in Judæa, out of Jerusalem, the only other instance, distinct from the first, is that which is specified at Jno. xi. 54, § 58: for though Ephraim might border upon Samaria, it was, notwithstanding, a city of Judæa.

'Besides these two instances, there is none other on record, either in St. John's Gospel, or out of it, during which there is any reason to suppose that our Saviour was residing in Judæa: for as to Bethabara, which is mentioned at Jno. x. 40, § 56, as the scene of a temporary residence also, it is proved, by a comparison with other passages, i. 28, § 10; iii. 23, .5, .6, § 13, to have been probably in Peræa, or, at least, in Galilee.

'The times and occasions of Jesus' attendances at Jerusalem were five; viz., two, of attendances at a passover, Jno. ii. 13, § 12, p. 81; xii. 1, § 81; one, of an attendance at a feast of tabernacles, Jno. vii. 2—10, § 51, .5; one, of an attendance at a feast of dedication, Jno. x. 22, .3, § 56; and one, which is left indefinite, Jno. v. 1, § 23; but besides these there are no more.

'The Gospel of St. John is supplementary to the rest not only in general, and even where they all relate to transactions in Galilee, or elsewhere out of Judæa, but especially so with respect to the transactions in Judæa. It was in this department of the gospel history that the preceding accounts were principally, or rather totally defective; since, with the exception of the history of passion week, that is, of seven or eight days before the close of our Lord's public ministry, it is a notorious fact that they nowhere speak of any visit to Jerusalem; they nowhere, except by implication, prove him to have been in Judæa at all. The reverse of this is true of St. John; the scene of whose accounts, with the same exception of a very little transacted in Galilee, or on the other side the lake of Tiberias, is placed in Judæa.

'These visits of our Lord were cardinal points in the discharge of the ministry in Judæa; the incidents which then transpired were always of a peculiar kind, and eminently deserving of record. They prove not merely the fact of our Lord's compliance with the legal requisitions, which enjoined such attendance, at stated times, on all the male Israelites, but what was still more to be expected from him, his anxiety to convince the Jews, strictly so called—his brethren according to the flesh—of the truth of his character by both his discourses, and his miracles, on the spot.'—*Greswell*, Vol. II. Diss. xxiii. pp. 245—.8.

'At the first passover, Jno. ii. 13, by the remarkable act of cleansing the temple, Jesus assumed and exercised an authority which he never assumed or exercised again, until the same time before the last; whereby he may justly be considered to have stamped this first passover with an importance, in the order of his ministry, scarcely inferior to that of the last. He predicted, at this early period, his death and resurrection, with a degree of significancy which he does not employ in alluding to them again until the last year of his ministry itself; and the words which he uttered now were remembered, and produced against him, three years afterwards. He wrought miracles *now* in the sight of all who attended the feast, both Jews and Galilæans; though a little before he had declined to work a miracle in private at Cana in Galilee. That *hour*, therefore, which was not come *then*, must have arrived *now*; and that evidence of his glory, with its effects in making him disciples, which had before been confined to his immediate friends, was now published to all the world. He held a discourse with Nicodemus on some of the most abstruse points of Christian doctrine. When he left Jerusalem, he began to baptize somewhere in Judæa; by the hands, at least, of his disciples; and to make converts in such numbers, as to eclipse the fame of John, and to divert the eyes of the Pharisees from John towards himself. And, finally, as he returned into Galilee, he declared himself more openly to the woman of Sychar than he ever declared himself afterwards, on any occasion but the last, when before the sanhedrim, or Pilate.

'The open assumption of the character of the Messias, and the beginning to act thenceforward in that character, which are in one sense the formal commencement of our Lord's ministry, must be dated from the passover, Jno. ii. 13,' *supra*, p. 81. —Vol. I. Diss. x. pp. 357, .8.

THE PASSOVER, p. 81.—(*Continued* from Sect. vi. p. 41.)

'The paschal lamb was to be eaten with unleavened bread, on pain of being cut off from Israel, or excommunicated; though some critics understand this of being put to death. The reason of this injunction was, partly to remind them of the hardships they had sustained in Egypt: unleavened bread being heavy, and less palatable than that which was leavened; on which account it is called the bread of affliction; De. xvi. 3, "*Thou shalt eat no leavened bread with it; seven days shalt thou eat unleavened bread therewith, even the bread of affliction; for thou camest forth out of the land of Egypt in haste: that thou mayest remember the day when thou camest forth out of the land of Egypt all the days of thy life;*" and partly to commemorate the speed of their deliverance or departure from thence, which was such, that they had not sufficient time to leaven their bread; Ex. xii. 39, "*And they baked unleavened cakes of the dough which they brought forth out of Egypt, for it was not leavened; because they were thrust out of Egypt, and could not tarry, neither had they prepared for themselves any victual;*" and on this account it was enacted into a standing law, De. xvi. 3. This rite, therefore, was not only observed at the first passover, but in all succeeding ages.

'The passover was likewise to be eaten " with bitter herbs:" this was doubtless prescribed as "a memorial of their severe bondage in Egypt, which made their lives *bitter* unto them." To this sauce the Jews afterwards added another, made of dates, raisins, and several ingredients beaten together to the consistence of mustard, which is called *charoseth*, and is designed to represent the clay in which their forefathers wrought while they were in bondage to the Egyptians.

'It was further prescribed, that they should eat the flesh of the lamb, without breaking any of his bones, Ex. xii. 46, "*In one house shall it be eaten; thou shalt not carry forth ought of the flesh abroad out of the house; neither shall ye break a bone thereof.*" This the later Jews understand, not of the smaller bones, but only of the greater which had marrow in them. Thus was this rite also intended to denote their being in haste, not having time to break the bones, and suck out the marrow.

'Lastly, it was ordered that nothing of the paschal lamb should remain till the morning; but, if it were not all eaten, it was to be consumed by fire, Ex. xii. 10, "*And ye shall let nothing of it remain until the morning; and that which remaineth of it until the morning ye shall burn with fire.*" The same law was extended to all eucharistical sacrifices, Le. xxii. 30, "*On the same day it shall be eaten up; ye shall leave none of it until the morrow: I am the Lord;*" no part of which was to be left, or set by, lest it should be corrupted, or converted to any profane or common use,—an injunction which was designed, no doubt, to maintain the honour of sacrifices, and to teach the Jews to treat with reverence whatever was consecrated more especially to the service of God.

'Such were the circumstances under which the first passover was celebrated by the Israelites; for, after they were settled in the land of Canaan, they no longer ate it standing, but the guests reclined on their left arms upon couches placed round the table, Jno. xiii. 23, § 87. This posture, according to the Talmudical writers, was an emblem of that rest and freedom which God had granted to the children of Israel by bringing them out of Egypt. This custom of reclining at table, over one another's bosom, was a sign of *equality* and strict union among the guests. This custom, Beausobre well observes, will explain several passages of Scripture, particularly those in which mention is made of Abraham's bosom, Lu. xvi. 22, § 69, and of the Son's being *in the bosom of the Father*, Jno. i. 18, § 7, p. 48, comp. with Ph. ii. 6, and Jno. xiii. 23, § 87.'—*Horne's Introduction*, Vol. III. pp. 309, .10.—*Continued*, Sect. lxxxvii.

SECTION 13.—AFTER THE PASSOVER, JESUS REMAINS IN JUDÆA;* HIS DISCIPLES BEGIN TO BAPTIZE; JOHN ALSO CONTINUES BAPTIZING. A DISPUTE HAVING ARISEN BETWEEN THE JEWS AND THE DISCIPLES OF JOHN, CONCERNING PURIFICATION JOHN RENDERS THE LAST, AND THE MOST EXPLICIT, OF HIS TESTIMONIES TO JESUS CHRIST. JESUS DEPARTS INTO GALILEE; AND, ON HIS WAY, ABIDES TWO DAYS AT SYCHAR, IN SAMARIA—JOHN NOT BEING YET CAST INTO PRISON. John iii. 22—iv. 42.

(G. 13,) No. 13. *Jesus' disciples baptize; John also continues baptizing. John iii. 22—.4.
Ænon, near to Salim.*

22 After these things came Jesus and his disciples into the land of Judæa; and there he-
23 tarried διετριβε with them, and baptized. And John also was baptizing in Ænon
near-to Salim, because there-was much water ὑδατα πολλα there· and they-came, and
24 were-baptized. For John was not-yet cast into prison.

(G. 14,) *John's last testimony to Jesus. John iii. 25—36.—The same.*

25 Then there-arose a-question between *some* of John's disciples and the Jews about
26 purifying. And they-came unto John, and said unto-him, Rabbi, he-that was with thee
beyond Jordan, to-whom thou barest-witness, behold, the-same baptizeth, and all *men*
27 come to him. John answered and said, A-man can receive nothing, except it-be given
28 him from heaven. Ye yourselves bear-·me·-witness, that I-said, I am not the Christ,
29 but that I-am sent before him. He that-hath the bride is the-bridegroom: but the

SCRIPTURE ILLUSTRATIONS.

22. *baptized*—that was said to be done by him, which was done by his disciples, see ch. iv. 2.
23. *Salim*, or Shalem—as Ge. xxxiii. 18.
24. *prison—see* as to the cause and result of John's imprisonment, Mt. xiv. 3—12, § 40.
26. *to whom thou barest witness*—John's witness to the excellency of Christ's baptism, and the purifying he will effect, Mt. iii. 11, .2, § 7, p. 54; Jno. i. 19—28, § 10, p. 68; 29—34, p. 69; 35, .6, p. 70.
27. *can receive, &c.*—similar confession by David, 1 Ch. xxix. 11—.5—the Spirit divideth 'to every man severally as he will, 1 Co. xii. 11—'by the grace of God I am what I am,' xv. 10; so Ga. i. 1.
29. . . . *the bride*— . . . . described, Ps. xlv. 9—17; Is. liv.; lxii. 4, 5—the church, 2 Co. xi. 2; Ep. v. 25—.7—the joy when the bride hath made herself ready, Rev. xix. 7—9—identified with outcast Israel, Is. liv. 4—8; Je. iii. 8—14—and with Jerusalem, Is. xlix. 14—.8—which as being given the name of her Husband is to be called 'The LORD our Righteousness,' Je. xxxiii. 16—identified with the New Jerusalem, Rev. xxi. 2—10.

NOTES.

22. *Land of Judæa;* i.e., the territory of Judæa, as distinguished from its metropolis.
And baptized. Jesus did not himself administer the sign—see ch. iv. 2. Thus what a king's servants do, is often spoken of as done by himself.
23. *Near to Salim.* Salim was a few miles west of Ænon.—See GEOGRAPHICAL NOTICE, p. 98.
Much water there, ὑδατα πολλα. 'Abundance of water.' 'A multitude of waters.' 'Many waters.'
24. *For John was not yet.*—See Lu. iii. 20, § 7, p. 55.
25. *A question.* Rather controversy; a dispute.
About purifying. [The methods of purification from ceremonial defilement were very different in form; but all represented the gradual purging of our conscience, heart, and life, by the word, the blood, and Spirit of Jesus Christ. He that offered the expiation-goat, or sprinkled his blood; he that led the scape-goat into the wilderness; he that burned the flesh of a sin-offering for the high priest or congregation; and the person or garment merely suspected of leprosy, was purified by a simple washing in water. The brazen pot wherein the flesh of a sin-offering had been boiled was to be *washed* and rinsed in water, Le. xvi., vi. 28, xiii., xiv. He that burned the red heifer, or cast the cedar-wood, scarlet, or hyssop into the fire; he that carried her ashes; he that sprinkled, or unnecessarily touched the water of separation; he that did eat or touch any part of the carcase of an unclean beast, washed himself in water, and continued unclean until the even, Nu. xix.; Le. xv.; De. xiv. xxiii.]
It would seem that the discussion was on the nature, efficacy, and necessity to Jews of baptismal purification, as καθαρισμος signifies in 2 Pe. i. 9: which, however, was closely connected with another, on the comparative efficacy of the baptism of John.

26. *Rabbi.* Master.—See ADDENDA, § 12, p. 87.
All men, παντες for οἱ πολλοι, 'very many;' by an hyperbole usual in the language of those who speak under the influence of passion and prejudice.
Come to him. Ερχονται προς αυτον, 'resort to him.'
27. *A man can receive nothing.* It is not from man, but from heaven, that the cleansing represented by baptism, and gift of the Spirit, must come. No one entrusted with a commission must exceed his commission.
28. *Bear me witness.* You remember that I told you I was not the Messiah, Mt. iii. 11, § 7, p. 54; Jno. i. 19, 20, § 10, p. 68. I came not to form *a separate party*, a peculiar sect, but that the people might be prepared for His coming; so far from indulging in envy, I greatly rejoice at his success.
29. *He that hath the bride, &c.* So the church, the bride of the Messiah, belongs to him—see Ep. v. 25—.7. It is *to be expected*, therefore, and *desired*, that the people should flock to him.

PRACTICAL REFLECTIONS.

22—.5 *ver.* Disputes about ceremonial purifying do not become the disciples of Jesus. It would have been well had they ended as they began, with John's disciples and the Jews.
[Soon may He give from above the washing of regeneration, and renewing of the Holy Ghost.]
26 *ver.* To the Jews, as being worldly-minded professors of religion, had they occupied John's position, the superior success of Jesus would have been a cause of great unhappiness; they would have deeply regretted having contributed to the introduction to public life of one who was likely to prove so powerful a supplanter. Let the servants of God beware of this spirit. Let us rather rejoice in seeing the work of God go forward, whether by means of ourselves, or others.
27 *ver.* With John, let us in all simplicity look up to our Father in heaven, from whom, through the Son of his love, the blessing alone can come.
[29 *ver.* Let the servants of the Lord beware of drawing attention to themselves, in place of introducing their hearers to Jesus.]

* Possibly Bethel, or Bethar, on the confines of Samaria and Judæa, twelve Roman miles from Jerusalem, and twenty-eight from Sychar.—See *Greswell*, Vol. II. Diss. xxi. pp. 210, .9.

A WORD SPOKEN IN DUE SEASON, HOW GOOD IS IT!—Prov. xv. 23.

JOHN iii. 30—.3.

friend of the bridegroom, which standeth and heareth him, rejoiceth greatly χαρα χαιρει
30 because of the bridegroom's voice: this my joy therefore is fulfilled. He must increase,
31 but I *must* decrease. He that cometh from above ανωθεν is above all: he that is of the earth is earthly, and speaketh of the earth: he that cometh from heaven is above all.
32 And what he hath seen and heard, that he testifieth; and no man receiveth his testi-
33 mony. He that hath received his testimony hath set to his seal εσφραγισεν that God is

SCRIPTURE ILLUSTRATIONS.

30. *he must increase*—' of the increase of his government and peace ... no end,' Is. ix. 7—'the stone that smote the image became a great mountain, and filled the whole earth,' Da. ii. 34, .5, 44, .5—the kingdom likened to a grain of mustard-seed, becoming the greatest of herbs, Mt. xiii. 31, .2, § 32—is to spread till 'the kingdoms of this world are become *the kingdoms* of our Lord, and of his Christ; and he shall reign for ever and ever,' Rev. xi. 14—.8.

I must decrease—John's baptism belonged to the ceremonial dispensation, Mt. xi. 11—.3, § 29—which was to pass away, He. ix. 10, *see* also xii. 27—' even that which was made glorious had no glory in this respect, by reason of the glory that excelleth,' 2 Co. iii. 10.

31. *from above*—so Jesus testified, Jno. viii. 23, § 55—' the second man is the Lord from heaven,' 1 Cor. xv. 47.

above all—*see* his exaltation as King over all, Ps. xlvii.—the four living creatures under the throne represent the hosts of Israel, Exc. i., x.—the children of Judah and of Israel to be gathered together, and appoint themselves one head, Ho. i. 11—'the LORD on the head of them,' Mi. ii. 13—'he is Lord of all,' Ac. x. 36—'over all, God blessed for ever,' Rom. ix. 5—'far above all principality, and power,' &c., Ep. i. 21—' a name which is above every name,'

Ph. ii. 9—11—' angels and authorities and powers being made subject unto him,' 1 Pe. iii. 22.

31. *earthly*—'as is the earthy, such are they also that are earthy,' 1 Co. xv. 48—'the natural man receiveth not the things of the Spirit of God; for they are foolishness unto him; neither can he know *them*, because they are spiritually discerned,' 1 Co. ii. 14—*see* as to 'carnal ordinances,' He. ix. 9, 10—'how turn ye again to the weak and beggarly elements?' Ga. iv. 9.

32. *no man receiveth his testimony*—although they were all baptized with John's baptism, Mk. i. 5, § 7, p. 52—but their observance of ceremonies had been like the conduct of children playing in the markets, Mt. xi. 16—.9, § 29—this neglect of Jesus' testimony had been predicted, Is. i. 2; liii. 1—3.

33. *set to his seal*—evidence or records were subscribed and sealed in the presence of witnesses, as Je. xxxii. 10—.2—God claims to have believing witnesses, as Is. xliii. 10—.2—*see* as to Abraham's faith, Rom. iv. 18—21—the apostle's trust in the Lord, 2 Ti. i. 12—'if we receive the witness of men, the witness of God is greater.... He that believeth on the Son of God hath the witness in himself,' 1 Jno. v. 9, 10—' with the heart man believeth unto righteousness; and with the mouth confession is made unto salvation,' Rom. x. 9, 10.

NOTES.

But the friend of the bridegroom. He whose office it is to attend him on the marriage occasion. This was commonly the dearest friend, and was a high honour.

[ὁ ἔχων τὴν νύμφην, &c. 'The subject is here *illustrated* by a similitude derived from common life, (as in Mt. ix. 15, § 36, und Mk. ii. 19, § 22,) in which the Baptist compares Christ to the *bridegroom* at a marriage feast, and himself to the παρανυμφος, or *brideman*; *i.e.*, a friend who had been employed to negociate the marriage, and had acted as his agent throughout the whole affair. The allusion at ἱστηκὼς χαίρει διὰ τὴν φωνὴν τοῦ νυμφίου is variously traced. But the words are, with most probability, supposed to allude to the ceremony of the formal interview, previous to marriage, of the betrothed pair; who were brought together by the brideman into a private apartment, at the door of which they were themselves stationed, so as to be able to distinguish any elevation of voice on the part of the future bridegroom in addressing his intended bride; from which, and from the *tone* of it, they would easily infer his satisfaction at the choice made for him by them, and feel corresponding joy.']

'The sense, then, may be thus expressed: "As at a marriage the bridegroom is the principal person, and his brideman willingly cedes to him the preference, and, rejoicing in his acceptance, is content to play an under part, so do I willingly sustain the part of an humble forerunner of Christ."'—*Bloomfield*.

30. *He must increase.* 'His kingdom and glory must increase to perfection, but my preparatory ministry will soon end.'

I must decrease. My teaching must *cease* when he is fully established, as the light of the morning star fades away and is lost in the beams of the rising sun.

31. *He that cometh from above.* The Messiah, represented as coming down from heaven.—*See* ver. 13, § 12, p. 85; ch. vi. 33, § 43; viii. 23, § 55.

He that is of the earth. He whose only origin or existence is in this world.

32. *And what he hath seen, &c.*—*See* ver. 11, § 12, p. 84. 'This is a beautiful instance of humility in John, and is his *third* testimony to the exalted character of Jesus, whom he had before pointed out as '*the Lamb of God, which taketh away the sin of the world.*' A man, though a prophet from God, can be of no greater dignity or authority than God has thought fit to confer on him. Jesus having entered upon his ministry, his kingdom and glory must increase to perfection; and John having fulfilled the office to which he was sent, a harbinger or messenger of the bridegroom, must retire and make room for Him whom the Father loveth, and into whose hands he hath given all things. The Baptist speaks officially, as it were, for the last time; he describes his own ministry as more than antiquated, and as almost superseded entirely: his own joy was now fulfilled; his proper part and province in a common work had been discharged, and were, therefore, to cease: Christ was to increase, and to go on increasing, while he was to decrease and to dwindle, in comparison to him, to nothing.'—*Grenvell*.

No man receiveth his testimony. The world flocked to a carnal ordinance, but few received 'the testimony of Jesus,' which 'is the spirit of prophecy,' Rev. xix. 10.

33. *He that hath received his testimony.* Hath received and fully believed his doctrine—hath yielded his *heart* to its influence.

PRACTICAL REFLECTIONS.

[30 ver. The more the true baptism, that of the Spirit, by Christ, does increase, the more will decrease a dependence upon outward ordinances.]

[31 ver. Carnal professors will have their minds occupied with carnal ordinances; and being themselves moved by earthly motives, will impute the same to others, as appears to have been the case with those Jews who thought to awaken discontent in the mind of John at the superior success of Jesus.]

He that is the true servant of God will both in his testimony and in his life acknowledge Christ as above all. And he that is risen with Christ will rise far above those mean and selfish considerations that keep in continual torment, envy, and enmity, the children of this world.

32 ver. Let every despised witness for the truth of God remember, that the truest and best accredited Witness that ever appeared in our world, was one whose message was least understood—was one who was himself the most despised and rejected of men.

A GRATEFUL MIND, IS A GREAT MIND.

PART II. JESUS DEPARTS INTO GALILEE. SECT. XIII.

JOHN iii. 34—iv. 3.

34 true. For he-whom God hath-sent speaketh the words of God: for God giveth not the
35 Spirit by measure *unto him*. The Father loveth the Son, and hath-given all-things
36 into his hand. He that-believeth on the Son hath everlasting life: and he that-
believeth-not the Son shall-·not·-see life; but the wrath of God abideth on him.

(G. 15.) *Jesus departs into Galilee; and,on his way, abides two days at Sychar in
Samaria—John not being yet cast into prison. John iv. 1—42.*

1 When therefore the Lord knew how the Pharisees had-heard that Jesus made and
2 baptized more disciples than John, (though Jesus himself baptized not, but his dis-
3 ciples,) he-left Judæa, and departed again into Galilee.

SCRIPTURE ILLUSTRATIONS.

God is true—so 2 Co. i. 18, .9—Christ is the 'truth,' Jno. xiv. 6, § 87—'was a minister of the circumcision for the truth of God, to confirm the promises made unto the fathers,' Rom. xv. 8—'all the promises of God in him *are* yea, and in him Amen,' 2 Co. i. 20— 'the faithful and true witness,' Rev. iii. 14.

34. *speaketh the words of God.*—' I will raise them up a Prophet from among their brethren, like unto thee, and will put my words in his mouth; and he shall speak unto them all that I shall command him,' De. xviii. 18—' he that sent me is true; and I speak to the world those things which I have heard of him.' Jno. viii. 26, 40, § 55—so again Jesus testified that he was that Prophet, who spake that which the Father had commanded him to speak, xii. 49, § 85; and again xiv. 10, 24, § 87.

giveth not the Spirit by measure unto him—the Spirit was seen descending upon him bodily, Lu. iii. 22, § 8, p. 59, and not like tongues of fire, representing individual members, as on the disciples, Ac. ii. 3, *comp.* 1 Co. xii.—' of his fulness have all we received, and grace for grace,' Jno. i. 16, § 7, p. 48—hath 'life in himself,' v. 26, § 23—' all fulness,' Col. i. 19—' all the fulness of the Godhead bodily,' ii. 9—' hath the seven spirits of God,' Rev. iii. 1, 5, 6.

35. *the Father loveth the Son*—so ch. v. 20, § 23—

'my beloved Son,' Mt. iii. 17, § 8, p. 60—'my beloved, in whom my soul is well pleased: I will put my spirit upon him,' xii. 18, § 26—*comp.* Is. xlii. 1— 'therefore doth my Father love me, because I lay down my life, that I might take it again,' Jno. x. 17, § 56—'as the Father hath loved me, so have I loved you,' xv. 9, § 87—the full enjoyment of the love, in the perfected unity, xvii. 23, .4, § 87.

all things—so Mt. xi. 27, § 29; Jno. xiii. 3, § 87; xvii. 2, § 10.—' Heir of all things,' He. i. 2—' for whom *are* all things,' ii. 10—as was predicted, Ps. ii. 8; viii. 5, 6; Da. vii. 14.

36. *he that believeth on the Son, &c.*—Ga. ii. 20, ' I live by the faith of the Son of God, who loved me, and gave himself for me.'—*See* the contrast of the case of the believer as viewed in the Son of God, to that of man as inheriting curse from the first Adam, Rom. v.

wrath—danger of incurring wrath for neglecting to embrace the Son, Ps. ii. 12—for holding the truth in unrighteousness, Rom. i. 18—for obeying not the truth, ii. 8, 9—coming wrath, 2 Th. i. 6, 9; Jude 15; Rev. vi. 15, .6; xiv. 9—11, .9, 20; xix. 15; xxi. 8.

iv. 2. *Jesus himself baptized not*—*see* also as to Paul, 1 Co. i. 10—.7.

NOTES.

33. *Hath set to his seal.* To seal an instrument is to make it sure, to acknowledge it as ours, to take it as ours, and to pledge our veracity that it is true and binding: as when a man seals a bond, a deed, or a will. Thus the meaning is: 'He who admits this doctrine doth thereby attest 'the truth of God in the fulfilment of his promises.' The sealing is by the Spirit through faith.

34. *Speaketh the words of God.* The *truth*, or substance of the law.

The Spirit. The Spirit of God. Though Jesus was God as well as man, yet as *Mediator* God anointed him, or endowed him with his Spirit, so as to be completely qualified for his great work.

[*By measure.* Not in a small degree. This is said with allusion to the *prophets*, the very greatest of whom were allowed by the Jewish rabbis to have only had the gifts of the Holy Spirit ἐκ μέρους. Nay, the law itself they considered as only given *ad mensuram*.]

35. *All things into his hand.* As king and judge universal.

36. *That believeth not.* ὁ ἀπειθῶν. The word includes both incredulity and disobedience. The full sense of the passage is well expressed by Bp. Jebb as follows: 'He who with his heart believeth in the Son is already in possession of eternal life; he, whatever may be his outward profession, whatever his theoretic or historical belief, who *obeyeth not* the Son, not only does not possess eternal life, he does not possess anything worthy to be called life at all. But this is not the whole; for as eternal life is the present possession of the faithful, so the wrath of God is the present and permanent lot of the disobedient; it abideth on him, not being removed by the atoning merits of the Redeemer.'

[iv. 2. *Though Jesus himself baptized not.* Had Jesus himself baptized with water, men might have been still more in danger of confounding John's baptism with that which it was promised Jesus should administer, ' *the baptism of the Spirit*.' As it is, there is no necessity for confounding the sign with the thing signified—' *the washing of regeneration, and renewing of the Holy Ghost.*']

PRACTICAL REFLECTIONS.

[33 *ver.* He that has truly received the testimony of Jesus thereby signifies his belief that God will prove true to all the promises—that the prophetic word is a great reality, of the full accomplishment of which the fullest pledge is given in the *first* coming of Christ.]

[34 *ver.* Jesus, the Sent of God, the Messenger of the covenant, had not come to set aside the words of God spoken in covenant unto the fathers, but to declare them more plainly. They do greatly err, who suppose that the words of Jesus are not according to the words of God by his servants the prophets.]

Although the several members of Christ are given the Spirit only in measure, it was not so with Him in whom dwelleth ' all the fulness of the Godhead bodily;' and from whom the body hath not yet received the fulness of the promised measure, which it is to receive when grown up unto the measure of the stature of the fulness of Christ.

35 *ver.* Although we do not yet see all things put under Christ, yet assuredly they shall be.

36 *ver.* How distinctive the state of him who believes on the Son. He hath everlasting life: and this must of course be manifested by his presenting a very different appearance from what he did when in spiritual death.

Let no man suppose that he can with impunity evade the great moral obligation of inquiring with sincerity and earnestness, what is truth. Life can only come through the belief of the truth. Men need not wait to know whether they will be condemned or not: already the wrath of God abideth on man; and from this he can be set free only through Him who hath borne the curse of the law for us.

iv. 1—3 *ver.* Let us learn, from the example of Jesus, to avoid giving occasion to the enemy to sow dissension among the children of God.

If baptizing with water had been in truth an introduction into the kingdom of God, it is not likely that Jesus would so easily have been induced to cease the practice of the rite. And we are to observe, that he was not only careful to give no occa-

DECLARE HIS GLORY AMONG THE HEATHEN, HIS WONDERS, ETC.—Psa. xcvi. 3.   [91

JOHN iv. 4—12.

4, 5 And he must-needs εδει go through Samaria. Then cometh-he to a-city of Samaria, which-is-called Sychar, near-to the parcel-of-ground that Jacob gave to his son Joseph.
6 Now Jacob's well was there. Jesus therefore, being-wearied κεκοπιακως with *his* journey, sat thus on the well: *and* it-was about the-sixth hour.
7 There-cometh a-woman of Samaria to-draw water: Jesus saith unto-her, Give me to-
8, 9 drink. (For his disciples were-gone-away unto the city to buy meat.) Then saith the woman of Samaria unto-him, How *is it that* thou, being a-Jew, askest drink of-me, which-am a-woman of-Samaria? for the-Jews have-'no-dealings συγχρωνται with-the-
10 Samaritans. Jesus answered and said unto-her, If thou-knewest the gift of God, and who it-is that saith to-thee, Give me to-drink; thou wouldest-have-asked-of him, and he-
11 would-have-given thee living water. The woman saith unto-him, Sir, thou-hast nothing to-draw-with, and the well is deep: from-whence then hast-thou that living
12 water? Art thou greater than our father Jacob, which gave us the well, and drank

SCRIPTURE ILLUSTRATIONS.

5. *Samaria*—built by Omri, 1 Kl. xvi. 23, 4—taken by the king of Assyria, 2 Kl. xvii. 5, 6; xviii. 9–12—given to be inhabited by the heathen, xvii. 24—6—its ruin had been predicted, Hos. viii. 5–7; Mic. i. 5–7—future restoration, Jer. xxxi. 4, 5—the gospel was to be preached in Samaria, Ac. i. 8; *fulfilm*. viii. 1, 4–25—churches edified therein, ix. 31.

Sychar—called Shechem, Ge. xxxiii. 18, 9—Joseph buried there, Jos. xxiv. 32.

that Jacob gave, &c.—this portion had been bought with money, Ge. xxxiii. 18–20; but had to be afterwards recovered with the sword—*see* Ge. xlviii. 22; also ch. xxxiv.

6. *wearied*—his becoming a wayfaring man predicted, Ps. cx. 7—'touched with the feeling of our infirmities,' He. iv. 15—able to succour,' ii. 18.

7. *draw water*—*see* case of Abraham's servant, Ge. xxiv. 11–3, 20, 43, 4; of Moses, Ex. ii. 15–7—joy at the drawing of water out of the wells of salvation predicted, Is. xii. 3.

9. *no dealings*—trading dealings they had, but not friendly intercourse: for the Samaritans were of foreign origin, superstitious, and idolatrous, 2 Kl. xvii. 24, 33–41; had ill-treated the Jews, Ezra iv. 1–6; Neh. vi. 1–14.

10. *gift of God*—the Father gives the Holy Spirit to them that ask him, Lu. xi. 13, § 62—not to be purchased with money, Ac. viii. 20—'is eternal life through Jesus Christ,' Rom. vi. 23.—See 'Notes,' ver. 14.

wouldest have asked—invitation to ask, Is. lv. 1, &c.; Zech. x. 1—'ask, and ye shall receive, that your joy may be full,' Jno. xvi. 24, § 87.

living water—God 'the fountain of living waters,' Jer. ii. 13—'fountain opened .... for sin and for uncleanness,' Zec. xiii. 1—foreshadowed by the water from the rock that followed Israel in the wilderness, 1 Cor. x. 4—'whosoever will, let him take the water of life freely,' Rev. xxii. 17.

NOTES.

5. *Sychar.* The place was originally called Σιχεμ, 'Shechem,' or 'Sychar,' from the name of the person of whose family Jacob bought the land.—*See* Ge. xxxiii. 18. The name is supposed to have been altered by the Jews to Σιχαρ, to denote the drunkenness or the idolatry of the inhabitants.

Near to the parcel of ground. πλησιον του χωριου, 'near the heritage.' The word means, 'an estate in land,' and is properly denominated 'heritage,' agreeably to what we are told, Jos. xxiv. 32.

6. *Jacob's well.*—See Geographical Notice, p. 98.

On the well. The Greek, επεκειτο, simply signifies he sat, not upon a stone, seat, or cushion, but as the circumstances of the case required, by the side of it, on the brink of it, upon the ground.

The sixth hour. 'According to St. John's computation of time, which is the modern, this would be at six o'clock in the evening; and this is the most usual time in the east for fetching water. After the autumnal equinox and near to midwinter, it would be necessarily dark; but after the vernal equinox and near to midsummer, it would still be open day.'—*Greswell*, Vol. II. p. 216.

7. *Of Samaria.* Not of the *city* of Samaria, but from the city of Sychar, in Samaria.

9. *No dealings.* The Jews say, 'It is an abomination to eat the bread or drink the wine of a Samaritan.'

Samaritans.—See Addenda, 'Samaritans,' p. 9ᵈ.

10. *Living water.* ὑδωρ ζων, i.e., 'running water,' as that of fountains, and rivers, in opposition to dead, i.e., stagnant pools of water.—*See* Ge. xxvi. 19; Le. xiv. 5. The sanctifying and comforting influences

of the Holy Spirit, conferring, sustaining, and perfecting spiritual life.

[11. *Hast nothing to draw with.* The woman understood it in its natural sense, but our Lord employed it figuratively for ζωοποιων; it being his custom, from things corporeal, to stir up the minds of his hearers to the study and knowledge of things spiritual. It is, indeed, common in the Scriptures and the rabbinical writers to liken unto spring water that which refreshes and blesses the souls of men.—See Pr. x. 11, *'The mouth of a righteous man is a well of life: but violence covereth the mouth of the wicked;'* and especially Je. ii. 13, which seems the origin of the expression: an image most apt and expressive; since, in the hot countries of the east, pure water is reckoned among the blessings of life.]

12. *Art thou greater?* This has reference to what our Lord had just before said, *'If thou knewest the gift of God, and who it is that saith to thee.'* The words following are as much as to say, 'It was good enough for our ancestor Jacob, who himself drank of it, &c.; which he would not have done, if he had known a better. If thou canst shew us a better, thou wilt, in that respect, be greater than Jacob.'

Our father Jacob. The Samaritans took it for granted that they were the children of Joseph; we have no evidence however that they were so: Ephraim had indeed been given this portion, but the whole seed of Ephraim had been cast among the Gentiles, Je. vii. 15; and these Samaritans who now dwell in the portion of Ephraim appear to have been of Gentile origin.

Which gave us, &c.—See Ge. xlviii. 22.

PRACTICAL REFLECTIONS.

sion to its being said that he made disciples by that rite, but began very sedulously to explain that the water which was truly efficacious was the living water—that which springeth up unto everlasting life; not by the mere water wherewith he washed his disciples' feet, but by the word which he spake unto them.—Those who hate the gospel will always be exasperated at its success. And, if duty do not require us to stand, it is best to avoid their resentment by flight.

6–10 *ver.* Let us admire and imitate the diligence of the great Shepherd of the sheep in the ministry of the gospel: although weary and hungry and thirsty,

he fully improves the opportunity given him of instructing a poor ignorant, superstitious, and sinful Samaritan woman.

Let us earnestly seek to know the gift of God, and Him through whom that gift is given, and we shall not fail to ask and obtain that rich consolation which can only come through the enjoyment of the Spirit of God in Christ Jesus.

11 *ver.* The woman of Samaria was a singular instance of mistaking the language of our blessed Lord when speaking of the living water—the Holy Spirit in his cleansing power and refreshing influence.

PART II.   JESUS AT THE WELL OF SYCHAR.   SECT. XIII.

JOHN iv. 13—21.

13 thereof himself, and his children, and his cattle? Jesus answered and said unto-her,
14 Whosoever drinketh of this water shall-thirst again: but whosoever drinketh of the water that I shall-give him shall-'never εις τον αιωνα'-thirst; but the water that I-shall-give him shall-be in him a-well of-water springing-up ἁλλομενου into everlasting life.
15 The woman saith unto him, Sir, give me this water, that I-thirst not, neither come
16 hither to-draw. Jesus saith unto-her, Go, call thy husband, and come hither.
17 The woman answered and said, I-have no husband. Jesus said unto-her, Thou-hast-
18 well'-said, I-have no husband: for thou-hast-had five husbands; and he-whom thou-
19 now'-hast is not thy husband: in that saidst-thou truly. The woman saith unto-him,
20 Sir, I-perceive θεωρω that thou art a-prophet. Our fathers worshipped in this moun-
21 tain; and ye say, that in Jerusalem is the place where *men* ought to-worship. Jesus

SCRIPTURE ILLUSTRATIONS.

14. *never thirst*—prediction as to deliverance from thirst, Is. xlix. 10—*confirm.*, Jno. vi. 35, § 43; Rev. vii. 16.

springing up—'rivers of living water,' Jno. vii. 38, 9, § 55—the Comforter, the Spirit of truth, xiv. 16, .7, § 87—'waters issued out from under the threshold of the house eastward,' &c., Eze. xlvii. 1—'a pure river of water of life, clear as crystal, proceeding out of the throne of God and of the Lamb,' Rev. xxii. 1.

15. *give me, &c.*—so had Jesus been misunderstood as to the new birth, Jno. iii. 4, § 12, p. 83; so as to the bread, Jno. vi. 31, § 43—'the natural man re-

ceiveth not the things of the Spirit of God: for they are foolishness unto him: neither can he know *them*, because they are spiritually discerned,' 1 Co. H. 14.

20. *this mountain*—Mt. Gerizim and Mt. Ebal were the places where the tribes made a public recognition of the blessing and the curse—(appointed, De. xxvii. 12, .3); Jos. viii. 32—.5.

in Jerusalem—a place west of Jordan, had been spoken of by Moses, as to be appointed for united worship, De. xii. 1—11—the Lord chose Jerusalem conditionally, 2 Ch. vii. 12—22—'shall choose Jerusalem again,' Zec. ii. 12—under the new covenant, Je. iii.14—.7.

NOTES.

12. *And his children.* οἱ υἱοί, *i.e.*, the family in general, including the servants, as in Ge. xiv. 11, '*And there will I nourish thee; for yet there are five years of famine; lest thou, and thy household, and all that thou hast, come to poverty.*' This, and the mention of the cattle conjoined, is agreeable to the simplicity of early times, especially in the east.

14. *The water that I shall give him.* Jesus here refers without doubt to his *teaching*, his *grace*, his *Spirit*, and the benefits which come into the soul that embraces his gospel. It is a striking image, and especially in eastern countries, where there are vast deserts and often a great want of water.

[*Shall never thirst.* οὐ μὴ διψήσῃ εἰς τὸν αἰῶνα, *i.e.*, shall have nothing more ever to desire.—See Rev. vii. 16. 'Meaning that the vivifying effect of the "word of life" shall be such as to satisfy the most ardent desires of the soul; which, placing its happiness in God and his worship, no other desire will be thought of. Also, that such is the nature of that truth, that by its purifying and sanctifying influence on the soul, it is, as it were, an ever-springing fountain of holy affections, producing comfort here, and everlasting happiness hereafter.']

16. *Go, call thy husband.* By thus shewing her that he knew her life, he convinced her that he was qualified to teach her the way to heaven.

[18. *Is not thy husband.* οὐκ ἔστι σ. ἀ. 'Is not [really] thy husband. It appears that the woman had been five times married; but whether those marriages had been dissolved by death, or by divorce, does not appear. Both might be the case; and as divorce was then shamefully prevalent, this implies no certainty of infidelity on the part of the woman.]

19. *I perceive...a prophet.* The woman is justly amazed that a *stranger* should be acquainted with the general tenour of her life—*see* ver. 29, p. 95. Such knowledge she knew could not be acquired but by Divine revelation, and therefore she justly inferred that Jesus must be at least a *prophet*; and, as such, be a proper authority to appeal to for the solution of the controverted question, as to the comparative holiness of the Jewish and the Samaritan places of common national worship.

20. *Our fathers.* The Samaritans: perhaps also

meaning to intimate that the patriarchs had done it also; Ge. xii. 6, 7, '*And Abram passed through the land unto the place of Sichem, unto the plain of Moreh,.. . there builded he an altar unto the* LORD.' And of Jacob it is said, xxxiii. 20, '*And he erected there an altar, and called it El-elohe-Israel.*'

In this mountain. Mount Gerizim, but a little way from Sychar.

[The Samaritans maintained that on this mountain Abraham and Jacob had erected an altar, and offered sacrifices to Jehovah—*see* above; and therefore, that the Deity had willed *blessing* to be pronounced from thence, and an altar to be erected, alleging in proof De. xxvii. 4, 12, .3, 4, '*Therefore it shall be when ye be gone over Jordan, that ye shall set up these stones, which I command you this day, in mount Ebal, and thou shalt plaister them with plaister.*' 12, .3, '*These shall stand upon mount Gerizim to bless the people, when ye are come over Jordan; Simeon, and Levi, and Judah, and Issachar, and Joseph, and Benjamin: and these shall stand upon mount Ebal to curse; Reuben, Gad, and Asher, and Zebulun, Dan, and Naphtali:*' and, in order to 'make surety doubly sure,' interpolating the word at ver. 4, and changing גריזים for עיבל, Gerizim. Hence they called it 'the blessed mount,' 'the holy place.' Not only did the Samaritans then worship on mount Gerizim, but the remnant of them yet subsisting continue to do so three times in the year, with great solemnity. On this mountain Sanballat had built a temple for his son-in-law Manasseh; it was destroyed by John Hyrcanus, the high priest. Sanballat was chief governor of the Cuthites, of the Samaritans, and a secret enemy to Nehemiah.]

Ye say. Ye Jews say.

In Jerusalem. As it was contemplated in the law of Moses that there should be but one place to offer sacrifice and to hold the great feasts, so it followed that the Samaritans were in error in supposing that *their* temple was the place.

21. *Worship the Father.* Both places were to be laid waste, as being neglected of God; the worship offered there being not '*in spirit and in truth.*' It is worthy of remark, that all worship is most carefully shut out from the place formerly occupied by the temple at Jerusalem, except that of Muhammed, which most expressly refuses to acknowledge God as a Father.

PRACTICAL REFLECTIONS.

12 *ver.* Our heavenly Father is not less provident with regard to his spiritual offspring who truly ask him for blessing, than was our father Jacob to his family, for whom it is said he provided the well at Sychar.

13, .4. Other delights perish in the using, and will be found wanting when those who have sought their enjoyment will stand most in need of comfort: but he who hath the Comforter hath that which shall rejoice him for ever.

We may learn here: 1st. That the Christian has a never-failing source of consolation, adapted to all times and circumstances.—2nd. That religion has its seat in the heart, and that it should constantly *live* there.—3rd. That it sheds its blessings on a world of sin, and is manifest by a constant *life* of piety, like an ever-bubbling spring.—4th. That its end is everlasting *life*. It will continue for ever; and *whosoever drinks of it shall never thirst*, for in him there is a pure fountain *springing up into everlasting life.*

I AM ALPHA AND OMEGA.—Rev. xxii. 13.   [93]

SECT. XIII.   JESUS MAKES HIMSELF KNOWN.   PART II.

JOHN iv. 22—.6.

saith unto-her, Woman, believe me, the-hour cometh, when ye-shall-·neither in this
22 mountain, nor-yet at Jerusalem,'-worship the Father. Ye worship ye-know not what:
we-know what we worship προσκυνουμεν ὁ οιδαμεν: for salvation σωτηρια is of the Jews.
23 But the-hour cometh, and now is, when the true worshippers shall-worship the Father
24 in spirit and in-truth: for the Father seeketh such to-worship him. God is a-Spirit:
25 and they that-worship him must worship him in spirit and in-truth. The woman
saith unto-him, I-know that Messias cometh, which is called Christ: when he is-come,
26 he-will-tell αναγγελει us all-things. Jesus saith unto-her, I that speak unto-thee am he.

SCRIPTURE ILLUSTRATIONS.

21. *this mountain, nor at Jerusalem*—' a great forsaking in the midst of the land,' Is. vi. 9—12—desolation both of Samaria and Jerusalem predicted, Mic. i. 5, 6; iii.

22. *ye worship ye know not what*—see as to the first institution of the Samaritan worship, 2 Ki. xvii. 24—41 —see Ezra iv. 2—the Athenians made an acknowledgment of similar ignorance, Ac. xvii. 23.

salvation is of the Jews—the Shiloh predicted to come of Judah, Ge. xlix. 10—' will place salvation in Zion for Israel my glory,' Is. xlvi. 13—' ten men shall take hold out of all languages of the nations, even shall take hold of the skirt of him that is a Jew,' Zec. viii. 23—' our Lord sprang out of Juda,' He. vii. 14—called ' Jesus: for he shall save his people from their sins,' Mat. i. 21, § 2, p. 13.

23. *true worshippers*—' open ye the gates, that the righteous nation which keepeth the truth may enter in,' Is. xxvi. 2—' desirest truth in the inward parts,' Ps. li. 6—*see* Zeph. iii. 9, 13.

spirit—' praying always with all prayer and supplication in the Spirit,' Eph. vi. 18—' worship God in the spirit,' Phil. iii. 3—' praying in the Holy Ghost,' Jude 20—*see* also Jno. vi. 63, § 43; Rom. viii. 1; 1 Cor. xiv. 15; 2 Cor. iii. 6—9; 1 Pet. iii. 18.

truth—' grace and truth came by Jesus Christ,' Jno. i. 17, § 7, p. 48—' I am the way, the truth, and the life: no man cometh unto the Father, but by me,' xiv. 6, § 87—' the LORD is nigh unto all them that call upon him, to all that call upon him in truth,' Ps. cxlv. 18—' whatsoever ye shall ask the Father in my name, he will give it you,' Jno. xvi. 23, § 87.

seeketh such to worship him—' a godly seed,' Mal. ii. 15—' ye are a chosen generation,' &c., 1 Pe. ii. 9—it had been predicted that the good Shepherd would seek out his sheep that had been scattered, Eze. xxxiv. 11—.3—' that which was lost,' ver. 16—' the Son of man is come to seek and to save that which was lost,' Lu. xix. 10, § 80—' the lost sheep of the house of Israel,' Mat. x. 6, § 39—of which, see, as contrasted with treacherous Judah, Je. iii. 11—.8.

24. *God is a Spirit*—' ye heard the voice of the words, but saw no similitude,' De. iv. 12—' the LORD, the God of the spirits of all flesh,' Nu. xxvii. 16—' the Father of spirits,' He. xii. 9—' no man hath seen God at any time,' 1 Jno. iv. 12—' now the Lord is that Spirit: and where the Spirit of the Lord is, there is liberty,' 2 Cor. iii. 17.

26. *I that speak unto thee am he*—' it is he that talketh with thee,' Jno. ix. 37, § 55—so when adjured by the high priest, Mk. xiv. 61, .2, § 89.

NOTES.

22. *Ye worship ye know not what.* Though the Samaritans received the five books of Moses, yet they rejected the prophets, and of course all that the prophets had said respecting the true God. Originally, also, they had joined the worship of idols to that of the true God.—*See* 2 Ki. xvii. 26—31.

Salvation is of the Jews. Christ the Saviour sprung of them, as also did the twelve apostles, and in general the first preachers of the gospel: the gospel proceeded from them to the Gentiles.

23. *And now is.* The old dispensation is about to pass away, and the new one to commence. *Already* there is so much light that God may be worshipped acceptably in any place.

The true worshippers. All who worship God with the *heart*, and not merely in *form*.

[*In truth.* Not through the medium of shadows and types; not by means of sacrifices and bloody offerings,' . . . . *a figure for the time then present*, in which were offered both gifts and sacrifices, that could not make him that did the service perfect, as pertaining to the conscience,' He. ix. 9: but in the manner represented or typified by all these—in the *true* way of direct access to God through Jesus Christ. ' *For Christ is not entered into the holy places made with hands, which are the figures of the true; but into heaven itself, now to appear in the presence of God for us,*' ver. 24, ib.]

For the Father seeketh, &c. Jesus came to fulfil his Father's will; he came ' *to seek and save that which was lost*,' Lu. xix. 10, § 80. ' Salvation ' was to be ' of the Jews,' unto a people who were to be sought out; that in them the Lord might more particularly manifest the wonders of redeeming love.

24. *God is a Spirit.* This is the *second* reason why men should worship him in spirit and in truth. ' *The Most High dwelleth not in temples made with hands*,' Ac. vii. 48; ' *neither is worshipped with men's hands, as though he needed anything, seeing he giveth to all life, and breath, and all things*,' xvii. 25. A pure, a holy, a spiritual worship, therefore, is such as he seeks—the offering of the *soul* rather than the *formal* offering of the *body*—the homage of the *heart* rather than that of the *lips*.

25. *I know that Messias cometh.* As the Samaritans acknowledged the five books of Moses, so they expected also the coming of the Messiah.

Will tell us all things. Jesus had decided the question proposed to him, ver. 20, in favour of the Jews. The woman seems not to have been fully satisfied, and therefore was disposed, as was customary in that age, to leave the matter undecided till the advent of the Messiah, who would finally determine these controversies.

26. *I am he.* I am the Messiah.—*See* Nathanael's concession, Jno. i. 49, § 10, p. 73.

PRACTICAL REFLECTIONS.

20 ver. Let us beware of making religion consist in attention to outward forms, instead of heart devotion to God, through the knowledge of his mercy and truth in the gift of his Son.

[21 ver. Let us see the truth of the Saviour of Israel confirmed, in the fulfilment of his prediction with regard to the ceasing of the true worship of God, even in the place he had himself specially appointed for meeting with his people.]

22, .3 ver. Let us never forget, that the salvation which hath been so remarkably manifested towards us was of the Jews, and that it was sent from them to us, that we might become the true worshippers, who should ' worship the Father in spirit and in truth.'

23 ver. Let us know, that as truly as the former prediction, with regard to the ceasing of true worship in the land, has been fulfilled, so truly will this purpose of God with regard to the true worshippers be fully accomplished also.

[24 ver. He who was sent of the Father to seek and to save the lost sheep of the house of Israel hath found as in the outward manifestation of his grace: may he also find in us the character of the people he hath for so long a time been forming for his praise.]

Let it be duly impressed upon us, that no mere outward ceremonies will suffice,—that God who is a Spirit can only be worshipped aright after his own nature, ' *in spirit and in truth.*'

25 ver. Let us beware of putting away from us that true knowledge of God and his ways which he is even now able and willing to bestow.

| PART II. | JESUS AT THE WELL OF SYCHAR. | SECT. XIII. |

JOHN iv. 27—37.

27 And upon this came his disciples, and marvelled that he-talked with the-woman: yet
28 no-man said, What seekest-thou? or, Why talkest-thou with her? The woman then
29 left her water-pot, and went-her-way into the city, and saith to-the men, Come, see a-
30 man, which told me all-things that-ever ὅσα I-did: is not this the Christ? Then
they-went out-of the city, and came unto him.
31, .2 In the mean-while *his* disciples prayed him, saying, Master, eat. But he said
33 unto-them, I have meat to-eat that ye know not-*of.* Therefore said the disciples one-to
34 another, Hath-·any-man·-brought him *ought* to-eat? Jesus saith unto-them, My meat
35 is to do ἵνα ποιῶ the will of him-that-sent me, and to-finish τελειώσω his work. Say
not ye, There-are yet four-months, and *then* cometh harvest? behold, I-say unto-you,
Lift-up your eyes, and look-on θεάσασθε the fields; for they-are white already to
36 harvest. And he that-reapeth receiveth wages, and gathereth fruit unto life eternal:
37 that both he that-soweth and he that-reapeth may-rejoice together. And herein is that

SCRIPTURE ILLUSTRATIONS.

34. *my meat, &c.*—so Job xxiii. 12, 'I have esteemed the words of his mouth more than my necessary *food*'—predicted of Christ, Ps. xl. 7, 8—*confirm.*, Lu. ii. 49, § 6, p. 41; Jno. vi. 38, § 43; xvii. 4, § 67—our example, He. xii. 2.

35. *harvest*—is the reaping time—promised continuance of, Ge. viii. 22—is a proper time for work, Pr. x. 5—is put for a people whose sins are ripe for judgment, Je. li. 33—and the gathering of the people to the gospel, Mt. ix. 36, .7, § 39; Lu. x. 2, § 60—the end of the world, or 'the day of the Lord,' Mt. xiii. 39, § 33; Joel iii. 13; Rev. xiv. 15.

36. *both he that soweth and he that reapeth*—'cast thy bread upon the waters: for thou shalt find it after many days,' Ecc. xi. 1—'blessed *are* ye that sow beside all waters,' Is. xxxii. 20—'they that sow in tears shall reap in joy,' Ps. cxxvi. 5, 6—'they that be wise shall shine as the brightness of the firmament; and they that turn many to righteousness is the stars for ever and ever,' Da. xii. 3—*see* as to Paul's service in the gospel, 1 Cor. ix. 19—23; Phil. ii. 15, .6; 1 Th. ii. 19, 20; 2 Tim. iv. 7, 8—the reaping, Rev. xiv. 14—.6.

NOTES.

27. *Marvelled.* Wondered. They wondered because the Jews had no intercourse with the Samaritans, and they were surprised that Jesus was engaged with her in conversation, for our Lord seemed rarely to converse with females, and the Jewish rabbies considered it indecorous for a doctor to hold public conversation with a woman, even though she were his wife, sister, or daughter.

What seekest thou? A popular expression, meaning, 'What is your purpose, or business?'

[29. *Is not this the Christ?* μήτι οὗτός ἐστιν ὁ Χρ. 'The woman seems to have meant, courteously, to propose this rather as a question for their *consideration,* than to *affirm* it, at least by implication. In short, the sense expressed in full would be, "Is this the Christ, or is he not?" The latter member being implied and suggested by the τι indefinite. which signifies *perhaps.* So I would understand Mt. xii. 23, μήτι οὗτός ἐστιν ὁ υἱὸς Δαυΐδ; besides other passages. The context, indeed, can alone, in such cases, decide whether belief or disbelief preponderated, and thus determine the exact sense.'—*Bloomfield.*]

32. *I have meat to eat.* 'I have mental and spiritual enjoyments.' In the scriptural and rabbinical phraseology that is said to be any one's meat or drink, whereby he is supported, refreshed, or delighted.

34. *My meat, &c.* Jesus here explains what he said in ver. 32. His great object—the great design of his life—was to do the will of God. He came to that place weary and thirsty; an opportunity of doing good presented itself, and he found comfort and joy in doing the will of God—of Him that sent him.

The will of him that sent me. The will of God in regard to the salvation of men.—*See* Jno. vi. 38, § 43.

To finish his work. To complete or fully to do the work which he has commanded in regard to the salvation of men. It is *his* work to provide salvation, and his to redeem, and his to apply the salvation to the heart. Jesus came to *do it* by teaching, by his example, and by dying to redeem.

35. *Four months, &c.* In Palestine there are about four months between the time of sowing and that of reaping; in other countries, generally more: but here the seed sown in the woman at the well immediately produces a plentiful harvest, in the many willing hearers who may now have been seen coming from the city to welcome the Saviour of the world. This was a most expressive answer to the question of the disciples, '*Why talkest thou with her?*' And thus were they taught to be diligent '*in season and out of season.*'—*And see* ADDENDA, p. 99, ' *On John* iv. 35.'

36. *He that reapeth.* Ὁ θερίζων. Meaning one employed in any sort of *harvest-work.* [Here we have, as Rosenmuller observes, a blending of the apodosis with the comparison. The sense being, 'As the agricultural labourer receives his wages, whether for ploughing and sowing, or for reaping and gathering the corn, so shall ye receive your reward for gathering men unto the kingdom of God; and whether your labour be only preparatory, or such as consummates the spiritual harvest, ye shall alike be blessed with an ample recompense.'—*Bloomfield.*]

Gathereth fruit unto life eternal. Converts souls, who shall inherit eternal life.

That both he that soweth, &c. It is the same work; and whatever part we may do, we should rejoice. God gives the increase, while Paul may plant, and Apollos water. The teacher in the Sunday school who sows the seed in early life shall rejoice with the minister of the gospel who may gather in the harvest; and if any good be effected, the praise is God's. To God belongs the praise.

PRACTICAL REFLECTIONS.

7—26 *ver.* 'From the whole of this discourse we may learn, 1st. The great art and wisdom of the Lord Jesus in leading the thoughts along to the subject of practical personal religion.—2nd. His knowledge of the heart and of the life; he must be, therefore, Divine. —3rd. He gave evidence here that he was the Messiah. —4th. We see *our* duty. It is to seize on all occasions to lead sinners to the belief that Jesus is the Christ, and to make use of all topics of conversation to teach them the nature of religion. There never was a model of so much wisdom in this as the Saviour; and we shall be successful only as we diligently study his character.—5th. We see the nature of true religion. It does not consist merely in external forms. It is pure, spiritual, active—a well, an ever-flowing fountain. It is the worship of a pure and holy God, where the *heart* is offered, and where the desires of an humble soul are breathed out for salvation.'

27 *ver.* Let us not question any of the words and works of Jesus.—Let us believe that he is right, even if we cannot fully understand all that he does.

29 *ver.* Let us, like the woman of Samaria, spread before others the evidence that Jesus is the Christ, and invite them to come and have personal knowledge of his being indeed the Sent of God.

31—*.4 ver.* Let us truly do the will of God from the heart, so shall we find the saying true, '*In the keeping of his commandments there is a great reward,*' and with Jesus say, '*My meat is to do the will of him that sent me.*'

34 *ver.* Let us not look for provision from God apart from the service unto which he hath called us, and let us be careful to finish the work he hath appointed us, ere we look for the full reward.

If he was so diligent for *our* welfare, if he bore fatigue and want to benefit *us,* then *we* should be diligent also in regard to our *own* salvation, and also in seeking the salvation of others.

JOHN iv. 38—42.

38 saying true, One soweth αλλος ὁ σπειρων, and another reapeth αλλος ὁ θεριζων. I sent you to reap that whereon ye bestowed-'no· labour: other-men laboured, and ye are-entered into their labours
39 And many of-the Samaritans of that city believed on him for the saying of-the woman, 40 which-testified, He-told me all that-ever ὁσα I-did. So when the Samaritans were-come unto him, they-besought him that-he-would-tarry with them: and he-abode there 41 two days. And many more believed because-of his-own word; and said unto-the 42 woman, Now we-believe, not because-of thy saying: for we-have-heard *him* ourselves, and know that this is indeed the Christ, the Saviour of-the world.

NOTES.

37. *One soweth, &c.* The application of the proverb is, that as Moses and the prophets, and finally John the Baptist, prepared the minds of men for receiving the gospel from Christ, so will the New Testament messengers reap the harvest of converts for which He had prepared.

40. *He abode there two days.* δύο ἡμέρας. He abode there *so long*, that he might not seem to slight persons desirous to learn.
41. *Many more believed.* ἐπίστευσαν, *i.e.*, professed to believe in him as the promised Messiah.
42. *The Saviour of the world.* σωτήρ του κοσμου, and not of the Jews only. So much more correct on this subject were the ideas of the Samaritans than those of the Jews.

PRACTICAL REFLECTIONS.

35, 6 *ver.* The word which was sown by the prophets began to be reaped in the days of the apostles. Then were the first fruits gathered, but the fulness of the harvest yet remains to be enjoyed; and when it is brought home, then both he that soweth and he that reapeth shall rejoice together.

37 *ver.* Let us duly regard the labours of others whilst diligent in our own measure of service; and in all things look to the great Lord of the harvest, who alone can rightly direct and fully support us, and unto whom all the glory is due.

Every part of the work of the ministry, and of teaching men, is needful, and we should rejoice that we are permitted to bear any part, however humble, in bringing sinners to the knowledge of our Lord and Saviour Jesus Christ, 1 Cor. xii. 21—.4.

We should never despair of doing good in the most unpromising circumstances; and we should seize upon every opportunity to converse with sinners on the great subject of their souls' salvation.

42 *ver.* Let us be able not merely to report what others say of Christ, but be able to speak from our personal knowledge of him.

From our blessed Lord's example, let us guard against sectarianism. ' Alas,' says Bishop Taylor, ' that men whom God hath made of the same flesh and blood—men on whom he daily causes his sun to rise and his rain to fall—men involved in the same condemnation, and dependent on the same revelation of mercy—alas! that such men, that any man, should dare to say to his fellow man, " Stand by, for I am holier than thou." Rather let us, like our Divine Master, *"be instant in season and out of season,"* going "*about doing good.*"'

GEOGRAPHICAL NOTICES.

SAMARIA.—See 'Historical Sketch,' p. ix.

ÆNON was about eight miles south of Scythopolis, and contiguous to Salim, where there was much water—probably a fountain divided into many streams. The word Ænon means fountain.

SALEM, or *Satim,* where John baptized, was probably a place near Shechem, whither Jacob came as he returned from Mesopotamia; but some commentators translate the word Shalem, *safe and sound*, or, *in peace*, Jno. iii. 23; Ge. xxxiii. 18. It was probably here that Melchisedek was king, and came to meet Abraham in his return southward, from smiting Chedorlaomer and his allies. It is certain Jerusalem, which was afterwards by contraction called *Salem*, Ps. lxxvi. 2, was then called Jebus, and was far off the way between Damascus and Sodom; whereas Shalem was directly on the way, when one came south by the west side of Jordan, Ge. xiv.

SHECHEM, SYCHEM, or SYCHAR.—*Neapolis, Naplouse, Napalose,* or *Nabulus.*

' SHECHEM was a very ancient place, though we do not find it mentioned as a city until the time of Jacob. *" And Abram passed through the land unto the place of Sichem, unto the plain of Moreh. And the Canaanite was then in the land,"* Ge. xii. 6. *" And Jacob came to Shalem, a city of Shechem, which is in the land of Canaan, when he came from Padan-aram ; and pitched his tent before the city.* (East of the latter city.) *And he bought a parcel of a field, where he had spread his tent, at the hand of the children of Hamor, Shechem's father, for an hundred pieces of money,"* xxxiii. 18, .9.

This corresponds to the present village of Salim, which lies east of Nabulus across the great plain. In this plain the patriarch encamped, and purchased the " parcel of ground," still marked by his well, and the traditional tomb of Joseph. It was here that Dinah was defiled by Shechem, the son of Hamor, prince of the country, and the city *Shechem*, with its gates, is spoken of, named probably after that prince. It would seem not then to have been large, inasmuch as the two sons of Jacob were able to overcome and slay all the males, *see* Ge. xxxiv. Jacob's field, as we have seen, was a permanent possession; and the patriarch, even when residing at Hebron, sent his flocks to pasture in this neighbourhood. It was on a visit to them in this region that Joseph was sold by his brethren: " *And his brethren went to feed their father's flock in Shechem. And Israel said unto Joseph, Do not thy brethren feed the flock in Shechem? come, and I will send thee unto them. And he said to him, Here am I. And he said to him, Go, I pray thee, see whether it be well with thy brethren, and well with the flocks; and bring me word again. So he sent him out of the vale of Hebron, and he came to Shechem,"* Ge. xxxvii. 12—.4.

' On the return of the Israelites from Egypt, after they had passed over Jordan, they were directed to set up great stones and build an altar on mount Ebal; and to station six of the tribes upon mount Gerizim to bless the people, and six upon mount Ebal to curse. Between these two mountains, according to Josephus, lay Shechem, having Ebal on the north and Gerizim on the south. In the division of the land, Shechem fell to the lot of Ephraim, but was assigned to the Levites, and made a city of refuge: *" For they gave them Shechem with her suburbs in mount Ephraim,* to be *a city of refuge for the slayer,"* Jos. xxi. 21.

' Here Joshua met the assembled people for the last time: *" And Joshua gathered all the tribes of Israel to Shechem, and called for the elders of Israel, and for their heads, and for their judges, and for their officers; and they presented themselves before God.* So Joshua made a covenant *with the people that day, and set them a statute and an ordinance in Shechem. And the bones of Joseph, which the children of Israel brought up out of Egypt, buried they in Shechem, in a parcel of ground which Jacob bought of the sons of Hamor the father of Shechem for an hundred pieces of silver: and it became the inheritance of the children of Joseph,"* Jos. xxiv. 1, 25, 32.

' In the days of the judges, Abimelech treacherously got possession of the city, which gave occasion for the beautiful parable of Jotham, delivered from mount

PART II.   SHECHEM—SYCHEM—SYCHAR.   SECT. XIII.

GEOGRAPHICAL NOTICES.—SYCHAR—(*continued.*)

Gerizim; the end the people proved treacherous to the usurp and he destroyed the city, Ju. ix.

'At Shechen all Israel came together to make Rehoboam king: "*And Rehoboam went to Shechem: for all Israel were come to Shechem to make him king,*" 1 Ki. xii. 1. Here the ten tribes rebelled, and the city became for a time the royal residence of Jeroboam: "*Then Jeroboam built Shechem in mount Ephraim, and dwelt therein; and went out from thence, and built Penuel,*" ver. 25.

'We hear nothing more of it before the exile; during which it seems still to have been inhabited: "*There came certain from Shechem, from Shiloh, and from Samaria, even fourscore men, having their beards shaven, and their clothes rent, and having cut themselves, with offerings and incense in their hand, to bring them to the house of the LORD,*" Je. xli. 5. After the exile, Shechem is mainly known as the chief seat of the people who thenceforth bore the name of Samaritans.

'Sichem, at the foot of Gerizim, became the metropolis of the Samaritans, and was inhabited by Gentiles, mixed with apostate Jews.

'The modern history of "*Shechem,*" "*Sichem,*" now Nabulus, and the surrounding region, is one of wars and rebellion. These districts were formerly regarded as among the most dangerous in Palestine.

'If of old the "Jews had no dealings with the Samaritans," the latter at the present day reciprocate the feeling; and neither eat, nor drink, nor marry, nor associate with the Jews; but only trade with them.'—*Robinson's Res.*, Vol. III. pp. 114—36.

'Sychar is nearly concealed by the thick olive groves of its walls, till you are within a few hundred yards of its walls, when it breaks upon the view—a charming object, with its graceful minarets embosomed in the richest foliage. Almonds, pomegranates, vines, figs, mulberries, apples, and orange trees, grow with the greatest luxuriance; while the cultivation of melons, cucumbers, &c., is abundant, and the produce carried as far as Jerusalem. The melons of Sychar are much esteemed. The garden hedges are for the most part formed of the prickly pear, (which is of the cactus *fam.*,) and often interlaced with the luxuriant vine.

'Sychar should be always viewed from without. The charm is lost when you enter into its miserable streets and offensive bazaars. Of its inhabitants, some were seated in groups, amidst piles of melons, cucumbers, and other fruits; some were engaged in cutting and preparing for sale large supplies of tobacco; others were carrying to and from the fountains water-bottles made of the untanned skins of sheep and goats; while veiled women were shuffling about in their yellow morocco boots, thrust into loose slippers, which gave them an awkward gait. In many of the houses and bazaars were extensive manufactures of cotton, in various stages; some were carding, others were spinning, and not a few weaving. There was a general appearance of activity, though in most streets were to be found large parties of those lovers of ease, whose day is spent reclining in the shade, and inhaling the fumes of Latakia.'—*A Pastor's Memorial, &c.*, pp. 312—.4.

The following particulars, from *Robinson's 'Researches,'* will perhaps be interesting.

'Travelling from Jerusalem to Nabulus, and after passing the village of Lubban, the ancient *Lebonah*, and proceeding some distance beyond it, we made,' Dr. Robinson writes, 'a very considerable descent along a steep, narrow Wady; and very soon reached the bottom of a large and very stony valley, running towards the W.S.W. . . . We could not learn the name of the valley . . . From this valley we had rather a steep ascent to the summit of the high ridge on the north. We reached the top . . . having just before passed the foundations of a ruined tower. Here we had our first view of the great plain of Mukbna, which stretches along for several hours on the east of the mountains among which Nabulus is situated. Those mountains were now before us in all their beauty; mount Gerizim, crowned by a Wely on its highest point, bearing north; just

beyond it the entrance of the valley of Nabulus . . . further north, the rugged heights of mount Ebal; and then the fine plain extending still beyond towards the N.N.E., skirted on its eastern side, in its whole length, by tracts of picturesque, though lower hills. . . . We could perceive our road forming a waving line along the foot of the high western hills, and under mount Gerizim, until it entered the valley of Nabulus, still two hours distant.

'A steep descent brought us in 20 m. to the southern extremity of the plain, near a cistern; in this part, indeed, the plain comes almost to a point . . (after a while,) the plain spreads out to a greater width, the eastern hills retiring somewhat more. On that side they are quite irregular and rocky, and often jut out into the plain; while, on the western side, the base of the slopes departs much less from a right line. The broad plain presented a beautiful appearance; it is everywhere cultivated, and was now covered with the rich green of millet, mingled with the yellow of the ripe grain, which the peasants were harvesting.

'Instead of keeping along at the foot of the mountain quite to the entrance of the valley of Nabulus, the road ascends and winds around the N.E. corner of mount Gerizim. We turned this point . . . and entered the narrow valley running up N.W. between mounts Gerizim and Ebal; thus leaving behind us the plain, which extends still further north. Below us, on the right, and just on the edge of the plain, are the ruins of a little hamlet, called Belat; (*see* p. 98, *of 'Jacob's well;'*) nearer at hand, and about in the middle of the mouth of the narrow valley, stands a small white building, a *wely*, called Joseph's tomb; while still nearer to the foot of Gerizim is the ancient well, known as that of Jacob. Directly opposite to the mouth of the valley, among the eastern hills, a beautiful smaller plain runs up eastward from the larger one; and on the low hills, near its entrance on the north, are seen . . . three villages, one of which is named Salim.—*See* Ge. xxxiii. 18—20.—*See* p. 96.

'After turning the point of the mountain, our path descended very little; yet so great is here the ascent of the narrow valley, that in a quarter of an hour we came out upon its bottom, near a fine copious fountain in its middle, furnished with a reservoir. At about half-past one o'clock, we were opposite the eastern end of the long narrow town, which we did not now enter. Keeping the road along its northern side, we passed some high mounds, apparently of rubbish; where, all at once, the ground sinks down to a valley running towards the west, with a soil of rich black vegetable mould. Here a scene of luxuriant and almost unparalleled verdure burst upon our view. The whole valley was filled with gardens of vegetables and orchards of all kinds of fruit, watered by several fountains, which burst forth in various parts, and flow westward in refreshing streams . . . We saw nothing to compare with it in all Palestine. Here, beneath the shade of an immense mulberry-tree, by the side of a purling rill, we pitched our tent for the remainder of the day and night.

'The city of Nabulus is long and narrow, stretching close along the N.E. base of mount Gerizim, in this small deep valley, half an hour distant from the great eastern plain. It has two long narrow streets running through the centre of the valley, intersected by several smaller, and contains about 10,000 inhabitants, chiefly Moslems; the houses high, and in general well-built, all of stone, with domes upon the roofs, as at Jerusalem. The valley itself, from the foot of Gerizim to that of Ebal, is here not more than some 500 yards wide, extending from S.E. to N.W. The city lies directly upon a water-summit in this valley, the waters in the eastern part . . . flowing off east into the plain, and so to the Jordan; while the fine fountains on the western side send off a pretty brook down the valley, N.W., towards the Mediterranean . . . Mounts Gerizim and Ebal rise in steep rocky precipices immediately from the valley (which runs nearly due east and west) on each side, apparently some 800 feet in height. Mount Ebal, or the mount of *cursing*, rises on the north side of the valley; and mount Gerizim, or the mount of *blessing*, on the south side of the valley. The sides

● 'After following the beautiful valley of Leban (old *Lebonah*), which we entered about eight hours and a half from Jerusalem, for rather more than three hours, it expanded into a magnificent plain, waving with corn—the parcel of ground, there can be no doubt, which Jacob gave to his son Joseph, and the gathering place, in every age of their history, of the clans of Israel: we saw camels and cattle winding their way through the corn fields far below us.'—*Lord Lindsay's Letters*, July, 1837, Vol. II. p. 73.

THE LORD SHALL REIGN FOR EVER.—Psalm cxlvi. 10.   [97

SECT. XIII.   ADDENDA.—THE SAMARITANS.   PART II.

GEOGRAPHICAL NOTICES.—SYCHAR—(continued.)

of both these mountains, as here seen, were, to our eyes, equally naked and sterile ... the only exception in favour of the former, so far as we could perceive, is a small ravine coming down opposite the west end of the town, which, indeed, is full of fountains and trees; in other respects, both mountains, as here seen, are desolate, except that a few olive-trees are scattered upon them. The side of the northern mountain, Ebal, along the foot, is full of ancient excavated sepulchres.

'Twenty minutes of ascent from the city ... led us to the top of Gerizim; which proved to be a tract of high table-land, stretching off far towards the W. and S.W. Twenty minutes more towards the S E., along a regular path upon the table-land, brought us to the Wely we had seen before, standing on a small eminence on the eastern brow of the mountain. Here is the holy place of the Samaritans, whither they still come to worship.

'The whole valley of Nabulus is full of fountains, irrigating it abundantly; and for that reason not flowing off in any large stream. The valley is rich, fertile, and beautifully green, as might be expected

from this bountiful supply of water. The sides of the valley, too, the continuation of Gerizim and Ebal, are studded with villages, some of them large; and these again are surrounded with extensive tilled fields and olive groves; so that the whole valley presents a more beautiful and inviting landscape of green hills and dales than perhaps any other part of Palestine * It is the deep verdure arising from the abundance of water which gives it this peculiar charm; in the midst of a land where no rain falls in summer, and where of course the face of nature, in the season of heat and drought, assumes a brown and dreary aspect.'—Vol. III. pp. 89—136.

Sychar is about forty miles north of Jerusalem. The cotton and soap manufactures are carried on there. In the town is a covered bazaar for fine goods, and an open one for provisions, and shops of every description; it is about ten miles S F. of the city Samaria. Lord Lindsay says, after leaving Nabulus, 'Two hours' ride, the following morning, through mule tracks, over the rocks, worn deep by the feet of centuries, took us to Subasta, the ancient Samaria, named by Herod Sebaste, in honour of Augustus.'—Letters, July, 1837, Vol. II. p. 74.

JACOB'S WELL, p. 92.

Jacob's well.—' It lies at the mouth of the valley, near the south side. We came to the opening of the valley on the north side, at the ruins of the little hamlet called " Belat." Joseph's tomb stands in the middle of the mouth of the valley; and the well is a little south of the tomb,† and just at the base of Gerizim, below the road by which we had passed along this morning. We were thirty-five minutes in coming to it from the city. It was now dry and deserted; but usually contains living water, and not merely to be filled by the rains. ... By dropping in stones, we could perceive that it was deep.‡ Maundrell describes it as dug in a firm rock, and about three yards in diameter, and thirty-five feet deep, five of which were full of water.

'I see much in the circumstances tending to confirm the supposition that this is actually the spot where our Lord held his conversation with the Samaritan woman. Jesus was journeying from Jerusalem to Galilee, and rested at the well, while "his disciples were gone away unto the city to buy meat," Jno. iv. 8. The well, therefore, lay apparently before the city, and at some distance from it. In passing along the eastern plain, Jesus had halted at the well, and sent his disciples to the city situated in the narrow valley, intending on their return to proceed along the plain on his way to Galilee, without himself visiting the city. All this corresponds exactly to the present character of the ground. A very

obvious question presented itself to us upon the spot, viz., how it can be supposed that the woman should have come from the city, now half an hour distant, with her water-pot, to draw water from Jacob's well, when there are so many fountains just around the city, and she must have also passed directly by a large one at mid-distance? The ancient city might probably lay in part nearer to this well than the modern one; and there is nothing improbable or unusual in the supposition, that the inhabitants may have set a peculiar value on the water of this ancient well of Jacob, and have occasionally put themselves to the trouble of going thither to draw. That it was not the ordinary public well of the city is probable from the circumstance, that there was here no public accommodation for drawing water, Jno. iv. 11. It was probably dug by the patriarch in some connexion with the possession of the "parcel of ground" bought of Hamor, the father of Shechem, which he gave to his son Joseph, and in which Joseph and probably his brethren were buried. The practice of the patriarchs to dig wells wherever they sojourned is well known; and if Jacob's field, as it would seem, was here before the mouth of the valley of Shechem, he might prefer not to be dependent for water on fountains which lay up that valley, and were not his own. I think we may thus rest with confidence in the opinion that this is Jacob's well, and here the parcel of ground which Jacob gave to his son Joseph.'—Robinson's Researches, Vol. III. pp. 107—13.

ADDENDA.

THE SAMARITANS, p. 92.

'The Samaritans, mentioned in the New Testament, are generally considered as a sect of the Jews. This appellation is, in the New Testament, given to a race of people who sprang originally from an intermixture of the ten tribes with Gentile nations. When the inhabitants of Samaria and of the adjacent country were carried into captivity by Shalmaneser king of Assyria, he sent in their place colonies from Babylonia, Cuthah, Ava, Hamath, and Sepharvaim;

..... Of them it is said, 2 Kl. xvii. 24, " And the king of Assyria brought men from Babylon, and from Cuthah, and from Ava, and from Hamath, and from Sepharvaim, and placed them in the cities of Samaria instead of the children of Israel: and they possessed Samaria, and dwelt in the cities thereof." An origin like this would, of course, render the nation odious to the Jews; and the Samaritans further augmented this cause of hatred by rejecting all the sacred books

---

* 'The valley of Naplous was, if possible, more beautiful by morning than by evening light, shaded by groves of figs, olives, almonds, and apricots. In full bloom, and bounded by lofty mountains, with a clear and beautiful stream winding and murmuring through its centre. For more than an hour we followed the coarse of the stream, and nothing could be more beautifully picturesque than the little mills on its banks, low, completely embosomed among the trees, and with their roofs covered with grass; and sometimes the agreeable sound of a waterfall was the first intimation we had of their presence.'—See Stephen's Incidents of Travel.

† Mr. Fisk thus describes it: 'About a quarter of a mile northward of Jacob's well stands a whited sepulchre. It consists of four walls, open at the top, and has a doorway opening to the north. On the left is a kind of covered sarcophagus, over which a wild vine clusters luxuriantly. Towards the right, is a raised piece of rude masonry, like the common coverings of Arab graves; undisputed tradition claims it as the tomb of Joseph.'—A Pastor's Memorial, &c. p. 311.

'There is a low pile of rude masonry, surrounded by large loose stones, and foundations of walls. A very ancient well is concealed by these remains, called by the Arabs, " Bir Yacob," the descent to which is through a narrow mouth in the stonework above, covered with a massive fragment of stone, too heavy for us to remove. In addition I learnt that the " well is deep," and I had " nothing to draw with."—Ibid. p. 339.

‡ Mr. Calhoun, a recent European traveller, ascertained its depth as 75 feet, with about twelve feet of water.

98]   MAN IS LIKE TO VANITY.—Psalm cxliv. 4.

ADDENDA.—THE SAMARITANS—(continued.)

of the Jews, except the Pentateuch, which they had received fr. the Israelitish priest who had been sent to them from Assyria to instruct them in the true religion. ver. 27, .8, "*Then the king of Assyria commanded, saying, Carry thither one of the priests whom ye brought from thence; and let them go and dwell there, and let him teach them the manner of the God of the land.* Then one of the priests whom they had carried away from Samaria came and dwelt in Beth-el, and taught them how they should fear the Lord." On the return of the Jews from the Babylonish captivity, when they began to rebuild Jerusalem and the temple, the Samaritans requested to be acknowledged as Jewish citizens, and to be permitted to assist in the work; but their application was rejected, Ezr. iv. 1—4, "*Now when the adversaries of Judah and Benjamin heard that the children of the captivity builded the temple unto the Lord God of Israel; then they came to Zerubbabel, and to the chief of the fathers, and said unto them, Let us build with you: for we seek your God, as ye do; and we do sacrifice unto him since the days of Esar-haddon king of Assur, which brought us up hither. But Zerubbabel, and Jeshua, and the rest of the chief of the fathers of Israel, said unto them, Ye have nothing to do with us to build an house unto our God; but we ourselves together will build unto the Lord God of Israel, as king Cyrus the king of Persia hath commanded us. Then the people of the land weakened the hands of the people of Judah, and troubled them in building.*" In consequence of this refusal and the subsequent state of enmity, the Samaritans took occasion to calumniate the Jews before the Persian kings, Ezr. iv. 5, "*And hired counsellors against them, to frustrate their purpose, all the days of Cyrus king of Persia, even until the reign of Darius king of Persia.*" Ne. iv. 1—8, "*But it came to pass, that when Sanballat heard that we builded the wall, he was wroth, and took great indignation, and mocked the Jews. And he spake before his brethren and the army of Samaria, and said, What do these feeble Jews? will they fortify themselves? will they sacrifice? will they make an end in a day? will they revive the stones out of the heaps of the rubbish which are burned? Now Tobiah the Ammonite was by him, and he said, Even that which they build, if a fox go up, he shall even break down their stone wall. Hear, O our God; for we are despised: and turn their reproach upon their own head, and give them for a prey in the land of captivity: and cover not their iniquity, and let not their sin be blotted out from before thee: for they have provoked thee to anger before the builders. So built we the wall; and all the wall was joined together unto the half thereof: for the people had a mind to work.* But it came to pass, that when Sanballat, and Tobiah, and the Arabians, and the Ammonites, and the Ashdodites, heard that the walls of Jerusalem were made up, and that the breaches began to be stopped, then they were very wroth, and conspired all of them together to come and to fight against Jerusalem, and to hinder it." Recurring to the directions of Moses, De. xxvii. 11—3, (*see* "in this mountain," "Notes," p. 93,) that on entering the promised land the Hebrews should offer sacrifices on mount Gerizim, they also erected a temple on that mountain, and instituted sacrifices according to the prescriptions of the Mosaic law.* From all these and other circumstances, the national hatred between the Samaritans and Jews increased to such a height, that the Jews denounced the most bitter anathemas against them, Ecclus. l. 26, and for many ages refused them every kind of intercourse. Hence the woman of Samaria was astonished that Jesus Christ, who was a Jew, should ask drink of her, Jno. iv. 9, p. 92. Hence also the Jews, when they would express the utmost aversion to Christ, said to him, "*Thou art a Samaritan, and hast a devil,*" Jno. viii. 48, § 55. The temple on mount Gerizim was destroyed by Hyrcanus, B.C. 129: but the Samaritans, in the time of Jesus, esteemed that mountain sacred, and as the proper place of national worship, Jno. iv. 20, 1, p. 93. At that time, also, in common with the Jews, they expected the advent of a Messiah, ver. 25, p. 91, and many of them afterwards became the followers of Jesus Christ, and embraced the doctrines of his religion: Ac. viii. 5, 12, "*Then Philip went down to the city of Samaria, and preached Christ unto them. But when they believed Philip preaching the things concerning the kingdom of God, and the name of Jesus Christ, they were baptized, both men and women.*" ix. 31, "*Then had the churches rest throughout all Judæa and Galilee and Samaria, and were edified; and walking in the fear of the Lord, and in the comfort of the Holy Ghost, were multiplied.*" xv. 3, "*And being brought on their way by the church, they passed through Phenice and Samaria, declaring the conversion of the Gentiles: and they caused great joy unto all the brethren.*"

'At present, the Samaritans are very much reduced in point of numbers. Their principal residence is at Sichem, or Shechem, now called Napolose, or Nabulus. In 1823, there were between twenty and thirty houses, and about sixty males paid the capitation tax to the Muhammedan government. Formerly they went four times a year, in solemn procession, to the old synagogue on mount Gerizim: and on these occasions they ascended before sunrise, and read the law till noon. The Samaritans have one school in Napolose, where their language is taught. The Samaritans at Napolose are in possession of a very ancient MS. Pentateuch, said to be nearly 3500 years old; but they reject the vowel points as a rabbinical invention.'—*Horne's Introd.* Vol. III. p. 371,..2.

' The Samaritans pretend to great strictness in their observance of the law of Moses, and account the Jews intolerably lax. From the letter of their high priest to Joseph Scaliger, about 200 years ago, and which was in the library of the French king, it appears that they profess to believe in God, and in his servant Moses, and in the holy law, the mount Gerizim, the house of God, and the day of vengeance and peace. They keep the Jewish sabbath so strictly, that they will not move out of their place, except to their synagogue. They always circumcise their children on the eighth day of their birth. They do not marry their own nieces nor allow a plurality of wives, as the Jews do. Their high priest still resides at Shechem, and offers their sacrifices at their temple on Mt. Gerizim.'—'No individual of the Samaritan faith, with whom they have any acquaintance, are supposed to be resident at any other place but Nabulus.'—*See Dr. Wilson's Lands of the Bible*, Vol. II. p. 64.

ON THE NATURAL INFERENCE OF JOHN iv. 35, p. 95.

[' Say not ye, There are four months, &c. ' The allusion is to a proverb; and its connexion with what follows may be thus explained:—When the seed is first sown, is it not a common saying, that there are yet four months, and the harvest or reaping time will come? Lift up your eyes, survey the country round about, and be convinced, by the whiteness of the fields, that the four months are drawing to a close; and that the season of reaping is at hand. The end which was proposed by the reference to this natural phenomenon may also be explained as follows:— This ripeness of the visible and the natural harvest, now that the period requisite to the maturity of he seed is accomplished, may be an earnest to you of the ripeness of that as yet unseen and spiritual harvest, to bring which to maturity will be the object of my personal labours; but to reap which will be the object of yours. ... Our Lord was speaking prophetically ... of what was still future, as if it were already past.'— *Gresswell*, Vol. II. Diss. xxi. pp. 222—..9.]

[If a figurative import is put upon this effect, however incongruous to the simplicity of the acts which precede, it can still signify only one thing, viz. that the fields were to be seen crowded with those among whom the spiritual harvest of our Saviour's ministry either had begun, or was about to begin; which crowding at least must have been a matter of fact. If so, the crowds of Samaritans were flocking from Sychar; for our Lord was now on Gerizim; and these inhabitants of Sychar were the proper subjects of our Saviour's ministry.—*Ibid*, p. 223.]

* The immediate occasion appears from Nehemiah, ch. xiii. 28, '*And one of the sons of Joiada, the son of Eliashib the high priest, was son in law to Sanballat the Horonite: therefore I chased him from me.*' And for whom Sanballat built the temple, and confederated with him high priest. ' According to Josephus, if a Jew at Jerusalem was called to an account for eating unclean food, or for breaking the sabbath, or for any similar crime, he fled to the Sichemites, declaring himself to be unjustly accused.'—*Robinson's Researches*, Vol. III. p. 117.

GREAT IS OUR LORD, AND OF GREAT POWER.—Psalm cxlvii. 5.

SECTION 14.—FROM SYCHAR JESUS PROCEEDS TO GALILEE; JOHN BEING NOW CAST INTO PRISON, JESUS AGAIN VISITS CANA. HE HEALS THE SON OF A NOBLEMAN, LYING SICK IN CAPERNAUM. John iv. 43—54.

(G. 16,) No. 14. *Jesus departs into Galilee. John iv. 43—.6.—Cana.*

43, .4 Now after two ras δυο days he-departed thence, and went into Galilee. For Jesus 45 himself testified, that a-prophet hath no honour in his-own country. Then when he-was-come into Galilee, the Galileans received him, having-seen all-the-things that he-did 46 at Jerusalem at the feast: for they also went unto the feast. So Jesus came again into Cana of Galilee, where he-made the water wine.

A nobleman's son healed. John iv. 46—54.

And there-was a-certain nobleman, whose son was-sick at Capernaum. 47, When-·he'-heard that Jesus was-come out-of Judæa into Galilee, he-went unto him, and besought him that he-would-come-down, and heal his son: for he-was-at-the-point-of 48 death ημελλε αποθνησκειν. Then said Jesus unto him, Except ye-see signs and 49 wonders, ye-will-'not'-believe. The nobleman saith unto him, Sir, come-down ere

SCRIPTURE ILLUSTRATIONS.

43. *after two days—see* ver. 40, § 13, p. 96. This allowed time for those who had seen his miracles in Jerusalem to return to Galilee, and prepare the minds of the people for him there, ver. 45.

44. *no honour in his own country—see* Mt. xiii. 57, § 37; Lu. iv. 24, § 15, p. 101.

45. *having seen—see* ch. ii. 23, § 12, p. 82.

46. *sick—see* other instances: woman of Canaan's daughter, Mt. xv. 22, § 45—Jairus' daughter, Mk. v. 22, .3, § 36—Lazarus, Jno. xi. 3, &c., § 58.

47. *besought*—Invitation to call upon the Lord in trouble: 'and call upon me in the day of trouble: I will deliver thee, and thou shalt glorify me,' Ps. l. 15 —case of centurion's servant at Capernaum, Mt. viii. 5—13, § 29.

48. *except . . . signs*—the Lord looks for faith in answer to his signs: 'and the Lord said unto Moses,

How long will this people provoke me? and how long will it be ere they believe me, for all the signs which I have shewed among them?' Nu. xiv. 11—willing to give them: 'ask thee a sign of the Lord thy God; ask it either in the depth, or in the height above,' Is. vii. 11—signs predicted: 'I and the children whom the Lord hath given me are for signs and for wonders in Israel from the Lord of hosts, which dwelleth in mount Zion,' viii. 18—*comp.* as to himself, Jno. ii. 18, .9, § 12, p. 81; Mt. xii. 40, § 31; xvi. 1—4, § 47—as to the children: 'after two days will he revive us: in the third day he will raise us up, and we shall live in his sight,' Ho. vi. 2.

49. *come down*—examples of earnest supplications: 'but I *am* poor and needy: make haste unto me, O God: thou *art* my help and my deliverer; O Lord, make no tarrying,' Ps. lxx. 5—'Lord, I cry unto thee: make haste unto me; give ear unto my voice, when I cry unto thee,' cxli. 1

NOTES.

44. *For Jesus himself testified, &c.* He did not immediately go into his own country, but delayed two days in Samaria. at Sychar, to allow time for those who witnessed his miracles at Jerusalem to return home, and prepare the minds of the people for a favourable reception of him. At Cana he spake the word which healed the nobleman's son at Capernaum, and led to his being more readily received as a prophet there and in the region around.

45. *Received him.* Gave him a favourable reception as a messenger from God. They had seen his miracles and believed on him.

46. *Cana of Galilee.—See* Geog. Notice, Sect. xi.

A certain nobleman. τις βασιλικός, 'ruler.'—*Tindal.* This is thought to have been Chuza, Herod's steward, whose wife became afterwards an attendant upon our Lord, Lu. viii. 3, § 30, and, it has been supposed, in consequence of the miracle wrought upon her son.

47. *He went unto him.* The rich and the poor, the high and the low, must come personally as humble suppliants; and must be willing to bear all the reproach that may be cast on them for thus coming to him. This man shewed strong faith in being willing thus to go to Jesus; but he had an erroneous view that Jesus could heal only by his being present with his son.

Come down. 'The whole route from Cana, according to the position of the place now so called, is a continued descent towards Capernaum.'—*E. D. Clarke.* The distance was about twelve or fourteen miles.

48. *Except ye see signs, &c.* This was spoken not to the nobleman only, but to the Galileans generally. The Samaritans had believed without any miracle. The Galileans, he said, were less disposed to believe him than even they were. And though he had wrought miracles *enough* to convince them, yet unless they continually saw them they would not believe.

49. *Come down, &c.* The earnestness of the nobleman evinces the deep and tender anxiety of a father.

PRACTICAL REFLECTIONS.

44 *ver.* Let us beware of despising those of the Lord's messengers with whose early history we are familiar.

43, .4 *ver.* How condescending was our Lord, in taking upon him, not only the form of a servant, but in also enduring the neglect, reproach, and suffering connected with his office! leaving us an example of patient labour, in the most trying circumstances.

[The servant of God must not shun to deliver his message, where he knows he will be slighted, as well as where he is favourably received; '*whether they will hear, or whether they will forbear,*' Eze. ii. 5: but he must be careful to use whatever means may be in his power for removing the obstacles to a favourable reception of his message.]

45 *ver.* God overrules man's evil for good. The rejection of the Lord's message in one place may be the occasion of its conveyance to another, from whence the manifestation of the truth may go forth

with greater power to the place of its first appearance.

46 *ver.* Let us, with our Lord, sympathize not only with the joys, but also with the sorrows of those around us.

47 *ver.* Let us have faith in Jesus, in his grace and power, so as to apply to him for healing, both for ourselves and those that are dear to us. Let us not, by our unbelief, limit him as to his power to relieve and to bless, but look for deeds to be done by him worthy of God.

48 *ver.* Let us beware of mistaking a looking to Jesus for temporal help as necessarily resulting from true faith in him as the promised Messiah: the temporal deliverances which Jesus effected were but signs of his still greater power to bless.

49 *ver.* Let us not, like the nobleman, restrict our Lord's healing power to his bodily presence.

HE IS NOBLY DESCENDED WHO IS BORN FROM ABOVE.

| PART II. | JESUS HEALS A NOBLEMAN'S SON. | SECT. XIV. |

JOHN iv. 50—4.

50 my child die. Jesus saith unto-him, Go-thy-way; thy son liveth. And the man 51 believed the word that Jesus had-spoken unto-him, and he-went-his-way. And as-he was-'now'-going-down, his servants met him, and told *him*, saying, Thy son liveth. 52 Then enquired-he of them the hour when he-began to-amend κομψοτερον εσχε. And 53 they-said unto-him, Yesterday at-the-seventh hour the fever left him. So the father knew that *it was* at the same hour, in the-which Jesus said unto-him, Thy son liveth: 54 and himself believed, and his whole house. This *is* again the-second miracle σημειον that Jesus did, when-he-was-come out-of Judæa into Galilee. [Ch. v. 1, ₰ 23.]

SCRIPTURE ILLUSTRATIONS.

50. *go thy way; thy son liveth—see*..... Jesus' miracle of healing the centurion's servant, Mt. viii. 13, § 28—woman of Canaan's daughter, xv. 28, § 45.

believed—such faith we find in the centurion, Mt. viii. 8, § 28—when Jesus was raised from the dead on the third day, and when thus the great predicted sign had been given, the disciples believed—*see* Jno. ii. 22, § 12, p. 82—*see* also Lu. xxiv. 8, § 93.

51. *thy son liveth*—the words of Jesus, ver. 50, used also by Elijah, upon raising the widow's son, 1 Ki. xvii. 23.

53. *same hour, &c.*—'he spake, and it was *done*; he commanded, and it stood fast,' Ps. xxxiii. 9—'he sent his word, and healed them, and delivered *them* from their destructions,' cvii. 20—*see* Mt. viii. 13, § 28, 'and Jesus said unto the centurion, Go thy way; and as thou hast believed, *so* be it done unto thee. And his servant was healed in the selfsame hour.'

himself believed, and his whole house—the mother supposed to be 'Joanna the wife of Chuza Herod's steward,' Lu. viii. 3, § 30, 'and Joanna the wife of Chuza Herod's steward, and Susanna, and many others, which ministered unto him of their substance.'—*See* as to whole households believing: that of Lydia, Ac. xvi. 15, 'and when she was baptized, and her household, she besought *us*, saying, If ye have judged me to be faithful to the Lord, come into my house, and abide *there*. And she constrained us,' —the jailor, ver. 31, 'and when he had brought them into his house, he set meat before them, and rejoiced, believing in God with all his house,'—Crispus, xviii. 8, 'and Crispus, the chief ruler of the synagogue, believed on the Lord with all his house; and many of the Corinthians hearing believed, and were baptized.'

54. *Galilee*—to which he had when a child been brought out of Egypt, Mt. ii. 23, § 5, p. 35, 'and he came and dwelt in a city called Nazareth: that it might be fulfilled which was spoken by the prophets, He shall be called a Nazarene.'—*See* Lu. i. 26, p. 9.

NOTES.

50. *Go thy way.* To shew that he could do even more than the father hoped for, and could heal the sick absent as well as present, (in order thereby effectually to remove any want of faith in the bystanders,) our Lord dismisses him with the assurance that his request is granted.

Thy son liveth. Thy son shall recover. Or he shall be restored to health according to thy request.

52. *The seventh hour.* According to St. John's computation of time, this would be either seven a.m., or seven p.m., and was most probably the latter.

53. *The same hour.* The time when Jesus spake.

The fever left him. It seems that it left him suddenly and entirely; so much so that they went to inform the father, and to comfort him; and also, doubtless, to apprize him that it was not necessary to ask aid from Jesus.

Himself believed. This miracle removed all his doubts, and he became a real disciple and friend of Jesus.

His whole house. His whole family. We may learn from this, 1st. That sickness or deep affliction is often the means of great good. Here the sickness of the son resulted in the faith of all the family. God often takes away earthly blessings for a time, that he may impart rich spiritual mercies.—2nd. The father of a family may be the means of the salvation of his children. Here the effort of a parent resulted in their conversion to Christ.—3rd. There is great beauty and propriety when sickness thus results in piety: for that, it is sent. God does not willingly grieve or afflict the children of men. And when afflictions thus terminate it will be cause of perfect joy, and ceaseless praise.—4th. There is a peculiar charm when piety thus comes into the families of the rich and the noble. It is so unusual; their example and influence go so far; it overcomes so many temptations; and affords opportunities of doing so much good, that there is no wonder that the evangelist selected this instance as one of the effects of the power and preaching of the Lord Jesus Christ.

54. *This is again the second miracle, &c.* That is, the second he did in that place, in Cana of Galilee; for otherwise, in Jerusalem and Judæa he had done many miracles, between the former and this.

In this miracle we see the following attributes of Jehovah plainly exhibited in our blessed Lord:—*First*, OMNIPOTENCE, in that he healed the sick man.—*Secondly*, OMNIPRESENCE, in that he healed the man who was sick at a distance of twelve or fourteen miles from the town where he then was.—*Thirdly*, OMNISCIENCE, in that he knew that his word was effectual, which was corroborated by the servants of the nobleman, who when he heard from them, '*Yesterday at the seventh hour the fever left him,*' ... '*knew that it was at the same hour, in which Jesus said unto him, Thy son liveth.*'

PRACTICAL REFLECTIONS.

50 *ver.* Jesus is as able to command blessing from Leaven as he was at *Cana* to command the healing of the nobleman's son at *Capernaum*.

[Let us not turn away from the weak in faith, but, like our Great Teacher, lead gently on to a firm reliance upon the word which Jesus hath spoken.—God will hear our prayers, and grant our requests, but often not in the precise *manner* in which we ask it. It is *his* to judge of the best way of doing us good.]

48—52 *ver.* Let us not put away the word, because it promises more than what we have yet experienced, but, like the nobleman, go at the bidding of Jesus, and we shall find his saying true, yea, we shall, like the noblemen, be met with the evidence of his being the Prince of life, whose omniscience, omnipresence, and omnipotence, mercy and truth, were all here manifested, as signs or indications of his greater power to save.

53 *ver.* Let affliction bring us to Jesus; and not only for temporal deliverance let us be brought individually, but as families may we be brought to place a firm and united reliance upon him, in thankful acknowledgment of his mercy.

GEOGRAPHICAL NOTICES.

CANA.—*See* Sect. xi. p. 79. | CAPERNAUM.—*See* Sect. xi. p. 79, and xvi. p. 109.

THE LORD IS GOOD TO ALL.—Psalm cxlv. 9.

SECTION 15.—JESUS VISITS NAZARETH; AND PREACHES THERE IN THE SYNAGOGUE ON THE SABBATH DAY. Luke iv. 14—30.

(G. 17,) No. 15. *At Nazareth.* [For ver. 13, see § ix. p. 66.]

14 And Jesus returned in the power of-the Spirit into Galilee: and there-went-out a-
15 fame of him through all the region-round-about. And he taught in their synagogues, being-glorified of all.
16 And he-came to Nazareth, where he-had-been brought-up: and, as his custom *was*,
17 he-went into the synagogue on the sabbath day, and stood-up for-to-read. And there-was-delivered unto-him the-book of-the prophet Esaias. And when-he-had-opened the
18 book, he-found the place where it-was written, The-Spirit of-the-Lord *is* upon me, because he-hath-anointed me to-preach-the-gospel to-the-poor; he-hath-sent me to-heal

SCRIPTURE ILLUSTRATIONS.

14. *power of the Spirit*—had been promised, Is. xi. 2; xlii. 1—the Spirit descended upon him, Lu. iii. 22, § 8—the disciples were to receive power by the Holy Ghost coming upon them, from their exalted Head, so were they to become witnesses for him 'unto the uttermost part of the earth,' Ac. i. 8—so Paul was directed in his ministry of the word, xvi. 6—10.

fame of him—the fame of Jesus 'went throughout all Syria,' Mt. iv. 24, § 18—'all the region round about Galilee,' Mk. i. 28, § 17—*see* the promise to Abraham, 'I will bless thee, and make thy name great,' Ge. xii. 2—'I will get them praise and fame in every land where they have been put to shame,' Zep. iii. 19.

16. *custom*—referred to by Jesus, Jno. xviii. 20, § 89—followed by the apostles, Ac. xiii. 5, 14—6; xvii. 1, 2; xix. 8, &c.—prediction, ' I will declare thy name unto my brethren: in the midst of the congregation will I praise thee,' Ps. xxii. 22—' I have preached righteousness in the great congregation: lo, I have not refrained my lips, O LORD, thou knowest,' xl. 9, 10.—*See* Se t. xvii. p. 110.

17. *opened the book*—*see* as to Ezra, Ne. viii. 5—it was after his death and resurrection more particu-larly that Jesus opened the Scriptures to his disciples, Lu. xxiv. 32, 45. §§ 94. 8—the Lamb as having been slain took the book, Rev. v. 7—at his opening of the first seal, of which (Rev. vi. 2) there went forth the white horse, expressive of the same glad tidings declared, Is. lxi. 1—3.

18. *anointed*—predicted also, Da. ix. 24—recognized, Jno. iii. 34, § 13; Ac. iv. 27; x. 38.

gospel to the poor—it had been predicted that 'the poor among men shall rejoice in the Holy One of Israel,' Is. xxix. 19—thus Jesus commenced his sermon on the mount, 'Blessed are the poor in spirit: for theirs is the kingdom of heaven,' Mt. v. 3, § 19—thus he characterised his ministry to John, 'The poor have the gospel preached to them,' xi. 5, § 29—*see* the invitation to the marriage, xxii. 9, 10, § 84—'hath not God chosen the poor of this world rich in faith?' Ja. ii. 5—instruments of his power in the gospel, 1 Co. i. 26, ,7—Israel, after being made poor, ch. 3, 13, was to have the words of comfort spoken to her in the wilderness, ver. 14—*comp.* Is. xl. 1—3, of which preaching, that of John was a pledge, Mk. i. 3, § 7, p. 49.

NOTES.

14. *In the power of the Spirit.* Under the powerful influence of the Spirit.

A fame. A report—*see* Mt. iv. 24, § 18.

16. *And, as his custom was, he went, &c.* From this it appears that our Lord regularly attended the service of the synagogue.

The synagogue. — See ADDENDA, 'Synagogue,' p. 106.

Stood up for to read. By standing up he shewed that he was ready to read the lesson of the day, if they would let him.

17. *There was delivered unto him.* By the minister of the synagogue, or the keeper of the sacred books. They were kept in an *ark*, or chest, not far from the pulpit, and the minister gave them to whomsoever he chose, to read them publicly.

The book. The volume containing Isaiah.

When he had opened. αναπτυξας, 'having unrolled;' for books formerly were written on rolls of paper or parchment, or vellum. These rolls were fastened to two laths with handles, by holding which in his hand the reader could roll or unroll the book.

18. *The Spirit of the Lord, &c.* The Holy Ghost, which had descended upon him in the form of a dove, abode upon him.

Anointed. The anointing of persons or things under the law imported the setting of them apart to the service of God, or to some noted office of prophet, priest, or king; and was typical of the communication of the Holy Ghost to Christ and his church, Ex. xxviii., xxix. The Holy Ghost is called an *unction*, or *anointing*. God's anointing of our Redeemer imports his calling him to the office of Mediator, Prophet, Priest, and King; hence the Son of God is called the *Messiah*, a Hebrew word signifying *the Anointed*; or the *Christ*, a Greek word signifying the same thing. Christ's unction was the descent of the Holy Spirit upon him at his baptism; whereby, as Peter says, Ac. x. 38, '*God anointed Jesus of Nazareth with the Holy Ghost and with power.*'

To preach the gospel to the poor. By the poor, are meant all those who are destitute of the comforts of this life; all those who are sensible of their sins, or are poor in spirit, Mt. v. 3, § 19; and all the miserable and the afflicted, described in Is. lviii. 7, as hungry, and cast out, and naked. Our Saviour gave it as one proof that he was the Messiah, or was from God, that he preached the gospel to *the poor*, Mt. xi. 5, § 29. The Pharisees and Sadducees despised the poor. Ancient philosophers neglected them. Riches too often fill the mind with pride, with self-complacency, and with a feeling that the gospel is not needed—*see* Rev. iii. 17. But the gospel pours contempt on all human greatness, and seeks, like God, to do good to those whom the world overlooks or despises.

PRACTICAL REFLECTIONS.

14 *ver.* Let us seek that the messengers of Jesus may go forth in the power of the Spirit, in the declaring of his message; earnestly desiring that the fame of Jesus may be spread abroad, in all the region around.

15 *ver.* Let us not mistake our glorifying the speaker for the being truly and permanently benefited by his message. Jesus was glorified of all in the synagogues, and yet, speedily, they cast him out.

16 *ver.* Let it be our custom, like that of Jesus, to go on the sabbath day where we may have an opportunity, along with others, of reading the Holy Scriptures.

['It is of vast importance that the public worship of God should be maintained; and it is our duty to assist in maintaining it, to shew by our example that we love it, and to win others to love it also.—See He. x. 25, '*Not forsaking the assembling of ourselves together, as the manner of some is; but exhorting one another: and so much the more, as ye see the day approaching.*' At the same time this remark cannot be construed as enjoining it as our duty to attend a place where the *true* God is not worshipped, or where he is worshipped by pagan rites and pagan prayers. As, therefore, the Unitarian does not worship the true God in Christ, and as the Roman Catholic worships God in a manner forbidden, and offers homage to the *creatures* of God also, thus being guilty of idolatry, it cannot be our duty to attend on such worship.']

PART II.   JESUS PREACHES AT NAZARETH.   SECT. XV.

LUKE iv. 18, .9.

the broken hearted συντετριμμενους την καρδιαν, to-preach deliverance αφεσιν to-the-captives, and recovering-of-sight to-the-blind, to-set at liberty them-that-are-bruised, 19 αποστειλαι τεθραυσμενους εν αφεσει, to-preach the-acceptable δεκτον year of-the Lord

SCRIPTURE ILLUSTRATIONS.

18. *heal the broken-hearted*—the Lord doth this, Ps. xxxiv. 18; cxlvii. 3—prayer for healing, xli. 4; Je. xvii. 14—the broken-heartedness of Israel, Eze. xxxvii. 11; Is. liv. 6—the promise of healing, ver. 7, 8; lvii. 18; Je. xxx. 17—' with his stripes we are healed,' Is. liii. 5.

deliverance to the captives—the Deliverer is called Jesus, because he saves his people from their sins, Mt. i. 21, § 2—delivers from the dominion of sin, Rom. vi. 11—23—gives men repentance to the acknowledging of the truth, ' that they may recover themselves out of the snare of the devil,' 2 Ti. ii. 25, .6—' by the blood of thy covenant I have sent forth thy prisoners out of the pit wherein *is* no water,' Zec. ix. 11—Israel's captivity predicted, Am. vii. 17—accomplished, 2 Ki. xvii. 18—23—deliverance predicted, Je. xxx. 8, 9; Ps. cii. 19—22; cvii. 10—6; cxxvi. 1—4; Is. xlii. 7; xlix. 9, 24—.6; lii. 2, 3—Israel to work deliverance for others as following Him who is their righteousness, Is. lviii. 6—8—so shall their own captivity be fully restored, ver. 11, .2; lxi. 1—3—' if thou forbear to deliver them that are drawn unto death,' &c., Pr. xxiv. 11, .2.

recovery of sight to the blind—Israel's blindness predicted, Is. xxix. 9—14—their foolishness in that blindness, ver. 15, .6—recovery of sight, ver. 18—what will then be seen, ver. 23—' yea, their children shall see,' Zec. x. 7—the great recovery of sight to be in connexion with Israel's restoration, Is. xxv. 7; xxxv. 5—10; xlii. 16—even the Lord's servant, who has been seeing many things, has been eminently blind, ver.

18—20—Israel to be emphatically the Lord's witnesses when they have recovered their sight, xliii. 8—10—Jesus confirmed these predictions by literally opening the eyes of the blind; 'two blind men,' Mt. ix 27—30, § 36—' blind and dumb,' xii. 22, .3, § 31—' the blind to see,' xv. 31, § 46—' blind man at Bethsaida,' was first partially restored, and then fully, so as to see every man clearly, Mk. viii. 22—.6, § 49—man at pool of Siloam, Jno. ix. 1—7, § 55—the danger of not knowing our blindness, ver. 39—41—Paul sent to the Gentiles ' to open their eyes, and to turn ... from darkness to light,' Ac. xxvi. 18—' blindness in part is happened to Israel, until the fulness of the Gentiles be come in,' Rom. xi. 25—Jesus entreats thee to ' anoint thine eyes with eye salve, that thou mayest see,' Rev. iii. 18, .9.

To set at liberty them that are bound—the scribes, &c., did ' bind heavy burdens and grievous to be borne, and lay *them* on men's shoulders,' Mt. xxiii. 4, § 85—the invitation of Jesus is, ' Come unto me, all ye that labour and are heavy laden, and I will give you rest,' &c., Mt. xi. 28—30, § 29—Israel appointed ' to undo the heavy burdens, and to let the oppressed go free, Is. lviii. 6—' the yoke of his burden, and the staff of his shoulder, the rod of his oppressor,' to be broken, ix. 4.

19. *acceptable year, &c.*—see as to the year of jubilee, Lev. xxv. 8—13—' In an acceptable time have I heard thee,' &c., Is. xlix. 8—13—subsequent return, ver. 17—22—comp. Rev. vii. 9—17—' behold, now *is* the accepted time,' 2 Co. vi. 2.

NOTES.

18. *To heal the broken-hearted.* To console those who are deeply afflicted, or whose hearts are broken by external calamities, or by a deep sense of their sinfulness.

Deliverance to the captives. Captive, one taken prisoner in war. There is a two-fold captivity—1. Natural, when men are apprehended by the enemy, and are carried out of their own land, and held in slavery, De. xxviii. 48, ' Therefore shalt thou serve thine enemies which the LORD shall send against thee, in hunger, and in thirst, and in nakedness, and in want of all things: and he shall put a yoke of iron upon thy neck, until he have destroyed thee.'—2. Sinful, when one is carried away, and oppressed or enslaved under the power of Satan, and his own inward corruption, Rom. vii. 23; 2 Tim. ii. 26.

[Israel had been led away captive by the Assyrian, 2 Ki. xvii. 6; and they had not been restored from captivity, ver. 23, as the Jews were from Babylon, 2 Ch. xxxvi. 22, .3. The Jews in Galilee were dwelling in the portion of cast-out Israel. A more important deliverance is provided for the captives, without which, a literal return from captivity can be of but little value.]

The gospel releases the mind which is held captive under sin.

Sight to the blind. This was often literally fulfilled, Mt. xi. 5, § 29—see ' Scrip. Illus.,' *supra.* [The restoration to spiritual vision is promised to Israel, Is. xxix. 18, ' *And in that day shall the deaf*

hear the words of the book, and the eyes of the blind shall see out of obscurity, and out of darkness; ' and is called for, xlii. 18—20, ' Hear, ye deaf; and look, ye blind, that ye may see. Who is blind, but my servant? or deaf, as my messenger that I sent? who is blind as he that is perfect, and blind as the Lord's servant? Seeing many things, but thou observest not; opening the ears, but he heareth not.']

To set at liberty them that are bruised. It means those who are pressed down by great calamity, or whose hearts are pressed or bruised by affliction or sin.

[Israel had, by the Assyrian, been given to be trodden under foot 'like the mire of the streets,' Is. x. 5, 6, ' *O Assyrian, the rod of mine anger, and the staff in their hand is mine indignation. I will send him against an hypocritical nation, and against the people of my wrath will I give him a charge, to take the spoil, and to take the prey, and to tread them down like the mire of the streets.*']

Bruised. Alludes to the pressure of the heavy chains.—See Judg. xvi. 21; 2 Ki. xxv. 7.—*Doddridge.*

19. *The acceptable year of the Lord.* There is here an allusion to the year of jubilee—the fiftieth year, when the trumpet was blown, and through the whole land proclamation was made of the liberty of Hebrew slaves, of the remission of debts, and the restoration of possessions to their original families, Lev. xxv. 8—13. Thus it is meant, that *the gospel is to the law* what the jubilee year was as compared to all others.

PRACTICAL REFLECTIONS.

17 ver. Let us beware, upon any pretence, of neglecting the written word, and especially the word of prophecy.—It was Jesus, the Son of God, who entered the synagogue, and he came there ' *in the power of the Spirit,*' and that in which we find him there engaged is, reading ' *the book of the prophet Isaiah.*'

18 ver. Let us not say that the Spirit is not needed now; it was upon Jesus as the Head of his body; and should be earnestly desired for the work of the ministry in every member of the body.

As we desire that Jesus may see of the travail of his soul, let us aid, to the utmost of our power, in preaching the glad tidings to the poor, in healing the broken-hearted, in setting at liberty the bound,

and those that are oppressed, and in doing good to all as we have opportunity, making the most destitute the special objects of our affectionate regard.

[And, that all this may be done most effectually, let us know our own blindness, depravity, and weakness; and seek first to have the enlightening, sanctifying, and enriching power of Jesus exerted upon ourselves; that we may, in his strength, and not in our own, engage in the work which is given us to do, and of which he must have all the glory.]

[19 ver. Let us earnestly pray and labour that the acceptable year of the Lord, the year of jubilee, may speedily be realized in the promised return of the redeemed of the Lord to the land of their inheritance, when those who have been indeed blind shall see.]

SECT. XV.   JESUS PREACHES AT NAZARETH.   PART II.

LUKE iv. 20—.7.

20 And he-closed the book, and-he-gave-*it*-again to-the minister, and-sat-down. And the eyes of-all-them *that were* in the synagogue were 'astened-on him ατενιζοντες αυτω. 21 And he-began to-say unto them, This-day is-'this scripture'-fulfilled in your ears. 22 And all bare-'him'-witness, and wondered at the gracious words λογοις της χαριτος 23 which proceeded out-of his mouth. And they-said, Is not this Joseph's son? And he-said unto them, Ye-will-'surely'-Παντως say unto-me this proverb, Physician, heal thyself: whatsoever we-have-heard done in Capernaum, do also here in thy country. 24 And he-said, Verily I-say unto-you, No prophet is accepted δεκτος in his-own country. 25 But I-tell you of-a-truth, many widows were in Israel in the days of-Elias, when the heaven was-shut-up three years and six months, when great famine was throughout all 26 the land; but unto none of-them was-'Elias'-sent, save unto Sarepta, *a city of* Sidon, 27 unto a-woman *that was* a-widow. And many lepers were in Israel in-the-time-of

SCRIPTURE ILLUSTRATIONS.

21. *scrip'ture ful'filled*—' Scriptures'—they which testify of Christ, Jno. v. 39, § 23—' the works' ' bear witness of me,' x. 25, § 56—' those things, which God before had shewed by the mouth of all his prophets, that Christ should suffer, he hath so fulfilled,' Ac. iii. 18—' and when they had fulfilled all that was written of him, they took *him* down from the tree, and laid him in a sepulchre,' xiii. 29.

22. *gracious words*—' the preacher sought to find out acceptable words: and *that which was* written *was* upright, *even* words of truth. 11, The words of the wise *are* as goads, and as nails fastened *by* the masters of assemblies, *which* are given from one shepherd,' Ec. xii. 10, .1—' His mouth *is* most sweet: yea, he *is* altogether lovely. This *is* my beloved, and this *is* my friend, O daughters of Jerusalem,' Cant.

v. 16—' the Lord GOD hath given me the tongue of the learned, that I should know how to speak a word in season to *him that is* weary: he wakeneth morning by morning, he wakeneth mine ear to hear as the learned,' Is. l. 4—' all that heard him were astonished at his understanding and answers,' Lu. ii. 47, § 6, p. 41—' never man spake like this man,' Jno. vii. 46, § 55—' whence hath this *man* this wisdom?' Mt. xiii. 54, § 37.

23. *in Capernaum*—such as that of the nobleman's son, Jno. iv. 46, § 14—see ii. 12, § 11; Mt. xi. 20, .3, § 29.

25. *widows in Israel in the days of Elias*—see the account of the dearth and of Elijah's raising the widow's son, 1 Ki. xvii. 1—16; 17—24—Elijah's power in prayer referred to, Ja. v. 17, .8.

NOTES.

20. *To the minister.* τω ὑπηρετη, ' to the servant,' who had brought it to him, a subordinate officer who attended on the minister.

And sat down. When the Jewish doctors taught the people, they sat down, Mt. xxiii. 2, § 85.

Were fastened on him. Expecting him to explain the passage.

21. *Fulfilled.* They had heard of his miracles.

22. *At the gracious words.* επι τοις λογοις της χαριτος, ' the graceful words;' literally, ' words of grace.' May refer both to his manner and the matter.

23. *Physician, heal thyself.* This proverb was probably in common use at that time.

Whatsoever we have heard done. Whatsoever we have heard that thou hast done. It would seem, from this, that Christ had *before* this wrought miracles in Capernaum. There had taken place the healing of the nobleman's son, and probably a remarkable change in his family, consequent upon their believing.

24. *No prophet.*—See Mt. xiii. 57, § 37. Has honour, or is acknowledged *as* a prophet; 'It is therefore much fitter for me to perform my miracles in other places than among a people whose prejudices will not give way even to conviction.'

[The prophets of God, however their words may have appeared to delight the ears of the Jews, among whom they lived, were not, as to the fulness of their message, received in their own country. This blessing was reserved for a people cast afar off, and unto whom the Lord was to be as a little sanctuary in the countries where they should come; a people despoiled, and who into captivity had been led away, broken-hearted, blind, and bruised; 'the lost sheep of the house of Israel,' Ezek. xi. 15, .6; xxxvii. 11.]

25. *Of a truth.* Truly, and therefore worthy of your observation. He calls attention to *two* cases

where *acknowledged* prophets had so little honour in their own nation that they bestowed their favours on foreigners.

Many widows, &c. God uses a holy sovereignty in the dispensation of his favours, not as man judges to be most likely, but as seems good in his sight; witness the widow of Sarepta, and Naaman the Syrian. This was a stab to their pride, and an intimation of the gracious regards of Heaven towards other nations.

In Israel. In the land of Israel. It was therefore the more remarkable, since there were so many in his own country whom he *might* have helped, that he should have gone to a heathen city, and aided a poor widow there.

The days of Elias. The days of Elijah; see the account of this in 1 Ki. xvii. 8—24. He was not a prophet in Judah, but in Israel; as was also Elisha, afterwards mentioned.

[*Three years and six months.* From 1 Kl. xviii. 1, 45, it would seem that the rain fell on the *third year.* That is, at the end of the third year after rain had ceased to fall at the usual time. There were two seasons of the year when rains fell in Judæa, in October and April, called the *early* and *latter* rain. Consequently, there was an interval between them of six months. To the three years, therefore, when rain was withheld *at the usual times*, are to be added the previous six months, when no rain fell as a matter of course; and consequently three years *and six months* elapsed without rain.]

Great famine. A great want of food, from long continued and distressing drought.

26. *Save unto Sarepta.* Sarepta was a town between Tyre and Sidon, near the Mediterranean sea. It was a Sidonian, and therefore a *Gentile* town.

27. *Many lepers.* For an account of the leprosy, see NOTE ou Lu. v. 12, § 21, p. 159, and ' ADDENDA,' p. 161, ' *Of leprosy.*'

PRACTICAL REFLECTIONS.

20 *ver.* Let us look to Jesus, not merely with wonder, or with the desire of selfish advantage, as did his countrymen, but with faith and hope in him as the promised Redeemer, and with earnest desire for the accomplishment of his gracious purposes with regard to his whole redeemed people.

21 *ver.* Let us see to it that the mission of Christ is not only fulfilled in our ears, but in our lives.

22 *ver.* Let us not merely wonder at the words of his grace, but receive them with faith, so as to be profited thereby.

[25—7 *ver.* The Lord early indicated his intention of communicating the blessing of his electing love north-westward, as with regard to the widow of Sarepta, by Elias; and northward, as in the instance of Naaman the Syrian, by Eliseus.]

HE THAT HATH EARS TO HEAR, LET HIM HEAR.—Matt. xi. 15.

PART II.   JESUS LED TO THE BROW OF A HILL.   SECT. XV.

LUKE iv. 27—30.

Eliseus the prophet; and none of-them was-cleansed, saving Naaman the Syrian. 28 And all-they in the synagogue, when-they-heard these-things, were-filled with-wrath, 29 and rose-up, and-thrust him out-of the city, and led him unto the brow of-the hill whereon their city was-built, that they-might-cast- him -down-headlong κατακρημνισαι. 30 But he passing through the-midst of-them went-his-way,

SCRIPTURE ILLUSTRATIONS.

27. *Eliseus*—appointment to the prophetic office, 1 Ki. xix. 16—.9—his curing Naaman, 2 Ki. v. 1—14.

28. *these things*—which went to shew that God chose Israel, not for blessing to themselves alone, but that they should dispense blessing to the nations, according to the original purpose, declared unto Abraham, Ge. xii. 3; xxii. 18.

filled with wrath—see Zechariah's martyrdom, 2 Ch. xxiv. 20, .1—' were filled with madness' against Jesus,

Lu. vi. 11, § 25—' ye seek to kill me,' Jno. viii. 37, 40, § 55—' hated both me and my Father,' xv. 24, .5, § 87.

30. *passing through, &c.*—other instances, Jno. viii. 59, § 55; x. 39, § 56.

In illustration of the supernatural power by which he was thus enabled to ' pass through the midst of ' his most deadly enemies unhurt, we have only to advert to the words of Jno. vii. 30, § 55, in a similar instance; and when in *Gethsemene* He said, ' I am he, they went backward,' &c., Jno. xviii. 6, § 88.

NOTES.

Time of Eliseus. Time of Elisha. The word *Eliseus* is the Greek way of writing the word Elisha; as *Elias* is of Elijah.

Saving Naaman the Syrian. Naaman, the general of Benhadad the Syrian's army. He was highly esteemed by his master, because he had saved Syria from ruin, probably in the battle where Ahab gave Benhadad his last defeat, or at the siege of Ramothgilead, when Ahab was slain. The account of his cure is contained in 2 Ki. v. 1—14.

25—27. God has a right to dispense his extraordinary favours as he pleases. He does this in a way which sometimes appears strange to man's judgment, but is nevertheless consistent with perfect wisdom and equity; as in the instances adverted to.

And they led him. και ήγαγον. Render: 'and they were leading or taking him,' &c.

To cast him down. ' Hurl him down the precipice.' A death sometimes, as among the Romans, adjudged by the law in the case of *sacrilege* ; of which, it seems, these superstitious zealots thought him guilty. This was the effect of a popular tumult.

PRACTICAL REFLECTIONS.

25—.8 *ver*. The words which to the Jews appeared gracious when they selfishly, and in the flesh, appropriated them to themselves, lost all their sweetness when Jesus pointed to the electing love of God to Gentiles.

[It may be noticed that the two instances of Divine favour, here referred to by our Lord, were both through the medium of prophets of Israel—of that house which had been long cast out among the Gentiles, and whose heritages in Galilee were now possessed by their brethren of the house of Judah. It is also to be observed, that the objects of favour were, the one in *Sarepta*, to the west, and the other from Syria, to the east, of Lebanon—' *the goodly mountain*,' De. iii. 25; ' *the holy mountain of God*,' ' *the mountain of the height of Israel*,' Eze. xx. 40; xxviii. 14.]

[The region of Tyre and Sidon, in the midst of which was *Sarepta*, and the region properly called *Syria*, of which Damascus was the capital, were both to the north of that portion of the promised land which was possessed by Israel under the law. Lebanon, between Damascus and Sarepta, se-ms to occupy the most central position, with regard to the whole land given by oath to Abraham, Ge. xv. It is midway between the river of Egypt and the great river Euphrates. This whole land is yet to be possessed by the children of promise, according to the everlasting covenant. * Then will be fulfilled the words of Isaiah, ii. 2, ' *And it shall come to pass in the last days, that the mountain of the* LORD'S *house shall be established in the top of the mountains, and shall be exalted above the hills; and all nations shall flow unto it*.' A pledge of the healing and help then to be freely bestowed upon the Gentiles, through the instrumentality of Israel, seems to have been given in the case of the widow of Sarepta and Naaman the Syrian.]

29 *ver*. How little do men know of themselves! How speedily were the worshippers in the synagogue, who had been listening with delight to the words of the evangelical prophet,—the great Teacher sent from God, of whom all the prophets testified !—how speedily, when their selfish nature and narrow sectarian prejudices were touched, were they turned into an infuriated rabble, hastening to hurl to destruction, out of their sight, Him upon whom their eyes had been, just before, in admiration fixed !

30 *ver*. The death of Jesus would at this time have been the act of individuals, but he was to be offered up in the view of the whole people, and by the authorities, civil and ecclesiastical, of the nation, and at the place and time appointed; therefore it was that passing through the midst of them he went his way.

The whole transaction shews: 1st. That the character given of the Galilæans elsewhere as being peculiarly wicked was a just one. 2od. It shews to what extremities the wickedness of the heart will lead men when it is acted out.

[There is in this narrative a very clear indication of the great purpose of God in revelation, as being especially designed for a people in another temper than the Jews, and dwelling in other countries than those in which the prophets prophesied.]

[The words were then closed up, and it is as vain to look for a true understanding of the prophets from the Jews, as it would have been to expect mercy at their hands for the meek and lowly Jesus.]

As Jesus who was of Judah hath shewn compassion to us, who were outcasts, let us shew compassion to his brethren according to the flesh, who are now suffering for their sin and folly, in rejecting Him, in whom we have been given to inherit blessing.

GEOGRAPHICAL NOTICES.

NAZARETH.—See §§ ii., vi., xxxvii., pp. 14, 43, 288.

GALILEE—A large and fertile territory of the north parts of Canaan. The Lower Galilee lay on the west of Jordan, and sea of Tiberias; and contained the portions of Issachar, Zebulun, Naphtali, and Asher. Upper Galilee lay eastward of the Jordan, and took in a great part of the lot of the eastern half-tribe of Manasseh.

Galilee of the Gentiles. So called, because it was inhabited by *Egyptians, Arabians*, and *Phœnicians*, according to the testimony of *Strabo*, and others. But it is, with a great degree of probability, referred to 1 Ki. ix. 11—.5. Solomon gave twenty cities of Lower Galilee, called the land of Cabul, to Hiram king of Tyre; '(Now *Hiram the king of Tyre had furnished Solomon with cedar trees and fir trees, and with gold, according to all his desire*,) . . . *king Solomon gave Hiram twenty cities in the land of Galilee*,' 1 Ki. ix. 11. From this circumstance

* *See* Dr. Keith's work on ' The Land of Israel according to the Covenant with Abraham, with Isaac, and with Jacob,' chap. ii. §§ 2, 3, 4, 5, pp. 57—164.

GEOGRAPHICAL NOTICES.—GALILEE—(continued.)

we may suppose this tract of country received the appellation 'Galilee of the Nations,' or of the Gentiles, Is. ix. 1. Benhadad, 1 Ki. xv. 20, and, long after, Tiglath-pileser, terribly ravaged the land of Galilee, 2 Ki. xv. 29. After the Jews returned from Babylon, the Samaritans kept possession of Samaria, or the portions of Ephraim and the western Manassites; but the Jews spread themselves into Galilee, and into the country called Peræa, beyond Jordan. In Galilee, our Saviour, and most of his disciples, were educated; and from this country he and they were sometimes called Galilæans. 'When Pilate heard of Galilee, he asked whether the man were a Galilæan,' Lu. xxiii. 6, § 90. 'And they were all amazed and marvelled, saying one to another, Behold, are not all these which speak Galilæans?' Ac. ii. 7.—See HISTORICAL SKETCH OF THE LAND OF PROMISE, p. ix.

SAREPTA.

SAREPTA, or ZAREPHATH.—A maritime city of Phœnicia, within the boundaries of the tribe of Asher, on the coast of the Mediterranean sea, Ju. v. 17, situate about midway between Tyre and Sidon, and is called 'a city of Sidon,' Lu. iv. 26. Dr. Robinson, describing his journey from Tyre to Sidon, at about four and three quarter hours from Tyre, says, ' We came to a wely, "tomb," near the shore, with a small khan close by, called el-Khudr, the Arab name of St. George. Five minutes beyond is a site of ruins on the left, indicating in themselves little more than a mere village. Opposite to this spot, high up on the southern slope of a partially isolated hill, and hardly half an hour distant, is a large village with two or three welys, bearing the name of Surafend. In this name we here have the Zarephath of the Old Testament, 1 Kl. xvii. 9, 10, and the Sarepta of the New, Lu. iv. 26, (see p. 104,) a place situated, according to Josephus and Pliny, between Tyre and Sidon, and belonging to the territory of the latter. Here Elijah dwelt long in the house of the widow, and miraculously continued to her the oil and meal, and restored her son to life, 1 KL xvii. 8—24. Eusebius and Jerome have the name, and the latter says Paula visited the spot. . . . The crusaders made it the seat of a Latin bishop, under the archbishop of Sidon; and erected near the port a small chapel over the reputed spot where Elijah dwelt, and raised the widow's son from the dead. The Christian chapel was doubtless succeeded by the mosk . . . and at the present day is probably found in the Wely el-Khudr. It would thus seem that the former city of Sarepta, or Surafend, stood near the sea shore; and that the present village, bearing the same name, upon the adjacent hills, has sprung up since the time of the crusaders. In the rocks along the foot of the hills are many excavated tombs, once doubtless belonging to the ancient city.'—*Robinson's Biblical Researches*, Vol. III. pp. 412—.4. The neighbouring scenery is described as 'exquisitely beautiful; the country rising gradually into hills of moderate height, and even to their summits covered with grain, and interspersed with olive trees.' Anciently, the wine of Sarepta was much celebrated.

ADDENDA.

'SYNAGOGUE,' p. 102.

SYNAGOGUE, the place where the Jews met for their public worship on ordinary occasions. When synagogues, properly so called, had their rise, we are uncertain. It is plain, that before the captivity the law was not read in them every sabbath, as it was afterwards; hence Jehoshaphat's reforming teachers had to carry a copy of it along with them, 2 Ch. xvii. 9, 'And they taught in Judah, and had the book of the law of the LORD with them, and went about throughout all the cities of Judah, and taught the people;' and its contents were much unknown in the time of Josiah, 2 Ki. xxii. 11, ' And it came to pass, when the king had heard the words of the book of the law, that he rent his clothes.' As most of the Jews, from the beginning of their settlement, attended the tabernacle or temple only at the three solemn feasts, it is probable they had a kind of synagogues, or schools, or proseuchæ, or prayer places, in one of which last our Saviour prayed all night, Lu. vi. 12, § 27. These differed from synagogues, as in them every one prayed by himself; they were in retired places, as by river sides, &c., Ac. xvi. 13, .6, and were uncovered, like groves; whereas synagogues were in elevated places, were covered with a roof, and one prayed as the mouth of the rest. Perhaps it was the proseuchæ that were the mohede (synagogues) of meeting-places, burned up by the Chaldeans, Ps. lxxiv. 8. Every trading fraternity had its synagogue, and companies of strangers, as Alexandrians, Cyrenians, and others, had theirs, for public prayer, and for the reading of the Scriptures. The scattered Jews, too, had theirs about Babylon; and almost everywhere in the eastern part of the Roman empire. The most famous synagogue the Jews ever had was the great synagogue of Alexandria.

Synagogues could only be erected where ten men of age, learning, piety, and easy circumstances, could be found to attend to the service which was enjoined on them. The erection of a synagogue being esteemed a mark of piety, they soon multiplied all over the land, and in Jerusalem alone, in our Saviour's time, there were from four hundred and sixty to four hundred and eighty. A council of *three* took cognizance of civil matters, and sometimes inflicted summary punishment; as we read in Mt. x. 17, § 39; Mk. xiii. 9, § 86.

The *sacrifices* of the Jews were appointed to be offered in *one* place, at Jerusalem. But there was nothing to forbid the other services of religion to be performed at any place. Accordingly the praises of God were sung in the schools of the prophets; and those who chose were assembled by the seers on the sabbath, and the new moons, for religious worship; see of the Shunammite woman's visit to Elisha, for her son; ' And he said, Wherefore wilt thou go to him today? it is neither new moon, nor sabbath, 2 Ki. iv. 23; 1 Sa. x. 5—11.

In the synagogues the *law*, i.e., the five books of Moses, divided into suitable portions, was read, prayers were offered, and the Scriptures were expounded. The Pentateuch was so distributed into portions for sabbath reading, that the whole might be gone through in the year; also that to them should be adjoined some such portion from the prophets as either had an affinity to the lesson from the Pentateuch, or was selected by the reader for edification. After reading the law and the prophets, the heads of the synagogue desired such learned and grave persons as happened to be there, to make a discourse to the people; and by virtue of this custom it was that our Saviour and the apostles were in the habit of attending at those places constantly, and of speaking to the people, Mk. vi. 2, § 37 Lu. iv. 15—22, pp. 102—.4; Ac. xiii. 14, .5, 44, &c. A short prayer concluded the service.

On the synagogue days the people assembled thrice: at the time of the morning and evening sacrifice, and in the dusk of the evening; and thither the devout persons oft retired for their secret prayers. There it was that the Pharisees stood, that their neighbours might hear them the better, Mt. vi. 5, § 19.

The synagogues were built in imitation of the temple, with a centre building, supported by pillars, with *courts* and porches. In the centre building, or chapel, was a place prepared for the reading of the law or the prophets. The law was kept in a chest, or ark, near to the pulpit. The chief seats, Mt. xxiii. 6, § 85, were those nearest to the pulpit. The people sat round, facing the pulpit. When the law was read, the officiating person rose; when it was expounded, he was seated. Our Saviour imitated their example, and was commonly seated in addressing the people, Mt. v. 1, § 19; xiii. 1, § 32.

PART II. JESUS CHOOSES CAPERNAUM TO DWELL IN. SECT. XVI.

SECTION 16.—JESUS MAKES CHOICE OF CAPERNAUM AS HIS PLACE OF ABODE; AND PREPARES TO ENTER THERE ON THE MINISTRY OF THE WORD OF THE KINGDOM, IN WHICH JOHN HAD PRECEDED HIM. JESUS CALLS FOUR DISCIPLES, SIMON AND ANDREW, AND JAMES AND JOHN, TO BE WITH HIM. Matt. iv. 12—22. Mark i. 14—20. Luke iv. 31.

(G. 18,) No. 16. *Jesus makes choice of Capernaum as his place of abode;* and prepares to enter on his public ministry, &c.—Line from Nazareth to Capernaum.*

MATT. iv. 12—7.   MARK i. 14, .5.   LUKE iv. 31.
[Ch. iv. 11, § ix. p. 66.]   [Ch. i. 13, § ix. p. 66.]   [Ch. iv. 30, § 15, p. 105.]
12 ªNow when- Jesus -had-   14 Now after that
heard that John was-cast-   John was-put-
into-prison παρεδοθη,   in-prison παραδοθηναι,
he-departed into Galilee;   Jesus came into Galilee.
13 and leaving Nazareth,
he-came and-dwelt in Capernaum,ᵇ   And came-down to Capernaum, 31
                                        ᵇa-city of Galilee.ᶜ
ᶜ*which is* upon-the-sea-coast, in the-borders   [For remainder, see p. 110.]
14 of Zabulon and Nephthalim: that it-might-
be-fulfilled which was-spoken by Esaias the
15 prophet, saying, The-land of-Zabulon, and
the-land of-Nephthalim, *by* the-way of-the-
sea, beyond Jordan, Galilee of-the Gentiles;
16 the people which sat in darkness saw great

SCRIPTURE ILLUSTRATIONS.

Mt. iv. 12. *John was cast into prison*—see the account of his being imprisoned and beheaded by Herod, Mt. xiv. 1—12, § 40.

13. *Zabulon*—'dwelling,'—see reference to the name by Leah: 'and Leah said, God hath endued me *with* a good dowry; now will my husband dwell with me, because I have born him six sons; and she called his name Zebulun,' Ge. xxx. 20—by the father: 'Zebulun shall dwell by the haven of the sea; and he shall be for an haven of ships; and his border *shall be* unto Zidon,' xlix. 13—allotment of the tribe, Jos. xix. 10—6.

Nephthalim—'wrestling:' 'and Rachel said, With great wrestlings have I wrestled with my sister, and I have prevailed: and she called her name Naphtali,' Ge. xxx. 8—by the father: 'Naphtali *is* a hind let

loose: he giveth goodly words,' xlix. 21—allotment of the tribe, Jos. xix. 32—.9.

14. *spoken by Esaias*—Is. ix. 1, 2—when contrasting the yet future invasion of Israel in the land, with the first and second invasions by the king of Assyria which had been predicted, viii. 7, 8, and the light of our Lord's first, with that of his second advent, ix. 2.

16. *region and shadow of death*—see the valley of dry bones described, Eze. xxxvii. 1—10—representing the case of the whole house of Israel, ver. 11, as contrasted with the case of Judah, ver. 16—the Jews were they who had sat in darkness, and whom the light had now visited; but rejecting that light, they have been left to wander in darkness, Jno. xii. 35, .6, § 82—see as to the light being more fully and gloriously displayed, Is. lx. 1—3, 19—21.

NOTES.

Mt. iv. 13. *Came and dwelt in Capernaum.* 'Dwelt.' Fixed on it to live there. It was conveniently situated for all parts, and well adapted to afford him opportunity to escape to the sea from the multitudes.

In this city, and its neighbourhood, Jesus spent no small part of the three years of his public ministry: it is hence called *his own city*, Mt. ix. 1, § 35. Here he headed the nobleman's son, Jno. iv. 47, § 14; Peter's wife's mother, Mt. viii. 14, .5, § 17; the centurion's servant, Mt. viii. 5—13, § 28; and the ruler's daughter, Mt. ix. 23—.5, § 36.—*See* GEOG. NOTICE, p. 109.

The sea coast. The only sea referred to in the gospel history is the 'sea of Galilee,' which is the same as the 'sea of Tiberias,' and 'lake Gennesaret.'

In the borders of Zabulon and Nephthalim. Jesus came and dwelt in the *boundaries* or *regions* of Zebulun and Naphtali.—*See* GEOGRAPHICAL NOTICES, p. 109.

15. *Beyond Jordan.* This does not mean on the east of Jordan, as the phrase sometimes denotes, but rather in the vicinity of the sources of Jordan, which were in Nephthalim.—*See* GEOGRAPHICAL NOTICES, Sect. xviii. ver. 25, p. 118.

16. *The people which sat in darkness, &c.* This is quoted from Is. ix. 2, where, instead of *sitting*, the prophet uses the word *walked*. The change of the term may be taken to point out the *increased* misery of these persons. *Sitting in darkness* expresses a greater degree of intellectual blindness, than *walking in darkness* does. Some commentators, however, affirm that the Hebrew phrases of *walked*, and *sat*, are only, to be or continue; καθημενος meaning no more than *degens*. The expression is evidently metaphorical, and represents the ignorance or spiritual darkness in which the people of that region, intermixed with the heathens, had lived, before they received the light of the gospel.

Saw great light. Christ himself, who came a light into the world.

The instruction which removes ignorance is called *light*—see Jno. iii. 19, § 12; 1 Jno. i. 5. As ignorance is often connected with crime and vice, so *darkness* is sometimes used to denote sin, 1 Th. v. 5; Ep. v. 11; Lu. xxii. 53, § 88.

PRACTICAL REFLECTIONS.

Mt. iv. 12. The good Shepherd, although he will not needlessly throw away his life, will yet be forward to place himself at the post of danger, when it can be of advantage to the flock. Thus Jesus came into the country which was ruled by the tyrant who had imprisoned John, his forerunner.

[13—16. Where judgment is to be the most intense, God mercifully vouchsafes, sometimes, the fullest offers of his grace, as was the case with regard to Capernaum, and the neighbouring countries, which afterwards were so severely devoted to destruction, and in which they still remain.]

Let us not flatter ourselves that because we have

been peculiarly favoured with God's messages of mercy, and because we are among those who have received them, we therefore may neglect them with impunity. The great scene of our Lord's ministry, GALILEE, and that wherefrom he gathered the greatest number of his early disciples, was, even before JUDÆA, given over to the sword of the Romans.

'Let us, like Jesus, prudently retire from the malice of those who wickedly oppose us, and from him learn, that when we have great duties to perform for the church of God, we are not wantonly to endanger our lives. When we can secure them without a sacrifice of principle, we are to do it.'

* Greswell, Vol. II. Diss. xxi. pp. 365—.70. On the choice of Capernaum.

WALK BEFORE ME, AND BE THOU PERFECT.—Gen. xvii. 1.   [107

SECT. XVI. JESUS BEGINS TO PREACH IN GALILEE. PART II.

MATT. iv. 16, .7.
light; and to-them which sat in the-region and shadow of-death light is-sprung-up ανετειλεν.
17 From that-time Jesus began to-preach,*
and to-say, Repent:
for the kingdom of heaven is-at-hand.

MARK i. 14, .5.
preaching
d the gospel of-the kingdom of God,*e*
and saying, 15
f The time καιρος is-fulfilled, and the kingdom of God is-at-hand: repent-ye, and believe ev the gospel.

(G. 19,) No. 16. *The four disciples, Simon and Andrew, James and John, are called by Jesus.*—At the sea of Galilee.

MATT. iv. 18—22.
18 *a* And Jesus, walking by the sea of Galilee, saw two brethren, Simon called Peter, and Andrew his brother, casting a-net into the sea: for they-were fishers.
19 And he-saith unto-them,
Follow me, and I-will-make you *b* fishers of-men.

MARK i. 16—20.
Now as-he-walked by the sea of Galilee, 16 he-saw Simon
and Andrew his brother casting a-net into the sea: for they-were fishers.
And Jesus said unto-them, 17
Come-ye after me, and I-will-make you
b to-become fishers of-men.*c*

SCRIPTURE ILLUSTRATIONS.

Mk. i. 14. *gospel of the kingdom of God*—referred to, Is. ix. 7; xxxii. 1; Da. vii. 13, .4; Je. iii. 12—.7—the coming of the king is to be greatly rejoiced in, Ps. xcvi., xcviii.; Zec. ix. 9—prediction as to the preaching of Jesus, Is. lxi. 1—3—fulfilment, Mt. iv. 23, § 18; ix. 35, § 38; Lu. viii. 1, § 30—carried out by his apostles, Mt. x. 7, § 39; Ep. iL 17—he speaketh to us from heaven, He. xii. 25—9.

15. *the time is fulfilled*—the coming of Shiloh predicted by Jacob, in the blessing of Judah, Ge. xlix. 9, 10—when the alternative would be given (as Is. i. 19, 20) to the Jews, of being willing and obedient, or of refusing and rebelling against ' Messiah the Prince,' Da. ix. 2—' the fulness of the time was come,' Ga. iv. 4—preparing for ' the dispensation of the fulness of times,' Ep. i. 10.

at hand—so John had preached, Mt. iii. 2, § 7, p. 50 —the seventy, ' the kingdom of God is come nigh unto you,' Lu. x. 9, 11, § 60—' the word is nigh thee,' Rom. x. 6—9—' the grace unto you,' 1 Pe. i. 10—' the true light now shineth,' 1 Jno. ii. 8—now was to be the entering into the sanctuary, (where were the seven golden candlesticks, as Rev. i. 12,) until unto the kingdom state, described in ch. iv., represented by the holy of holies, in which was the mercy seat, or throne of the Lord—*see* Is. vi. 1—4; Heb. ix. 1—5.

Repent ye—' wash you, make you clean; put away the evil of your doings from before mine eyes; cease to do evil; learn to do well; seek judgment, relieve

the,' &c., Is. i. 16, .7—' let the wicked forsake his way,' &c., iv. 7—' repent, and turn *yourselves* from all your transgressions; so iniquity shall not be your ruin,' Eze. xviii. 30—' if thou wilt return, O Israel, saith the LORD, return unto me: and if thou wilt put away thine abominations out of my sight, then shalt thou not remove,' Je. iv. 1—the repentance of Israel contemplated by Moses, Le. xxvi. 40—.2—by Solomon, 1 Ki. viii. 47—9—repentance of Ephraim, Je. xxxi. 18—20—Jesus came to call 'sinners to repentance,' Mt. ix. 13, § 36—' Him hath God exalted with his right hand... a Prince and a Saviour, for to give repentance to Israel, and forgiveness of sins,' Ac. v. 31—' repent ye therefore, and be converted,' iii. 19—the goodness of God leadeth to repentance, Rom. ii. 4—repentance to salvation, 2 Co. vii. 9—11—repentance to the acknowledging of the truth,' &c., 2 Ti. ii. 25, .6—the Lord is longsuffering, &c., 2 Pe. iii. 9—James, in his Epistle ' to the twelve tribes scattered abroad,' especially calls for repentance: ' Cleanse &c.' Ja. iv. 8. . . . . this washing by the word was represented by the washing of the priesthood in the laver, made of looking-glasses—comp. Ex. xxxviii. 8, with Ja. i. 21—7.

16. *sea*—Jesus was accustomed to minister the word by the sea of Galilee, Lu. v. 1, § 20; Mk. iL 13, § 22; iii. 7, § 26; Mt. xv. 29, § 46; Jno. vi. 1, § 40—after his resurrection, he there shewed himself to his disciples, Jno. xxi. 1, § 97.

NOTES.

Light is sprung up. The heathen writers represented the arrival of a public benefactor in a place as a new light sprung up in the midst of darkness.—The blessed hope of Israel, the long-expected Messiah, was come—Christ, who came to give the light of the gospel, that we might have the light of life.

Mk. i. 14. *The gospel.* The glad tidings respecting the full and free remission of sins through Jesus Christ, and his coming kingdom.

Of the kingdom of God. God is about to take the government more manifestly into his own hands.

15. *The time is fulfilled.* ' The time of my kingdom, foretold by Daniel, and expected.'

' The time here spoken of,' says Campbell, ' is that which, according to the predictions of the prophets, was to intervene between their days, or between any period assigned by them, and the appearance of

the Messiah. This had been revealed to Daniel, as consisting of what, in prophetic language, is denominated seventy weeks, that is (every week being seven years) four hundred and ninety years; reckoning from the order issued to rebuild the temple at Jerusalem. However much the Jews misunderstood many of the *other* prophecies relating to the reign of Messiah, what concerned both the time and the place of his first appearance seems to have been pretty well apprehended by the bulk of the nation.'—*Comp.* Gal. iv. 4; Eph. i. 10; and *see* Da. ix. 25.

Repent, &c. In submitting to the government of Christ, men must renounce the dominion of sin.—*See* ' Note' on Lu. iii. 3, § 7, ' *The baptism of repentance*,' p. 50.

Mt. iv. 19. *Casting a net into the sea.* Αμφίβληστρον, answers to that kind of net which we call a *drug-net*.

PRACTICAL REFLECTIONS.

17 *ver.* Jesus shunned not to identify himself with the imprisoned servant of God; taking up the message which John had not now power to deliver, he proclaimed the words of warning and of grace, ' *Repent: for the kingdom of heaven is at hand.*'

[Mk. i. 15. The time was come for men to cease from looking to rites performed for them according to the law, and when they should place their imme-

diate dependence upon God, through the one Mediator of the new covenant.]

Those who would enjoy the kingdom of God in glory, must now become the subjects of that kingdom, through grace, and have the law of that kingdom, which is love, written upon their hearts, and put in their inward parts—no longer regarding the words of Jesus as hard sayings, but as gospel, as ' glad tidings of great joy.'

* In the vicinity of Capernaum, Greswell, Vol. II. p. 280. On this call, *see* § xx. ADDENDA, p. 157.

MY SON, GIVE ME THINE HEART.—Prov. xxiii. 26.

PART II. FOUR DISCIPLES CALLED. SECT. XVI.

MATT. iv. 20—2.	MARK i. 18—20.
20 *And they straightway left *their* nets, and-followed him. 21 And going-on*d* from-thence, he-saw *other two brethren, James the son of Zebedee, and John his brother, in a ship with Zebedee their father, mending their nets;/ and he-called them. 22 *g*And they immediately ευθεως left the ship and *h* their father, and-followed him. [Ver. 23, ? xviii. p. 115.]	And straightway they-forsook their nets, 18 and-followed him. And when-he-had-gone 19 *d* a-little farther-thence, he-saw*e* James the son of Zebedee, and John his brother, who also *were* in the ship mending *their* nets. /And straightway ευθεως he-called them:*g* 20 and they-left *h* their father Zebedee in the ship with the hired-servants, and-went after him.

SCRIPTURE ILLUSTRATIONS.

Mt. iv. 19. *follow me*—Jesus had already called Peter by a new name, Jno. i. 42, § 10, p. 71—call of Philip, ver. 43—the same call to Matthew, Mt. ix. 9, § 22, or

Levi, Lu. v. 27, § f&.—through suffering, the followers of Jesus are being led into glory, Mt. xvi. 24—.7, § 50. —*See* also xix. 27—30, § 75; Lu. xxii. 28—30, § 87.

NOTES.

Mk. 1. 20. *Hired servants.* The disciples laboured for their daily bread; but the sacrifice they made was of some worldly property; they were not mere labourers, but had 'hired servants' under them.

PRACTICAL REFLECTIONS.

Mt. iv. 19. How prone are men to be cumbered with the world, and to depart from the rule, ' Seek ye *first the kingdom of God!*' Although Peter had already been called, Jno. i. 42, § 10, p. 71, yet here we find him as having returned to his fishing.

[How much in contrast to their previous employment was that to which Simon and Andrew were invited! It was not to draw unto death, but out of overwhelming cares of this life, into a peaceful trust in God, and joyful hope of the world to come—out of that perdition into which their countrymen were fast sinking, and through the sure protection of Almighty God, in all the trials through which they had to pass in preparation for the kingdom.]

Let us not stop to calculate the worldly loss to which we may be called in obeying the command of

Christ; but straightway leaving all to which we may previously have looked for support, let us in all simplicity of heart follow Jesus.

Neither let the claims of natural relationship, any more than mere selfish considerations, prevent our entire devotedness to the service of our Lord, who is equally able to provide for those we leave behind, as he is for us, in his more immediate service. At the same time, let us beware of mistaking the suggestions of our own vain imaginations for the call of our Divine Master, who has a right to dispose of us as seemeth to him good.

Let us not despise the poor: such the Lord chose to be his more privileged associates upon earth: nor has he ceased to honour such in his service now that he is in heaven.

GEOGRAPHICAL NOTICES.

GALILEE OF THE GENTILES.—*See* Sect. xv. p. 105.

CAPERNAUM. — The denunciation of our blessed Lord against this city, pronounced Mt. xi. 20—4, § 29, has been awfully fulfilled, so that, of it, and the other cities, Chorazin and Bethsaida, upbraided at the same time, no traces of former grandeur can be found. Capernaum must have been a city of vast importance: for the form of our Lord's imprecation was, 'And thou, Capernaum, which art exalted unto

heaven, shalt be brought down to hell.' It was highly favoured above all the neighbouring cities; being chosen as the dwelling place of the Son of God, and as the city which had numberless opportunities of witnessing his Divine power and mercy.—*See* Sect. xi. p. 79.

An awful voice rises from the ruined heaps of Gennesaret, warning the cities of our favoured land, that a despised gospel will bring them low as Capernaum.—See Sect. xx. ' *Lake Gennesaret.*'

ZEBULUN, p. 107,

Or *Zabulon,* the tenth son of Jacob, the sixth by Leah, Ge. xxx. 20. From his three sons, Sered, Elon, and Jahleel, sprung three numerous families. When this tribe came out of Egypt their fighting men amounted to 57,400 men, (*see* Nu. i. 31,) commanded by Eliab the son of Elon, ver. 9: they increased 3100 in the wilderness, xxvi. 26, .7. Their spy to search Canaan was Gaddiel the son of Sodi, xiii. 10; and their prince to divide it was Elizaphan the son of Parnach, xxxiv. 25. They had their inheritance on the south of the tribes of Asher and Naphtali, and north of Issachar, and had the sea of Galilee on the east, and the Mediterranean on the west; theirs was an eminently flourishing portion: they enriched themselves by their fisheries, their sea trade, and making

of glass; they did not drive out the Canaanites from Kitron or Nahalol, Ju. i. 30. But they and the Naphtalites, under Barak, were very active in routing the host of Jabin, iv. 14, .8. They assisted Gideon against the Midianites, vi. 35. ' *Elon, a Zebulonite, judged Israel; and he judged Israel ten years,*' xii. 11. And 50,000 of them attended at David's coronation to be king over Israel, and brought large quantities of provision, 1 Ch. xii. 33, 40. They partly joined with Hezekiah in his reformation, 2 Ch. xxx. 11. Perhaps there was also a city called *Zebulun,* near Accho, which is said to have been built in the form of Tyre and Sidon, and to have been taken and burned by Cestius the Roman about A.D. 66, Jos. xix. 27.

NAPHTALI, p. 107.

NAPHTALI.—The sixth son of Jacob, and by Bilhah, the handmaid of Rachel, Ge. xxx. 8. His sons were Jahzeel, Guni, Jezer, and Shillem, xlvi. 24, all of them parents of a numerous progeny. When this tribe came out of Egypt, it consisted of 53,400 fighting men, *see* Nu. i. 42, .3; ii. 29, 30, under the command of Ahira, the son of Enan, ver. 29; x. 27; but they decreased in the wilderness to 45,400, xxvi. 50. They encamped on the north of the tabernacle, and

marched in the rear of the Hebrew host, in the camp of Dan. Their spy to search Canaan was Nahbi, the son of Vophsi, xiii. 14; and their agent to divide it was Pedahel, the son of Ammihud, xxxiv. 28. Their inheritance was the ' *west and the south,*' along the south of Lebanon; on the east were the seas of Merom and Tiberias; on the west lay Asher. Their inheritance was extremely fertile, De. xxxiii. 23; Jos. xix. 32, .3.

[109

SECTION 17.—JESUS TEACHES FOR THE FIRST TIME IN THE SYNAGOGUE OF CAPERNAUM ON THE SABBATH DAY; THE PEOPLE ARE ASTONISHED AT HIS MANNER OF TEACHING; HE CASTS OUT A DEVIL. THE SAME DAY HE HEALS SIMON'S MOTHER-IN-LAW. AND AFTER SUNSET PERFORMS DIVERS MIRACLES OF HEALING AND DISPOSSESSION. Matt. viii. 14—17. Mark i. 21—34. Luke iv. 31—41.

(G. 20.) No. 17. *Jesus teaches for the first time in the synagogue of Capernaum on the sabbath day;* the people are astonished at his manner of teaching; he casts out a devil.

MARK i. 21—.8.

21 *And they-went into Capernaum; and straightway on-the sabbath-day he-entered into the synagogue, and-taught.*
22 And they-were-astonished at his doctrine: *for he-taught them as one-that-had authority, εξουσιαν, and not as the scribes.*

23 And there-was in their synagogue a-man with εν an-unclean spirit; and he-cried-out,
24 saying, Let-us-alone; what *have* we *to do* with thee τι ημιν και σοι, *thou* Jesus of-Nazareth? art-thou-come to-destroy us? I-know thee who thou-art, the Holy One of God.

LUKE iv. 31—.7.
[For preceding part, see p. 107.]

and taught them on the sabbath-days. 31

And they-were-astonished at his doctrine: 32 for his word was with power.
εν εξουσια.

*And in the synagogue there-was a-man, 33 which-had a-spirit of-an-unclean devil, and cried-out with-a-loud voice, saying, Let-us-alone; what *have* we *to do* 34 with thee, *thou* Jesus of-Nazareth? art-thou-come to-destroy us? I-know thee who thou-art; the Holy One of God.

SCRIPTURE ILLUSTRATIONS.

Mk. i. 21. *synagogue—see custom*, Lu. iv. 16, § 12, p. 102; Mt. iv. 23, § 18; Lu. 25, § 38; xiii. 54, § 37; Lu. xiii. 10, § 65; Juo. vi. 59, § 43.

22. *astonished—*so at the conclusion of his sermon on the mount, Mt. vii. 29, .9, § 19—*see* prediction, 'Behold, I and the children,' &c., Is. viii. 18—*confirm*, 'Whence hath this *man* this wisdom, and *these* mighty works?' Mt. xiii. 54, § 37.

23. *an unclean spirit*—*see* the remarkable instance of Saul, as falling a prey to an evil spirit, upon the spirit of the Lord departing from him, 1 Sa. xvi. 14,.5—David was given power to drive away from him, for a time, that evil spirit, ver. 23—the true David did cast out the evil spirits, as Mt. viii. 2—31, § 35—he gave the like power to his twelve disciples, x. 1, § 39—and to the seventy, Lu. x. 17, § 60—promised to them that believe, Mk. xvi. 17, § 98 —this power exercised by Philip in Samaria, Ac. viii. 5—7—*see* the case of a damsel at Philippi, xvi. 16—8.

24. *let us alone*—the language of the wicked, 'Depart from us,' &c., Job xxi. 14—so Ahab to Elijah, 'Art thou he that troubleth Israel?' &c., 1 Ki. xviii. 17,.8—so the Jews spoke of Paul and Silas, 'These that have turned the world upside down,' Ac. xvii. 6 —'the devils also believe, and tremble,' Ja. ii. 19.

destroy us—the Holy One of God took on him our nature, that he might destroy not only the devil, He. ii. 14, but ' the works of the devil,' 1 Jno. iii. 8—if the devil being bound for a thousand years, *see* Rev. xx. 2 —and his subsequent destruction, ver. 10.

Holy One—the true High Priest, to whom in perpetuity belong the Thummim and Urim, represented by those which Aaron wore, De. xxxiii. 8—'wilt thou suffer thine Holy One to see corruption,' Ps. xvi. 10 —'light of Israel shall be for a fire, and his Holy One for a flame,' Is. x. 17—'I am the Lord thy God, the Holy One of Israel, thy Saviour,' xliii. 3, 14—'the Redeemer of Israel, his Holy One,' xlix. 7—the Jews denied the Redeemer of Israel, 'the Holy One and the Just,' and desired a murderer, Ac. iii. 14.

NOTES.

Mk. i. 21. *Straightway*. On the following sabbath.
The synagogue.—See ADDENDA, Sect. xv. p. 106.

22. *At his doctrine.* επι τη διδαχη αυτου, *at his manner of teaching.* The word διδαχη denotes often *the doctrine* taught, sometimes *the act* of teaching, and sometimes even *the manner* of teaching.

As one that had authority, and not as the scribes. The scribes were the learned men and teachers of the Jewish nation, and were principally Pharisees. They taught chiefly the sentiments of their rabbins, and the traditions which had been delivered; they consumed much of their time in useless disputes and 'vain jangling.' Jesus was open, plain, grave, useful; delivering truth as *became* the oracles of God, not trifling; and confirming his doctrine by miracles and argument; teaching *as having power*, as it is in the original, and not in the vain and foolish manner of the Jewish doctors.—*See* ADDENDA, 'On Christ's manner of teaching,' p. 113.

Scribes.—See ADDENDA, Sect. v. p. 39.

23 *A man with an unclean spirit.* εν, 'in an unclean spirit,' for the spirit had the man in his possession.—*Henry.*

It is probable that this man had lucid intervals, or he would not have been admitted into the synagogue.

24. *What have we to do with thee?* Jesus came to destroy the works of the devil, and he had a right, therefore, to liberate the captive, and to punish him who had possessed him. Satan still considers it an infringement of his rights, when God frees a sinner from bondage, and destroys his influence over the soul.

To destroy us? The Jews had a tradition that the Messiah would destroy Galilee; this, therefore, ought to be considered as spoken by the man, as a Galilean; and by such representations Satan may have intended to excite such fears in the Galileans as would stir them up to enmity against Jesus, as at Nazareth.

PRACTICAL REFLECTIONS.

[The word of Jesus was with power, but there was another and an adverse spiritual power in the same synagogue. And it was the duty of the hearers not to confound the two powers, so as to blame Jesus for the confusion that resulted. It would not have become them to be scandalized at all extraordinary manifestation of spiritual power, but carefully to survey the facts, and honestly and clearly to distinguish between things that so widely differ.—*See* Mt. xii. 24, .5, § 31; Lu. iv. 34, *supra*.]

Mk. i. 21. Let us improve the sabbath day, as our Lord so frequently gave us example, by frequenting the house of prayer, and engaging in religious instruction, either as teachers or as taught.

22 *ver.* How different is the teaching of one who knows his mission is from God, and is well acquainted with the truth of his message, from that of the scribes, who doubtfully reported the conflicting opinions of the doctors!

*June 5, the first sabbath after the day of Pentecost, May 30, A.U. 780. Vol. II. Diss. xxiii. p. 260.

PART II. JESUS CASTS OUT AN UNCLEAN SPIRIT.

MARK i. 25—.8.

25 And Jesus rebuked him, saying, Hold thy-peace φιμωθητι, and come-out of him
26 And when-· the unclean spirit · -
*had-torn σπαραξαν, him *
*and cried with-a-loud voice,
he-came-out of him.*

27 * And they-were-· all ·-amazed, εθαμβηθησαν, insomuch-that they-questioned συζητειν among themselves, saying, What-thing is this?
what new doctrine *is* this?* for with authority commandeth-he επιτασσει *even the unclean spirits, and they-do-obey him.*

28 " And immediately his fame ἡ ακοη spread-abroad throughout all the region* - round-about *Galilee.

LUKE iv.

And Jesus rebuked hi thy-peace, and cum
And when-· th ſhad-thrown ριψαν h

he-came-out
* and-hurt him not *
And they-were *
*εγενετο θαμβος,
συνελαλουν among th

* What a word *is* authority and power δυν the unclean
" and they-co
And the-fame of *n went-o
*into every place o round-ab

SCRIPTURE ILLUSTRATIONS.

25. *rebuked*—' the LORD said unto SATAN, The LORD rebuke thee, O Satan; even the LORD that hath chosen Jerusalem rebuke thee: *is* not this a brand plucked out of the fire?' Zec. iii. 2—' when Jesus saw that the people came running together, he rebuked the foul spirit, saying unto him, Thou dumb and deaf spirit, I charge thee, come out of him, and enter no more into him. And *the spirit* cried, and rent him sore, and came out of him: and he was as one dead; insomuch that many said, He is dead. But Jesus took him by the hand, and lifted him up; and he arose,' Mk. ix. 25—.7, § 51—also the fever, Lu. iv. 39, p. 112—and 'the winds and the sea,' Mt. viii. 26, § 31.

27. *amazed*—same at casting out of a dumb devil: 'and when the devil was cast out, the dumb spake: and the multitudes marvelled, saying, It was never so seen in Israel,' Mt. ix. 33, 'and all the people were a this the son of David?' xii.

Lu. iv. 38. *besought him* faults one to another, and p ye may be healed. The effe righteous man availeth me tenel to such prayer for c Jairus' daughter: 'and, bel the rulers of the synagogu when he saw him, he fell a him greatly, saying, My litt point of death: *I pray thee* on her, that she may be hea And *Jesus* went with him; a him, and thronged him,' M vii. 2—10, § 29.

NOTES.

25. *And Jesus rebuked him.* This was not the man that he rebuked, but the *spirit*, for he instantly commanded the same being to come out of the man. His conversation was with the *evil spirit*; proving conclusively that it was not a mere disease, or derangement—for how could the Son of God hold converse with *disease*, or *delirium*?—but that he conversed with a *being*, who also conversed, reasoned, cavilled, felt, resisted, and knew him.

Hold thy peace. Greek. '*Be muzzled.*' Restrain thyself. Cease from complaints, and come out of the man. This was a very signal proof of the power of Jesus.

26. *And when the unclean* pant, though doomed to ol he was obliged, not because lust power, inflicted all the bowel to the Son of God, the nature of an evil disposi

Torn. σπαραξαν, 'convul lent convulsions and spasms

27. *And they were all ame* imports a mingled feeling It was done by a word. He and by his own authority. *superior* to all the unclean s

PRACTICAL REFLECTIONS.

Lu. iv. 34. How opposite the call of Jesus, and that of the unclean devil! Jesus called for change of heart and life, saying, '*Repent ye.*' But the unclean spirit cried out with a loud voice, '*Let us alone.*'

Jesus had invited us to a blessed and eternal union with himself in the kingdom of God, Mk. i. 15, § 16, p. 108; but the devil cried out, '*What have we to do with thee, thou Jesus of Nazareth?*'

[How crafty was Satan in uniting the name of Jesus with a place which had just recently been the scene of confusion and outrage, in connection with his preaching, and which had repudiated him even so as to seek his destruction! The name 'Jesus of Nazareth,' also, covered over the most important truth, that Jesus had, according to the promises, been born in Bethlehem ;

Jesus had come preaching the gospel, or glad tidings, but Satan insinuates that his coming was for a very different purpose: '*Art thou come to destroy us?*' It is true that the word preached is either the savour of life unto life, or of death unto death.

The devil may acknowledge Jesus as '*the Holy* One *of God*,' but it is only in truth to confess Christ a *the flesh,* and to give thank his holiness, in place of desi alone.'

[35 ver. Let us not be dec but examine every manifes ther it be of God or not, an made, be not only truth, but blessed Redeemer, as being our redemption, who should as Lord and Christ.]

Mk. i. 26 Satan is not t overcome, when he makes th gle to retain possession, and power in opposition to the cl

Lu. iv. 36, .7. The efforts the cause of truth are som for its furtherance. The cu a deeper search into the w *word is this?*' and the natu immediately his *fame spread* the region round about Galil

SECT. XVII. JESUS HEALS VARIOUS DISEASES. PART II.

(G. 21,) No. 17. *The same day he heals Simon's mother-in-law of a fever.—At Capernaum.*

MATT. viii. 14, .5. [Ch. viii. 13, & xxviii.]	MARK i. 29—31.	LUKE iv. 38, .9.
14 And when Jesus was come into Peter's house, he saw his wife's-mother laid, βεβλημενην and sick-of-a-fever.	29 ᵃ And forthwith, when-they-were-come out of the synagogue, they-entered into the house of Simon and Andrew, with James and John.ᵇ 30 But Simon's wife's-mother lay κατεκειτο sick of a-fever, ᶜ and anon they-tell him of her.ᵈ	And 38 he-arose out-of the synagogue, and-entered into Simon's house. ᵇ And Simon's wife's-mother was taken-with συνεχομενη a-great fever;ᶜ ᵈ and they-besought him for her. And he-stood over her, 39 and-rebuked the fever;ᵉ
15 And he-touched her hand, and the fever left her: ƒ and she-arose, and ministered unto-them.	31 ᵉ And he-came and-took her by-the hand, and-lifted her up; and immediately the-fever left her,ƒ and she-ministered unto-them.	and it-left her: and immediately she-arose and-ministered unto-them.

After sunset Jesus performs divers miracles of healing and dispossession.

MATT. viii. 16, .7.	MARK i. 32—4.	LUKE iv. 40, .1.
16 When the-even 'οψιας δε γενομενης was-come, they-brought unto-him many that-were-possessed-with-devils:	22 ᵃ And at-even,ᵇ when the sun did-set, ᶜ they-brought unto him all that-were diseased, and them that-were-possessed-with-devils. ᵈ 33 ᵉ And all the city was gathered-together at the door.ƒ 34 And he-healed many that-were sick of-divers diseases, and cast-out many devils; of many, crying-out, and saying, Thou art Christ the Son of God. And he-rebuking	Now 40 ᵇ when the sun-was-setting,ᶜ Δυνοντος δε του ηλιου all-they that had any-sick with-divers diseases brought them unto him; ᵈ and he laid *his* hands on-every one of-them, and-healed them.ᵉ ƒ And devils also came-out 41

33 ᵉ And all the city was gathered-together at the door.ƒ
and he-cast-out the spirits 34 And he-healed many
with-*his*-word, and healed that-were sick of-
all that-were sick: divers diseases, and
                              cast-out many devils;   ƒ And devils also came-out 41
                                                     of many, crying-out, and saying, Thou art
                                                     Christ the Son of God. And he-rebuking

SCRIPTURE ILLUSTRATIONS.

Mk. i. 31. *took her by the hand*—so he raised up Jairus' daughter, Mk. v. 41, .2, § 36—so Peter lifted up the lame man, Ac. iii. 7.

Lu. iv. 40. *when the sun was setting*—the day was from evening to evening, as Ge. i. 5, and the sabbath had expired on which the immediately preceding acts of mercy had taken place, Mk. i. 29—31—as the Jews were superstitiously scrupulous with regard to the sabbath, Mk. iii. 1—5, § 25; Lu. xiii. 14, § 65—but our Lord held that it was lawful to do good on the sabbath, Mt. xii. 12, § 25; Lu. xiii. 16, § 65.

41. *thou art Christ*—this confession he even forbade his disciples to make, until they were better instructed, Mt. xvi. 20, § 50—it is the special office of the Holy Ghost, the Comforter, to testify of Jesus, as being the Christ, Jno. xv. 26, § 87—with which being anointed, the disciples were to bear witness of Christ, Ac. i. 4, 8. Evil spirits still being forbid to testify of Christ, this is a criterion whereby they may be distinguished from the Spirit of God: 'Hereby know ye the Spirit of God: Every spirit that confesseth that Jesus Christ is come in the flesh is of God: and every spirit that confesseth not that Jesus Christ is come in the flesh is not of God: and this is that *spirit* of antichrist, whereof ye have heard that it should come; and even now already is it in the world,' 1 Jno. iv. 2, 3—' wherefore I give you to understand, that no man speaking by the Spirit of God calleth Jesus accursed: and *that* no man can say that Jesus is the Lord, but by the Holy Ghost,' 1 Co. xii. 3.

NOTES.

Mt. viii. 14. *Peter's house.* That Peter lived at Capernaum, and that Christ lodged with him, is evident from this verse compared with ch. xvii. 24, § 52. Grotius, however, conjectures that, as Peter and Andrew were of Bethsaida, see Jno. i. 44, § 10, p. 72, the house of Peter's mother-in-law at Capernaum was only a temporary residence, to which Christ and his apostles sometimes resorted. But Drs. Lightfoot and Macknight suppose that Peter and Andrew his brother had removed to this city for the convenience of their trade, after Peter's marriage. Mark adds that Simon and Andrew lived together, and that James and John went with them into the house.

Fever. A disease, consisting in a fermentation of the blood, accompanied with a quick pulse.

15. *And he touched her hand.* The miracle here recorded did not, as in some other cases, consist in the cure of an incurable disorder, but in the *mode* of cure, instantly and by a touch.

Mk. i. 32. *And at even, when the sun did set.* ὀψιας. The Hebrews reckoned two ὀψιαι, the *early*, from the ninth hour to our six o'clock, or sunset, and the *late*, from sunset to nightfall. From Mk. i. 32 it appears that the *later* one is here meant; namely, after sunset. Thus the sabbath (for we find from Mk. i. 21 that it was a sabbath day) had ended when the sick were brought; and hence they did it without scruple.

33. *All the city.* A great part of the city. A great multitude from the city. All that were brought to him he healed. This was proof of two things; first, his great benevolence; and, secondly, his Divine mission.

PRACTICAL REFLECTIONS.

Mk. i. 29. Although Jesus was now so great in the eyes of the people, he shunned not to acknowledge the most intimate fellowship with his humble disciples, the four fishermen of Galilee.

Lu. iv. 39. Although Jesus had called Peter from his fishing, he gave no intimation that he should put away his wife, as his pretended successors have commanded with regard to the Romish priesthood. Our Lord rather honoured the relation, by going so publicly into Peter's house and healing his wife's mother.

PART II. CHRIST SUFFERS NOT THE DEVILS TO SPEAK. SECT XVII.

MATT. viii. 17.	MARK i. 34.	LUKE iv. 41.
17 *that it-might-be-fulfilled which was-spoken by Esaias the prophet, saying, Himself took our infirmities, and bare εβαστασε our sicknesses. [Ch. viii. 18, § xxxiv.]	and suffered not the devils to-speak, because they knew him.	them suffered them not to-speak: for they knew that-he was(τον)Christ.⁶

SCRIPTURE ILLUSTRATIONS.

Mt. viii. 17. *fulfilled*—'surely he hath borne our griefs, and carried our sorrows: yet we did esteem him stricken, smitten of God, and afflicted,' Is. liii. 4 —'who his own self bare our sins in his own body on the tree, that we, being dead to sins, should live unto righteousness: by whose stripes ye were healed,' 1 Pe. ii. 24—he even bore the punishment that was to be inflicted upon the most vile--upon one prophesying by an unclean spirit—and on whom his nearest friends were commanded to use violence: ' And one shall say unto him, What *are* these wounds in thine hands?' Then he shall answer, *Those* with which I was wounded *in* the house of my friends,' Zec. xiii. 6—*comp.* with ver. 2, 3—' For he hath made him *to be* sin for us, who knew no sin; that we might be made the righteousness of God in him,' 2 Co. v. 21.

NOTES.

34. *And suffered not the devils to speak, because they knew him.* The sense is, ' He would not suffer them to speak, because they knew, and would address him as Messiah;' a title to which our Lord as yet made no public claim, lest he should excite tumult among the people.

Mt. viii. 17. *That it might be fulfilled, &c.* The word translated 'griefs' in Isaiah, and 'infirmities' in Matthew, means properly diseases of the body. To bear those griefs, is clearly to bear them away, or to remove them. This was done by his miraculous power in healing the sick. The word rendered 'sorrows' in Isaiah, and 'sicknesses' in Matthew, means pains, griefs, or anguish of mind. To carry them, is to sympathize with the sufferers; to make provision for alleviating those sorrows, and to take them away. This he did by his precepts and his example: the cause of all sorrows—sin, he removed by his atonement.

PRACTICAL REFLECTIONS.

Mt. viii. 15. When having experienced the healing power of Jesus, let us, after the example of our heavenly Benefactor, use all our strength and means in ministering to the wants and otherwise shewing kindness to his disciples.

Mk. i. 32. Jesus had both cast out a devil and exercised his healing power on the sabbath, but it was not until the sun was setting and their sabbath was past that the inhabitants of Capernaum brought their sick to be healed—they seem slavishly to have observed the letter of their law; he as a son obeyed, in the spirit of it, the commandment which teaches to shew mercy.

[Lu. iv. 41. How near to the full testimony of the truth did the devils at length come! and if they had been allowed to proceed, how hard indeed would it have been, for a simple child of God to distinguish between the voice of the Spirit of God and the confession of devils! but Jesus rebuking them, would not allow them to confess that Jesus is the Christ, the Son of God.]

The confession, 'Thou art the Christ, the Son of the living God,' is the great foundation truth, as pointed out, Mt. xvi. 16—8, § 50. And the injunction upon evil spirits to keep silence with regard to Jesus, as being both truly God and truly man, appears to have been continued, 1 Jno. iv. 2, 3.

Mt. viii. 17. When Jesus took to him our infirmities, and bare our sicknesses, it was not merely that he might bear them, but take them away; and as truly as the cures were performed at Capernaum, so in Jerusalem '*the inhabitant shall not say, I am sick: the people that dwell therein* shall be *forgiven* their *iniquity,'* Is. xxxiii. 24.

ADDENDA.

ON CHRIST'S MANNER OF TEACHING.
' *He taught them as one that had authority,*' Mark i. 22, p. 110.

' He taught them and spake as a prophet having authority from God.

' His matter and manner were infinitely beyond anything that the people had heard before. He did not, like the heathen philosophers, entertain his hearers with dry metaphysical discourses on the nature of the supreme good, and the several divisions and subdivisions of virtue; nor did he, like the Jewish rabbies, content himself with dealing out ceremonies and traditions, with discoursing on mint and cummin, and estimating the breadth of a phylactery; but he drew off their attention from these trivial and contemptible things, to the greatest and noblest objects.

' That there was something peculiarly striking in our Lord's method of teaching, may be inferred from the surprise which it excited, and the effect which it produced, as "*the officers answered, Never man spake like this man,*" Jno. vii. 46, § 55. Again: " *Jesus, therefore, knowing all things that should come upon him, went forth, and said unto them, Whom seek ye?* 5, *They answered him, Jesus of Nazareth. Jesus saith unto them, I am he. And Judas also, which betrayed him, stood with them.* 6, *As soon then as he had said unto them, I am he, they went backward, and fell to the ground,*" xviii. 4—6, § 88.

' In confirmation of the judgment repeatedly passed upon the matchless character of our Lord's teaching, the evangelists have sometimes detailed its features according to their apprehension; and remarked, "*He taught them as one having authority.*" The negative, he taught them, "*not as the scribes,*" leaves us much to supply. He reversed all the haughty, censorious, obscure, and careless habits of that degenerate class of teachers. His *condescension* was manifest, in addressing the multitude, whom they treated with contempt, and left to be destroyed by vice and ignorance. He sympathized with the privations of the poor, elevated their hopes, imparted to them knowledge, and soothed their afflictions. He listened to their inquiries, resolved their doubts, bore with their infirmities, and was unwearied in his communications. He spake a language which they understood, and chose subjects which they felt. His *gentleness* was apparent in all his addresses. He entreated, persuaded, wept— quenching the lightning of his eyes in tears of love; and silencing the thunders of heaven, that the whispers of mercy might be heard.

' The *earnestness* and energy of our Lord's teaching also formed a strong contrast to the supineness and indifference of the scribes. Where could they look for a faithful shepherd, when the whole priesthood was alike corrupt? " He can teach in any place, and at any time; he is found labouring in season and out of season; he preaches from a boat, on the side of a hill, in the desert, by the wayside—he consecrates every spot by his doctrines and prayers." Such being some of the characters of our Lord's teaching, no wonder that " *the common people heard him gladly.*"'

THE LORD GIVETH WISDOM, ETC.—Prov. ii. 6.   [113

SECTION 18.—EARLY IN THE MORNING OF THE NEXT DAY, THAT IS, OF THE FIRST DAY OF THE WEEK, JESUS DEPARTS FROM CAPERNAUM TO A DESERT PLACE TO PRAY:* HIS DISCIPLES FOLLOW HIM THITHER: ATTENDED BY WHOM HE SETS OUT ON THE FIRST GENERAL CIRCUIT OF GALILEE, PREACHING THE GOSPEL OF THE KINGDOM, TEACHING, AND WORKING MIRACLES OF HEALING AND DISPOSSESSION EVERY-WHERE.

(G. 22,) No. 18. *See line from Capernaum going Northward, Westward, Southward, Eastward, and to the North of the Lake of Galilee.*

MATT. iv. 23—.5. MARK i. 35—.9. LUKE iv. 42—.4.
[Ch. iv. 22, § xvi. p. 109.]

35 *And in-the-morning, πρωι rising-up a-great-while before-day εννυχον λιαν,*

b And when-it-was day, 42 he-departed and-went into a-desert place:

*c he-went-out, and departed into a-solitary place, and-there prayed.

36 And Simon and they *that were* with him followed-
37 after him. And when-they-had-found him, they-said
38 unto-him, All men seek-for thee. And he-said unto-them, Let-us-go into the next towns, that I-may-preach there-also: for therefore came-I-forth.*d*

SCRIPTURE ILLUSTRATIONS.

Mk. i. 35. *morning*—Jesus was an early riser—see Jno. viii. 2. § 55; Lu. xxi. 38, § 86—and so he would have his disciples to be, vi. 13, § 27—the women were early at the sepulchre, xxiv. 1, § 93—in the morning the pentecostal anointing was given: 'and when the day of Pentecost was fully come, they were all with one accord in one place,' Ac. ii. 1; 'for these are not drunken, as we suppose, seeing it *is but* the third hour of the day,' ver. 15—and by Divine command the apostles entered into the temple early in the morning and taught: 'but the angel of the Lord by night opened the prison doors, and brought them forth, and said, Go, stand and speak in the temple to the people all the words of this life. And when they heard *that*, they entered into the temple early in the morning, and taught,' Ac. v. 19—21.

solitary place— . . . . to Jacob: 'and Jacob was left alone; and there wrestled a man with him,' Ge. xxxii. 24—30— . . . . . Ho. xii. 3—5. . . . . in the wilderness, Jesus wrestled with the enemy, Mk. i. 12, .3, § 9, p. 63—'and he withdrew himself into the wilderness, and prayed,' Lu. v. 16, § 21—immediately before sending forth the twelve, Lu. vi. 12, § 27—and

In a solitary place also was his last severe wrestling with the Father, in the garden, immediately before his apprehension, Mt. xxvi. 36—45, § 88—*see* direction to his disciples regarding prayer, vi. 6, p. 131.

prayed—' my voice shalt thou hear in the morning, O Lord; in the morning will I direct *my prayer* unto thee, and will look up,' Ps. v. 3—*see* the prayer which Jesus taught his disciples, Mt. vi. 9—13, § 19—his intercessory prayer for his disciples, Jno. xvii. § 87—in the garden, Lu. xxii. 40—.6, § 85—upon the cross, Lu. xxiii. 34, § 91; Ps. xxii. . . . . —earnest continuous prayer becomes the followers of Jesus: 'praying always with all prayer and supplication in the Spirit, and watching thereunto with all perseverance and supplication for all saints,' Ep. vi. 18.

38. *therefore came I forth*—' but thou, Bethlehem Ephratah, *though* thou be little among the thousands of Judah, yet out of thee shall he come forth unto me *that is* to be Ruler in Israel; whose goings forth have been from of old, from everlasting,' Mi. v. 2—' I came forth from the Father, and am come into the world: again, I leave the world, and go to the Father,' Jno. xvi. 28, § 87.

NOTES.

Mk. i. 35—.7. *And in the morning, rising up a great while before day.* Luke says, ch. iv. 42, '*when it was day.*' The passage in Mark is, in the original, not literally *a great while before day,* but very early, or while there was yet *much appearance of night*. The place in Luke means *at daybreak*, at the beginning of day. Then also there is much appearance of night; and Luke and Mark, therefore, refer to the same time—before it was fully light, or just at daybreak. It was customary with the Jews to resort early in the morning to prayers, and our Lord has left us on ex-mple that, before entering upon any undertaking, we should ask God's counsel and blessing. The object of this prayer is reasonable to presume was preparation for the circuit of Galilee.

[M. And Simon and they *that were with him*. *corrobofee*. 'This word not only signifies *persequi*, but *mirquoi*—see Ho. ii. 7, "And she shall follow after her lovers, but she shall not overtake them; and she shall seek them, but shall not find them: then shall she say, I will go and return to my first husband; for then was it better with me than now." It here implies the ardent desire which Simon had for finding and accompanying his Master. In the passage of Luke this is ascribed to οἱ ὄχλοι: "the people." Yet there

is, in effect, no discrepancy; since the two circumstances may both have taken place. First, it should seem, his disciples "hunted him out," as *ανεδιωξαν* literally means, and said what is recorded in Mark; and then the multitudes, coming up, said what is recorded in Luke.'—*Bloomfield.*]

37. *All men seek for thee.* The inquiry after him was general. They told him this evidently with a view to induce him to leave his place of retirement, and to prevail upon him to appear publicly, to instruct the multitudes. Many wished to be instructed, and others to be healed by him.

38. *Towns.* The word here rendered *towns*, denotes places in size between *cities* and *villages*, or large places, but without walls.—*See* ADDENDA, '*Jesus' first general circuit of Galilee,*' p. 118, third paragraph.

That I may preach, &c. This was part of his office for which he came into the world: to proclaim the mercy of God, and direct men in the way of everlasting life.

For therefore came I forth. That is, came forth from God, or was sent by God. Luke says, ch. iv. 43, '*for therefore am I sent.*' Making known God's mercy was his business, to which his miracles gave witness.

PRACTICAL REFLECTIONS.

Mk. i. 35. Let us be followers of Jesus: he went out as soon as it was day, and had been up a great while before the sun, even although the preceding day had been one of constant occupation, in his great work of delivering men, from both their spiritual and bodily ills.

Let us learn from the example of Jesus, not only

to join in the public worship of God, and reading of his word, but to seek, in solitude also, communion with our heavenly Father.

[Those especially who are much outwardly engaged in the work of God, as had been Jesus, have need to follow his example, as to secret prayer, that, having done all, they may stand: receiving from God, and giving to men, should go hand in hand.]

* See ADDENDA, p. 118.

PART II.　　　JESUS' FIRST GENERAL CIRCUIT OF GALILEE.　　　SECT. XVIII.

MATT. iv. 23.	MARK i. 39.	LUKE iv. 42—.4.
23 *And Jesus went-about all Galilee, teaching in their synagogues, and preaching the gospel of-the kingdom, and healing all-manner-of sickness πασαν νοσον and all-manner-of disease πασαν μαλακιαν among the people./	39　And he-preached in their synagogues, throughout all Galilee,	*and the people sought him, and came unto him, and stayed κατειχον him, that-he-should-not'-depart from them. And he said unto 43 them, I must preach the kingdom of God to-other cities also: for therefore am-I-sent.' And he-preached 44 in the synagogues of Galilee. [Ch. v. 1, ? xx. p. 153.]

ƒ and cast-out devils.*
[For Mark i. 40, ? xxi. p. 159.]

SCRIPTURE ILLUSTRATIONS.

Lu. iv. 43. *therefore am I sent*—he is the Shiloh, or Sent of the Father, the Apostle of our profession, (He. iii. 1,) the Messenger of the Covenant, (Mal. iii. 1,) the *Sent*, Jno. viii. 42, § 55—to bring unto us peace, he was given of the Father and sent into the world: ' The sceptre shall not depart from Judah, nor a lawgiver from between his feet, until Shiloh come; and unto him *shall the gathering of the people be*,' Ge. xlix. 10 —which gathering is through the power of ' the gift of Christ:' 'but unto every one of us is given grace according to the measure of the gift of Christ,' Ep. iv. 7; 'and he gave some, apostles; and some, prophets; and some, evangelists; and some, pastors and teachers; for the perfecting of the saints, for the work of the ministry, for the edifying of the body of Christ: till we all come in the unity of the faith, and of the knowledge of the Son of God, unto a perfect man, unto the measure of the stature of the fulness of Christ,' ver. 11—.3; 'from whom the whole body fitly joined together and compacted by that which every joint supplieth, according to the effectual working in the measure of every part, maketh increase of the body unto the edifying of itself in love,' ver. 16 —' say ye of him, whom the Father hath sanctified, and sent into the world, Thou blasphemest; because I said, I am the Son of God?' Jno. x. 36, § 56—he 'said, I am not sent but unto the lost sheep of the house of Israel,' Mt. xv. 24, § 45—' many nations shall be joined to the LORD in that day, and shall be my

people: and I will dwell in the midst of thee, and thou shalt know that the LORD of hosts hath sent me unto thee,' Zec. ii. 11—' the word which God sent unto the children of Israel, preaching peace by Jesus Christ: (he is Lord of all),' Ac. x. 36—so Jesus sent forth the apostles, Mt. x. 5, 6, &c., § 39—'in this was manifested the love of God toward us, because that God sent his only begotten Son into the world, that we might live through him,' 1 Jno. iv. 9—Jesus said unto his disciples, ' Peace be unto you: as my Father hath sent me, even so send I you,' Jno. xx. 21, § 95.

Mt. iv. 23. *teaching—see* ' custom,' Sect. xv. p. 102.

preaching the gospel of the kingdom—see ' Scripture Illustrations,' Mk. i. 14, § 16, p. 108.

healing — usually accompanied the preaching of Jesus, and of his apostles—*see* § 17, p. 112; Lu. v. 15, § 21; vi. 17—49, § 27; vii. 19—23, § 29—*see* his second general circuit, § 30—his third, § 34—the apostles' mission, § 39—preceded the feeding of the 5000, Lu. ix. 11, § 40—the mission of the seventy, Lu. x. 1—24, § 60—so Philip at Samaria, Ac. viii. 5—7........ —and Paul at Lystra, to Lycaonia, chv. 7—10—' God also bearing *them* witness, both with signs and wonders, and with divers miracles, and gifts of the Holy Ghost, according to his own will,' He. ii. 4.

Mk. i. 39. *cast out devils—see* ' an unclean spirit,' Sect. xvii. p. 110.

NOTES.

Mt. iv. 23. *All Galilee.—See* ADDENDA, ' *Jesus' first circuit of Galilee*,' p. 118.

Synagogues. Places where the Jews met to pray, and hear the reading of the Law and the Prophets. The heads of the synagogue desired such learned and grave persons as happened to be there, to give a discourse to the people. The fame of Jesus' miracles obtained for him ready admission to preach.— *See* ADDENDA, '*Synagogue*,' Sect. xv. p. 106.

Preaching.—See ' Came preaching,' ch. iii. 1, § 7, p. 50.

The gospel of the kingdom. The good news respecting the kingdom which he was about to set up; or the good news respecting the coming of the Messiah, and the nature of his kingdom.—*See* 'Notes,' '*The beginning of the gospel*,' § 7, p. 49; and ' Scripture Illustrations,' Mk. i. 14, § 16, p. 108.

PRACTICAL REFLECTIONS.

35. 'Jesus knew the value of the morning hours— he rose while the world was still—he saw when the light spread abroad from the east with fresh tokens of his Father's presence, and joined with the universal creation in praising the everywhere present God.'

'If Jesus prayed in the morning, how much more important is it for us, before the world gets possession of our thoughts—before Satan fills us with unholy feelings; when we rise fresh from beds of repose, and while the world around us is still!'

' This will be found to be true, universally, *that the pious feelings—the religious enjoyment through the day, will be according to the state of the heart in the morning, and can therefore be measured by our faithfulness in early, secret prayer.*'

[36—.8 ver. Let us, with the disciples, follow after Jesus early to the place of retirement and prayer; and, not contented with the good which has been done, let us, with Jesus, contemplate the much that remains to be accomplished, as to the making known of his truth upon the earth.]

[Lu. iv. 42, .3. As Jesus could not be driven from the work which he came forth to do, so neither could he be drawn therefrom, into a corner, by the kindly

solicitations of friends, who would have detained him in Capernaum.]

From the example of Jesus, let us direct the attention of others, as frequently as we have opportunity, to the coming kingdom : by keeping this constantly in view, we shall bear the more cheerfully with the evils of the present time, and become assimilated to those who through faith and patience inherit the promises.

Mt. iv. 23, Mk. i. 39. Jesus did not let one work prevent his doing another; he both taught in their synagogues, and proclaimed the gospel of the kingdom in other places; and, at the same time, healed all manner of sickness and disease, and cast out devils. He is our example, with regard to diligence in service, as well as watchfulness in prayer.

[24, .5 ver. Beside those that came to him from Syria, there were many that came to him from all the quarters around, except from Samaria, the portion of Ephraim—plainly intimating that this was not yet the great gathering of the people unto Shiloh, when the adopted firstborn will be found in possession of the birthright, which can only be had in Christ—' *In him all the promises are Yea and Amen.*']

HE 'WENT ABOUT DOING GOOD.'—Acts x. 38.　　　[115

SECT. XVIII. JESUS' FIRST GENERAL CIRCUIT OF GALILEE. PART II.

MATT. iv. 24, .5.	MARK.	LUKE.

24 *And his fame went throughout all Syria: and they-brought unto him all sick-people that-were-taken συνεχομενους with-divers diseases and torments βασανοις, and those-which-were-possessed-with-devils, and those-which-were-lunatick, and those-that-had-the-25 palsy; and he-healed them. And there-followed him great multitudes *of people* from Galilee, and *from* Decapolis, and *from* Jerusalem, and *from* Judæa, and *from* beyond Jordan.

SCRIPTURE ILLUSTRATIONS.

Mt. iv. 24. *those which were possessed with devils*—Christ and the apostles spoke *to* them, and *of* them, *as* under the influence of evil spirits. They spake, conversed, asked questions, gave answers, and expressed their knowledge of Christ, and their fear of him; things that certainly could not be said of *diseases*, Mt. viii. 28—32, [Mk. v. 1—13, Lu. viii. 27—33,] § 35. They are represented as going out of the persons possessed, and entering other bodies, Mt. viii. 32, *ib.* He threatened them, commanded them to be silent, to depart, and not to return, Mk. i. 25, § 17, p. 111; v. 8, § 35; ix. 25, § 51. Christ says, he cast out devils by the Spirit of God, Mt. xii. 25—8, § 31. Those possessed are said *to know Christ; to be acquainted with the Son of God*, Mk. i. 24, [Lu. iv. 34,] § 17, p. 110: this could not be said of diseases.—*See 'unclean spirit*,' Sect. xvii. p. 110, ver. 23.

those that had the palsy—one carried by four, and let down to Jesus, Mk. ii. 3, 4, [Lu. v. 18, .9,] § 22.

25. *great multitudes*—at the conclusion of this circuit, 'seeing the multitudes, he went up into a mountain,' Mt. v. 1, § 19, p. 120—having ended his sermon on the mount, 'it came to pass, that, as the people pressed upon him to hear the word of God, he stood by the lake of Gennesaret,' Lu. v. 1, § 20—when withdrawn from the malice of the Pharisees, 'great multitudes followed him, and he healed them all,' Mt. xii. 15, § 26—after the ordination of the twelve apostles, 'he came down with them, and stood in the plain, and ... a great multitude ... came to hear him, and to be healed,' Lu. vi. 17—9, § 27—so on his second circuit of Galilee 'the multitude cometh together again, so that they could not so much as eat bread,' Mk. iii. 20, § 30—as he went to raise Jairus' daughter, 'much people followed him, and thronged him,' Mk. v. 24, § 36—and on his *third* circuit of Galilee, Mt. ix. 35, .6, §§ 38, .9.

—see the miracles of feeding multitudes, §§ 40, .6—and as Jesus went up to the last passover, 'they trode one upon another,' Lu. xii. 1, § 63—and when he had finished his sayings, 'he departed from Galilee, and came into the coasts of Judæa beyond Jordan; and great multitudes followed him; and he healed them there,' Mt. xix. 1, 2, § 71—and 'as he was come nigh unto Jericho,' Lu. xviii. 35, .6, § 78—and having passed through Jericho, Zaccheus 'sought to see Jesus ... and could not for the press,' Lu. xix. 3, 4, § 80 —' and when he was come into Jerusalem, all the city was moved,' Mt. xxi. 10, .1, § 82—a few days after, this same multitude cried out, 'Crucify him,' Mk. xv. 11, .3, .4, § 90—and as he hung on the cross, 'they that passed by railed on him.' ver. 29, 30, § 91—' Let him save himself, if he be Christ, the chosen of God,' Lu. xxiii. 35, § 93.—When he comes again it will be with multitudes of angels, as he said: ' The Son of man shall come in the glory of his Father with his angels ; and then he shall reward every man according to his works,' Mt. xvi. 27, § 50 —' whosoever therefore shall be ashamed of me and of my words in this adulterous and sinful generation; of him also shall the Son of man be ashamed, when he cometh in the glory of his Father with the holy angels,' Mk. viii. 38, § *ib.*—' when the Lord Jesus shall be revealed from heaven with his mighty angels, in flaming fire taking vengeance on them that know not God, and that obey not the gospel of our Lord Jesus Christ,' 2 Th. i. 7, 8.

Galilee—N.W. part of the land, wherein his disciples were mostly gathered : ' and they were all amazed and marvelled, saying one to another, Behold, are not all these which speak Galilæans?' Ac. ii. 7.

Decapolis—N.E., referred to, Mk. v. 20, § 35—and vii. 31, § 46.

NOTES.

24. *Fame.* Sometimes signifies common talk, public report, Gen. xlv. 16, ' *And the fame thereof was heard in Pharaoh's house, saying, Joseph's brethren are come : and it pleased Pharaoh well, and his servants ;*' but ordinarily it means a wide-spread report of one's excellency and glorious deeds, Zep. iii. 19, ' *Behold, at that time I will undo all that afflict thee ; and I will save her that halteth, and gather her that was driven out; and I will get them praise and fame in every land where they have been put to shame.*'

And his fame went throughout all Syria. It is not easy to fix the exact bounds of Syria in the time of our Saviour, of which the country of the Jews and the Samaritans was but a very small part. It was, perhaps, the general name for the country lying between the Euphrates on the east, and the Mediterranean on the west; and between mount Taurus on the north, and Arabia on the south—but more properly referred to the region N.E. of Palestine.—*See* GEOGRAPHICAL NOTICES, '*Syria,*' p. 117.

Possessed with devils. 'Persons possessed by evil spirits. It is evident from Scripture, and the writings of primitive Christians, that *evil spirits, devils, or some of those angels who kept not their first estate, and which are called by the collective name Satan, and Διαβολος the Devil,* were permitted about the time of our Saviour's appearance in the world to possess, and in various and dreadful manners to torment, the bodies of men, by which their malice to mankind was manifestly displayed, as well as our Saviour's Divine power and benevolence demonstrated in casting them out.'

[Δαιμονιζομενοι, 'devils,' is not the strictly correct rendering. The word διαβολοι, 'devil,' is not found in the plural in any part of the sacred writings; evil spirits are called demons, of which there are multitudes, Mk. v. 9, § 35, ' *And he asked him, What is thy name? And he answered, saying, My name is Legion : for we are many ;*' but there is but one devil, supreme or head over the rest.—*Clarke.*]

Those that were lunatic. Literally, 'moon-struck, but *fg.* denoting 'epileptic persons ;' so called from the common notion that the disorder was aggravated by, and returned upon them with the increasing moon. It is mentioned only in this place, and in Mt. xvii. 15, § 51.

And those that had the palsy. Many infirmities were included under this general name of *palsy*, in the New Testament. 1st. The apoplexy, or paralytic shock, affecting the whole body. 2nd. The hemiplegy, affecting only one side of the body; the most frequent form of the disease. 3rd. The paraplegy, affecting all the system below the neck. 4th. The catalepsy. This is caused by a contraction of the muscles in the whole or a part of the body, and is very dangerous. The effects are very violent and fatal. For instance, if, when a person is struck, he happens to have his hand extended, he is unable to draw it back; if not extended, he is unable to stretch it out. It appears diminished in size, and dried up in appearance. Hence it was called *the withered hand*, Mt. xii. 10—3, § 25. 5th. The cramp. This, in eastern countries, is a fearful malady, and by no means unfrequent. It originates from chills in the night. The limbs, when seized with it, remain unmovable, and the person afflicted with it resembles one undergoing a torture. This was probably the disease of the servant of the centurion, Mt. viii. 6, [Lu. vii. 2,] § 23. Death sometimes follows from this disease in a few days.

LET THY MERCY, O LORD, BE UPON US.—Psalm xxxiii. 22.

GEOGRAPHICAL NOTICES.
DECAPOLIS, p. 116.

DECAPOLIS.—A country of Palestine, which was mainly in the half-tribe of Manasseh, so called from its containing ten cities; about the names of which the learned are not agreed.

'The city of Bethshan, or Bethsean, *Bysan*, was in the N. E. corner of Samaria, on the borders of Galilee and Peræa, and close to the river Jordan: to this place the Philistines brought the body of Saul after the battle in Gilboa, and fastened it to a wall. It was afterwards called Scythopolis, from the Scythians, who, during the time of the Medes, overran all Asia, and advanced as far as the limits of Egypt. It became subsequently a very flourishing place, being the metropolis of the Decapolis, or those ten cities, which were chiefly inhabited by Syrians, and united themselves in a league to resist the oppressions of the Maccabees.

'The other nine cities which constituted the Decapolis are supposed to have been all on the eastern side of the Jordan: they were Capitolias, Canatha, Abila, Hippos, Gadara, Pella, Dium, Gerasa, and Philadelphia. The whole of these belonged to the kingdom of Israel, prior to the captivity, but they were subsequently reckoned as belonging to *Syria*: the Romans included them in their province of *Cœle-Syria*, and though they gave Herod some of them, yet, upon his death, they were withheld from his heirs. A few miles to the south of Scythopolis was Bezec, where the men of Judah defeated the Canaanites with great slaughter, Ju. i. 4, and where also Saul mustered his army prior to giving the Ammonites a signal overthrow, 1 Sa. xi. 8. To the eastward of this stood Ænon, near to Salim, where John baptized after he quitted Bethabara,' Jno. iii. 22—4, § 13, p. 89.—*Arrowsmith's Ancient and Modern Geog.*

SYRIA.

'SYRIA, or *Sham*, as it is called by the natives, was bounded on the west by the Mediterranean; on the north by mount Amanus, and by mount Taurus; on the east by the river Euphrates, and the desert of Palmyra; and on the south by the river Arnon, the Dead Sea, and the torrent of Egypt. To the north it touched upon Asia Minor, to the east on Mesopotamia, and to the south on Arabia and Egypt: it contained 55,800 square miles, and was divided into the three great divisions of Syria Superior, or Syria properly so called; Phœnice; Palestina, or Judæa. Syria is also called Assyria, as forming part of that great empire, and the two names, though sufficiently defined in geography, are often used indiscriminately in history.

'The name of Syria, which seems to have been derived from *Sora*, or *Tyre*, does not appear to have been applied to the country until this city had arrived at the pre-eminence it enjoyed, which was long after the time of Homer, who mentions neither the one nor the other. The old Greeks called the inhabitants of Syria, Arminia, and Mesopotamia, *Arimœi*, or *Arimi*, a name derived from *Aram*, one of the sons of Shem, to whose lot these countries first fell (except Phœnice and Palestine, which came into the possession of Canaan); they seem, also, to have extended the appellation to the Leuco-Syri of Asia Minor. Syria, prior to Assyrian invasion, does not appear to have been governed by one king; for besides the Phœnicians and the Israelites, who were a people distinct from all others, there were also the kingdoms of Damascus, of Hamath, and probably other dynasties in the northern part of the country. From the hands of the Assyrians and Medes, the whole of Syria fell under the Persian yoke, to which it remained subject until wrested from it by Alexander the Great, after whose death, Seleucus Nicanor, one of his generals, received this province as part of his lot in the division of the Macedonian dominions: he raised it B.C. 312 to an empire, which is known in history as the kingdom of Syria or Babylon. The Seleucidæ, or successors of this prince, governed the country for more than two hundred years, during which they contested parts of it with the Egyptians, the Parthians, and the Jews; the last of their race was Antiochus Asiaticus, who was dethroned by Pompey, B.C. 65; and from that time Syria became a Roman province. The new conquerors allowed the ancient divisions of the country to remain, and kept possession of it until it was reduced by the *Saracens*, A.D. 640.'—*Arrowsmith's Ancient and Modern Geography*, p. 497.

'Its excellent soil and agreeable rivers, the Euphrates, Orontes, Cassimire, Adonis, Barrady, &c., rendered it a most delightful country. It was anciently divided into a variety of cantons, as Aram-naharaim, Aram-zobah, Aram-maachah, Aram-rehob, and Aram of Damascus. Zobah, Damascus, Hamath, Geshur, &c., were its most noted states about the time of David, who conquered it, 2 Sa. viii.—x. About sixty years after, Rezin, who had fled from Hadadezer his master, erected a kingdom at Damascus. He, and his successors, Benhadad and Hazael, did much mischief to the Hebrews, 1 Ki. xv., xx., xxii.; 2 Ki. vi., viii., x.; but Joash and Jeroboam, kings of Israel, sufficiently resented these injuries, and brought the Syrian kingdom to the point of ruin, 2 Ki. xiii., xiv. They recovered themselves, and under Rezin they made a consider-

able figure, and terribly harassed Ahaz and his subjects, and even took Elath, on the Red Sea. But Tiglath-pileser, instigated by Ahaz, ravaged their country, demolished their cities, and carried the inhabitants to Media. During the decline of the Assyrian empire, the Syrians returned, and recovered themselves not a little; but Nebuchadnezzar again reduced them. In the end of the 11th century, the Seljukian Turks seized on it, and erected one of their four sultanies at Aleppo, and another at Damascus. Soon after, the European croisaders took the most of it, and after terrible struggling were, about an hundred years after, driven out of it, by Saladin, sultan of Egypt, and his successors. In the beginning of the sixteenth century it was seized by the Ottoman Turks, who retain it to this day. We know no place in it at present of note, except Aleppo and Damascus. Its principal rarities are the ruins of noted buildings, especially those of Tadmor and Baalbek. A Christian church was early planted here, and was famous at Antioch, and other places of the country: and there is still a shadow of Christianity with not a few.—Ac. xv. 23, 41. 23, 'And they wrote *letters* by them after this manner; The apostles and elders and brethren *send* greeting unto the brethren which are of the Gentiles in Antioch and Syria and Cilicia.' 41, 'And he went through Syria and Cilicia, confirming the churches.'

The following are some of the prophecies concerning Syria:—

Am. i. 3—5. 3, 'Thus saith the LORD; For three transgressions of Damascus, and for four, I will not turn away *the punishment* thereof; because they have threshed Gilead with threshing instruments of iron: 4, but I will send a fire into the house of Hazael, which shall devour the palaces of Ben-hadad. 5, I will break also the bar of Damascus, and cut off the inhabitant from the plain of Aven, and him that holdeth the sceptre from the house of Eden: and the people of Syria shall go into captivity unto Kir, saith the LORD.'

Am. iii. 12, 'Thus saith the LORD; As the shepherd taketh out of the mouth of the lion two legs, or a piece of an ear; so shall the children of Israel be taken out that dwell in Samaria in the corner of a bed, and in Damascus in a couch.'

Is. vii. 4, 'And say unto him, Take heed, and be quiet; fear not, neither be fainthearted for the two tails of these smoking firebrands, for the fierce anger of Rezin with Syria, and of the son of Remaliah.'

Is. viii. 4, 'For before the child shall have knowledge to cry, My father, and my mother, the riches of Damascus and the spoil of Samaria shall be taken away before the king of Assyria.'

Is. ix. 11, .2. 11, 'Therefore the LORD shall set up the adversaries of Rezin against him, and join his enemies together; 12, the Syrians before, and the Philistines behind; and they shall devour Israel with open mouth. For all this his anger is not turned away, but his hand *is* stretched out still.'

Is. xvii. 1—3. 1, 'The burden of Damascus. Behold, Damascus is taken away from *being* a city, and it shall be a ruinous heap. 2, The cities of Aroer are forsaken: they shall be for flocks, which shall lie down, and none shall make *them* afraid. 3, The fortress also shall cease from Ephraim, and the kingdom from Damascus, and the remnant of Syria: they shall be as the glory of the children of Israel, saith the LORD of hosts.'

YE SHALL KNOW THAT I AM THE LORD.—Ezek. xi. 10. [117

GEOGRAPHICAL NOTICES—(continued).

JUDÆA, properly so called, was the south division of the Holy Land.—*See* HISTORICAL SKETCH OF THE LAND OF PROMISE, p. ix.

FROM BEYOND JORDAN, p. 116.—Probably including the parts about and east of the sources of the Jordan.—*See* GEOGRAPHICAL NOTICE, Sect. x. p. 74; also ADDENDA, Sect. vii. '*On the ministry of John the Baptist*,' p. 56, commencing at The scene of this ministry, &c.

ADDENDA.

'ON JESUS' FIRST GENERAL CIRCUIT OF GALILEE,' p. 114.

'The next morning ... Jesus retired early to a solitary place, for the sake of private prayer, Mk. i. 35—9, [Lu. iv 42—.4] ... With this time, then, that is, with the morning of the first day of the week, answering to Sunday with us, and, probably, within seven days since the recurrence of the feast of Pentecost, consequently on June 6, we must date the commencement of a circuit of Galilee; which evidently set out from Capernaum, and though it was confined to Galilee, yet was general in that country, and on all these accounts the first of its kind, and as complete as any. The intention of making such a progress, in his departure from Capernaum itself, is implied by his answer to Simon, and the people, when they would have detained him, or prevailed upon him to return to that city; Let us go to the neighbouring *κωμοπόλεις—(κώμας καὶ πόλεις)* towns or cities—that I may preach there also; for, for this purpose am I come forth, Mk. i. 38. ... This circuit is also described by St. Matthew, iv. 23—5. St. Luke says, the work of the circuit was discharged in the synagogues of Galilee; St. Mark, in their synagogues unto all Galilee; and St. Matthew, that it went round all Galilee; and each of them, that it consisted in teaching, and preaching, that is, proclaiming; and performing miracles. ...

'The expediency of undertaking such a progress, as soon after the public commencement of the ministry in Galilee as possible, must be undeniable; ... and whatever length of time might have been occupied by such circuit, the same, it may be supposed, would be taken up by another. ... Every circuit, whether in Galilee or elsewhere, undertaken in the course of our Lord's ministry, having been undertaken for the benefit of the inhabitants, ... must be determined by the number of places which he would visit, and the length of the stay which he would make in each. ... It is not to be supposed that he would merely perambulate Galilee in a circle, and, consequently, pass through such towns and villages only as lay on the line of his route: the expression, *περιῆγεν ὅλην τὴν Γαλιλαίαν*, in reference to this circuit, must be understood and interpreted, conformably with others, *περιῆγεν ὁ Ἰησοῦς τὰς πόλεις πάσας καὶ τὰς κώμας*, Mt. ix. 31, § 3*—and, διώδευε κατὰ πόλιν καὶ κώμην*, Lu. viii. 1, § 30, in reference to circuits subsequently undertaken. ...

'The number of towns and villages—*πόλεις καὶ κώμας*—which Galilee contained is estimated by Josephus, *Bell. Jud.* iii. iii. 2, at 204, and the population of each, upon an average, at not less than 15,000 souls.'—*Greswell*, Vol. II. Diss. xxiii. p. 289—92.

'Many of them, especially the cities, as we may presume, would contain much more. To assume, however, the average population of every town or city as only 15,000—and to understand the specified number of such towns as intended of both the Galilees; on these suppositions the population of all Galilee amounted to 3,060,000 souls.

'The whole extent of Palestine from Dan to Beersheba, that is, from Beersheba to Cæsarea Philippi, is estimated by Reland, ii. cap. v. 423, at 156 Roman miles; of which 52 miles, or one third, at least, must be assigned to the length of Galilee, Upper and Lower, in particular. And as the breadth of the country (that is, of the habitable part of the country, on the west of the Jordan), was sufficiently uniform, if the population of every part had been on an equal scale, the population of the whole in general would have been three times the population of a third part in particular. On this principle the whole population of Palestine, west of the Jordan, must have been estimated at 9,180,000 souls. In this number, however, the inhabitants of Judæa, east of the Jordan, are not included; and their country, which was once adequate to the support of the two tribes, and one half, out of the twelve, would probably supply a million of souls additional. The population of all Palestine, then, both west and east of Jordan, would appear to be, on this principle, not less than ten millions of souls.

'The populousness of Judæa is a circumstance often insisted on by profane writers, *Diod. Sic. lib.* xl. *Ecloga I., Operum* x. 215—.9; *Tac. Hist.* v. 5; and there is little doubt that, in proportion to its size, it was the most abundant in numbers of any country within the Roman dominions; and Strabo tells us, that in his time, the small district of Jamnea and its suburbs could bring into the field an army of 40,000 men, *Lib.* xvi. 2, § 28, 347, which implies a general population of at least 160,000.'—*Ibid.* Vol. IV., *App. Diss.* xxiii. p. 491, ..2.

'We will assume that our Lord would visit only one half of the towns and villages; and, what is no extravagant supposition, that he would pass, upon an average, one day in each. We will assume also that, for every week of the continuance of the progress, he would necessarily be stationary somewhere during the four and twenty hours of the sabbatic rest. Even upon this calculation, which every one will allow to be moderate and reasonable, the duration of a circuit would never be less than three months, and probably never less than four. This, then, we may assume, in every instance of what is perceived to have been a general circuit, not otherwise limited, as the nearest approximation to the exact measure of its continuance. Consequently, the circuits which began about the feast of Pentecost would be over about the feast of Tabernacles; of which fact we shall find incidental notices supplied, on more than one occasion, by the gospel narrative itself. And it is a general argument in favour of its truth, first, that on this principle a circuit would commonly begin after wheat-harvest was over, and terminate when seed-time was ready to arrive; the effect of which would be that the people in the interval would be enabled to attend upon our Saviour with the least inconvenience to themselves: and, secondly, that it would coincide with the period of the year when travelling could best be performed only in the morning and the evening of the day, and when resting throughout the day, so obviously necessary for the purpose of teaching, would not be more necessary for that purpose than expedient in itself.

'The course of the present circuit, we may conjecture from *St. Matthew*, iv. 24, .5, was, upon the whole, as follows—first, along the western side of the Jordan, northward; which would disseminate the fame of Jesus in Decapolis; secondly, along the confines of the tetrarchy of Philip, westward; which would make him known throughout Syria; thirdly, by the coasts of Tyre and Sidon, southward: and, lastly, along the verge of Samaria, and the western region of the lake of Galilee—the nearest points to Judæa Proper, and to Peræa—until it returned to Capernaum. In the course of the progress, if he visited Bethsaida, he might be joined by Philip, Jno. i. 44, § 10, p. 72; if he visited Cana, by Nathanael, xxi. 2, § 97; and if there was such a village as Iscarioth, Chrys. *Oper.* 219; *Theophyl. Comm. in Matt.* bl. 160, by Judas Iscariot also. All our Lord's disciples were natives of Galilee, and, probably, first became disciples in Galilee. No incident, however, is expressly recorded as having transpired on the circuit itself; a circumstance by no means more peculiar to this first, than to any other of the number, except the last; for these periods in our Lord's ministry, though in themselves integral portions of its whole duration, and as full of action and employment as any part of it, are invariably the least related in detail of all.'—*Ibid.* Vol. II. Diss. xxiii. pp. 292, ..3

PART II. THE SERMON ON THE MOUNT. SECT. XIX.

SECTION 19.—WHEN THE CIRCUIT WAS DRAWING TO AN END, AND THE CONCOURSE OF THE PEOPLE WAS GREATEST, JESUS TEACHES HIS DISCIPLES FROM SOME MOUNTAIN IN THE NEIGHBOURHOOD OF CAPERNAUM.* Matt. v.—viii. 1

INTRODUCTION AND ANALYSIS.

The Sermon on the Mount may be viewed as consisting of *ten* divisions; these are generally distinguished, each from the others, by some peculiarity of form as well as of subject.

The *first* portion, ch. v. ver. 3—12, consists of Beatitudes, describing the Christian life from its commencement to its consummation.

The *second*, ver. 13—,6, calls for the manifestation of that life, for the good of man, unto the glory of God.

The *third*, ver. 17—20, points to the truth and importance of that whereby the life divine is nourished, the word of righteousness as fulfilled by Christ.

The *fourth*, ver. 21—48, consists of *six* paragraphs, each beginning with '*Ye have heard*,' or, '*It hath been said*.' In each, there is a contrast between the law, as viewed by them '*of old time*,' and the truth of the word, as revealed by Him who introduces us into the perfect law of liberty.

The *fifth*, ch. vi. ver. 1—18, consists of *four* paragraphs, warning against formalism; and directing to the true manner of serving or worshipping God, our Father '*who seeth in secret*.'

The *sixth*, ver. 19—34, shews the reasonableness of faith in God, and exposes the folly of that worldly wisdom which is most destructive to the spiritual life.

The *seventh*, ch. vii. ver. 1—6, forbids presumption in judging, and also the prostituting that which is holy.

The *eighth*, ver. 7—14, invites us to '*ask—seek—knock*,' giving the assurance of a favourable answer. It then speaks more fully as to what, and of whom, we are to ask. Then we have the golden rule, the practical use of the Law and the Prophets, as read in the light of the Gospel. Then, as to where we are to knock—it is '*at the strait gate*.' We must practise self-denial, if we would fully participate in the blessings of the life everlasting.

The *ninth*, ver. 15—20, bids us beware of false prophets; and tells us how they, as well as the true witnesses, may be known; and intimates that, however men may deceive others now, the faithful Judge will give a true witness hereafter.

In the *tenth*, ver. 21—7, we are told that nothing can stand the trial, except that which is in truth built upon the Rock. It is only as standing in the grace of God, that faith can endure the trials to which it is, and will be, subjected.

These ten sections of our Lord's exposition of the new covenant may be viewed as exhibiting the manner in which God, by his gospel, writes his law (see the ten commandments, Ex. xx. 3—17) in its spirituality upon the fleshly tables of the heart.

I. In the Beatitudes, ch. v. ver. 3—12, is described the character of those who truly take the Lord to be their God. '*The poor in spirit*,' ver. 3, are they who, being divested of every other dependence, are brought into obedience to the first commandment, Ex. xx. 3, '*Thou shalt have no other gods before me*.' To such the King, '*THE PRINCE OF PEACE*,' makes promise of '*the kingdom of heaven*.'

It is to those who '*mourn*,' ver. 4, that the Eternal, '*THE EVERLASTING FATHER*,' proves the Father of mercies, and the God of all consolation.

It is '*the meek*,' ver. 5, that the Immortal, '*THE MIGHTY GOD*,' will exalt in resurrection glory, to '*inherit the earth*.'

It is for those that '*hunger and thirst after righteousness*,' ver. 6, that the '*COUNSELLOR*,' who hath for us entered within the vail, will procure that which shall fully and for ever satisfy.

It is to '*the merciful*,' ver. 7, that the '*WONDERFUL*,' '*the only wise God*,' will abound in the marvellous displays of his mercy.

Such having been made '*pure in heart*,' ver. 8, '*shall see God*,' being joined to Him in an everlasting covenant.

They are engaged in bringing others within the bond of the covenant, through the peace-speaking blood of Jesus, ver. 9, and are thus made like unto the Son of God

They '*are persecuted for righteousness' sake*,' ver. 10; but '*theirs is the kingdom of heaven*.' Such may meet with but an ill reward from men, ver. 11, for all their labour of love, in manifesting the truth respecting Him who is the '*Wonderful, Counsellor,*

The mighty God, The everlasting Father, The Prince of Peace;' '*the King eternal, immortal, invisible;*' '*the only wise God*;' comp. Is. ix. 6, 1 Ti. i. 17, with ver. 3—7, as above; but great is their reward in their Father's house above: their portion is with those whom nothing could separate from the love of God.

II. Ver. 13—.6. Those who are thus joined unto the Lord as their God are to manifest the life and light into which they are introduced, through Christ Jesus their Lord, the image of the invisible God, and after whose image they are to be formed anew.

They are made one with Him who is '*the Light of the world*;' eschewing all the darkness of idolatry, they are to be for light unto others, being as stars in the right hand of their Redeemer, to reflect the glorious light of that '*Sun of Righteousness*.' They are to let their light so shine, as that not their works, however good, may arrest the attention of men, but that men may be led to *glorify their Father who is in heaven*; compare Ex. xx. 4—6, with Mt. v. 13—.6.

III In order that we thus in truth manifest the Name of the Lord, it is needful that we have a due regard to, and a right understanding of, that whereby God hath made himself known. He hath magnified his word above all his name. He hath made himself known in the Son of his love, as foreshewn by the Law and the Prophets; and we must duly prize the Scriptures of truth, as revealing the purpose for which Christ came into the world—He' is *the end of the law for righteousness to every one that believeth*,' Rom. x. 4. He also came to seal the testimony of the prophets with his blood. Let us beware of making a vain use of Holy Scripture, which is thus so wondrously confirmed. And men must not esteem it a light thing to take upon them the name of Christ: we are taking '*the Lord's name in vain*,' if, while professing to belong to the family of God, we yet are conformed to the world—think lightly of God's manifestation of love in the gift of his Son, and care not to manifest that love to others; compare Ex. xx. 7, with Mt. v. 17—20.

IV. Ver. 21—48. Those '*of old time*' had been labouring to work out a righteousness of their own, according to the law; but we, who trust in the Son of God, by whom the law has been most perfectly fulfilled, do enter with him into rest; as is taught us in the exposition of the fourth commandment, He. iv. 10, '*He that is entered into his rest, he also hath ceased from his own works, as God did from his*.' Thenceforth the law is life, and his commandments are not grievous, but are rest and peace. It is as reaching the heart, that our Lord here presents a view of the second table of the law, as with regard to the *sixth* commandment, ver. 21—.6, and the *seventh*, ver. 27—32; and as to the *eighth*, we are taught not to subtract from that which is vowed or promised, but to act in all simplicity toward man, the same as if under a vow to God, ver. 33—.7. So far from bearing false witness, against which we are warned in the *ninth*, we are not even to prosecute according to the strict rigour of justice, ver. 38—42; and, so far from wishing evil to our neighbour, as forbidden in the *tenth* commandment, we are even to love our enemies, and do them all the good we are able: and as being made one with the Son of God. We are thus to bring forth the fruit of the perfect work of Christ, even as our Father in heaven continues to bestow the blessings of his completed work of creation, 43—.8.

These, the *sixth, seventh, eighth, ninth,* and *tenth* commandments, viewed in relation to our neighbour, we are to obey, as being brought into obedience to the *fifth* commandment, viewed as reaching to the highest relation of parent and child. Those of old time had been claiming the honour that belongs to God. These fathers were heard and obeyed, to the making void the word of the everlasting Father. He is honoured by our listening to the voice of his '*well-beloved Son*,' and by our thus becoming conformed to his image, according to his word: '*Be ye therefore perfect, even as your Father which is in heaven is perfect*.'

It is only as resting in the perfect work of Jesus, the Son of God, who hath for us brought in everlasting righteousness, that we can rejoice in the spirituality of the law, become followers of God as dear children, and serve him in the Sonship, ver. 21—48.

* See ADDENDA, '*On this Sermon and that in St. Luke* vi. 20—49,' § 27, pp. 211, .3.

THOU SHALT LOVE THY NEIGHBOUR AS THYSELF.—Mark xii. 31. [119

SECT. XIX.   THE SERMON ON THE MOUNT.   PART II.

(G. 23,) No. 19. *Mountain North of Capernaum.*

1 And seeing the multitudes, he-went-up into a mountain: and when-'he'-was-set, his disciples came-unto him:
2, 3 And he-opened his mouth, and-taught them, saying, Blessed Μακαριοι *are* the poor
4 in spirit: for their's is the kingdom of heaven. Blessed *are* they that-mourn: for they
5, 6 shall-be-comforted. Blessed *are* the meek: for they shall-inherit the earth. Blessed

SCRIPTURE ILLUSTRATIONS.

1. *set*—the posture in which instruction was given—*see* Mt. xiii. 2, § 32; Lu. iv. 20, § 15, p. 101; v. 3, § 20; Jno. viii. 2, § 55—so Paul at Antioch in Pisidia: 'but when they departed from Perga, they came to Antioch in Pisidia, and went into the synagogue on the sabbath day, and sat down,' Ac. xiii. 14—and by the river side at Philippi: 'and on the sabbath we went out of the city by a river side, where prayer was wont to be made; and we sat down, and spake unto the women which resorted *thither*,' xvi. 13—*see* § 6, p. 41, Note, Lu. ii. 46, '*in the midst.*'

3. *poor in spirit*—the humble heart is the throne in which the King of heaven delighteth to dwell: 'For thus saith the high and lofty One that inhabiteth eternity, whose name *is* Holy; I dwell in the high and holy *place*, with him also *that is* of a contrite and humble spirit, to revive the spirit of the humble, and to revive the heart of the contrite ones,' Is. lvii. 15— 'Hearken, my beloved brethren, Hath not God chosen the poor of this world rich in faith, and heirs of the kingdom which he hath promised to them that love him?' Ja. ii. 5—'I will also leave in the midst of thee an afflicted and poor people, and they shall trust in the name of the LORD,' Zep. iii. 12.

4. *mourn*—occasioned by the prevalence of evil and absence of the Lord Jesus: 'verily, verily, I say unto you, That ye shall weep and lament, but the world shall rejoice: and ye shall be sorrowful, but your sorrow shall be turned into joy.' 'And ye now therefore have sorrow: but I will see you again, and

your heart shall rejoice, and your joy no man taketh from you,' Jno. xvi. 20, .2, § 87.

comforted—'If I go not away, the Comforter will not come unto you; but if I depart, I will send him unto you,' Jno. xvi. 7, § 87—*see* as to the Comforter, Jno. xiv. 16—20, § ib.—' The Lord hath anointed me . . . to appoint unto them that mourn in Zion,' &c., Is. lxi. 1—3 . . . . —comfort promised in Zion, Is. xxx. 18, .9 . . . . —the comforting acknowledged, Ps. cxlv.— . . . . ; exlviii. . . . ; Is. xii. —. . . . &c.—'all ye that mourn for her'—'ye shall be comforted in Jerusalem,' Is. lxvi. 10, .3—*see* ch. lxvi.

5. *the meek*—'the meek shall inherit the earth; and shall delight themselves in the abundance of peace,' Ps. xxxvii. 11—'the man Moses *was* very meek, above all the men which *were* upon the face of the earth,' Nu. xii. 3—he however came short as to this virtue: 'And the LORD spake unto Moses and Aaron, Because ye believed me not, to sanctify me in the eyes of the children of Israel, therefore ye shall not bring this congregation into the land which I have given them,' xx. 12—Jesus our example, 'meek and lowly in heart,' Mt. xi. 29, § 29.—' Rejoice greatly, O daughter of Zion; shout, O daughter of Jerusalem: behold, thy King cometh unto thee: he *is* just, and having salvation; lowly, and riding upon an ass, and upon a colt the foal of an ass,' Zech. ix. 9—'Be patient therefore, brethren, unto the coming of the Lord,' Ja. v. 7—11. . . . . 'speak evil of no man, . . . be no brawlers, *but* gentle, shewing all meekness unto all men,' Tit. iii. 2.

NOTES.

1. *Seeing the multitudes.* 'Seeing so great a concourse of people.' This is commonly called the sermon on the mount. It is not improbable that it was repeated, in substance, on different occasions.—*See* Lu. vi. 17—19, § 27. The design of our Lord in this discourse was to make known the *nature* of that kingdom he had announced as being about to be established, and to rescue the moral law from the false glosses put upon it by the Pharisees.

Set. The master sat in the chief place, and the disciples before him in a circuit—*see* Lu. ii. 46, § 6, p. 41.

His disciples came unto him. The apostles, or the peculiar disciples of Christ, may be principally concerned. From Lu. vi. 13, .7, § 27, and Jno. vi. 66, .7, § 43, all who followed our Saviour, and heard him favourably, were called 'his disciples.'

2. *Opened his mouth.* This phrase is expressive of free and full discourse, Ep. vi. 19, '*And for me, that utterance may be given unto me, that I may open my mouth boldly, to make known the mystery of the gospel,'* of some weighty and important matter, uttered with great alacrity of spirit.

[3. *Blessed are the poor in spirit.* Μακάριοι, '*Happy.*' The best commentators generally render μακάριοι, *happy*, and εὐδαίμονες, and εὐδαιμονές, *blessed.* The several blessings here pronounced appear to have some opposition to the vices to which the Jews were chiefly addicted.]

Such are truly happy who are sensible of their own ignorance, sinfulness, and insufficiency, and who depend on God's free grace for instruction, forgiveness, and supply: and whose hearts are so weaned from the riches, honours, and pleasures of this life, that they readily submit to God's disposal, and part with everything temporal for the gospel's sake;—such only have a full and everlasting interest in all the riches and honours of the kingdom of grace here, and of the kingdom of glory that is about to come.

Theirs is the kingdom of heaven. That is theirs, as a *gift*, which cannot be procured by purchase. They are, through Divine grace, constituted heirs of a kingdom which shall fully satisfy, and that for ever.

[4. *Blessed are they that mourn.* All kinds of mourning cannot be here intended; '*for the sorrow of the world worketh death.*']

[Our Lord predicted that the days were coming when the Bridegroom would be taken from his disciples, and then should they fast or mourn; and when he did make them understand that he was indeed going away, sorrow filled their heart. But he did not leave them comfortless: he left the promise of his return; to apply which promise was one of the special purposes for which the Comforter was to be sent.]

5. *The meek; i.e.*, 'the gentle and forgiving.' It is not apathy which is enjoined, but a regulation of passion, as, '*Be ye angry, and sin not: let not the sun go down upon your wrath*,' Ep. iv. 26. Not such as are constitutionally meek, but made so by grace, made so under injuries, &c., by faith and in answer to prayer; those who, from principle, patiently submit to the will of God, whether it be as to suffering, or doing.

They shall inherit the earth. This might have been translated the land. It was promised to Israel that they should inherit the *land* of Canaan. The patriarchs looked forward to this—*see* Ga. xv. 7, 8. 7. '*And he said unto him, I am the LORD that brought thee out of Ur of the Chaldees, to give thee this land to inherit it.* 8. *And he sa.'d, Lord GOD, whereby shall I know that I shall inherit it?*' and Ex. xxxii. 13, '*Remember Abraham, Isaac, and Israel, thy servants, to whom thou swarest by thine own self, and saidst unto them, I will multiply your seed as the stars of heaven, and all this land that I have spoken of will I give unto your seed, and they shall inherit it for ever.*' Yet they did not possess it till after the Exodus from Egypt. Moses, although the meekest of men, did not enter into the land, although he led the children of Israel to the borders of it. Abraham, Isaac, and Jacob, although they sojourned in the land, were not given it in possession, notwithstanding their being given it in promise. Nevertheless, those who patiently wait for God will find his promise sure. '*The meek shall inherit the earth,*' when the wicked are cut off.

PART II. BLESSED ARE THE PEACEMAKERS. SECT. XIX.

MATT. v. 7—9.

7, 8 Blessed *are* the merciful: for they shall-obtain-mercy ελεηθησονται. Blessed *are* are they which-do-hunger and thirst-after righteousness: for they shall-be-filled. 9 the pure in heart: for they shall-see God. Blessed *are* the peacemakers: for they

SCRIPTURE ILLUSTRATIONS.

6. *hunger and thirst after, &c.*—such as keep judgment and do mercy, Is. lvi. 1—3, . . . —*see the contrast*, ver. 9—12, and lxv. 11—.6, . . . —such as truly 'keep judgment and do justice say, 'As for me, I will behold thy face in righteousness: I shall be satisfied, when I awake, with thy likeness,' Ps. xvii. 15.

shall be filled—' Ho, every one that thirsteth,' &c., Is. lv. 1—3, . . . —' whosoever drinketh,' &c., Jno. iv. 14, § 13, p. 93—'if any man thirst,' &c., vii. 37, .8, § 55—' the bread of God is he which cometh down from heaven,' &c., vi. 33—.5, § 43—' *When* the poor and needy seek water, and *there is* none, *and* their tongue faileth for thirst, I the LORD will hear them, *I* the God of Israel will not forsake them.' Is. xli. 17 —*see* Lu. i. 53, § 2, p. 12. . . . . 'As new born babes, desire the sincere milk of the word, that ye may grow thereby,' 1 Pe. ii. 2—Let us with Job say, ' I have esteemed the words of his mouth more than my necessary *food*,' xxiii. 12—and we shall be able to say, ' Thy words were found, and I did eat them; and thy word was unto me the joy and rejoicing of mine heart,' Jer. xv. 16.

7. *the merciful*—' With the merciful thou wilt shew thyself merciful,' 2 Sa. xxii. 26—the righteous is 'ever merciful, and lendeth; and his seed *is* blessed,' Ps. xxxvii. 26—blessings promised to Israel when he sheweth mercy, Is. lviii. 6—12.

shall obtain mercy—mercy with men when they need it, but especially mercy with God: ' For if ye forgive,' &c., ch. vi. 14, p. 133—supplying mercy: ' He that hath pity upon the poor lendeth unto the LORD; and that which he hath given [or, *his deed*] will he pay him again,' Pr. xix. 17—mercy in that day: ' The Lord grant unto him that he may find mercy of the Lord in that day: and in how many things he ministered unto me at Ephesus, thou knowest very well,' 2 Ti. i. 18—' for God *is* not unrighteous to forget your work and labour of love, which ye

have shewed toward his name, in that ye have ministered to the saints, and do minister,' He. vi. 10.

8. *pure in heart*—' With the pure thou wilt,' &c., 2 Sa. xxii. 27—Job was 'perfect and upright,' Job i. 1—8 . . . . —such shall abide in the tabernacle of God, Ps. xv. 1—4 . . . . —and 'receive the blessing from the LORD,' xxiv. 4, 3, . . . —Purity necessary to seeing God in his word: ' Many shall be purified, and made white, and tried; but the wicked shall do wickedly: and none of the wicked shall understand; but the wise shall understand,' Da. xii. 10—and in his works, Ps. cxi. . . . . —' Follow peace with all *men*, and holiness, without,' &c., He. xii. 14.

9. *peacemakers*—' Abram said unto Lot, Let there be no strife,' &c., Ge. xiii. 7, 8—Moses was a peacemaker, Ex. ii. 13—*comp.* Ac. vii. 26—' Love your enemies,' &c., Lu. vi. 27, § 27—' Bless them which persecute you: bless, and curse not,' Rom. xii. 14—21; xiv. 1—19, ... 16, ' For where envying and strife *is*, there *is* confusion and every evil work. But the wisdom that is from above is first pure, then peaceable, gentle, *and* easy to be intreated, full of mercy and good fruits, without partiality, and without hypocrisy. And the fruit of righteousness is sown in peace of them that make peace,' Ja. iii. 16—.8—Christians to seek that men may be reconciled to God: ' *how* then we are ambassadors for Christ, as though God did beseech *you* by us: we pray *you* in Christ's stead, be ye reconciled to God,' 2 Co. v. 20—and to one another in the Lord, Ep. iv. . . . . *see* as to the disposition in which this peace is to be sought, ver. 1—3—the power to accomplish it, ver. 4—10—the ministry appointed for the purpose, ver. 11, .2—and the grand result contemplated, ver. 13—6—the obstructions to be removed out of the way, ver. 17—31—the example of forgiveness in the Father, ver. 32—and of sacrifice in the Son, ch. v. ver. 2. . . . . to be followed by the sons of God, ver. 1.

NOTES.

6. *Blessed are they which do hunger, &c.* Hunger and thirst here are expressive metaphors of ardent desire. The hungry desire food; the thirsty, drink: gold is despised for bread. The words are descriptive of a holy ardour of soul, in pursuit of the most eminent attainments in universal goodness.

They shall be filled. χορτασθησονται, 'satisfied,' so as to desire nothing more. It is derived from χορτος, 'grass,' or 'herbage;' and is a figure taken from cattle in a good pasture, fed till they are satisfied, and graze no longer.

7. *Blessed are the merciful.* In nothing do we imitate God more than in shewing mercy. He specially appointed the 'mercy seat,' saying, '*there I will meet with thee*,' Ex. xxv. 21, .2.

[8. *Pure in heart*. Those, in whose souls all carnal, sinful, and sensual desires are mortified; who are inwardly replenished with holy natures and affections, and influenced by the fear and love of God in their habitual conduct. In opposition to the Pharisees, who affected outward purity, while their hearts were full of corruption and defilement.]

' The clean in heart,' οι καθαροι τη καρδια, an allusion to the ancient ritual. The laws in regard to the cleanliness of the body, and even of the garments, if neglected, excluded a person from the temple.

[*Shall see God*. The words are a Hebraism, signifying, ' they shall possess God,' enjoy his felicity:—(seeing a thing was used among the Hebrews for possessing it.)—See Ps. xvi. 10, ' *For thou wilt not leave my soul in hell; neither wilt thou suffer thine Holy One to see corruption.*'—Jno. iii. 3, 16, § 12, pp. 83, .6.]

9. *Blessed are the peacemakers.* Ειρηνοποιοι. This word is not found in any other part of Scripture, but (which is nearly the same) the verb ειρηνοποιεω, of the same origin, occurs Col. i. 20, where the connexion shews that it signifies *actively to reconcile, to make peace*; ' *And, having made peace through the blood of his cross, by him to reconcile all things unto himself; by him*, I say, *whether they* be *things in earth, or things in heaven*.' Etymology and classical use, also, concur in affixing the sense of *reconciler, peacemaker*, to ειρηνοποιος.]

PRACTICAL REFLECTIONS.

[3—8 *ver*. The *first* pre-requisite to blessing, is to know our need of it, that we have nothing to purchase it, and that it must be of *grace*—the *next* is, to mourn the absence of Him, in whom the fulness of blessing is to be found—the *third* is, quietly to submit to the will of God, in patient waiting for the fulfilment of his promise—the *fourth* is, the preparation for it, in the most earnest desire after righteousness —the *fifth* is, that, knowing our own shortcomings, and the forgiving grace and enriching goodness of God, we act in mercy toward others—and the *sixth* is, that our clemency be not extended to our own faults, no, not even as to secret thought or motive; but, that we be pure in heart. Such shall see God; a people thus prepared will be delighted in by him as his chosen bride.]

9 *ver*. God sent his Son into the world, to reconcile sinners unto himself. And those who *follow the Lamb whithersoever he goeth*, willing to be at any sacrifice as loving the truth and the peace, are those who will be found standing with the Lamb upon mount Sion, having his Father's name written on their foreheads, manifesting as sons of the living God, His Name, which is LOVE.

[* The Jews look for Messiah to lead them to *war* and victory. Happy shall they be, who, being reconciled to God through Christ, have his peace filling their hearts, and rendering them earnestly diligent to maintain and promote peace, consistently with truth and holiness; such shall enjoy all the privileges that belong to the adoption of sons.']

A TENDER HEART IS LIKE MELTING WAX. [121

SECT. XIX. THE SALT OF THE EARTH. THE LIGHT OF THE WORLD. PART II.

MATT. v. 10—.4.

10 shall-be-called the-children υἱοὶ of-God. Blessed *are* they which-are-persecuted for-
11 righteousness'-sake: for their's is the kingdom of heaven. Blessed are-ye, when *men* shall-revile you, and persecute *you*, and shall-say all-manner-of evil παν πονηρον ῥῆμα
12 against you falsely ψευδομενοι, for-·my·-sake. Rejoice, and be-exceeding-glad: for great *is* your reward in heaven: for so persecuted-they the prophets which *were* before you.
13 Ye are the salt of-the earth: but if the salt have-lost-his-savour μωρανθῃ, wherewith shall-it-be-salted? it-is-·thenceforth·-good ισχυει ετι for nothing, but to-be-cast out, and
14 to-be-trodden-·under·-foot of men. Ye are the light of-the world. A-city that-is-set on

SCRIPTURE ILLUSTRATIONS.

9. *children of God*—as bearing resemblance to God: 'Be perfect, be of good comfort, be of one mind, live in peace; and the God of love and peace shall be with you,' 2 Co. xiii. 11—see Hos. i. 10.

10. *persecuted for righteousness' sake*—to be willing to suffer for the Son of man's sake, Lu. vi. 22, § 27— 'All that will live godly in Christ Jesus shall suffer persecution,' 2 Ti. iii. 12—' If we suffer, we shall also reign with *him*: if we deny *him*.' &c., ii. 12— the heirs of the kingdom are described as those who had lost their lives 'for the witness of Jesus,' &c.: ' And I saw thrones, and they sat upon them, and judgment was given unto them: and *I saw* the souls of them that were beheaded for the witness of Jesus, and for the word of God, and which had not worshipped the beast, neither his image, neither had received his mark upon their foreheads, or in their hands; and they lived and reigned with Christ a thousand years,' Rev. xx. 4; xi. 16.

12. *so persecuted they the prophets*—see the case of Joseph as to persecution, Ge. xxxvii. 8, 18—28; and blessing—comp. xlix. 26—Jezebel persecuted the prophets: 'For it was so, when Jezebel cut off the prophets of the LORD, that Obadiah took an hundred prophets, and hid them by fifty in a cave, and fed them with bread and water,' 1 Ki. xviii. 4—so Ahab, xxii. 8—27—Zechariah stoned. 2 Ch. xxiv. 20, .1—.. . . . . . ver. ' —last col. last l. 'they were disobedient, and rebelled against thee, and cast thy law behind their backs, and slew thy prophets which testified

against them to turn them to thee, and they wrought great provocations,' Ne. ix. 26—so Jeremiah, ch. xxvi. 8, 9, 20—.3 - see the parallel passage, Luke vi. 23, § 27—our Lord twice bewailed Jerusalem, on account of her hardness of heart, in slaying the prophets, Lu. xiii. 34, § 66: Mt. xxiii. 37, § 85—so Stephen accused the Jewish sanhedrim: 'Ye stiffnecked and uncircumcised in heart and ears, ye do always resist the Holy Ghost: as your fathers *did*, so do ye. Which of the prophets have not your fathers persecuted? and they have slain them which shewed before of the coming of the Just One; of whom ye have been now the betrayers and murderers,' Ac. vii. 51, .2 —comp. 1 Th. ii. 14, .5, and He. xi. 36, .7.

13. *ye are the salt, &c.*—salt was to be offered with the meat offering, Le. ii. 13—' Let your speech be alway with grace, seasoned with salt, that ye may know how ye ought to answer every man.' Col. iv. 6—Christians are said to escape ' the pollutions of the world through the knowledge of the Lord and Saviour Jesus Christ,' 2 Pe. ii. 20.

14. *ye are the light*—Christians are individually to shine as 'lights in the world;' 'blameless and harmless, the sons of God, without rebuke, in the midst of a crooked and perverse nation, among whom ye shine as lights in the world,' Ph. ii. 15—as John, who was a 'burning and a shining light,' Jno. v. 35, § 22—also collectively, as 'light in the Lord,' Eph. v. 8—21 . . . . . Christ is the 'true Light, which lighteth,' &c., Jno. i. 9, § 7, p. 47.

NOTES.

9. *Children of God.* It is here *implied* that they will, by the Father, be loved and blessed with a truly paternal affection; they being made conformable to his dear Son, who came to make ' peace *through the blood of his cross*,' Col i, 20.—See p. 121.

10. *Persecuted.* δεδιωγμενοι. They who are hard pressed upon, and pursued with repeated acts of enmity.

[11. *And persecute you.* The persecution in the preceding verse signifies that of the hand; this of the tongue, as calumny, &c.; but as *διωκειν*, which we render 'to persecute,' is a forensic term, and signifies 'legal persecutions and public accusations,' our Lord probably refers to such in relation to the primitive Christians.—*Clarke*.]

12. *Great is your reward.* A patient and cheerful suffering for Christ in this life will certainly be rewarded in the blessedness of the life to come. Not a reward of debt, but of grace; ' For our *light affliction, which is but for a moment, worketh for us a far more exceeding and eternal weight of glory*,' 2 Co. iv. 17.

13. *Salt.* This is the grand preservative from corruption in the material world. Salt is a common symbol of wisdom. The disciples and ministers of Christ are, by their doctrine, conversation, example, labours, and prayers, to oppose the progress of sin and impiety, and season men's minds with holiness.

[*If the salt have lost his savour.* As salt which has lost its savour is useless, so Christ's disciples will be

worthless and contemptible, even in the most eminent stations, if by their conduct they maintain not their character for real and vital religion. In eastern countries salt is found in the earth in veins or layers, and when exposed to the sun and rain loses its saltness entirely.]

[*But to be cast out.* ' Who shall teach the teacher?' εἰ μὴ βληθῆναι ἔξω. A sort of rustic proverb, signifying ' *to be good for nothing.*']

14. *Light of the world.* τὸ φῶς τοῦ κόσμου, i. e., 'the means by which God is pleased to enlighten the minds of men with true religion, as the globe is enlightened by the rays of the sun; which is, in the *proper sense,* τὸ φῶς τοῦ κόσμου. The term was applied by the Jews to their rabbins, as among the Greeks and Romans celebrated persons were called *lights of the world.*'— *Bloomfield.* Christ is the true Light, but Christians shine by the light of knowledge and holiness derived from him.

A city set on a hill. Not far from the Mount of Beatitudes is *Saphet*, supposed to be the ancient *Bethulia.* It stands on a very conspicuous mountain, and might easily be seen from the mountain on which our Lord made this discourse. Many writers have justly observed that *Christ* takes his *similes* from the most obvious things, familiarly known to his hearers, and often before their eyes, even while he was speaking. See this beautifully illustrated by Sir Isaac *Newton in his Work on the Prophecies.*

PRACTICAL REFLECTIONS.

10 *ver.* Those who are espoused unto Jesus, the Lord our Righteousness, are not to be discouraged, on account of their being hated of the world.

[11, .2 *ver.* Christians must not be surprised, although they should be reviled for their work of faith and labour of love, and although they should have their motives misrepresented; they must have the patience of hope, looking for their reward, not from man or in time, but from God, and in the coming kingdom, like the prophets who have gone before them.]

13 *ver.* As salt was of old a token of friendship, and actually brings more closely together, so as to

preserve from putrefaction, the several particles of the substances into which it is put—so should true believers exhibit the power of the salt of his covenant, in diffusing his purifying, healing, and preserving grace around them.

[14 *ver.* Christians should not merely be as lights; they should, in Christ, concentrate their efforts, so as to be like one great light, for the enlightenment of the world. They should not be as dwelling in scattered tents, they should be as fellow-citizens, combining their efforts for the common good, and as an open example to the world, not merely of individual holiness, but of social harmony, beauty, and blessing.]

IS THE EYE OF PROVIDENCE EVER SHUT?

PART II.   CHRIST CAME TO FULFIL THE LAW.   SECT. XIX.

MATT. v. 15—.9.
15 an-hill cannot be-hid. Neither do-*men*-light a-candle, and put it under a bushel, but
16 on a candlestick; and it-giveth-light unto-all that *are* in the house. Let-'your light
so'-shine before men, that they-may-see your good works, and glorify your Father
which *is* in heaven.
17 Think not that I-am-come to-destroy καταλυσαι the law, or the prophets: I-am-'not'-
18 come to-destroy, but to-fulfil πληρωσαι. For verily I-say unto-you, Till heaven and
earth pass παρελθῃ, one jot ιωτα or one tittle κεραια shall-'in-no-wise'-pass from the
19 law, till all be-fulfilled. Whosoever therefore shall-break one of-these least command-

SCRIPTURE ILLUSTRATIONS.

15. *on a candlestick*—churches likened to candlesticks—*see* Rev. i. 20, ...Christians to attach themselves to the assemblies of the saints, for the purpose of unitedly and openly exhibiting the light, Ile. x. 23—.5. . . . . . . *see* as to the armour of light, with which the darkness and the powers of darkness are to be opposed, Ep. vi. 11—.9 . . . . .—'What I tell you in darkness, *that* speak ye in light,' &c., Mt. x. 27, § 39.

16. *let your light*—even those who occupy the lowest stations may 'adorn the doctrine of God our Saviour in all things,' Tit. ii. 10—.2—Christians are practically to exhibit the light, so that their enemies may be led to glorify God, 1 Pe. ii. 12. . . . . thus even in this life are the meek to be beautified with salvation, whether as subjects, ver. 13—.7—or as servants, ver. 18—25—or as wives and husbands, iii. 1—7. . . . .'a chosen generation, a royal priesthood' . . . to 'shew forth the praises of him who hath called you out of darkness into his marvellous light,' 1 Pe. ii. 9—' God is light,' and we are to walk in the light, 1 Jno. i. 5—7.

good works—Tabitha, Ac. ix. 36—'we are his workmanship, created in Christ Jesus unto good works, which God hath before ordained that we should walk in them,' Ep. ii. 10—through the Scripture, the man of God is 'throughly furnished unto all good works,' 2 Ti. iii. 17—a doer of the word : 'But he ye doers of the word, and not hearers only, deceiving your own selves,' Ja. i. 22—God is glorified in such as bear much fruit, Jno. xv. 8, § 87.

17. *think not . . . to destroy the law*—'Do we then make void the law through faith ?' God forbid : yea,

we establish the law,' Rom. iii. 31—'For Christ *is* the end of the law for righteousness to every one that believeth,' x. 4—' Jesus Christ . . . a minister of the circumcision for the truth of God, to confirm the promises *made* unto the fathers,' xv. 8—' the covenant, that was confirmed,' &c., Ga. iii. 17,. . . . . 'The LORD is well pleased for his righteousness' sake; he will magnify the law, and make *it* honourable,' Is. xlii. 21

18. *till heaven and earth shall pass*—' For ever, O LORD, thy word is. settled in heaven,' Ps. cxix. 89, 152. —' The grass withereth, the flower fadeth: but the word of our God shall stand for ever,' Is. xl. 8—' And it is easier for heaven and earth to pass, than one tittle of the law to fail,' Lu. xvi. 17, § 69; xxi. 33, § 86; Mt. xxiv. 35, § *ib.*—it is not in order to make void his word, that God hath become incarnate, Nu. xxiii. 19 . . . . ver. 51, under ' THE SON OF MAN,' but in order to make it sure; ' He that spared not his own Son, but,' &c., Rom. viii. 32.

19. *whosoever . . . shall break*—the word of the Lord, given to Moses, to be kept in integrity : 'What thing soever I command you, observe to do it : thou shalt not add thereto, nor diminish from it,' De. xii. 32—the Pharisees made ' the commandment of God of none effect by . . . . tradition,' Mt. xv. 3—6, § 44—' Take heed and beware of the leaven,' &c., Mt. xvi. 6, § 48—the church at Pergamos reproved: ' But I have a few things against thee, because thou hast there them that hold the doctrine of Balaam, who taught Balac to cast a stumblingblock before the children of Israel, to eat things sacrificed unto idols, and to commit fornication,' Rev. ii. 14—' Abstain from all appearance of evil,' 1 Th. v. 22.

NOTES.

15. *Light a candle, &c.* λυχνον, 'a lamp.' Their houses were illuminated all night by LAMPS placed on a large stand, here rendered 'candlestick,' fixed in the ground, from which the smaller lamps used in the apartments were lighted.

Under a bushel. ὑπο τον μοδιον, 'under a corn measure;' a bushel was unknown to the Jews. A proverbial saying, illustrative of the folly of depriving anything of its utility, by putting it to a purpose the farthest from what it was intended for.

16. *Let your light so shine.* Ὁυτω λαμψατω το φως, 'thus let your light shine,' 'the light of your example,' ' unequivocal profession of the truth.'

That they may see your good works. This is not the *motive* to influence us, simply that we *may be seen* —*see* ch. vi. l. p. 131—but that our heavenly Father may be glorified. The Pharisees acted to be *seen of men*; true Christians act to glorify God ; and care little what *men* may think of them, except as by their conduct others may be brought to honour God.

[17. *Think not that I am come to destroy the law, &c.* As if he had said, ' I am not come to make the law of none effect—to dissolve the connexion which subsists between its several parts, or the obligation men are under to have their lives regulated by its moral pre-

cepts; nor am I come to dissolve the *connecting* reference which it has to the *good things promised*. But I am come, πληρωσαι, *to complete*—to perfect its connexion and reference, to ratify and accomplish everything shadowed forth in the Mosaic *ritual*, to fill up its great design.']

18. *Verily.* 'Αμην. [The proper signification of this word is *true*,—*verus*, as spoken of things; *observant of truth, verax*, as spoken of persons; sometimes *truth* in the abstract. In the New Testament it is frequently used in affirmation.]

[*Jot*, ιωτα, answers to the Hebrew letter י, *yod*, which, being the least letter of the alphabet, might be proverbially used on this occasion. Thus our Lord means to express, in addition to the *eternal obligation*, the *boundless extent* of the moral law, as demanding the utmost purity of *thought*, as well as innocence of action.]

One tittle—see ADDENDA, p. 123.

Till all be fulfilled. ἑως αν παντα γενηται, ' till all things which it requires or foretells shall be effected.'

19. *Break.* 'Shall neglect, or transgress,' in his practice, or pervert and weaken by his doctrines; violate or disobey.

PRACTICAL REFLECTIONS.

[15 ver. God, the great Giver of light, gives the knowledge of his truth, not in order that it may lie in concealment, but in order that the whole household of faith may be benefited thereby. The Christian must endeavour to dispel the surrounding darkness.]

16 *ver.* We should seek that our light may be put forth in such a way as to prove that it proceeds from the God of truth and love—that it exhibit in us, not the deformities of sin, or the infirmities of the flesh, but the beauties of holiness, the fruits of the Spirit, not as seeking the praise of men, but their good, and the glory of our Father which is in heaven.

[17 *ver.* Let us not dishonour Christ, by having imperfect views of his mission. Let us not dishonour God, by thinking that he sent his Son to undo all that he had been doing before; to gainsay what he had said, and had solemnly confirmed by oath—the coming of Christ is rather the assured pledge that all shall be accomplished.]

18 *ver.* God is a great lawgiver, and we may not trifle with his commands: his word must stand, and he will do all his pleasure. The threatened judgment must fall, the promised blessing will come; as God hath from the beginning appointed.

BE SURE YOUR SIN WILL FIND YOU OUT.—Numb. xxxii. 23.

SECT. XIX. WHAT IT IS TO KILL. PART II.

MATT. v. 19—22.

ments, and shall-teach men so, he-shall-be-called the-least in the kingdom of heaven: but whosoever shall-do and teach *them*, the-same shall-be-called great in the kingdom
20 of heaven. For I-say unto-you, That except your righteousness shall-exceed περισσευσῃ πλειον *the righteousness of*-the scribes and Pharisees, ye-shall-'in-no-case'-enter into the kingdom of heaven.
21 Ye-have-heard that it-was-said by-them of-old-time, Thou-shalt-'not'-kill; and who-
22 soever shall-kill shall-be in-danger-of ενοχος the judgment: but I say unto-you, That whosoever is-angry with his brother without-a-cause εικη shall-be in-danger-of the judgment: and whosoever shall-say to his brother, Raca, shall-be in-danger-of the

SCRIPTURE ILLUSTRATIONS.

19. *whosoever shall do and teach*—'They that be wise shall shine as the brightness of the firmament; and they that turn many to righteousness as the stars for ever and ever,' Da. xii. 3.—'Study to shew thyself approved unto God, a workman that needeth not to be ashamed, rightly dividing the word of truth,' 2 Ti. ii. 15—following righteousness—' In meekness instructing those that oppose,' ver. 22.—6—'In all things shewing thyself a pattern of good works: in doctrine *shewing* uncorruptness, gravity, sincerity, sound speech, that cannot be condemned; that he that is of the contrary part may be ashamed, having no evil thing to say of you,' Ti. ii. 7, 8.

20. *except your righteousness shall exceed, &c.*—so John warned the Pharisees and Sadducees, who had merely an outward formal righteousness, performed as in the sight of man, Mt. iii. 7—10, § 7—the Pharisee and publican, Lu. xviii. 9—14, § 73—no deceiver can enter the kingdom of heaven: ' And there shall in no wise enter into it anything that defileth, neither *whatsoever* worketh abomination, or *maketh* a lie: but they which are written in the Lamb's book of life,' Rev. xxi. 27—'and be found in him, not having mine own righteousness, which is of the law, but that which is through the faith of Christ, the righteousness which is of God by faith,' Ph. iii. 9—*see also* Rom. i. 16—8, ' For I am not ashamed of the gospel of Christ: for it is the power of God unto salvation to every one that believeth; to the Jew first, and also to the Greek. For therein is the righteousness of God revealed from faith to faith: as it is written, The just shall live by faith. For the wrath of God is revealed from heaven against all ungodliness and unrighteousness of men, who hold the truth in unrighteousness.'

21. *thou shalt not kill*—'Whoso sheddeth man's blood, by man shall his blood be shed,' Ge. ix. 5, 6; Ex. xx. 13—'he that killeth any man shall surely be put to death,' Le. xxiv. 17.

22. *angry without cause*—Cain, Ge. iv. 1—8—Joseph's brethren hated him, xxxvii. 4—8 . . . —*see* the case of Miriam and Aaron, Nu. xii.; Korah, Dathan, &c., xvi.—Saul: ' And Saul was very wroth, and the saying displeased him; and he said, They have ascribed unto David ten thousands, and to me they have ascribed *but* thousands: and *what* can he have more but the kingdom? And Saul eyed David from that day and forward,' 1 Sa. xviii. 8, 9—the Jews hated Jesus, Jno. xv. 25, § 87—as having just cause we may be angry; but the sun is not to go down upon our wrath; and we are not to 'give place to the devil,' the suggester of dark suspicions and distrust, Ep. iv. 26, 7—' be ye,' &c. comp. Ge. iii. 1—6, ... 'Now the serpent was more subtil than any beast,' &c.—' Ye are of *your* father,' &c., Jno. viii. 44, § 55.

Raca—such language may not be used unjustly, or without cause; it is used, but not without cause, Ja. ii. 20, ' But wilt thou know, O vain man, that faith without works is dead?'

the council—see Nu. xi. 16, ' And the Lord said unto Moses, Gather unto me seventy men of the elders of Israel, whom thou knowest to be the elders of the people, and officers over them; and bring them unto the tabernacle of the congregation, that they may stand there with thee '—Jesus foretold that the apostles should be delivered up to councils, Mt. x. 17, § 39—sought to put Jesus to death, Mt. xxvi. 59, § 89.

NOTES.

19. *These least commandments*. The Pharisees, it is probable, divided the precepts of the law into *lesser* and *greater*, teaching that they who violated the former were guilty of a trivial offence only; distinguishing between what is called, by the corrupt Romish church, *mortal* and *venial* sins—*see* Mt. xxiii. 23, § 85.

Shall be called least. ' The farthest from attaining heaven;' *i. e.*, ' he shall not attain it at all.'—*Bloomf*.

[20. *The righteousness of the scribes and Pharisees*. They made no small part of the law void by their traditions and divisions, Mt. xxiii. 23, § 85; xv. 3—9, § 44. Christ meant to say that he would not own for his disciple the man who gave a relaxed view of the law, as did the scribes, ver. 20—the righteousness required is that perfect righteousness which can only be found in Christ, The Lord our Righteousness; by submitting to whom we are also made holy in heart and life.]

21. *Thou shalt not kill*. The Jews understood the law, ' Thou shalt not kill,' only of actual murder, and that committed by a man's own hand. But such is the spirituality and extent of this commandment, that whosoever indulges rash, wrathful, and causeless anger, or a malicious and revengeful temper, is, in God's account, guilty of murder in his heart, and thereby exposed to his righteous judgment.

[The *judgment* means an inferior court, consisting of twenty-three members; from it an appeal might be made to the *council*, the supreme court, or sanhedrim, composed of seventy-two elders.]

22. *With his brother*; *i.e.*, with any one. With the Jewish writers, a 'brother' is, *Ben Berith*, a son of the covenant; *i.e.*, an Israelite. A 'neighbour' was a proselyte, in opposition to a heathen. In the church, a 'brother' is a Christian, Mt. xviii. 15, ,7, § 53; 1 Co. v. 11, ' *But now I have written unto you not to keep company, if any man that is called a brother be a fornicator, or covetous, or an idolater, or a railer, or a drunkard, or an extortioner; with such an one no not to eat*.' A neighbour is any one we can assist, Lu. x. 29—37, § 60.

Shall be in danger of the judgment. Shall be liable to a worse punishment from God.

Raca. (That is, without cause.) This is a Syriac word, expressive of great contempt. It comes from a verb signifying to be *empty*, *vain*; and hence, as a word of contempt, denotes *senseless*, *stupid*, *shallow-brains*. Jesus teaches us that to use such words unjustly is a violation of the sixth commandment.

[*Danger of the council*; *i.e.* ' of the sanhedrim,' whose business was to judge in the most important affairs of the nation; for instance, in all matters relative to religion, as when any person pretended to be a prophet, or attempted to make innovations in the established worship. Possibly, this court always consisted of *seventy-one* members, in imitation of the elders appointed by Moses, but with very varying powers.—*See* Addenda, ' *The council*,' p. 129.]

PRACTICAL REFLECTIONS.

19 *ver*. We must be careful not only to avoid committing great sins, but the least sins; and especially of justifying ourselves therein before men, thus teaching them to act in opposition to our God. And we must be heedful not only to do the will of God ourselves, but to communicate the knowledge thereof to others.—' Wouldest thou know if thou lovest God, be frequent in exercises of love and charity.'

[20 *ver*. The Christian's righteousness must not be merely that which consists in an orthodox creed, even when combined with a punctilious observance of religious ordinances. It must be the righteousness which is of God by faith; faith in Christ, as the end of the law for righteousness, must be in the heart, working by love, so as to bring the soul and the life into a living conformity to the will of God.]

DOEST THOU WELL TO BE ANGRY?—Jonah iv. 4.

MATT. v. 23—.9.

council: but whosoever shall-say, Thou-fool μωρε, shall-be in-danger-of hell fire εις
23 την γεενναν του πυρος. Therefore if thou-bring thy gift to the altar, and-there remem-
24 berest that thy brother hath ought against thee; leave there thy gift before the altar,
and go-thy-way; first be-reconciled to thy brother, and then come and-offer thy gift.
25 Agree with thine adversary quickly, whiles thou-art in the way with him; lest-at-any-
time the adversary deliver thee to-the judge, and the judge deliver thee to-the officer,
26 and thou-be-cast into prison. Verily I-say unto-thee, Thou-shalt by-no-means·-come-
out thence, till thou-hast-paid the uttermost farthing.
27 Ye-have-heard that it-was-said by-them of-old-time, Thou-shalt·'not'-commit-adul-
28 tery: but I say unto-you, That whosoever looketh-on a-woman to lust-after her hath-
29 committed-adultery-with her already in his heart. And if thy right eye offend thee,

SCRIPTURE ILLUSTRATIONS.

22. *thou fool*—'The fool hath said in his heart, There is no God,' Ps. xiv. 1—this word is used by our Lord himself, but not 'without cause,' as Mt. xxiii. 17, § 85.

23. *bring thy gift*—'And Samuel said, Hath the Lord *as great* delight in burnt offerings and sacrifices, as in obeying the voice of the Lord? Behold, to obey *is* better than sacrifice. *and* to hearken than the fat of rams,' 1 Sa. xv. 22—God turned away from the sacrifices of the Jews, as offered by hands stained with blood, Is. i. 11—.5 . . . . —they were first, to do justice to those who had only God to plead for them, ver. 16, .7, *ib.*—and then, he would be gracious to them, ver. 18, *ib.*

24. *be reconciled*—Laban warned of God to be reconciled to Jacob, Ge. xxxi. 24—.9—Christians are to be willing to suffer wrong: 'Now therefore there is utterly a fault among you, because ye go to law one with another. Why do ye not rather take wrong? why do ye not rather *suffer yourselves* to be defrauded?' 1 Co. vi. 7—'be ye all of one mind, having compassion one of another,' 1 Pe. iii. 8—11.

25. *agree with, &c.*—Jacob sought agreement with his brother Esau, Ge. xxxii. 3—5 . . . . —'Take,

I pray thee, my blessing that is brought to thee; because God hath dealt graciously with me, and because I have enough. And he urged him, and he took *it*,' xxxiii. 11—' Seek ye the Lord while he may be found,' Is. lv. 6, 7 . . . .—' Kiss the Son, lest he be angry,' Ps. ii. 12 . . . .—' To-day if ye will hear his voice, harden not your hearts,' &c., He. iii. 7—13. . . . . . .—*see* the case of Balaam, Nu. xxii. 31, .2; xxxi. 8; Rev. ii. 14—*see* p. 123, ver. 19.

26. *thou shalt by no means come out, &c.*—the servant who would not forgive his fellow servant, Mt. xviii. 34, § 53.

27. *thou shalt not commit adultery*—Ex. xx. 14—such to be put to death, Le. xx. 10—' whoso committeth adultery with a woman lacketh understanding: he *that* doeth it destroyeth his own soul,' Pr. vi. 32—' whoremongers and adulterers God will judge,' He. xiii. 4—the adulteress 'forsaketh the guide of her youth, & forgetteth the covenant of her God,' Pr. ii.17.

28. *whosoever looketh, &c.*—thus Shechem sinned, Ge. xxxiv. 2—so Potiphar's wife, xxxix. 7—so David, 2 Sa. xi. 2—' Lust not after her beauty,' Pr. vi. 25—' every man is tempted, when he is drawn away of his own lust, and enticed,' Ja. i. 14, .5.

NOTES.

22. *Thou fool*. μωρε. A term of the greatest abhorrence,—'thou impious wretch,' folly and impiety being equivalent with the Hebrews.—*Bloomfield.*

[*Hell-fire*. γεενναν, the Gehennah of fire. The place referred to is supposed to have been a beautiful spot at the foot of mount Moriah, lying partly within the mouth of Hinnom, and partly in the valley of Jehoshaphat, and irrigated by the waters of Siloam. It was called Tophet because of the sacrifices that were offered there to the god Molech, by beat of drum, which in Hebrew is called *Toph* (תף). The statue of Molech was of brass, hollow within, with its arms extended, and stooping a little forward. They lighted a great fire within the statue, and another before it. They put upon its arms the child they intended to sacrifice, which soon fell into the fire at the foot of the statue. To stifle the noise of these cries, they made a great rattling of drums and other instruments, that the spectators might not be moved with compassion. And this, as they say, was the manner of sacrificing in Tophet.—*See* ADDENDA, '*Tophet*,' p. 129.]

23. As the former verse forbids *ill-timed* and *excessive anger and hatred*, so this and the following enjoin *love to our neighbour*, and a *placable spirit*. And since the Pharisees reckoned anger, hatred, and reviling among the slighter offences; and thought that they would not incur the wrath of God, if sacrifices and other external rites were accurately observed; so here we are taught that external worship is not pleasing in the sight of God, unless it be accompanied by a meek and charitable spirit.

[23, .4. *Therefore, if thou bring thy gift, &c.* The scribes required restitution in money-matters; yet otherwise held, that gifts and sacrifices would expiate all offences not amenable to the judge.]

25. *Adversary.* αντιδικος. 'one going to law with another.' It here means a *creditor*; a man who has a just claim on us. It is wrong to carry the contention to a court of law—*see* 1 Co. vi. 7, ver. 24,' Sc. Illus.'

Whiles thou *art in the way*. According to the

Roman custom, an aggrieved person could compel the party to go with him before the prætor, unless he agreed by the way to adjust the matter.

26. *Farthing.* κοδραντην. A word formed from the Latin *quadrans*, which (*from quatuor*, four,) denotes a Roman coin, made of brass or lead, the fourth part of an *as*, and equal in value to about three-fourths of our farthing. There was a smaller coin than this in use among the Jews.—*See* Mt. xii. 42, § 85.

[28. *Looketh, &c.* ὁ βλεπων γυναικα. 'Gazeth on a woman.' Indulges unchaste imaginations, desires, and intentions. Such was the guilt of David—*see* 2 Sa. xi. 2. 'Our Lord means to say, that it is not the *act* only, but the *unchaste desire* also, (what is called at 2 Pe. ii. 14, "eyes full of adultery,") which is included in the commandment. 'Επιθυμια may be defined, "such a desire as gains the full consent of the will, and would certainly terminate in action, did no impediments from other causes arise;" thus making the essence of the vice to be in the *intention.*'—*Bloomfield.*]

[29. ει δε ὁ ὀφθαλμος-σκανδαλιζει σε. 'If thy right eye prove a stumblingblock to thee,' 'occasion thee to stumble,' 'lead thee into sin.' It is used as a metaphor for whatever proves the occasion of the commission of sin. The Hebrews were accustomed to compare lusts and evil passions with members of the body; for example, an evil eye denoted envy, Mt. xx. 15, § 76; the bowels denoted compassion; the heart, affection, &c. So Paul writes to the Romans, ch. vi. 13. ' *Neither yield ye your members* as *instruments* of *unrighteousness unto sin*: but yield *yourselves* unto God, as those that are alive from the dead, and your *members* as *instruments of righteousness unto God.*' Thus, to pluck out the eye, and cut off the hand, is equivalent to crucify '*the flesh with the affections and lusts*,' Ga. v. 24; and Col. iii. 5, ' *Mortify therefore your members which are upon the earth.*']

Why the *right* eye is mentioned, may be that *that* was essentially necessary to the purposes of *war*, as it was then carried on.

PRACTICAL REFLECTIONS.

21—.6 *ver.* Justice must be observed in thought and word, as well as in deed. Without cause, we must neither be angry, nor at any time speak despitefully of others. 'Other men's failings should be our warnings.'

If we would desire our gifts to be accepted of God, we must first render justice to man; and no delay is to be made in satisfying all just demands. The longer the injustice is continued, the greater is the difficulty in procuring a discharge.

MATT. v. 30—.7.

pluck-·it·-out, and cast *it* from thee: for it-is-profitable συμφερει for-thee that one of-thy
30 members should-perish, and not *that* thy whole body should-be-cast into hell. And if
thy right hand offend thee, cut-·it·-off, and cast *it* from thee: for it-is-profitable for-thee
that one of-thy members should-perish, and not *that* thy whole body should-be-cast
into hell.
31   It-hath-been-said, Whosoever shall-put-away his wife, let-him-give her a-writing-of-
32 divorcement: but I say unto-you, That whosoever shall-put-away his wife, saving-for
the-cause-of παρεκτος λογου fornication, causeth her to-commit-adultery: and whosoever shall-marry her-that-is-divorced committeth-adultery.
33   Again, ye-have-heard that it-hath-been-said by-them of-old-time, Thou-shalt-·not·-
34 forswear-thyself, but shalt-perform unto-the Lord thine oaths: but I say unto-you,
35 Swear not at-all; neither by heaven; for it-is God's throne: nor by the earth; for it-is
36 his footstool: neither by Jerusalem; for it-is the-city of-the great King. Neither shalt-
37 thou-swear by thy head, because thou-canst not make one hair white or black. But

SCRIPTURE ILLUSTRATIONS.

30. *if thy right hand offend thee*—Mt. xviii. 8, 9, § 53;
Mk. ix. 43—8, § 52.

31. *whosoever shall put away, &c.*—permitted by
Moses, De. xxiv. 1; comp. Mk. x. 5—12, § 74—the
Pharisees tempted Jesus with this question, Mt. xix.
3, *ib*.

32. *but I say unto you, &c.*—so Paul advised the
Corinthians: 'And unto the married I command, yet
not I, but the Lord, Let not the wife depart from *her*
husband,' 1 Co. vii. 10.

33. *thou shalt not forswear, &c.*—Ex. xx. 7—' And ye
shall not swear by my name falsely, neither shalt thou
profane the name of thy God: I am the Lord,' Le.
xix. 12—they who swear to their own hurt and change
not, shall be blessed, Ps. xv. 4—' When thou shalt
vow a vow unto the Lord thy God, thou shalt not
slack to pay it: for the Lord thy God will surely require it of thee; and it would be sin in thee,' De.
xxiii. 21—' When thou vowest a vow unto God, defer
not to pay it; for *he hath* no pleasure in fools: pay
that which thou hast vowed,' Ec. v. 4—' O Judah,
keep thy solemn feasts, perform thy vows,' Na. i. 15.

34. *swear not at all*—Jesus himself did not refuse to
take an oath in a court of law, Mt. xxvi. 63, .4, § 80—
so Paul often *called God to witness* his sincerity, which
is all that is meant by an oath, Rom. i. 9, ' For
God is my witness, whom I serve with my spirit in the
gospel of his Son, that without ceasing I make mention of you always in my prayers'—ix. 1, ' I say the

truth in Christ, I lie not, my conscience also bearing
me witness in the Holy Ghost.'—The Lord, speaking
of New Testament times, Is. xlv. 22—.5, . . . swears
'unto me every knee shall bow, every tongue shall
swear,' ver. 23. To Israel it is said, Je. iv. 2, ' Thou
shalt swear, The Lord liveth, in truth, in judgment,
and in righteousness; and the nations shall bless
themselves in him, and in him shall they glory.'

34. *neither by heaven; for it, &c.*—Thus saith the
Lord, The heaven *is* my throne,' Is. lxvi. 1 . . .
. . .—' he that shall swear by heaven, sweareth by the
throne of God,' Mt. xxiii. 22, § 95.

35. *nor by the earth; for it is, &c.*—' Exalt ye the
Lord our God, and worship at his footstool; *for he is*
holy,' Ps. xcix. 5.

neither by Jerusalem—' the holy city,' Mt. iv. 5, § 9,
p. 64—' Beautiful for situation, the joy of the whole
earth, *is* mount Zion, on the sides of the north, the
city of the great King,' Ps. xlvii. 2—' Glorious things
are spoken of thee, O city of God,' lxxxvii. 3—unto
which the kingdom is to come: ' And thou, O tower of
the flock, the strong hold of the daughter of Zion,
unto thee shall it come, even the first dominion; the
kingdom shall come to the daughter of Jerusalem,'
Mi. iv. 8—Je. iii. 12, .4, .7 . . . .—for a description of 'the holy city, New Jerusalem,' *see* Rev.
xxi., .ii.

36. *neither . . . by thy head, &c.*—' Which of you by
taking thought,' &c., Mt. vi. 27, p. 135; Lu. xii. 25, § 63.

NOTES.

[31. *It hath been said.* Having before adverted to
the seventh commandment, our Lord takes occasion
to allude to that abuse of the judicial law, which,
though intended to regulate and repress divorces,
had rendered them more frequent, and become almost as pestilent to good morals as adultery itself.
We are to bear in mind,—1, that the Jews were permitted to divorce their wives without assigning any
cause;—2, that our Lord, neither here nor at Mt. xix.
3, § 74, meant to do away *political* directions;—3, that he,
moreover, did not contradict Moses, who even himself never approved of the arbitrary divorces of his
times—*see* xix. 8, § *ib.*;—and, 4, that the Jewish doctors in the age of Christ were not agreed on the sense
of the passage of De. xxiv.;—*see* 'Scrip. Illus.']

[32. *Saving for the cause of fornication.* παρεκτος
λογου πορνειας. *Except for whoredom.* The Jews had
extended it to any cause, and to such an extent, that
Rabbi Akiba said, ' A man may put *away his wife, if*
he see another woman that pleases him better.']

33—7. *Thou shalt not forswear thyself.* Christ here
proceeds to correct another false interpretation of the
law.—*See* ' Scripture Illustrations,' ver. 33.
An oath is a solemn act wherein we swear by God,
or call on him to witness the truth of what we assert

or promise; and to avenge us in time and eternity, if
we swear what is false or unknown to us, or if we do
not perform what we engage. An oath was not to
be taken but in the name of the one true God: De.
vi. 13, ' *Thou shalt fear the Lord thy God, and serve
him, and shalt swear by his name*;' Jos. xxiii. 7,
' *neither make mention of the name of their gods, nor
cause to swear* by them, *neither serve them, nor bow
yourselves unto them*;' Ja. v. 12—*see* ver. 37, ' Scripture Illustrations;' *see* ver. 31, 5; oaths are not to
be taken irreverently, without godly fear and awe of
the Most High.

Perform unto the Lord thine oaths. The morality
of the Jews on this point was truly reverable; they
maintained, that a man might swear with his lips,
and annul it at the same moment in his heart.

36. *Thy head.* This was a practice common to both
Greeks and Romans. The hand, it should seem, was
placed on the head during swearing; implying imprecation in case of perjury, since the *head* was peculiarly spoken of in such imprecations. To swear
by the *head* was the same as to swear by the *life*; or
to say, ' I will forfeit my *life* if what I say is not true.
God is the author of the life, and to swear by *that*,
therefore, is the same as to swear by *him*.

PRACTICAL REFLECTIONS.

[27—32 *ver.* The stability of our Christian character is manifested not merely by standing the force of
great trials, but by resisting the first approaches of
evil, and is is secured by denying ourselves to everything that may be likely to lead into sin, although
the thing should in itself be lawful.]
But though dear as is a right eye, or necessary as

is a right hand, let it be parted with rather than that
it should sink us in perdition.

[Let our firmness be manifested, not merely by
the resisting of evil in ourselves, but in bearing with
the infirmities of others, and in our being constant
to our engagements in the several relations of life, as
here with regard to the marriage covenant.]

PART II.   CHRIST EXHORTETH TO SUFFER WRONG.   SECT. XIX.

MATT. v. 38—43.

let your communication be, Yea, yea; Nay, nay: for whatsoever is more περισσον than these cometh of evil, εκ του πονηρου.
38 Ye-have-heard that it-hath-been-said, An-eye for αντι an-eye, and a-tooth for a-tooth:
39 but I say unto-you, That-ye-resist not evil: but whosoever shall-smite thee on thy
40 right cheek, turn to-him the other also. And if-any-man will sue-·thee·-at-the-law, and
41 take-away thy coat, let·him·-have thy cloke also. And whosoever shall-compel-·thee·-
42 to-go αγγαρευσει a mile, go with him twain. Give to-him that-asketh thee, and from him that-would borrow of-thee turn-·not·-thou-away.
43 Ye-have-heard that it-hath-been-said, Thou-shalt-love thy neighbour, and hate thine

SCRIPTURE ILLUSTRATIONS.

37. *yea, yea; nay, nay*—' putting away lying, speak every man truth with his neighbour: for we are members one of another,' Ep. iv. 25.—' above all things, my brethren, swear not, neither by heaven, neither by the earth, neither by any other oath: but let your yea be yea; and your nay, nay; lest ye fall into condemnation,' Ja. v. 12.

38. *an eye for an eye*—' And thine eye shall not pity; but life shall go for life, eye for eye, tooth for tooth, hand for hand, foot for foot,' De. xix. 21; Ex. xxi. 24; Le. xxiv 20

39. *resist not evil*—' Thou shalt not avenge, nor bear any grudge,' &c., Le. xix. 18—*see* ver. 43—'he is brought as a lamb to the slaughter, and as a sheep before her shearers is dumb, so he openeth not his mouth,' Is. liii. 7—' Recompense to no man evil for evil,' Rom. xii. 17—9. . . . . ' See that none render evil for evil unto any man; but ever follow that which is good, both among yourselves, and to all

men,' 1 Th. v. 15—' Ye have condemned and killed the just; and he doth not resist you,' Ja. v. 6—' not rendering evil for evil, . . . but contrariwise blessing,' 1 Pe. iii. 9.

whosoever shall smite thee, &c.—' and when they had blindfolded him, they struck,' &c., Lu. xxii. 61, § 89—' who did no sin,' 1 Pe. ii. 22, .3.

42. *give*—to ' thy poor brother' ' thou shalt open thine hand wide,' &c., De. xv. 7—10 . . . . 'do good, and lend, hoping for nothing again,' Lu. vi. 35, § 27.

43 *ye have heard, &c.*—' Thou shalt not avenge, nor bear any grudge against the children of thy people, but thou shalt love thy neighbour as thyself: I am the LORD,' Le. xix. 18—but as to the Moabites and Ammonites, it was commanded, ' Thou shalt not seek their peace nor their prosperity all thy days for ever,' De. xxiii. 6.

NOTES.

[37. *Yea, yea. Nai, val*, ... The Hebrew repeats the affirmative, to give it more strength. It was a proverbial manner among the Hebrews of characterizing a man of strict probity and good faith, by saying, ' *his yes is yes, and his no is no*.']

[*Of evil. εκ του πονηρου*. ' Of the evil one.' And there is not in the universe more cause of amazement at his forbearance, than that God does not, in vengeance, smite the profane swearer at once to hell.]

38. *An eye for an eye, &c.* By the Mosaic law, retaliation was permitted.—*See* ' Scripture Illustrations.' There was a rule given to regulate the decision of the judges, but the Jews made it a rule to take private revenge. Greeks and Romans had the same law. The savage nations in America, as well as in almost every other part of the world, set no bounds to the cool, deliberate indignity, with which they will pursue, for years together, not only the person himself, from whom they have received an injury, but sometimes every one related to or connected with him. The Arabs are equally implacable in their resentments; and the Koran itself, in the case of murder, allows private revenge. Christianity only is powerful to overcome evil with good.

39. *Whosoever shall smite thee. ῥαπίσει.* The word corresponds to our *rap* or *slap*; and was chiefly, as here, used of striking on the *face*; which was regarded as an affront of the worst sort; and was severely punished both by the Hebrew and Roman laws.

Turn to him the other also. A proverbial phrase, to express a meek submission to injuries and affronts: ' I gave my back to the smiters, and my cheeks to them that plucked off the hair; I hid not my face from shame and spitting,' Isa. l. 6; ' He giveth his cheek to him that smiteth him: he is filled full with reproach,' La. iii. 30—*see* Mt. xxvi. 67, .8; Jno. xviii. 22, .3, § 89. So the heathen writers, Liv. iv. 35; and Tacit. Hist. iii. 31.

40. *Coat. χιτωνα.* The linen tunic encircling the body. The Jews wore two principal garments, an interior and an exterior. The *interior*, here called the *coat*, or the *tunic*, was made commonly of linen, and encircled the whole body, extending down to the knees. Sometimes beneath this garment, as in the case of the priests, there was another garment corresponding to pantaloons. The coat, or tunic, extended to the neck, and had long or short sleeves. Over this was commonly worn an *upper* garment, here called *cloak*, or mantle. It was made commonly nearly square, of different sizes, five or six cubits long, and as many broad, and wrapped around the body, and thrown off when engaged in labour.

[' By ιματιον is denoted the *under* garment; and by *ενδντον* the *upper*, usually of greater value than the former. Indeed, from the circumstance of its being used as a blanket, to wrap the person in by night, it was not allowed by the law to be taken by the creditor, though the χιτων might, Ex. xxii. 26, ' *If thou at all take thy neighbour's raiment to pledge, thou shalt deliver it unto him by that the sun goeth down*.']

41. *Whosoever shall compel thee to go a mile.* Αγγαρεύσει (from ' *hangar*,' a dagger, which the couriers wore as a mark of authority;—Chardin, Tav. vol. II. 242; Michaelis, part I. c. iv. Sect. ix. p. 159, Clark's Trav.) is a Persian word used to express the obliging of men to carry burthens from stage to stage. In order that the royal commands might be delivered with safety and dispatch in different parts of the empire, Cyrus stationed horsemen at proper intervals on all the great public highways. One of these delivered the message to another, and intelligence was thus rapidly and safely communicated. These *Angari* are now termed ' Chappars,' and serve to carry dispatches between the court and provinces. When a chappar sets out, the master of the horse furnishes him with a single horse, and when that is weary he dismounts the first man he meets, and takes his. There is no pardon for a traveller that refuses to let a *chappar* have his horse, nor for any other who should deny him the best in his stable. The Jews and other provinces were compelled by the Roman governors, or tetrarchs, to furnish horses, and themselves to accompany them (Plin. Epist. x. 14, 121.) The practice is still retained by the Turks.

a mile. Μιλιον. A word formed from the Latin *mille*, a thousand; for a Roman mile consisted of a thousand paces, each of which was nearly equal to five English feet.

43. *Ye have heard, &c.* Their malevolence toward all mankind except their own nation was so remarkable, that the heathens took notice of it :—Tacit. Hist. v. 5, ' Their fidelity is inviolable, and their pity ready

PRACTICAL REFLECTIONS.

33—.7 ver. [Cunning is to be eschewed by the Christian, and especially in matters so solemn as that of calling God to witness.—He is not the less a witness and the avenger because we do not choose to recognise his presence & his power in our making of covenants.] We are honestly to say what we mean, and promise what, God willing, we intend to perform; saying and doing all as in the sight, and under the power of God.

TURN THOU US UNTO THEE, O LORD.—Lam. v. 21.   [127

SECT. XIX.　　　　　　　TO LOVE OUR ENEMIES.　　　　　　　PART II.
MATT. v. 44—.8.

44 enemy. But I say unto-you, Love your enemies, bless them that-curse you, do good to-
them that-hate you, and pray for them which-despitefully-use επηρεαζοντων you, and
45 persecute you; that ye-may-be the-children of your Father which *is* in heaven: for he-
maketh-*his sun*-to-rise on the-evil and *on* the-good, and sendeth-rain on the-just and
46 *on* the-unjust. For if ye-love them which-love you, what reward have-ye? do not even
47 the publicans the same? And if ye-salute your brethren only, what do-ye more περισσον
48 *than others?* do not even the publicans so? Be ye therefore perfect τελειοι, even-as
your Father which *is* in heaven is perfect.

SCRIPTURE ILLUSTRATIONS.

44. *but I say, &c.*—he 'having abolished in his flesh the enmity, *even* the law of commandments contained in ordinances; for to make in himself of twain one new man, so making peace; and that he might reconcile both unto God in one body by the cross, having slain the enmity thereby,' Ep. ii. 15, .6.

love your enemies—so did Jesus—' when we were enemies, we were reconciled to God by the death of his Son,' Rom. v. 10—and so he hath commanded his followers, ' Love,' &c., ' do good to them which hate you,' Lu. vi. 27, .8 § 27—' Bless them which persecute you,' Rom. xii. 14—20—as Christ, 'Father, forgive, &c., Lu. xxiii. 34, § 91—so Stephen, Ac. vii. 60—and, so should all that truly would act as followers of the Lamb, 1 Pe. iii. 9—*see* ver. 39, p. 127.

45. *that ye may be*—the children of God are not to imitate the world—' be not conformed to this world: but be ye transformed by the renewing of your mind, that ye may prove what *is* that good, and acceptable, and perfect, will of God,' Rom. xii. 2—but to take the Most High for their example as to holiness, 1 Pe. i. 14—.6 . . . .—as to love, 1 Jno. iv. 7, 8 . . . . .—his love was manifested in the most costly sacrifice for us, ver. 9, 10, *ibid.*—and it is by acting out our love in like manner, that we truly confess the truth respecting the Father and the Son, ver. 11—.7, *ibid.*

his run—' upon whom doth not his light arise?' Job xxv. 3—' Nevertheless he left not himself without witness, in that he did good, and gave us rain from heaven, and fruitful seasons, filling our hearts with food and gladness,' Ac. xiv. 17.

46. *what reward*—the reward is of grace, according to the grace manifested—' So speak ye, and so do. as they that shall be judged by the law of liberty. For he shall have judgment without mercy, that hath shewed no mercy; and mercy rejoiceth [or, *glorieth*] against judgment,' Ja. ii. 12, .3.

47. *what do ye more?*—the children of God are not to content themselves with merely receiving from God—' For unto whomsoever much is given, of him shall be much required,' Lu. xii. 48, § 63.

48. *be ye therefore perfect*—' And when Abram was ninety years old and nine, the LORD appeared to Abram, and said unto him, I *am* the Almighty God; walk before me, and be thou perfect,' Ge. xvii. 1—so to Israel, ' And ye shall be holy unto me: for I the LORD *am* holy, and have severed you from *other* people, that ye should be mine,' Le. xx. 26—so to the disciples: ' Be ye therefore merciful, as your Father also is merciful,' Lu. vi. 36, § 27—Christians must aim high: ' Be ye therefore followers of God, as dear children; and walk in love, as Christ also hath loved us, and hath given himself for us an offering and a sacrifice to God for a sweetsmelling savour,' Ep. v. 1, 2— . . . . . 'whom we preach, warning every man, and teaching every man in all wisdom; that we may present every man perfect in Christ Jesus,' Col. i. 28.

NOTES.

toward one another; but unto all others they bear an implacable hatred.' It is evident, that by 'neighbour' they understood *a Jew*; and that by 'enemy' they understood *heathens* in general. It is to be remarked, that the clause, *hate thine enemy*, is not in the law—*see* Lev. xix. 18, ' Scrip. Illus.;' but the Rabbins pretended, that it was deducible from the first part of the precept, which seems to limit forgiveness to Israelites.

44. *Bless them that curse you*. Implying such a sincere disposition to do them good as shall *shew* itself in *actions*; done to them not indeed as enemies, but as *fellow creatures*. It is said of Theodosius the emperor, that being urged to execute one who had reviled him, he answered, ' So far from gratifying your wish; were it in my power, if he were dead, I would raise him to life again; rather than, being alive, to put him to death.'

45. *That ye may be the children, i.e.,* ' assimilated to him by conformity of disposition,' as children usually are to their parents—*see* ' Scrip. Illus.'

[48. *Be ye therefore perfect, even as your Father, &c.* ' Not children of mammon like the publicans (τελωναι), but ' *Be ye perfect* ' (τελειοι); and, so, the children of ' *your Father which is in heaven*,'—perfect in goodness, exercising longsuffering and patience, while working good for others; fully resolved to carry out your Father's purposes of love, notwithstanding all outward discouragements, persevering in kindness, not only to the good, but also to the unthankful.]

PRACTICAL REFLECTIONS.

36—48 *ver.* We are not to imitate the world in returning evil for evil; but rather to rejoice in opportunities of benefiting or obliging those who seek to do us hurt.

Of the good which God hath given us, we are to dispense to others to the utmost of our power. Thus should we act, not only like forgiven sinners, but like Him who forgives, like our heavenly Father; who, when we were yet enemies, not only gave us the temporal blessing we enjoyed, but gave us his Son, the dearest object he had, that we might be made most blessed in him by the power of his Holy Spirit.

So let us be willing to part with what is dearest to us that others may be with us reconciled unto God.

[Our standard of perfection is not presented from among the mighty and honourable of the earth: it is to be seen in the condescending mercy and longsuffering kindness of our Father in heaven.]

ADDENDA.

ONE TITTLE, ch. v. ver. 18, p. 123.

' *One tittle.*—The Hebrew letters were written with small points or apices, which serve to distinguish one letter from another. To change a small point of one letter, therefore, might vary the meaning of a word, and destroy the sense. It might have been correctly rendered, "*not the least letter, or stroke*," &c.; and the more so, as *jot* and *tittle* in English signify much the same. Hence the Jews were exceedingly cautious in writing these letters, and considered the smallest change or omission a reason for destroying the whole manuscript, when they were transcribing the Old Testament. The expression, "one jot or tittle," became proverbial, and means that the *smallest part* of the law shall not be destroyed.

' The laws of the Jews are commonly divided into moral, ceremonial, and judicial. The moral laws are such as grow out of the *nature of things*, which cannot, therefore, be changed, such as the duty of loving God and his creatures.

' Those requiring *love and obedience to God*, and love to men, could not be changed, and Christ did not attempt it, Mt. xix. 19, § 75; xxii. 37—9, § 85; Lu. x. 27, § 60; Rom. xiii. 9.

' Of this kind are the ten commandments. The ceremonial laws are such as are appointed to meet certain states of society, or to regulate the religious rites and ceremonies of a people. These can be

128]　　　　　　　LET US SEARCH AND TRY OUR WAYS.—Lam. iii. 40.

PART II. THE COUNCIL—TOPHET—VALLEY OF HINNOM. SECT. XIX.

ADDENDA—(continued.)

changed when circumstances are changed, and yet the moral law be untouched. A parent might suffer his children to have fifty different dresses at different times, and love them equally in all. The dress is a mere matter of ceremony, and may be changed. The child, in all these garments, is bound to love and obey his father: this is a moral law, and cannot be changed. So the laws of the Jews.

'A third species of law was the judicial, or those regulating courts of justice, contained in the Old Testament. These were of the nature of the ceremonial law, and might also be changed at pleasure.

'The ceremonial law was fulfilled by the coming of Christ; the shadow was lost in the substance, and ceased to be binding. The moral law was confirmed and unchanged.'—Barnes.

THE COUNCIL, ver. 22, pp. 124, ..5.

The seventy-two members were made up of the chief priests and elders of the people, and the scribes. The chief priests were such as had discharged the office of the high priest, and those who were the heads of the twenty-four classes of priests, who were called, in an honorary way, high or chief priests—see Mt. ii. 4, § 5, p. 32. The elders were the princes of the tribes, or heads of the family associations. — See § 25, p. 199, ADDENDA, 'Scribes.'

Till the time when Judea was subjected to the Romans, this council had the power of life and death. It still retained the power of passing sentence, though the Roman magistrate held the right of execution.— See Mt. xxvii. 1, 2, § 89; [Mk. xv. 1; Lu. xxiii. 1; Jno. xviii. 28], 31, § 90.

The situation of the great Sanhedrim, or, as the Jews speak, the House of Judgment, was partly within the priests' court, and partly within that of the Israelites; and the time that this supreme court usually assembled was, after the morning daily sacrifice, to the afternoon daily sacrifice. It was not necessary that all the members should be present, but no business could be done unless there were twenty-three assembled. The head of this council was called Hanasci, i.e. president; and he who supplied his room in his absence was called the Ab, i.e. the father of the council, and always sat at the president's right hand. It was before this tribunal that our Saviour was tried. It was then assembled in the palace of the high priest, Mt. xxvi. 3—5; 57; §§ 86, .9; Jno. xviii. 24, § 89—see also Ac. iv., v.

TOPHET, ver. 22, p. 125.

Tophet.—It is thought that Tophet was the butchery, or place of slaughter, at Jerusalem, lying to the south of the city, in the valley of the children of Hinnom. It is also said that a constant fire used to be kept there, for burning the carcasses, and other filthiness, that were brought thither from the city. It was in the same place that they cast away the ashes and remains of the images of false gods, when they demolished their altars, and broke down their statues. King Josiah defiled the place of Tophet, where the temple of Molech stood, that nobody might go thither any more to sacrifice their children to that cruel heathenish deity, 2 Ki. xxiii. 6—10. Those guilty of certain crimes were, according to the law, to be burned with fire—Le. xx. 14, 'And if a man take a wife and her mother, it is wickedness: they shall be burnt with fire, both he and they; that there be no

wickedness among you.' Also xxi. 9. 'And the daughter of any priest, if she profane herself by playing the whore, she profaneth her father: she shall be burnt with fire.' If any were thus executed, this accursed place may have been the spot of ground on which they were consumed. It seemed, both with regard to its former state, when Molech was worshipped, and after Josiah had polluted it, a fit emblem of hell itself; Is. xxx. 33, ... Je. vii. 32, 'Therefore, behold, the days come, saith the LORD, that it shall no more be called Tophet, nor the valley of the son of Hinnom, but the valley of slaughter: for they shall bury in Tophet, till there be no place.'

Jeremiah upbraids the Israelites with having built temples to Molech, in the valley of Hinnom, in Tophet, to burn their children in the fire, Je. vii. 31.

VALLEY OF HINNOM.

From Dr. Robinson's 'Biblical Researches in Palestine,' Vol. I. pp. 402—..4.

Valley of Hinnom.—This valley is so called in the Old Testament; though more commonly in the fuller form, 'Valley of the son of Hinnom.' הנם ‏‎בן‎‏ Jos. xv. 8. בן הנם ‏‎גי‎‏ Je. xix. 2, 6. Hence are derived the Greek Γίεννα, and the corresponding English forms Gehinnom, Gehenna. The Arabian writer, Edrisi, in the twelfth century, apparently includes the lower part of it under the name Wady Jehennam; and this is the usual name for the whole Wady among the Arabs at the present day. Other Arabic writers apply this name to the valley of Jehoshaphat. Its commencement is in the broad sloping basin on the west of the city, south of the Yafa road, extending up nearly to the brow of the great Wady on the west. The large reservoir, commonly called the Upper Pool, or Gihon, may be regarded as a sort of central point in this basin; from which the land slopes upwards by a gentle acclivity on every side except the east. On this side the ground descends towards the Yafa Gate, forming a broad hollow or valley between the two swells on the N. and S. This part might, perhaps, not improperly be termed the valley of Gihon; though the name Gihon in Scripture is applied only to a fountain.

From the eastern side of the said Upper Pool, the course of the valley is S. 51° E. for the distance of 1,900 feet, to the bend opposite the Yafa Gate. The valley is here from 50 to 100 yards in width. The bottom is every where thickly covered with small stones; but is nevertheless sown, and a crop of lentils growing upon it. From this point up to the Yafa Gate was a distance of 400 feet; viz., 130 in the valley, 200 on the steep slope, at an angle of 20°, and 100 on the level of the gate above. Hence the depth of the valley is here 44 feet below the gate. The valley now descends on a course S. 10° W. for 2,107 feet, to

the bend at the S.W. corner of * Zion. In this distance, 875 feet brings us to the aqueduct as it crosses the valley; at 220 feet further is the upper end of the Lower Pool, the length of which in the middle is 592 feet, and the remaining 420 feet lie between the pool and the angle of the valley. In this part the valley continues about the same breadth, grows deeper, is planted with olive and other fruit trees, and is in some places tilled. A new course of S. 40° E. strikes the south side at the distance of 700 feet; and then another of S. 75° E. carries us 625 feet further. In this last, at 130 feet, a path crosses the valley leading up over the hills towards Bethlehem, and 75 feet below this road is the point to which we measured in order to determine the height of Zion; which last is here 154 feet.† From the end of this course, the valley runs due east, for the space of 1,140 feet. For about 400 feet of this distance, the breadth remains the same as above; and the fruit trees and tillage continues. The southern hill is steep, rocky, and full of tombs. At 440 feet the valley contracts, becomes quite narrow and stony, and descends with much greater rapidity. Towards the end of the course it opens again, and meets the gardens in the oblong plat, where it forms a junction with the valley of Jehoshaphat. The S.E. corner of Zion here runs down and out in a low point. From the end of the last course to the well of Nehemiah, is a distance of 480 feet, measured on a course S. 30° E.

In these gardens, lying partly within the mouth of Hinnom, and partly in the valley of Jehoshaphat, and irrigated by the waters of Siloam, Jerome assigns the place of Tophet, where the Jews practised the horrid rites of Baal and Molech, and burned their sons and their daughters in the fire.

* Of that which some now call Zion.
† The height above the valley at the S. W. corner of the wall of the city is 104 feet.

FEAR GOD, AND GIVE GLORY TO HIM.—Rev. xiv. 7.

SECTION 19.—THE SERMON ON THE MOUNT—(continued.)
MATTHEW vi. chap.*

RECAPITULATION AND ANALYSIS.

I. Having in the Beatitudes shewn what it is to take our Lord alone to be our God—the self-denial and alienation from the world which it implies, and the blessing which it brings, Mt. v. 3—12—p. 119.

II. Having shewn that his disciples are to be made in the image of Him who is the Preserver of men, the Light of the world, and the Producer of good, whom, and not their own works, they are to endeavour to glorify, ver. 13—6.—*ib.*

III. Having shewn how the Name of the Lord is to be reverenced; viz., by seeing 'the Law and the Prophets,' as testifying of Christ; and by rightly regarding the purpose for which he came into the world, as the Fulfiller of all righteousness, ver. 17—20.—*ib.*

IV. Having also shewn what it is to cease from our own works, and rest in the finished work of the Son of God; that it is to be as our Father who is in heaven, who continues to bestow the blessing of his completed creation, even upon the evil and unthankful; so should his children, as having entered upon the finished work of the Son, continue to bring forth, for the benefit of men, the fruits of the new creation—'*Be ye therefore perfect, as your Father which is in heaven is perfect*,' ver. 21—48.—*ib.*

V. Having thus led us into the adoption of sons, the Great Teacher next instructs us in the spirituality of the *fifth* commandment. If God be our Father, honour belongs to him in that relation: if we have been made the sons of God, who is just and good, omniscient and omnipotent, we should honour him, the Father of our spirits, by ever acting as in his sight; and *that* to God as a Father, and as having a regard to the *honour* that cometh from God only, vi. 1—18.—*ib.*

Ch. vi. 1—4. It is thus that, in our contributions, whether for religious or charitable purposes, we are to act as under the eye of our Father who seeth in secret.

Ver. 5, 6. So are we to acquaint ourselves with God, as that our prayers will be for communion with Him, and not for display before men.

Ver. 7—15. Prayer is to be made with holy reverence and childlike confidence, in communion with the saints, for God's kingdom of righteousness and peace to come upon earth; and it is to be made with the ascription of glory to God, and with good-will towards men.

Ver. 16—8. Our Heavenly Father is to be *honoured* by our having such a regard to the happiness of his creatures, as that even, when most sad within ourselves, and most deeply humbled before Him, we shall endeavour to put on a pleasing exterior before them

Thus are we to worship God—to love, the brotherhood: thus are we to become truly obedient to the *fifth* commandment, as applied to the highest relation of parent and child.

It may be remarked, that in the form of prayer taught us in the third of the four paragraphs of this FIFTH section of the 'Sermon on the Mount,' are *six petitions*, ver. 9—13, which are the last SIX COMMANDMENTS, or second table of the Law, spiritualized and presented in the form of prayer. It is thus we are to *honour* OUR HEAVENLY FATHER, by seeking not the gratification of our selfish wishes, but the accomplishment of his will for the good of men.

The NAME of the Lord, or that by which he is made known, or brought to remembrance, had been the subject of the first four commandments; and God claims that the filial piety called for in the *fifth* commandment should be especially rendered to Him.

Having been given the Spirit of adoption, and being thereby taught, as before, to clear ourselves from all malevolence against our neighbour, we, as in communion with the whole household of faith,

pray, '*Our Father which art in heaven, Hallowed be thy name.*'

In praying, *Thy kingdom come,*' we pray that his kingdom's law, which is 'LOVE,' may prevail; that righteousness and peace, and joy in the Holy Ghost, may abound: so will the being angry without cause, and all other breaches of the *sixth* commandment, cease.

In praying, '*Thy will be done in earth, as it is in heaven,*' we pray that his people may be 'holiness unto the Lord;' that the Bride may not longer submit to other lords; that the great and the manifold spiritual adultery may be done away; which cannot be until human *will* ceases to have sway in the church of God, and there results a holy keeping of the *seventh* commandment.

In praying, '*Give us this day our daily bread,*' we cast ourselves fully upon our Father's care, and that simply for what we need; knowing that what is good, the Lord will give: so are we freed from all transgression of the *eighth* commandment.

In praying, '*Forgive us our debts, as we forgive our debtors,*' we express a disposition the very reverse of that which leads to a breach of the *ninth* commandment: so far from witnessing falsely against our neighbour, we, as truly witnessing of the grace of God, are willing to forgive our neighbour that which is justly our due.

In praying, '*Lead us not into temptation, but deliver us from evil: For thine is the kingdom,*' &c., we renounce all covetousness—all desire for any thing apart from the will of our God. An entire recognition of the divine sovereignty is one of the best means whereby we may repel every approach of the deceiver, and all attacks of the adversary.

VI. Having taught us how to hold fellowship with the great Author of life and Giver of all good—our Lord next directs us to the conservation of the life which is given; how to avoid the worst kind of murder—the killing of the spiritual life. We avoid this—

By having our treasure in heaven, ver. 19—21.

By being single-eyed in the service of God, 22—4.

By having an entire trust in the good providence of God, 25—30.

By resisting the common example—a seeking the things belonging to the present life, 31—4.

The '*life which we now live in the flesh*' must be a life of faith upon the Son of God—a life in which we honour God, by reposing in him a child-like confidence. It is thus only that we can escape a breach of the *sixth* commandment.

The life of the soul is destroyed by worldly anxiety about the life of the body. '*He that loveth his life shall lose it*;' and he that, for the kingdom of heaven's sake, '*hateth his life,*' '*shall keep it unto life eternal,*' Jno. xii. 25, § 82. Let us beware that we kill not the life, either in ourselves or in others, by departing from the living God, through a love for the service of mammon, or through a want of confidence in the almighty God, as if he had not power to support the life he has given.

Upon the folly of this sin which doth so easily beset us, and whereby so much spiritual murder is perpetrated, our Lord powerfully reasons in ver. 19—31.

It was by inducing distrust in God, that the father of lies, who '*was a murderer from the beginning,*' brought death into the world, and all our woe; and his kingdom of darkness and of death is upheld by the same means whereby it had its commencement amongst men: in opposition to which we are given directions, '*Seek ye first the kingdom of God,*' &c., ver. 33—*For* ch. vii. *see* p. 137.

---

* This is LESSON XX. (*First Part*) in the First, Second, and Third Grades of '*The System of Graduated Simultaneous Instruction.*'—Matt. vi, vii.

THE SERMON ON THE MOUNT—(continued.)
MATTHEW vi. 1—7.

1 TAKE-heed that-ye-do not your alms before men, to be-seen θεαθηναι of-them: other-
2 wise ye-have no reward of your Father which *is* in heaven. Therefore when thou-
doest *thine* alms, do-·not·-sound-a-trumpet before thee, as the hypocrites do in the
synagogues and in the streets, that they-may-have-glory of men. Verily I-say unto-you,
3 They-have απεχουσι their reward. But when-·thou·-doest alms, let-·not thy left-
4 hand·-know what thy right-hand doeth: that thine alms-may-be in secret: and thy
Father which seeth in secret himself shall-reward thee openly.
5 And when thou-prayest, thou-shalt-·not·-be as the hypocrites *are:* for they-love to-
pray standing in the synagogues and in the corners of-the streets, that they-may be-
6 seen of men. Verily I-say unto-you, They-have their reward. But thou, when thou-
prayest, enter into thy closet, and when-thou-hast-shut thy door, pray to thy Father
which *is* in secret; and thy Father which seeth in secret shall-reward thee openly.
7 But when-ye-pray, use-·not·-vain-repetitions βαττολογησητε, as the heathen do: for

SCRIPTURE ILLUSTRATIONS.

1. *alms*—or righteousness; the returning of the pledge to a poor brother, although kindness to him, was to be reckoned as justice in the sight of God—'It shall be righteousness unto thee before the LORD thy God,' De. xxiv. 13—of the man who hath dispersed and given to the poor it is said, 'his righteousness endureth for ever,' Ps. cxii. 9.

2. *sound a trumpet*—gifts were deposited in a chest —see 'Notes '—'Jehoiada the priest took a chest, and bored a hole in the lid of it, and set it beside the altar, on the right side as one cometh into the house of the LORD: and the priests that kept the door put therein all the money *that was* brought into the house of the LORD,' 2 Ki. xii. 9; 2 Ch. xxiv. 8—11— 'Jesus . . . . beheld how the people cast money into the treasury: and many that were rich cast in much,' Mk. xii. 41, § 85.

they have their reward—'thou in thy life time receivedst thy good things . . . . but now,' &c., Lu. xvi. 25, § 69.

3. *let not thy left hand know, &c.*—'ne that giveth, *let him do it* with simplicity,' Rom. xii. 8—to do good to the poor, not as seeking a reward in time, or from man, 'for thou shalt be recompensed at the resurrection of the just,' Lu. xiv. 14, § 67.

4. *shall reward thee openly*—such as have acknowledged Christ in his poor brethren, shall be honoured by him, when he comes 'in the glory of his Father

with his angels,' Mt. xvi. 27, § 50; xxv. 31—40, § 86— 'in the day when God shall judge the secrets of men by Jesus Christ according to my gospel,' Rom. ii. 16.

5. *pray standing—see* Mk. xi. 25, § 84; Lu. xviii. 11—3, § 73.

may be seen of men—the Lord will turn such worldly wisdom into foolishness: 'Forasmuch as this people draw near me with their mouth, and with their lips do honour me, but have removed their heart far from me, and their fear toward me is taught by the precept of men:' . . . 'the wisdom of their wise *men* shall perish,' Is. xxix. 13, 4. . . . 'Every one *that is* proud in heart *is* an abomination to the LORD,' Pr. xvi. 5—'God resisteth the proud, but giveth grace unto the humble,' Ja. iv. 6.

6. *enter into thy closet, &c.*—so Elisha: 'he went in therefore, and shut the door upon them twain, and prayed unto the LORD,' 2 Ki. iv. 33—it is the living presence which is to be felt, as expressed in Ps. cxxxix. 1—12.

shall reward—'The eyes of the LORD *are* upon the righteous, and his ears *are* open unto their cry,' Ps. xxxiv. 16—see the cry, xxxii. 5—7, . . .—and the answer, 8—11.

7. *vain repetitions*—repetitions, but not *vain* repetitions, may be used in the praise of God, as in Ps. cvii. 8, 15, 21, 31 . . . —and in prayer, Mt. xxvi. 39, 42, 4, § 88.

NOTES.

2. *Do not sound a trumpet.* The trumpet referred to seems to have been the mouth of the chest or box into which the worshippers dropped their contributions. These were placed in the synagogues, and at the corners of streets. They were trumpet-formed, narrowing inwardly, and the money dropped therein could be made to '*sound*' upon the side if the contributor wished to make a display of his liberality. Dr. Lightfoot affirms, that in all his researches he has not been able to find that they had the custom of otherwise sounding a trumpet when they gave alms.

Hypocrites, υποκριται, is well known to signify 'players' disguised, as the Grecian actors used to be, in masks. A hypocrite is one who feigns himself to be what he is not.—*See* on ver. 16, p. 133.

Have their reward. απεχουσι τον μισθον αυτων. 'Have already received it, have had all that they will have.'

3. *Let not thy left hand know, &c.* A proverbial expression signifying to conceal an action.

5. *Love to pray standing.* The Jews of old observed stated hours of prayer, as the Mahommedans do at this day. The Scriptures mention three of them:

the *third hour*, answering to our nine o'clock, when the morning sacrifice was offered: the *sixth hour*, answering to our twelve o'clock; at this hour Peter prayed on the house-top, Ac. x. 9, 30: the *ninth hour*, answering to our three o'clock in the afternoon, at which time the apostles Peter and John are said to have gone up to the temple, Ac. iii. 1. The three are mentioned together, Ps. lv. 17, ' *Evening, and morning, and at noon, will I pray, and cry aloud: and he shall hear my voice.*' It is also recorded of Daniel, that he prayed three times a day. Da. vi. 10, ' *Now when Daniel knew that the writing was signed, he went into his house; and his windows being open in his chamber toward Jerusalem, he kneeled upon his knees three times a day, and prayed, and gave thanks before his God, as he did aforetime.*'

At these hours, the Pharisees and hypocrites took care to be in some public meeting or other, εν συναγωγαις, perhaps in the market-place, or in some court of justice, or in a corner of a street where they might be seen at a considerable distance, and where there was a concourse of passengers to behold them.

7. *Vain repetitions.* The Jewish rabbins lay down as maxims, that 'every one that multiplies prayer

PRACTICAL REFLECTIONS.

1—4 *ver.* We should take heed as to the hope we set before us, and ask ourselves, whether it be '*the hope set before us in the gospel,*' or whether we are not rather influenced by things present and temporal. Those who act with a view of obtaining the praise of men have now their reward. They have nothing farther to look for. But those who, moved by his grace, do good, simply as in the sight of God, have still their reward to look forward to.

5, 6 *ver.* We are to pray as worshipping God, not that we may be worshipped ourselves.

[We are to pray as supplicating pardon and blessing from God, not as making a display of our piety before men. In prayer more especially let us be able to say, '*Whom have I in heaven but thee? And there is none upon earth that I desire beside thee,*' Ps. lxxiii. 25.]

NATURAL WORKS SHALL HAVE NATURAL WAGES.

SECT. XIX. OUR LORD GIVES A FORM OF PRAYER. PART II.

MATTHEW vi. 7—11.

they-think that they-shall-be-heard εισακουσθησονται for their much-speaking εν τη
8 πολυλογια. Be-'not'-ye-'therefore'-like unto-them: for your Father knoweth what-
9 things ye-have need-of, before ye ask him. After-this-manner therefore pray ye: Our
10 Father which *art* in heaven, Hallowed-be thy name. Thy kingdom come. Thy will
11 be-done in earth, as *it is* in heaven. Give us this-day our daily τον επιουσιον bread.

SCRIPTURE ILLUSTRATIONS.

their much speaking—so the prophets of Baal cried 'from morning even until noon, saying, O Baal, hear us,' 1 Ki. xviii. 26.

8. *knoweth, &c.*—' Thou understandest my thought afar off; ' ' not a word in my tongue, but, lo, O LORD, thou knowest it altogether,' Ps. cxxxix. 2—4 . . . . . .—' before they call, I will answer; and while they are yet speaking, I will hear,' Is. lxv. 24.

9. *after this manner*—in the same form, Lu. xi. 2—4, § 62.

Our Father—' The LORD *is* my portion, saith my soul; therefore will I hope in him,' Lam. iii. 24—' the LORD *is* the portion of mine inheritance and of my cup: thou maintainest my lot,' Ps. xvi. 5—' ye [Gentiles] have received the Spirit of adoption, whereby we [Jews] cry, Abba, Father' . . . ' and if children, then heirs; heirs of God, and joint-heirs with Christ,' Rom. viii. 15—.7.

in heaven—whilst we approach him with filial confidence, let it be with reverence, and godly fear: 'let us lift up our heart with our hands unto God in the heavens,' Lam. iii. 41—' our God *is* in the heavens,' Ps. cxv. 3.

hallowed be thy name—' let them praise thy great and terrible name; *for* it *is* holy,' Ps. xcix. 3—' holy and reverend *is* his name,' cxi. 9—hath been leading his people, to make to himself 'a glorious name,' Is. lxiii. 14, .4, .6 . . . . —' and, lo, a Lamb stood on the mount Sion, and with him an hundred forty *and* four thousand, having his Father's name written in their foreheads,' Rev. xiv. 1.

10. *thy kingdom come*—' the Son of man shall send forth his angels, and they shall gather out of his kingdom all things that offend.' &c.—' then shall the righteous shine forth as the sun in the kingdom of their Father,' Mt. xiii. 41—.3, § 33—see also Da. vii. 9—12 . . . . —' and the Father shall give the kingdom to the Son, ver. 13, .4—' and when all things shall be subdued unto him, then shall the Son also himself be subject unto him that put all things under him, that God may be all in all,' 1 Co. xv. 28—*comp.* Rev. xx. 4—*see* § 2, Lu. i. 33, ... —' hast made us unto our God kings and priests: and we shall reign on the earth,' Rev. v. 10.

thy will be done in earth, &c.—as to how the will of God is done in heaven, *see* Ps. ciii. 20, .1, . . . —it was done upon earth by Jesus, Mt. xxvi. 39, 42, § 88—' by the which will we are sanctified through the offering of the body of Jesus Christ once *for* all,' He. x, 10—by the renewing of your mind, 'prove what *is* that good, and acceptable, and perfect, will of God,' Rom. xii. 2—' All the ends of the world shall remember and turn unto the LORD: and all the kindreds of the nations shall worship before thee. For the kingdom *is* the LORD's: and he *is* the governor among the nations,' Ps. xxii. 27, .8.

11. *daily bread*—the Lord gave daily bread to the Israelites, Ex. xvi. 4, 21—that they might ' know that man doth not live by bread only, but by every *word* that proceedeth out of the mouth of the LORD doth man live,' De. viii. 3—Jesus said, ' I am the living

NOTES.

shall be heard, and that the prayer which is long shall not return empty.' In one place of the Greek poet Eschylus nearly a hundred verses are filled with a repetition of the same invocation to the gods. The *vain repetitions*, which Christ forbids his disciples to use in their prayers, were such as proceeded from an opinion that they were *to be heard for* πολυλογια *their much speaking*, after the manner of the heathens.

9. *After this manner.* That is, with that reverence, humility, seriousness, confidence in God, zeal for his glory, love to mankind, submission and moderation in temporal, and earnestness about spiritual things, which it inculcates; avoiding vain repetitions, and using grave and comprehensive expressions. The whole of this prayer, with the exception of the clause, ' as *we forgive our debtors*,' is, in substance, found in the nineteen prayers of the Jewish Liturgy.

Our Father. It was a maxim of the Jews, that a man should, whether alone or with the synagogue,

use the *plural* number, as comprehending all the followers of God.—*See* ' Scripture Illustrations.'

[πατερ-ουρανοις. This prefatory address (frequent in the Jewish forms of prayer) is expressive of the deepest reverence; and by εν τοις ουρανοις are *implied* all the attributes of that glorious Being who inhabiteth heaven, but whom the heaven of heavens cannot contain; namely, his omnipresence, omniscience, omnipotence, and infinite holiness. He is styled ' our Father,' being such by right of creation, preservation, adoption, and grace.—*Bloomfield.*]

10. *Thy kingdom come.* The kingdom of God, under the Messiah.—*See* § 7, p. 50, 'Notes,' Mt. iii. 2, ' *Kingdom of heaven.*' *See* also p. 83, 'Notes,' ver. 3. The ancient Jews affirmed, that, ' He prays not at all, in whose prayers there is no mention of the kingdom of God.' Hence they were accustomed to say, ' Let him cause his kingdom to reign, and his redemption to flourish; and let the Messiah speedily come, and deliver his people.'

PRACTICAL REFLECTIONS.

7, 8 ver. Our desires are to be presented to God for things agreeable to his will; we may not think, by making many prayers, to purchase the objects of our desire, but we may prepare ourselves for their enjoyment, as asking in submission to the divine will.

9 ver. We are to pray as in communion with Christ, our Elder Brother, in whom we are presented before the Heavenly Majesty, and as in communion with all our brethren in Christ. Thus let us be able to say, ' *Our Father which art in heaven.*'

— *The poor in spirit*' will rejoice in Christ Jesus, asking only in his name, of whom the Father hath said, ' *My name is in him,*' Ex. xxiii. 21; and who himself hath said, ' *Whatsoever ye shall ask the Father in my name, he will give it you,*' Jno. xvi. 23. Well indeed may we, as knowing our own unworthiness, desire that the Name may be hallowed, through which alone we can approach the Father with acceptance, and be constituted heirs of the kingdom.

10 ver. Those who ' *mourn*' over the evils that prevail, and who are comforted with words respecting the kingdom, when Satan shall be bound, and the saints shall be given the dominion under their Lord, who

will put an end to the groaning of creation, and make sin and sorrow give place to his own most blessed reign of righteousness and peace: those who thus mourn the darkness and distress that prevail, until their Lord's return, cannot but with earnestness ask, ' *Thy kingdom come.*'

—The ' *meek,*' who ' *shall inherit the earth,*' are they who are willing to be denied a portion here, and who patiently submit to the providence of God, desirous, through his grace, to be made meet for his glory. Such can with fervour ask, ' *Thy will be done in earth, as it is in heaven.*' Those who thus yield up their own wills to the will of God, shall find the will of God good towards them—' *they shall inherit the earth.*'

11 ver. They who ' *hunger and thirst after righteousness*' will not be easily induced to fast whole weeks or even days at a time. They know their need of a continual use of the bread of life; and consistently they pray, as in the fourth petition, ' *Give us this day our daily bread.*' They hear the injunction, ' *Labour not for the meat which perisheth, but for that meat which endureth unto everlasting life, which the Son of man shall give unto you,*' Jno. vi. 27, § 43,p.326.

132] LABOUR NOT TO BE RICH: CEASE FROM THINE OWN WISDOM.—Prov. xxiii. 4.

PART II.   OF FORGIVING OUR BRETHREN—OF FASTING.   SECT. XIX.

MATTHEW vi. 12—.7.

12, .3 And forgive us our debts αφες τα οφειληματα, as we forgive our debtors. And lead us not into temptation, but deliver us from evil απο του πονηρου: for thine is the 14 kingdom, and the power, and the glory, for ever εις τους αιωνας. Amen. For if ye-15 forgive men their trespasses, your heavenly Father will-'also'-forgive you: but if ye-forgive not men their trespasses, neither will-'your Father'-forgive your trespasses. 16 Moreover when ye-fast, be not, as the hypocrites, of-a-sad-countenance σκυθρωποι: for they-disfigure αφανιζουσι their faces, that they-may-appear unto-men to-fast. Verily 17 I-say unto-you, They-have their reward. But thou, when-thou-fastest, anoint thine

SCRIPTURE ILLUSTRATIONS.

bread which came down from heaven,' Jno. vi. 19—51, § 43—' I have esteemed the words of his mouth more than my necessary food' [MARG. 'my appointed portion']. Job xxiii. 12—we are to ask from God our bread, both temporal, ('remove far from me vanity and lies: give me neither poverty nor riches; feed me with food convenient for me,' Pr. xxx. 8)—and spiritual, Mt. vii. 7—11, pp. 138, ..9.

12. *forgive us our debts, as we, &c.*—'be ye kind one to another, tenderhearted, forgiving one another, even as God for Christ's sake hath forgiven you,' Ep. iv. 32—it is only in the spirit of forgiveness to one another, that we can look for forgiveness from God, ver. 14, .5, above—see ch. xviii. 21—35, § 53.

To *forgive sin* is the prerogative of God only. When the Pharisees, who denied the Divinity of Christ, heard him forgiving sins, they said, 'This man blasphemeth,' Mt. ix. 3, § 22, and agreeably to this, the God of Jacob says, 'I, even I, am he that blotteth out thy transgressions,' Is. xliii. 25. It was the ground of worship in the Old Testament church, that there was *forgiveness* with God: 'but *there is* forgiveness with thee, that thou mayest be feared,' Ps. cxxx. 4—and to exercise this attribute of Godhead Jesus Christ is exalted: ' Him hath God exalted with his right hand *to be* a Prince and a Saviour, for to give repentance to Israel,' &c., Ac. v. 31.

13. *temptation*—Eve was led into temptation when she began 'to parley with the deceiver, Ge. iii. 2—6 . . . . . .—Jesus repeatedly warned his disciples that they had need to watch and pray, lest they should enter into temptation, Mt. xxvi. 41, § 88; Lu. xxii. 40—.6, § *ib.*—but Peter, too much in his own strength, risked himself in the place of trial, and was shamefully overcome, Mk. xiv. 66—72, § 89—to those who take the guidance of God, it is said, 'God is

faithful, who will not suffer you to be tempted above that ye are able; but will with the temptation also make a way to escape, that ye may be able to bear *it*,' 1 Cor. x. 13—such as keep the word of his patience, Jesus has promised to keep 'from the hour of temptation, which shall come upon all the world,' &c., Rev. iii. 10—Jesus 'gave himself for our sins, that he might deliver us from this present evil world,' Gal. i. 4.

the kingdom—the right to command, and that in all things, is his, 'King of kings, and Lord of lords,' 1 Tim. vi. 15—this name given to the WORD: 'and he hath on *his* vesture and on his thigh a name written, KING OF KINGS, AND LORD OF LORDS,' Rev. xix. 16—and in this name the Lamb will triumph: ' these shall make war with the Lamb, and the Lamb shall overcome them: for he is Lord of lords, and King of kings: and they that are with him *are* called, and chosen, and faithful,' xvii. 14—those who are wise among the kings of the earth will acknowledge his claim, Ps. ii. 10—.2.

the power—the power to do that which is commanded must come from Him: 'it is God which worketh in you both to will and to do of *his* good pleasure,' Ph. ii. 13.

the glory—all the honour is due unto him: 'for of him, and through him, and to him, *are* all things: to whom *be* glory for ever. Amen,' Rom. xi. 36.

14, .5. *if ye forgive, &c.*—see above, ver. 12, and after, on Mt. xviii. 21—35, § 53.

16. *when ye fast, &c.*—the Lord despises such fasting as is calculated only to annoy our neighbours, Is. lviii. 3—and requires the exercise of good will to men, the renunciation of selfishness, as the best evidence of our contrition before God, and preparation for blessing, ver. 6—12.

NOTES.

12. *And forgive us our debts, &c.* The word *debts* is here used figuratively, and signifies withholding from God his due honour and love—offences which God only can forgive.

[13. *And lead us not into temptation.* πειρασμον not only implies violent assaults from *Satan*, but also sorely afflictive circumstances, none of which we have as yet grace or fortitude sufficient to bear.]

Amen, אמן, signifies, in Hebrew, 'true,' 'faithful,' 'certain.' It is used likewise in affirmation, and was often thus employed by our Saviour, 'amen, amen,' rendered ' verily, verily.'

14. *Your heavenly Father will also forgive you.* Not that the forgiveness of others is the procuring cause of the forgiveness of God.

16. *Hypocrites*. A hypocrite is one who learns his postures, has his tongue tipped with Scripture language, and walks in the habit of a Christian. This is taking up God's arms, and using them in the devil's service.—See ver. 2, p. 131.

They *disfigure their faces*. It was the custom anciently to express bitter sorrow by sprinkling ashes

and earth upon the head, 2 Sa. i. 2; Es. iv. 1, ' *When Mordecai perceived all that was done, Mordecai rent his clothes, and put on sackcloth with ashes, and went out into the midst of the city, and cried with a loud and a bitter cry;*' also Eze. xxvii. 30. Or if their griefs were of a lesser kind, they shewed them by neglecting to wash and anoint themselves, Da. x. 3, ' *I ate no pleasant bread, neither came flesh nor wine in my mouth, neither did I anoint myself at all, till three whole weeks were fulfilled;*' a custom which it is probable our Lord had now in view—see ver. 17.

17. *Anoint thine head, and wash thy face*. These were forbidden, in the Jewish canon, on days of fasting and humiliation; and hypocrites availed themselves of this ordinance, that they might appear to men to fast.

The Jews and all neighbouring nations were much in the habit of washing and anointing their bodies. This washing was performed at every meal; and where it could be effected, the head, (or other parts of the body,) was daily anointed with sweet or olive oil.—See Ps. xxiii. 5; Lu. vii. 46, § 29, p. 231; Mk. vi. 13, § 39, p. 303; vii. 2, 3, § 44, p. ; Jno. xii. 3, § 81.

PRACTICAL REFLECTIONS.

12 ver. ' *The merciful* . . . *shall obtain mercy;*' they who are convinced of the forgiving grace of God, and who become conformed unto him, unto whom their affections are drawn forth in grateful love, can sincerely pray, ' *Forgive us our debts, as we forgive our debtors.*'

13 ver. ' *The pure in heart*' are they who, distrustful of themselves, seek none other to whom to avoid sin, but the first approaches to it: who are able, consistently with their daily life, to pray, ' *Lead us not into temptation, but deliver us from evil;*' who, with their whole hearts, devote themselves and their all unto God;

acknowledging in all things the law of his kingdom, which is LOVE; acknowledging that the power is alone of him, and that to him should be given all the glory.—*And see* Lu. xi. 2—4, § 62.

14 ver. Let us not rigidly exact from others, but forgive as we expect to be ourselves forgiven.

[16—.9 ver. Let us not lay the punishment of our sins upon others, but even when most afflicted within ourselves, because of that in which we have come short or transgressed, let us be careful not to mar their happiness. We must commend our religion by kindness, even in trifles.

FIGHT THE GOOD FIGHT OF FAITH.—1 Tim. vi. 12.

SECT. XIX.   WHERE OUR TREASURE IS TO BE LAID UP.   PART II.

MATTHEW vi. 18—24.

18 head, and wash thy face; that thou-appear not unto men to-fast, but unto thy Father which *is* in secret: and thy Father, which seeth in secret, shall-reward thee openly.
19 Lay-'not'-up for-yourselves treasures upon earth, where moth and rust doth-corrupt
20 αφανιζει, and where thieves break-through and steal: but lay-up for-yourselves treasures in heaven, where neither moth nor rust doth-corrupt, and where thieves do-'not'-
21 break-through nor steal: for where your treasure is, there will-'your heart'-be also.
22 The light λυχνος of-the body is the eye: if therefore thine eye be single απλους, thy
23 whole body shall-be full-of-light φωτεινον. But if thine eye be evil πονηρος, thy whole body shall-be full-of-darkness σκοτεινον. If therefore the light that is in thee *be*
24 darkness, how-great *is* that darkness! No-man can serve two masters: for either he-will-hate the one, and love the other; or-else he-will-hold-to the-one, and despise the

SCRIPTURE ILLUSTRATIONS.

19. *lay not up, &c.—see* Lu. xii. 33, § 63; xvi. 9, § 69—'labour not to be rich,' Pr. xxiii. 4—riches a hinderance to entering the kingdom, Lu. xviii. 24, .5, § 75—dangers into which those that will be rich are apt to fall: 'But they that will be rich fall into temptation and a snare, and *into* many foolish and hurtful lusts, which drown men in destruction and perdition.' 'Charge them that are rich in this world, that they be not highminded, nor trust in uncertain riches, but in the living God, who giveth us richly all things to enjoy,' 1 Ti. vi. 9, 17—the loss to which those who disregard our Lord's direction will be exposed in the last days, Ja. v. 1—3. . . . *see* the loss which Lot sustained: 'and they took Lot, Abram's brother's son, who dwelt in Sodom, and his goods, and departed,' Ge. xiv. 12; xix. 12—.7, 26.

20. *lay up, &c.—see* as to the riches of him who 'feareth the Lord—delighteth greatly in his commandments,' Ps. cxii. . . . —'he that hath pity upon the poor lendeth unto the Lord; and that which he hath given will he pay him again,' Pr. xix. 17—'be rich in good works. . . laying up in store . . against the time to come,' 1 Ti. vi. 18, .9—the earthly inheritance 'fadeth away,' Is. xxiv. 4, . . . —'is defiled,' ver. 5—corrupted, ver. 6—but the children of God have 'an inheritance incorruptible, and undefiled, and that fadeth not away,' 'reserved' for them 'in heaven,' 1 Pe. i. 3, 4.

21. *where your treasure is, &c.*—so Lu. xii. 34, § 63 —'remember Lot's wife,' Lu. xvii. 32, § 72—*see* above on ver. 19; Ge. xix. 26—Judas had his treasure in the bag, Jno. xii. 4—6, § 81—and it drew him into perdition, Mt. xxvi. 14—.6, § 86; Ac. i. 16—.8 . . . . —Peter prized his fishing apparatus, which he had left for the sake of Jesus, and he so acted that our Lord had to ask, 'Simon, son of Jonas, lovest thou me more than these?'—*comp.* Mt. iv. 20, § 16, p. 109; Lu. v. 1—11, § 20, p. 152; Mt. xix. 27, § 75; Jno. xxi. 3, 11, .5, § 97.

22. *eye be single, &c.*—Lu. xi. 34—.6, § 62—*see* this single-eyedness to the word of the Lord, in order to know and do his will, expressed at large in Ps. cxix. —and called for in Pr. iv. 20—.7 . . . . —Jesus testified, 'I am the light of the world,' Jno. viii. 12, § 55—we are to 'run with patience the race that is set before us, looking unto Jesus the author and finisher of our faith,' He. xii. 1, 2.

23. *eye be evil—darkness*—as contrasted with the path of the righteous, Pr. iv. 18, .9, . . . and *see* the border of this page—Jesus left in darkness the men whose eyes were evil, Mt. xxi. 23—.7, § 84; Jno. xii. 35, .6, § 82—Saul, although a blasphemer and a persecutor and injurious, being single-eyed, was not left in the darkness which befell his nation—*comp.* 1 Ti. i. 13, ... (Mt. L 19, § 2, 'Paul;') 1 Th. ii. 14—.6.

how great is that darkness.—'Christ *is* the end of the law for righteousness to every one that believeth,' Rom. x. 4—'the children of Israel could not stedfastly look to the end of that,' &c., 2 Co. III. 13, .4—so also many professing Christians have been left to 'strong delusion, that they should,' &c., 2 Th. ii. 11, 12—'and his kingdom was full of darkness; and they gnawed their tongues for pain,' Rev. xvi. 10.

24. *no man, &c.*—'no servant can serve,' &c., Lu. xvi. 13, § 69—Joshua would have the people clear as to whom they would choose to serve, Jos. xxiv. 14—25—so Elijah: 'How long halt ye between two opinions? if the Lord *be* God, follow him: but if Baal, then follow him,' 1 Ki. xviii. 21—so Paul, 1 Ti. vi. 17—*see first column, ver.* 19—'the friendship of the world is enmity with God,' Ja. iv. 4—'if any man love the world, the love of the Father is not in him,' 1 Jno. ii. 15—Jesus plainly testified, 'Whosoever he be of you that forsaketh not all that he hath, he cannot be my disciple,' Lu. xiv. 33, § 67.

NOTES.

19. *Treasures, &c.* Their treasures consisted much in changes of raiment; in beautiful and richly-ornamented articles of apparel—*see* Gen. xlv. 22, here Joseph gave to his brethren *changes of raiment*;—and Jos. vii. 21, Achan coveted and secreted *a goodly Babylonish garment; see* also Ju. xiv. 12, *'And Samson said unto them, I will now put forth a riddle unto you: if ye can certainly declare it me within the seven days of the feast, and find it out, then I will give you thirty sheets and thirty change of garments.'* This last will account for the use of the word *moth.*

22. *The light of the body is the eye; if therefore thine eye be single, &c.* Here is an apt comparison, in which the duty of fixing the attention on heavenly things is illustrated by reference to the case of the eye in the body: 'As the natural eye, when healthy, regulates the motions of the body, so does the mental eye direct the soul.'

[It has been well observed by Olearius, that the whole passage is *adagial*; of which the *first* part forms the *adage* itself: ' The eye is the light of the body.' The *second* supplies the *deduction*, by consequence: 'If then thine eye be healthy and clear,'

&c. The *third* the *application*: 'If therefore the light (or what *should* be so) within thee be darkness, how great must be that darkness!']

—*Thy...body shall be full of light.* All that is needful to direct the body is that the eye be fixed right. So all that is needful to direct the *soul* and the *conduct* is that the eye of faith be fixed on Christ. A man crossing a stream on a log. If he will look across at some object steadily, will be in little danger. If he looks down on the dashing and rolling waters, he will become giddy.

23. *If therefore the light that is in thee, &c.* 'If therefore the maxim, you lay down for yourselves are wrong, how very erroneous must your conduct be!' Avarice darkens the mind, obscures the view, and brings in a gloomy night over all the faculties.

24. *Mammon*. A Syriac word for *riches*, which our Lord beautifully represents as a *person*, whom the folly of men had deified.

[Dr. Castel deduces these words from the Hebrew אמן *aman, to trust, confide;* because men are apt to trust in riches. Mammon may, therefore, be considered anything earthly in which a man *confides.*]

PRACTICAL REFLECTIONS.

22—4 ver. Let us look simply to God for direction, support, motive, and reward; we may not expect that we can please God whilst we are looking for these from the world.

LAY HOLD ON ETERNAL LIFE.—1 Tim. vi. 12.

PART II.   NOT TO BE CAREFUL FOR WORLDLY THINGS.   SECT. XIX.

MATTHEW vi. 25—32.

25 other. Ye-can not serve God and mammon. Therefore διὰ τοῦ͂ο I-say unto-you, Take-'no'-thought for your life, what ye-shall-eat, or what ye-shall-drink; nor-yet for-
your body, what ye-shall-put-on. Is not the life more than-meat, and the body than-
26 raiment? Behold εμβλεψατε the fowls of-the air ουρανου: for they-sow not, neither do-
they-reap, nor gather into barns; yet your heavenly Father feedeth them. Are-'ye not
27 much'-better διαφερετε than-they? Which of you by-taking-thought can add one cubit
28 unto his stature? And why take-ye-thought for raiment? Consider καταμαθετε the
29 lilies of-the field, how they-grow; they-toil not, neither do-they-spin: and-yet I-say
unto-you, That even Solomon in all his glory was-'not'-arrayed like one of-these.
30 Wherefore, if God so clothe the grass of-the field, which-to-day is, and to-morrow is-cast
31 into the-oven, *shall he* not much more *clothe* you, O-ye-of-little-faith? Therefore take-
no'-thought, saying, What shall-we-eat? or, What shall-we-drink? or, Wherewithal
32 shall-we-be-clothed? (For after-'all these-things-'do'-the Gentiles'-seek:) for your

SCRIPTURE ILLUSTRATIONS.

25. *take no thought, &c.*—'the LORD was with Joseph, and he was a prosperous man;'... 'the LORD
made all that he did to prosper in his hand,' Ge.
xxxix. 2, 3—and although he was wrongfully cast
into prison, 'the Lord was with Joseph, and shewed
him mercy;' and he prospered. ver. 21—.3—and the
Lord not only fed him, but gave him the power of
feeding all Egypt, and the countries around, xli. 56,.7.

is not the life more than meat—'I am fearfully and
wonderfully made,' &c., Ps. cxxxix. 14—.6 . . .
. .—we are simply to do what is right, and leave
the result with Him—'commit thy way unto the
LORD: trust also in him; and he shall bring it to
pass,' Ps. xxxvii. 5—'cast thy burden upon the LORD,
and he shall sustain thee: he shall 'never suffer the
righteous to be moved,' lv. 22—'commit thy works
unto the LORD, and thy thoughts shall be established,' Pr. xvi. 3—'be careful for nothing; but in
everything by prayer and supplication with thanksgiving let your requests be made known unto God,'
Ph. iv. 6—*see* Lu. xii. 22, .3, § 63—*see* on ver. 19, p. 134.

26. *behold the fowls*—'provideth for the raven his
food,' Job xxxviii. 41—' the fowls of the heaven,' &c.
—'these wait all upon thee; that thou mayest give
them their meat in due season,' Ps. civ. 12, 27—'Consider the ravens,... how much more are ye better
than the fowls?' Lu. xii. 24, &c., § 63.

27. *cubit unto his stature*—'Lord, make me to know
mine end, and the measure of my days'.... 'behold, thou hast made my days *as an* handbreadth'
.... 'surely they are disquieted in vain,' Ps. xxxix.
4—6.

28. *raiment*—our Lord had spoken of sustenance

for the life, ver. 26, .7—and now he speaks of clothing
for the body, ver. 28—30.

29. *Solomon*—'king Solomon exceeded all the
kings of the earth for riches and for wisdom,' 1 Ki.
x. 23—*see* the queen of Sheba's testimony, ver. 1—10
—Solomon, whose name means *peace-maker*, was but
a type of the children of God, referred to Mt. v. 9, p.
121—the sons of the true David referred to, Ps. lxxxix.
27—37.

30. *the grass*—*see* Ps. xc. 5—8—'in the morning it
flourisheth, and groweth up; in the evening it is cut
down, and withereth,' ver. 6—*see* the cause of our
nakedness: 'Thou hast set our iniquities before
thee, our secret *sins* in the light of thy countenance,'
ver. 8—as to the clothing: 'Let the beauty of the
LORD our God be upon us,' ver. 17—*comp.* with Ph.
iii.—at his coming in his kingdom, our Lord Jes s
Christ 'shall change our vile body, that it may be
fashioned like unto his glorious body, according to
the working whereby he is able even to subdue all
things unto himself,' ver. 20, .1.

31. *take no thought*—'casting all your care upon
him; for he careth for you,' 1 Pe. v. 7—*see* before,
'what ye shall eat,' ver. 25, .6—'wherewithal be
clothed,' ver. 28—30.

32. *the Gentiles, &c.*—the disciples of Jesus, like
ancient Israel, are called to be a peculiar people, to
shew forth his praise, 2 Co. vi. 14—.8; 1 Pe. ii. 9—
to whom the example of the heathen is presented for
warning, and not for imitation: 'learn not the way
of the heathen,' &c., Je. x. 2—*see* their foolishness,
and the wisdom of choosing the portion of Jacob,
ver. 3—16—*see* the evil of conformity to the ways of
the Gentiles, Nu. xxv. 1—9.

NOTES.

Is not the life more than meat, &c. Of riches Henry
somewhere says, 'the trouble of getting them, the
care of keeping them, and the fear of losing them,
takes away all the pleasure of using them.' Men can
trust God with their soul, but scarcely do so with
their body! but surely He who so wondrously formed
the body, contrived its curious mechanism, and set it
in motion, is able to provide for its sustenance in his
own appointed service.

26. *Behold the fowls.* From the power thus manifested in providing for the wants of the physical creation, we may argue as to the power he is willing to
put forth in support of his moral government.

27. *One cubit.* The cubit was originally the length
from the elbow to the end of the middle finger. The
cubit of the Scriptures is not far from twenty-two
inches. Terms of *length* are often applied to life;
and it is thought by many to be so here.—*See*
'Scripture Illustrations.'

28. *Consider the lilies.* Lilies are very high flowers,
and many spring from one root: they are no less
fragrant, comely, and medicinal, especially the roots
of white lilies. Tournefort mentions forty-six kinds
of lilies. Lilies were so plentiful in Canaan, that, it

seems, they heated their ovens with withered ones,
ver. 28, 30. The white lily is, probably, here alluded
to, as the eastern princes were often clothed in white
robes; and Josephus states, that Solomon was usually clothed in white. We are, however, told, that
the white lily is not known in Palestine; and that
the fields of the Levant are overrun with a species of
lily whose golden flowers in autumn afford one of the
most brilliant and gorgeous objects in nature.

29. *Even Solomon in all his glory, &c.* Glory is taken
for worldly splendour and magnificence, which make
kings glorious before men. Thus-riches, authority,
sumptuous buildings and garments, which men are
ready to praise, are called in Scripture, glory—*see*
Ps. xlix. 16.

30. *So clothe.* αμφιεννυσιν, expresses 'the putting
on a complete dress,' 'covering all sides.'
The grass. Let reason judge, if He who has done
so much to beautify inanimate matter, may not be
expected to provide sufficient covering for his own
obedient children.

Cast into the oven. Dr. Shaw tells us, that the
chief consumption of fuel in Arabia and Judæa is for
their ovens, which they heat with grass, rosemary,
myrrh, and other plants.

PRACTICAL REFLECTIONS.

25—30 *ver.* God, who hath given life, is able to
support the life he hath given. He whose matchless
wisdom formed the human frame can surely clothe
the body with raiment. He who feeds the fowls of
the air can provide food for his servants. He who
clothes the lilies of the field is the same God who

hath promised to provide covering for his obedient
children. Let us trust in him, being simply desirous
to do his will, leaving the result to his infinite wisdom and almighty power; so will the Cause of all
goodness not fail to produce good for us.

REMEMBER LOT'S WIFE.—Luke xvii. 32.   [135

SECT XIX. TO SEEK FIRST THE KINGDOM OF GOD. PART II.

MATTHEW vi. 33, 4.

33 heavenly Father knoweth that ye-have-need of-all these-things. But seek-ye first the kingdom of God, and his righteousness; and all these-things shall-be-added unto-you. 34 Take-therefore no-thought for the morrow: for the morrow shall-take-thought for-the-things of-itself. Sufficient unto-the day is the evil thereof.

SCRIPTURE ILLUSTRATIONS.

Father knoweth—'Like as a father pitieth,' &c., Ps. ciii. 13, 4.

33. *seek ye first, &c.*—'If ye then be risen with Christ, seek those things which are above, where Christ sitteth on the right hand of God. Set your affection on things above, not on things on the earth. For ye are dead, and your life is hid with Christ in God. When Christ, *who is* our life, shall appear, then shall ye also appear with him in glory,' Col. iii. 1—4; 1 Th. i. 9 10.

his righteousness—the righteousness of the kingdom must be sought, ere its peace can be enjoyed: 'first being by interpretation King of righteousness, and after that also King of Salem, which is, King of peace,' He vii. 2—*see* the preceding darkness of unrighteousness described, Is. lix. 1—15—the cutting off in righteousness, &c., ver. 16—21—the peace and prosperity, ch. lx. . . . —when the people shall be all righteous, ver. 21—the foundation of all that temporal as well as spiritual blessing to be in righteousness, ch. liv. 14 . . . —'and their righteousness is of me, saith the Lord,' ver. 17.

34. *sufficient*—'the time past of *our* life may suffice us to have wrought the will of the Gentiles,' 1 Pe. iv. 3.

the evil thereof—'Go to now, ye that say, To day or to morrow we will go into such a city, and continue there a year, and buy and sell, and get gain' . . . 'all such rejoicing is evil,' Ja. iv. 13—6—*see* the murderous tendency of this evil described, Hab. ii. 4—13 it will be put to shame, when 'the earth shall be filled with the knowledge of the glory of the Lord, as the waters cover the sea,' ver. 6, 14.

HABAKKUK II. I will stand upon my watch, and set me upon the tower, and will watch to see what he will say unto me, and what I shall answer when I am reproved. 2, And the Lord answered me, and said, Write the vision, and make *it* plain upon tables, that he may run that readeth it. 3, For the vision *is* yet for an appointed time, but at the end it shall speak, and not lie: though it tarry, wait for it; because it will surely come, it will not tarry. 4, Behold, his soul *which* is lifted up is not upright in him: but the just shall live by his faith.

5, Yea also, because he transgresseth by wine, *he is* a proud man, neither keepeth at home, who enlargeth his desire as hell, and *is* as death, and cannot be satisfied, but gathereth unto him all nations, and heapeth unto him all people: 6, shall not all these take up a parable against him, and a taunting proverb against him, and say, Woe to him that increaseth *that which* is not his! how long? and to him that ladeth himself with thick clay! 7, Shall they not rise up suddenly that shall bite thee, and awake that shall vex thee, and thou shalt be for booties unto them? 8, Because thou hast spoiled many nations, all the remnant of the people shall spoil thee; because of men's blood, and *for* the violence of the land, of the city, and of all that dwell therein.

9, Woe to him that coveteth an evil covetousness to his house, that he may set his nest on high, that he may be delivered from the power of evil! 10, Thou hast consulted shame to thy house by cutting off many people, and hast sinned *against* thy soul. 11, For the stone shall cry out of the wall, and the beam out of the timber shall answer it.

12, Woe to him that buildeth a town with blood, and stablisheth a city by iniquity! 13, Behold, *is it* not of the Lord of hosts that the people shall labour in the very fire, and the people shall weary themselves for very vanity? 14, For the earth shall be filled with the knowledge of the glory of the Lord, as the waters cover the sea.

15, Woe unto him that giveth his neighbour drink, that puttest thy bottle to *him*, and makest *him* drunken also, that thou mayest look on their nakedness! 16, Thou art filled with shame for glory: drink thou also, and let thy foreskin be uncovered: the cup of the Lord's right hand shall be turned unto thee, and shameful spewing *shall be* on thy glory. 17, For the violence of Lebanon shall cover thee, and the spoil of beasts, *which* made them afraid, because of men's blood, and for the violence of the land, of the city, and of all that dwell therein.

18, What profiteth the graven image that the maker thereof hath graven it; the molten image, and a teacher of lies, that the maker of his work trusteth therein, to make dumb idols? 19, Woe unto him that saith to the wood, Awake; to the dumb stone, Arise, it shall teach! Behold, it *is* laid over with gold and silver, and *there is* no breath at all in the midst of it. 20, But the Lord *is* in his holy temple: let all the earth keep silence before him.

NOTES.

32. *Your heavenly Father knoweth.* It is unbecoming the child of God to be anxious, as if he had no heavenly Father to care for him.

33. *Seek ye first, &c.* Anxiety about the things of this life is unbecoming us, not only as being witnesses for God among the nations, and as having the Almighty to care for us, but also is unbecoming us as expectants of the kingdom.

The kingdom of God.—See § 7, p. 50, 'Note,' Mt. iii. 2, 'Kingdom of heaven;' also, Jno. iii. 3, § 12, p. 83.

And his righteousness. It seems most natural to interpret this of that way of becoming righteous which the gospel proposes, called by St. Paul the righteousness of God, Ph. iii. 9, '*And be found in him, not having mine own righteousness, which is of the law, but that which is through the faith of Christ, the righteousness which is of God by faith.*'—As it is a sin to divide grace from glory, and to seek the one without the other; so it is also a sin to look *first* for happiness, and *then* after holiness.'

PRACTICAL REFLECTIONS.

[31]—4 *ver.* It is unbecoming the sons of God to be anxious for the present life, as if they knew not God—the Omniscient, the Almighty, our Father in heaven. Let our first aim be the securing for ourselves and others an interest in the kingdom, and, therewith, a preparation in ourselves and them for that kingdom, by the possession of righteousness; and what else is needed the Lord will add.]

END OF LESSON XX. PART I.*

* This Lesson XX., in the '*System of Graduated Simultaneous Instruction*,' in the first, second, and third grades, embraces Matt. ch. vi. and vii. The classes of the first, second, and third grades must therefore recapitulate the lesson, and be examined in the preceding lessons, on the second sabbath, by the teachers.

THE BLESSING OF THE LORD, IT MAKETH RICH.—PROV. X. 22.

SECTION 19.—THE SERMON ON THE MOUNT—(continued.)
LESSON XX., part 2.—MATTHEW, chap. vii.

RECAPITULATION AND ANALYSIS.

In the *first* part of the Sermon on the Mount, ch. v. ver. 3–12, we were shewn the blessedness of those whose life is hid with Christ in God.

In the *second*, ver. 13—6, the manifestation of this life, in our being made after the likeness of Him, who is our Light and our Salvation.

In the *third*, ver. 17—20, we were warned not to think lightly of the Ground of this life: it is Christ himself, the Fulfiller of all righteousness, according as God had before declared in Old Testament type and prophecy. There is no other Name given under heaven whereby we must be saved, than that of the Lord our Righteousness.

In the *fourth*, ver. 21—48, we were taught that perfect grace and truth which the Son of God alone can teach, and which the Mediator of the New Covenant does teach to all who enter into his rest; all who, through his redeeming love, are enabled to look up unto God as their Father.

In the *fifth*, ch. vi. ver. 1—18, we were instructed as to the manner in which the Father of our spirits is by us to be honoured, especially in those exercises that more immediately belong to his worship.

In the *sixth*, ver. 19—34, we were shewn how the life we live in God is to be maintained—the excellency of a simple trust in God is pointed out: this we are to have, not only as to spiritual matters, but also as to the things belonging to the natural life: worldlymindedness, either as to object or means, destroys the spiritual life.

VII. We now come to the *seventh* portion of our Lord's discourse, ch. vii. ver. 1—6, which warns against spiritual uncleanness—the interposing mere human will in place of the Divine, in the government of the Lord's people—the seeking to have others conformed to our *darkness*, in place of being brought into GOD'S LIGHT—the exercising upon them our own evil passions, in place of seeking that they '*may be presented, holy and without blame before him in love;*' or, on the other hand, the prostituting that which is holy to those who are as natural brute beasts, so that waste and defilement are brought into the house of God.

VIII. In the *eighth* portion, ver. 7—14, we are taught how to avoid a breach of the 8th commandment, '*Thou shalt not steal.*' What we need we are to ask of God, in the assurance that he will give what is good. The good things we are to prize are the gifts of God; and the being by his Holy Spirit enabled to learn from the Law and the Prophets the golden rule of doing to others the things that we would they should do unto us; and we are also to exercise self-denial, as entering

in *by the strait gate*: so looking to God for all we need; to our neighbour, as to one who is to receive from us favour; and to ourselves, that we be ready to part with every encumbrance, we shall give liberally to others, rather than take from them unjustly.

IX. In the *ninth* portion, ver. 15—20, we are shewn, that not only is it our duty to avoid bearing false witness ourselves, but to discourage it in others; and especially are we to beware of false prophets, of those who speak falsely in the name of God. And equally are we to be careful not to neglect the words of the true prophet. Neither are we to say that it is impossible to discern the true prophet from the false. This would be to contradict *Him* who is emphatically the TRUE WITNESS, for he hath said, '*By their fruits ye shall know them.*' They who *say*, and yet *do not* the truth, are warned, that however they may obtain place in the church upon earth, they will fail of an entrance into the kingdom of heaven. However men may deceive their fellow men, or even themselves, true witness will be borne of them in the judgment.

X. The *tenth* and last portion, ver. 21—7, teaches the danger of making our own use of the words of Scripture, and thus of building upon our own opinions, or others' interpretations, in place of building upon Christ the Rock, of whom the Scriptures testify. Covetousness is the cause of that perversion of the words of God; men wish to have, in some respect, the kingdom, the power, or the glory to themselves, without ascribing all to God, and without being entirely devoted to his service, in all good-will to man; they thus enter into temptation, and are by the evil one led to wrest the Scriptures to their own wishes, which is, to their own destruction. In order that we be safe for time and for eternity, we must '*beware of covetousness,*' and most earnestly seek to have no wish but according to the will of God, and so be willing to be saved by free grace unto perfect holiness of heart and of life. We must be careful to build not only with good materials, but upon the '*One Sure Foundation.*' It is He alone that can effectually teach us the great commandment like unto the first, '*Thou shalt love thy neighbour as thyself.*' Early was the falling away, in consequence of building upon the many or the great, in place of resting simply in '*THE FAITHFUL AND THE TRUE.*' Every system built upon mere human opinion or support must ultimately fall; nay, it may be expected that every refuge of lies will be undermined and swept away amid the storms that have already begun to sweep around us.

ch. vii. 1, 2 Judge not, that ye-be-·not-·judged. For with what judgment ye-judge, ye-shall-be-judged : and with what measure ye mete, it-shall-be-measured-·to-you·-again.

SCRIPTURE ILLUSTRATIONS.

Ch. vii. 1. *judge not, that ye be not judged*—similar words, Lu. vi. 37, § 27, p.20 the Lord called for one, who was himself without sin, to judge the adulteress, Jno. viii. 7, § 55—' We shall all stand before the judgment seat of Christ... Let us not therefore judge one another any more,' Rom. xiv. 10, .3.

2. *with what judgment, &c.*—*see* the case of Adonibezek—' But Adoni-bezek fled; and they pursued after him, and caught him, and cut off his thumbs and his great toes. And Adoni-bezek said. Threescore and ten kings, having their thumbs and their great toes cut off, gathered *their meat* under my table: as I have done, so God hath requited me,' Ju. i. 6, 7 —*see* David's psalm of thanksgiving: ' With the merciful thou wilt shew thyself merciful, *and* with the upright man thou wilt shew thyself upright. With the pure thou wilt shew thyself pure; and with the

froward thou wilt shew thyself unsavoury,' 2 Sa. xxii. 26, .7—*see* the judging of the Assyrian: ' Am I now come up without the LORD against this land to destroy it ? the LORD said unto me, Go up against this land, and destroy it,' Is. xxxvi. 10—and the judgment upon him: ' Then the angel of the LORD went forth, and smote in the camp of the Assyrians a hundred and fourscore and five thousand: and when they arose early in the morning, behold, they *were* all dead corpses,' Is. xxxvii. 36—.8—and the degradation and diminishing of Egypt: Eze. xxix. 15—which had sought to degrade and diminish Israel, Ex. i. 13—.6—' He shall have judgment without mercy, that hath shewed no mercy,' Ja. ii. 13—' He that leadeth into captivity shall go into captivity: he that killeth with the sword must be killed with the sword,' Rev. xiii. 10.

NOTES.

2. *With what judgment, &c.* This was a *proverb* among the Jews. It refers no less to the way in which *men* will deal with us, than to the rule by which God will judge us. The Christian should be more engaged in searching his own heart, than in censuring others.

PRACTICAL REFLECTIONS.

vii. 1, 2. *ver.* When we take the place of judge, let us recollect that we ourselves are before the judgment seat of Christ, and let us deal mercifully with others, as we expect to be mercifully dealt with of God.

SECT XIX.   NOT TO JUDGE—NOT TO PROSTITUTE HOLY THINGS.   PART II.

MATTHEW vii. 3–8.

3 And why beholdest thou the mote that *is* in thy brother's eye, but considerest κατανοεις
4 not the beam that *is* in thine-own eye? Or how wilt-thou-say to thy brother, Let-me pull-out αφες εκβαλω the mote out-of thine eye; and, behold, a beam *is* in thine-own eye?
5 Thou-hypocrite, first cast-out the beam out-of thine-own eye; and then shalt-thou-see-clearly διαβλεψεις to-cast-out the mote out-of thy brother's eye.
6 Give not that which-is-holy unto-the dogs, neither cast-ye your pearls before swine, lest they-trample them under their feet, and turn-again and-rend you.
7 Ask, and it-shall-be-given you; seek, and ye-shall-find; knock, and it-shall-be-opened
8 unto-you: for every-one that asketh receiveth; and he that-seeketh findeth; and to-

SCRIPTURE ILLUSTRATIONS.

3. *why beholdest thou the mote, &c.*—' Behold, thou art called a Jew,'... 'and art confident that thou thyself art a guide of the blind, a light of them which are in darkness,'—'thou therefore which teachest another, teachest thou not thyself?' &c., Rom. ii. 17, .9, 21.

considerest—' Stand in awe, and sin not: commune with your own heart upon your bed, and be still. Selah. Offer the sacrifices of righteousness, and put your trust in the Lord,' Ps. iv. 4, 5—' Brethren, if a man be overtaken in a fault, ye which are spiritual, restore such an one in the spirit of meekness; considering thyself, lest thou also be tempted,' Ga. vi. 1.

5. *first cast out, &c.*—God takes time to prepare the instruments he intends to make use of in the delivering of others—so Moses, Ex. ii. 11—25; iii. &c.—so Israel in the wilderness, De. viii. 2—6—so are the people who are to be employed as the Lord's witnesses to the nations, to be convinced of their own blindness, Is. xliii. 7—12 . . . . —and sinfulness, ver. 22—4—and the Lord's forgiveness, ver. 25, .6—and the folly of creature dependence, ver. 27, .8—Having obtained his Holy Spirit, xlv. 3, . . —and had the Lord's name put upon them, ver. 5—then they shall truly be witnesses for God, ver. 6—8—comp. Rev. xiv . . . —so Jesus commanded his disciples to wait In Jerusalem, until they were baptized, Ac. i. 4, 5, 8, § 98.

6. *dogs, &c.*— 'Ignorant, dumb dogs,' Is. lvi. 10—'greedy dogs which can never have enough,' ver. 11—'grievous wolves .... not sparing the flock,' Ac. xx. 29—' Beware of dogs, beware of evil workers, beware of the concision,' Ph. iii. 2; Jas. iii. 6—8.

neither cast ye your pearls, &c.— 'Speak not in the ears of a fool: for he will despise the wisdom of thy words,' Pr. xxiii. 9—' We speak wisdom among them that are perfect:'—'the wisdom of God in a mystery, even the hidden *wisdom*,' 1 Co. ii. 6, 7.

swine—men of a grovelling nature, 'whose god *is* their belly, and *whose* glory *is* in their shame, who mind earthly things,' Ph. iii. 19—'sensual,' Ja. iii. 15.
—The precious things of God are withheld from such, for 'the words of the Lord *are* pure words:' ... 'thou shalt keep them, O Lord, thou shalt preserve them from this generation for ever,' Ps. xii. 6, 7—

' Unto the pure all things *are* pure: but unto them that are defiled and unbelieving *is* nothing pure; but even their mind and conscience is defiled,' Tit. i. 15—the Christian teacher is rightly to divide the 'word of truth,' 2 Ti. ii. 15, .6.

rend you—see the fearful rending by the evil beasts, who got into the professing church, Rev. xiii. 7, 15—'7—and Comp. xvii. 16—Phil. iii. 2. ' Beware of dogs, beware of evil workers, beware of the concision, &c,'

7. *ask, &c.*—see ver. 9—11, p. 139—' If his son ask bread, will he give him a stone?' ver. 9.

seek, &c.—see ver. 12, p. 139, for the golden rule, which is to be found in what God hath given us to search: 'Search the scriptures,' Jno v. 39, § 23, p. 180.

knock, &c.—see ver. 13, .4, p. 139, as to the gate at which an entrance is to be sought, Jno. x. 9, § 55; xiv. 6, § 87—the same words, Lu. xi. 9, § 62.

8. *for every one that asketh, &c.*— Ho, every one that thirsteth,' &c., Is. lv. 1, . . —we are not to go to a limited source, where all comers, and that at all times, *cannot* be supplied: 'Behold, I am against the prophets, saith the Lord, that steal my words every one from his neighbour,' Je. xxiii. 30—' If any of you lack wisdom, let him ask of God, that giveth to all men liberally, and upbraideth not; and it shall be given him,' Ja. i. 5, 6—Solomon, when bid to ask what he would have of God, 2 Ch. i. 7, made his request for wisdom and knowledge to guide him in the duties of his office, ver. 10—and God gave him what he asked, and unequalled riches, wealth, and honour beside, ver. 11, .2—God, in faithfulness to his promise of saving us from our sins, may sometimes refuse us what we ask, Ja. iv. 3—the way to be prepared for an unlimited supply, is the being cleansed from all our filthiness, and having a simple and entire trust in Jesus, Jno. xiii. 8, § 67; xiv. 12—4, § ib.— ' Whatsoever ye shall ask the Father in my name, he will give it you,' xvi. 23—7, § 87—ask that ye 'may be able to comprehend with all saints what *is* the breadth, and length, and depth, and height; and to know the love of Christ . . . that ye might be filled with all the fulness of God '—' Now unto him that is able to do exceeding abundantly above all that we ask or think, according to the power that worketh in us,' &c., Ep. iii. 14—21.

NOTES.

3. *The mote.* The word αδρφος, which we render *mote*, signifies a *little splinter of wood*, and this with great propriety is opposed to *δοκοs*, a large *beam.*

The beam. Δοκος, a *beam* or *rafter;* used figuratively in this place to signify a *great fault*, or something which blocks out the light, as did the Jewish trust in the flesh, and in carnal ordinances.

[6. *Unto the dogs.* By *dogs* and *swine* are meant respectively the brutal and ferocious, and the gross and licentious; those brutal and sensual persons, who,

far from exhibiting the graces which adorn the gospel of our Lord Jesus Christ, will, if given the outward privileges proper to the children of God, only use them, and the body of Christ.

7. *Knock.* Implies faith, constancy, importunity.

8. *Every one that asketh receiveth.* That is, every one that asks aright, that prays in faith, and in submission to the will of God. Paul asked that the thorn in his flesh might be removed. God did not literally grant the request, but told him that his grace should be *sufficient* for him, 2 Co. xii. 7—9.

PRACTICAL REFLECTIONS.

3 *ver.* Let us first know our own darkness, before we severely scrutinize the faults of others. Let us be careful lest the imperfections in our own power of vision prevent us from seeing excellence in others, and dispose us to see faults where they do not exist.

[4, 5 ver. Let us not be in too great haste to effect reform in others, lest we do more harm than good; but first having known our own evil, and how it can be eradicated, let us then allow others to have the benefit of our experience. Let the divine precept be illustrated in our own example. God takes time to work, and his instruments must be carefully prepared.]

[6 ver. In endeavouring to benefit others, let us observe the order which becomes the house of God, giving to each that which is appropriate to their se-

veral conditions. The dogs must not be given that which is holy, nor must pearls be cast beneath the filthy feet of swine. The most precious gifts of the Spirit, which delight and adorn the true child of God, would be but despised and degraded as being forced upon the carnally minded.]

7, 8 *ver.* How large is the promise, 'Ask, and it *shall be given* you !' How widely extended the invitation, '*For every one that asketh receiveth!*' Let us ask wisdom, seek opportunities of separating ourselves unto his glory in the good of men; and, having asked and found entrance by Him who is the door, let us, by the manifestation of his grace, knock patiently at the hearts of others as God hath given us example.

VAIN MAN WOULD BE WISE.—Job xi. 12.

MATTHEW vii. 9–14.

9 him that-knocketh it-shall-be-opened. Or what man is-there of you, whom if his son 10 ask bread, will-he-give him a-stone? Or if he-ask a-fish, will-he-give him a-serpent? 11 If ye then, being evil πονηροι, know how to-give good gifts unto your children, how-much more shall-'your Father which *is* in heaven'-give good-things to-them that-ask him?
12   Therefore all-things whatsoever ye-would that men should-do to-you, do ye even-so to-them: for this is the law and the prophets.
13   Enter-ye-in at the strait gate: for wide *is* the gate, and broad ευρυχωρος *is* the way, 14 that leadeth to destruction, and many there-be which go-in thereat δι'αυτης:* because strait *is* the gate, and narrow τεθλιμμενη *is* the way, which leadeth unto life, and few there-be that find it.

* MARGINAL READING:—'*through it.*

SCRIPTURE ILLUSTRATIONS.

9. *ask bread, &c.*—Ln. xi. 11, § 62—Satan, in tempting our Lord, seems to insinuate that the Father had given nothing but stones, in place of bread, to his Son—see Mt. iv. 3, § 9, p. 61—Jesus answered by referring to that which is to be esteemed more than our necessary food, ver. 4, *ib.*

10. *a serpent*—the spirit of evil is sometimes represented by this reptile, Rev. xx. 2, ... A stone may have the same form as a loaf of bread, but is very different in substance. Jesus, however, has both characteristics: 'If so be ye have tasted that the Lord *is* gracious. To whom coming, *as unto* a living Stone,' 1 Pe. ii. 3, 4, ... a serpent also may have much the same form as a fish, but it is very different from it in character; and Satan may be 'transformed into an angel of light,' 2 Co. xi. 14—but, however God may allow to be deceived '*them that are* wise in their own eyes,' Is. v. 21, .4. he will not fail those that truly seek him, La. iii. 24—.6.

11. *being evil*—see the heart of man recognised as evil, before the flood, Ge. vi. 5, and after, viii. 21.

give good things, &c.—'give the Holy Spirit to them that ask him,' Lu. xi. 13, § 62—'Thy spirit *is* good; lead me into the land of uprightness,' Ps. cxliii. 10—'The Spirit searcheth all things, yea, the deep things of God,' 1 Co. ii. 10—'Now we have received, not the spirit of the world, but the spirit which is of God; that we might know the things that are freely given to us of God,' &c., ver. 12—*see* the excellency of these things, Pr. viii. 6—19, . . . The bestowment of good is more especially promised, in connection with Israel's restoration, Je. xxxii. 37—41, . . . —and the Holy Spirit is to be abundantly given, Is. xxxii. 15, .6. . . . Es. xxxvi. 27, .8.

12. *whatsoever ye would, &c.*—'as ye would,' &c., Lu. vi. 31, § 27—Jacob deceived his father, Ge. xxvii. 6—24—and he was himself deceived as to his wife, xxix. 21—.5—Pharaoh made a law that the Hebrew male children should be thrown into the river, Ex. i. 22—and in due time, Israel had to sing 'Pharaoh's chariots and his host hath he cast into the sea,' &c., xv. 4, 5—said to Edom, 'As thou hast done, it shall be done unto thee: thy reward shall return upon thine own head,' Ob. 15; see Ps. cxxxvii. 7—9.

this is the law and the prophets—these testify of Jesus, Jno. v. 39, § 23; Lu. xiv. 27, § 94—who hath done for us, what he requires of us, Mt. xvi. 21—.4, § 50—' Hereby perceive we the love *of God*, because he laid down his life for us: and we ought to lay down *our* lives for the brethren,' 1 Jno. iii. 16.

13. *strait gate*—'Strive to enter in at the strait gate,' &c., Lu. xiii. 24, § 66—Jesus is the door, Jno. x. 7, § 55—to enter by that strait gate requires self-denial, Lu. xiv. 26—33, § 67—it was too strait for the rich man, Mk. x. 22, § 75—' It is easier for a camel to go through the eye of a needle [*a wicker gate*], than for a rich man to enter,' &c., ver. 25—Moses chose this entrance: 'choosing rather to suffer affliction,' &c. . . . . 'esteeming the reproach of Christ greater riches than the treasures in Egypt,' He. xi. 25, .6—entering by this gate requires a distrust in our own righteousness, as well as every claim in the flesh, and is exemplified in Paul, Ph. iii. 3—9. . . . . . Rev. xxi. 27.

wide is the gate, &c.—'Be not deceived: neither fornicators, nor idolaters,' &c., 1 Co. vi. 9, 10.

leadeth to destruction—' The sun is no sooner risen with a burning heat, but it withereth the grass, and the flower thereof falleth, and the grace of the fashion of it perisheth: so also shall the rich man fade away in his ways,' Ja. i. 11.

14. *leadeth unto life*—' Blessed . . . the man that endureth temptation,' Ja. i. 12, ... *see* as to those who chose the way that holy prophets went—a way which, although it may be rough and thorny, leads to glory, He. xi. &c.—*see* the glory, unto which leads the path of the lowly, Ps. cxxxviii.: 'Though I walk in the midst of trouble, thou wilt revive me,' ver. 7.

few, &c.—'Fear not, little flock; for it is your Father's good pleasure to give you the kingdom,' Lu. xii. 32, § 63—and that kingdom will ultimately embrace all nations, Ps. lxxii. 8—10, .7, .9, ... Ps. cxxxviii. 4.

NOTES.

10. *Or if he ask a fish.* Bread and fish was the common food of the people in that part of Galilee. [The examples taken from a *stone* and a *fish* are derived from two *ainogia* found also in all the classical writers (Αντι τέρας εαφμιον) representing, by a familiar illustration, those who disappoint the just expectations of others, by giving them not the thing they ask for and need, but something else, which, though similar to it in form, as a serpent is to some sorts of fish (eel and perch), or a stone to a cake or biscuit, yet it is not only *not* the thing, but wholly useless, or even noxious.'—*Bloomfield.*

12. *Whatsoever ye would that men, &c.* The whole of the Scripture record contains the development of the principle—just recompence. ' *With the merciful thou wilt shew thyself merciful.*' So with the upright and pure. ' *And with the froward, thou wilt shew thyself froward,*' Ps. xviii. 25, .6. ' *A just weight and balance* are *the LORD'S,*' Pr. xvi. 11. And no power of man can prevent the just award of Him whose counsel, judgment, and understanding are perfect. ' *The way of the just is uprightness: thou, most upright, dost weigh the path of the just,*' Is. xxvi. 7. ' *The liberal deviseth liberal things; and by liberal things shall he stand,*' Is. xxxii. 8.—See the conduct of Abram, in parting with Lot Ge. xiii. 8, 9. Abram gave Lot his choice of the land, ver. 9; and the Lord gave Abram the whole, ver. 14—.7.

13. *The strait gate.* The comparison is to a gate opening into a road leading up to a citadel. The *τῃ* implies that there is *another* gate, leading to the broad road, which we are *not* to enter. ' * Jere is no entering into the King of heaven's privy chamber without passing through the strait gate of purity.'

PRACTICAL REFLECTIONS.

[9—11 *ver.* God, in his Word, and by his Spirit, hath not merely given the form of good, but the very substance of blessing. Let us not through our unbelief allow the bread of life to be unto us as a stone. Let not that which should have been for blessing, be through our own evil nature turned into a curse.]

12 *ver.* Let us weigh in an even balance what we give, with what we would take from others: God in Christ hath given Himself, and upon this ground he calls upon us to give ourselves to Him. ' *This is the law and the prophets.*'

13, .4 *ver.* Let us not be caught by first appearances, or think that safety is to be found in following a multitude to do evil. The brightness of heaven may shine upon the end of that path which is difficult at first; whilst the blackness of darkness may close upon that which is the most easy of entrance.

IT IS GOOD FOR A MAN THAT HE BEAR THE YOKE IN HIS YOUTH.—Lam. iii. 27.   [139

| SECT. XIX. | TO BEWARE OF FALSE PROPHETS. | PART II. |

MATTHEW vii. 15—21.

15 Beware of προσεχετε απο false-prophets, which come to you in sheep's clothing, but
16 inwardly they-are ravening wolves. Ye-shall-know them by their fruits. Do-*men*-
17 gather grapes of thorns, or figs of thistles? Even-so every good tree bringeth-forth
18 good fruit; but a corrupt tree bringeth-forth evil fruit. A-good tree can not bring-forth
19 evil fruit, neither *can* a-corrupt tree bring-forth good fruit. Every tree that-bringeth-
20 not-forth good fruit is-hewn-down, and cast into the-fire. Wherefore by their fruits
ye-shall-know them.
21 Not every-one that saith unto-me, Lord, Lord, shall-enter into the kingdom of heaven;

SCRIPTURE ILLUSTRATIONS.

15 *beware of false prophets*—' They speak a vision of their own heart, and not out of the mouth of the Lord,' Je. xxiii. 16—' Take heed that no man deceive you,' &c., Mt. xxiv. 4 24, § 86.

which come, &c.—' Such *are* false apostles, deceitful workers, transforming themselves into the apostles of Christ,' 2 Co. xi. 13—' H :ving a form of godliness, but denying the power thereof,' 2 Ti. iii. 5.

ravening wolves—' Prophets that make my people err, that bite with their teeth, and cry, Peace; and he that putteth not into their mouths, they even prepare war against him,' Mi. iii. 5—Paul warned the Ephesians : 'I know this, that after my departing shall grievous wolves enter in among you, not sparing the flock,' Ac. xx. 29—see, in the truly apostolic example of Paul, the fruits of disinterested love, with which the conduct of the ravening wolves is in contrast, ver. 31—.5.

16. *ye shall know them, &c.*—there are sure indications whereby they may be known—' Some men's sins are open before hand, going before to judgment ; and some *men* they follow after. Likewise also the good works *of some* are manifest before hand,' &c., 1 Ti. v. 24, .5.

by their fruits—false spirits may be known by their deficiency of testimony to Jesus Christ, as come in the flesh, 1 Jno. iv. 3, ... and the men themselves may be known by their deficiency of the fruit of the Spirit, which is contrasted with the works of the flesh, Ga. v. 19—26, ... ' who can bring a clean,' &c., Job xiv. 4.

grapes of thorns, &c.—see Lu. vi. 43—.5, § 27. p. 210.

17, .8. *every good tree—corrupt tree—see* Mt. xii. 33, § 31, p. 237—the good fruit is only to be found in the good tree—the Man, Christ Jesus, Jno. xv. 1—8,

§ 87—in contrast is the woman described, Rev. xvii. 3—6—whose bitter fruit is alluded to, Ec. vii. 26—.9 —saith the Lord to Ephraim, ' From me is thy fruit found,' Ho. xiv. 8.

19. *hewn down*—the king of Babylon, as taking the glory to himself in place of acknowledging God. Da. iv. 30, was hewn down, ver. 31—.3, until he had learned to bring forth fruit unto God, by giving praise unto his name, ver. 34—.7.

cast into the fire—the Jews, as trusting in the flesh, Mt. iii. 9, § 7, p. 53, and so failing to bring forth good fruit, were threatened by John with being hewn down and cast into the fire, ver. 10. The Romans were forewarned of similar judgment to be executed upon them, should they boast as they have done, Rom. xi. 17—24, ... ' that great city,' Rev. xvii. 18—' hath glorified herself . . . . and she shall be utterly burned with fire : for strong *is* the Lord God who judgeth her,' Rev. xviii. 7, 8.

20. *wherefore by their fruits, &c.*—by their deadly, destructive influence upon individuals, churches, and nations they may be known. ' What fruit had ye then in those things whereof ye are now ashamed ? for the end of those things *is* death,' &c , Ro. vi. 21— let us take warning, so as to obey the exhortation to the Hebrew disciples of Jesus : ' By him therefore let us offer the sacrifice of praise to God continually, that is, the fruit of *our* lips giving thanks to his name,' He. xiii. 15.

21. *Lord, Lord*—' Israel shall cry unto me, My God, we know thee. Israel hath cast off . . . . good : the enemy shall pursue him,' Ho. viii. 2, 3—the foolish virgins are represented as saying, ' Lord, Lord ;' but are refused admission, Mt. xxv. 11, .2, § 86—*see* also Lu. vi. 46, § 27 ; viii. 21, § 33, p. 262; xiii. 25, § 66.

NOTES.

15. *False prophets.* The expression may be taken to denote, in a general way, those who falsely pretend to have a Divine commission.

Which come to you in sheep's, &c. 'Ενδύμασι προβάτων has an allusion to the *μηλωτη* (sheep-skin, or sometimes a cloak made of fleece roughly worked up), with which the false prophets clothed themselves, in imitation of the true ones ; and also, as it seems, the false teachers among the Pharisees. — *Bloomfield.* ' Hypocrites have nothing of the sheep but its skin.'

Ravening wolves. Rapacious, or disposed to plunder. Applied to the false teachers, it means that they assumed the appearance they did in order that they might the more readily get the *property* of the people. They were full of extortion and excess.—*See* Mt. xxiii. 25, § 85.

16. *Ye shall know them by their fruits.* Men do not judge of a tree by its leaves, or bark, or flowers, but by the fruit which it bears. The flowers may be handsome and fragrant; the foliage thick and green ; but these are merely ornamental. The fruit is that to which regard should be had.

Grapes of thorns, &c. Men of proud, unsanctified minds, tempers, and dispositions, cannot be expected to sow the fruit of righteousness in others, Ja. iii. 13.

19. *Hewn down, &c.* However fair men's professions and appearances be, ye<, if their inward principles of action are unsound, their doctrines erroneous, and their lives immoral, they shall in the righteous judgment of God be cast into everlasting burnings.

[21]. *Not every one.* οὐ πᾶς, a Hebraism for *no person.* The sense of this verse seems to be this:—No person by merely acknowledging my authority, with calling upon my name with a seeming zeal and fervour, much less he who does these things only in a cold and formal manner, shall enter ' *the kingdom of heaven.*'—*See* Rom. ix. 6.]

PRACTICAL REFLECTIONS.

[15, .6 *ver.* The words of God's true prophets are precious : and we must not be robbed of them by mere human teaching, or by those who are sent by the father of lies. These may not be known by any want of mere outward credentials : these the enemy of souls will in general try to secure. It is not by the clothing, but by the fruits, that we are called to judge.]

[17, .8 *ver.* Although the children of God are not to be rash in judging, still they are to judge, after a patient examination, of the fruits of the teaching, as to whether it be of God. Our Great Teacher has pointed us to the credentials of his servants. It is simply a life evincing the goodness, and illustrating the beauty of the doctrine which they teach.]

19, 20 *ver.* Let not the unfruitful think that because they do not bring forth bad fruit, they shall escape the judgment which shall fall upon the evil. The judgment was sorely executed upon the whole body of the Jewish teachers in the land. ' *Every tree that bringeth not forth good fruit is hewn down, and cast into the fire,*' and thus their ignorant followers were dealt with. Wherefore, seeing that so great is the responsibility as to hearing, let us take heed as to what we hear, and let us seek discernment for ourselves from God. Let us obey the precept and enjoy the promise, ' *By their fruits ye shall know them !*' Let us see that their lives are in harmony with their doctrine, and both with the word of God.

21 *ver.* It is not being busy in the verbal acknowledgment of Christ, as Lord, that will prove any one an heir of the kingdom of heaven. It is the practical, the heart and life confession, that God delights in.

PART II. NOT TO BE MERELY HEARERS, BUT DOERS OF THE WORD. SECT. XIX

MATTHEW vii. 22—.7.

22 but he that-doeth the will of my Father which *is* in heaven. Many will-say to-me in that day, Lord, Lord, have-we-'not'-prophesied in thy name? and in thy name have-23 cast-out devils? and in thy name done many wonderful-works δυναμεις? And then will-I-profess unto-them, I-never'-knew you: depart from me, ye-that work iniquity.
24 Therefore whosoever heareth these sayings of-mine, and doeth them, I-will-liken him 25 unto-a-wise man, which built his house upon a rock: and the rain descended, and the floods came, and the winds blew, and beat-upon that house; and it-fell not: for it-was-26 founded upon a rock. And every-one that heareth these sayings of-mine, and doeth them not, shall-be-likened unto-a-foolish man, which built his house upon the sand:
27 and the rain descended, and the floods came, and the winds blew, and beat-upon that house; and it-fell: and great was the fall of-it.

SCRIPTURE ILLUSTRATIONS.

doeth the will, &c.—' This is the work of God, that ye believe on him whom he hath sent,' Jno. vi. 29, § 43—' And this is the will of him that sent me, that every one which seeth the Son, and believeth on him, may have everlasting life,' ver. 40—' If ye live after the flesh, ye shall die: but if ye through the Spirit do mortify the deeds of the body, ye shall live,' Ro. viii. 13—' for this is the will of God, *even* your sanctification,' 1 Th. iv. 3—' He that walketh uprightly, and worketh righteousness, and speaketh the truth in his heart,' &c. . . . ' He that doeth these things shall never be moved,' Ps. xv. 2—5, . . . —' Be ye doers of the word, and not hearers only, deceiving your own selves,' &c., Ja. i. 22.

22. *in that day*—' He hath appointed a day, in the which he will judge the world in righteousness, by *that* man whom he hath ordained,' Ac. xvii. 31.

cast out devils—there were certain of the vagabond Jews, that attempted this in the name of Jesus, Ac. xix. 13—but though one were successful in the exercise of any or all the gifts, and have not the life of Christ in him, he is nothing, 1 Co. xiii. 2.

23. *depart from me*—those who will not, in heart and life, be separated unto Christ now, may most assuredly lay their account with being separated from him hereafter; for, ' without (holiness) no man shall see the Lord,' He. xii. 14—*see* Lu. xiii. 25—.7, § 66—also the judgment, Mt. xxv. 31—46, § 86—' Depart from me,' &c.—*see* on ver. 21, p. 140.

24. *heareth, &c.*—It is by hearing that we come to build upon the Sure Foundation—' Hear, and your s ul shall live; and I will make an everlasting covenant with you,' &c., Is. lv. 3—' Faith *cometh* by hearing,' Ro. x. 17—' The just shall live by faith,' Ga. iii. 11—' and faith . . worketh by love,' ch. v. 6—' and love *is* the fulfilling of the law,' Rom. xiii. 10—thus the apostle

could say, ' I live by the faith of the Son of God, who loved me, and gave himself for me,' Ga. ii. 20.

sayings of mine—it is not enough that words are heard, and worship given: the Lord will not accept of that fear toward him, which is taught ' by the precept of men,' Is. xxix. 13, . . .—his word must be received ' not *as* the word of men, but as . . . the word of God,' 1 Th. ii. 13—and it is Jesus, of whom the Father hath said, ' Hear ye him,' Mt. xvii. 5, § 51—' Him shall ye hear in all things whatsoever he shall say unto you. And it shall come to pass, *that* every soul, which will not hear that prophet, shall be destroyed from among the people,' Ac. iii. 22, .3.

Doeth them, &c.—see as before, ver. 21, p. 140—doing is very much insisted upon in both the Old Testament and the New; as Ps. ciii. 18, . . . Mt. xii. 50, § 31; Lu. xi. 28, § 62; Jno. xiii. 17, § 87; 1 Jno. iii. 7—(*see* § 9, p. 65. *border*)—' Blessed *are* they that do his commandments, that they may have right to the tree of life, and may enter in through the gates into the city,' Rev. xxii. 14.

wise man, &c.—' The fear of the LORD,' &c., Ps. cxi. 10; Pr. ix. 10—(*see the border*)—' The fear of the Lord, that *is* wisdom; and to depart from evil *is* understanding,' Job xxviii. 28.

25. *founded upon a rock*—' Other foundation can no man lay than that is laid, which is Jesus Christ,' 1 Co. iii. 11—build upon this Rock: ' the Rock . . . His work *is* perfect,' De. xxxii. 3, 4. . . . —see how secure in the midst of storm and tempest is the glorious structure reared upon this Foundation, Is. xxvi. 9—17. . . . —' He *is* my rock, and *there is* no unrighteousness in him,' Ps. xcii. 13—.5; *see* Ep. ii. 18—22. . . —' We are made partakers of Christ, if we hold the beginning of our confidence stedfast unto the end,' He. iii. 14.

NOTES.

[22. *Prophesied.* There have been instances of men who were separated unto the exercise of the gift of prophecy, who yet gave no evidence of being separated in holiness unto the kingdom of God. Such was Balaam, in the time of Moses, Nu. xxiv. 4; and Caiaphas the high priest, in the time of our Saviour's sojourn upon earth, Jno. xi. 51, § 58. Saul also was among the prophets, 1 Sa. x. 5—13.]

23. *Will I profess.* ἀπολογήσω, 'I will fully and plainly tell them.'

24. *Whosoever, &c.* This is the grand point to be attended to. It makes no matter what may be his condition, race, or attention to outward forms and ceremonies. Ga. iii. 28, .9; vi. 15, *compare* with 1 Co. vii. 19.—' *Whosoever cometh to me, and heareth my sayings, and doeth them, I will shew you to whom he is like,*' &c., Lu. vi. 47, .8, § 27, p. 210.

25. *And the rain descended, &c.* The rain, floods, and winds of an eastern monsoon strikingly illustrate this passage. When people in those regions speak of the strength of a house, it is not by saying

it will last so many years, but it will outstand the rains; it will not be injured by the floods. Houses built of the best materials, and having deep foundations, in a few years often yield to the rains of a monsoon. The house founded upon a rock can alone stand the rains and floods of a wet monsoon.—*Roberts.*

26. *Foolish man.* ' The fool hath said in his heart, . . . no God,' Ps. xiv. 1—' *A fool also is full of words.*'—he despises the warning voice of the great Prophet, and says, ' *A man cannot tell what shall be; and what shall be after him, who can tell?*' Ec. x. 14—' *Lo, they have rejected the word of the Lord; and what wisdom is in them?*' Je. viii. 9.

[27. *And great was the fall of it.* Britain, although great, not only as to temporal advantages, but especially as to the unspeakable privilege of hearing the word of the Lord, has no small cause to stand in awe. The case described is not that of those from whom the word of God is entirely withheld; it is that of a people, who hear these sayings of Christ, but do them not.]

PRACTICAL REFLECTIONS.

22, .3 ver. It matters not how near we come to the true disciples of Christ as to outward sign: if we are not made one with Him by a pure and living faith, we cannot be united with them in glory. We must have holy fellowship with Christ now, if we would not have the shame of being put far from him when he comes in the glory of his kingdom.

[' Many souls not only perish praying, repenting, believing, after a sort; but they perish by their praying and repenting, because they trust in them.']

[24, .5 ver. Let the power of the anointing, the wisdom that cometh down from above, and of which we are made partakers in Christ; let this be manifested both in our choosing the Rock whereon to build, and in our building upon the Rock we have been given the wisdom to choose. Our safety is in building, not upon human opinion, but upon the Rock of eternal truth.]

SIN IS THE TRANSGRESSION OF THE LAW.—1 John iii. 4. [141]

THE RECOGNITION OF THE LAW AND THE PROPHETS

MATTHEW vii. 28, 9; viii. 1.

28 And it-came-to-pass, when Jesus had-ended συνετελεσεν these sayings, the people were-astonished at his doctrine: for he-taught them as one having authority εξουσιαν, and not as the scribes.

viii. 1 When-he'-was-come-down from the mountain, great multitudes followed him.
[Ch. viii. 2, ? xxi. p. 159.]

SCRIPTURE ILLUSTRATIONS.

27. *the floods came, &c.*—after the promise, 'Behold, I lay in Zion for a foundation a stone, a tried stone, a precious corner stone, a sure foundation;' It is said, 'And the hail shall sweep away the refuge of lies, and the waters shall overflow the hiding place,' &c.— 'When the overflowing scourge shall pass through, then ye shall be trodden down by it,' Is. xxviii. 16—22.

and great was the fall of it—let us bear the words of warning, Is. x. 1—4. 'Woe unto them that decree unrighteous decrees,' &c., indulging their own covetousness, in neglect of the great law of love, ver. 2— 'And what will ye do in the day of visitation, and in the desolation *which* shall come from far? to whom will ye flee for help? and where will ye leave your glory? Without me they shall bow down under the prisoners, and they shall fall under the slain,' ver. 3, 4 —' Woe to him that coveteth an evil covetousness to his house, that be may set his nest on high, that he may be delivered from the power of evil !' . . . ' For the stone shall cry out of the wall, and the beam out of the timber shall answer it,' Hab. ii. 9—11—*see* also ver. 12—4.—the curse, Zec. v. 1—3—' It shall enter into the house of the thief, and into the house of him that sweareth falsely by my name: and it shall remain in the midst of his house, and shall consume it with the timber thereof and the stones thereof,' ver. 4.

29. *having authority*—as the Prophet foretold by Moses, De. xviii. 15—9—. . . . . and referred to, Ac. iii. 22—6.

NOTES.

[28. *When Jesus had ended these sayings.* This plainly intimates that all *this discourse* was delivered at once; and, consequently, that several passages related by St. Luke, as spoken at different times, are repetitions of it; compare Mt. v. 3, and seq., § 19, p. 120, with Lu. vi. 20, and seq., § 27; Mt. v. 13, § 19, p. 122, with Lu. xiv. 31, 5, § 67; Mt. v. 25, § 19, p. 125, with Lu. xii. 58, § 63; Mt. vi. 2, § 19, and seq., p. 132, with Lu. xi. 2, and seq., § 52; Mt. vi. 20, .1, § 19, p. 131, with Lu. xii. 33, .4, § 63; Mt. vi. 24, § 19, p. 134, with Lu. xvi. 13, § 69; and Mt. vii. 13, .4, § 19, p. 139, with Lu. xiii. 24. § 66.}

Were astonished at his doctrine. τῇ ἰδαχῇ. The word may denote either the *doctrine taught*, or the *manner of teaching*. The latter is probably meant.
—*See* Greswell on the Parables, vol. i. Introd.

PRACTICAL REFLECTIONS.

26, 7 ver Although without *hearing* it cannot be expected we shall *do*, yet it is quite possible we may *hear* the sayings of Christ, and not *do* them. An awful time of trial is approaching, when those who have not been building upon the Rock Christ will be found like the man who built his house upon the sand.*

28. Let us not be merely astonished at the doctrine of Christ, but let us mingle faith with what we hear; a faith which worketh by love, and purifieth the heart; and let us never forget that ' *This is the work of God, that ye believe on Him whom He hath sent,'* Jno. vi. 29, § 43, p. 327.

ADDENDA.

THE RECOGNITION OF THE LAW AND THE PROPHETS, BY OUR LORD, IN HIS SERMON ON THE MOUNT.—MATTHEW, ch. v. 1—vii. 29.

[We have before seen that the SERMON ON THE MOUNT is an exposition of the LAW, ACCORDING TO THE GOSPEL—shewing how, by the provisions of the New Covenant, the Law is to be written upon the fleshy tables of the heart. It is also important to observe that, in the same order, it makes a very distinct recognition of the books of 'THE LAW AND THE PROPHETS.' These are *twice* distinctly referred to, in the course of the Sermon.

The Sermon divides itself into two halves.

First, ch. v. 1, to vi. 18.

Second, ch. vi. 19—vii. 29.

At the commencement of the central portion of the Sermon, ch. v. ver. 17—20, of the first half, (ch. v. 1—18,) our Lord says, ver. 17: ' *Think not that I am come to destroy the Law, or the Prophets: I am not come to destroy, but to fulfil.*' And near the end of the central part, vii. 7—14, of the second half, (vi. 19—vii. 29,) he says, ver. 12: ' *Whatsoever ye would that men should do to you, do ye even so to them: for this is the Law and the Prophets.*'

In the *first* case, he gives us the sum of divine revelation as to doctrine; and in the *second*, as to practice.

Let us now see how the same discourse, which is an exposition of the Decalogue, is also an epitome of ' *the Law and the Prophets.*'

I. In the Beatitudes, Mt. v. 3—12, the Mediator of the New Covenant describes the character and blessedness of those who, obedient to the *first* commandment, take the Lord alone to be their God.

In GENESIS, the first book of the Law and Prophets, we have the characters described, which are here referred to, as in the cases of Abel, Noah, Abraham, Jacob, and Joseph. ' *By faith Jacob, when he was a dying, blessed both the sons of Joseph,*' Heb. xi. 21—comp. Gen. xlviii. 14—20. . . . *and they which be of faith are blessed with faithful Abraham,*' Gal. iii. 9, whose history, and that of his more immediate descendants, occupies so large a portion of the first book of the Law and Prophets, Gen. xii. 1. And the blessing of Abraham, who gave such an example of obedience to the first commandment, was to come upon the Gentiles through Jesus Christ.

II. In Mt. v. 13—.6, Jesus requires that his disciples be made after the image of Him who is ' *the Saviour of all men,*' 1 Tim. iv. 10; ' *the Light of the world,*' Jno. viii. 12, § 55. They are to keep the second commandment by being made in the likeness of the Lord from heaven, who descended in order to give us light and life, that God might be glorified thereby.

In EXODUS we have an illustration of this. There is described how the Lord came down to deliver Israel, to be a light to enlighten, and as well to protect. He appeared in a flame of fire to Moses in the bush, ch. iii. 2—10. Afterwards, when there was darkness that might be felt over the whole land of Egypt, ' *all the children of Israel had light in their dwellings,*' ch. x. ver. 21—3. Israel were protected through the Red Sea by the 'pillar of the cloud,' which gave them light by night, ch. xiv. ver. 19, 20. He brought them to the mount, on which he descended in fire, and whence, amid lightnings, he delivered them that law which especially witnessed against idolatry, ch. xix. 16—8; xx. 4—6; and the punishment of a breach of which is recorded, ch. xxxii. In this book is described the beautiful workmanship of all belonging to the tabernacle, and especially of the candlestick, which was ever to give light in the Lord's house, as representing the church, which is designed to minister light to all around; not that men may be induced to worship the candlestick, but be led to glorify our Father which is in heaven.

III. In Mt. v. 17—20, we are warned not to think lightly of the Law and the Prophets, or fail of rightly apprehending the purpose for which the Son of God came into our world. He who came in the name of the Lord to save us, came as the Fulfiller of all that had been written of him, as being the chosen One, who should bring in everlasting righteousness.

*Since writing the above the time seems to have commenced.

LOOK TO YOURSELVES.—2 John 8 ver.

And in LEVITICUS, we have the types of the 'One Sacrifice' he was to make for our sins. The actings of the high priest, who, on his heart and upon his shoulders, was to bear the names of the children of Israel before the Lord, represented the working of the Lord our Righteousness, by whom we have entrance into the kingdom of heaven: '*Christ is the end of the law for righteousness to every one that believeth*,' Rom. x. 4.

That the Lord would not allow those ordinances which pointed out the way of approach to him to be broken with impunity, was early made manifest in the case of the sons of Aaron, Nadab and Abihu, Lev. x. 1—11. It is in this book also that we find recorded the punishment for breaking the *third* commandment, or blaspheming the Name of the Lord, xxiv. 10—,6; and as well do we find here predicted the punishment, long and severe, which was to come upon the people, as not properly regarding that whereby he made himself known, xxvi. 3—39, and the favour reserved for them when, confessing their iniquity, they would accept of the punishment thereof, ver. 40—.3, as typified by the sacrifices prescribed in this book, and fulfilled in Christ. '*For by one offering he hath perfected for ever them that are sanct.*,' He. x. 14.

IV. In Mt. v. 21—48, we see Jesus calling the attention of his disciples from the teaching of those who had been in vain labouring to work out a righteousness of their own. Our attention is directed to that exhibition of the law which was given in himself, who, in fulfilling the law for us, hath left us an example that we should follow his steps, 1 Pe. ii. 21. It is as being made sons of God in him, who in his work of redemption hath manifested perfect love, and taught us the forgiveness here required, that we can hear the command, '*Be ye therefore perfect, even as your Father which is in heaven is perfect.*' The forbearance, forgiveness, and kindness of the Father of Israel, as procured by the intercession of the typical mediator, Moses, are most strongly manifested in the book of NUMBERS, as describing the journeyings of Israel in the wilderness.

In the *fourth* commandment the Lord was presented as their example, both as to labour and rest.

In this *fourth* book of the LAW, NUMBERS, we have the Lord leading about the children of Israel, after all the work of the tabernacle was finished, which represented the perfect work of the Son of God: wherever, and so long, as the Lord led, Israel were to follow; and when the cloud rested they were to rest; and when they rested, it was as being concentrated around that which had led them in all their journey, and which represented Him in whom we have guidance and rest.

When encamped and at rest around the tabernacle, then by observing those ordinances as typical of the perfect work of Christ, they were taught the holiness, forbearance, truthfulness, forgiveness, and love, which we more plainly read in the life and death, as well as in the words, of the Son of God, who most perfectly did the will of the Father, not only for us, but for our example; which example we are enabled to follow, only as having faith in his perfect work, in his divine wisdom to lead, in his power to protect, and in his goodness to bless. It may also be observed, that it is in this *fourth* book of the Law that the punishment for a breach of the fourth commandment is noticed, xv. 32—6.

V. In Mt. vi. 1—18, we have directions given as to the manner in which we are to honour the Father of our spirits, in the expectation of living hereafter in the enjoyment of that enduring inheritance, with which he will honour those that honour him. We are to do all as in his sight, and, before all things, seek that his name may be hallowed—that his kingdom may come, and his will be done upon earth as, &c.

In DEUTERONOMY, we have the illustration of this. In this repetition of the Law, the Lord by Moses addresses Israel as a father doth his children, and calls for that reverential regard to his voice which becomes the relationship; and especially are they called to be attentive to his voice, in the view of being prepared to receive aright that Great Prophet, the Mediator of the New Covenant, with regard to whom the Father hath said, '*Hear ye him,*' and without honouring whom, we honour not the Father which hath sent him.

In this *fifth* book of the Law is described the punishment of the breaker of the *fifth* commandment, De. xxi. 18—21. Often in this book are the people reminded of the promise annexed to the keeping of the fifth commandment. Their casting out of the land, in the case of disobedience to God as their Father, is described; and also the rich inheritance, which in the Lord their Saviour the Israel of God are to obtain.

It is here plainly shewn that the Lord delighteth not in dead and gloomy forms of religious service. He calls upon his children to know, and thence to love him, and to serve him with gladness of heart, as children a father whom they reverence and love, ch. xxvi. 10, .1; xxviii. 47, .8; xxxii. 6—9.

VI. In Mt. vi. 19—31, we bear the Lord warning against those things that go more immediately to destroy the spiritual life, which can only be maintained by faith, by simplicity of trust, by childlike confidence in God. In JOSHUA was exemplified all this: he was remarkable for not only a meek submission to the will of God, but a ready acquiescence in all his appointments. There is no instance of his heart fretting against the Lord, however trying his situation, or painful the work he had to perform. JOSHUA was privileged to lead the hosts of Israel into the land of promise—the waters of the Jordan dividing, to let them pass over, ch. iii. iv. '*By faith the walls of Jericho fell down,*' He. xi. 30; as if to teach Israel by what they should continue to live and triumph. By the same God, who had so marvellously sustained them in the wilderness, they were still to live. Here also, in the case of Achan, ch. vii., we see that seeking to lay up treasures upon earth, not trusting to the Lord's provision, brought destruction upon many, as well as disgrace and death to himself. He would have served God and mammon, but it could not be. In the destruction of the nations of Canaan we more especially see the evil case of those who say, What shall we eat? and, What shall we drink? and, Wherewithal shall we be clothed? They were only as dead men before Joshua; who, as seeking first the kingdom of God, and his righteousness, had fulfilled unto him the promise, '*All these things shall be added unto you.*' Joshua was as remarkable for living the life of faith, as for being the executioner of the sentence of death, which the Lord had pronounced upon the wicked nations of Canaan.

In this *sixth* book of the Law and Prophets, it is abundantly shewn that all killing was not a breach of the *sixth* commandment. Here is recorded the divinely directed killing, not only of individuals, but of nations, ch. i.—xii. Here also is the appointment of cities of refuge, unto which he might flee, who killed any person at unawares, ch. xx., &c.

VII. In Mt. vii. 1—6, we have the rule, '*Judge not, that ye be not judged,*' &c.

We find this rule exemplified in the book of JUDGES, ch. i. 7. See also the case of Abimelech and the men of Shechem, ch. ix. 56, .7. So in the case of Samson, ch. xv., xvi.; and in that of all Israel, as executing judgment upon the tribe of Benjamin, ch. xx. Israel, as described in this book, early and frequently went a whoring from the Lord, and thereby were allowed to fall into other uncleanness; aud, for both, the Lord allowed them to be punished, by their falling under the dominion of cruel lords. But according to the measure these dealt out to Israel, was it measured out to them again. The judgment may be just, but he that casts the first stone should himself be without sin. Equally must care be taken, not to prostitute to the profane the portion of the Lord's people. It was by allowing the heathen to become mixed up with Israel in the possession of the land, that Israel became torn, trampled upon, and debased; and in place of shining forth in the midst of the nations, as a holy nation, a peculiar people, they were as a woman who hath forsaken her own husband, and is despised of her lovers, and hated of all around. *See* for illustration their history as contained in JUDGES.

VIII. In Mt. vii. 7—14, the Lord directs us how to avoid a breach of the *eighth* commandment. What we need we are freely to ask of God, being assured that he will give what is good. We are to learn from the Law and Prophets that golden rule, ver. 12, by acting according to which, we shall carefully avoid breaking this commandment. And finally, we are not to take our rule of duty from the multitude who seek their own things. We are to take Christ as our pattern, and so exercise self-denial as we are exhorted, ver. 13, .4.

HE THAT HATH AN EAR, LET HIM HEAR.—Rev. iii. 6. [143

SECT. XIX. SERMON ON THE MOUNT, INTRODUCTORY TO PAUL'S EPISTLES. PART II.

In the *eighth* book of the Law and Prophets, SAMUEL (*asked of God*), we have the illustration of this eighth portion of our Lord's discourse, Mt. vii. 7—14, ' *Ask, and it shall be given you.*' Thus Samuel received his name, 1 Sa. i. 20, .7, as having been asked of the Lord by Hannah, his mother, whose song is a rejoicing in the truth that our God is a prayer-hearing God, who giveth to the needy, ch. ii. And the same truth was exemplified in the case of David; and by him also celebrated in song, to the praise of the Giver of all good, as 2 Sa. xxii. The punishment of a breach of the eighth commandment, or taking for ourselves, not according to the divine appointment, was punished upon the family of Eli by the loss of the priesthood—*comp.* 1 Sa. ii. 12—.7, 27—36; iii. 11—.4; and upon the house of Saul, by the loss of the kingdom, xv. 10—28.

David, toward his enemy Saul, observed the golden rule, and he met with his reward. But having done all, we have need to ask that we may be able to stand; and not, like David, fall, when the victory seems to be won, 2 Sa. xi. His sin, it may be observed, is spoken of by Nathan, in the language of the eighth commandment, 2 Sa. xii. 4—10, as he was in that case judged according to the golden rule and found wanting.

The last fact recorded in this book is to the honour of David, as being scrupulously observant of the commandment; and as presenting an offering to the Lord on account of deliverance, which he had earnestly asked of God, 2 Sa. xxiv.

IX. In Mt. vii. 15—20, the Faithful and True Witness warns his disciples with regard to false prophets, and tells us how we may form a correct judgment as to who are appointed to speak forth the mind of God to his people; and it is intimated, that many may not only deceive others, but also themselves, who will, at the last, be rejected by the righteous Judge.

The illustration of this *ninth* part of our Lord's discourse we have in the BOOKS OF KINGS, which describe the sin and punishment of bearing false witness, as in the matter of Naboth's vineyard, 1 Ki. xxi. Here we have abundant proof of the truth of the warning which God by his prophet had given, 1 Sa. viii., with regard to their king. Here also we see, that when Israel was faithful, in their witness for God, against the lying vanities of the heathen around them, they were eminently prosperous: 1 Ki. i.—x. But when they fell from their testimony, and treated truth and error as alike worthy of their regard, Israel and Judah soon came to variance, and were brought to ruin as the prophets had forewarned. It is here also that we have the most striking type of the prophetic office in Elijah, 1 Ki. xxi., whose rough garment, or sheep's clothing, appears to be alluded to by our Lord, as being that which could be affected by pretended successors, whilst having not his spirit. *Comp.* 2 Ki. i. 8, with Matt. vii. 15, p. 140. It is not by outward credentials, such as man may fabricate, but by the fruits of the Spirit, that the true

witnesses for God are to be known, as distinguished from the false prophets, who may give abundant evidence of their sincerity, as did the prophets of Baal. There was abundance of crying, ' O Baal (or Lord), hear us,' 1 Ki. xviii., whilst they were leading the people astray—were bringing down upon their land the just judgment of Heaven, to the entire destruction of their nation, according as God had forewarned, 2 Ki. xvii. 5—23. The warnings of the true prophets having been slighted, they were given a commission to execute judgment upon Israel, 1 Ki. xix. 9—17. The case of that nation may well serve for warning to individuals to prepare for the judgment to which our attention is here directed, Mt. vii. 22, .3, by the Faithful Witness.

X. In Mt. vii. 21—.7, which is the *tenth* and last portion of the Sermon on the Mount, we are warned that the words here spoken regard the hearers of Christ; and that his word must not only be heard, but be understood and obeyed. If we merely attend to the outward letter, and then attach to that letter the thoughts of other men, or of our own minds, without seeking to know what is really the mind of God, as expressed by his word, we are guilty of the worst kind of *covetousness*; we are perverting the words of God to our own purposes; the folly as well as sin of which the Lord will doubtless make evident, as forewarned by all the prophets; when also the security of those who have in truth built simply upon the Rock will be the more evident by the storms that prevail around, and the trials with which the righteous may themselves be tried, but through which they will be brought with songs of everlasting joy.

Not only are the larger prophets, Isaiah, Jeremiah, Ezekiel, full of this subject, but the minor prophets also, as Hab. ii. 4—11; Zec. v. 1—4. When God reclaims his own word from the perversions thereof by man—from every appropriation thereof to selfish or sectarian purposes, great must be the confusion of many. Let us avoid that fall by building, and that in truth, upon the Rock; and this we may be the better enabled to do, as seeing that by the Gospel we do not make void the Law, but establish it upon the only true Foundation upon which we with it can stand.

It may also be noticed, that when the Lord, according to his promise by the prophets, claims the possession of his people, his redeemed inheritance, then those who have been looking upon that inheritance as theirs, and who have in too many cases been acting as lords over God's heritage, will find that they have built upon a false foundation: and all their souls lusted after, and for which they so perverted the words of truth, will pass away from them, and leave them to shame and everlasting contempt. Then will those, who have chosen their portion with Mary,* rejoice, in beholding the wonders of His grace, and the glory of His power, in whom they have an unfailing refuge and fulness of blessing for ever.]

* Lu. x. 42, § 6L.

See 'THE MINOR PROPHETS AND THE DECALOGUE,' comp. p. 171.

THE SERMON ON THE MOUNT, INTRODUCTORY TO ST. PAUL'S EPISTLES.

It may be observed, that the *ten* divisions of ' THE SERMON ON THE MOUNT,' which give a recognition of ' THE LAW AND THE PROPHETS,' are also correspondent to the ministration of THE LAW, according to the NEW COVENANT, AS GIVEN BY THE SPIRIT, THROUGH PAUL IN HIS FIRST TEN EPISTLES. To his appointment to this service for the church, Paul seems to make frequent allusion throughout these Epistles, as—Rom. i. 1—5; iii. 31; xvi. 25, .6; 2 Co. iii. . . . Ep. iii. 1—11, &c. . . . Col. i. 25, .6, . . . 1 Ti. i. 5, 12—7. . . . vi. 13—.6.

I. In the EPISTLE TO THE ROMANS there is, in ch. i., an exposure of the unreasonableness of not acknowledging the one true God, and of the evils resulting from a breach of the *first* commandment.

Having cut off every false ground of confidence, ch. ii., iii., there is afterwards shewn the blessedness of taking the Lord alone to be our God, according as he is presented in the gospel, and enjoyed by those who possess the characteristics described in the ' Beatitudes,' Mt. v. 3—12, pp. 120—.2—*see* Rom. iv., v., viii. The hindrances on the part of Israel, to this simplicity of trust in God, are noticed, ch. ix.,

x., xi., and afterwards is described simple devotedness to God, according to the great law of LOVE, and in the observance of all relative duties, ch. xii., xiii. Communion with God leads to forbearance, brotherly kindness, and charity, ch. xiv., xv., &c.

II. In the FIRST EPISTLE TO THE CORINTHIANS our attention is more particularly directed to the *second* commandment, which forbids idolatry; and to the subject of the *second* part of ' *The Sermon on the Mount,*' which requires that we be made in the image of HIM who is our Light and Salvation.

The *idolatry* of teachers is noticed, ch. i. ver. 12, .3, of human wisdom and worldly greatness, ver. 18—29. The danger of defiling the temple of God, ch. iii. ver. 17, by giving undue honour to the creature, ch. iv. ver. 6, which is too often attended with other uncleanness, ch. v.—*see* also ch. vi. ver. 9, 10, .8—20. Then *idolatry* commonly so called, ch. viii. x. 7, 14—21. Thou how God is to be glorified in his house, by the man as the image and glory of God, and by the woman as representing the church, ch. xi. ver. 1—15; and by the church, in the unity of faith and love observing the ordinances of Christ, ver.

144] THAT WHICH YE HAVE . . . HOLD FAST TILL I COME.—Rev. ii. 25.

18—31; and in the diversities of gifts, &c., glorifying the Triune God, ch. xii. The spirit of love in which only this can be done, ch. xiii. The manner, ch. xiv. The light of the glorious gospel, exhibiting our transformation into the image of 'the second Adam, the Lord from heaven,' ch. xv. The becoming manner in which liberality, &c., is now to be exercised, and the vast importance of that love which alone can transform us into the likeness of Christ, ch. xvi.

III. In Paul's *third* Epistle, the SECOND TO THE CORINTHIANS, is an illustration of the *third* commandment, and a farther development of the *third* part of '*The Sermon on the Mount*.' Paul did not take the NAME of God in vain; he recognises the solemnity of an oath—the calling God to witness, ch. i. ver. 17—23. He speaks of the ministration of righteousness, for which Christ had come into the world, and of which Paul was made a minister, so that the Law, in the spirit of it, might be fulfilled, ch. iii. See how he speaks as if upon oath, ch. ii. 17; iv. 1, 2. He was willing to confirm the testimony, by enduring suffering, as looking to the glorious purpose which God had in view with regard to it, ver. 8—15; and also the eternal reward, ver. 16—8. He speaks as in the view of the coming judgment, and as having a sense of the awful importance of his position, as being given to speak in the name of the Lord, or in Christ's stead, ch. v. Declares again his willingness to sacrifice all for the name's sake of Christ, and calls upon those to whom he writes to be in truth that which they were called, the people of the Lord, ch. vi. He acknowledges the truthfulness, so far, of their profession, ch. vii., and calls for the farther evidence of liberality to the poor, as the fruits in them of righteousness, and of God's unspeakable gift, ch. viii., ix. Paul, for their sakes, and the sake of Him whose NAME he bore, clears his own name from the several false aspersions that had been cast upon him among the Corinthians, and fully vindicates his apostleship, ch. x.—xii. He farther refers to his sincerity, and the proof of Christ speaking in him; or, in other words, his not taking '*the name of God in vain;*' and calls upon them to examine themselves, and see that Christ is in them; that is, that they have not in vain taken upon them the Name of the Lord, but are in truth his people, ch. xiii.

IV. In Paul's *fourth* Epistle, that to the GALATIANS, we find the correspondence to the *fourth* commandment, and the *fourth* part of '*The Sermon on the Mount*,' Mt. v. 21—48. The raising of Jesus Christ from the dead, on account of which we observe the Christian Sabbath on the first day of the week, is referred to in the first verse of the Epistle, as in the end of it our attention is directed to the new creation, ch. vi. ver. 15. It is upon the production of this new creation that we cease from our own works, as God did from his; and enjoy a blessed *rest* in Jesus, while continuing to bring forth the fruits of faith in him. Rest in the finished work of the Son of God, as opposed to labouring in order to work out a righteousness for ourselves according to the Law, is emphatically the subject of the Epistle as a whole. Thus, see as to justification through Christ, and life in the Son of God, ch. ii. ver. 16—21. It is through faith in Christ that the Spirit is ministered, the blessing promised to Abraham is enjoyed, ch. iii.; and not only the blessing of the children of Abraham, ver. 15—29, but the privileges of the sons of God, ch. iv. ver. 1—7. There is not to be a turning back unto the beggarly elements of the ceremonial law, ver. 8—18. The spirit of bondage must be cast out, ver. 19—31, and we must 'stand fast . . . in the liberty wherewith Christ hath made us free,' ch. v. ver. 1—11. It is only by our being in Christ, that there can be fulfilled in us that in which all the Law is fulfilled, 'Thou shalt love thy neighbour as thyself.' It is as knowing the love that the Father hath towards us in his dear Son, that we are enabled to crucify the flesh, and bring forth the fruits of the Spirit, as ver. 12—26.

If we are indeed new created in Christ Jesus, we follow the example of Him who hath borne our burden and 'so fulfil the law of Christ,' ch. vi. ver. 1—11. Nothing can avail but a new creation. When we are one with the Son of God, we have a joyful rest, even though the outward world should speak trouble. To our enjoyment of this Christian Sabbath it is necessary that we cease to have any dependence upon either our observance or non-observance of ceremonial religion, ver. 12—8. That which we are to see after is, *that Christ be formed in us the hope of glory*.

V. In Paul's *fifth* Epistle, that to the EPHESIANS, we have the exposition of the *fifth commandment*, and the amplification of the *fifth* portion of *The Sermon on the Mount*,' Mt. vi. 1—18. The reward of inheritance in the land, in the view of which the children of Israel were to be observant of this '*first commandment* with promise, Ep. vi. 1—3, shadowed forth the more enduring inheritance unto which the children of God are appointed; which inheritance is here often referred to, ch. i. 1—14. There is to be, without ceasing, thanksgiving and supplication to God as a Father, as ver. 15—23. Indeed the whole Epistle breathes the spirit of devotion—of filial piety —of childlike gratitude and submission. All is ascribed to the grace of God in Christ Jesus, ch. ii. 1—10. He that loves Him that begat, loves those also that are begotten of him, and accordingly there is the greatest willingness expressed to receive into fellowship all whom the Father receives into his family, ch. ii. 11—22. The purpose of God with regard to his household is contemplated as being an eternal purpose—a mystery, in the ministry of which Paul had a special appointment, ch. iii. 1—13—*see* also the prayer unto the Father of our Lord Jesus Christ, 'of whom the whole family in heaven and earth is named,' ver. 13—21. The oneness of spirit, with which, by the diversity of gifts, the children of God are, in the unity of the faith, to grow up unto Him which is the Head, Christ, ch. iv. 1—16. The dispositions with which they are to honour their kind, forgiving Father, as contrasted with those that characterize the old man, ver. 17—32; ch. v. 1. The walk which becomes the children of light, ver. 2—21. God is to be *honoured* in all the relations of life, as in those of wife and husband, child and parent, servant and master, ver. 22—33; ch. vi. 1—9. So also is he to be *honoured*, by our making a diligent use of all the means he hath provided for the spiritual conflict. We may not think we are wiser than He; that we can with safety dispense with any part of the spiritual armour He hath seen meet to provide. So are we also to *honour* his power, by our using every weapon in a prayerful dependence upon his strength. And especially is God as a Father to be *honoured*, by a due regard being had to his children, our brethren in Christ, our associates in the spiritual warfare, ver. 10—24.

VI. In Paul's *sixth* Epistle, that to the PHILIPPIANS, we have the ministration of the *sixth commandment*, correspondent to our Lord's teaching in '*The Sermon on the Mount*,' on the same subject, Mt. vi. 19—34.

The same elevation of mind above the things belonging to the temporal life, and the same earnest desire after the things that are above, to which our Lord exhorts, are here manifested to the degree of giving a desire to die, 'and be with Christ; which is far better:' only that the expectation of being of use to others gives a willingness to live. There must be care to live as becomes the gospel, but anxiety about the life of the body there is to be none, ch. i. Our life is to be in the Triune God, and as having a care for each other in the Lord, ch. ii. 1—4. Christ is our example as to denying ourselves; yea, as to the laying down our lives for others, ver. 5—11. As having our life in the God of love, we are to hold forth the word of life to others, ver. 12—8. Our fellowship in the Spirit is to be such, that we are to feel the sorrows or joys of our brethren in Christ as if they were our own, ver. 19—30. The things that cut off from the full enjoyment and communication of spiritual life are warned against, ch. iii. These are, a trust in external or ceremonial religion, or other supposed advantages of a carnal nature, impairing our simple trust in Christ, ver. 1—11; a resting in the things whereunto we have attained, ver. 12—6; a minding earthly things, so as to be unwilling to bear the cross—forgetting the treasure we have above—our citizenship in heaven—the coming of the Saviour, 'who shall change our vile body,' &c., ver. 17—21. Again, the manifestation of the life of love, as having trust in God, so as to be careful for nothing, is exhorted to, ch. iv. 1—7. The things that are truly of value, and are really beautiful, belong to that life, ver. 8, 9. That spirit of simple dependence upon Divine Providence, as seeking first the kingdom of God, to which our Lord exhorts his disciples in '*The Sermon on the Mount*,' Paul was himself enabled to enjoy, ver. 10—23.—*Comp.* the whole Epistle with Mt. vi. 19—34.

VII. In Paul's *seventh* Epistle, that 'to the saints and faithful brethren in Christ which are at Colosse,' we have that which is correspondent to the *seventh* commandment, and the *seventh* part of '*The Sermon on the Mount*,' Mt. vii. 1—6.

It warns against all usurpation of the Headship, which belongs to Christ as the Husband of the church. Wives are to submit themselves to their own husbands, as it is fit in the Lord. His Bride in particular is to submit herself to her own Husband. The reverse is spiritual *adultery*. All *adulterations* of the truth, whether by heathen philosophy, or Judaizing teaching, are here also earnestly deprecated. It may be premised, that the 'Mystery' so frequently referred to throughout this Epistle is explained as being the marriage union of Christ with his church.—*See* Eph. v. 3], .2.

The church, the Lamb's wife, is herself to be characterised as possessing faith, love, and hope; as having received the truth, and bringing forth fruit, &c., ch. i. 3—6.

The knowledge of her Lord's will is to be desired for her, that she may 'walk worthy of the Lord unto all pleasing,' &c., ver. 9—11.

In Him is her Inheritance, for which she is made meet, as having been redeemed by his blood, ver. 12—4.

What Adam was typically, Jesus is really — 'the Image of the invisible God, the Firstborn of every creature,' the Head of the woman, his body, the church, ver. 15—9. She is being brought into conformity to his Image, in order to be presented (as Eve was to Adam) holy and unblameable and unreproveable in his sight,' ver. 20—2.

To further the purposes of God with regard to this glorious mystery of the Bridegroom and Bride—of Christ and his church, Paul was appointed to a special ministry, ver. 23—9.

All the endeavours of those who are fitted for the ministry, are to be for the purpose of enabling the church the more clearly to see that her all is in Christ, ch. ii. 1—7.

The church is to be beware of being spoiled, either through vain philosophy on the one hand, or Pharisaism on the other. It was as being dead in their sins that the Gentiles were quickened by Christ: and the Jewish ordinances, so far from giving to the Jews a claim to blessing, were as a handwriting or bill of divorce against them, which had to be taken out of the way, in order that the marriage union might take place, which is to be consummated in resurrection glory. Worship is to be given to Christ the Head, not to his messengers, ver. 8—23.

The church's affection is to be where her risen Lord is, at the Father's right hand. Her life is to be there; and bodily uncleanness, and all breaches of the commandment in any respect, are most carefully to be avoided. She is to be made after the image of her Husband, the second Adam, ch. iii. 1—11.

She is to be clothed as becomes 'the Elect of God, holy and beloved,' &c., having the peace of God ruling in her heart, and the word of Christ indwelling richly, as was shadowed forth by the ark of the testimony: in which was the word, expressive of the will of God, and upon which was the mercy seat, the throne of Him who had espoused Israel to himself, ver. 12—7.

In the several relations of life the pleasure of the Lord is to be done, ver. 18—25; ch. iv. 1.

The mystery of Christ (shadowed out by the marriage relation) is that which it is the great business of the Christian ministry to bring to light. This is that which is most earnestly to be desired, 'that ye may stand perfect and complete in all the will of God,' ver. 2—18.

It may be noticed that 'Nymphas' (a spouse), mentioned ver. 15, appears to be the same with 'Philemon,' a name of similar import; and that the Epistle mentioned, ver. 16, appears to be the same with that to Philemon.

VIII. In Paul's *eighth* Epistle, the FIRST TO THE THESSALONIANS, we are directed to the right keeping of the *eighth* commandment, correspondent to the *eighth* part of '*The Sermon on the Mount*,' Mt. vii. 7—14.

We are best saved from a breach of the *eighth* commandment when, having known the grace of God to ourselves, we are, like Paul, given thankfulness to God for the favours bestowed upon others; and when our asking is for blessing upon them—ever remembering in the sight of God, not our own necessities only, but others' 'work of faith, and labour of love, and patience of hope in our Lord Jesus Christ,' ch. i. 1—3.

That which we are to prize for ourselves, with regard to others, is the privilege of communicating unto them the gospel in power, &c., and teaching them, by example, to become ensamples to others, sacrificing all for the word of truth, ver. 4—8.

We are to seek, not that men may be drawn to us, but that they may be turned to the living and true God, and '*to wait for his Son from heaven*,' &c., 9, 10.

The gospel is not ours, so that we may traffic therewith for temporal gain; we are put in trust with it, that we may dispense it freely, as in the sight of God, using no cloak of covetousness. Let us be willing to impart to men, '*not the gospel of God only*,' they being dear to us, ch. ii. 1—8.

Paul was an example of what the servant of the Lord ought to be, as to disinterested labour for the benefit of others. He did not, by looseness of conduct, deprive himself of the power of consistently exhorting the church to '*walk worthy of God*,' ver. 9—12.

When the Word of God is received as such, there is that for which to give thanks without ceasing, even though the greatest worldly loss should be incurred. Those who hinder the spiritual enriching of others, do, as has been abundantly evident in the case of the Jews, treasure up wrath for themselves. The Christian's rich reward—his crown of rejoicing, is having those to whom he ministers enriched with all spiritual grace '*in the presence of our Lord Jesus Christ*,' ver. 13—20.

The comfort of the Christian minister is the seeing the children of God comfortably sustained, in the faith, through trial and temptation. His prayer is, that they may be prepared for the full fruition of their glorious hope—'*the coming of our Lord Jesus Christ with all his saints*,' ch. iii.

We are earnestly to desire the being preserved in holiness to the Lord, '*that no man go beyond and defraud* [MARG. '*oppress*,' or, '*overreach*'] *his brother in any matter;*' and that, avoiding all lustfulness, we abound in all love, quietly labouring with our own hands, that we '*may walk honestly*,' &c., ch. iv. 1—12.

Those who have their treasure in Christ may not, at the most painful bereavements, sorrow as those that have no hope. Not with expectations of worldly gain or glory, but with words respecting our Lord's second and glorious appearing, are the saints to '*comfort one another*,' ver. 13—8.

To those who purloin, to purposes of selfish ease and indulgence, that of which they have been made stewards, '*the day of the Lord . . . cometh as a thief in the night*.' Let us be prepared for that day, by being found diligent in comforting and edifying one another, ch. v. 1—11.

Although those who labour in the gospel are to labour as to the Lord only, yet is there to be in those to whom they minister a kindly remembrance of them. To them also the commandment is to be observed—they are not to be defrauded, but rather are they to be honourably sustained in their work. Their work is great and various, according to the variety of character and condition of those among whom they may labour. Each member of the flock has to be remembered for good, according as his different case may require, ver. 12—5.

Brief exhortations, opposed to a murmuring, self-seeking disposition; and directing to the free exercise of the graces and gifts of the Spirit of God; and prayer for entire separation unto God; with expressions of holy love unto all the holy brethren, close the Epistle, ver. 16—28.

IX. In Paul's *ninth* Epistle, the SECOND TO THE THESSALONIANS, is the correspondence to the *ninth* commandment; and further intimations respecting the false prophets of which our Lord had forewarned his disciples, in the *ninth* part of '*The Sermon on the Mount*,' Mt. vii. 15—20.

The true witnesses are they whose faith groweth, whose charity aboundeth, who are willing patiently to endure tribulation and persecution for the truth's sake, ch. i. 1—4.

PART II. SERMON ON THE MOUNT, INTRODUCTORY TO PAUL'S EPISTLES. SECT. XIX.

They warn of coming wrath, as well as point forward to the glory that awaits those who receive the Divine testimony. They labour as looking for their rest, '*when the Lord Jesus shall be revealed from heaven,*'... '*when he shall come to be glorified in his saints, and to be admired in all them that believe,*' ver. 5—10.

It is earnestly to be desired that our God would vouchsafe a thorough meetness for their calling, unto all who have been intrusted with the testimony of Jesus—who have been called to glorify his name, ver. 11, .2.

It is not only necessary that we be ourselves true witnesses, but that we should beware of false prophets, and especially of those pretending to have apostolic authority. Here we are most expressively forewarned of that gigantic system of falsehood and wickedness, which, under the name of Christianity, but really antichrist, was afterwards to arise, and against which, as well as for Christ, the true witnesses are to be bold in bearing their testimony. There was first a falling away, and then appeared '*the son of perdition,*' '*who opposeth,*' &c.—who, in place of witnessing of Jesus, sheweth forth himself as if he were God, ch. ii. 1—4.

The rise of antichrist had been much the subject of the Spirit's faithful forewarning; and it only required the farther development of a principle which was already at work among the disciples, and which would come forth into full operation so soon as circumstances allowed; but the Christian was to feel certain, that so surely as the predicted '*wicked*' was revealed, would he be destroyed by the brightness of the coming (*parousia*), by the full and true witnessing, preparatory to the appearing of the Lord. Those who love not the truth are the most in danger of believing a lie; and those who believe not the truth, having pleasure in unrighteousness, are ripening for destruction. Their cunning, in contriving and contending for what is false, will be found folly in the end, ver. 5—12.

Believers in Christ are, in opposition to the slaves of antichrist—brethren, for whom thanks are to be given to God for their being made Christians; and the means of their salvation in Christ are not carnal ordinances, but the '*sanctification of the Spirit and belief of the truth:*' being called by the gospel to the obtaining of the glory, &c., ver. 13, .4.

We are not merely ourselves to hold firmly the truth, but we are to be much in prayer that the word of the Lord, as witnessed by others, may both have free course, and be productive of fruit; and that the work of God may be free from the interference of unreasonable and wicked men, ch. ii. 15—.7; iii. 1, 2.

It is in trusting in a faithful God, as having our hearts directed into his love, and the patient waiting for Christ. that we are enabled to continue unwavering in our testimony, ver. 3—5.

The faithful witnesses for the truth must not associate with those who walk disorderly. Paul denied himself even that which was justly his due, in order to avoid any appearance of being burdensome to the churches, ver. 6—9.

Those who act according to the apostolic rule, '*with quietness work, and eat their own bread,*' ver. 10—2.

Those who are themselves unwearied in welldoing are not to be identified with any who bring reproach on the cause of truth by seeking to make a gain of godliness, ver. 13—5.

The peace-bestowing witness of the Lord of peace himself, by whatever means he is pleased to express his will, is that which is to be desired. That which was ministered by epistle, through Paul, may be *known* by his peculiar salutation, ver. 16—8.

X. In the *tenth* Epistle of Paul, the FIRST to TIMOTHY, we have ample illustration both of the *tenth commandment*, and of the *tenth and last* portion of '*The Sermon on the Mount,*' Mt. vii. 21—7.

1. At the commencement of the Epistle, the apostle recognises our having come to '*the end of the commandment,*' which '*is charity, out of a pure heart, and of a good conscience, and of faith unfeigned,*' 1 Tim. i. 5.

It is only as being right in doctrine that we can be right in practice. The RIGHTEOUSNESS required by the Law can only be truly learned in the light of '*the glorious gospel of the blessed God,*' ch. i. 1—11.

2. Paul reckoned himself a signal example of Divine mercy, that in him Jesus Christ might exhibit a PATTERN of faithfulness, grace, and especially longsuffering, ver. 12—.6.

3. The NAME to which we are to be faithful; and the necessity of '*holding faith, and a good conscience,*' if we would not, '*concerning faith,*' make shipwreck, are next spoken of, ver. 17—20.

4. Love for our fellow-men is to be expressed in our approaches to God. The reconciling grace taught in the mediatorial work of Christ, is to be exhibited by us, in all our communications both with God and with man, chap. ii. 1—7.

5. We are to exercise longsuffering towards each other, and submission to the sovereign appointments of God, '*every where lifting up holy hands,*' to heaven, not usurping, &c., ver. 8—15.

6. Meekness, or an imperturbable determination to do what is right and kind, keeping in due restraint every inordinate desire, is a principal characteristic required in those who are to exercise rule, ch. iii. 1—13.

7. The great mystery, the church of the living God, for becoming service in which we are to be prepared; and the spiritual wickedness, against which the true church of God would have to contend, ch. iii. 14—.6; iv. 1—6.

8. The things—those belonging to eternal life—upon which the desires are to lay hold, and in which the man of God may indeed be profitably exercised, ver. 7—16.

9. The carefulness that was to be used in order to avoid the alloy of covetousness in church arrangements, and especially in those offices by which the love and truth of Christianity were to be exhibited to the world, so that these might bear true witness for Christ, ch. v.

10. Covetousness, or unlawful desire, producing partiality, discontent with one's situation, and '*many foolish and hurtful lusts, which drown men in destruction and perdition,*' is most earnestly to be avoided, ch. vi. 1—10.

The apostle here, ch. vi. 3, as at the close of the *first* of these Epistles, Ro. xvi. 25—7, seems to recognise the connection between '*the preaching,*' or words of *Jesus Christ,* and the teaching which Paul himself was empowered to give '*according to godliness.*'

The danger of not doing these things, after having heard them, is here pointed out, ch. vi. 3—10, as at the close of '*The Sermon on the Mount,*' Mt. .6. 26, .7. Here is also shewn the manner in which, fleeing covetousness, we may safely build upon the Rock; by which, even the rich in this world may be found '*laying up in store for themselves a good foundation against the time to come, that they may lay hold on Eternal Life,*' 1 Tim. vi. 11—.9; *comp.* Mt. vii. 24, .5.

Mammon, as promising a command over the enjoyments generally of the present world, is that which chiefly interposes so as to prevent a simple trust in HIM, whom the word reveals as the Rock, in whom our entire confidence should be placed. Mammon, or money, is accordingly warned against: '*For the love of money is the root of all evil: which while some coveted after, they have erred from the faith, and pierced themselves through with many sorrows,*' ver. 10.

SUMMARY OF THE CONTENTS OF THIS EPISTLE, AND OF THE EPISTLES OF PAUL GENERALLY, IN THE CHARGE TO THE '*MAN OF GOD,*' GIVEN 1 TIM. vi. 11—.6.

The apostle, in directing to flee from covetousness, gives a brief recapitulation of the contents of this Epistle, as presenting the things opposed to covetousness, and according to the commandment, ver. 11, '*But thou, O man of God, flee these things; and follow after righteousness, godliness,*' &c.

BE THOU INSTRUCTED.—Jer. vi. 8. [147

SECT. XIX.   SERMON ON THE MOUNT, INTRODUCTORY TO PAUL'S EPISTLES.   PART II.

1. 'RIGHTEOUSNESS'—*see* this and its contrast described, 1 TIM. 1—11; and in the Epistle to the ROMANS throughout.

2. 'GODLINESS'—being like God, or after the Divine pattern—*comp.* ver. 12—6, and the FIRST EP. TO THE CORINTHIANS.

3. 'FAITH'—a truthful profession of the NAME of the Lord—*comp.* 17—20, and the SECOND EP. TO THE CORINTHIANS.

4. 'LOVE'—the great lesson taught in the work of redemption—*comp.* ch. ii. 1—7, and GALATIANS.

5. 'PATIENCE'—prayerful submission to our Father in heaven, in the exercise of mutual forbearance—*comp.* ver. 8—15, and EPHESIANS.

6. 'MEEKNESS'—or self-restraint, necessary especially in those who are called to feed and be ensamples to the flock—*comp.* ch. iii. 1—13, and PHILIPPIANS.

7. 'FIGHT THE GOOD FIGHT OF FAITH'—*comp.* ver. 14—.6; ch. iv. 1—6, and COLOSSIANS.

8. 'LAY HOLD ON ETERNAL LIFE, WHEREUNTO THOU ART ALSO CALLED'—*comp.* ch. iv. 7—16, and the FIRST EP. TO THE THESSALONIANS.

9. As to professing 'A GOOD PROFESSION BEFORE MANY WITNESSES'—*comp.* ch. v., and the SECOND EP. TO THE THESSALONIANS.

10. 'THAT THOU KEEP THIS COMMANDMENT, WITHOUT SPOT, UNREBUKEABLE,' &c., ch. vi. 1—12.—*See* the EPISTLES to TIMOTHY, TITUS, and PHILEMON.

THE CHARGE TO THE 'MAN OF GOD,' WHICH MAY THUS BE VIEWED AS CONTAINING A SUMMARY OF THE PRECEDING EPISTLES OF PAUL, GIVES, AT THE SAME TIME, A RECOGNITION OF 'THE WORDS OF OUR LORD JESUS CHRIST,' AS PRESENTED IN 'THE SERMON ON THE MOUNT.'—*Comp.* 1 TIM. vi. 11—.6, *with* MATT. v.—vii.

1. 'RIGHTEOUSNESS' before God, is described in the Beatitudes, Mt. v. 3—12.

2. 'GODLINESS'—or being made in the likeness or image of Him who is our Light and Salvation. ver. 13—.6.

3. 'FAITH'—a truthful reception and profession of what God hath revealed respecting the great object of our faith, and the righteousness which is of God by faith, ver. 17—20.

4. 'LOVE'—is the great lesson taught by the Mediator of the new covenant, ver. 21—48.

5. 'PATIENCE'—a prayerful submission to the will of our Heavenly Father in the exercise of forgiveness one towards another, ch. vi. 1—18.

6. 'MEEKNESS'—quietude of spirit as to all those matters that occasion worldly trouble, and that prevent our attending to that whereby the spiritual life is sustained, ver. 19—34.

7. 'FIGHT THE GOOD FIGHT OF FAITH' — the strife is to be for the being found first in serving one another—behaving ourselves well in the house of God—giving to each his portion of meat in due season, ch. vii. 1—6.

8. 'LAY HOLD ON ETERNAL LIFE'—the call to this, 'Ask, and it shall be given you,' &c., ver. 7—14.

9. 'A GOOD CONFESSION'—is required from those whom men may receive as God's witnesses, and whom Christ will acknowledge before all, ver. 15—20.

10. 'THE CHARGE'—to keep the commandment, not in word only, but in very deed, as building simply upon the Rock, ch. vii. 21—.7.

AN APPLICATION OF THE COMMANDMENT TO THE CASE OF 'THE RICH IN THIS WORLD,'—*Compare* 1 TIM. vi. 17—.9, *with* MATT. v.—vii.

After having given directions with regard to the poor, as to how they should eschew covetousness (1 Ti. vi. 1—10), and content themselves with being followers of Him, who, although the blessed and only Potentate, stood as a poor man before the tribunal of Pilate, confessing that his kingdom was not of this world, ver. 11—6, the apostle proceeds, 17—9, to deliver a charge for the benefit of the rich, which gives a brief summary of the contents of our Lord's discourse; and in which is shewn the connection between securing a good foundation against the time to come, and denying ourselves of a covetous appropriation of wealth; against which, as well as in favour of an earnest search after the true riches, the sayings of Christ were throughout chiefly directed.

1. The words, '*Charge them that are rich in this world, that they be not high-minded,*' immediately suggest the commencement of our Lord's discourse, Mt. v. 3—12, '*Blessed are the poor in spirit,' &c.* By following the apostle's advice, those who are not literally poor as to this world, may possess the blessedness described in the Beatitudes, otherwise their fancied elevation will be found deceptive indeed.

2. The words that follow, '*nor trust in uncertain riches,*' may well be connected with the *second* part of '*The Sermon on the Mount,*' Mt. v. 13—6, as nothing is so apt to deprive of godliness—to render insipid and dark, and timid in the cause of God, as that against which we are warned by the apostle—a cleaving to the earth.

3. The direction to trust '*in the living God*' is correspondent to the *third* part of '*The Sermon on the Mount,*' Mt. v. 17—20, which speaks of the better righteousness, 'the righteousness which is of God by faith,' as contrasted with the dead formality of the scribes and Pharisees.

4. He '*who giveth us richly all things to enjoy,*' hath taught us forgiveness, truthfulness, and grace; not only by fulfilling his covenant mercy as to sunshine and shower, both of which are implied in the rainbow, the token of the covenant, and adverted to Mt. v. 45. He hath given us the still more assured pledge of our enjoying all things, in his having given his own Son, to teach in deed as well as in word the lessons contained in the *fourth* part of '*The Sermon on the Mount,*' Mt. v. 21—48.

5. '*That they do good*'—that they be truly obedient children—doing good simply as in the sight of God, is that which our Lord requires of his disciples in the *fifth* portion of his discourse, Mt. vi. 1—18.

6. '*That they be rich in good works,*' is the same as that given, Mt. vi. 19—34, where we are directed not to lay up for ourselves treasures upon earth, but in heaven—to live above the world.

7. The being '*ready to distribute,*' is that which should characterise the Bride, the Lamb's wife; and it is that to which our Lord directs, Mt. vii. 1—6. As dissuading from the opposite spirit, a readiness to judge, he shews that there must first be a preparedness in ourselves, and then in others, for enjoying in light the blessings of God; and next, that discrimination must be used, both as to what is distributed, and those to whom distribution is made.

8. That we be '*willing to communicate*' we require to have communion with the great Giver of Good, and that disposition to reciprocate, as well as that exercise of self-denial, to which our Lord directs in the eighth part of '*The Sermon on the Mount,*' Mt. vii. 7—14.

9. The '*laying up in store for themselves a good foundation against the time to come,*' requires that attention to the true testimony of God, and that faithful reception thereof, which can alone avail us in trial, temptation, and judgment. If we would indeed stand our ground, the word of God must not be merely in our mouths; it must be laid up in our hearts, and practised in our lives, as taught by our Lord in Mt. vii. 15—20.

10. '*That they may lay hold on eternal life.*' That they may indeed be found fixed upon the Rock, Mt. vii. 24, .5, the Rock of Ages, that Eternal Rock, upon which all who truly build are everlastingly secure, it is necessary that all intervening ground of trust should be entirely renounced, and that the Saviour be trusted in simply and entirely; and that we be sure that this is our own case, we must be willing to deny ourselves to covetousness. *See* ver. 20, .7.

168]   QUENCH NOT THE SPIRIT.—1 Thess. v. 19.

PART II. THE ROCK OF OUR SALVATION EXHIBITED IN THE BOOKS, &c. SECT. XIX.

THE SAME PASSAGE WHICH RECOGNISES THE CONTENTS OF 'THE SERMON ON THE MOUNT,' MAY BE VIEWED AS SKETCHING THE GENERAL CONTENTS OF THESE EPISTLES OF PAUL.

1. The being '*highminded*,' is that against which the apostle warns in the EPISTLE TO THE ROMANS, as ch. xi. 20—2.

2. The folly of trusting '*in uncertain riches*,' he exposes in his FIRST EPISTLE TO THE CORINTHIANS, as ch. i. 26—31; iii. 16—23; iv. 8—13, &c.

3. Trust '*in the living God*,' is most strongly expressed in the SECOND EPISTLE TO THE CORINTHIANS, as ch. i. 9; iii. 3—6, &c.

4. God's giving us '*richly all things*' in Christ, and these '*to enjoy*' in the liberty of the Sonship, is expressed in the EPISTLE TO THE GALATIANS, ch. i. 4; ii. 20; iv. 4—7; v. 1, 13.

5. The desirableness of being led to '*do good*' according to the good pleasure of the Father of glory, is intimated in the EPISTLE TO THE EPHESIANS, as ch. i. 4, 5, 15—20; ii. 10; v. 1, 2, 8—10, &c.

6. As to being '*rich in good works*'—forwarding, whether by suffering or by doing, the message of salvation—see the EPISTLE TO THE PHILIPPIANS, as ch. i. 3—11, 27; ii. 1—17; iv. 1—9.

7. The being '*ready to distribute*,' as knowing Him in whom all fulness is to be found, and as being fully equipped for service, is that for which the apostle prays, and to which he exhorts in the EPISTLE TO THE COLOSSIANS, ch. i. 9—11; ii. 1—3; iii. 12—7.

8. A willingness '*to communicate*' is that which is recognised, as belonging both to Paul and those to whom he had communicated the gospel among the THESSALONIANS, and to which he exhorts still farther, FIRST EPISTLE, ch. i. 2—8; ii. 8—12; iii. 10—2; iv. 9, 10; v. 14—23.

9. The '*laying up in store . . . a good foundation against the time to come*,' so as to be able to resist the devil, the world, and the flesh, and remain faithful witnesses for Christ against all intruders, is called for, in the SECOND EPISTLE TO THE THESSALONIANS.

10. It is perhaps superfluous to say that the EPISTLES to TIMOTHY and TITUS most strongly oppose the sin of *covetousness*, and point out the propriety of our loosening our hold of this world, and of every false ground of confidence, that we may freely and fully '*lay hold on eternal life*.'

THE 'ROCK,' MATT. vii. 24.—THE 'NAME,' ISAIAH ix. 6, EXHIBITED IN THE BOOKS OF THE NEW TESTAMENT.

'*Whosoever heareth these sayings of mine, and doeth them, I will liken him unto a wise man, which built his house upon a rock*,' Mt. vii. 24. Christ is the 'Rock,' confessed by Peter, Mt. xvi. 16—8, § 50, p. 37.—'*the Spiritual Rock*,' from which, even under the law, Israel was refreshed in the thirsty wilderness, 1 Cor. x. 4. He is the only Rock upon which we can safely build. '*Other foundation can no man lay than that is laid, which is Jesus Christ*,' 1 Cor. iii. 11. He is '*the Foundation of the apostles and prophets*,' even '*Jesus Christ himself*.' He being also '*the chief Corner Stone*,' Eph. ii. 20. The ministration of the Spirit was promised to publish the NAME—to testify of Jesus as the ROCK, De. xxxii. 1—4:

'Give ear, O ye heavens, and I will speak;
And hear, O earth, the words of my mouth.
My doctrine shall drop as the rain,
My speech shall distil as the dew,
As the small rain upon the tender herb,
And as the showers upon the grass:
Because I will publish the NAME of the LORD:
Ascribe ye greatness unto our God.
He is THE ROCK, *his work is perfect*:
For all his ways *are* judgment:
A God of truth and without iniquity,
Just and right *is* he.'

It is by simple faith in God, through Christ, by hearing, so as to obey, the words of our blessed Redeemer, revealed by his Holy Spirit, that we build upon the Rock; and it is worthy of observation, that the writings of the New Testament, which present unto us '*the ministration of the Spirit*,' in manifestation of Christ as the one sure Foundation, are a publication, in order, of the NAME of the Lord, according as that Name is declared by Isaiah, ch. ix. 6. That Name we have already noticed, in connection with the first five Beatitudes, which describe the disposition with which we may successfully lay hold upon eternal life—build upon Christ the Rock—and become prepared to see God with gladness, when those who have built upon the sand will be swept from his blissful presence. It is only as building upon this Rock that acceptable obedience can by man be rendered unto God—that the commandment can be kept 'without spot, unrebukeable, until the appearing of Jesus Christ: which in his times he shall shew,

The blessed and only Potentate,
The King of kings, and Lord of lords;
Who only hath immortality,
Dwelling in the light which no man can approach unto;
Whom no man hath seen, nor can see:
To whom be honour and power everlasting.
Amen.'—1 Tim. vi. 15.

1. He is the WONDERFUL, the Unsearchable One, who is past finding out:

'Whom no man hath seen, nor can see.'

We cannot comprehend the Infinite. We can but feebly apprehend the truth respecting him. He is 'Immanuel, God with us,' in whom the marvellous lovingkindness of the Father hath been declared.

In the *Gospel according to Matthew*, we have his wondrous incarnation. Here also he is presented as the Revealer of secrets; his discourses, especially those of a prophetic nature, being given in Matthew. In this first book of the New Testament is also displayed his wisdom, as concealing in parables; and in replying to his opposers, as well as in revealing to his disciples.

In *Mark* we have more fully brought before us the wonders of his working; his power in casting out devils, and his miracles of healing; his unwearied diligence in doing good to both the souls and bodies of men.

In both Matthew and Mark we contemplate his marvellous endurance of suffering and reproach, as having undertaken our redemption, and as giving us an example that we should follow his steps. Blessed are they who are thus led; 'they shall understand the lovingkindness of the Lord.' To them will be opened up the wonders of redeeming love.

II. He is the COUNSELLOR—our Mediator, God-man, through whom we have reconciliation with God. In order to this, he partook of our nature, and was verily man, as is more particularly shewn out in the *Gospel according to Luke*. At the same time, he is verily God, as is most fully manifested in the *Gospel according to John*.

In both these books we see him indicating the way of approach to the Father, and giving us example of communion with him by prayer. In Luke, repentance, and submission to the Divine way of being reconciled, are called for; and in John, we are led into the very bosom of eternal love, to rest in the embrace of the everlasting arms, whilst rejoicing in the abundance of the peace and truth, which are, by 'THE WONDERFUL COUNSELLOR,' unfolded to our view. In these two Gospels, we have more fully shewn to us the one atoning Sacrifice, on the ground of which we are thus brought nigh unto God; also the evidence that He who suffered is risen, and hath the same interest in the welfare of his disciples, as when before his death he tabernacled with them upon earth. He hath ascended to exercise his priestly office at the right hand of the Father in

BE NOT HIGHMINDED, BUT FEAR.—Rom. xi. 20. [149

heaven. Our Counsellor hath for us entered within the vail, and dwelleth in the light which no man can approach unto. Blessed are they who hunger and thirst for God, the living God—who earnestly desire the blessings procured by the intercession of Christ, and who long for his appearing: they shall be filled.

III. He is THE MIGHTY GOD: He hath burst the bonds of death, and triumphed over hell and the grave; ascended to the throne of the Father, and become possessed of all power in heaven and in earth; bestowing upon his chosen witnesses power to preach to all men the forgiveness of sins; to proclaim to all nations the gospel, for the obedience of faith; ministering the Spirit, for the renewing of man after the Divine image, in order to make meet for the inheritance of the saints in light. All this, the proof of his being the 'IMMORTAL,' 'THE MIGHTY GOD,' 'who only hath immortality,' to bestow, we have most fully presented to us in *the Acts of the Apostles,* and *the Epistles of Paul.* With regard to the apostle of the Gentiles, the mighty power of the Redeemer—of Jesus, whom he had persecuted, was indeed marvellously displayed. Paul was emphatically an apostle of Christ, to give witness of the resurrection. It was as having risen and ascended, that the Lord appeared to him, on his way to Damascus.

And the resurrection-life was made manifest in his mortal flesh: 'Through mighty signs and wonders, by the power of the Spirit of God,' he could say, ' *I have fully preached the gospel of Christ,*' Rom. xv. 19. When the ministration of the gospel, by the apostle of the Gentiles, is effectual in the raising up of Israel, the people of the God of Abraham, new created in Christ Jesus, through the word of the truth of the gospel which Paul preached—the word of the Lord spoken over the '*bones very many and very dry,*' Eze. xxxvii. 1—14—when that which Paul contemplated is realized, ' *Howbeit for this cause I obtained mercy, that in me first Jesus Christ might shew forth all long suffering for a pattern to them which should hereafter believe on Him to lift everlasting;*' then will the mighty power of God be made manifest, both in them and for them. Then he will indeed appear as The mighty God, '*the King eternal, immortal, invisible, the only wise God;*' and as truly will he prove himself faithful and powerful to fulfil his promise, '*Blessed are the meek; for they shall inherit the earth.*'

IV. He is THE EVERLASTING FATHER—the Eternal, the Father of a royal priesthood.

In *the Epistle to the Hebrews* is shewn that it is by him men have been made the partakers of eternal life, in any age, under any dispensation. He is the great federal Head, in whom all new covenant mercy has been enjoyed, from Abel downwards. He is the Author of eternal life to all that obey him; his throne is for ever and ever, and his is an everlasting priesthood. He ever liveth to procure for us the nourishment meet for the life which we have in him—'*Jesus Christ, the same yesterday, to-day, and for ever.*'

In *the Epistle of James,* we are still farther reminded that he is indeed a Father to Israel; that he hath loved us with an everlasting love. It is addressed, not to the Jews, the remnant of Israel, but to their brethren, '*the whole house of Israel,*' who had been cast out among the Gentiles, and who were to human appearance lost, Eze. xl. 13—21. It is addressed '*to the twelve tribes scattered abroad,*' and clearly recognises us as being still the peculiar objects of the truly parental care and tenderness of our everlasting Father. '*Of his own will begat he us with the word of truth, that we should be a kind of firstfruits of his creatures,*' Ja. i. 18; and correspondent admonition and encouragement, together with a most remarkably minute description of our character and condition, are given throughout the epistle, all belonging to us at this time when '*the coming of the Lord draweth nigh,*' ch. v. 8. He hath ever been mindful of his covenant. He hath been a Father of the fatherless, ' *very pitiful, and of tender mercy;*' so that we may truly say, '*Doubtless thou art our Father, though Abraham be ignorant of us, and Israel acknowledge us not: thou, O Lord, art our Father. our Redeemer; thy Name . . . from everlasting.*' ' *Return for thy servants' sake, the tribes of thine inheritance,*' &c., Is. lxiii. 16—9. They who thus mourn

shall be comforted. The people who had been scattered throughout the countries, are '*begotten again unto a lively hope, by the resurrection of Jesus Christ from the dead,*' Pe. i. 1—3. ' *Born again, not of corruptible seed, but of incorruptible, by the word of God, which liveth and abideth for ever,*' ver. 23—' *A chosen generation, a royal priesthood, an holy nation, a peculiar people; that ye should shew forth the praises of him who hath called you out of darkness into his marvellous light; which in time past*' (as forewarned by the prophet, Hos. i. 6—11) were made ' *not a people, but are now the people of God; which had not obtained mercy, but now have obtained mercy,*' 1 Pe. ii. 9, 10.

In *the Epistles of Peter,* the first of which is more particularly upon the sufferings of Christ, and the second upon the glory that should follow, are presented the keys of the kingdom of heaven,—a description of which, first as to grace, and then as to glory, we have in the remaining books of the New Testament.

V. He is the PRINCE OF PEACE. Even in the midst of trouble, and as enduring affliction, his people can now enjoy peace. The manner in which they may do so, and the profitable use which, in the view of the coming kingdom, is to be made of present suffering, are described in *the First Epistle of Peter;* as in the *second* epistle we are shewn by what power, and against what enemies, the spiritual warfare is now to be maintained; how we may rest in the day of the Lord, a day of trouble and alarm to those who have chosen their portion amid the changeful things of time; who have been at ease in rejection of the Divine testimony respecting the coming of the Lord.

The Epistles of John shew us the law of the kingdom, which is LOVE, in obedience to which we enjoy peace; they also contain warning against all that would mar that peace, and render us exposed to the attacks of the adversary, through our succumbing to the enemy, and yielding up our rights and privileges as sons of God. They also teach us properly to discriminate between friend and foe.

Jude shews that there is indeed to be no peace with the enemy, but that we must '*earnestly contend for the faith which was once delivered unto the saints,*' looking '*unto him that is able to keep you from falling, and to present you faultless before the presence of his glory with exceeding joy, to the only wise God our Saviour, be glory and majesty, dominion and power, both now and ever. Amen,*' Jude 3, 24, 5

The Apocalypse is emphatically the revelation of the PRINCE OF PEACE. In it are described the successive revolutions through which he is reaching forward to the full establishment of his kingdom of righteousness and peace. As our Prince, the Prince of the kings of the earth, he is spoken of in the very beginning of the book; and as our Peace, he is described, ch. i. 12—20. And as preparing his people for its enjoyment, he addresses them in ch. ii., iii. A glimpse of the glorious rest that awaits them in the kingdom, ch. iv. His procuring it for them in heaven, ch. v. His removing their crown, and consequently peace, from the earth; his giving to his saints rest in trouble; and the awful tribulation which is coming upon the world, are referred to, ch. vi. The transmission of the gospel westward, and the abundant peace his people are to enjoy standing before the throne, ch. vii. The seven prophetic trumpets, giving warning of the King's approach, and the triumph of his kingdom, ch. viii.—xi. The church and her beastly adversaries, the devil, the world, and the flesh, ch. xii., xiii. The Lamb on the mount Sion, the universal preaching of the gospel, the last warnings to Babylon and the world, and the speedy accomplishment of the judgment upon those who have refused the proffered peace, ch. xiv. The triumph in trial of those that overcome, who sing the song of Moses and the Lamb, ch. xv. And the pouring out of the seven vials full of the seven last plagues—intimations that there is to be no peace to the wicked, ch. xv., xvi. The last plague upon Babylon and all the enemies of the King, which had been announced in ch. xiv., and samples of which are given, ch. xvi., are more fully described, ch. xvii. —xix. Now the Lord is manifested as indeed the Prince, ch. xix. 11—6; and the peace into which He is leading those that are '*called, and chosen,* and

[150] I WILL CONFESS TO THEE . . . . AND SING UNTO THY NAME.—Rom. xv. 9.

faithful,' is described, ch. xxi., xxii. Then is Jerusalem—the Seeing of Peace—

'And there shall be no more curse:
But the throne of God and of the Lamb shall be in it;
And his servants shall serve him:
And they shall see his face;
And his name *shall be* in their foreheads.
And there shall be no night there;
And they need no candle,
Neither light of the sun;
For the Lord God giveth them light:
And they shall reign for ever and ever.'
—*Rev.* xxii. 3—5.

Then will be seen the fulfilment of the promise, '*Blessed* are *the poor in spirit; for theirs is the kingdom of heaven.*' Then shall they rejoice to celebrate the praises of our King—

'Unto him that loved us,
And washed us from our sins in his own blood,
And hath made us kings and priests unto God and his Father;
To him *be* glory and dominion for ever and ever. Amen.'—*Rev.* i. 5, 6.

Compare 1 Ti. i. 17; Is. ix. 6, 7; and 1 Ti. vi. 15, .6.—

1. He is 'THE KING'—'the Prince of Peace'—'the blessed and only Potentate.'

2. 'ETERNAL'—'the Everlasting Father'—the Father of a royal priesthood—'the King of kings, and Lord of lords.'

3. 'IMMORTAL'—'the Mighty God'—who hath for us conquered death and hell—'who only hath immortality.'

4. 'INVISIBLE'—'the Counsellor'—whom now we see not, He having for us entered within the vail—'dwelling in the light which no man can approach unto.'

5. 'THE ONLY WISE GOD'—the 'Wonderful'—whose wisdom is unsearchable—the depth of whose working is beyond the reach of human eye—'whom no man hath seen, nor can see.'

CONCLUDING REMARKS.

When the Lord spake, in Horeb, the words of the Decalogue, Israel had said, De. xviii. 16, 'Let me not hear again the voice of the LORD my God, neither let me see this great fire any more, that I die not.' 'And the LORD said unto' Moses, ver. 17—9, 'They have well spoken *that* which they have spoken. I will raise them up a Prophet from among their brethren, like unto thee, and will put my words in his mouth; and he shall speak unto them all that I shall command him. And it shall come to pass, *that* whosoever will not hearken unto my words which he shall speak in my name, I will require *it* of him.' Moses, the mediator of the national covenant made with Israel, was a type of the Mediator of the new covenant, never to be broken. Jesus hath come near and spoken, to our better understanding, the words of the Law. In '*The Sermon on the Mount*,' he hath given, as we have seen, an evangelical exposition of the Decalogue.

We have seen that the law of the Ten Commandments, which the Lord delivered in the ears of the children of Israel, and which twice with his own finger he wrote upon two tables of stone, he caused also to be written in the books of the LAW and the Prophets, and that in the same order as these are presented in the Hebrew Scriptures: the five books of Moses being correspondent to the *first* five Commandments; while the other five Commandments have their illustration in Joshua, Judges, Samuel, Kings, and the Prophets.

We have seen that our Lord, in the *ten* portions of his '*Sermon on the Mount*,' made a recognition of those books, in the same order, and gave a renewal of the Law, according to the New Testament. We have seen that not only did he speak thus on earth, but that from heaven he hath, by his Spirit, through the instrumentality of the apostle of the Gentiles, ministered the Law in the fulness of Gospel light;

that the ten Epistles of Paul, from Romans to First Timothy, contain a further development and application of the Law in its spirituality, as presented in '*The Sermon on the Mount*.' The tenth of these Epistles we have seen to be a kind of recapitulation of the whole; while at the end of it there is a measure according to Paul's gospel, and '*the words of our Lord Jesus Christ*,' first, for '*the man of God*,' who is rich as having only God for his portion, 1 Ti. vi. 11—.6; and next for those who may be also rich in the things of this world, ver. 17,—9.

It remains that we in all simplicity of purpose, with an earnest desire to know and do the will of God, present ourselves before him, in order that he may accomplish his promise, Je. xxxi. 31—.3, 'Behold, the days come, saith the LORD, that I will make a new covenant with the house of Israel, and with the house of Judah: not according to the covenant that I made with their fathers, in the day *that* I took them by the hand to bring them out of the land of Egypt; which my covenant they brake,' &c.; 'But this *shall be* the covenant that I will make with the house of Israel; After those days, saith the LORD, I will put my law in their inward parts, and write it in their hearts; and will be their God, and they shall be my people.'

Then will be better understood the words of the apostle, 2 Co. iii. 5—8, 'Our sufficiency *is* of God; who also hath made us able ministers of the new testament; not of the letter, but of the spirit: for the letter killeth, but the spirit giveth life. But if the ministration of death, written *and* engraven in stones, was glorious, so that the children of Israel could not stedfastly behold the face of Moses for the glory of his countenance; which *glory* was to be done away; how shall not the ministration of the Spirit be rather glorious?'

'Now to Him that is of Power to stablish you
According to my Gospel,
And the Preaching of Jesus Christ,
According to the Revelation of the Mystery,
Which was kept secret since the world began,
But now is made manifest,
And by the Scriptures of the Prophets,
According to the Commandment of the Everlasting God,
Made known to all nations
For the Obedience of Faith:
To God only Wise,
Be glory through Jesus Christ for ever. Amen.'—Rom. xvi. 25—.7.

HALLOWED BE THY NAME.—Matt. vi. 9.

www.ingramcontent.com/pod-product-compliance
Lightning Source LLC
Chambersburg PA
CBHW020911230426
43666CB00008B/1406